![Country Living Magazine]

GUIDE TO RURAL ENGLAND

THE WEST COUNTRY

By Peter Long

Published by:

Travel Publishing Ltd

7a Apollo House, Calleva Park

Aldermaston, Berks, RG7 8TN

ISBN 1-904-43409-6

© Travel Publishing Ltd

Country Living is a registered trademark of The National
                                          pany Limited.

Second Edition: 2004

Scotland
The South of England
The South East of England
The West Country
Wales

All advertisements in this publication have been accepted in good faith by Travel
Publishing and they have not necessarily been endorsed by *Country Living*
Magazine.

All information is included by the publishers in good faith and is believed to be
correct at the time of going to press. No responsibility can be accepted for errors.

Editor: Peter Long

Printing by: Scotprint, Haddington

Location Maps: © Maps in Minutes ™ (2004)   © Crown Copyright, Ordnance Survey 2004

Walks: Walks have been reproduced with kind permission of the internet
                 walking site www.walkingworld.com

Walk Maps: Reproduced from Ordnance Survey mapping on behalf of the
                 Controller of Her Majesty's Stationery Office, © Crown Copyright.
                 Licence Number MC 100035812

Cover Design: Lines & Words, Aldermaston

Cover Photo: Thatched Cottage, East Quantoxhead, Somerset © www.britainonview.com

Text Photos: Text photos have been kindly supplied by the Britain on View photo library
                 © www.britainonview.com

Foreword

From a bracing walk across the hills and tarns of The Lake District to a relaxing weekend spent discovering the unspoilt hamlets of East Anglia, nothing quite matches getting off the beaten track and exploring Britain's areas of outstanding beauty.

Each month, *Country Living Magazine* celebrates the richness and diversity of our countryside with features on rural Britain and the traditions that have their roots there. So it is with great pleasure that I introduce you to the *Country Living Magazine Guide to Rural England* series. Packed with information about unusual and unique aspects of our countryside, the guides will point both fair-weather and intrepid travellers in the right direction.

Each chapter provides a fascinating tour of the West Country area, with insights into local heritage and history and easy-to-read facts on a wealth of places to visit, stay, eat, drink and shop.

I hope that this guide will help make your visit a rewarding and stimulating experience and that you will return inspired, refreshed and ready to head off on your next countryside adventure.

Susy Smith

Susy Smith
Editor, Country Living magazine

PS To subscribe to *Country Living Magazine* each month, call 01858 438844

Introduction

This is the fourth Country Living Magazine rural guide edited by Peter Long, an experienced travel writer who spent many years as an inspector and writer with Egon Ronay's Hotels & Restaurants Guides before joining the Travel Publishing editorial team. Peter has ensured that the West Country edition of our popular rural guides series is packed with vivid descriptions, historical stories, amusing anecdotes and interesting facts on hundreds of places in Cornwall, Devon, Somerset and Dorset

The coloured advertising panels within each chapter provide further information on places to see, stay, eat, drink, shop and even exercise! We have also selected a number of walks from walkingworld.com (full details of this website may be found to the rear of this guide) which we highly recommend if you wish to appreciate fully the beauty and charm of the varied rural landscapes and coastlines of the West Country.

The guide however is not simply an "armchair tour". Its prime aim is to encourage the reader to visit the places described and discover much more about the wonderful towns, villages and countryside of the West Country. In this respect we would like to thank all the Tourist Information Centres who helped us to provide you with up-to-date information. Whether you decide to explore this region by wheeled transport or on foot we are sure you will find it a very uplifting experience.

We are always interested in receiving comments on places covered (or not covered) in our guides so please do not hesitate to use the reader reaction form provided at the rear of this guide to give us your considered comments. This will help us refine and improve the content of the next edition. We also welcome any general comments which will help improve the overall presentation of the guides themselves.

Finally, for more information on the full range of travel guides published by Travel Publishing please refer to the details and order form at the rear of this guide or log on to our website at www.travelpublishing.co.uk

Travel Publishing

Locator Map

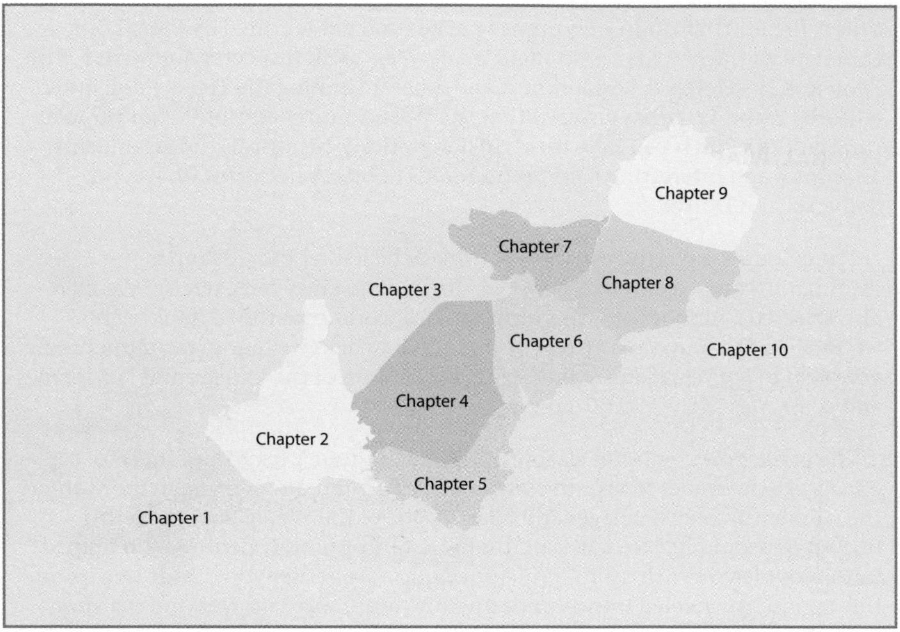

Chapter 9

Chapter 7

Chapter 3

Chapter 8

Chapter 6

Chapter 10

Chapter 4

Chapter 2

Chapter 5

Chapter 1

Contents

FOREWORD   III

INTRODUCTION   V

REGIONAL MAP   VI

CONTENTS   VII

GEOGRAPHICAL AREAS:

Chapter 1:   West Cornwall   3

Chapter 2:   East Cornwall   71

Chapter 3:   North Devon   113

Chapter 4:   In and Around Dartmoor   147

Chapter 5:   Plymouth and the South Hams   185

Chapter 6:   Exeter and East Devon   227

Chapter 7:   Exmoor and the Quantock Hills   263

Chapter 8:   South Somerset   285

Chapter 9:   Bath and the Mendips   317

Chapter 10:   Dorset   359

INDEXES AND LISTS:

Tourist Information Centres   416

Alphabetic List of Advertisers   423

List of Walks   429

Order Form   434

Reader Comment Forms   435

Index of Towns, Villages and Places of Interest   437

LOCATOR MAP

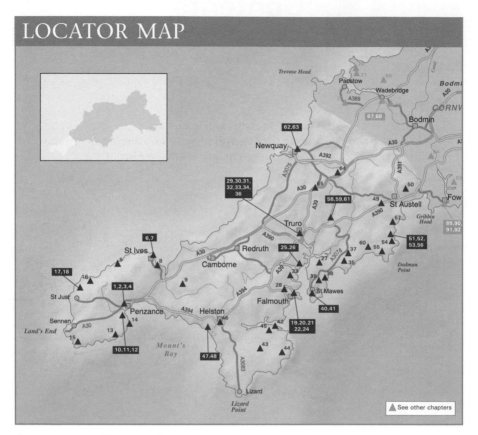

ADVERTISERS AND PLACES OF INTEREST

1	Cornish Farm Holidays	page 5
2	Little Jem's Jewellers, Penzance	page 6
3	The Goldfish Bowl, Penzance	page 6
4	Enys Wartha Tea Rooms, Penzance	page 7
5	Wayside Folk Museum, Zennor, St Ives	page 9
6	Garrack Hotel & Restaurant, St Ives	page 10
7	New Millenium Gallery, St Ives	page 12
8	Rotorua Apartments, Carbis Bay	page 12
9	Alicium Ceramics, St Erth Praze, Hayle	page 13
10	Badcock's Gallery, Newlyn, Penzance	page 15
11	The Pilchard Works, Tolcarne, Newlyn	page 16
12	Smugglers Restaurant, Newlyn	page 17
13	Lamorna Cove, West Penwith	page 18
14	Sandpiper Gallery, Mousehole	page 19
15	The Minack Theatre, Porthcurno	page 20
16	Yew Tree Gallery, Morvah, Penzance	page 21
17	North Inn, Pendeen, Penzance	page 24
18	Gem & Jewellery Workshop, Pendeen	page 25
19	The Sticky Prawn, Falmouth	page 29
20	Tall Ships Trading, Falmouth	page 30
21	Beside The Wave Gallery, Falmouth	page 30
22	National Maritime Museum, Falmouth	page 31
23	Pandora Inn, Mylor Bridge, Falmouth	page 32
24	The Tony Warren Maritime Gallery, Falmouth	page 33
25	Penhale Cottages, Feock, Truro	page 34
26	Come to Good Farm, Feock, Truro	page 34
27	Smugglers Cottage of Tolverne, Philleigh	page 35
28	Prospect House, Penryn	page 35
29	Gili Trading, Truro	page 38
30	Saffron, Truro	page 39
31	Cliftons Guest House, Truro	page 40
32	Phoenix, Truro	page 40
33	Hall for Cornwall, Truro	page 41

WEST CORNWALL 1

"An isolated beauty that contains some of the most dramatic and spectacular scenery in the country." This is an apt description of Cornwall, a land of strong Celtic heritage and ancestry, a place dotted with monuments such as crosses, holy wells and prehistoric sights and where legends of old still have a strong romantic appeal among the Cornish people. Surrounded by rugged coastline, Cornwall has often been referred to as the English Riviera,

encompassing pretty little fishing ports, secluded picturesque villages, narrow winding lanes and romantic seafaring traditions.

Land's End, where Cornwall's granite meets the Atlantic Ocean in a dramatic series of steep cliffs, is one of the most famous places in the country. On a journey of discovery

Coverack Harbour

ADVERTISERS AND PLACES OF INTEREST

34 2wentythree, Truro   page 42
35 Veryan Gallery, Veryan Green, Truro   page 42
36 Trewithen Gardens & Nurseries, Truro   page 43
37 Trenona Farm Holidays, Ruan High Lanes,
        Truro   page 44
38 Roseland Holiday Cottages, Portscatho   page 45
39 The Royal Standard, Portscatho, Truro   page 45
40 The Rising Sun, St Mawes   page 46
41 The Green Lantern, St Mawes   page 47
42 St Anthony Holidays & Sailaway St Anthony,
        Manaccan, Helston   page 48
43 F N Gardner Rocking Horses, St Martin   page 49
44 Roskilly's, St Keverne, Helston   page 50
45 The New Inn, Manaccan, Helston   page 51
46 Flambards Theme Park, Helston   page 54
47 The Net Loft Gallery, Porthleven   page 56
48 Julia Mills Gallery & Workshop,
        Porthleven   page 56

49 Bosinver Farm Cottages, Trelowth   page 57
50 The Eden Project, Bodelva, St Austell   page 58
51 Cofro, Mevagissey   page 60
52 The Harbour Tavern, Mevagissey   page 60
53 In Your Dreams, Mevagissey   page 61
54 Bodrugan Barton, Portmellon   page 62
55 The Granary, Boswinger, Mevagissey   page 62
56 Mevagissey Model Railway, Mevagissey   page 63
57 Lost Gardens of Heligan, Pentewan   page 63
58 Gulshan Indian Cuisine, Probus, Truro   page 64
59 Trudgian Farm Shop, Probus, Truro   page 64
60 Caerhays Castle Gardens, Gorran   page 65
61 Probus Gardens, Probus, Truro   page 65
62 Finn's at the Old Boathouse, Newquay   page 66
63 Blue Reef Aquarium, Newquay   page 67
64 Fraddon Pottery, Fraddon   page 68
65 The Plume of Feathers, Mitchell, Truro   page 69

through the West Country to this most south-westerly point of mainland Britain, visitors will pass many places of equal beauty and charm, and throughout the region there are numerous prehistoric relics including the ancient tomb of Zennor Quoit and Carn Euny Iron Age village.

Throughout history the western region of Cornwall has been mined – for tin, copper and, latterly, china clay, and the marks left by this industry are everywhere. Around St Just, close to Penzance, one of the last tin mines to close, Geevor Mine, has been preserved as a heritage centre while, nearby, an old mine steam engine, perched high on the cliff top, still produces power. Further east lie the towns of Redruth and Camborne, which were once at the centre of the mining industry. The land around St Austell is somewhat different and was at one time dubbed the Cornish Alps due to the spoil heaps from the china clay industry. At St Blazey, one china clay pit has been converted into the Eden Project – massive conservatories that aim to promote the vital relationship between plants, people and resources.

Cornish Tin Mines

Elsewhere, the old ports and harbours, which exported the minerals and where the county's great catches of pilchards were once landed, are now sailing and yachting centres.

Finally there is Falmouth, which lies on the Fal estuary, known as Carrick Roads, and which has the third largest natural harbour in the world. To the south of Falmouth, which is now becoming a fashionable and expensive yachting centre, lies the unique Lizard Peninsula. To the east is the unspoilt countryside of Roseland. In the 18th and 19th centuries Cornwall's mild climate encouraged the creation of numerous gardens stocked with exotic trees and shrubs from newly explored lands. One of the most impressive is the Lost Gardens of Heligan, which were lost under weeds and ivy for over 70 years before being restored to their former world-renowned glory.

CORNISH FARM HOLIDAYS

Brochure 01872 510050
e-mail: enquire@cornish-farms.co.uk
website: www.cornish-farms.co.uk

The members of **Cornish Farm Holidays** offer high-quality bed & breakfast and self-catering accommodation, with friendly, helpful service, on some of the most beautiful farms in Cornwall. Visitors can look forward to a warm welcome and good company, enjoying a quiet retreat in the country air, with exceptional value for money, and often with delightful bonuses such as helping to feed the farm animals. All the accommodation is of a very high standard, and the owners take great pride in the service they provide and their excellent local knowledge.

Each property - there are 64 in all - is individual and each is situated in attractive, largely unspoilt countryside - and since this is Cornwall, the sea is never far away, so visitors get the best of both worlds. For B&B guests, a delicious breakfast of local farm-fresh produce starts the day, and some hosts can provide evening meals. If the accommodation is self-catering, it will be fully equipped and the host will usually be close at hand. The 30 properties in West Cornwall sleep from 2 to 12 and range from converted stables and barns just off the St Ives-Land's End coast road to a Georgian farmhouse at Lanivet south of Bodmin. Most are open all year round.

PENZANCE

For centuries a remote market town that made its living from fishing, mining and smuggling, Penzance today is popular with holidaymakers as well as being the ferry port for the Isles of Scilly. Along with its near neighbours, Newlyn and Mousehole, Penzance was sacked by the Spanish in 1595. Having supported the Royalist cause during the Civil War, it suffered the same fate again less than 60 years later. A major port in the 19th century for the export of tin, the fortunes of Penzance were transformed by the railway's arrival in 1859. Not only could the direct despatch of early flowers, vegetables and locally caught fish to the rest of Britain be undertaken but the influx of holidaymakers boosted the town's fledgling tourist industry. Still a busy town and harbour, Penzance is home to Cornwall's only promenade

stretching south-westwards to Newlyn. On the promenade the wonderful open-air sea water pool, the **Jubilee Swimming Pool**, retains its original art deco styling.

Most of the town's more interesting buildings can be found on Chapel Street, which leads down from the domed **Market House** (built in 1836) to the quay. Outside Market House is a statue to Penzance's most famous son, Sir Humphry Davy, the scientist best remembered for inventing the miners' safety lamp. Born close to Market House, Davy was one of the foremost chemists of the 19th century and, along with his contribution to miners' safety, he also founded both the Athenaeum Club and London Zoo. Also along this thoroughfare is the exotic **Egyptian House**, created from two cottages in the 1830s by John Lavin, to entice customers into his shop. Although the designer of

LITTLE JEM'S JEWELLERS

41 Market Place, Penzance, Cornwall TR18 2JG
Tel: 01736 351400

When Jamie Lagden moved to Penzance from the Southeast several years ago, she brought with her many years' experience gained among the big names in the jewellery trade. **Little Jem's Jewellers**, which she established in 1988 in the heart of one of the town's

main shopping areas, has become one of the region's major buyers and sellers of antique and modern jewellery. Rings to suit all ages and budgets, in all sorts

of styles and from all periods - Georgian, Victorian, art nouveau and modern - are Jamie's speciality, and her collection is probably the largest in the Southwest.

The window display makes it hard to walk past this splendid little place, and once inside, visitors are certain to find just the right ring for any special occasion among the spotlit counters and cabinets. The stock also includes necklaces, brooches and other items of jewellery, and Jamie offers an exchange service and undertakes repairs and commission work. Such has been the success of Little Jem's Jewellers that she now has a second shop in town.

GOLDFISH CONTEMPORARY FINE ART

56 Chapel Street, Penzance, Cornwall TR18 4AE
Tel: 01736 360573
e-mail: mail@goldfishfineart.co.uk
website: www.goldfishfineart.co.uk

After recent relocation from St Ives to Penzance, **Goldfish Contemporary Fine Art** (formerly The Goldfish Bowl), seems to go from strength the strength. This prestigious contemporary fine art gallery, spread over two floors of open display space, features a varied

display of the highest quality painting, sculpture, ceramic and jewellery from artists of both national and local renown; these include symbolic abstracts by David Briggs, Kenneth Spooner, Paul Wadsworth,

strong figurative work by Andrew Litten, Zoe Cameron, Joseph Clarke, and the late Julian Dyson, contemporary landscapes by Kerry Harding and Shirley Foote, nude drawing by Barbara Karn and Judy Symons and ceramics by Emma Johnstone, sculpture by Jane Muir and Alex Smirnoff, to name a short few of the many artists on show. The gallery has a timetable of exhibitions throughout the year, as well as a permanent mix of general work on show, ensuring that this space continues to remain a must see when in West Cornwall. As well as offering a comprehensive website , newsletters and mailing list facility with the aim of keeping clients in the picture at all times.

Penzance Harbour

the victory of Trafalgar and the death of Lord Nelson. Chapel Street was also the childhood home of Marie Branwell, the mother of the Brontë sisters.

Penzance has not forgotten its long-standing links with the sea. At the **Maritime Museum** there is a fascinating collection of artefacts that illustrate the ferocity of the waters along this stretch of coast, while down at the harbour, at the

the magnificent facade is unknown, it is believed to have been inspired by the Egyptian Hall in Piccadilly, London. Opposite this splendid building lies **The Union Hotel**, whose Georgian facade hides an impressive Elizabethan interior. From here was made the first announcement in mainland England of

Trinity House Lighthouse Centre, the story of lighthouse keeping is told. Opened by Prince Andrew in 1991, the centre has assembled what is the probably the largest and finest collection of lighthouse equipment in the world. Elsewhere in Penzance, local history and the work of the Newlyn School of artists

can be seen at the **Penlee House Art Gallery and Museum**. The county's long association with the mining industry is highlighted at the **Cornwall Geological Museum**. Just to the northwest of the town, and close to the village of **Madron**, lie **Trengwainton Gardens**, the National Trust-owned woodland gardens that are known for their spring flowering shrubs, their exotic trees and the walled garden that contains plants that cannot be grown in the open anywhere else in the country. The walled garden was built in the early 19th century by the then owner Sir Rose Price, the son of a wealthy Jamaican sugar planter.

AROUND PENZANCE

ZENNOR

5½ miles N of Penzance on the B3306

This delightful ancient village, situated between moorland and coastal cliffs, shows evidence of Bronze Age settlers. It also has a 12th century church, famous for its bench end, depicting a mermaid holding a comb and mirror. A local legend tells of a mysterious young maiden who was drawn to the church by the beautiful singing of a chorister, the church warden's son Matthew Trewhella. An enchanting singer herself, the maiden lured Matthew down to nearby Pendour Cove where he disappeared. On warm summer evenings, it is said that their voices can be heard rising from the waves. By the porch in the church is a memorial to John Davey, who died in 1891, stating that he was the last person to have any great knowledge of the native Cornish language Kernuack. It is said that he remained familiar with the language by speaking it to his cat. There has recently been a revival of interest in Kernuack, and visitors to Cornwall who

chance upon a Kernuack speaker might impress him by asking "Plema'n diwotti?" and with any luck being directed to the nearest pub. Another useful entry in the Cornish phrasebook is "Fatell yu an pastyon yn gwerthji ma? A wrons I ri dhymn drog goans?", which means "What are the pasties like in this shop? Will they give me indigestion?"

For an insight into the history of Zennor and the surrounding area, the **Wayside Folk Museum** (see panel opposite) has numerous exhibits that tell of this region's tin mining industry. This is also referred to in the name of the local inn, The Tinners. DH Lawrence spent many hours at this pub, while living in the village with his wife Frieda during World War I. It was during his stay here, under police surveillance, that Lawrence wrote *Women in Love*. However,

Chysauster Ancient Village

WAYSIDE FOLK MUSEUM

Zennor, Nr St Ives, Cornwall TR26 3DA
Tel: 01736 796945

It was in the 1930s that Colonel 'Freddie' Hirst started a collection of relics peculiar to Zennor. That collection was the basis of the **Wayside Folk Museum**, a privately owned museum which portrays the lives of ordinary people in the area through its displays of artefacts, stories and photographs. Although it appears small from the outside, the museum has something of the tardis about it, and the 16 display areas contain more than 5,000 items, from maps and archaeological exhibits to blacksmith's and wheelwright's equipment, a cobbler's shop, an 18th century kitchen,

relics of local mining and quarrying and early agricultural implements.

In 1997 the old piggery was incorporated into the museum and contains displays on 'Childhood Memories', 'The Sea' and ' Village Dairy'. 'People of Past Zennor' is an exhibition of photographs and text depicting the lives of its inhabitants. In the grounds are two waterwheels from the mining industry and a unique collection of corn grinding querns and stone tools dating back as far as 3000BC. Bridge House Gift & Book Shop specialises in things Cornish as well as providing light refreshments.

his pacifist tendencies and Frieda's German heritage (her cousin was the flying ace the Red Baron) caused them to be 'moved on' in October 1917.

To the southeast of the village lies the Neolithic chamber tomb, **Zennor Quoit**. One of the many ancient monuments in the area, the tomb has a huge capstone that was once supported on five broad uprights.

A couple of miles to the south of Zennor, on a windy hillside, lies **Chysauster Ancient Village**, a Romano-Cornish village, built around 2,000 years ago, which has one of the oldest identifiable streets in the country. The site was only discovered during archaeological excavations in the 1860s but the villagers here were farmers, as cattle sheds have been unearthed. They also worked tin beside the nearby stream. Their housing consisted of stone-walled homesteads, each with an open central

courtyard surrounded by several circular living rooms topped with thatch or turf.

ST IVES

7 miles NE of Penzance on the A3074

With five sandy beaches, a maze of narrow streets and a picturesque harbour, this lovely old fishing town manages to retain its charm despite being deluged by tourists from late spring until early autumn. The original settlement takes its name from the 6th century missionary St Ia, who is said to have landed here from Ireland on an ivy leaf. The 15th century parish church bears her name along with those of the two fishermen Apostles, St Peter and St Andrew.

One of the most important pilchard fishing centres in Cornwall until the early 20th century, St Ives holds a record dating back to 1868 for the greatest number of fish caught in a single seine

The Garrack
Hotel & Restaurant

Burthallan Lane, St Ives,
Cornwall TR26 3AA
Tel: 01736 796199
Fax: 01736 798955

e-mail: clenquiry@garrack.com
website: www.garrack.com

Mature gardens overlooking Porthmeor Beach, The Island and the impressive sweep of St Ives Bay provide a scenic, secluded setting for the **Garrack Hotel**, where resident proprietors the Kilby family have been welcoming guests for 40 years. Bedrooms in the main house are in character with the

traditional look of the hotel, while those in the sea-facing lower ground floor wing are more modern in style. All rooms have a private bathroom, direct-dial telephones, baby monitoring, TV and beverage tray, and some boast four-poster or half-tester beds and spa baths. Three ground-floor rooms with level access to the public areas are suitable for less mobile guests, and one of them is specifically designed with wheelchair users in mind. Two en suite rooms are located in a cottage annexe in the grounds.

The comfortable lounges, kept warm and cosy by open fires, are well stocked with books, magazines and board games for all ages, and the bar is open throughout the day for coffee and tea, drinks and snacks. In a separate building is a leisure centre containing a pool with spa and counter-current swim jet, a sauna and a small gym area, a seating area and ladies' and gentlemen's changing rooms.

As well as providing excellent accommodation, the Garrack is rightly proud of the reputation it has earned for the quality of its cuisine. Local produce is used whenever available. Both carnivores and vegetarians are very well catered for, and seafood comes

sparkling fresh from the port and market at Newlyn; smaller quantities are landed at St Ives, and the hotel has its holding tank for keeping fresh locally caught lobsters. The fine food is complemented by an extensive, wide-ranging wine list that offers exceptional value for money, particularly among the better quality wines.

St Ives needs plenty of time to explore, and the Garrack is an ideal base from which to do it. Apart from the town itself, there are miles of inland footpaths, and the coastal path passes along the end of the lane in which the hotel stands.

Tate Gallery, St Ives

and two widows would dance around the Steeple.

The decline of the fishing and mining industries in the late 19th century saw St Ives develop as an artists' colony. The special quality of the light drew painters such as Turner, Whistler, Sickert, McNeill, Munnings and Hepworth to the town. Art still dominates and, along with the numerous private galleries, there is the **Tate Gallery**, where the work of 20th century painters and sculptors is permanently on display in a superb modern three-storey building backing directly into the cliff face. The gallery offers a unique introduction to contemporary and modern art, and many works can be viewed in the surroundings that inspired them. The Tate also manages the **Barbara Hepworth Sculpture Garden and Museum** at Trewyn Studio, where she

net. Known locally as **The Island**, St Ives Head is home to a Huer's Hut, from where a lookout would scan the sea looking for shoals of pilchards. A local speciality, heavy or *hevva* cake, was traditionally made for the seiners on their return from fishing. As well as providing shelter for the fishing fleet, the harbour was also developed for exporting locally mined ores and minerals. The town's two industries led the labyrinthine narrow streets to become divided into two communities: *Downalong* where the fishing families lived and *Upalong*, the home of the mining families.

Housed in a building that once belonged to a mine, **St Ives Museum** displays a range of artefacts chronicling the natural, industrial and maritime history of the area. There is also a display dedicated to John Knill, mayor of the town in the 18th century. A customs officer by profession, he was also rumoured to be an energetic smuggler. Certainly one of the town's most memorable citizens, he built the Steeple monument to the south of the town to be his mausoleum, but it also served to guide ships carrying contraband safely to the shore. Knill left a bequest to the town so that, every five years, a ceremony would be held when ten girls

Barbara Hepworth Sculpture Garden

NEW MILLENNIUM GALLERY

Street-an-Pol, St Ives, Cornwall TR26 2DS
Tel/Fax: 01736 793121
e-mail: stives@newmillenniumgallery.co.uk
website: www.newmillenniumgallery.co.uk

Centrally located opposite the Guildhall and Tourist Information centre, the **New Millennium Gallery** is the largest privately owned art gallery in St Ives. Opened in 1996 by much-travelled director David Falconer, the slate-fronted building houses three floors of spacious, well-lit art space. A large light space on the ground floor is devoted to a changing display of gallery artists' work selected by David, and the

gallery is the product of 20 years of collecting that reflects his love of highly abstract and innovative contemporary art work. One of his favorite artist's is Neil Canning, who is a colourist who uses vivid colour and bold gesture to convey an emotional and elemental view of the landscape. His third one man show at the gallery will be 9th April - 11th May 2004. Other shows scheduled for 2004 include: Judy Buxton, Jeremy Annear, Mark Surridge, Sax Impey.

The New Millennium Gallery is open 10.30am to 4.30pm Monday to Saturday or by appointment.

ROTORUA APARTMENTS

Trencrom Lane, Carbis Bay, St Ives,
Cornwall TR26 2TD Tel/Fax: 01736 795419
e-mail: rotorua@btconnect.com
website: www.stivesapartments.com

In a quiet wooded lane just off the main St Ives road, **Rotorua Apartments** provide an ideal base for exploring the many delights of this lovely part of the world. Eight one or two-bedroom apartments in what was once a family hotel are very warm and comfortable, with double glazing and central heating, full bathroom facilities and all the amenities needed for a relaxing, go-as-you-please holiday. The kitchens are both practical and attractive, with light oakwood units, electric cooker, microwave oven, dishwasher, fridge-freezer, coffee-maker, toaster and ample pots and pans, crockery, cutlery and glasses.

Each also has TV/video in the living area and TV in the bedrooms, and the shared facilities comprise a heated outdoor swimming pool (May to September), a fully equipped laundry room, a children's play area and a barbecue area. Cots are available on request. Owners Linda and Nicky Roach, who live next door to the apartments, are committed to personal service to each and every guest. Carbis Bay and other excellent beaches are a short walk away, it's a five minute drive to St Ives, and the A30 is only a few miles away, giving easy access to the rest of Cornwall.

both lived and worked until her tragic death in a fire in 1975.

It is not only artists who have been inspired by the beautiful surroundings of St Ives: Virginia Woolf recaptures the happy mood of the childhood holiday here in her novel *To the Lighthouse*, and Rosamunde Pilcher, famous for her books set in Cornwall, was born near here in 1924.

Carbis Bay

Just to the southeast of St Ives, easy to reach on foot and a great favourite with families, lies the sheltered beach of **Carbis Bay**, where various water sports are also available. To the west of St Ives is a wonderful and remote coastline of coves, cliffs and headland that provides a wealth of wildlife and archaeological interest. Following the network of footpaths from St Ives to Pendeen, walkers can discover small wooded valleys, rich bogs, old industrial remains and prehistoric features such as the cliff castles at Gurnard's Head and Bosigran.

HAYLE

7½ miles NE of Penzance on the B3301

Established in the 18th century as an industrial village, Hayle was also a

ALICIUM CERAMICS

2 Steppy Downs Road, St Erth Praze, Hayle, Cornwall TR27 5EF
Tel: 01736 755301/01736 851090
website: www.alicium-pottery.co.uk

For more than 30 years, Anthony Swanson has been practising his trade as a master potter, making fine quality ceramic giftware in his workshop in Hayle, West Cornwall. He uses traditional casting methods in the meticulous production of everything from kitchenware to chamber pots and vases. Visitors can see the kilns and the mouldings in the workshop as well as the pottery in various stages of production. The finished articles are on display in the showroom. All ware is individually hand decorated. Anthony's mother creates the designs, while his wife assists within the workshop as well as with the administration of the business. The pottery supplies businesses both large and small, as well as private customers. Much of the collection has been purchased by people from all over the world.

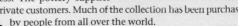

The client portfolio has been built up over the years with the unchanging quality of the products and the friendly, personal service offered by the family. Favourites in his repertoire include tea and coffee sets, beautiful hive-shaped honey pots, cheese bells and fish-shaped serving platters. Opening hours are 10am to 5pm Monday to Friday, and Sunday in high season. They also do mail orders. Alicium Ceramics is located at the corner of Steppy Downs Road and the B3302 Hayle-Helston road.

seaport with harbour in the natural shelter of the Hayle estuary. It was here, in the early 1800s, that the Cornish inventor Richard Trevithick built an early version of the steam locomotive. A short time later, one of the first railways in the world was constructed here to carry tin and copper from Redruth down to the port. With its industrial past, Hayle is not a place naturally associated with cosmetics, but it was Hayle-born Florence Nightingale Graham who set up her own beauty parlour on New York's Fifth Avenue under the name Elizabeth Arden.

On the southern outskirts of the town lies **Paradise Park**, a leading conservation zoo, which is home to some of the world's rarest and most beautiful birds. The Hayle estuary and sands around the town are an ornithologist's delight.

Across the estuary lies **Lelant**, a thriving seaport in the Middle Ages that lost its traffic as the estuary silted up. Now a popular holiday village, with a golf course, Lelant is particularly loved by birders, who come to watch the wide variety of wildfowl and waders on the mud and salt flats.

GODOLPHIN CROSS
9 miles E of Penzance off the B3302

To the northwest of the village lies **Godolphin House**, an exceptional part Tudor, part Stuart house that still retains its original Elizabethan stables. The former home of the Earls of Godolphin, the house has many splendid features. However the family, who made their fortune in mining, are more interesting; Sidney the poet was killed during the Civil War while on the side of the king; Sidney, the 1st Earl was a Lord High Treasurer; the 2nd Earl imported the famous Godolphin Arabian, one of three stallions from which all British

thoroughbreds are descended. While the house remains in private ownership, the Godolphin estate is owned by the National Trust and this historic landscape includes more than 400 recorded archaeological features.

To the south of Godolphin lies the hamlet of **Rinsey** where evidence of tin mining can be seen in the restored 19th century engine house of **Wheal Prosper** and the ruins of the copper mine, **Wheal Trewavas**. Just to the west of Rinsey two headlands enclose the mile long crescent of **Praa Sands**, one of the finest family beaches in Cornwall. Further west again lies **Prussia Cove**, a clifftop settlement, named after a notorious 18th century smuggler, John Carter, who modelled himself on Frederick the Great.

MARAZION
3 miles E of Penzance off the A394

Cornwall's oldest charter town (dating from 1257), Marazion was for many centuries the most important settlement around Mount's Bay. The legacy of this harbour town is its fine old inns and residential houses overlooking the sandy beach. The town is now a windsurfing and sailing centre, but to the northwest is **Marazion Marsh & RSPB Reserve**, an extensive area of wetland and reed beds behind Marazion Beach on the Penzance road. Over 450 plant species have been recorded here, and the reserve is home to many nesting and roosting birds, including herons, reed and sedge warblers and Cetti's warbler.

Situated a third of a mile offshore, **St Michael's Mount** rises dramatically out of the waters of Mount's Bay. It is connected to Marazion by a cobbled causeway that is exposed at high tide. Inhabited since prehistoric times, this granite rock is named after the Archangel St Michael who, according to legend, appeared to a party of fishermen in a

St Michael's Mount

buildings are incorporated into the marvellous **St Michael's Mount Castle** owned by the St Aubyn family from 1660 until the 1950s, when it was donated to the National Trust. Along with the impressive medieval remains, the castle incorporates architectural styles from the 17th to the 19th century. Open from April until the end of October, this is a place of history, charm and intrigue that,

vision in the 5th century. In the 11th century, Edward the Confessor founded a priory on the mount, which had become a place of pilgrimage, in tribute to the famous Benedictine Mont St Michel in Normandy. The remains of these

to this day, remains the home of the St Aubyn family.

NEWLYN

1 mile SW of Penzance on the B3315

The largest fish landing port in England

BADCOCK'S GALLERY

The Strand, Newlyn, Penzance, Cornwall TR18 5HW
Tel: 01736 366159
website: www.badcocksgallery.co.uk

In the four years since they set up in business, Fiona Gray and Mimi Connell have established **Badcock's Gallery** as one of the leading contemporary art galleries in the West Country. The gallery, which is

located on a corner site opposite the fish market and harbour, is both intimate and

beautifully light and sunny, and the atmosphere informal yet always very professional. It shows a monthly changing exhibition of paintings and prints alongside ceramics, contemporary jewellery and unique crafts and gifts.

Fiona and Mimi make a point of getting to know their clients' tastes and are always actively looking for work on their behalf. They also cultivate relations with the artists. World renowned artists such as Sir Terry Frost have shown their work here, but the owners are always interested in showcasing new talent. 80% of the artists are from the West Country, reflecting the standard of excellence that has become the hallmark of Cornish art and which brings collectors from all over the world. Badcock's also shows in other locations, most recently the Affordable Art Fair in London's Battersea Park.

THE PILCHARD WORKS

Tolcarne, Newlyn, Cornwall TR18 5QH
Tel: 01736 332112 Fax: 01736 332442
website: www.pilchardworks.co.uk

In the busy fishing port of Newlyn, near Penzance, is **The Pilchard Works**, Britain's only working salt pilchard factory. On the same site is a museum that has won two national awards, for "Outstanding Presentation of Britain's Heritage" and the Shoestring Award for "Brilliant Presentation of a Tiny Enterprise". Visitors can see traditional salt fish processing using ancient presses that are used to pack the fish into wooden boxes ('coffins') for export to Italy and other European countries. The museum contains many paintings, photographs and artefacts from a bygone age, including Britain's oldest pilchard net making machine. The pilchard was once Britain's best-loved fish, and a century ago in Newlyn alone 16,000 tonnes were landed each year. In 1905 an estimated 13 million pilchards were landed in a single night, and in that year exports to Italy started. But fashions changed and demand gradually dwindled, even though there were plenty of pilchards in the sea.

The factory, and to a large extent the industry, have been rescued by the efforts of Nick Howell, who bought the Pilchard Works (once a Shippam's Paste factory) in 1992, modernising much of the factory but maintaining some of the traditional methods. Small local boats using nets specially designed not to catch other fish operate in the evening, landing their catch directly to the factory, where they are immediately layered with salt in tanks. When some weeks later they are cured, they are pressed to extract excess water and oil and transferred in blocks to the wooden boxes. The range has recently been expanded to include fillets packed in jars with olive oil and, during the summer, fresh whole fish are sold chilled to grill or barbecue and fillets to marinate. This side of the business has grown rapidly, with supermarkets showing great interest, and both Newlyn and Mevagissy now have boats dedicated to this catch.

Pilchards are really just grown-up sardines and are cooked in the same way. Fresh pilchards can be rolled in sea salt and simply grilled, or coated in egg, breadcrumbs and flour and fried. The salt variety have attracted recipes from many sources at home and overseas: grilled, flaked and served on bruschetta with garlic, tomatoes and red onion; marinated with olive oil, garlic, chilli, herbs and sun-dried tomatoes; in a salad with orange wedges; or as an alternative to the anchovy in spaghetti alla puttanesca.

The museum and factory are open for visits on weekdays from Easter to the end of October.

and Wales, this town has a long association with fishing. Its massive jetties, built in the 1880s, embrace not only the existing 15th century harbour but also 40 acres of Mount's Bay. The arrival of the railway in 1859 allowed the swift transportation of fresh fish and seafood to London and beyond. Newlyn is still a base for around 200 vessels. The **Pilchard Works Heritage Museum** (see panel opposite) offers a unique insight into the fascinating history of the industry in Cornwall. The company can speak with authority, as it is the sole producer and exporter of the county's traditional salted pilchards.

However, it was not fish but the exceptionally clear natural light that drew Stanhope Forbes to Newlyn in the 1880s. He was soon joined by other artists, keen to experience the joys of painting outside. The **Newlyn School** of art was founded with the help of other artists such as Lamorna Birsh, Alfred Munnings and Norman Garstin, and, today, it is art that brings most visitors to the town.

A mile down the coast lies **Mousehole** (pronounced 'Mowzel') which was described by Dylan Thomas, who honeymooned here in 1937, as "the loveliest village in England". Though peaceful and picturesque today, Mousehole has a history that is both long and, at times, turbulent. Visited by the Phoenicians in 500 BC, the village

Smugglers Restaurant

12-14 Fore Street, Newlyn,
Cornwall TR18 5JN
Tel: 01736 331501
e-mail: smugglersnewlyn@btconnect.com

When the Turner family relocated from London to Cornwall in 2003, they fulfilled two ambitions, to live by the sea and to open their own restaurant. On the quayside next to the harbour and the fishing fleet, **The Smugglers Restaurant** provides a warm, traditional ambience, with fine linen and sparkling crystal, for enjoying some of the best food in the region. With the fishing boats landing their catch just moments

away, it is not surprising that seafood is the speciality, and the kitchen is equally adept at preparing simple classics and dishes with Mediterranean or eastern influences.

Typical choices on the mouthwatering menu run from oak smoked fish cake with rocket salad and rémoulade sauce or a classic fish and shellfish soup with rouille and garlic bread for starters to grilled megrim sole with parsley butter, whole John Dory with capers, anchovy, rosemary and lemon, or steamed salmon with pak choi, five spiced potted crab and sesame seed soy dressing. A vegetarian main course is always available, along with meaty options such as rib eye steak or Cornish chicken breast with swede fondant and cassoulet of beans.

LAMORNA COVE

West Penwith, Cornwall TR19 6XQ
Tel: 01736 731734 Fax: 01736 732560

Situated between the beautiful beach of Porthcurno and the picturesque village of Mousehole, **Lamorna Cove** is a wonderful, rugged, short coastline that remains privately owned. Famous in the past for its granite quarry, this isolated hamlet was immortalised by the artist Lamorna Birch who was one of the Newlyn School of Artists attracted to this cove between 1880 and 1910. It was also a beloved place for Alfred Mullings, Nancy Mitford, John le Carré the spy novelist and the author Derek Tangye.

Today, the tiny hamlet and the cove remain in private hands and the owners, welcome visitors to enjoy this jewel of the South West Cornish coast. For holidaymakers, there are two holiday homes here: Sunny Vale 2 and Harbour View. Overlooking the famous little harbour, from where the granite

was shipped years ago, Harbour View is a spacious first floor flat, very comfortable for four adults, although not suitable for young children. In addition to two guest bedrooms, there is a fully fitted kitchen, a large bathroom and a sitting room with picture windows and a patio so that guests can look out over the beautiful cove whatever the weather.

Meanwhile, Sunny Vale 2 lies not far away on rising ground. From here too, there are glorious views out across this beauty spot. A semi-detached cottage dating back to the mid 19th century, this attractive holiday home, with two bedrooms and two bathrooms, provides spacious and luxurious accommodation of the same high standard as Harbour View but with the added advantage of a small garden.

The ground floor of the building that houses the Harbour View flat is taken up with the celebrated Lamorna Cove Café and the cove's Gift Shop. Described by one of the national Sunday newspapers as having the "best crab and fish soup in England", this is no ordinary café where a cup of tea and a sticky bun are all that is on offer. The bracing sea air is enough to give anyone an appetite and not only does the café offer a wonderful menu of tasty dishes but everything here is prepared in-house

using only the very best of local produce. As well as the savoury dishes, there is Penzance cake – a rich fruit cake flavoured with cinnamon, ginger and rum – and a wonderful home-made apple and blackberry pie, served hot with clotted cream, that is to die for! A very popular place with walkers making their way along the South West Coastal Path, this well-recommended café alone is enough to encourage discerning diners to make their way to Lamorna Cove.

SANDPIPER GALLERY

2 Carn Topna, Mousehole, Penzance, Cornwall TR19 6QE
Tel: 01736 732441
e-mail: sandpiper@blue-earth.co.uk

A beautifully renovated cottage overlooking the harbour is the setting for one of the most interesting galleries in the whole region. **Sandpiper Gallery** is owned by Sue Marshall, a talented weaver and craftswoman whose sons and daughter-in-law are skilled in many arts and crafts, including painting, photography, pottery, jewellery and furniture making. The open-plan ground floor is a showcase for an eclectic range of work in various media, much of it by local artists, and the ever-changing display is supplemented by regular exhibitions.

These have recently included Landscapes of Cornwall and Wales by Peter Perry; Domestic Pottery by David Garland; Woven Tapestry by Sue Spooner and others; Moving Magic, with a fascinating collection of automata; and Four Marshalls - three generations of artists-craftsmen from St Ives. Dylan Thomas, who honeymooned in Mousehole in 1937, described it as "the loveliest village in England". Countless visitors since then would not disagree with this view, and Sandpiper Gallery provides one more reason to spend time in this delightful place.

was ransacked some 2,000 years later by the Spanish in 1595. The villagers saw the attack as the fulfilment of the prophecy inscribed on **Merlin's Rock**:

> *There shall land on the Rock of Merlin*
> *Those who shall burn Paul, Penzance*
> *and Newlyn.*

ST BURYAN

5 miles SW of Penzance on the B3283

The landscape around this village is dominated by the 14th century tower of one of the finest churches in Cornwall. It also provides a day mark for shipping around Land's End. To the north of St Buryan is the isolated **Boscawen-Un Stone Circle**, whose central standing stone is an attractive leaning pillar of sparkling quartz.

To the southwest and sheltered in a shallow valley is the unspoilt hamlet of **Treen**. A short walk away is the spectacularly sited Iron Age coastal fort, **Tretyn Dinas**. Also on this headland lies the famous **Logan Rock**, a massive 60-ton granite boulder that was once so finely balanced that it could be rocked by hand.

PORTHCURNO

7½ miles SW of Penzance off the B3315

Protected by **Gwennap Head** and **Cribba Head**, it was from this dramatic cove, in 1870, that the first telegraph cable was laid linking Britain with the rest of the world. The **Porthcurno Wartime Telegraph Museum**, housed in a secret underground wartime communications centre, explains the technology that has been developed from Victorian times to the present. This interesting village is also home to the **Minack Theatre** (see panel on page 20), founded by Rowena Cade in the 1930s, an open-air amphitheatre cut into the cliff.

THE MINACK THEATRE

Porthcurno, Penzance, Cornwall TR19 6JU
Tel: 01736 810694 Fax: 01736 810779
e-mail: info@minack.com
website: www.minack.com

Surely one of the most spectacular and unusual theatres in the world, the **Minack Theatre** is an open-air amphitheatre cut into the cliffs at Porthcurno. The place has the look of something the Romans might have built above the rocky crag ('Minack' in Cornish means 'a rocky place'), but Minack was the brainchild of one very determined lady, Rowena Cade. Between 1931 until her death in 1983 she planned, built and financed the theatre. She had built a house for herself and her widowed mother on the headland, and used the garden for plays and entertainment by her family and friends. She had a strong ambition to stage more ambitious productions, and looking down into the gulley below the house she envisaged a stage and some simple seating.

Over the next decades, World War II intervening, the stage and the seating took shape, hewn by Rowena and a handful of helpers from granite. Since The Tempest was first produced in 1932, the plays of Shakespeare have provided a central focus to every season, but Minack has seen, and continues to see, a great variety of summer productions, with the Pirates of Penzance a great favourite. A Visitor Centre selling refreshments and gifts is open throughout the year.

LAND'S END

9 miles SW of Penzance on the A30

Mainland Britain's most westerly point and one of the country's most famous landmarks, it is here that the granite of Cornwall finally meets the Atlantic Ocean in a series of savage cliffs, reefs and sheer-sided islets. It is officially 874 miles from John O'Groats in the far north of Scotland, and both locations are part of the Heritage Great Britain plc Group. Land's End has been a tourist destination since the early 19th century, and down the years an ever-expanding complex of man-made attractions has been added to the majestic scenery that nature has

Sunset at Land's End

Lanyon Quoit

Rock **Lighthouse**, seven miles away. Over the centuries this has become a place of legends, believed to be the entrance to Lyonesse, the fertile kingdom that stretches from here to the Isles of Scilly.

SANCREED

3½ miles W of Penzance off the A30

The best example of an ancient Celtic Cross in Cornwall stands nine feet high in the churchyard of 15th century **St Credan's Church**. In the surrounding area are two Bronze Age monuments, the **Blind Fiddler** and the **Two Sisters**. Like many Cornish menhirs, they are said to represent humans turned to stone for committing irreligious acts on the Sabbath.

provided. Notable among these are an exhibition telling the story of the men of the RNLI and state-of-the-art displays of local tales and legends and the lives of the Cornish farmers and craftsmen. From this headland can be seen **Longships Lighthouse**, just off shore, and **Wolf**

YEW TREE GALLERY

Keigwin Farmhouse, Morvah, Penzance,
Cornwall TR19 7TS   Tel: 01736 786425
website: www.yewtreegallery.com

Close to the rugged coastline of southwest Cornwall, on a former farm near the tiny hamlet of Morvah, is a gallery unlike any other. **Yew Tree Gallery** is the creation of Gilly Wyatt Smith and is its third incarnation. Gilly first opened in Derbyshire in 1971 and later moved to Gloucestershire. On a visit to an artist friend near Zennor she became convinced that she had to be in Cornwall

and set about looking for premises. She came across Keigwin Farmhouse quite by chance and proceeded to transform the semi-derelict buildings into the gallery, which opened to visitors in the spring of 2002. The Gallery is open during exhibitions - please ring to check.

Her holistic approach gives the gallery a truly distinctive feel, and the nucleus of the regularly changing exhibitions is usually an artist whose work explores the relationship with the environment. Once that is in place she looks for complementary work by artists in other media to complete the exhibition. The two light, bright indoor spaces are just part of the gallery experience, as the garden and grounds are also full of interest, with some very special features including an organic potager and a duck pond. Sculptures are displayed on the lawns, and there are more to discover in the secret walled garden.

Bosllow

Distance:	4.0 miles (6.5 kilometres)
Typical time:	180 mins
Height gain:	70 metres
Map:	Explorer 102 & Landranger 203
Walk:	www.walkingworld.com ID:1052
Contributor:	Dennis Blackford

Access Information:

From Penzance take the B3311 road to Madron and continue towards Trevowhan. 2½ miles along this road look for the 'Men-an-Tol' studio on your left and park in the parking area on the opposite side of the road. On this road you will pass the ancient healing well just outside Madron and Lanyon Quoit a bit over one mile further on.

From the St Just to St Ives road - turn at Trevowhan (approximately five miles from St Just) onto the Madron road. Approx one mile along this road look for the 'Men-an-Tol' studio on your right.

Description:

This walk takes you up onto Ding Dong Moor and visits ancient stone monuments. The first is The Men-an-Tol which is an ancient healing site about 6,000 years old and where sick or infertile people pass through the holed stone. Secondly we visit Men Scyfa. This is an inscribed stone marking the grave of a warrior killed near this spot around 500AD. Next we pass the group of stones known as the 'Nine Maidens', which would have been used for various religious rites throughout the year. The age of this stone circle is unknown but is thought to have been redundant by 1250BC. The more modern building of Ding Dong Mine is next, although there has been a mine here for over 2,000 years and legend has it that the young Jesus was brought here by his uncle Joseph of Arimathea. Finally we visit Lanyon Quoit, a

classical monument whose massive stones were erected over 6,000 years ago. Those who are interested can also visit the ancient healing well just outside Madron, where even today hundreds of people tie tokens on the branches (please use biodegradable ones, plastics do not work!)

Additional Information:

This walk is on open moor so be sure to take 'moor care' and wear stout walking shoes and take an extra layer of clothing; a thin waterproof cagoule is most useful to keep out wind or rain. There are many old mine shafts and cave-ins in this area, so keep to the paths and be careful with children and dogs.

Features:

Hills or fells, wildlife, birds, flowers, great views, butterflies, industrial archaeology, moor, ancient monument.

Walk Directions:

1 From the car park go through the gate leading to a farm track.

2 About one kilometre up the track, go over the small stone bridge and steps signed 'The Men-an-Tol'. After visiting the Men-an-Tol return to the farm track and continue on up the track. The Men-an-Tol is an ancient healing site about 6,000 years old where sick or infertile people pass through the holed stone.

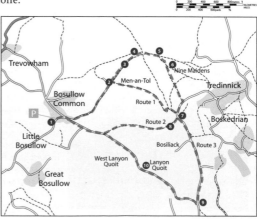

3 About another ½km up the track there is a stone stile to the left of a metal gate; this leads to Men Scyfa. This is an inscribed stone marking the grave of a warrior killed near this spot around 500AD. This 1.8-metre stone is the same height as the warrior, although part is now underground. Return to the track and continue on up.

4 The track now curves to the left, but you should take the path leading straight on past a ruined building on the left and up to a metal gate. Pass through the gate and follow the path straight on up and over the moor.

5 The track is well-worn so is easy to follow. Remember that there are many old mine shafts and cave-ins in this area, so keep to the paths and be careful with children and dogs.

6 On the bend, look for the small path between the large rock and the small tree on your left; this will lead you up to the tor. After exploring the tor return to Dr Blackall's Drive and continue along it. A few hundred metres further on you will pass Aish Tor up on your left.

7 Having reached the engine house of Ding Dong Mine and looked around, there are three ways back. The shortest and best route is to walk to the end of the spoil heap in front of the mine and find the well-worn path to the NW of it (right-hand side when facing the heap from the engine house). This path

meanders back to the Men-an-Tol, which, although out of sight for most of the way, is in line with the farm on the valley wall roughly midway between the farm on the horizon left and the tor on the right. From the Men-an-Tol, retrace your steps back to the car park. To visit Lanyon Quoit drive towards Madron, where you can also visit the Holy Well and Celtic Chapel.

8 The second route is very rough going especially in late summer and autumn, due to bracken and brambles. Take the smaller track past the engine house entrance and pass under the wooden pole onto a grassy path. Pass through the gate at the end and follow the field boundary on your left, down to the bottom of the hill and then another field boundary wall on your right as you ascend the hill to Lanyon Quoit. After visiting the Quoit go over the stone stile to the road and turn right to follow the road back to the car park (approx 1 kilometre).

9 The third route is the longest and has a lot of road walking. Follow the wide farm track past the mine and onto the metalled farm road down to the main road from Madron (approx 1.5 kilometres).

10 Turn right and follow the road back to the car park (approx 2.5 kilometres), passing Lanyon Quoit on your right about halfway along (see picture on page 21).

To the southwest of the village is **Carn Euny**, a fascinating Iron Age courtyard farming settlement that was founded in 200 BC. By far the most impressive building here is the **Fogou** which was first discovered by miners in the 19th century and takes its name from the Cornish for 'cave'. This underground chamber was constructed in three separate stages, and the 65ft room was entered by a low 'creep' passage at one end. Immediately west of Carn Euny is **Bartinney Downs**, a large area of heathland where programmes are in place to preserve both wildlife habitats and archaeological sites and historic features, including old china clay works,

abandoned quarries and the ruins of Bartinney Castle.

St Just

6½ miles NW of Penzance on the A3071

The westernmost town in mainland Britain, St Just was a copper and tin mining centre and the surrounding area is littered with industrial remains. A narrow road leads from this rather sombre town westwards to **Cape Cornwall**, the only cape in England, passing the last remains of Cape Cornwall mine – its tall chimney. On the southern side of this headland lies **Priest's Cove**, a quiet boulder strewn beach while, further along, the **South**

NORTH INN

The Square, Pendeen, Penzance,
Cornwall TR19 7DN
Tel: 01736 788417
e-mail: ernestjohncoak@aol.com

The **North Inn** is a 17th century hostelry with a creeper-covered front and an open-plan bar running the whole width of the building. It's carpeted throughout, with lots of beams and panelling, exposed stone and a mixture of traditional furnishings. John Coak, the experienced host, is a local man with a very friendly, sunny disposition that pervades the whole place, and he has made the inn a great favourite with the locals and the large number of tourists who come to this lovely part of the world. Darts and euchre are the favourite pub games, and major sporting events are shown on

a TV screen. The North Inn is CAMRA's Cornwall Pub of the Year for 2003, so real ale enthusiasts will always find plenty of choice, including many ales from the St Austell Brewery.

Comprehensive menus cater for all tastes and appetites, from bar snacks to full meals, and the curry nights are always guaranteed to bring in the crowds. Food is served from noon - 2.30pm and from 6.30pm - 8.30pm, and there's a non-smoking eating section at the back of the bar. There's plenty of off-road parking at the front, while out at the back, the seaward side, the large lawn is dotted with picnic benches.

The inn has recently added another string to its bow. A separate new building houses four en suite guest bedrooms, all with TV, tea tray, hairdryer, - everything for a comfortable stay, whether on a business visit or on holiday. Also available are camping facilities with toilets. The coast is very close by,

with magnificent views and wonderful walks towards St Just and Land's End in one direction and Zennor and St Ives in the other. Pendeen itself is a very interesting place with a tin mining heritage that goes back to prehistoric times. Its many attractions include the Geevor Tin Mine and Heritage Centre, the Levant Steam Engine, Pendeen Lighthouse and the 19th Century Church of St John the Baptist, built of local stone by local hands and modelled on the cathedral on the Isle of Iona.

West Coast Path follows the cliff tops.

St Just marks the start (or the end) of **The Tinners' Way**, an ancient track way between the town and St Ives. The track follows ancient moorland paths that were certainly used more than 2,000 years ago and may originally have been part of a network of paths dating to Neolithic times.

To the northwest of the town lies **Botallack**, where the remains of Three Crowns Mine stand on the picturesque clifftop. Here, tunnels were cut over half a mile out to sea, under the seabed, to extract rich copper lode.

To the northeast lies **Pendeen**, where tin has been mined since prehistoric times. The last of 20 or so mines in this area, **Geevor Tin Mine and Heritage Centre**, was a working mine until as recently as 1990. It not only preserves the mine but offers visitors the chance to experience the conditions of miners underground. Close by, housed in a tiny building perched high on the cliff, is the National Trust-owned **Levant Steam Engine**, once again producing power. Further to the north, on the slate promontory of **Pendeen Watch**, stands **Pendeen Lighthouse**, which has been guiding ships for nearly a century.

REDRUTH

This market town owes its past prosperity to its location at the heart of Cornwall's mining industry. Some pockets of Victorian, Georgian and earlier buildings can still be found. Redruth was also the home of the Scottish inventor William Murdock, who is famous for such innovations as coal-gas lighting and vacuum powered tubes. His home was the first private house to have gas lighting, in 1792.

THE GEM & JEWELLERY WORKSHOP

St Johns Terrace, Pendeen, Penzance,
Cornwall TR19 7DP
Tel: 01736 788217

On the B3306 coast road between St Ives and Land's End, the **Gem and Jewellery Workshop** is located in traditional stone buildings that were once stables and farm premises. Rodney and Maureen Hobbs came to Pendeen at the heart of the Granite Kingdom many years ago and have developed the workshop into one of the most important heritage attractions in the area.

In his workshop, Rodney, a Somerset man and an engineer of great talent in many aspects of craftwork, uses granite and gemstones and silver to produce beautiful jewellery and high-quality gifts, and in the adjoining shop rock and mineral specimens are for sale, along with rock tumblers, geology hammers and books and maps pertaining to the locality and its minerals.

In the same group of buildings is the Pendeen Mining Museum, where visitors can see working models of local mines and trace the history of mine production in the Pendeen area. The workshop and exhibition are open all year except Sundays and entrance is free.

Immediately south of the town lies dramatic **Carn Brea**, a granite hill that rises some 738 feet above sea level and crowned by a 90-foot monument to Francis Basset, a local, benevolent mine and land owner. Once the site of an early Neolithic settlement, Carn Brea is also home to a small, part-medieval castle and it is still the site of the pagan ritual of the Midsummer Bonfire ceremony.

To the north, along the coast, lie the two thriving holiday centres of **Porthtowan** and **Portreath**. Although they developed as a copper mining village and ore exporting port respectively, they are now both the preserve of surfers and families during the summer season.

Just to the southeast of Redruth is the mysterious **Gwennap Pit**, a round, grass-covered amphitheatre, thought to have been created by the collapse of a subterranean mine shaft. Once used as a pit for the staging of cock fights, this curious theatre is sometimes known as the 'Methodist Cathedral' as John Wesley preached here on many occasions.

AROUND REDRUTH

St Agnes
6 miles NE of Redruth on the B3285

Once known as the source of the finest tin in Cornwall, this old village still retains many of its original miners' cottages and grander mine owners' houses. Of particular interest is the steeply terraced row of 18th century cottages known as **Stippy-Stappy**. Surrounding the village are the ruins of old mine workings including the clifftop buildings of one of Cornwall's best known mines – **Wheal Coates**. Now in the hands of the National Trust, the

mine operated between 1860 and 1890 and the derelict **Engine House** is one of the more exceptional landmarks along this stretch of coast. Walkers should beware of the mass of abandoned mine shafts that litter the area but the walk to the remains of **Wheal Kitty** provides panoramic views over this once industrial area. Visitors coming to this now popular seaside resort can learn more about the village's heritage through the displays on mining, seafaring and local natural history at the **St Agnes Parish Museum**. Visitors with an interest in learning about the tin production processes should take one of the guided tours around **Blue Hills Tin Streams** at nearby **Trevellas**.

Renowned as the birthplace of the Georgian society painter, John Opie, St

Wheal Coates

Agnes was also introduced to thousands through the Poldark novels of Winston Graham – in which the village appeared as *St Ann*. From the village a footpath takes walkers out to **St Agnes Head** and **St Agnes Beacon**. Here there are spectacular views over the old mine workings and also remains from both the Bronze and Iron Ages. Now the home of some rare and localised plants and a wide variety of bird life, this area is criss-crossed by footpaths and is owned by the National Trust.

For industry of a very different kind, the **Cider Farm** just south of nearby **Penhallow** offers a tour of the orchards. Visitors can sample some of the over 40 fruit products made here, including jams, country wines and both cider and traditional scrumpy. The **Cider Museum** tells the history of cider making through displays of old equipment and artefacts.

PERRANPORTH

8½ miles NE of Redruth on the B3285

This pleasant holiday resort, with its three-mile stretch of golden sand, was, at one time, a pilchard fishing and mining village that also harboured smuggling gangs. Though little has survived from those days, the small town's Celtic heritage is still remembered during the annual **Lowender Peran Festival**, which brings all the Celtic nations together through music and dance.

High up in the dunes overlooking Penhale Sands, **St Piran's Oratory**, a ruined 6th or 7th century building constructed on the site of St Piran's grave, lay beneath the sand until it was uncovered in 1835. The shifting sands have once again claimed the remains and a simple plaque now marks the burial place of the saint, who is said to have travelled from Ireland to the Cornish coast on a millstone.

ST ALLEN

9½ miles NE of Redruth off the A30

As with many parts of the country with a Celtic tradition, Cornwall has its own 'little people' – the *piskies*.

One legend tells of a boy from St Allen who failed to return home after going out to pick flowers in a nearby wood. His frantic mother began a search and eventually he was found, three days later, dazed but unharmed. All the boy could remember was being led deep into the forest, to a fantastic cave filled with jewels, and being fed the purest honey by the piskies.

Just to the north of St Allen, at the village of **Zelah**, lies **Chyverton Garden** which is centred around the grand Georgian house of a wealthy local mine owner. The garden is renowned for its rhododendrons, the first of which were planted in 1890, and its magnolias, camellias and conifers.

POOL

2 miles W of Redruth on the A3047

Now consumed into the Camborne and Redruth conurbation, this village was very much at the heart of Cornwall's mining industry. The **Cornish Mines and Engines**, owned by the National Trust, shows the two huge engines that were used to pump water from the mines. At the **Industrial Discovery Centre**, the secrets of the county's dramatic heritage are revealed.

Before the days of steam, heavy work was carried out by horses, and the **Shire Horse Farm and Carriage Museum**, at nearby **Treskillard**, pays a living tribute to these gentle giants. The Museum has an interesting collection of private carriages and horse-drawn commercial vehicles, farming implements and hand tools from days gone by.

CAMBORNE

3 miles W of Redruth on the A3047

Once the capital of Cornwall's tin and copper mining area, in the 19th century the land around Camborne was the most intensely mined in the world. In the 1850s, over 300 mines were producing some two thirds of the world's copper. However, the discovery of extensive mineral deposits in the Americas, South Africa and Australia led to the industry's decline in Cornwall in the early 20th century when it became no longer economically viable. Before the industry took off in the 18th century, Camborne was a small place and the traces of rapid expansion can still be seen in the numerous terraces of 18th and 19th century miners' houses.

As the town's livelihood has depended on mining for several hundred years, it is not surprising that Camborne is home to the world famous **School of Mining**. Its **Geological Museum** displays rocks and minerals from all over the world. Outside the town's library is a statue to Richard Trevithick, a talented amateur wrestler known as the Cornish Giant, who was responsible for developing the high pressure steam engine, the screw propeller and an early locomotive that predated Stephenson's Rocket by 12 years.

To the northwest of Camborne lies **Godrevy Point**, whose low cliffs mark the northern edge of St Ives Bay, a well-known beauty spot from where seals can be sighted offshore. Just off the point lies **Godrevy Island** with the lighthouse that featured in Virginia Woolf's novel *To the Lighthouse*. Much of the coastline from Godrevy eastwards to **Navax Point** is owned by the National Trust and the clifftops support some of the botanically richest maritime heath in Europe.

FALMOUTH

A spectacular deep-water anchorage that is the world's third largest natural harbour, Falmouth lies in Britain's Western Approaches and guards the entrance into Carrick Roads. First settled centuries ago, it was not until the 17th century that the port was properly developed, although Henry VIII, a hundred years earlier, sought to defend the harbour from invasion. Standing on a 200ft promontory overlooking the entrance to Carrick Roads, Henry's **Pendennis Castle** is one of Cornwall's great fortresses. Along with St Mawes Castle on the opposite bank, it has protected Britain's shores from attack ever since its construction. Strengthened further during the threat of a second Spanish Armada, Pendennis was one of

Godrevy Point and Island

Pendennis Castle

fortress is explained.

During its heyday in the early 19th century, Falmouth was the home of almost 40 packet ships, which carried cargo to every corner of the globe. The introduction of steam-powered vessels put paid to Falmouth's days as a major port and, by the 1850s, the packet service had moved to Southampton. Although the docks continue to be used by merchant shipping, the town's traditional activities are being overshadowed by yachting and tourism. Falmouth's nautical and notorious past is revealed at the **National Maritime Museum Cornwall** (see panel on page 31), where the wealth of displays explain the rise in popularity

the last Royalist strongholds to fall during the Civil War. It remained in use until the end of World War II. Now under the ownership of English Heritage, the castle is a fascinating place to visit. Through a variety of displays and exhibitions, the 450-year history of the

THE STICKY PRAWN

Flushing Quay, Falmouth, Cornwall TR11 5TY
Tel: 01326 373734 Fax: 01326 373698
e-mail: paullight@hotmail.com

Londoner Paul Lightfoot is putting years of international experience in the catering and hospitality business to excellent use at **The Sticky Prawn**, which he has owned and run since 1999. A great favourite with both locals and visitors, it stands on the water's edge, overlooking the River Fal on a jetty built centuries ago by the Dutch. It serves as bar, café and restaurant, open for morning coffee, lunch and dinner. Inside, stone walls, beams, simple wooden furniture and nautical bric-a-brac create a friendly, inviting ambience, and when the weather is kind, the outside tables are in great demand. Paul's sons give him fine support, and one of them, Ben, is the senior chef.

Not surprisingly, Ben's menu puts the emphasis on fish, landed daily by local boats, but there's no

shortage of choice for meat-eaters, with raw materials sourced as far as possible from Cornish suppliers. Oysters, mussels and superb crevettes are always popular among the daily specials, which might also include grilled lemon sole, halibut, medallions of monkfish and sea bass with a red pepper dressing. There are always some imaginative meaty options, and in season nothing can beat a finale of Cornish strawberries with Cornish clotted cream! Parking is available right outside, but a delightful alternative is to arrive by water taxi – pick-ups can be arranged from various local points.

TALL SHIPS TRADING

49 Church Street, Falmouth, Cornwall TR11 3DS
Tel: 01326 318888
e-mail: info@tallshipstrading.co.uk
website: www.tallshipstrading.co.uk

The sea-blue frontage with a nautical flag fluttering over the door gives a strong hint of what **Tall Ships Trading** is all about. John and Louise Spargo transformed what used to be a travel agency into a delightful shop selling a wide range of things nautical. With their background in interiors and their passion for Cornwall, they have made a wonderful job of the conversion, and their shop has become a focal point for both local people and visitors to the town.

The stock includes items large and small, from seascapes and paintings of racing yachts to model yachts, ships in bottles, flags and pennants, mobiles and hanging ornaments, pine and custom-painted furniture, globes of all sizes, telescopes, brass clocks and barometers, lifeboat mirrors and casual outdoor wear. The goods are displayed in cabinets, on dressers and shelves and counters – even on an old rowing boat which stands tipped on its end against a wall, its seats now a charming and appropriate display case for craftwork and bric-a-brac. Opening hours are 10am to 5pm Monday to Saturday, also 11am-4.30pm on Sundays in high season.

BESIDE THE WAVE GALLERY

10 Arwenack Street, Falmouth, Cornwall TR11 3JA
Tel: 01326 211132 e-mail: gallery@beside-the-wave.co.uk
Fax: 01326 212212 website: www.beside-the-wave.co.uk

Beside the Wave Gallery is located in one of the main streets of Falmouth opposite the church. Housed in a Regency building overlooking the sea, the business was started in 1989 by Lesly Dyer and her family, providing a new venue to show the work of leading contemporary artists and potters. Several of Cornwall's best-known artists now exhibit regularly at the

gallery, including John Dyer, Ted Dyer, Mike Hindle, Amanda Hoskin, Paul Jackson, Robert Jones, Sue McDonald, Neil Pinkett, Joanne Short, Andrew Tozer, Richard Tuff and Andrew Waddington. Impressions of Cornwall through these and many other artists have drawn customers from far and wide to the gallery.

For anyone who loves art and Cornwall, Beside the Wave always has a great deal to offer. Special exhibitions are held throughout the year; some feature the work of individual artists, while others are mixed shows by selected gallery artists – these are the Easter, Summer and Christmas Exhibitions. Opening times are 9am to 5.30pm Monday to Saturday, also 10am to 4pm on Sunday in July and August. The gallery manager is Dr Ryya Saunders. Many of the artists whose work is shown here also feature in London exhibitions: in 2003 Beside the Wave held London exhibitions at Gallery 27 in Cork Street and at the Affordable Art Fair in Battersea Park.

Falmouth Beach

of the town due to the packet ships. Pirates and smugglers were also drawn to Falmouth and, on **Custom House Quay**, stands an early 19th century brick-built incinerator known as the **Queen's Pipe**. It was here that contraband tobacco seized by Falmouth's customs men was burnt. As well as carrying cargoes around the world, the ships coming into Falmouth also brought

NATIONAL MARITIME MUSEUM

Discovery Quay, Falmouth,
Cornwall TR11 3QY
Tel: 01326 313388 Fax: 01326 317878
e-mail: enquiries@nmmc.co.uk
website: www.nmmc.co.uk

December 2002 saw the opening of a major new attraction on the waterfront at Falmouth. The **National Maritime Museum** has been designed for broad appeal, with a wide range of hands-on displays, a superb collection of small boats, demonstrations of boat-building, lectures, a research library, a meteorology gallery, remote-control scale-model boats, exhibitions that tell the story of Cornwall's unique maritime heritage and a waterside café. For many, the highlight will naturally be the Museum's collection of 120 historic British and international boats, many of which had been in storage for years; these are supplemented by contemporary vessels, prototypes and future designs. 30 of these craft will routinely be sailed from the NMMC's own jetties.

PANDORA INN

Restronguet Creek,
Mylor Bridge, Nr Falmouth,
Cornwall TR11 5ST
Tel: 01326 372678

General Manager David Adams and his staff welcome friends old and new at the **Pandora Inn**, one of the best-known inns in Cornwall, set in the beautiful surroundings of Restronguet Creek. The setting is superb and the ambience inside the thatched inn is splendidly traditional, with lots of snug corners, low wooden ceilings, panelled walls, flagstone floors, a log fire in winter, an ancient black kitchen range and a variety of maritime memorabilia. When the sun shines, the tables and chairs on the pontoon outside come into their own.

A full range of drinks is served in the bars, and food is served either in the bars or upstairs in the more formal surroundings of the restaurant. Food is taken very seriously here, and the lunchtime and evenings menus are supplemented by daily specials chalked up on blackboards. Old Pandora favourites that are always on the menu are crab cakes, crab thermidor, Mediterranean fish stew, chicken curry and Mylor Bridge sausages served with Cornish apple chutney and French fries. These are the choice of many, while others consult the blackboards for specials such as cod in beer batter, fillets of sea bass with a basil and asparagus sauce, mushroom stroganoff, beef lasagne or breast of Barbary duck with a red wine and sour cherry sauce.

Parts of the inn date back to the 13th century, when there was a farm on the site. The building later became known as the Passage House, and a 15th century document notes that a passing-boat was kept here, it being the post-road and the nearest cut from Falmouth to Truro. After an accident in which the ferry boat sank with the loss of several lives, the inn changed its name to The Ship. It was renamed the Pandora in memory of the naval ship sent to Tahiti to capture the Bounty mutineers. The

vessel struck a remote part of the Great Barrier Reef in 1791 and sank with the loss of many lives, both crew and mutineers. The Captain was court-martialled on his return to England and retired to Cornwall, where he is alleged to have bought the inn. This wonderful old hostelry lies at the end of a series of narrow lanes off the A39, but the superior way to arrive is by boat, tying up at the pontoon that extends out into the creek. The Pandora Inn and the Rising Sun at St Mawes are the jewels in the crown of the St Austell Brewery.

THE TONY WARREN MARITIME GALLERY

32 Arwenack Street, Falmouth, Cornwall TR11 3JB
Tel/Fax: 01326 313929 e-mail: PeterSoden@mns.com
website: www.tonywarrengallery.co.uk

Peter and Teresa Soden moved from Oxfordshire to run this delightful shop specialising in gifts with a maritime theme. **The Tony Warren**

Maritime Gallery is located on one of the town's main streets. Inside you will find an amazing range of all things nautical, from many beautiful Tony Warren prints to an extensive range of model ships, yachts, and canal boats. You will also discover lighthouses, seagulls, lamps, clocks, bells, barometers and lobster pots, plus many other gifts.

The shop, which trades all year, retains the name of Tony Warren, who was a Falmouth artist renowned for his beautiful paintings of ships and the sea. Tony died in the 1994, but many fine quality prints are always available framed or unframed and occasionally originals are offered for sale. The business offers a mail order facility. Opening hours are 10am to 8pm during the summer and 10am to 5.30pm the rest of the year.

exotic plants from the Far East, Australia and the Americas; these have found their way into many private gardens as well as the town's four public gardens.

AROUND FALMOUTH

MYLOR

2 miles N of Falmouth off the A39

The two attractive villages of **Mylor Churchtown** and **Mylor Bridge** have now blended into one another as a yachting and water sports centre. It was at Mylor Churchtown that the packet ships called and in the village's ancient churchyard lie the graves of many sea captains. In the churchyard, too, by the south porch, stands a 10-foot **Celtic Cross** which is one of the tallest in Cornwall. Just to the southwest lies another popular yachting centre,

Flushing, which was given its distinctive look by Dutch settlers from Vlissingen who arrived here in the 17th century.

FEOCK

4 miles N of Falmouth off the B3289

This is one of the prettiest small villages in Cornwall, and there is a pleasant creekside walk to the west. This follows the course of an old tramway, which dates from the time when this area was a bustling port. To the south of the village lies **Restronguet Point** and the 17th century Pandora Inn, named after the ship sent out to capture the mutineers from the *Bounty*.

From **Tolverne**, just north of Feock, Allied troops left for the Normandy coast during the D-day landings. On the shingle beach the remains of the concrete honeycombed mattresses can still be seen. While in the area General Eisenhower stayed at **Smugglers Cottage**

PENHALE COTTAGES

Trevilla House, Feock, Truro, Cornwall TR3 6QG
Tel: 01872 862369 Fax: 01872 870088
e-mail: jinty@trevilla.com
website: www.trevilla.clara.net

Penhale Cottages lie within a quiet country estate in an Area of Outstanding Natural Beauty next to the National Trust's Trelissick Gardens. Approached along a secluded drive shared with the privately occupied Penhale House, the charming traditional Cornish stone cottages

offer comfortable, characterful self-catering accommodation for 2, 4 or 6 guests. Each of the adjacent cottages is attractively decorated, with simple furnishings and fitted carpets, and fully equipped with nightstorage heaters, TVs, videos, microwaves and open fires - wood is provided. They share a garden and a laundry room, and other amenities include a table tennis table (bats and balls provided in each cottage); dinghy facilities can be provided by arrangement.

The south-facing cottages are in a courtyard that originally contained the coach house and stable yard of the former dower house to Trelissick. The famous King Harry Ferry is close by, and the cottages are an excellent base for exploring the many gardens and the scenic, historic and sporting and leisure attractions the region has to offer. Owner Mrs Copeland welcomes well-behaved children, but pets are not allowed.

COME TO GOOD FARM

Feock, Truro, Cornwall TR3 6QS
Tel/Fax: 01872 863828
e-mail: sue.james1@tesco.net

Come to Good Farm is situated in a beautiful valley between Truro and Falmouth. It is the home of Sue and Robin James, along with hundreds of sheep, two sheepdogs, a cat and numerous chickens and ducks. The farmhouse is a converted barn with guest accommodation in a warm, comfortable en suite double bedroom with TV and tea/coffee making facilities. Another guest bedroom is available in a separate outbuilding. Breakfast is served in the farmhouse kitchen, and guests have the use of a lounge in which to relax and plan the day's activities.

This is excellent walking country, and a footpath through the valley follows an old road between Penelewey and Penpol Creek. Other attractions include several interesting Cornish gardens close by, and the farm itself is a birdwatcher's delight, with blue and great tits, song thrushes, tawny owls and buzzards all regular visitors, and ravens nesting each year in the pine trees in the old quarry. The farm is diagonally opposite the famous Come to Good Quaker Meeting House, which holds services each Sunday morning.

SMUGGLERS COTTAGE OF TOLVERNE

Tolverne, Philleigh, Nr Truro, Cornwall TR2 5NG
Tel: 01872 580309
website: www.tolverneriverfal.co.uk

Smugglers Cottage, a lovely Grade II listed thatched cottage dating back over 500 years, stands in a unique and stunning location on the River Fal. Between mid-May and mid-October the cottage and gardens offer morning coffee, home-made light lunches, home-made cream teas and Pasty Suppers (during high season only). Much of the food has that lovely "home-baked" touch, earning the Cottage a superb reputation. Its history goes back to the 15th century, when it was the home of Bessie who operated the ferry on this river crossing on the London-Penzance route. However the Cottage is now the home of Peter and Elizabeth Newman and their son Rhos runs the passenger boat "Cornish Belle" from Tolverne to Falmouth and back, three times daily (except Sunday) with a very informative commentary about the history of the river and places of interest.

In the Second World War as part of the build-up to the D-Day invasion. Tolverne, with its deep-water facilities, was chosen as a place where allied forces could load troops, guns, tanks and other equipment in preparation for the D-Day landings, and the road, the hard and the slipway were all constructed for the occasion. The cottage was requisitioned by the Admiralty and Eisenhower visited the troops at the cottage. The Newmans have assembled a fascinating collection of maritime paintings, prints and other memorabilia, much of it relating to the D-Day episode. One room is given over to the *SS Uganda*, which saw service as a hospital ship in the Falklands conflict after being an educational cruise ship for many years.

PROSPECT HOUSE

1 Church Road, Penryn, Cornwall TR10 8DA
Tel: 01326 373198
e-mail: prospecthouse@cornwall-selectively.co.uk
website: www.cornwall-selectively.co.uk

If the idea of a relaxing holiday in a lovely part of the world appeals, Mrs Carolyn Hartley will offer you a warm welcome and pleasant stay at **Prospect House**. It has three en suite bedrooms for bed & breakfast accommodation, two doubles, and a twin with TV, tea/coffee making

facilities and very comfortable furnishings. A handsome breakfast room looks out on to the walled garden, with small lawns, shrubs and roses; a separate Victorian greenhouse can also be enjoyed within the garden. The house, which is set back from the road on the edge of the town centre, was built in Georgian style in 1840.

Carolyn's husband is a Merchant Navy Officer, so it is appropriate that the house was originally built for a seafaring captain at a time when Penryn was a busy seaport. At one time, locally quarried granite was shipped from here to all parts of the world and was also used for many fine Tudor, Jacobean and Georgian houses that can be seen in Penryn. A leisurely stroll around the town's conservation area is well worth while, and tourists will find Prospect House an ideal base, with Falmouth, Truro and the delights of coast and countryside in easy reach.

Trelissick Gardens

Distance:	4.4 miles (7.0 kilometres)
Typical time:	180 mins
Height gain:	50 metres
Map:	Explorer 105
Walk:	www.walkingworld.com ID:1513
Contributor:	Jim Grindle

Access Information:

Trelissick is four miles south of Truro on the B3289. Buses T7 and 89B run from Truro where there is a railway station.

Description:

Trelissick House is in an enviable position with rivers on three sides, and this walk will enable you to see all of them - Lamouth Creek to the north; the Fal to the east; and Carrick Roads to the south, all three part of the complex Fal estuary. You begin by entering the park and dropping to the river which is followed through woods to King Harry Ferry. Further woodland paths are succeeded by open views of the estuary before a gentle climb back through the park to the starting point.

Additional Information:

The first house was built here in about 1750 and went through many hands with much development of the gardens which were acquired by the National Trust in 1955. Among the notable restoration by the Trust has been the re-planting of the once famous orchards with many old Cornish varieties of apple . The best place for seeing birds is between Waymarks 6 and 7. Between 7 and 8 is a sizeable Iron Age Promontary Fort, while at 8 is Roundwood Quay. This was built in the 18th century to ship tin and copper, and in past days there were buildings for smelting and refining and many wharves. There was a malt house, lime-kilns and ship-building yards, a busy place compared to the tranquillity that you will find there now. Since 1888 the King Harry Steam Ferry Company has operated a ferry which pulls itself across the

Fal by chains but the motive power is now diesel. It is thought that a ferry has existed since the Norman Conquest. Between Waymarks 10 and 11 watch for large sea-going vessels at anchor; some are waiting repair, others are more permanently anchored for economic reasons or because they have been impounded by customs for drug smuggling for instance, or are the subject of litigation.

Features:

River, toilets, stately home, National/NTS Trust, wildlife, birds, flowers, great views, butterflies, cafe, gift shop, food shop, good for kids, industrial archaeology, nature trail, restaurant, tea shop, woodland, ancient monument.

Walk Directions:

1 The kiosk is where you pay for car parking. Take the tarmac path next to it - it is signposted 'Woodland Walks.' Go through a gate next to a cattle-grid (Waymark 12) and follow the tarred path to a junction.

2 Turn right and stay on this driveway until at the edge of a wood you reach another cattle-grid.

3 Go through the gate at the left of the grid and then turn to the right on a path going

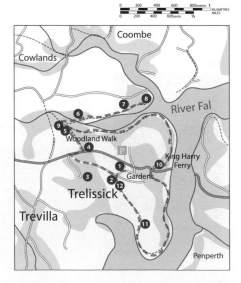

uphill. This will bring you to one of the lodge-gates on the estate.

4 Pass the lodge and go through the green gate. Cross the road and go through the matching gate on the other side. Follow a gravel track which zig-zags downhill, passing a bench on one corner. When it straightens out there is a stream on the left, with pools made for the cultivation of water-cress. In a few metres you meet another track at right-angles. At this point is a low notice in cast metal with directions - for people going the other way.

5 Turn left and you will see a footbridge over the stream that you have been following. Cross it, and on the other side the track forks again.

6 Take the right fork which follows Lamouth Creek which is below you on your right. (When the tide is out this is a good spot for waders and where we saw the egret more than once.) The woods become no more than a strip of trees with a field visible on the left, until you reach the next wood. There is an entrance of kinds here formed from two low stone banks.

7 There are several unmapped paths here. The simplest way is to take the right fork beyond the entrance. The path goes over the ditch and then straight through the rampart of the Iron Age fort before joining the other track

where you turn right. Just before the quay you go down a few steps and emerge into the open.

8 This is a magical spot and you could spend some time here looking for the remains of the old industries. When you have had enough, retrace your steps over the bridge back to Waymark 5.

9 Now continue with the river on your left for 1.5km. You will reach a steep flight of steps leading down to the road you crossed earlier. The ferry is just to your left, and opposite is a white house with a flight of steps going up on its right.

10 This is Bosanko's Cottage. The track that you have been on continues on the far side. Only one track branches off to the right away from the river and your way is signposted. This is the section where you might see the anchored boats; in fact you are quite likely to hear their auxiliary engines first. The track clears the woods to give beautiful views of the river, much of it used for rehearsing the D-Day landings of 1944. 1.5km from the ferry you leave the woods by a kissing gate.

11 This is where you re-enter the parkland. Go up the hill with the iron fence on your right and at the top cross the drive which enters Trelissick House. In a few moments you will reach the exit from the car park, recognised by the cattle grid.

12 Go through the gate on the right to complete the walk.

Trelissick Gardens

(see panel on page 35) and today this simple house holds a large collection of memorabilia from that era.

Close by lies the estate of **Trelissick**, a privately owned 18th century house, surrounded by marvellous gardens and parkland with wonderful views over Carrick Roads. While the house is not open to the public, the estate, which is owned by the National Trust, offers

GILI TRADING

10 Cathedral Lane, Truro, Cornwall TR1 2QS
Tel: 01872 263030 Fax: 01872 263737
e-mail: info@gilitrading.com
website: www.gilitrading.com

Gili Trading is a very special shop. It is special because it sells beautiful unique furniture. It is also special because it brings Indonesian culture and craftsmanship into the heart of Truro.

Gili is the Indonesian word for island and Debbie Harris, who established and runs Gili Trading with her husband Arie, chose the name because her home is on Lombok - an island to the east of Bali.

Inspired by the beauty of the Indonesian islands and their way of life, Debbie and Arie have worked hard to develop a business that literally spans the globe. Using highly skilled local craftsmen in village cooperatives and their own employees in a Bali workshop, they manage a production process that starts with the purchase of reclaimed or otherwise certified timber from responsibly harvested plantations and ends, some months later, in a spectacular display of high quality, competitively-priced, furniture and handicrafts in a two-storey shop in Cornwall.

All the wood used in the manufacture of each Gili piece has, where necessary, been seasoned and kiln-dried to a moisture content appropriate for the UK environment.

Debbie and Arie visit Britain regularly but, whilst they are busy in Indonesia, management of the Truro shop is overseen by Debbie's parents - making Gili Trading a truly trans-world family concern .

Customers to the Truro shop are encouraged to browse and touch the wide variety of furniture available. The range includes beds, dining suites, chests, desks and cabinets. Items in glass, wrought iron and other materials are also on display - as are accessories and handicrafts personally chosen by Debbie to complement the furniture.

Gili Trading is the only link between its island craftman and the UK customer, so personal service is a vital part of the business. Gili staff will always do their best to help anyone with a particular requirement and there is no obligation to buy a product that has been requested if it doesn't wholly satisfy.

Nor is there any need for a Gili customer to worry about getting their purchases home. Deliveries can be arranged throughout the UK and - fittingly for a business that unites two cultures - can also be arranged worldwide.

So, when you're in Truro, do call in: you won't be hassled - but you will undoubtedly be impressed.

visitors tranquil gardens of exotic plants and the chance to walk the miles of paths through its extensive park and woodland. Various outbuildings have been converted into restaurants, an art and craft gallery and a gift shop.

TRURO

8 miles NE of Falmouth on the A39

This elegant small town at the head of a branch of the River Fal is the administrative and ecclesiastical centre of Cornwall. It expanded from its ancient roots in medieval times on the prosperity originating from local mineral extractions. It was one of the first towns to be granted the rights of stannary, and several small medieval alleyways act as a reminder of those busy times before the silting up of the river saw Truro decline

Truro Cathedral

as a port and be overtaken by Falmouth. It was a fashionable place to rival Bath in the 18th century, and the short-lived recovery in mineral prices at that time saw the creation of the charming Georgian streets and houses that are still so attractive today.

The arrival of the railway in 1859 confirmed Truro's status as a regional

SAFFRON

5 Quay Street, Truro, Cornwall TR1 2HB
Tel: 01872 263771
e-mail: saffronrestaurant@btconnect.com
website: www.saffronrestauranttruro.co.uk

A passion for food and drink led Nik and Traci Tinney to open **Saffron** in January 1999, since when their style of cooking, their eclectic menu and the informal, welcoming ambience have made it a popular venue for locals as well as visitors to Truro. In a side

street just off the centre, in an old part of town, the cheerful flower-decked frontage promises a warm welcome, and inside, the scene is set by flagstone floors, mirrors and straight-backed chairs set at scrubbed wooden tables. All the dishes are cooked to order from fresh seasonal ingredients, including the best available Cornish produce, and the keen owners offer a menu that keeps an eye on healthy eating – they are fully paid-up members of the Campaign for Real food.

Everything tempts on menus that are excitingly and intriguingly different, as shown by roast garlic and patty pan soup, twice-baked spider crab soufflé with chive clotted cream and roast loin of lamb with beetroot mousse and rosemary jus. The enjoyment level stays sky high right to the end with scrumptious desserts, and the brilliant food is complemented by interesting wines and beers. Summer Seafood Specials feature oysters, mussels, tiger prawns, langoustines, lobsters and spider crabs. Saffron is a non-smoking restaurant.

CLIFTONS GUEST HOUSE

46 Tregolls Road, Truro, Cornwall TR1 1 LA
Tel/Fax: 01872 274116
e-mail: enquiries@cliftonsguesthouse.co.uk
website: www.cliftonsguesthouse.co.uk

After spending 27 years in the Isles of Scilly , Peter and Sarah Conisbee now run a delightful guest house in a quiet location back from the main access road into Truro from the east (A390). **Cliftons Guest House** is a distinguished greystone Victorian house offering bed & breakfast accommodation in six well appointed bedrooms – two

doubles, three twins and a single, one of the doubles is situated on the ground floor. All are en suite and have TV, radio-alarm clock, hairdryer and decent toiletries.

A comfortable residents' lounge is available throughout the day, and guests wake up to an excellent breakfast with plenty of choice – the full English with hash browns and black pudding, smoked haddock, bagels with smoked salmon and scrambled eggs, vegetarian sausages, or a light Continental with croissants and preserves. Cliftons is a very pleasant and civilised base for discovering the delights of Truro at leisure or for venturing further afield to the county's top attractions such as the Eden Project, Tate St Ives and Cornwall's spectacular gardens. The owners operate a no smoking policy.

PHOENIX

Quay Street, Truro, Cornwall TR1 2GA
Tel: 01872 277666 Fax: 01872 276111
e-mail: dbg321@hotmail.com

David Blackman changed direction in the early 1990s when he gave up a career in the upmarket side of engineering to open **Phoenix** with his wife Lolly. Located in one of the older shopping areas of Truro, now largely pedestrianised, this delightful shop stocks an amazing variety of household goods and gifts to suit all pockets, ages and occasions.

The windows displays attract many passing strollers inside, where they will find the stock on show on shelves and tables, on the floor – even hanging on hooks from the ceiling.

The range really is impressive, from greetings and special occasion cards to prints and pictures, photo frames, pots and bowls and vases, fashion jewellery, candles, traditional and contemporary lighting, soft furnishings and imported furniture. With many years in a professional environment, David and Lolly know the importance of customer service, and the care and concern they show guarantees that a visit here will always be a pleasure. The owners have four other outlets in the county.

HALL FOR CORNWALL

Back Quay, Truro, Cornwall TR1 2LL
Tel: 01872 262466 Fax: 01872 760246
e-mail: admin@hallforcornwall.demon.co.uk
web: www.hallforcornwall.co.uk

In 1991 Cornwall started a campaign for its own professional theatre, and today **Hall For Cornwall** attracts theatre- and concert-goers from all over the south west. Dance, music, theatre and children's shows all feature on the bill in the 1,000-seat auditorium, which has seen visits from the likes of Coldplay, the Royal Shakespeare Company, the Rambert Dance Company and top West End shows, plus the very best local productions. *Joseph and the Amazing Technicolor Dreamcoat*, by Tim Rice and Andrew Lloyd Webber, was the first West End musical to be staged here, in 2001, and returned in triumph in the summer of 2003. Other West End hits performed here to sell-out crowds include Willy

Russell's *Blood Brothers*, the blockbuster *Buddy* and the award-winning comedy *Stones in his Pockets*. Fascinating Aida were here as part of their farewell tour, and other recent highlights included Tasmin Little with the European Union Chamber Orchestra and the second annual *Last Night of the Cornish Proms*.

Every year there are 250 to 300 performances, with over 150,000 tickets sold every year. The venue has a strong commitment to education, and every week it stages three youth workshops, voice workshops and dance workshops. The aim is to involve people of all ages from all over Cornwall in arts and theatre-making activities, and the schools programme offers workshops, projects, forums and resource materials throughout the year. As well as all the live shows, the workshops and all the other events, Hall for Cornwall has a fine restaurant and bustling coffee shop and is also host to the city's popular flea markets.

The present building, on the site of Truro's first market hall, dates from 1846, with remodelling in 1925 to accommodate a stage. Through the 1960s and 1970s the hall deteriorated and Carrick District Council broached the idea of selling the site for redevelopment. A campaign led by the distinguished singer Benjamin Luxon, Chris Warner and some Carrick councillors resulted in Carrick granting a lease on the Hall and in 1991 the group took over the property, which was in an advanced state of decay. In 1996 the contractors moved in to work on the high-tech venue. The work took 18 months and the inaugural performance took place in November 1997.

2WENTYTHREE

23 River Street, Truro, Cornwall
Tel: 01872 223003

Close to Truro's Museum on River Street there is **2wentythree**, a fabulous new boutique specialising in women's clothing.

Every piece is individually picked by Ali and Jenna who both have a background in design and a passion for wearable clothes.The look is smart casual with clothes and bags from Orla Kiely, linens and fine knits from Marilyn Moore, nostalgic prints from Saltwater, a selection from Denmark with CCDK and 120% Lino famous for excellent cut linen in sublime colours.

The delicious display of jewellery, made by local jewellery designers, works well alongside current clothing collections.

An exciting shopping experience is in store for you at 2wentythree! Open from 9.30am to 5.30pm Monday to Saturday.

VERYAN GALLERIES

Veryan Green, Truro, Cornwall TR2 5QQ
Tel: 01872 501469
e-mail: info@veryangalleries.co.uk
website: www.veryangalleries.co.uk

Anthony and Yvonne Allkins came to the area several times on holiday, and when they visited **Veryan Galleries** they immediately fell in love with it. They found that it was for sale, so they bought it and gradually moulded it to their style and personality. It is a thriving centre for arts and crafts and a showcase for the work of artists and craftspeople, most of them from Cornwall or Devon. The impressive Long Gallery attached to the owners' thatched residence is a lovely display area with a stunning trompe

l'oeil mural at one end by Alldex Murals-commissions can be arranged .

The ever-changing items on display cover a wide variety of media and subject matter, including landscape, marine, mining, botanical, figurative and abstract. Besides the paintings, the Gallery displays prints, cards, ceramics, pottery, silks, woodcraft and garden sculpture. Solo exhibitions are held on a regular basis throughout the year, there is a delightful informality about the gallery, which is situated on the eastern side of the charming village of Veryan. Opening times are 10am to 5.30pm Tuesday to Saturday. Closed January.

TREWITHEN GARDENS & NURSERIES

Grampound Road, Truro, Cornwall TR2 4DD
Tel: 01726 883647 Fax: 01726 882301
e-mail: gardens@trewithen-estate.demon.co.uk
website: www.trewithengardens.co.uk

On the A390 midway between Truro and St Austell, **Trewithen Gardens** are internationally famous for the superb collections of magnolias, camellias and rhododendrons, but the visitor will find many other attractions. Trewithen was developed by George Johnstone at the time of the great plant hunting expeditions in the first decades of the 20th century, and the astonishing seed collections obtained on these expeditions were the basis of the magical 28-acre woodland garden seen today. George Johnstone's greatest gardening achievement is the Main Lawn, where besides the glorious magnolias and rhododendrons are numerous rare and interesting shrubs and trees.

But at Trewithen there are highlights at every turn, including a camellia walk, a sunken garden, a walled garden, a beech wood and a beautiful magnolia fountain. The nurseries produce some of the finest quality plants and shrubs in Cornwall, and the 1,500 varieties include many bred from the original species introduced to the garden. The garden is open Monday to Saturday March to September, also Sundays in April and May. The formal walled garden and the outstanding 18th century house are open Monday and Tuesday afternoons April to July. The Nurseries are open all year.

capital. In 1877, it became a city in its own right when the diocese of Exeter was divided and Cornwall was granted its own bishop. The foundation stone of **Truro Cathedral** was laid by the future Edward VII in 1880. This splendid Early English style building, with its celebrated Victorian stained glass window, was finally completed in 1910. Housed in one of Truro's fine Georgian buildings, the **Royal Cornwall Museum** covers the history of the county from the Stone Age to the present day. At the city's **Art Gallery**, Cornwall's links with the art world are maintained.

Truro combines a pleasant modern city with an attractive shopping centre with living historic traditions. During Advent, wassailers continue the age-old custom of circulating through the streets, drinking from a decorated wassail bowl and collecting money for charity.

VERYAN

8 miles NE of Falmouth off the A3078

Set within a wooded hollow, this charming village is famous for the five **Roundhouses** that lie at its entrance. Built in the early 19th century for the daughters of the local vicar, the cottages'

TRENONA FARM HOLIDAYS

Trenona Farm, Ruan High Lanes,
Nr Truro, Cornwall TR2 5JS
Tel/Fax: 01872 501339
e-mail: info@trenonafarmholidays.co.uk
website: www.trenonafarmholidays.co.uk

Trenona Farm is a 250-acre working mixed farm run by David and Pamela Carbis with their two young children. David runs the farm, while Pamela takes excellent care of her guests, offering the choice of bed & breakfast accommodation in the farmhouse or self-catering in two cottages within the grounds. Guests are welcome to see the farm's beef cattle and breeding ewes at close quaters and to explore the woodlands and streams that run through the land. A network of paths lead inland and to the coast (three miles), and most of Cornwall's major attractions are within an easy drive.

Bed & Breakfast is available in the farmhouse, which dates from around 1850, where there are four guest bedrooms, all of which are doubles or family rooms sleeping up to four guests. All the rooms have TV, clock radios and tea/coffee making facilities and three have en suite bathrooms whilst the fourth has a private bathroom adjacent. Downstairs there is a guest lounge with TV and board games, and a separate dining room where a full English or Continental breakfast is served around the large antique dining table. Guests have the use of the garden and patio area with picnic benches. Smoking is restricted to this area. Children and pets are welcome.

Self-catering accommodation is available throughout the year in two renovated barns centrally situated near the main farmhouse. Both have wheelchair access and pets are also welcome by prior arrangement. **Chy Tyak** sleeps up to eight guests (plus cot). There is a double master bedroom with en suite bathroom and two twin-bedded rooms upstairs. Downstairs, all the modern comforts and conveniences are provided, from comfortable, high-quality furnishings to pro-logic TV, video, CD player, payphone on private line, dishwasher, fridge/freezer, washer/drier, coffee maker, microwave and full electric fan oven. The kitchen is resplendent in hand-made fitted pine, and the lounge has a double bed settee and matching suite. **Chy Whel** is a single storey cottage and sleeps up to six guests in three en suite bedrooms (a double and two twin bedded rooms). The open plan lounge/kitchen/diner has all the modern comforts as in Chy Tyak. Both properties also have private gardens with patio and lawn areas and ample parking nearby with room for boats or trailers and under cover storage for bicycles.

ROSELAND HOLIDAY COTTAGES

Crab Apple Cottage, Portscatho, Nr Truro,
Cornwall TR2 5ET
Tel/Fax: 01872 580480
e-mail: enquiries@roselandholidaycottages.co.uk
website: www.roselandholidaycottages.co.uk

Fifty prime properties sleeping from two to 12 are on the
books of **Roseland Holiday Cottages**, a holiday letting
and management agency run by a young team headed
by Leonie and Rick Iddison. They all have excellent local
knowledge and can guide visitors to the perfect choice
in this very pleasant and beautiful part of the country. There are historic towns and villages to discover,
miles of countryside to explore and plenty of safe sandy beaches for families with children.

At many points along the coast, boats and moorings
can be hired. The area covers St Mawes, St Just in Roseland,
Portscatho, Gerrans, Veryan and Portloe, each of which
has its own charm and character. The same is true of the
cottages, all of which are provided with everything needed
for an independent, carefree holiday. The majority have
gardens and private parking. At either end of the range are
The Beach House (sleeps two, in an exceptional location
above sandy Porthcurnick Beach, and Cuilan (sleeps 12), a
large modern house overlooking the Percuil River, with
large gardens, a games room, steps down to the beach, a
private foreshore and moorings available to rent.

THE ROYAL STANDARD

5 The Square, Gerrans, Portscatho, Nr Truro,
Cornwall TR2 5EB Tel: 01872 580271
e-mail: mikeroyalstandard@supanet.com

Boxes and baskets of geraniums adorn the attractive cream
and red frontage of **The Royal Standard**, where Welshman
Mike Davies and his family have a warm greeting for all
their customers. The atmosphere inside the 18th century
premises is friendly and cosy, and among the decorative
features are period pictures and prints, coins and
banknotes, badges and trophies, ceramic and glass
measuring jugs and a framed collection of beer taps.
Outside, picnic benches are set out on the lawn at the back. Two real ales and a guest head the drinks
list, and other offerings include a large selection of single malts.

No one ever goes hungry at the Royal Standard, as an
excellent choice of food is available that caters for all
appetites, from lunchtime sandwiches and jacket potatoes
to light meals such as steak or cheese pasty, ham, egg and
chips or homemade Lamb Rogan Josh. Full meals are also
served throughout the day, and the main menu,
supplemented by a specials board, offers classics such as
garlic mushrooms, grills and steak & kidney pie, along
with such delights as pan-fried mussels with coriander,
chilli, lemon grass and garlic, or chicken in a mild coconut
and red pepper sauce.

THE RISING SUN

The Square, St Mawes, Cornwall TR2 5DJ
Tel: 01326 270233 Fax: 01326 270198
e-mail: therisingsun@btclick.com
website: www.innsofcornwall.com

Luxury, elegance, personal service and superb cuisine are just some of the many qualities that have made the **Rising Sun** one of the most sought after places to stay in the whole of the county. The inn enjoys an unrivalled location right by the water's edge, and the high standards for which it has become renowned are maintained by the top team of John Milan, proprietor of several top St Austell Brewery houses, experienced General Manager Roy Readman and master chef Ann Long.

The eight en suite bedrooms, each with its own individual character and named after famous local gardens, provide style, comfort and the modern conveniences expected by today's guests; some enjoy

glorious sea views. The inviting bar offers three draught ales, lagers and keg beers and an excellent range of wines and spirits, along with more than two dozen single malt whiskies and very good bar lunches. On fine days the terrace is a perfect spot for enjoying a drink while watching the world sail by, and at any time the residents' lounge is a civilised, peaceful retreat for reading a book, writing a letter or planning the day's activities.

The non-smoking restaurant, with its pastel green decor, spotless table linen and comfortable wicker chairs, is a bright, convivial setting in which to relish the delicious food prepared by Ann Long and her kitchen brigade. Ann has for many years been at the top of her profession, and her reputation has spread far beyond Cornwall. She is constantly seeking to provide new and innovative dishes, and her cooking is based on the finest available fresh West Country produce including locally landed fish and shellfish. Typical dishes on her fixed-price two or three

course menus run from kedgeree cake with a quail's egg centre to a puff-pastry topped fish pie with cod, brill and salmon; best end of lamb with chargrilled vegetables and couscous; and, for dessert, vanilla and lavender pannacotta set on mango and raspberries. The fine food is complemented by a well-chosen wine list that includes a good choice of house wines by bottle or glass.

The Rising Sun is a superb base for a holiday, whether for touring, for total relaxation, for gentle strolls round the local sights or for something more active: St Mawes is a popular sailing centre, and sailing lessons and various water sports can be arranged at reception.

circular shape is believed to guard the village from evil as there are no corners in which the Devil can hide.

Eastwards, on the coast, lies the unspoilt fishing village of **Portloe** whose tiny harbour is completely overshadowed by steep cliffs. To the south lies **Carne Beacon**, one of the largest Bronze Age burial mounds in the country.

PORTSCATHO
4½ miles NE of Falmouth off the A3078

This pleasant, unspoilt fishing village, with its sandy beach on Gerrans Bay, may appear familiar to anyone who watched the TV drama, *The Camomile Lawn*, as it was used as a location. To the west, at **St Just in Roseland**, lies an exquisite 13th century church, surrounded by gardens containing many subtropical trees and shrubs, first planted by the botanist John Treseder at the end of the 19th century.

ST MAWES
2 miles E of Falmouth on the A3078

This charming town, a popular and exclusive sailing centre in the shelter of Carrick Roads, is dominated by its artillery fort, **St Mawes Castle**. Built in the 1540s as part of Henry VIII's coastal defences, it is a fine example of Tudor military architecture. The castle's cloverleaf, or trefoil, design ensured that, whatever the direction of an attack, the castle could defend itself. However, a shot was never fired from here in anger and today visitors can look around the Tudor interiors which are in remarkably good condition.

From the town, ferries take passengers across the river to Falmouth and, during the summer, a boat also takes passengers down the river to the remote and unspoilt area of Roseland around **St Anthony**. From **St Anthony Head**, the

THE GREEN LANTERN

6 Marine Parade, St Mawes, Cornwall TR2 5DW
Tel: 01326 270878 Fax: 01326 270594
e-mail: info@thegreenlantern.uk.com
web: www.thegreenlantern.uk.com

The Green Lantern offers the double delights of superb food and a charming location on the seafront just out of the busy town centre. Christopher Waite, his wife Carolyn, and Chef de Cuisine Andy Mason opened the restaurant in the summer of 2002, and soon established it as a favourite destination of discerning diners. Behind a pretty flower-decked frontage, the room is elegant and relaxing, with pastel colours, lightwood furnishings and stylish table settings.

The menu makes exciting reading, and the food does not disappoint. The chef combines technical perfection with a well-judged sense of adventure in superb dishes such as pan-roasted duck foie gras and vanilla-poached rhubarb with watercress and crisp shoestring celeriac cake, or pan-fried scallops and Cornish lobster with spring peas, butterbean and Jurusalem artichoke fricassee and Champagne sauce. Desserts such as Braeburn apple and almond galette bring a memorable meal to a perfect conclusion, and the fine food is accompanied by an expertly selected choice of wines. The restaurant is open for dinner and also for Cornish cream teas during the summer. Booking for dinner is strongly recommended.

St Mawes Castle

walks, St Anthony Head, owned by the National Trust, is also home to the remains of a military battery in use right up until the 1950s.

MAWNAN SMITH

3 miles SW of Falmouth off the A39

Just to the west of this pretty village lies **Glendurgan Garden**, created in the 1820s in a wonderful wooded valley that drops down to the shores of the Helford estuary. Containing many fine trees and exotic plants, children will enjoy the famous **Heade Maze**, created in 1833 from laurels, and the **Giant's Stride** – a maypole.

southernmost tip of the Roseland peninsula, there are wonderful views across Carrick Roads. At the foot of the headland lies **St Anthony's Lighthouse**, built in 1834 to warn sailors off the notorious Manacles rocks. An excellent starting point for a number of coastal

To the southeast, the tower of the 15th century church at **Mawnan** has been a local landmark for sailors for centuries. An excellent place from which to take in

ST ANTHONY HOLIDAYS & SAILAWAY ST ANTHONY

St Anthony, Manaccan, Helston, Cornwall TR12 6JW
Tel/Fax: 01326 231357
e-mail: info@stanthony.co.uk
website: www.stanthony.co.uk

Anthony Jenkin has restored old barns and cottages surrounding St Anthony's beautiful Norman church to provide comfortable, relaxing self-catering accommodation in the most delightful setting. The properties range from The Chalet, a single-level wooden chalet sleeping four to an old coastguard cottage with three bedrooms, and Lantinning Farmhouse, a Grade II listed farmhouse sleeping eight, located between the church on one side and the beach and creek on the other. The cottages are very comfortable and well equipped for all-year comfort; several have log fires and provide ideal accommodation for a winter break.

St Anthony, nestling in a suntrap on the shores of Gillan Creek, is a popular spot for a sailing holiday, and Sailaway St Anthony can provide sailing, motor and rowing boats for hire from St Anthony or Helford. These range from rowing dinghies and Wayfarer, Laser and Topper sailing dinghies to Drascombe Longboat sailing cruisers and diesel launches. Sailing tuition is available and moorings and launching facilities may be provided for guests bringing their own boats. The chandlers stock a super selection of the very best in sailing and summer clothing.

Boats at Helford

exotic plants and trees collected from around the world. Reaching maturity in the early 1930s and regarded at the time as one of the most beautiful in England, the garden was sold in 1939. Then began over 40 years of neglect before a massive restoration programme in the 1980s returned it to its original impressive state.

HELFORD
5½ miles SW of Falmouth off the B3293

the sweeping coastline, the tower was also used as a lookout post during times of war. Further up Helford Passage is the tiny fishing hamlet of **Durgan** along with the **Trebah Garden** that has often been dubbed the 'garden of dreams'. On land originally owned by the Bishop of Exeter, the owner at the time Charles Fox set out to create a garden of rare and

A picture-postcard village standing on the secluded tree-lined southern banks of the Helford estuary, Helford must have one of the most attractive settings in the whole of the county. Once the haunt of smugglers who took advantage of the estuary's many isolated creeks and inlets, this is now a popular sailing centre. During the summer, it is linked to

F N GARDNER ROCKING HORSES

New Inn Farmhouse, Traboe, St Martin, Nr Helston,
Cornwall TR12 6EA
Tel/Fax: 01326 231053
e-mail: fngardner@tiscali.co.uk
website: www.qualityrockinghorses.co.uk

Nick Gardner, whose varied working life includes a long period as a farmer, gave up the land some years ago to develop a new career as a maker of hand-crafted rocking horses. He runs **F N Gardner Rocking Horses** from his farmhouse home, which is set among rambling gardens in

the village of Traboe, a few miles southeast of Helston near the Helford River. In his workshop, he carries out the whole process, from bulk timber to the completed horse, making horses to order in various sizes, various woods and two basic styles – traditional dapple or natural wood which are french polished and waxed and come on bow rockers or safety swingers.

The bow rocker enables the horse to have a more stretched stance than when mounted on swinger. The horses can have either traditional fixed tack or fully removable saddle and bridle, and customers can specify certain details such as the colour of the mane and tail. Hand-tooled , no two horses are exactly alike, so a horse from the F N Gardner stable is truly unique, a wonderful gift that will last a lifetime.

ROSKILLY'S

Tregellast Barton, St Keverne,
Helston, Cornwall TR12 6NX
Tel: 01326 280479
Fax: 01326 280320
e-mail: admin@roskillys.co.uk
website: www.roskillys.co.uk

A splendid day out is for all the family is guaranteed at **Roskilly's**, a working dairy farm with a restaurant, ice-cream parlour, craft shop and accommodation. It has been in the Roskilly family since 1948, when Joe Roskilly came here to help his godmother. He married Rachel in 1960, and their three children, sons Jacob and Toby and daughter Bryn, all work on the farm, helping to run the business, making furniture and stained glass. The farm, which is located just south of St Keverne, occupies 130

acres made up of 33 little fields bounded by stone-faced hedges that are home to a wide variety of birds, bats, reptiles and unusual plants.

The farm's resident herd of 95 Jersey cows is bred for the high-quality milk used for the cream and ice cream for which the name of Roskilly has become renowned. The ice cream is made in the finest Italian machines in a variety of mouthwatering flavours, and skimmed milk is used to make low-fat yoghurt and yoghurt ices. Clotted cream also goes into the farmhouse fudge and the chocolate truffles that are on sale in the shop, along with apple juice and cider, jams, marmalades, mustards and chutneys, all made on the farm. Also on sale are the furniture and stained and moulded glass made by the family, and even the furniture polish is home-made, using wax from the farm's bees. A viewing gallery in the upper part of the farm allows visitors to watch the milking, and the old milking parlour has been turned into an excellent restaurant open every day in summer and at weekends during the winter. Roskilly's ponds and woodland provide leisurely walks that are filled with interest, and a well-defined circular walk takes in the ponds, the woodland, the old orchard and the meadows.

Roskilly's is a place where visitors can spend not just many a happy hour but many a happy day, and self-catering accommodation is provided in four cottages dotted about the farm, quite separate from one another and each with its own character. The cottages, sleeping from four to six or seven guests, are well equipped and very comfortable, and the open fires, with coal and wood supplied, keeps things snug even on chilly days. Just up the road from the farm is a caravan club site in a flat meadow with firm standings.

Helford Passage, on the northern bank, by a ferry that has been in existence since the Middle Ages. The deep tidal creeks in the area have given rise to rumours that this is the home of Morgawr, the legendary Helford monster. The first recorded sighting of Morgawr was in 1926 and ever since there have been numerous people who claim to have seen this 'hideous, hump-backed creature with stumpy horns'.

From the village, the five-mile **Helford River Walk** takes in several isolated hamlets and a 200-year-old fig tree in the churchyard at **Manaccan** before returning to the tea rooms and pubs of Helford. The rich mud of the Helford River, revealed at low tide, is a wonderful feeding ground for many birds including heron, cormorant and curlew, while the ancient natural woodlands along the shores support a wealth of plants and wildlife.

ST KEVERNE
7 miles SW of Falmouth off the B3293

Something of a focal point on this part of the Lizard Peninsula, the pleasant village of St Keverne is rare in Cornwall in that it has a handsome village square. Its elevated position has led to its church spire being used as a landmark for shipping attempting to negotiate the treacherous rocks, **The Manacles**, which lie offshore. In the churchyard, there are some 400 graves of those who have fallen victim of the dangerous reef. Just outside the village a statue commemorates the 500th anniversary of the **Cornish Rebellion** of 1497, while the church has a plaque in memory of the executed rebel leaders. Although St Keverne has been dominated by the sea for centuries, its agricultural heritage is continued in the ancient custom of 'Crying the Neck'. It was believed that

THE NEW INN

Manaccan, Nr Helston, Cornwall TR12 6HA
Tel: 01326 231323

The New Inn is a delightful thatched hostelry dating from the 16th century and set in a pleasant garden in the middle of the village of Manaccan. Inside, exposed stone, black-painted half-panelling, sturdy beams, scrubbed wooden tables and sporting prints create an atmospheric setting, and the warm, inviting feel is reinforced by the tenants Penny and Mark Williams, who have run the inn since 1996 with the essential

presence of Morsel the terrier – a real character ands very much part of the charm of the place. Real ales and other brews from the St Austell Brewery offer plenty of variety for quenching thirsts, and there's also an impressive choice of food on the printed menu and specials board, sourced locally as far as possible.

At lunchtime, the sandwiches are a popular quick snack, and the choice of almost 30 runs from old favourites such as cheddar cheese or egg mayonnaise to smoked salmon, ham with coleslaw and roast beef or chicken (depending on the Sunday roast served lunchtime and evening with all the trimmings). Other popular orders are smoked fish, pasties and pies, crab cakes, fish & chips, bangers & mash, sole and sea bass, with desserts ranging from lemon sorbet to sticky toffee pudding and strawberries & cream.

the corn spirit resided in the last wheatsheaf cut, which was plaited and hung over the fireplace until spring.

LIZARD

14 miles SW of Falmouth on the A3083

The most southerly village in mainland Britain, Lizard is a place of craft shops, cafés and art galleries and lends its name to the **Lizard Peninsula**. Physically separate from mainland Cornwall, the peninsula's unique attraction has caused it to be designated an Area of Outstanding Natural Beauty. The **South West Coast Path** follows the coastline, much of which is in the hands of the National Trust providing many opportunities for walkers of all abilities. In particular, there is a nine-mile, and sometimes strenuous, walk to Mullion that takes in some of the most spectacular scenery as well as passing lowland Britain's largest National Nature Reserve.

The Lizard is also known for its unique Serpentine rock, a green mineral that became fashionable in the 19th century after Queen Victoria visited Cornwall and ordered many items made from the stone for her house, Osborne, on the Isle of Wight. The village is still the centre for polishing and fashioning the stone into souvenirs and objets d'art.

To the south of the village lies **Lizard Point**, the tip of the peninsula, whose three sides are lashed by waves whatever the season. There has been a form of lighthouse here since the early 17th century. The present **Lighthouse** was built in 1751 despite protests from locals, who feared that they would lose a regular source of income from looting wrecked ships. It now houses a light that is one of the most powerful in the world.

Just to the northeast of Lizard is the very picturesque fishing village of **Cadgwith**. With its cluster of pastel coloured thatched cottages and two shingle beaches, it is everyone's idea of a typical Cornish village. Life has not always been so peaceful here as, in the 19th century, this was a busy pilchard fishing centre. In 1904, a record catch of nearly 1.8 million pilchards was landed in just four days! However, a small fleet of boats still sails from here, though their catch now is mainly lobster, crab, shark and mullet. Separating the main cove from Little Cove is **The Todden**, a grass covered mushroom of land. Nearby is the curiously named **Devil's Frying Pan**, a collapsed sea cave filled with water at high tide.

To the northwest lies the famous beauty spot, **Kynance Cove**, whose marvellous sandy beach and dramatic offshore rock formations have been a favourite destination ever since Prince Albert visited here with his children in 1846. The cove is the site of the largest outcrop of the Lizard Peninsula's curious Serpentine rock and the caves to the west of the cove can be explored, with care, at low tide.

Lizard Lighthouse

Kynance Cove

in telecommunications – the **Earth Satellite Station**. The largest such station in the world, there have been few world events that have not been transmitted or received through here since it opened in the 1960s. The guided tour around the station, which takes in all manner of telecommunications including the internet and videophone links, is a fascinating and rewarding experience.

MULLION
12 miles SW of Falmouth on the B3296

The largest settlement on the peninsula, Mullion is an ideal base from which to explore this remarkable part of Cornwall. A mile to the east lies the pretty, weather-worn harbour of **Mullion Cove**, and just up the coast is the popular sandy beach of **Poldhu Cove**. It was from the clifftops above the beach that, in 1901, the radio pioneer, Guglielmo Marconi, transmitted the first wireless message across the Atlantic. His Morse signal, the letter 's' repeated three times, was received in St John's, Newfoundland, quelling the doubts of the many who said that radio waves could not bend round the Earth's curvature. In 1903 Marconi was honoured with a visit by the future King George V and his wife, and in 1905 a daily news service for ships was inaugurated. In 1910 a message from Poldhu to the *SS Montrose* led to the arrest of the murderer Dr Crippen. A small granite obelisk, the **Marconi Monument**, was unveiled on the site of the wireless station by his daughter after the inventor's death.

Just a couple of miles inland, on the windswept heathland of **Goonhilly Downs**, is a monument to the very latest

GWEEK
8 miles SW of Falmouth off the A394

Gweek grew up as an important commercial port after Helston harbour became silted in the 13th century. The same fate befell Gweek years later although it retains its links with its maritime past and the old harbour is very much alive with craft shops and small boatyards. Just a short distance from the centre of the village along the north side of the creek, is the **National Seal Sanctuary**, the country's leading marine rescue centre established over 40 years ago. The sanctuary cares for sick, injured and orphaned seals, and visitors can witness the joyful antics of the seals at feeding time and explore the **Woodland Nature Quest** around an ancient coppiced wood.

HELSTON
10 miles SW of Falmouth on the A394

Dating back to Roman times, when it was developed as a port, Helston is the westernmost of Cornwall's five medieval stannary towns. During the Middle Ages, tin was brought here for assaying and taxing before being shipped. However, in the 13th century a shingle bar formed across the mouth of the River Cober, cutting off the port's access to the sea. Helston's long history has left it with a legacy of interesting buildings. **The Blue Anchor Inn** was a hostel for monks in the 15th century, while the 16th century **Angel House** was the former town house of the Godolphin family. In the 1750s, the Earl of Godolphin rebuilt the parish church. In the churchyard lies a memorial to Henry Trengrouse, the Helston man who invented the rocket-propelled safety line that has saved so many lives around the British coast. Elsewhere, there are a surprising number of Georgian, Regency and Victorian buildings, which all help to give Helston a quaint and genteel air. Housed in one of the town's old market halls, close to the classical 19th century **Guildhall**, is the **Helston Folk Museum**, which covers many aspects of the town's and the local area's history. The displays range from

FLAMBARDS THEME PARK

Helston, Cornwall TR13 0QA
Tel: 01326 573404
website: www.flambards.co.uk

An intriguing and unique attraction, **Flambards** has been entertaining visitors of all ages for more than 30 years with its award-winning exhibitions, exciting rides, family shows and glorious gardens. At the centre of the complex is the Victorian village, a faithfully re-created collection of lamplit streets and alleyways where visitors can peer into over 50 shops, watch traders at work and see how life both above and below stairs was carried on more than a century ago.

Each of the lifelike characters is authentically dressed in genuine Victorian costume, and the houses and shops are equipped and furnished with thousands of antique items. The famous chemist shop time capsule is particularly intriguing with its old medicines and cures that give a unique glimpse of dispensing long before the NHS. These fascinating displays are augmented by an audio tour that tells about the magic and misery of life in Victorian times.

Another top attraction here is an undercover life-size re-creation of a World War II blitzed street, avowed chillingly authentic by those old enough to remember those dark days and a source of wonder for others. This remarkable exhibition was opened by Dame Vera Lynn in 1984. 'Wedding Fashions

Down the Years' features a romantic assembly of changing styles, a collection of wedding dresses and wedding cakes from 1870 to 1970.

Rides and slides that range from the gentle to the adventurous keep the youngsters happy, and for older children and adults the figure-of-eight karting circuit offers the opportunity to put driving skills to the test. Some of nature's less cuddly creatures - birds, snakes and large spiders - can be seen close up at the Creepy Crawly Show, and the among the other attractions - the list is almost endless - are boats and bumper cars, fun buggies for toddlers and a science centre, and after all the excitement a stroll round the lovely gardens and the plant centre is the perfect way to end a visit.

archaeological finds and mineral specimens to the reconstruction of a blacksmith's shop, an 18th century cider mill and a farm wagon from 1901.

Still very much a market town serving much of the Lizard Peninsula, Helston has managed to escape from the mass tourism that has affected many other Cornish towns. However, the famous **Festival of the Furry**, or **Flora Dance**, a colourful festival of music and dance, does bring people here in droves. The origins of the name are unknown but it is clear that the festival has connections with ancient pagan spring celebrations as it is held in early May.

Just to the northwest of the town lies **Trevarno Estate and Gardens**, a beautiful and rare estate with a long history stretching back to 1296 when Randolphus de Trevarno first gave the land its name. Over the intervening centuries the gardens and grounds have been developed and extended so that, today, Trevarno is known as one of the finest gardens in a county, with a great gardening tradition. The estate's **Gardening Museum** complements the grounds and highlights the ingenuity of gardeners down the ages by the range of gardening implements exhibited.

To the east of the town lies another interesting and award-winning family attraction, **Flambards** (see panel opposite). Based around a faithful recreation of a Victorian street, it has numerous attractions for all the family. Close by is the Royal Navy's land and sea rescue headquarters at **Culdrose**, one of the largest and busiest helicopter bases in Europe. Since the base was established here in 1947 as *HMS Seahawk*, it has carried out a great many successful search and rescue operations. There are guided tours and a special viewing area from which the comings and goings of

the helicopters can be observed.

When the shingle bar formed to the west of the town in the 13th century and dammed the River Cober, it created the largest freshwater lake in Cornwall, **Loe Pool**. This is now owned by the National Trust and is a haven for sea birds as well as waterfowl such as mallard, mute swan, coot, teal and red-necked grebe. A Cornish folk tale links Loe Pool with the Arthurian legend of the Lady of the Lake. As at Bodmin Moor's Dozmary Pool, a hand is said to have risen from the depths of the water to catch the dying King Arthur's sword. Another local story connects **Loe Bar** with the legendary rogue, Jan Tregeagle, who was set the task of weaving a rope from its sand as a punishment.

PORTHLEVEN
12 miles SW of Falmouth on the B3304

This pleasant fishing town developed from a small village in the 19th century. In 1811, London industrialists built its three-section harbour to export tin and china clay and import mining machinery, and also to protect the growing fishing fleet. Although this scheme to establish Porthleven as a major tin-exporting centre failed, the inner basin of the harbour can still be sealed off to protect boats from the worst of the southwesterly gales. A number of the town's old industrial buildings have been converted into handsome craft galleries, restaurants and shops, and the charming old harbour is overlooked by an assortment of attractive residential terraces and fishermen's cottages. A popular and attractive town today, Porthleven is gaining a gastronomic reputation on account of the many excellent and tempting restaurants, cafés and inns to be found in such a small area.

THE NET LOFT GALLERY

The Harbour, Porthleven, Cornwall TR13 9JD
Tel: 01326 564010
e-mail: netloft@cornwall-art.co.uk
website: www.cornwall-art.co.uk

Since its opening on Boxing Day 1999, the **Net Loft Gallery** has established itself as a major focal point for connoisseurs of Cornish art. Situated in the courtyard to the rear of The Old Customs House Studio right beside the picturesque fishing harbour of Porthleven.

The Net Loft Gallery attracts the eye with its display of elegant stone sculptures and continues to impress with its unique selection of paintings by leading Cornish artists. The original contemporary art depicts landscapes, seascapes, abstracts and figurative

work in different styles and media by David Hosking, Andrew Giddens, award-winning Roy Lang, William Waite, Robert Bell, David Gray, Alec Oliver, Matthew Hedges, Lucy Russell as well as an "Artist of the Month" highlighting new paintings by a selected artist. Atmospheric photographs by Clive Vincent complement the gallery's exhibition as do the limited edition bronze sculptures by Sue Rhodes (Associate of the Royal Society of British Sculptors), Dorothy Brook and Len Gifford. Glass bowls and vases in vibrant colours, elaborate ceramics and designer jewellery for day or evening wear all add to the ambiance of The Net Loft Gallery.

JULIA MILLS GALLERY & WORKSHOP

Fore Street, Porthleven, nr Helston, Cornwall TR13 9HH
Tel: 01326 569340

A short distance from the charming old harbour at Porthleven lies **Julia Mills Gallery & Workshop**, which has attracted a steadily growing number of visitors since being set up in December 2000. A diverse and ever-changing range of contemporary art, ceramics, glass, jewellery and sculpture is on display. Julia's own speciality is working

with hand-blown glass and from this she creates atmospheric panels in a vast range of chiefly pastel colours. Inspired not only by the Cornish landscape but by Kaffe Fassett, Jane Ray and fairytale folklore, the panels are beautifully produced, very decorative and highly desirable.

Also on display are the works of associate Catherine Hyde, whose paintings combine symbolism derived from Greek, Norse, European and Welsh myths. The fish, stag and hare – ancient symbols with multiple layers of meaning – represent wildness, fertility and permanence; soaring between earth, sea and air, they leap through her landscapes, which resound with the profound connection between all living things. Catherine Hyde produces giclee prints from her paintings, printed in limited editions using light fast ink on high-quality acid-free papers.

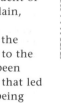

The town was visited on holiday by Guy Gibson, wartime commander of 617 Squadron, the renowned Dam Busters. A street in the town is named after him.

WENDRON

8½ miles W of Falmouth on the B3297

Close to this bleak village is one of the many mines that have been worked in this area since the 15th century. It has now re-opened as the **Poldark Mine Heritage Complex**, and visitors to this interesting attraction can take an underground tour of the tunnels, see the famous 18th century Poldark village and wander around the machinery exhibits, some of which are in working order.

ST AUSTELL

This old market town had for centuries been at the centre of the tin and copper mining industries. It was transformed in 1748, when William Cookworthy, a chemist from Plymouth, discovered large deposits of kaolin, or china clay, here. Cookworthy realised the importance of the china clay, which is a constituent of many products other than porcelain, including paper, textiles and pharmaceuticals. Over the years, the waste material from the clay pits to the north and west of the town has been piled up into conical spoil heaps that led to these bare, bleached uplands being nicknamed the **Cornish Alps**. More recently the heaps and disused pits have been landscaped with acid-loving plants, such as rhododendrons, and they now have gently undulating footpaths and nature trails.

Although china clay has dominated St Austell since it was first discovered, the town is also the home of another

THE EDEN PROJECT

Bodelva, St Austell, Cornwall PL24 2SG
Tel: 01726 811911
website: www.edenproject.com

Since its opening in May 2001, the **Eden Project** has been a huge international success, bringing many thousands of visitors and much needed revenue to Cornwall. It began with the simple idea of telling the story of how the whole world relies heavily on plants, and from that has sprung what has been called one of the wonders of the modern world.

The Project is the brainchild of a former record producer Tim Smit, who started to formulate the idea when driving around the china clay district in 1994. An abandoned china clay pit just outside St Austell has become home to the largest conservatories ('biomes') in the world where, in the space of a day, visitors can walk from steamy rain forests to the warmth of the Mediterranean in a project that aims to "promote the understanding and responsible management of the vital relationship between plants, people and resources". In the huge Humid Tropic Biome, 787 feet in length and 180 feet high, orchids, sugar cane, rubber trees, tea and coffee plants, bananas and pineapples flourish, fed by water from a waterfall that drops from the top of the biome into pools below.

The second covered biome, the Warm Temperate Biome, is filled with plants from temperate zones, including olive trees and fruits and flowers from the Mediterranean, California and South Africa. The Roofless Biome contains plants from our own temperate climate. A third covered biome, already at the planning stage, will be dedicated to plants from arid zones and will show how plants and humans manage to survive in areas where there is almost no water. Keeping this biome dry for the desert plants will be a major drainage operation, and when it opens it will, says Tim Smit, further enhance Eden's progress towards the status of one of the world's 'must see' tourist destinations. Outside the biomes, the gardens at the Eden Project are planted with many plants that are native to Cornwall. In each area, visitors will learn about the intimate connection between the plants and the human population. There are many other attractions, too, including some fine sculptures. The aim of this most exciting and ambitious project has always been both to entertain and to educate.

Regular talks, workshops and demonstrations take place in the Living Theatre of Plants and People, with different themes for each month, and in the Eden Arena some of the world's most famous and talented musicians and performers help to raise funds for the Eden Trust, supporting artists from developing countries. Three restaurants offer a wide range of dishes that reflect the enormous variety of the ingredients grown on site, and there are juice bars and small refreshment outlets around the site. The scope of this global garden for the 21st century, the facts and figures and the impact it has had on the county are staggering: the site area covers 50 hectares and could hold 35 football pitches; the biomes, which are covered not in glass but in EFTE, a transparent high-tech foil, contain more than 100,000 plants from 5,000 species; £86 million has been spent up to autumn 2002; staff have almost doubled to over 650; the site has attracted more than two million visitors in less than two years; a benefit of £1.8 billion to the Cornish economy is predicted for the period 2001-2011.

important local business – the St Austell Brewery. Founded by Walter Hicks in 1851, the brewery flourished as the town expanded on the prosperity of the kaolin. Still flourishing today, it remains a family business. The history of the company and an insight into the brewing process can be found at the informative **St Austell Brewery Visitor Centre**, from where visitors are also taken on a guided tour of the brewery.

Just to the north of the town, in the heart of the Cornish Alps, lies Wheal Martyn, an old clay works, now home to the **Wheal Martyn China Clay Museum**. This open air museum tells the 200-year story of the industry in Cornwall through a wide variety of displays. The land around this once busy mine has been replanted and it now has a unique range of habitats. The nature trail through the surrounding countryside offers visitors the opportunity to discover many different birds, small mammals, plants and insects.

AROUND ST AUSTELL

St Blazey
3½ miles NE of St Austell on the A390

To the west of the village in the heart of the china clay area, lies the **Eden Project** (see panel opposite), an unmissable attraction that aims to "promote the understanding and responsible management of the vital relationship between plants, people and resources."

Charlestown
1 mile SE of St Austell off the A390

This small fishing village, once named West Polmear, was transformed in the 1790s by Charles Rashleigh, a local mine owner, who built a harbour here to support the flourishing china clay

industry. Charlestown's harbour declined in the 19th century as other ports, such as Fowey and Plymouth, developed better facilities. However, what has been left is a harbour and village in a Georgian time capsule. As well as providing a permanent berth for square-rigged boats, it is a popular destination with holidaymakers and has been used as the location for TV series such as *Poldark* and *The Onedin Line*. Close to the docks is the **Charlestown Shipwreck, Rescue and Heritage Centre**. This offers an insight into the town's history, local shipwrecks and the various devices that have been developed over the years for rescuing and recovering those in peril at sea.

Just to the northeast of Charlestown, close to **Tregrehan Mills** is **Tregrehan Gardens**, where visitors can not only see many mature trees from as far afield as North America and Japan but also rhododendrons and a range of Carlyon Hybrid Camellias. The house and estate has been the home of the Carlyon family since 1565.

Mevagissey
5 miles S of St Austell on the B3273

Once aptly known as *Porthilly*, Mevagissey was renamed in the 14th century after the saints: St Meva and St Issey. The largest fishing village in St Austell Bay, Mevagissey was an important centre of the pilchard industry and everyone who lived here was linked in some way with either the fishing boats or processing the catch. This has led to a labyrinth of buildings all within easy reach of the harbour. The **Inner Harbour** of today dates from the 1770s while the **Outer Harbour**, built to increase the size of the port, was finally finished at the end of the 19th century.

Housed in a harbour building dating from 1745, the **Mevagissey Folk**

COFRO

14 Fore Street, Mevagissey, Cornwall PL26 6UQ
Tel: 01726 842249
e-mail: sales@cofro.co.uk website: www.cofro.co.uk

Cofro is a Cornish Art Coffee House situated in the picturesque fishing village of Mevagissey just a few steps from the harbour.

In these refitted double fronted corner premises, which were once fishermen's cottages and date back to the 18th century, visitors can browse through a wide range of affordable contemporary arts, crafts and different ideas for gifts.

Cofro which means keepsake or memento in Cornish, is the perfect place to find that unusual object, which has been made in Cornwall. Cofro specialises in the work of local artists including paintings, prints, photography, pottery, glass, jewellery, wood and

metal sculpture. As the pieces are all made in the region, many are inspired by the beautiful Cornish countryside and seascape.

Visitors can also take time out to enjoy a cup of coffee or tea with local farmhouse or home baked cakes and biscuits, or try a traditional Cornish cream tea with Mevagissey strawberry jam. The beans used for the coffee are the best, 100% Arabica and produce a fantastic espresso, cappuccino or latte using a stylish new Italian espresso machine.

There is much to interest the visitor in Mevagissey and Cofro provides yet one more reason to linger in this delightful place.

THE HARBOUR TAVERN

Jetty Street, Mevagissey, Cornwall PL26 6UH
Tel/Fax: 01726 842220

The Harbour Tavern enjoys an unbeatable location right on the harbourfront in the bustling fishing village of Mevagissey. The Tavern, whose origins can be traced back to the 14th century, is in the excellent care of Chris and Susannah Macklin, who took over the reins in 2002 and have refitted the whole place from top to bottom, to the very highest standards. Good food, generously served, from hot and cold snacks to full meals, is served all day, and the impressive range of drinks includes real ales and draught ciders, wines and spirits.

Families are always welcome, and for visitors staying overnight the Tavern has three en suite

bedrooms with TV and tea trays, with irons and hairdryers available on request. There could not be a more pleasant and more convenient place to choose as a base for enjoying the delights of Cornwall. In high season, the scene outside the Tavern is one of colourful activity, with little fishing and pleasure boats coming and going in the harbour, and at any time of year the village has much to offer the visitor. The South West Coast Path offers mile after mile of bracing walks and stunning scenery, the sandy beaches of Gorran Haven are a short distance away, and it's only a very short drive to the renowned Lost Gardens of Heligan.

Mevagissey Harbour

Museum has a broad collection of artefacts that includes not only the pilchard industry but agricultural machinery, early photographs of village life and the story of Pears soap – originally created by Cornishman Andrew Pears in the 18th century. Elsewhere around the harbour, visitors can see the fascinating displays and models at the **World of Model Railway Exhibition** (see panel on page 63). The old lifeboat station that was built on the quayside in 1897 has now become **The Aquarium**. In the 1750s, when John Wesley first came to Mevagissey to preach, he was greeted with a barrage of rotten eggs and old fish and had to be rescued from the crowd and taken to safety. In return for their hospitality, Wesley gave his hosts James and Mary Lelean his silver shoe buckles.

To the northwest of Mevagissey lie the famous **Lost Gardens of Heligan** (see

IN YOUR DREAMS

9 Fore Street, Mevagissey, Cornwall PL26 6UQ
Tel: 01726 844600

In the centre of the bustling fishing village of Mevagissey, **In Your Dreams** is a delightful treasure chest of beautiful things to add personality and colour to a home or to make a special present. The exterior, painted in bright orange and blue, is very inviting, and the irresistible window display makes it very difficult not to be drawn inside.

Here, the extrovert, affable owner Helen Angrave has filled every inch of wall, floor and ceiling space in assembling more things than you can dream of, including pictures and prints, greetings cards, trinket boxes and trinkets of all kinds, pottery

and ceramics, cuddly toys, bags, wooden figures and children's puzzles, vases, hanging decorations and handicraft kits. Here, too, are toiletries and fragrances, among them the 'kindest soap on planet Earth', Double Bubble Scent Balls, Manor House pot pourri and Yankee Candles. If ever a place was made for browsing and buying, it is In Your Dreams, which really does have something to appeal to anyone who drops in. Opening hours are 10am to 5.30pm, with evening extension in high season.

BODRUGAN BARTON

Bodrugan Manor, Portmellon, Mevagissey,
Cornwall PL26 6PT
Tel: 01726 842094 Fax: 01726 844378
e-mail: bodruganbarton@ukonline.co.uk

Bodrugan Barton is the family home of Tim and Sally Kendall, who welcome guests into an ambience of friendly relaxation and generous hospitality. Accommodation at Bodrugan is delightfully warm and comfortable, whether in the large rooms in the main house or in an en suite study bedroom in the converted barn at the centre of the 400-acre farm. The latter are used for the courses which Sally runs: these comprise management courses and courses in various aspects of arts and handicrafts.

Home-made bread, local bacon and sausages, locally smoked salmon and free-range eggs make the best possible start to a day's painting, working or sightseeing. Everyone eats in the large dining room with its imposing archway fireplace, woodburner and sofas. Bodrugan is not licensed, but guests can bring their own wine for dinner. The farm, which boasts an indoor heated swimming pool and sauna, stands in a particularly beautiful part of the county between Mevagissey and the Roseland Peninsula; an ancient path leads to secluded Colona Bay, connecting with the South West Coast Path.

THE GRANARY

Boswinger, Nr Mevagissey, Cornwall PL26 6LL
Tel: 01726 844381
e-mail: holidays@thegranary.boswinger.freeserve.co.uk
website: www.cornwallbandb.co.uk

Sandra Chubb moved from the Cotswolds several years ago after spending many holidays in Cornwall. She now lives at **The Granary**, where she offers bed & breakfast accommodation in comfortably appointed bedrooms

with TV and tea trays. Guests have the use of a well-furnished lounge, and when the weather is kind the garden, with its pond and wildlife, is a very pleasant place to sit at the end of the day.

The handsome house - a converted barn - enjoys a superb setting that affords terrific views across fields to the cliffs and the open sea. The South West Coast Path is nearby, and local attractions include the picturesque fishing village of Mevagissey, many sandy beaches, the Lost Gardens of Heligan, Caerhays Castle and the Eden Project.

MEVAGISSEY MODEL RAILWAY

Meadow Street, Mevagissey, Cornwall
Tel: 0800 298 5525
website: www.model-railway.co.uk

Situated 130 metres from the picturesque harbour of Mevagissey, the World of Model Railways is an exhilarating experience into a miniature world. Up to 40 trains run in computerised sequence through fine detailed scenery and the displays include an indoor garden layout and an interactive fairground. An extended model shop holds a comprehensive range for both the enthusiast and the beginner. Open daily from 10am.

panel below), one of the country's most interesting gardens. Originally laid out in 1780, the gardens lay undisturbed, or 'lost', for 70 years before being rediscovered in 1990. Today, this beautiful and intriguing place is once again attracting visitors from all over the world.

Gorran Haven, to the south of Mevagissey, was once a settlement to rival its neighbour. Those days were long ago and it is now an unspoilt village with a sandy beach, sheltered by **Dodman Point** – a prominent headland where the remains of an Iron Age defensive earthwork can be seen.

To the west of Mevagissey lies **Caerhays Castle Gardens** (see panel on page 65), set in one of only a few remaining examples of a castle built by John Nash.

PROBUS

8 miles SW of St Austell off the A390

This large village is famous for having the tallest parish church tower in the county. Built of granite in the 16th century and richly decorated, it stands 124 feet high. The village is also home to 'the really useful garden'. **Probus Gardens** (see panel on page 65) were established to show local gardeners what could be achieved in a domestic garden with a climate as mild as Cornwall's.

Just west of the village lies another place of interest to gardeners – **Trewithen House and Gardens**. The early Georgian house, whose name literally means 'house of the trees',

THE LOST GARDENS OF HELIGAN

Pentewan, St Austell, Cornwall PL26 6EN
Tel: 01726 845100
website: www.heligan.com

Recently voted "The Nation's Favourite Garden" by Gardeners' World viewers, the award-winning restoration of Heligan's productive gardens is only one of many features which combine to create a destination with a breadth of interest around the year: Victorian pleasure grounds with spring flowering shrubs, summerhouses, pools and rockeries; a sub-tropical jungle valley brimming with exotic foliage; woodland and farm walks through beautiful Cornish countryside, where sustainable management practices promote habitat conservation and a pioneering new project offers visitors a close-up view of native wildlife on site. Free access to parking, toilets, licensed restaurant/tearoom and Heligan Shop and Plant Sales.

GULSHAN INDIAN CUISINE

Fore Street, Probus, Nr Truro, Cornwall TR2 4JL
Tel: 01726 882692/882679

The large village of Probus is famous for its lovely gardens and for having the tallest parish church tower in the county. These two attractions are popular with locals and tourists alike, and the same can be said for the **Gulshan Indian Restaurant** at the heart of the village where a warm welcome awaits you. The restaurant exterior is painted cream, with a wonderful display of hanging baskets, and an inviting patio area to dine on weather permitting.

The interior is warm and welcoming, the restaurant with its spotless ivory linen is no smoking, but you can enjoy a drink and smoke in the bar area. The owner, Ali, has practiced the art of Indian cuisine for over 20 years. Every region has its own individual style and the Gulshan has tried to include the best of these dishes in the menu. In addition to the menu, Ali says "If there is a particular dish you would like which is not on the menu we will do our best to provide it for you. We are happy to cater for individual preferences and our dishes include fish and vegetarian choices." Gulshan India Cuisine is open Tuesday to Sunday, all Bank Holiday Mondays 5.30pm to 11.30pm.

TRUDGIAN FARM SHOP

Church Terrace, Probus, Nr Truro, Cornwall TR2 5JN
Tel: 01726 883946   website: www.Trudgianfarm.co.uk

Margaret Richards, a local lady and a farmer's wife, owns and runs **Trudgian Farm Shop**, a well-established and well-respected supplier of home-produced meat and vegetables. Behind the white-painted frontage of the shop - originally two little houses - is an impressive array of foodstuffs, and it is the owner's proud boast that 90% of the fresh produce on display is home-grown. The layout is traditional, with shelves and racks throughout and the freezers and butchery at the far end. The meat and the fruit and vegetables are the main attraction, but

the shop also sells a wide range of everyday foodstuffs, from chocolate bars to canned soups, oils and pickles, preserves and soft drinks.

The shop has established itself not only as a source of prime fresh produce but as one of the hubs of the community, where the villagers meet to chat as well as shop. The farm is within easy reach of the shop, which is situated in the centre of the village of Probus. It's a very short walk from the shop to the village square and the famous 16th century church, which has the distinction of possessing the tallest and most richly ornamented tower in the county.

CAERHAYS CASTLE GARDENS

Gorran, Nr St Austell, Cornwall PL26 6LY
Tel: 01872 501310/501144
Fax: 01872 501870
e-mail: estateoffice@caerhays.co.uk

Caerhays is an informal 60-acre woodland garden on the coast by Porthluney Cove. The garden can be traced back to the end of the 19th century, and many of the plants and shrubs to be seen today were introduced by Chinese plant hunters. The garden is best known for its huge Asiatic magnolias, which are in their prime in March and April, and is the holder of the NCCPG National Magnolia Collection. It is also home to the x williamsii camellia hybrids and to many varieties of rhododendron. The house, built in the gothic style by John Nash between 1805 and 1807, is open for conducted tours on certain days.

stands in glorious woods and parkland and has gardens containing many rare species laid out in the early 20th century by George Johnstone.

To the southeast lies **Tregony**, a small village that was an important river port long before Truro and Falmouth were developed; it is often called the 'Gateway to the Roseland Peninsula'. This indented tongue of land, which forms the eastern margin of the Fal estuary, is always known by its Cornish name **Carrick Roads**. It has a network of footpaths that take in not only the craggy cliffs with their nesting seabirds but also the grasslands dotted with wildflowers and the ruined military fortresses that go back to the time of the Armada and beyond.

NEWQUAY

Despite first appearances, Newquay is an ancient settlement. There is evidence of an Iron Age coastal fort among the cliffs and caves of **Porth Island** – the outcrop connected to the mainland by an elegant suspended footbridge. For centuries, the

PROBUS GARDENS

Probus, Nr Truro, Cornwall TR2 4HQ
Tel: 01726 882597 Fax: 01726 883868

Established in the 1970s with the aim of encouraging local gardeners to take advantage of Cornwall's mild climate, **Probus Gardens** is a domestic garden on a grand scale, unique in its relationship to the everyday experience of gardeners everywhere.

The eight acres are divided into areas of varying sizes separated by hedges that are resistant to the salt-laden winds that include an organic fruit and vegetable garden, a butterfly garden, a low allergen garden, a winter garden, a seaside garden tended by local schoolchildren and the Millennium herbaceous garden based on a Celtic design.

The glasshouse area has units devoted variously to plant propagation, cacti, exotic species and plants that need winter protection. A unusual feature that always commands great interest is a model 60 feet long that shows the geological structure of the county of Cornwall, with samples of the rocks found in each area. The head gardener and his staff are happy to give advice on gardening problems, and weekly lectures take place from September to April. The gardens lie 100 yards off the A390 east of Probus village.

harbour lay at the heart of this once important pilchard fishing village. The town takes its name from the 'New Kaye' that was built in the mid-15th century by the villagers who wanted to protect the inlet here. On Towan Headland, the **Huer's Hut** can still be seen; this was where the Huer would scan the sea looking for shoals of red pilchards. Once spotted, he would cry "hevva" to alert the fishing crews and then guide them to the shoals using a pair of bats known as 'bushes'. As the fishing industry declined, Newquay became a major port for both china clay and mineral exports. However, today, its beautiful rocky coastline and acres of golden sands has seen it develop into a popular seaside resort, famed throughout the world for its surfing. Although there is some Regency architecture here, the rise of the town's fortunes in the 19th century saw a rapid expansion and many of the large

Victorian hotels and residential houses still remain. The **Trenance Heritage Cottages**, Newquay's oldest dwellings, date to the town's distant past and are now home to the work of local craftsmen and artists. This is a traditional English resort and there are a wide variety of attractions in and around the town. In Towan Bay, the **Blue Reef Aquarium** (see panel opposite) is home to a wide variety of creatures that live beneath the waves. At **Newquay Zoo**, where conservation, education and entertainment go hand in hand, visitors can see creatures from the land and sky as well. The characters and events that have shaped the history of this part of Cornwall can be discovered at **Tunnels Through Time**: more than 70 realistic life-size figures set in carefully constructed tableaux bring the days of smugglers and highwaymen, plague victims and miners, King Arthur and Merlin vividly to life. The scariest part is

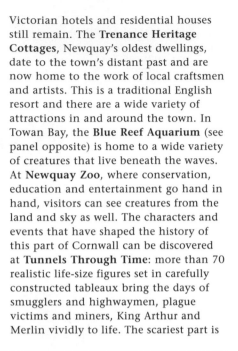

the Dungeon of Despair, where visitors can hear the screams of prisoners being tortured in the name of old-time 'justice'. At the indoor **Water World** complex, the whole family can enjoy a range of pools and water activities in a tropical climate.

Newquay Harbour

To the southwest of Newquay's famous beaches, **Towan Beach** and **Fistral Beach**, between the headlands of Pentire East and Pentire West, lies the quieter **Gannel**, home to notable populations of waders and wildfowl, which feed off the mudflats and saltings. Just a short distance further on is the pretty hamlet of **Holywell** with its attractive beach, towering sand dunes and **Holywell Bay Fun Park** offering a whole range of activities for young and old.

Inland from Newquay lie the imposing engine house and chimney stack of **East Wheal Rose** mine, Cornwall's richest lead mine that was the scene, in 1846, of the county's worst mining disaster. 39 miners were drowned in a flash flood caused by a sudden, unexpected cloudburst. The village cockpit, where cockfighting had taken place for centuries, was restored as a memorial to the dead; the mine was re-opened a year after the tragedy but closed for good in 1885.

Close by, hidden in the lanes two miles west of Kestle Mill, is the delightful small Elizabethan manor house, **Trerice**, now owned by the National Trust. A real architectural gem, it was built in 1571 for the influential Arundell family. As well as the hint of Dutch styling in the gables

BLUE REEF AQUARIUM

Towan Promenade, Newquay,
Cornwall TR7 1DU
Tel: 01637 878134 Fax: 01637 872578
website: www.bluereefaquarium.co.uk

Blue Reef Aquarium takes visitors on an undersea voyage that explores the amazing range of marine life from around the world, from the beaches and cliffs of the local Cornish coastline to the spectacular 'underwater gardens' of the Mediterranean and the dazzling beauty of exotic tropical reefs. The centrepiece of the museum is a stunning coral reef display housed in a giant 250,000 litre ocean tank that is home to hundreds of brightly coloured reef fish, puffer fish and black tip reef sharks.

This amazing spectacle can be seen from a boardwalk overlooking the atoll, from inside a glass cave or from inside an underwater walk-through tunnel. Open daily from 10 o'clock, the Aquarium has more than 30 living displays - the sea horses and the friendly rays are great favourites - and holds regular talks and feeding demonstrations.

and the beautiful window in the Great Hall with 576 small panes of 16th century glass, Trerice is noted for its huge, ornate fireplaces, elaborate plasterwork and fine English oak and walnut furniture. Several rooms contain superb English and Oriental porcelain, and among the more esoteric collections are clocks and drinking glasses. There are portraits by the renowned Cornish painter John Opie and an unusual set of early wooden skittles. The grounds are equally charming, and another attraction is the **Lawnmower Museum**, which traces the history of the lawnmower and contains more than 100 machines. Nearby is a very different family attraction that has seen more than two million visitors since opening in 1975. **DairyLand Farm World** is a working dairy farm where visitors can see the 140 cows being milked to music; try their hand at milking a life-size model

cow; explore the nature trail and look around the Heritage Centre and Alternative Energy Centre. The farm is located on the A3058 four miles east of Newquay.

AROUND NEWQUAY

INDIAN QUEENS
6 miles SE of Newquay off the A30

Close to an area dominated by china clay quarries, this chiefly Victorian village is home to the **Screech Owl Sanctuary**, just to the northeast. A rehabilitation, conservation and education centre, the sanctuary has the largest collection of owls in the southwest of England. As well as offering visitors the chance to see hand-tame owls at close quarters, the Centre runs courses on owl welfare; Harry Potter would approve.

FRADDON POTTERY

Fraddon Hill, Fraddon, Cornwall TR9 6QU
Tel: 01726 860206

Frances Osborne and her daughter Rachel make fine pottery and jewellery at their studio in the garden at **Fraddon Pottery**. Frances uses local clay to make a variety of pieces that are both practical and decorative, with beautiful glazes to finish what are certainly destined to be heirlooms of the future.

All the pieces are hand-painted with metal oxides in blues, pinks and greens, and some are fired with a

special gold lustre. Rachel creates her beautiful and unique jewellery using sterling silver, and many of her pieces are adorned with beads made by Frances.

The pottery, which is located close to the A30 midway between Bodmin and Truro, is open from 10am to 4pm every day except Monday. The studio and showroom with work on display are accessible to visitors in wheelchairs. Frances also teaches her craft and would be delighted to hear from those who wish to learn.

St Columb Major

6 miles E of Newquay off the A39

Once in the running for consideration as the site of Cornwall's cathedral, this small town has an unusually large and flamboyant parish church where monumental brasses to the influential Arundell family can still be seen. In the 14th century Sir John Arundell was responsible for the town receiving its market charter. In 1850 the town's officials constructed a bishop's palace in anticipation of the county's cathedral being built here. Now called the **Old Rectory**, it retains much of its grandeur though it does not play host to its originally intended guests. The town has preserved the tradition of 'hurling the silver ball', in which the ball, cased in real silver, is thrown from person to person up and down the street in an attempt to score a goal.

A couple of miles south-east of St Columb Major, on **Castle Downs**, lie the remains of a massive Iron Age hill fort. **Castle-an-Dinas** was a major defence of the Dumnonia tribe, who were in the area around the 2nd century BC. The earthwork ramparts enclose an area of over six acres, and anyone climbing to the gorse-covered remains will be rewarded with panoramic views over the leafy Vale of Mawgan to the northwest and the unearthly landscaped created by china clay extraction to the south.

To the northeast of St Columb Major, at **Winnards Perch**, lies the **Cornish Birds of Prey Centre** where visitors can see hawks, falcons and buzzards fly freely during demonstrations. There are also waterfowl, ducks, pheasants, emus, rheas, kookaburras, fallow deer, dwarf zebus and Shetland ponies. Also in the centre are three well-stocked fishing lakes.

The Plume Of Feathers

Mitchell, Nr Truro, Cornwall TR8 5AX
Tel: 01872 510387 Fax: 01872 511124

Martyn Warner and his family have regenerated a run-down local into a fine destination pub and restaurant. The **Plume of Feathers** is a handsome 16th century building with a distinctive pillared entrance above which John Wesley once preached his Methodist views. Inside, where the atmosphere is always warm and welcoming, the main attraction is the excellent cuisine produced by Martyn and his team. Their menus, for which they have been voted County Dining Pub of the Year in the Good Pub Guide 2004, are a fusion of classical British and modern European dishes, with an emphasis on fresh fish and the best Cornish ingredients. The extensive seasonal menu is supplemented by a frequently changing specials board, and a typical meal could be pan-fried Cornish scallops with a fresh herb salsa to

start, honey-glazed lamb shank for a main dish and home-made sticky toffee & banana pudding with butterscotch sauce to round off in style.

The Plume of Feathers is definitely a place for lingering, and the old stables and a barn have been superbly converted to provide five bed & breakfast rooms, all with bath or shower en suite, and a two-bedroom self-catering holiday cottage with its own garden. The B&B rooms are equipped with terminals for lap-tops, TV and hairdryer and tea/coffee making facilities. All rooms have wrought iron bedsteads and are non-smoking; no pets.

LOCATOR MAP

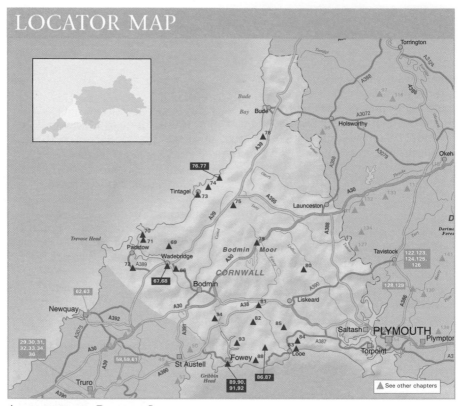

ADVERTISERS AND PLACES OF INTEREST

66 Trelawney Garden Leisure, Sladesbridge,
    Wadebridge   page 72
67 Cornish Farm Holidays   page 73
68 The Bear and Dolls House Company,
    Wadebridge   page 74
69 The Olde House, Chapel Amble,
    Wadebridge   page 74
70 Finn's, Polzeath, Wadebridge   page 75
71 Mowhay Gallery, Trebetherick,
    Wadebridge   page 76
72 The Old Mill House, Little Petherick,
    Wadebridge   page 78
73 Tintagel Castle, Tintagel   page 79
74 Rocky Valley Gallery, Rocky Valley,
    Tintagel   page 81
75 St Kitts Herbery, Starapark, Camelford page 83
76 Lower Meadows, Boscastle   page 84
77 The Old Mill, Boscastle   page 85
78 Quinceborough Farm & Cottages,
    Widemouth Bay, Bude   page 86

79 Jamaica Inn & Museums, Bolventor,
    Launceston   page 89
80 Sterts Theatre, Upton Cross, Liskeard   page 92
81 Caradon Country Cottages, East Taphouse,
    Liskeard   page 93
82 Porfell Animal Land Wildlife Park,
    Lanreath, Liskeard   page 94
83 Trehaven Manor Hotel, East Looe   page 98
84 Bucklawren Farm, St Martin By Looe   page 98
85 Cornish Orchards, Duloe   page 100
86 Pitt House, Pelynt, Looe   page 102
87 Trenderway Farm, Pelynt, Looe   page 102
88 Lesquite Farm, Lansallos, Looe   page 104
89 The Romantic Englishwoman, Fowey   page 105
90 Old House of Foye, Fowey   page 106
91 Pink Kite Interiors, Fowey   page 106
92 Constables Studio, Fowey   page 107
93 St Veep Riding Stables, St Veep, Lerryn page 108
94 Restormel Castle, Lostwithiel   page 109

EAST CORNWALL 2

This eastern region of Cornwall has, like much of the rest of the county, managed to maintain its Celtic heritage and the most common reminders are in the place names – those beginning with Tre, Pol and Pen – but there are also many ancient monuments to discover. Along with providing a boundary, the River Tamar, which for much of its length is now an Area of Outstanding Natural Beauty, was also dotted with river ports that transported mineral ores and other goods down to the seaports and beyond.

The Tamar Valley also hides one of the best-preserved late medieval estates in the country, Cotehele House, once the principal home of the Earls of Edgcumbe.

Along the south coast, to the west of Saltash, whose two magnificent bridges now carry both the major road and rail links into the county, there are numerous picturesque fishing towns and villages, such as Looe, Fowey and Polperro, which once prospered on the back of first the pilchard fishing industry and then the mining and china clay industries. In contrast, the north coast is much harsher and harbours are few and far between as the Atlantic Ocean continues to pound

Widemouth Bay

the rugged coastline. However, there is some respite, and Bude was the birthplace of British surfing, as well as being a popular holiday destination.

At the centre of eastern Cornwall lies the mysterious Bodmin Moor, the inspiration for Daphne du Maurier's famous novel, *Jamaica Inn*. An isolated expanse of bleak moorland and a place once frequented by smugglers, it has a wealth of prehistoric monuments and several natural features that have given rise to many legends - none more famous than lonely Dozmary Pool, believed to be home to the Lady of the Lake of the Arthurian legends. Stories of Arthur continue at Tintagel, a small coastal village whose romantic castle ruins, situated on a craggy headland, are thought to be the birthplace of the legendary king.

TRELAWNEY GARDEN LEISURE

Sladesbridge, Nr Wadebridge,
Cornwall PL27 6JA
Tel: 01208 893030
Fax: 01208 814798
e-mail: enquiries@trelawney.co.uk
website: www.trelawney.co.uk

Trelawney Garden Leisure, just outside Wadebridge on the A389 in the beautiful Camel valley, was founded in 1970 by Frank and Marion Danning. At that time it was a small roadside stall selling home-grown fruit and vegetables to local customers as they passed by. As time progressed the business flourished, and with the help of their son David and long-time family friend David Symonds Trelwaney Garden centre grew and became renowned for the quality and variety of its products and its friendly family atmosphere. The centre steamed ahead in 2000, incorporating an endearing new image to suit

the new look garden centre by recreating the original siting of the London & South Western Railway which ran through the land up until the 1960s. April 2003 saw the completion of an extended undercover Planteria filled with locally grown seasonal plants, shrubs and trees and pots, and major redevelopment of the outside plant area, which includes an adventure play park and avery.

The plant side is just one aspect of a business developed by over 30 years of hard work that also contains three fantastic shopping platforms and a restaurant. Platform 1 specialises in quality garden products, with themed shops supplying everything needed for tending a garden. The outlets on Platform 2 are stocked with quality clothing, books, household goods, and gifts in all shapes and sizes, and the florists here can design and make exquisite bouquets and arrangements for any special occasion. Platform 3 steams into action in spring and summer with garden and patio furniture and the latest barbecues and accessories; at Christmas time the whole area is decorated and themed for Christmas, becoming Santa's Grotto and Winter

Wonderland. Carriages Restaurant and Coffee Shop, also with a railway theme, serves anything from hot and cold snacks and Cornish cream teas to a full English breakfast, classic roasts and scrumptious hot puddings. Trelawney Garden Leisure has recently won for the second time the prestigious Garden Centre Association regional South West and Wales region winners 2002/3/4 award. This achievement, which included the highest number of certificates (15) for a single garden centre, qualifies it for entry into the final for Best Garden Centres in the UK.

Cornish Farm Holidays

Brochure Tel: 01872 510050
e-mail: enquire@cornish-farms.co.uk
website: www.cornish-farms.co.uk

The members of **Cornish Farm Holidays** offer high-quality bed & breakfast and self-catering accommodation, with friendly, helpful service, on some of the most beautiful farms in Cornwall. Visitors can look forward to a warm welcome and good company, enjoying a quiet retreat in the country air, with exceptional value for money, and often with delightful bonuses such as helping to feed the farm animals. All the accommodation is of a very high standard, with everything provided for a comfortable stay, and the owners take great pride in the service they provide and their excellent local knowledge.

Each property - there are 64 in all - is individual and each is situated in attractive, largely unspoilt countryside - and since this is Cornwall, the sea is never far away, so visitors get the best of both worlds. For B&B guests, a delicious breakfast of local farm-fresh produce starts the day, and some hosts can provide evening meals. If the accommodation is self-catering, it will be fully equipped and the host will usually be close at hand with help and advice. There are 34 properties in East Cornwall, ranging from award-winning farm cottages at Lostwithiel to an organic dairy farm at Woolley, near Bude. Most are open all year round.

WADEBRIDGE

Standing at the historic lowest bridging point on the River Camel, this ancient port and busy market town is now a popular holiday centre which is not only attractive but also is renowned for its craftware. Linking the north and south coasts of Cornwall and the moorland with the sea, Wadebridge has always been a bustling place and its establishment as a trading centre began in earnest in the 15th century. The Rev Lovibond, the vicar of St Petroc's, was looking for a means of conveying his flock of sheep safely across the river and in the 1460s he built the 320-feet-long and now 14-arched bridge which can still be seen today. One of the longest bridges in Cornwall, it originally had 17 arches and it is said that this bridge, nicknamed the **Bridge on Wool**, was constructed on bridge piers that were

sunk on a foundation of woolsacks. The bridge still carries the main road that links the town's two ancient parishes.

With a permanent river crossing there was a steady growth in trade through the town and its port but the arrival of the railway in the 19th century saw Wadebridge really thrive. As a result, much of the town's architecture dates from the Victorian era. Wadebridge maintains its links with farming and each June to the west of the town centre the **Royal Cornwall Agricultural Show** is held. Another popular annual event is the Wadebridge Folk Festival, a feast of dance, music and fun that takes place on August Bank Holiday. The town's former railway station is now home to the **John Betjeman Centre**, dedicated to the life and work of the much-loved Poet Laureate. Among the tributes and intimate artefacts on display there are, in

THE BEAR AND DOLLS HOUSE COMPANY

Foundry Court, Wadebridge,
Cornwall PL27 7QN Tel: 01208 816849
website: www.bearsanddollshouses.co.uk
e-mail: sales@bearsanddollshouses.co.uk

When Jackie's father made her first doll's house, little did they both realise that her hobby would turn into a thriving business. Situated in a lovely

courtyard in the heart of historic Wadebridge, the first thing that catches your eye about **The Bear and Dolls House Company** is the beautiful window display. Jackie's window changes with the seasons, always wonderfully themed, it has become a "must see".

Her shop is filled with everything for the teddy bear and doll's house enthusiast, from garden furniture, to carpets, to lighting. Any item not stocked is easily obtained and Jackie can advise you on anything you may need to know. Visit Jackie's website which displays her lovely houses with their interiors. Please call, e-mail or best of all pay her a visit, the promise is that you won't be disappointed.

THE OLDE HOUSE

Chapel Amble, Wadebridge, Cornwall PL27 6EN
Tel: 01208 813219 Fax: 01208 815689
e-mail: info@theoldehouse.co.uk
website: www.theoldehouse.co.uk

The comfortable self-catering cottages are a mixture of purpose built houses and converted farm buildings on a 500 acre working farm set in and around the hamlet of Chapel Amble. There is a leisure centre with an indoor heated pool, toddlers pool, sauna, jacuzzi, full size snooker table, darts and colour TV. There is also a small paperback and children's library for guests use. Outside there are two tennis courts. For younger guests ther is an outdoor adventure playground and a farm trail. The indoor

playbarn has a ballpool, wendy house, ropes to climb and slides to use, together with the indoor pets corner. Laundry facilities are included and a baby sitting service is available by arrangement.

Nearby are the sandy beaches at Rock, Daymer Bay and Polzeath, ideal for all the family, for surfing, sailing, swimming and golf, also the famous Camel Cycle Trail which is great fun for everyone. Only a short drive away is the spectacular Eden Project. A warm welcome awaits you at The Olde House-telephone for details of a family holiday to remember. Open all year - short breaks and long weekends usually available by request.

the memorabilia room, the poet's desk, his chair and drafts of his books.

Although the railway line, which opened in 1899, closed in the 1960s, a stretch of the trackbed has been used to create the superb **Camel Trail**, a footpath and cycleway that leads up into the foothills of Bodmin Moor to the east and westwards, along the River Camel, to Padstow.

Just to the west of Wadebridge, close to the hamlet of **St Breock**, lies **St Breock Downs Monolith**, a striking Bronze Age longstone that is also known as the Men Gurta (the Stone of Waiting). Other prehistoric remains, such as the Nine Maidens stone row, can also be found on St Breock Downs.

AROUND WADEBRIDGE

POLZEATH AND NEW POLZEATH
6 miles NW of Wadebridge off the B3314

Surfers and holidaymakers flock to these two small resorts as the broad west-facing beach is not only ideal for surf, but the fine sands, caves and tidal rock pools make it a fascinating place for children. This was also a place much loved by Sir John Betjeman and, to the north of the villages, is a beautiful coastal path that takes in the cliffs and farmland of **Pentire Point** and **Rumps Point** – where stands **Rumps Cliff Castle**, an Iron Age fortification where the remains of four defensive ramparts

FINN'S

Beach Road, Polzeath, Nr Wadebridge, Cornwall PL27 6SP
Tel/Fax: 01208 863472
e-mail: david@finnscafe.co.uk
website: www.finnscafe.co.uk

The original concept of **Finn's** was established in the mid-1990s in this wonderful setting right by the beach. From the start, David and Neal Spurrell and their father Roger brought in the crowds with a menu of seafood that was prepared without frills or frippery, with clean,

uncomplicated flavours and simple, beautiful presentation. The concept was commonly known as 'sexy fish & chips' and that philosophy is still the driving force behind menus that combine classic simplicity and innovative modern influences.

Superb dishes such as chargrilled lobster, moules marinière and whole roasted sea bass with garlic and herbs share the main list with such temptations as pan-fried swordfish with merguez or halibut steak with aubergine caviar, crispy ham and white butter sauce. Meat-eaters and vegetarians are also well catered for, and children can choose from their special section on the menus. Lighter dishes, snacks, salads and afternoon tea make up the daytime menu, and before that a breakfast menus offers toast and preserves, hot sandwiches and Finn's Full Grill - also with a vegetarian option. The wines, all organic, are supplied by Wine World of Cornwall. A second Finn's opened in Newquay in 2001 (see separate advertisement).

can still be seen. The area is known for its wild tamarisk, an elegant flowering shrub that is more commonly found around the shores of the Mediterranean Sea.

In the 1930s, Pentire Head was saved from commercial development by local fund raisers, who bought the land and donated it to the National Trust.

This stretch of dramatic coastline that runs round to **Port Quin** includes sheltered bays and coves, ancient field patterns, old lead mines and Iron Age defensive earthworks. It is ideal walking country, and there are numerous footpaths taking walkers on circular routes that incorporate both coastal countryside and farmland.

The tiny hamlet of Port Quin suffered greatly when the railways took away the slate trade from its once busy quay and the demise was so swift that, at one time, outsiders thought that the entire population had been washed away by a great storm. Overlooking the now re-populated hamlet is **Doyden Castle**, a squat 19th century castellated folly that is now a holiday home.

To the southwest of Polzeath lies the delightful **Church of St Enodoc**, a Norman building that has, on several occasions, been virtually submerged by windblown sand. At these times the congregation would enter through an opening in the roof. The sand was finally cleared away in the 1860s, when the church was restored, and the bell in the tower, which came from an Italian ship wrecked nearby, was installed in 1875. The beautiful churchyard contains many graves of shipwrecked mariners but what draws many people to this quiet place is the grave of the poet Sir John Betjeman, who is buried here along with his parents. Betjeman spent many of his childhood holidays in the villages and coves around the Camel Estuary, and his affection for the local people and places

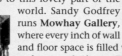

MOWHAY GALLERY

Top of Daymer Lane, Trebetherick, Nr Wadebridge, Cornwall PL27 6SE
Tel: 01208 863634

Handsome old farm buildings have been developed over a period of years into a delightful family-run enterprise comprising craftware gallery and shop, tea room and accommodation for visitors to this lovely part of the world. Sandy Godfrey runs **Mowhay Gallery**, where every inch of wall

and floor space is filled with pictures and prints and contemporary craftware and giftware. These range from beautiful fabrics and fashions to vases, bowls and tableware, clocks, carved wooden animals and hanging ornaments - yes, even the ceilings are used to display some of the items!

Sandy's daughter Amie runs the café, which has space for 30 inside and a few tables and chairs under parasols in a charming little garden. Visitors can enjoy morning coffee, snacks and light lunches, and the café is licensed. Above the gallery and tea room are two one-bedroom self-catering apartments that provide a quiet, civilised base for a pilgrimage to Betjeman country, to the Norman Church of St Enedoc, for a beach or golfing holiday, and to browse at leisure for the perfect gift in the Gallery. Normal opening hours at Mowhay Gallery are from 10.30am to 5pm between Easter and October.

was the inspiration for many of his works. The church is reached across a golf course that is regarded as one of the most scenic links courses in the country.

Porthcothan

6 miles W of Wadebridge on the B3276

This tiny village overlooks a deep, square, sheltered cove, with a sandy beach, which was once the haunt of

Bedruthan Steps

smugglers but today is just one part of a stretch of coastline owned by the National Trust. A footpath over the southern headland leads to **Porth Mear**, another secluded cove beyond which, on a low plateau, is a prehistoric earthwork of banks and ditches. Further south again lie the **Bedruthan Steps** (not National Trust) a curious beach rock formation that is best viewed from the grassy clifftops. The giant slate rocks have been eroded over the centuries and their uniform shape has caused them, according to local legend, to be thought of as the stepping stone used by the Cornish giant Bedruthan.

To the north, the **South West Coast Path** leads walkers around **Constantine Bay** and past a succession of sandy beaches which are ideal for surfing, but unfortunately the strong currents along this stretch make swimming hazardous. Beyond Constantine Bay lies the remote headland of **Trevose Head** from where there are wonderful views down the coast, taking in bay after bay. At the tip of the headland stands **Trevose Lighthouse**, which has been warning mariners away from its sheer granite cliffs since 1847 with a beam that, today, can be seen up to 27 miles away.

Padstow

6 miles W of Wadebridge on the A389

Padstow's sheltered position, on the western side of the Camel estuary, has made it a welcome haven for vessels for centuries and the area has been settled by many different people over the years, including the prehistoric Beaker folk, Romans, Celtic saints and marauding Vikings. Originally named Petroc-stow, it was here that the Welsh missionary St Petroc landed in the 6th century and, before moving on to Bodmin Moor to continue his missionary work, founded a Celtic Minster. Beginning at the door of the town's 13th century parish Church of St Petroc, the **Saints' Way** is a middle distance footpath that follows the route taken by travellers and pilgrims crossing Cornwall on their way from Brittany to Ireland.

However, the silting up of the River Camel in the 19th century and the evocatively named Doom Bar, which restricts entry into the estuary mouth, put paid to Padstow continuing as a major port. Today the harbour still teems with people and the influence of the sea is never far away, as more recently Padstow has become linked with seafood

Padstow Harbour

and the famous chef and restaurateur Rick Stein. A popular attraction is the **National Lobster Hatchery** on South Quay. The Harbour remains the town's focal point and here too can be found many of Padstow's older buildings including **Raleigh Cottage**, where Sir Walter Raleigh lived while he was

Warden of Cornwall, and the tiny **Harbour Cottage**.

As well as the annual Fish and Ships Festival, Padstow continues to celebrate **May Day** in a traditional manner that has it roots back in pagan times. Beginning at midnight on the eve of May Day and lasting throughout the next day, the townsfolk sing in the new morning and then follow the 'Obby 'Oss through the town until midnight when the 'Obby 'Oss dies.

It was while visiting Padstow in 1842 that Charles Dickens was inspired to write *A Christmas Carol* in which he mentions a lighthouse - the one at Trevose Head. His good friend, Dr Miles Marley, whose son, Dr Henry Marley, practised in Padstow for 51 years, provided the surname for Scrooge's

THE OLD MILL HOUSE

Little Petherick, Wadebridge, Cornwall PL27 7QT
Tel: 01841 540388 Fax: 01841 540406
website: www.theoldmillhouse.com

New owners Paul and Hanna Charlesworth have taken over **The Old Mill House**, a Grade II listed building whose oldest parts go back to the 16th century. Their charming house is open from February through to the end of November, and the seven tastefully decorated en suite bedrooms provide very comfortable accommodation with colour TV, telephone and data ports. Four of the rooms are overlooking the picturesque garden, while the other three are in front of the house overlooking the pretty stream that runs into the Camel Estuary. Guests can enjoy a leisurely breakfast and superb dinner in the Mill Room while watching the old mill wheel turning. They can relax and take an aperitif in the welcoming bar area or in the cosy lounge.

The attractive hamlet of Little Petherick lies on the A389 between Wadebridge and Padstow in the designated Area of Outstanding Natural Beauty with some lovely walks: Saints Way footpath goes past the gate, along the creek, through woods and over fields and hills into Padstow. There are many idyllic beaches and coves nearby, and many of the region's scenic and historic attractions are within an easy drive. The Old Mill House is a non-smoking establishment and children over 14 are welcome, but no pets.

partner, Jacob. Dr Henry Marley died in 1908, at the age of 76, at his home in Mellingey, at nearby St Issey and his funeral took place in the local parish church.

On the northern outskirts of the town and built on the site of St Petroc's monastery lies **Prideaux Place**, a magnificent Elizabethan mansion which has been the home of the ancient Cornish Prideaux-Brune family for over 400 years. Along with family portraits and memorabilia the house is home to many artefacts that tell of the history of this area and the country. The mansion is surrounded by glorious gardens and parkland that were laid out in Capability Brown style in the 18th century.

TINTAGEL

The romantic remains of **Tintagel Castle** (see panel), set on a wild and windswept headland that juts out into the Atlantic, are many people's image of Cornwall. Throughout the year, many come to clamber up the wooden stairway to **The Island** to see the castle that is thought to be the birthplace of King Arthur. The legends are thought to have been started by Geoffrey of Monmouth in the mid-12th century and became particularly popular during the Romantic era of the 19th century. The village, of course, owes much of its popularity to its Arthurian connections and one of its other

TINTAGEL CASTLE

Tintagel, Cornwall
Tel: 01840 770328 website: www.english-heritage.org.uk

For over 800 years the tale has been told that **Tintagel Castle** was the birthplace of King Arthur, born to the beautiful Queen Igerna and protected from evil by the magician Merlin, who lived in a cave below the fortress. But the history of the site goes back even further. Fragments of a Celtic monastic house dating from the 6th century have been unearthed on the headland and their origins certainly coincide with the activities of the Welsh military leader on which the Arthurian legends are thought to be based. The castle was, in fact, built in the 12th century, some 600 years after the time of King Arthur, by Reginald, Earl of Cornwall, the illegitimate son of Henry I. Whatever the truth behind the stories, the magic of this site, with Atlantic breakers crashing against the cliffs, certainly matches that of the tales of chivalry and wizardry.

In 1998 the discovery of a 6th century slate bearing the Latin inscription 'Artognov' - which translates as the ancient British name for Arthur - renewed the belief that Tintagel was Arthur's home. The cave, found at the foot of The Island, is known as **Merlin's Cave** and is said still to be haunted by a ghost. Tintagel is also of great interest to nature-lovers: the cliffs are at the heart of a Site of Special Scientific Interest, providing breeding grounds for sea birds, lizards and butterflies. Tintagel Castle is one of over 400 historic sites in the care of English Heritage.

interesting attractions along this theme is **King Arthur's Great Hall**. In the series of vast halls the story of the chivalrous deeds of the king and his Knights is told. Seventy-two stained glass windows depict their coats of arms and some of their adventures.

Tintagel Castle

Distance:	3.8 miles (6.0 kilometres)
Typical time:	170 mins
Height gain:	100 metres
Map:	Explorer 111
Walk:	www.walkingworld.com ID:1095
Contributor:	Dennis Blackford

Access Information:

From Tintagel, take the Boscastle road for about 1 km until you come to Bossiney car park on your left. Look for the mast!

Description:

The walk takes us through the village of Tintagel and out along the cliff path to visit the legendary castle of King Arthur and Merlin's Cave. All along the path you will find wonderful views and a wealth of wildlife.

Additional Information:

There are toilets at the start point. Toilets, food and drink are available at Tintagel and the castle visitor centre.

Features:

Hills or fells, sea, toilets, castle, National Trust/NTS, wildlife, birds, flowers, great views, butterflies, cafe, gift shop, food shop, public transport, restaurant, tea shop, ancient monument

Walk Directions:

❶ After parking in the car park, turn right onto the main road and walk into Tintagel Village, about 0.7 kilometre away.

❷ Walk through the village until reaching the 'no through road' to 'Glebe Clif' at the side of the 'Cornishman's Inn'. Turn into this road.

❸ Follow this road almost one kilometre down to the car park at the end. Follow the church wall around to the right and on to the coast path. The corner of the road may be cut off by going through the churchyard, which is being kept rough as a nature reserve.

❹ After a few hundred metres you will be looking out over the ruins of the castle. Follow the path down.

❺ When you have reached the paved path to the castle, take the path to your right which zigzags down to the visitor centre. At low tide you can, with care, go to the beach and visit Merlin's Cave. Cross over the little bridge and up the steep flight of steps, or go past the cafe (which is an easier path) to continue on the coast path up the other side of the valley.

❻ 200 metres further on after crossing a little wooden bridge, the path branches and you can go left or right; left goes up onto the point of 'Barras Nose' and is well worth the detour for a spectacular view over the cove and the castle. Continue on the coast path.

❼ About 1 km further on and you pass through a gate which will lead you to the headland known as 'Willapark'.

❽ After the path passes through the gap in the wall it branches. Left takes you out onto the point and is a very pleasant place to visit and relax before finishing your walk. After visiting the point, return to this junction and continue on the path to the right of the gap, which will take you down into the valley.

❾ Steps up the other side of the valley bring you to a stone stile. Cross the stile down to the track. Turn right to return to the starting point. Alternatively, turn left down into the secluded cove of Bossiney Haven, which is popular for swimming at low tide (the sand is covered at high tide).

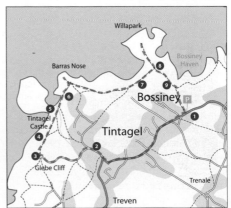

However, there is more to Tintagel than King Arthur. In the High Street, is the weather-beaten **Old Post Office** – a 14th century small manor house that first became a post office in the 19th century. Purchased by the National Trust in 1903 for £100, the building still has its original stone paved medieval hall and ancient fireplace along with the ground-floor office of the postmistress. The early 15th century tower of the parish church, set some distance from the centre of the village on an exposed cliff, has long been used as a landmark by sailors.

To the north of the village lies the mile-long **Rocky Valley**, a curious rock-strewn cleft in the landscape which has a character all of its own. In the wooded upper reaches can be found the impressive 40-foot waterfall known as **St Nectan's Kieve**. This was named after the Celtic hermit whose cell is believed to have stood beside the basin, or kieve, at the foot of the cascade. Here, too, can be seen the **Rocky Valley Carvings**, on a rock face behind a ruined building. Though it is suggested that the carvings date from early Christian times, around the same time that St Nectan was living here, it is impossible to be accurate and other suggestions range from the 2nd century BC to the 17th century!

A little further north, and reached by a short footpath from the village of **Bossiney** is the beautiful, sheltered beach of **Bossiney Haven**, surrounded by a semi-circle of cliffs. The views from the cliff tops are spectacular but only the fit and agile should attempt to scramble down to the inviting beach below. Inland, at **Bossiney Common**, the outlines of ancient field patterns, or lynchets, can still be traced.

ROCKY VALLEY GALLERY

Rocky Valley, Tintagel, Cornwall PL34 0BB
Tel: 01840 779245
website: www.rocky-valley-gallery.co.uk

Rocky Valley Gallery stands at the head of a picturesque wooded valley near the beautiful, rugged Cornish coastline. The setting is the inspiration for many of the local artists whose worked is displayed in this modern stone building run by young, energetic and enthusiastic owners Keiron and Alison Chatterjea. The wonders of coast and countryside are close at hand both literally and in the high-quality oils, the watercolours, the prints and

the sculptures that are the basis of the regularly changing displays and exhibitions hosted by the Gallery.

Everything on display is for sale, which apart from the major pieces includes, cards, books, ceramics, clothing and jewellery - in fact, something to suit most tastes and pockets. The Gallery and the area surrounding it are well worth more than a fleeting visit. The valley itself, a curious rock-strewn cleft in the landscape, has many interesting features, including an impressive 40-foot waterfall and the intriguing labyrinthine rock carvings by the ruins of Trewethett Mill. The Gallery is located on the B3263 a mile from Tintagel, down the hill from Bossiney towards Boscastle. It's open every day in season except for some Tuesdays.

AROUND TINTAGEL

PORT ISAAC

6 miles SW of Tintagel on the B3267

A wonderful fishing village that has retained much of its ancient charm, Port Isaac is surrounded by open countryside, Heritage Coast and an Area of Outstanding Natural Beauty. A busy port since the Middle Ages, during its heyday in the 19th century, fish along with cargoes of stone, coal, timber and pottery were loaded and unloaded on Port Isaac's quayside. Following the arrival of the railways, pilchards were landed here in great numbers, gutted and processed in the village's many fish cellars before being packed off to London and beyond by train. The centre of this conservation village is concentrated around the protected harbour where old fish cellars and fishermen's cottages line the narrow alleys and 'opes' that wend their way down to the coast.

Just to the east lies **Port Gaverne**, another busy 19th century fishing port, where, in one season, over 1,000 tons of pilchards were landed and processed in the village's fish cellars or 'pilchard palaces'. Today, most of the large stone buildings, including some of the old fish cellars, have been converted into holiday accommodation. Tourism has prospered as the village has one of the safest beaches along the North Cornwall coast.

Just inland from the village can be found the double ramparts of **Tregeare Rounds**. This Celtic hill fort was excavated in 1904. Among the finds uncovered were pottery fragments thought to be around 2,000 years old. It is believed to be the Castle Terrible in Thomas Malory's 15th century epic, *Morte D'Arthur*. Here Uther Pendragon laid siege and killed the Earl of Cornwall because he had fallen in love with the earl's beautiful wife, Igerna.

Just over a mile inland, close to the village of Trelights, lies the only public garden along this stretch of North Cornwall coast – **Long Cross Victorian Gardens**, a real garden lover's delight. Imaginative planting and superb panoramic views make this a very special place, and other attractions include a secret garden and a fascinating Victorian maze.

DELABOLE

3 miles S of Tintagel on the B3314

Home to the most famous slate quarry in Cornwall, Delabole, is, almost literally, built of slate. It has been used here for houses, walls, steps and the church. The high quality dark blue slate has been quarried here, uninterrupted, since Tudor times and it is known that, in around 2000 BC Beaker Folk on Bodmin Moor used slate as baking shelves. The huge crater of **Delabole Slate Quarry** is over half a mile wide and 500 feet deep – making it the largest man-made hole in the country. Although the demand for traditional building materials declined during the 20th century, the quarry is still worked and there are occasional slate splitting demonstrations.

To the southwest of the village lies the first wind farm in Britain, **Delabole Wind Farm**, which produces enough power each year to satisfy over half the annual demands of both Delabole and Camelford. The tall turbines provide an unusual landmark and at the heart of the farm is the **Gaia Energy Centre**, where visitors can learn all about the past, present and future of renewable energy. One of the many striking exhibits is a giant steel and glass waterwheel. The Centre has a café and shop, a picnic area and easy access and facilities for disabled visitors.

CAMELFORD

4 miles SE of Tintagel on the A39

This small and historic old market town, on the banks of the River Camel, prospered on the woollen trade. Around its central small square are some pleasant 18th and 19th century houses. The **North Cornwall Museum and Gallery**, housed in a converted coach house, displays aspects of life in this area throughout the 20th century as well as the reconstruction of a 19th century moorland cottage. Just to the north of the town is the **British Cycling Museum**, whose exhibits include over 400 cycles, an old cycle repair shop, a gallery of framed cycling pictures, an extensive library and a history of cycling from 1818. Close by, on the riverbank at **Slaughterbridge**, lies a 6th century slab that is said to mark the place where King Arthur fell at the Battle of Camlann in AD 539. The **Arthurian Centre** houses the Land of Arthur exhibition and also contains an information room (including brass rubbing and a video presentation), a play area, a refreshment area and a shop stocked with Arthurian books and gifts.

BOSCASTLE

3 miles NE of Tintagel on the B3263

This ancient and picturesque fishing village stands in a combe at the head of a remarkable S-shaped inlet that shelters it from the Atlantic Ocean. The only natural harbour between Hartland Point and Padstow, the inner jetty was built by the renowned Elizabethan, Sir Richard Grenville, when the village was prospering as a fishing, grain and slate port. The outer jetty, or breakwater, dates from the 19th century when Boscastle had grown into a busy commercial port handling coal, timber, slate and china clay. Because of the dangerous harbour

---

ST KITTS HERBERY

Starapark, Camelford, Cornwall PL32 9XH
Tel/Fax: 01840 213442
e-mail: enquiries@stkittsherbery.co.uk
website: www.stkittsherbery.co.uk

Paul and Susan Johnson turned a deep personal interest into a most unusual cottage industry when they opened **St Kitts Herbery**, a fascinating nursery and shop located on the A39 2 miles north of Camelford. The herb nursery has a large selection of medicinal, culinary and ornamental herb plants for sale, many of them unusual and all hand-reared in as natural a way as possible, without the use of pesticides and other chemicals. The range is growing all the time, and if a customer wants something not currently in the repertoire the owners will do their best to sow it for the following season.

The shop stocks a wide range of home-produced herb-related products, including herbal tinctures, oils, creams and toiletries, and a selection of books, candles and gifts. The newly introduced food range, with herb oils and vinegars, olives, sun-dried tomatoes, honey, mustard and dry mixes, has proved a great success. Paul and Susan's other offerings include aromatherapy treatments, reflexology and workshops on topics such as making cosmetics, cooking with herbs and dyeing with herbs; they also plan to plant a herbal wood that will be open for the interest and enjoyment of visitors.

Boscastle

lives, their spells, their charms and their curses.

The spectacular slate headlands on either side of the harbour mouth provide some excellent, if rather demanding, walking. This stretch of tortuous coastline is not only of ecological importance but also historic. An Iron Age earthwork can be seen across the promontory at Willapark, and there is a 19th century lookout tower on the summit.

entrance, ships were towed into it by rowing boats and a blowhole in the outer harbour still occasionally sends up plumes of spray. Next to the slipway where the River Valency meets the sea is the **Museum of Witchcraft**, where visitors will learn all about witches, their

From the village there is a footpath that follows the steep wooded Valency Valley to the hidden hamlet of **St Juliot**. Appearing as 'Endelstow' in one of Thomas Hardy's novels, St Juliot is home to the church on which a young Hardy worked as an architect during its

LOWER MEADOWS

Penally Hill, Boscastle, Cornwall PL35 0HF
Tel: 01840 250570
e-mail: stay@lowermeadows.co.uk
website: www.lowermeadows.co.uk

Set in dramatic wooded countryside close to historic Boscastle harbour and the coastal path. Anne and Adrian Prescott offer you a friendly, comfortable and relaxing stay at **Lower Meadows**. Comprising of four double en-suite rooms (one with balcony) and one en-suite twin, all rooms have tea/coffee making facilities and colour TV. Daily Local and National Newspapers are available and the Guest Lounge has a selection of local information, books, videos and colour TV. A full English

breakfast is served or you may order any variation to suit your own requirements. Ample car parking available.

Lower Meadows is adjacent to the National Trust's steep, wooded Valency Valley, where there is a footpath to the hidden hamlet of St Juliot and the church where the writer Thomas Hardy was an assistant architect and where he married his sweetheart Emma. The Trust owns much of the land hereabouts, including the cliffs of Penally Point and Willapark, which guard the entrance to the harbour, once a thriving trading port and now used by local fishermen and visitors to this lovely part of the world. Lower Meadows is a non-smoking establishment.

THE OLD MILL

Boscastle, Cornwall PL35 0AQ
Tel: 01840 250230 website: www.boscastleoldmill.com

The Old Mill looks towards the harbour in Boscastle, and was a working corn mill as recently as 1920. It still retains the water wheel, once driven by a leat from the Valency River. The stone flagged courtyard is filled with flowers in the summer, and visitors can sit and enjoy home-cooked food from the Millers Pantry. Steps lead up onto four floors of shops, offering a great variety of unusual and fascinating items. Customers can browse among displays of antiques - furniture, glass and jewellery. There are secondhand books, a den of teddy bears and animal gifts, and also soaps, scents, prints, cards and beautiful linens.

restoration and where he also, in 1870, met his future wife, Emma Gifford, the rector's sister-in-law. Emma later professed that the young architect had already appeared to her in a dream and wrote how, on first meeting him, she was "immediately arrested by his familiar appearance." Much of the couple's courtship took place along this wild stretch of coastline between Boscastle and Crackington Haven and, when Emma died over 40 years later, Hardy returned to St Juliot to erect a memorial to her in the church. Following his death in 1928 a similar memorial was erected to Hardy.

CRACKINGTON HAVEN

7 ½ miles NE of Tintagel off the B3263

One of the most dramatic places along this remarkable stretch of coastline, this tiny port is overlooked by towering 400-foot cliffs, which make it Cornwall's highest coastal point. The small and narrow sandy cove is approached, by land, down a steep-sided wooded combe. It is difficult to see how sizeable vessels once landed here to deliver their cargoes of limestone and Welsh coal. Just to the south of Crackington Haven the path leads to a remote beach, curiously named **The Strangles**, where at low tide, large patches of sand are revealed amongst the vicious looking rocks. During one year

alone in the 1820s, some 20 ships were said to have come to grief here. The undercurrents are strong and swimming is always unsafe.

BUDE

Bude is a busy north Cornwall port, which expanded rapidly after the opening of the canal to Launceston in 1820. The arrival of the railway brought Victorian holidaymakers looking for fresh, bracing sea air. A traditional seaside resort with sweeping expanses of sand, rock pools and Atlantic breakers, Bude has plenty to offer holidaymakers and coastal walkers. A popular surfing centre, said to be where British surfing began, the town is a much favoured holiday destination in summer. However, during the winter, gales can turn this into a remote and harsh environment.

The **Bude Canal** was an ambitious project that aimed to connect the Atlantic with the English Channel via the River Tamar. However, the only stretch to be finished was that between Bude and Launceston. It was a remarkable feat of engineering as the sea lock at the entrance to the canal was the only lock even though it ran for 35 miles and rose to a height of 350 feet in six miles. In order to achieve the changes in level a series of inclined planes, or ramps, were used between the different levels and a wheeled tub boat was pulled up the ramps on metal rails. It finally closed to commercial craft in 1912 and now the **Bude Canal Trail** follows this tranquil backwater right into the heart of Cornwall.

Close to the entrance to the canal stands **Bude Castle**, an unusually small fortification with no towers or turrets, designed by the local 19th century physician, scientist and inventor, Sir Goldsworthy Gurney. It is now an office building but is particularly interesting because it is thought to be the first building in Britain to be constructed on sand. In this case, it rests on a concrete raft - a technique developed by Gurney. Among his other inventions were a steam jet, a musical instrument consisting of glasses played as a piano, and the Bude Light, an intense light obtained by introducing oxygen into the interior flame and using mirrors. He used this to light his own house and also to light the House of Commons, where his invention replaced 280 candles and gave rise to the expression 'in the limelight'. This earned Gurney a knighthood and served the House of Commons for 60 years. To celebrate the new millennium, Carole Vincent and Anthony Fanshawe designed the Bude Light 2000, the first large-scale public sculpture to combine coloured concrete with fibre optic lighting. It stands close to the Castle. The history of the town and its canal can be explored in the **Town Museum**, which stands on the canal side in a former blacksmith's forge. The story of Bude and the surrounding area, including shipwrecks, railways, farming and geology, is told in a series of vivid displays. One of the high spots in the Bude calendar is the annual jazz festival, held in August and featuring numerous

---

QUINCEBOROUGH FARM & COTTAGES

Widemouth Bay, Bude, North Cornwall EX23 0NA
Tel: 01288 361236
website: www.quinceboroughfarmcottages.co.uk

Quinceborough Farm is a mixed working farm of 120 acres situated half a mile from the sandy surfing beach of Widemouth Bay. In 1980, a redundant hay barn was sympathetically converted into three cottages, each of them offering excellent, well-heated self-catering accommodation for up to seven guests. The spacious lounges, which have the original beams and stone walls of the old barn, provide splendid views over the fields and down to the sea. Each has a TV and video, and a spare double bed; they open on to modern fitted kitchens. Downstairs are two pretty bedrooms and a bathroom. The cottages share a laundry room, and among other amenities are a heated outdoor swimming pool, tennis court, putting green and games room. Guests are welcome to join the 'Kids' Patrol' in the morning, helping with feeding the farm animals.

Even closer to the sea are Lower Quinceborough, a two-bedroom bungalow with a front lawn and

an enclosed rear garden; Longstone, with two bedrooms and front and rear gardens; and Driftwood (two bedrooms) and Westhaven Cottage (three bedrooms), which share a walled garden with a built-in barbecue and a summer house.

Patricia Rowland, who owns and runs the cottages, also offers bed & rreakfast accommodation in the farmhouse.

Shore Line at Bude

performances, street parades, jazz workshops - even jazz church services.

Just inland from Bude, in an area, characterised by small fields, old farmsteads, hamlets and isolated churches, lies **Stratton**. This ancient market town and one time port is believed to have been founded by the Romans. During the Civil War, the town was a stronghold of the Royalists and their commander, Sir Bevil Grenville, made **The Tree Inn** his centre of operations. In May 1643, at the Battle of Stamford Hill, Grenville led his troops to victory over the Parliamentarians and the dead of both sides were buried in unmarked graves in Stratton churchyard. The battle is re-enacted in mid-May each year. The Tree Inn was also the birthplace of the Cornish giant, Anthony Payne, Sir Bevil's bodyguard who stood over seven feet tall. They fought together both here and later at Lansdown Hill, near Bath, where Grenville was killed. After helping Grenville's son lead the Royalists to

victory, Payne carried his master's body back to Stratton. After the Civil War, Payne continued to live at the Grenville manor house until his death. When he died, the house had to be altered to allow his coffin to pass through the doorway.

AROUND BUDE

LAUNCELLS
2½ miles E of Bude off the A3072

Set in a delightful wooded combe lies the 15th century Church of St Swithin, declared by Sir John Betjeman as 'the least spoilt church in Cornwall'. The church is notable for its fine Tudor bench-ends and for 15th century floor tiles made in Barnstaple. In the churchyard is the grave of the remarkable Sir Goldsworthy Gurney of Bude.

KILKHAMPTON
4 miles NE of Bude on the A39

The tall and elegant Church of St James contains monuments to the local Grenville family, many of them the work of Michael Chuke, a local man and a pupil of Grinling Gibbons. Equally notable are the magnificent carved bench-ends, and the organ is the one played by Henry Purcell when it was in Westminster Abbey.

MORWENSTOW
5 miles N of Bude off the A39

Used to taking the full brunt of Atlantic storms, this tiny village lies on the harshest stretch of the north Cornwall coast. Although it can sometimes seem rather storm-lashed, it is a marvellous place from which to watch the changing moods of the ocean. Not surprisingly shipwrecks have been common along this stretch of coast. Many came to grief in storms, but it was not unknown for local criminals to lure unsuspecting ships onto the rocks by lighting lanterns on the cliff tops or the shore.

The village's most renowned inhabitant was its eccentric vicar and poet, the Reverend Robert Stephen Hawker, who came here in 1834 and remained among his flock of "smugglers, wreckers and dissenters" until his death in 1875. A colourful figure dressed in a purple frock coat and fisherman's jersey, Hawker spent much of his time walking through his beloved countryside. When not walking he could often be found writing verses and smoking, opium by some accounts, in the driftwood hut that he built 17 steps from the top of the precipitous **Vicarage Cliff**. Though a bizarre character, Hawker was also one of the first people to show concern at the number of ships coming to grief along this stretch of coastline. He spent hours monitoring the waves and would often climb down the cliffs to rescue shipwrecked crews or recover the bodies of those who had perished among the waves. After carrying the bodies back to the village he would give them a proper Christian burial. One of the many ships wrecked off Sharpnose headland was the *Caledonia*, whose figurehead stands above the grave of her captain in Morwenstow churchyard.

Hawker's other contribution to Morwenstow was the rectory, which he built at his own expense and to his own design. As individual as the man himself, the chimneys of the house represent the towers of various churches and Oxford colleges; the broad kitchen chimney is in remembrance of his mother. His lasting contribution to the church was to reintroduce the annual Harvest Festival and his most famous poem is the rousing Cornish anthem, *The Song of Western Men*. The National Trust-owned land, between the church and the cliffs, is dedicated to this remarkable man's memory.

To the north of village lies **Welcombe Mouth**, the graveyard of many ships that came to grief on its jagged rocks. Set back from the shore are the **Welcombe and Marsland Valleys** that are now a nature reserve and a haven for butterflies. To the south are the headlands, **Higher** and **Lower Sharpnose Points**. Rugged rocks, caused by erosion, lie above a boulder-strewn beach, while some of the outcrops of harder rock have begun to form tiny islands.

BODMIN MOOR

BOLVENTOR

In the centre of Bodmin Moor off the A30

Situated at the heart of Bodmin Moor, this scenic village is the location of the former coaching inn, immortalised by Daphne du Maurier in her famous novel, *Jamaica Inn*. During the 18th and 19th centuries this isolated hostelry, on the main route across the bleak moorland, provided an ideal meeting place for smugglers and other outlaws as well as legitimate travellers journeying between Cornwall and the rest of England.

Daphne du Maurier first came to Cornwall in 1926 when she travelled to Fowey with her mother and sisters. While crossing Bodmin Moor she fell in love with its windswept yet romantic landscape and it became the inspiration for many of her novels. Little changed, **Jamaica Inn** still welcomes visitors,

JAMAICA INN AND MUSEUMS

Bolventor, Launceston, Cornwall PL15 7TS
Tel: 01566 86250 Fax: 01566 86177

Built in the mid-18th century to serve travellers making the journey on the new turnpike road between Launceston and Bodmin, **Jamaica Inn** has become one of the best known hostelries in the country if not the world thanks to novelist Daphne du Maurier. Whilst staying here in the 1920s, she was not only taken with the romance of the surrounding bleak moorland but also fascinated by the tales of smugglers and other rogues who made the inn their meeting place.

Today, the inn still serves travellers who can enjoy a drink in the Smugglers bar, dinner in the du Maurier Restaurant, relax by a roaring log fire before retiring to one of the inn's comfortable guest rooms. However, there is much more here that an atmospheric inn that retains much of its 300 year old character. Tales of smugglers and the arch villain, Demon Davey the vicar of Altarnun, are told through a theatrical presentation at the Smugglers at Jamaica Inn exhibition whilst more can be learnt of Daphne herself at the Daphne du Maurier Room. Basing many of her novels in Cornwall where she came to live with her husband in the 1930s, the room here is filled with memorabilia including her Sheraton writing desk, a packet of du Maurier cigarettes that were named after her famous actor father, Sir Gerald, and a dish of glacier mints – her favourite sweets.

Finally, there is Mr Potter's Museum of Curiosity, a fascinating collection of tableaux that were created by the Victorian taxidermist, Walter Potter. Visitors can see not only Steptoe and Son's bear, but also Walter's first tableau, the Death and Burial of Cock Robin, along with smoking memorabilia, Victorian toys and dolls' houses and some curious oddities.

seeking refreshment and accommodation as they have done for centuries. They are joined today by those in search of the secrets of the moors or details of the life and works of du Maurier (see panel above).

Bodmin Moor, the bleak expanse of moorland, surrounding Bolventor, is the smallest of the three great West Country moors and an Area of Outstanding Natural Beauty. Its granite upland is characterised by saturated moor land and weather-beaten tors. From here the rivers Inny, Lynher, Fowey, St Neot and De Lank flow to both the north and south coasts of Cornwall.

At 1377 feet, **Brown Willy** is the highest point of Bodmin Moor, and Cornwall, while, just to the northwest, lies **Rough Tor** (pronounced 'row tor' to rhyme with 'now tor'), the moor's second highest point. Standing on National Trust owned land, Rough Tor is a magnificent viewing point and also the site of a memorial to the men of the Wessex Regiment who were killed during World War II.

Throughout this wild and beautiful moor land, there are remains, left behind by earlier occupiers. There are scattered Bronze Age hut circles and field enclosures and Iron Age hill forts. Many villages in and around the moor grew up around the monastic cells of Celtic missionaries and took the names of saints. Others were mining villages where ruined engine houses still stand out against the skyline.

To the south of Bolventor is the mysterious natural tarn, **Dozmary Pool**, a place, strongly linked with the legend of King Arthur. Brought here following his final battle at Slaughterbridge, King Arthur lay dying at the water's edge when he is said to have asked his friend, St Bedivere, to throw his sword,

Excalibur, into the centre of the pool. As the knight did so a lady's hand rose from the waters to receive the sword. However, this is not the only lake to claim the Lady of the Lake – Loe Pool at Mount's Bay and Bosherstone and Llyn Llydaw in Wales are put forward as alternative resting places for Excalibur.

This desolate and isolated place is also linked with Jan Tregeagle, the wicked steward of the Earl of Radnor whose many evil deeds included the murder of the parents of a young child whose estate he wanted. As a punishment, so the story goes, Tregeagle was condemned to spend the rest of time emptying the lake with a leaking limpet shell. His howls of despair are still said to be heard to this day. By tradition, Dozmary Pool is bottomless, although it did dry up completely during a prolonged drought in 1869. Close by is the county's largest man-made reservoir, **Colliford Lake**. At 1,000 feet above sea level, it is the perfect habitat for long tailed ducks, dippers and grey wagtails.

TREWINT

3 miles N of Bolventor off the A30

This handsome village often played host to John Wesley, the founder of Methodism, on his preaching tours of Cornwall. One of the villagers, Digory Isbell, built an extension to his house for the use of Wesley and his preachers, and **Wesley Cottage** is open for visits. The rooms, thought to be the smallest Methodist preaching place in the world, have been maintained as they were in the 18th century, and visitors can see the prophets' room and the pilgrims' garden. Digory Isbell and his wife are buried in Trewint churchyard.

ALTARNUN

4 miles NE of Bolventor off the A30

This moorland village, charmingly situated in a steep-sided valley, is home

to a splendid, 15th century parish church that is often referred to as the **'Cathedral of the Moors'**. Dedicated to St Nonna, the mother of St David of Wales, the church has a 108-feet pinnacled tower that rises high above the river. Inside, it is surprisingly light and airy, with features ranging from Norman times through to 16th century bench end carvings. In the churchyard stands a Celtic cross, thought to date from the time of St Nonna's journey here from Wales in around AD 527. The waters of nearby St Nonna's well were once thought to cure madness and, after immersion in the waters, lunatics were carried into the church for mass. The process was repeated until the patient showed signs of recovery.

Just to the northwest, near the peaceful village of **St Clether**, lies another holy well, standing on a bracken-covered shelf above the River Inny beside its 15th century chapel. While, to the north, lies **Laneast**, where yet another of Bodmin Moor's holy wells is housed in a 16th century building, close to a tall Celtic cross and the village's original Norman church. Laneast is also the birthplace of John Adams, the astronomer who discovered the planet Neptune.

MINIONS

6 miles SE of Bolventor off the B3254

Boasting the highest pub in Cornwall, this moorland village was a thriving mining centre during the 19th and early 20th centuries with miners and quarrymen extracting granite, copper and lead from the surrounding area. It was also the setting for EV Thompson's historical novel, *Chase the Wind*. One of the now disused mine engine houses has become the **Minions Heritage Centre**. It covers over 4,000 years of life on the moor land, including the story of mining along with the life and times of much earlier settlers.

Close to the village stands the impressive **Hurlers Stone Circle**. This Bronze Age temple comprising three circles takes its name from the ancient game of hurling, the Celtic form of hockey. Legend has it that the circles were men who were caught playing the game on the Sabbath. As a punishment, they were turned to stone. The **Cheesewring**, a natural pile of granite slabs whose appearance is reminiscent of a cheese press, also lies close to the village. Again, legends have grown up around these stones. One, which is probably true, involves Daniel Gumb, a local stonecutter who was a great reader and taught himself both mathematics and astronomy. He married a local girl and they supposedly made their home in a cave under the Cheesewring. Before the cave collapsed, numerous intricate carvings could be seen on the walls, including the inscription "D Gumb 1735". Another story tells that the Cheesewring was once the haunt of a Druid who would offer thirsty passers-by a drink from a golden chalice that never ran dry. The discovery at nearby Rillaton Barrow, in 1837, of a ribbed cup of beaten gold lying beside a skeleton gives credence to the story. The chalice, known as the Rillaton Cup, is displayed in the British Museum.

Just to the northeast lies **Upton Cross**, the home of **Cornish Yarg Cheese**. Made since 1983 in the beautiful Lynher Valley, this famous cheese with its distinctive flavour comes wrapped in nettle leaves. The local delicacy reaches many of the best restaurants and delicatessen counters in the country. Visitors can watch the milking of the dairy herd and the cheesemaking process, follow the pond and woodland trails and enjoy cheese tastings.

South of Minions and not far from the sizeable moorland village of **St Cleer**, is another holy well, **St Cleer's Holy Well**, also thought to have curative powers. There are several other reminders of the distant past. Dating back to Neolithic times, **Trethevy Quoit** is an impressive enclosed chamber tomb that originally formed the core of a vast earthwork mound. The largest such structure in Cornwall, this quoit is believed to be over 5,000 years old. Just to the west lies a tall stone cross, **King Doniert's Stone**, erected in memory of King Durngarth, a Cornish king, believed to have drowned in the River Fowey in AD 875. Downstream from the Stone the River Fowey descends through dense broadleaved woodland in a delightful series of cascades known as **Golitha Falls**. This outstanding and well-known beauty spot is a National Nature Reserve.

Golitha Falls

STERTS THEATRE

Upton Cross, Liskeard, Cornwall PL14 5AZ
Tel/Fax: 01579 362962/362382
website: www.sterts.co.uk

Sterts Theatre was the brainchild of Ewart and Anne Sturrock, who began to develop an arts centre from the outbuildings of their farmhouse. That was more than 20 years ago, and in that time the centre, with its theatre, studio and gallery, has enabled many thousands of people from all sections of the community to take part in creating music, drama, dance, opera, writing, painting, sculpture and pottery. Ewart's and Anne's

© Sterts Theatre

successors, led now by Jonathan Lewsey, hold firmly to Ewart's belief that 'everyone is creative', and continue to provide a unique experience in a unique venue. The variety of performances held in the summer in the spectacular canopied open-air amphitheatre offers something for all tastes, and visitors can make the most of the beautiful surroundings with a family picnic before the show. Alternatively, they can enjoy a meal in the cosy Bistro and Café Bar, or tuck into a burger or hot dog straight from the barbecue.

© Sterts Theatre

The 450-seat amphitheatre was built in only 6 weeks in 1990, and opened with a production of *Othello* directed by Ewart. It was played to an audience of 300 sheltering under umbrellas (the canopy was only added in 1994!). In-house productions for 2003 included *Bugsy Malone*, *Cold Comfort Farm*, *Don Giovanni* and *The Lion in Winter*, while included past touring companies have been Miracle Theatre, Ophaboom, Heartbreak Productions and the Théâtre de Complicité. There are regular music evenings, too, from folk nights to concerts and operas. 2004/2005 will be just as exciting and varied, and every performance will involve the special atmosphere and the feeling of intimacy and involvement that only an outdoor show can evoke.

The lovely art gallery (open from

© Sterts Theatre

9am to 5pm Monday to Friday) features an eclectic range of exhibitions throughout the year, and the displays include jewellery, ceramics and craft items for sale. Sterts also offers various workshops and classes, ranging from StageKids (a youth drama theatre class), ballet and contemporary dance to piano and voice training. Craft workshops run throughout the year and include stained glass, living willow, garden chair and raku pottery workshops.

Set in 11 acres of grounds, Sterts has plenty of car parking space and ample room for picnics, for strolling and for children to romp; but above all it provides a unique opportunity to experience the performing arts in natural surroundings. Other leading attractions in the vicinity include the Cornish Yarg Cheese Farm and the Minions Heritage Centre, but on a summer's evening it's definitely Sterts that takes centre stage.

© Sterts Theatre

LISKEARD

9 miles SE of Bolventor on the B3254

Situated on the undulating ground between the valleys of the East Looe and Seaton Rivers, this picturesque and lively market town was also one of Cornwall's five medieval stannary towns – the others being Bodmin, Lostwithiel, Truro and Helston. The name comes from the Latin for tin, 'stannum', and these five towns were the only places licensed to weigh and stamp the metal. Liskeard had been a centre for the mining industry for centuries. However, by the 19th century, after the construction of a canal linking the town with Looe, vast quantities of copper ore and granite joined the cargoes of tin. In the 1850s, the canal was replaced by the Looe Valley branch of the Great Western Railway. A scenic stretch of the **Looe Valley Line** is still open today though the industrial wagons have long since been replaced with passenger carriages.

Although it is a small town, Liskeard does boast some public buildings that act as a reminder of its past importance and prosperity. The **Guildhall** was constructed in 1859 while the **Public Hall**, opened in 1890, is still used as offices of the town council as well as being home to a local **Museum**. Adjacent to the Passmore-Edwards public library stands **Stuart House**, a handsome Jacobean residence where Charles I stayed in 1644 while engaged in a campaign against Cromwell at nearby Lostwithiel. Finally, in Well Street, lies one of Liskeard's most curious features – an arched grotto that marks the site of **Pipe Well**, a medieval spring reputed to have had curative powers.

To the west of Liskeard is an attraction that will please all the family. **Dobwalls Family Adventure Park** has a miniature steam railway based on an old North American railroad, woodland play areas and a restaurant as well as a charming Edwardian countryside museum with a permanent exhibition on the life and works of wildlife artist Archibald Thorburn. Another top attraction is **Porfell Animal Land Wildlife Park** (see panel on page 94).

ST NEOT

6 miles S of Bolventor off the A38

Once a thriving centre of the woollen industry, St Neot is famous for the splendid 15th century Church of St Anietus and, in particular, its fabulous early 16th century stained glass. Of the many beautiful scenes depicted here, perhaps the most interesting is that of St

Neot, the diminutive saint after whom the village is named. Although only 15 inches tall, the saint became famous for his miracles involving animals. One story tells of an exhausted hunted doe, which ran to St Neot's side. A stern look from the saint sent the pursuing hounds back into the forest while the huntsman dropped his bow and became a faithful disciple. Another tale – the one that can be seen in the church window – tells of an angel giving the saint three fish for his well and adding that as long as he only eats one fish a day there will always be fish to eat. Unfortunately, when St Neot fell ill his servant took two fish and prepared them for his master. Horrified, Neot prayed over the meal, ordering the fish be returned to the well and, as they touched the water, they came alive again.

Tied to the tower outside the church is an oak branch that is replaced annually on Oak Apple Day. The ceremony was started by Royalists wishing to give thanks for the oak tree that hid Charles II during his flight from the country.

To the south of St Neot are the **Carnglaze Slate Caverns** where slate for use in the building trade was first quarried in the 14th century. Today, visitors can journey underground and see the large chambers that were once used by smugglers as rum stores and the subterranean lake that is filled with the clearest blue-green water.

WARLEGGAN
5 miles SW of Bolventor off the A38

The remote location of this tiny hamlet has led to it been acknowledged as a haunt of the Cornish 'piskies' but Warleggan's most eccentric inhabitant was undoubtedly Rev Frederick Densham, who arrived here in 1931. Immediately alienating his parishioners by closing the Sunday school, Densham continued by putting barbed wire around the rectory and patrolling the grounds with a pack of German Shepherd dogs. In response, his flock stayed away from his church and one record in the parish registry reads, "No fog. No wind. No rain. No congregation." Unperturbed, the rector fashioned his own congregation from cardboard, filled the pews and preached on as normal. It would, however, appear that Densham did have a kinder side to his nature, as he built a children's playground in the rectory garden.

To the north and west lie the peaceful backwaters of **Cardinham Woods**, enjoyed by both walkers and cyclists. Acquired by the Forestry Commission in 1922, this attractive and varied woodland is a haven for a wide variety of wildlife as well as

PORFELL ANIMAL LAND WILDLIFE PARK

Trecangate, Nr Lanreath, Liskeard, Cornwall PL14 4RE
Tel: 01503 220211

The peace and tranquillity of the Cornish countryside combine with the exotic world of wild animals at **Porfell Animal Land Wildlife Park**. In 15 acres of fields bounded by streams and woodland, visitors can meet wallabies, marmosets, lemurs, zebra, meerkats and

porcupines, and feed the deer, goats, ducks and chickens. After a stroll through the woods, visitors can relax and enjoy some refreshments in the cosy Peacock Tea Room, housed in an attractive old barn. The Park is signposted on the B3359 south of the A390 St Austell-Liskeard road.

producing high quality Douglas fir for the timber industry. In medieval times, the woods were the location of an important Norman castle belonging to the Cardinham family but all that remains today are an earthwork mound and a few traces of the original keep.

BODMIN

10 miles SW of Bolventor on the A38

Situated midway between Cornwall's two coasts and at the junction of two ancient trade routes, Bodmin has always been an important town used, particularly, by traders who preferred the overland journey to the sea voyage around Land's End. **Castle Canyke**, to the southeast, was built during the Iron Age to defend this important route. A few centuries later, the Romans erected a fort (one of a string they built to defend strategic river crossings) on a site here above the River Camel. The way-marked footpath, the **Saints' Way**, follows the ancient cross-country route. In the 6th century, St Petroc, one of the most influential of the early Welsh missionary saints, visited Bodmin. In the 10th century, the monastery he founded at Padstow moved here as a protection against Viking raiders. The town's impressive church is dedicated to the saint and in the churchyard can be found one of the many holy wells in Bodmin – **St Goran's Well** – which dates from the 6th century.

The only market town in Cornwall to appear in the Domesday Book, Bodmin was chiefly an ecclesiastical town until the reign of Henry VIII. However, this did not mean that this was a quiet and peaceful place. During the Tudor reign, it was the scene of three uprisings: against the tin levy in 1496, in support of Perkin Warbeck against Henry VII in 1597 and, in 1549, against the imposition of the English Prayer Book. The town's failure to flourish when the railways arrived in Cornwall was due to its decision not to allow the Great Western Railway access to the town centre. Not only did it fail to expand as other towns did but, when Truro became the seat of the new bishopric, Bodmin missed out again.

The Crown Jewels and the Domesday Book were hidden at **Bodmin Jail** during World War I and this former county prison, dating from 1776, is an interesting place to visit. The Shire Hall, built in 1837, served as the County Court until 1988. Now restored (it was officially opened by the Queen in 2000), it brings to life in **The Courtroom Experience** the notorious murder in 1844 of Charlotte Dymond on lonely Bodmin Moor and the trial of Matthew Weeks for the crime. **Bodmin Town Museum** provides an insight into the town's past and that of the surrounding area. Just a short distance from the town centre lies **Bodmin Beacon Local Nature Reserve**. From the beacon summit, on which stands the 114-foot **Gilbert Memorial**, there are splendid views over the town and moor. Also easily reached from Bodmin is the **Camel Trail**, a walking and cycling path along the River Camel to Padstow following the track bed of one of the country's first railways.

Housed in The Keep near the railway station in Bodmin, the **Duke of Cornwall's Light Infantry Regimental Museum** covers the military history of the County Regiment of Cornwall, The Duke of Cornwall's Light Infantry.

To the south of the town, near the village of Cutmadoc, lies one of the most fascinating late 19th century houses in England, the spectacular **Lanhydrock House**. Now owned by the National Trust and surrounded by wonderful formal gardens, woodland and parkland, it originally belonged to Bodmin's Augustinian priory. This large estate was bought, in 1620, by Sir Richard Robarts

Lanhydrock House

Distance:	4.1 miles (6.5 kilometres)
Typical time:	150 mins
Height gain:	115 metres
Map:	Explorer 107
Walk:	www.walkingworld.com ID:1514
Contributor:	Jim Grindle

Access Information:

The estate is just under two miles from Bodmin Parkway railway station from which the no. 55 bus runs. It is signposted from the A30, the A38 and the B3268.

Description:

This is an excellent walk for anybody with an interest in natural history. The trees in the parkland have on them over 100 species of lichens and there are also mosses, beetles and birds, including treecreeper, tawny owl, nuthatch and all three British woodpeckers. Nine of the 14 British bats can be found here and there is an abundance of grassland flowers. On the River Fowey are otters and we saw lots of dippers and grey wagtails, more of the latter than I have seen anywhere else. You could spend a long time getting round! The walk is a mixture of woodland and river with a steady climb back uo to the house.

Additional Information:

The National Trust describes the house as, "One of the most fascinating late 19th century houses in England, full of period atmosphere and the trappings of a high Victorian country house." There is enough time to visit the house and do this walk in a day, but obviously there is a lot to see both indoors and out.

Features:

River, toilets, stately home, National Trust/ NTS, birds, flowers, butterflies, cafe, gift shop, good for kids, nature trail, restaurant, tea shop, woodland.

Walk Directions:

1 From the car park go back to its entrance and look for a path on the left. The low signpost directs you to reception and the house. Just out of sight is a gate giving access to a road. (There are toilets in the car park and a refreshment kiosk with limited opening hours.)

2 From here you can see the award-winning reception building. Cross the road and pass to the right of it. You do not have to pay if you just intend doing the walk and you will be on a public footpath. Follow the main drive to the gatehouse outside the main house.

3 Pass the gatehouse and follow the tarmac to the right where you will see a wooden gate in a corner.

4 Go through and follow this drive. Don't take any of the smaller paths that join it, including the one immediately to the left behind the gate. You will pass a house with the estate's kitchen gardens and go through a red gate. Almost 1km from this Waymark a track goes off to the right.

5 Pass by it and where the main track curves right there is another which you also ignore. A few metres past this bend, though, a track joins from the left.

6 This one you do want. Turn left and pass an old quarry as it leaves the wood to enter meadows. At the entrance to another wood is a gate.

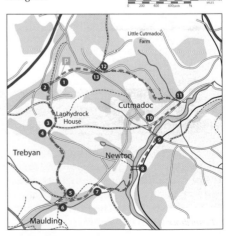

7 Go through and turn right. The track leads down, with more gates, to the banks of the River Fowey.

8 Turn left and follow the river until you see a bridge. This is Kathleen Bridge that was built in 1991 by the Royal Engineers. Cross and turn left following the river to an ancient stone bridge.

9 Once over the bridge turn to the right into the car park and cross to a little footbridge.

10 Go over the bridge onto Station Drive, a stone track. You will pass a large Giant Redwood just across the stream. Turn right and follow the track for 1km until you see a red, signposted metal gate on your left.

11 Go through onto a lane and turn left - you will see a similar gate a few metres along on the far side of the road. This gives access to the wood. Turn left on any forks in the path - there are lots of yellow arrows on this stretch - so that you keep to the edge of the wood - you will be able to see the meadows outside for most of the way. When the path levels out it meets a forestry track at right angles. Turn left and follow it until you reach a road.

12 Cross to the minor road directly opposite. Almost on the corner (on the right) is another of the red gates.

13 Go through this - a path goes to the left, passing around the edge of a cricket field and then following a wall all the way round to the left to enter the back of the car park.

(who made his fortune in tin and wool) and his family lived here until the estate was given to the Trust in 1953. Partially destroyed by fire in 1881, this mansion is probably the grandest in Cornwall. Visitors can see that many of the rooms combine the building's original splendour with the latest in Victorian domestic comforts and amenities. One special bedroom belonged to Tommy Agar-Robarts, who was killed at the Battle of Loos in 1915; it contains many of his personal possessions. The grounds are equally magnificent and are known for the fabulous springtime displays of rhododendrons, magnolias and camellias, a superb avenue of ancient beech and sycamore trees, a cob-and-thatch summer house and a photogenic formal garden overlooked by the small estate church of St Hydroc. In the woods are many unusual flowers and ferns as well as owls, woodpeckers and many other birds.

BLISLAND

6 miles W of Bolventor off the A30

Hidden in a maze of country lanes, this moorland village has a tree-lined village green that has stayed true to its original Saxon layout – an unusual sight on this side of the River Tamar. The part Norman parish church, dedicated to St Protus and St Hyacinth, was one of Sir John Betjeman's favourites, described by the poet as "dazzling and amazing". On the moorland to the north of the village are numerous ancient monuments

Lanhydrock Gardens

TREHAVEN MANOR HOTEL

Station Road, East Looe, Cornwall PL13 1HN
Tel: 01503 262028 Fax: 01503 265613
e-mail: enquiries@trehavenhotel.co.uk
website: www.trehavenhotel.co.uk

Once the vicarage to St Mary's Church in Looe, this mid-19th century building in traditional Cornish stone is now a very comfortable, quiet and civilised hotel. **Trehaven Manor Hotel** is set in an elevated position along a sweeping driveway, and the views from the approach over the everchanging estuary, the picturesque harbour and beyond are just one of its many special attractions. The views are shared by most of the beautifully decorated, spacious bedrooms, which all boast en suite facilities, TV, radio/alarm clock and beverage tray.

Breakfast, with fresh local produce to the fore, is served in the beautiful bay-fronted dining room (more stunning views) and a splendid tea with home-made scones and Cornish clotted cream is a treat served on arrival in the elegant lounge. Though surrounded by peace and tranquillity, Trehaven Manor is only a three-minute walk from the centre of the fishing port, and just a couple more to the beach. It is an ideal base for exploring Looe, whose many attractions include the famous Banjo Pier, as well as the varied delights of the nearby coast and countryside.

BUCKLAWREN FARM

St Martin by Looe, Cornwall PL13 1NZ
Tel: 01503 240738 Fax: 01503 240481
e-mail: bucklawren@btopenworld.com
website: www.bucklawren.com

On the site of a manor mentioned in the Domesday Book, **Bucklawren** is a working farm with 500 acres of arable and beef farmland set in the lovely Cornish countryside with beautiful sea views. The Henly family offer the warmest of welcomes and a choice of either bed & breakfast or self-catering accommodation. Family, twin and double en suite bedrooms in the farmhouse are individually decorated and generous in homely comforts, and guests staying here start the day with a traditional farmhouse breakfast. The sunny conservatory is a great place to while away a winter's afternoon with a good book, while there are many beautiful gardens, National Trust properties and country houses within an easy drive.

The self-catering option offers a choice of cosy stone cottages set in large, well-kept gardens with fine views of the countryside and coast. Combining original character with modern amenity, they comprise the two-storey Hayloft, which sleeps up to eight in comfort; the Horseshoe (sleeps six), the Forge (four) and Tackroom (four), all converted from the farmhouse stables; and The Lodge, with two bedrooms and two bathrooms, designed for ease of use by disabled visitors. Also on the farm is the Granary Licensed Restaurant, whose lunch and dinner menus make excellent use of prime local produce including fish and shellfish from Looe.

including the stone circle of **Blisland Manor Common** and **Stipple Stone Henge Monument** on Hawkstor Down.

LOOE

The tidal harbour at Looe, created by the two rivers the East Looe and West Looe, made this an important fishing and sea-faring port from the Middle Ages through to the 19th century. Originally, two separate towns on either side of the estuary, East and West Looe were first connected by a bridge in the early 15th century. In 1883, they were officially incorporated. The present day seven-arched bridge, dating from the 19th century, carries the main road and links the two halves of the town. Something of a jack-of-all-trades, over the years Looe has had a pilchard fishing fleet, it has served the mineral extractors of Bodmin Moor and is has also been the haunt of smugglers. However, it is only the fishing industry that remains from the town's colourful past. Looe is still Cornwall's second most important port with fish auctions taking place at East Looe's busy quayside market on the famous **Banjo Pier**.

Of the two distinct parts, East Looe, with its narrow cobbled streets and twisting alleyways, is the older. Here, housed in one of the town's several 16th century buildings, is the **Old Guildhall Museum**, where can be seen the old magistrates' bench and original cells as well displays detailing much of Looe's history. In 1800, a bathing machine was built overlooking East Looe's sandy beach. After the opening of the Looe Valley Line to passengers in 1879, the development of the twin towns as a holiday resort began. Fortunately, the character of East Looe has been retained

while West Looe is, essentially, a residential area.

The Looe Valley Line railway replaced the Liskeard to Looe canal and today the same journey can be made by following the **Looe Valley Line Footpath**. A distance of 10 miles, the walk takes in some of Cornwall's most beautiful woodlands as well as the 'Giant's Hedge', a seven-foot earth embankment. For an all round view of the area's flora and fauna, the **South East Cornwall Discovery Centre**, in West Looe, introduces visitors to the wealth of wildlife, plant life and scenery in the southeastern region of the county.

More recently, Looe has established itself as Britain's major shark fishing centre and regularly plays host to an International Sea Angling Festival. At the **Aquarium** fish and other curious creatures from the deep can be seen. Once a refuge for one of Cornwall's most notorious smugglers, Black Joan, **Looe Island**, just off the coast, is now home to a bird sanctuary. The island was made famous by the Atkins sisters who featured it in their books, *We Bought an Island* and *Tales from our Cornish Island*.

AROUND LOOE

ST KEYNE

5 miles N of Looe on the B3254

Named after one of the daughters of a Welsh king who settled here during the 5th century, St Keyne is home to the famous holy well – **St Keyne's Well** – that lies a mile from the village. Found beneath a great tree, newly married couples came here to drink as the first to taste the waters was said to be the one to wear the trousers in the marriage. Romanticised by the Victorians, the custom is still carried out by newly-weds today. One of the more curious episodes in St Keyne's history took place during the reign of Catholic Mary Tudor, when the local rector and his wife (who were married during the reign of Protestant Edward VI) were dragged from their bed in the middle of the night and placed in the village stocks.

Though a small village, St Keyne sees many visitors during the year as it is home to **Paul Corin's Magnificent Music Machines**, a wonderful collection that opened in 1967. Housed in the old mill buildings, where Paul was the last miller, this collection of mechanical instruments covers a wide range of sounds and music from classical pieces to musicals. It has featured on numerous radio and television programmes. Paul's grandfather was Bransby Williams, the only great star from the Music Hall days to have his own BBC television show, in the early 1950s.

Just to the south of St Keyne, and in the valley of the East Looe river, is a **Stone Circle** of eight standing quartz stones, said to be older than Stonehenge.

St Germans

7 miles NE of Looe on the B3249

Before the Anglo Saxon diocese of Cornwall was incorporated with Exeter in 1043, this rural village was a cathedral city and the present **St Germans' Church** stands on the site of the Saxon cathedral. Dating from Norman times, it was built as the great church for the Augustinian priory founded here in 1162. As well as curiously dissimilar towers dating from the 13th and 15th centuries, the church contains several striking monuments to the Eliot family. This family bought the priory shortly after its dissolution under Henry VIII and renamed their new estate Port Eliot. Also in the church is an old chair that

---

Cornish Orchards

Westnorth Manor Farm, Duloe, Cornwall PL14 4PW
Tel: 01503 269007 Fax: 01503 263373
e-mail: apples@cornishorchards.co.uk
website: cornishorchards .co.uk

Cornwall may not be well known for its cider making but, like all rural areas, it has long practised the art. The county once boasted extensive orchards however these have reduced to small isolated pockets of trees - harvests were often left to rot for lack of a market. **Cornish Orchards**, located at the head of the unspoilt wooded Looe Valley, now uses the harvests of these old orchards to produce quality apple juices and ciders.

Started in 1999 as a farm diversification, Cornish Orchards at Westnorth Manor Farm has fifteen acres of its own traditional variety apple orchards. The processing of lesser known apple varieties such as Lord of the Isles, Collogett Pippin, Tommy Knight and The Rattler is labour intensive and does not lend itself to substantial mechanisation. The products are 'hand made' and as a small operation the collection of the harvest, its handling, processing, blending and final juice or cider creation can be controlled and managed to suit the readiness of the fruit.

The ciders and apple juices contain no artificial sweetners, preservatives or colouring, allowing the true taste of the harvest to remain. Varieties of juice can be changed season on season depending on harvest quality and quantity. Craftmanship is needed to achieve the best products from the resources available. With up to eight varieties of apple juice and five types of cider available, the Farm Shop provides an opportunity to sample and enjoy the high quality of goods that can be created by a small producer. Call 01503 269007 for opening times.

bears a series of carvings depicting Dando, a 14th century priest from the priory. According to local stories, one Sunday Dando left his prayers to go out hunting with a group of wild friends. At the end of the chase, the priest called for a drink and was handed a richly decorated drinking horn by a stranger on a black horse. While quenching his thirst Dando saw the stranger stealing his game. Despite his calls, the horseman refused to return the game. In a drunken frenzy, Dando swore that he would follow the stranger to Hell in order to retrieve his prizes, whereupon the stranger pulled Dando up onto his horse and rode into the River Lynher. Neither the stranger on the horse nor the priest was ever seen again.

SALTASH

11½ miles NE of Looe on the A38

A medieval port on the River Tamar, Saltash was once the base for the largest river steamer fleet in the southwest. Today, it remains the 'Gateway to Cornwall' for many holidaymakers who cross the river into Cornwall via one of the town's mighty bridges. Designed by Isambard Kingdom Brunel in 1859, the iron-built **Royal Albert Bridge** carries the railway while, alongside, is the much more slender **Tamar Bridge**, a suspension road bridge that was opened in 1961 replacing a ferry service that had operated since the 13th century.

Though older than Plymouth, on the other side of the Sound, Saltash is now becoming a suburb of its larger neighbour, following the construction of the road bridge. However, Saltash has retained much of its charm and Cornish individuality. The 17th century **Guildhouse** stands on granite pillars and close by is **Mary Newman's Cottage**, a quaint 15th century building that was the home of Sir Francis Drake's first wife.

TORPOINT

11½ miles E of Looe on the A374

This small town grew up around a ferry service that ran across the **Hamoaze** (as the Tamar estuary is called at this point) to Devonport in the 18th century. From here there are excellent views over the water to the Royal Navy Dockyards and *HMS Raleigh*, the naval training centre for ratings and artificer apprentices. Commissioned in 1940, *HMS Raleigh* is also the home of the Royal Marine Band (Plymouth).

To the north of the town, overlooking the River Lynher as it meets the Tamar, is **Antony House**, a superb example of early 18th century architecture, now in the hands of the National Trust. Although the estate has been owned by the influential Carew family for nearly 600 years, the neo-classical house was built of pale silver-grey stone between 1718 and 1729.

It remains home to a wonderful collection of paintings (many by Sir Joshua Reynolds), tapestries and furniture. Surrounding the house are the gardens and grounds landscaped by Humphry Repton in the late 18th century, including the delightful **Antony Woodland Gardens**, which are at their best in the spring and autumn. The formal gardens contain the National Collection of Day Lilies.

CREMYLL

12½ miles E of Looe on the B3247

Linked to Plymouth by a foot ferry, Cremyll is an excellent place from which to explore **Mount Edgcumbe House** , the 16th century home of the Earls of Edgcumbe. They moved here from Cotehele House after Piers Edgcumbe married Jean Durnford, an heiress with considerable estates including the Cremyll ferry.

PITT HOUSE & COTTAGE

Nr Looe/Polperro
Fowey
Log on to website: www.pittstops.co.uk
or for more information Tel: 01503 264571

- Private Location
- Peaceful & Relaxing Atmosphere
- Well Equipped & Comfortably Furnished
- Quality Homes for your stay
- Sleeps 6 & 4
- Regret no pets

For those of you that appreciate the tranquility of the country side, Pitt is an ideal choice for a self-catering holiday. Situated in one of Cornwalls hidden valleys Pitt lies nestled at the top of the Looe river surrounded by farm and woodland. This rural hideaway set in two and a half acres of gardens and grounds is close to all amenities, country inns and well stocked shops are but 2 miles in the local villages of Pelynt and Duloe. The historic fishing coves of Looe and Polperro with an abundance of restaurants are a short car drive of 5 miles.

Pitt is very fortunate in it's position to be blessed with the availability of many local activities and places of interest. The Lost Gardens of Heligan, The Eden Project and the Maritime Museum to mention but a few. Whatever your interests you are sure to find them catered for.

However you may find yoursleves forgetting the rest of the world exsists and truly relax in the lovely landscaped gardens and grounds of Pitt.

A special retreat where time gives way for thought

TRENDERWAY FARM

Pelynt, Nr Polperro, Cornwall PL13 2LY
Tel: 01503 272214 Fax: 01503 272991
e-mail: trenderwayfarm@hotmail.com
website: www.trenderwayfarm.co.uk

Owner Lynne Tuckett's flair for interior design is evident throughout **Trenderway Farm**, a working mixed farm lying on gentle western slopes at the head of the Polperro Valley. The 16th century farmhouse is surrounded by a huddle of barns and outbuildings in local stone, and the four superior

guest bedrooms are divided between the main house and one of the adjacent barns. The bedrooms are not only elegant and stylish but also very generous in size, and contain separate shower cabins as well

as baths. One of the rooms in the barn boasts a four-poster, and all have TV, tea/coffee-making facilities and central heating. Breakfast with eggs from the farm's free-range eggs and sausages from an excellent local butcher is served in the conservatory, and guests can while away a relaxing hour or two by the fire in the sitting room, meeting the other guests or planning the day's activities.

Lakes have recently been created from the stream that runs to Polperro, and a rowing boat is available for guests staying at the farm, which is signposted off the A387 Looe-Polperro road.

To the southwest of Cremyll are the two small and attractive villages of **Cawsand** and **Kingsand** that, for centuries, by some administrative quirk were placed in different counties: Cornwall and Devon respectively. Though it is hard to believe today, it was from here that one of the largest smuggling fleets in Cornwall operated. At the peak of their activities in the late 18th and early 19th centuries, thousands of barrels of brandy, silk and other contraband were landed here in secret and transported through sleeping villages to avoid the attentions of the revenue men. It was also at **Cawsand Bay** that the Royal Navy fleet used to shelter before the completion of the **Plymouth Breakwater** in 1841, leaving a legacy of a large number of inns that still welcome locals and holidaymakers alike.

Further southwest again and at the southernmost point of Mount Edgcumbe Country Park lies the spectacular **Rame Head**, which guards the entrance into Plymouth Sound. From the 400-foot cliffs there are superb views but this beautiful headland has its own special feature – the ruined 14th century St Michael's Chapel, from which a blazing beacon warned of the coming of the Armada. In the little hamlet of Rame itself is the older Church of St Germanus, which is still lit by candles; for centuries its west tower and spire acted as a landmark for sailors.

The **Eddystone Lighthouse**, which can be seen on a clear day, lies 10 miles offshore from Rame Head. It was from here, in July 1588, that the English fleet had their first encounter with the Spanish Armada.

WHITSAND BAY

8 miles E of Looe off the B3247

Running between Rame Head and the hamlet of **Portwrinkle**, this bay has an impressive stretch of beach that is more a series of coves that one continuous expanse of sand. The seaside village of Portwrinkle developed around its medieval harbour. Further west along the coast, at the coastal village of **Murrayton**, lies the famous **Monkey Sanctuary**, the world's first protected colony of Amazonian woolly monkeys. The sanctuary was set up in 1964 to provide a safe environment for monkeys rescued from zoos or abandoned as pets, and its inhabitants roam freely in the gardens of the outdoor enclosures. Plants for the monkeys to eat are grown in a forest garden, while the Tree Top Café takes care of hungry humans.

POLPERRO

3½ miles SW of Looe off the A387

Polperro is many people's idea of a typical Cornish fishing village as its steep, narrow streets and alleyways are piled high with fisherman's cottages built around a narrow tidal inlet. All routes in this lovely village seem to lead

Polperro

down to its beautiful Harbour. It is still a busy fishing port, where there is normally an assortment of colourful boats to be seen. For centuries dependent on pilchard fishing for its survival, Polperro also has a long association with smuggling. During the 18th century, the practice was so rife that nearly all of the inhabitants were involved in the shipping, storing or transporting of contraband. To combat this widespread problem, HM Customs and Excise established the first 'preventive station' in Cornwall here in the 1800s. At the **Museum of Smuggling** a whole range of artefacts and memorabilia are used to illustrate the myths, legends surrounding the characters, who dodged the government taxes on luxury goods. A model of *Lady Beatrice*, a traditional gaff-rigged fishing boat, can also be seen.

Other interesting buildings to be seen include the **House on Props** and **Couch's House**, the 16th century dwelling where Dr Jonathan Couch, the naturalist and grandfather of author Sir Arthur Quiller-Couch, lived.

FOWEY

8 miles W of Looe on the A3082

Guarding the entrance to the river from which it takes is name, Fowey (pronounced Foy) is a lovely old seafaring town with steep, narrow streets and alleyways leading down to one of the most beautiful natural harbours along the south coast. An important port in the Middle Ages, though it was certainly occupied by the Romans, the town exhibits architectural styles ranging from Elizabethan to Edwardian. As a busy trading port, Fowey also attracted pirates and it was the home of the 'Fowey Gallants', who preyed on ships in the Channel and engaged in raids on the French coast. Brought together during

LESQUITE FARM

Lesquite, Lansallos, Looe, Cornwall PL13 2QE
Tel: 01503 220315
website: www.lesquite-polperro.fsnet.co.uk
e-mail: lesquite@farmersweekly.net

Owners Richard and Annette Tolputt combine growing organic vegetables and beef with running a successful bed & breakfast business at their farm in a quiet, secluded setting. The guest accommodation comprises three bedrooms in the part 17th century stone-faced farmhouse, all with large shower units, full central heating, TV and beverage tray; one room features a bed hand-made from Cornish oak. Breakfast, based around home-grown and local produce, is served in a sunny room with doors opening on to the patio and gardens, and guests have the use of a sitting room with a log burner.

Alternative self-catering accommodation is offered in Little Cottage, a converted coach house and

stable with its own patio sheltered by a beautiful copper beech. The owners have not only sympathetically extended and modernised the farmhouse but have greatly enhanced the grounds, creating a haven for wildlife among the lawns and gardens that run down to ancient oak woodland and a tributary steam of the River Fowey. With the help of the Cornwall Wildlife Trust they are also extending the nature trail that runs through the grounds. Standing on one lawn is an old cider press, a reminder of a traditional local industry - it is now filled with flowers.

the Hundred Years War to fight the French, these local mariners did not disband at the end of the hostilities but continued to terrorise shipping along this stretch of coast and beyond. A devastating raid by the French in 1457, that saw much of Fowey burnt to the ground, was in direct retaliation for attacks made by the Gallants.

Later, in the 19th century, much of the china clay from St Austell was exported through Fowey. It is still a busy place as huge ships continue to call at this deep water harbour alongside fishing boats and pleasure craft. The town's **Museum** is an excellent place to discover Fowey's colourful past, from the days of piracy through to the china clay exports of the 19th century. Naturally,

Fowey

there are many inns here including the **King of Prussia**, named after an 18th century smuggler, and the **Ship Inn**,

The Romantic Englishwoman

5-7 Lostwithiel Street, Fowey,Cornwall PL231BD
Tel: 01726 833855

33 Fore Street, Lostwithiel, Cornwall PL22 OBN
Tel: 01208 873818

8 Molesworth Street, Wadebridge, Cornwall PL27 7DA
Tel: 01208 815880

website: www.romanticwomen.co.uk

The Romantic Englishwoman are shops like few others - treasure troves filled with beautiful quilts, cotton bedlinens, tablelinens, french soaps and lots more. Temptingly displayed are a range of

beautiful, romantic items for the home. Here the customer will find practical items such as a superb range of linen clothes and cotton sweaters but also special gifts for weddings, christenings, anniversaries and of course Christmas is a must.

To compliment both the traditional and the modern home there are unusual tablelamps, pictures, frames and all of the furniture is for sale including the superb antique French beds, reuphostered antique chairs, pine dressers, boxes and chest of drawers.With an excellent reputation that extends far beyond Cornwall the company has recently expanded into the world of interiors and a new shop has opened in Wadebridge

OLD HOUSE OF FOYE

31-35 Fore Street, Fowey, Cornwall PL23 1 AH
Tel: 01726 833712
e-mail: oldhouse@foye.co.uk
website: www.foye.co.uk

When visitors step inside **Old House of Foye** they can look forward to a unique shopping experience. The goods on sale complement its unique character, and behind its whitewashed frontage almost every available inch is filled with interesting and exotic things to buy. The owner Rosemary Blackstock has preserved many original features, including low ceilings, original beams, and the old kitchen complete with slate floor, a section of which has been cut away to reveal the 15th century cobbles. The stock includes rugs and other merchandise from the Middle and Far East blending with top-quality Cornish arts

PAINTING BY SIMON POWELL

and crafts, including limited edition Kate Glanville pottery celebrating the annual Daphne du Maurier Festival. Also to be found are beautifully glazed pots and bowls by Anthony Richards; pottery by Heather Swain; hand-painted silks, bowls and glassware by Rita Williams; the striking Exmoor Cranberry glass by James Adlington and his team; and beautiful stained glass by Deborah Martin.

Quality cards cater for most occasions, with appropriate Biblical quotations, and there's a small assortment of books, mostly with a spiritual theme.

PINK KITE INTERIORS

Quayhouse, 4 Fore Street, Fowey, Cornwall PL23 1AQ
Tel/Fax: 01726 833784
e-mail: jane@pinkkite.co.uk
website: www.pinkkite.co.uk

Fabulous fabrics and furnishings and an eclectic mix of unusual, stylish accessories for the home are to be found at the two branches of **Pink Kite Interiors**, one newly opened in Fowey, the other in Polruan. Owner and interior designer Jane Wheeler has assembled a

collection of desirable items that can be cool, colourful, classic or contemporary, and she and her staff are always ready with a friendly welcome and helpful advice in surroundings that are pleasantly relaxing and just made for browsing - and the cool background music helps the mood along!

A sweet little heart-shaped hot water bottle; a glitzy, funky handbag; colourful glasses and tableware; vacuum flasks in various hues; soft toys to cuddle and cherish; flowerpots and planters - the selection is wide-ranging and everything has Jane's seal of approval, so it's all sure to please and delight, whether it's bought as a gift or for a personal treat. The local residents have taken both places to their hearts, and visitors to the region are sure to be equally taken with these most individual shops.

The Polruan outlet is at 3 Fore Street, Tel: 01726 870100

originally a town house built by the influential Rashleigh family in the 15th century.

Fowey has two important literary connections: with Daphne du Maurier, who lived at Gribbin Head (the Daphne du Maurier Literary Centre is next to the church); and with Sir Arthur Quiller-Couch (or 'Q'), who lived for over 50 years at **The Haven**, on the Esplanade just above the Polruan ferry. Sir Arthur was a Cambridge professor, sometime Mayor of Fowey, editor of the *Oxford Book of English Verse* and author of several books connected with Fowey - he called it Troy Town. He died in 1944 after being hit by a car and was buried in St Fimbarrus churchyard.

To the south of Fowey lies **Readymoney Cove**, whose expanse of sand acts as the town's beach. Further along, lies **St Catherine's Castle**, part of a chain of fortifications, built by Henry VIII to protect the harbours along the south coast. From Readymoney Cove the **Coastal Footpath** is clearly marked all the way around to **Polkerris** and the walk takes in many fine viewpoints as well as the castle and the wonderful daymark on **Gribbin Head**. The beacon on Gribbin Head was built in 1832 to help seafarers find the approaches into Fowey harbour. But the craggy headland is best known as the home of Daphne du Maurier, who lived at the still private house of **Menabilly**, which featured as Manderley in her most famous novel *Rebecca*.

Facing St Catherine's Castle across the mouth of the River Fowey, **Polruan** is a pretty village that can be reached by ferry from Fowey. Beside the harbour, busy with pleasure craft and some industrial vessels, lies the late 15th century **Polruan Blockhouse**, one of a pair of artillery buildings constructed to

control the entrance into Fowey.

Just to the north of Polruan and also facing Fowey lies the pretty hamlet of **Bodinnick**, which was home to Daphne du Maurier before her marriage and where she wrote her first novel *The Loving Spirit*. Sir Arthur Quiller-Couch is remembered by a monolithic memorial that stands on the coast facing Fowey. It was close to the site of this monument that, in 1644, Charles I narrowly escaped death from a sniper's bullet while making a survey of Cromwell's forces at Fowey. From the Bodinnick ferry there is a delightful walk across mainly National Trust land that leads up to the 'Q' memorial and then back via the Polruan ferry back to Fowey.

GOLANT

8 miles W of Looe off the B3269

Close to this delightful waterside village, which is home to yet another of Cornwall's many holy wells, lies the **Castle Dore Earthworks**. This densely overgrown Iron Age lookout point is thought to be the site of King Mark's castle and is, therefore, linked with the legend of Tristan and Iseult.

Upriver and found in a sleepy creek is the quiet village of **Lerryn** that was once a busy riverside port. Those familiar with Kenneth Grahame's novel, *The Wind in the Willows*, may find the thickly wooded slopes of Lerryn Creek familiar as they are believed to have been the inspiration for the setting of this ever-popular children's story.

LOSTWITHIEL

10 miles NW of Looe on the A390

Nestling in the valley of the River Fowey and surrounded by wooded hills, Lostwithiel's name – which means 'lost in the hills' – perfectly describes its location. This small market town was the 13th century capital of Cornwall. As one of the stannary towns, tin and other raw materials were brought here for assaying and onward transportation until the mining activity cause the quay to silt up and the port moved further down river.

Lostwithiel was also a major crossing point on the River Fowey and the bridge seen today was completed in Tudor times. Beside the riverbank lies the tranquil **Coulson Park**, named after the American millionaire, Nathaniel Coulson, who grew up in Lostwithiel. On the opposite bank of the river from the town lies **Bonconnoc Estate**, the home of the Pitt family who gave Britain two Prime Ministers: William Pitt the Elder and his son, William Pitt the Younger.

Throughout the town there are reminders to Lostwithiel's once important status including the remains of the 13th century **Great Hall**, which

RESTORMEL CASTLE

Off the A390 1½ miles N of Lostwithiel
Tel: 01208 872687
website: www.english-heritage.org.uk

High on a moated mound overlooking the River Fowey, **Restormel Castle** is one of the former strongholds of the Earls of Cornwall, whose number included Edward, the Black Prince. Dating from the 11th century, it was one of the first motte and bailey castles to be raised in the West Country, and in the next century its original wooden defences were replaced with stone and a full set of domestic buildings added. In 1272 Restormel was inherited by Edmund of Almaine, Earl of Cornwall, whose builders constructed a miniature palace within its walls; this provided lavish accommodation for the Earl and his guests, who could look out on to a deer park created for their favourite pursuit.

The Black Prince stayed here in 1354 and 1365, but with the loss of Gascony soon after, most of the contents of value were removed, and the Castle fell into ruin. Today, the ruins survive in this tranquil hilltop setting. In spring the banks are covered in daffodils and bluebells, and in summer the site is one of the best picnic spots in Cornwall, boasting stunning views of the peaceful countryside.

served as the stannary offices, and the early 18th century **Guildhall**. Built by Richard, Lord Edgcumbe, this building, today, is home to the **Lostwithiel Museum**. It tells the story of this interesting town as well as displaying photographs of everyday life from the late 19th century to the present day.

Lostwithiel's strategic position as a riverside port and crossing place, led to the construction of **Restormel Castle** (see panel above), upstream from the town high on a mound overlooking the wooded Fowey valley. In summer, the site is one of the best picnic spots in Cornwall, boasting stunning views of the peaceful surrounding countryside.

LANREATH

5½ miles NW of Looe off the B3359

This pretty village of traditional cob cottages is home to the **Lanreath Folk and Farm Museum**, found in Lanreath's old tithe barn. There are numerous vintage exhibits here, many of which can be touched, including old agricultural implements, mill workings, engines, tractors, a traditional farmhouse kitchen and a bric-a-brac shop. Craft workshops and a pets' corner complete the museum.

LAUNCESTON

Situated on the eastern edge of Bodmin Moor close to the county border with Devon, Launceston (pronounced locally Lawnson) is one of Cornwall's most pleasant inland towns and was a particular favourite of Sir John Betjeman. The capital of Cornwall until 1838, it guarded the main overland route into the county. Shortly after the Norman Conquest, William I's half-brother, Robert of Mortain, built the massive **Launceston Castle** overlooking the River Kensey. Visited by the Black Prince and seized by Cornish rebels in 1549, the castle changed hands twice during the Civil War before becoming an assize court and prison. George Fox, the founder of the Society of Friends was detained here in 1656. The court was famous for imprisoning and executing 'on the nod'. Although now in ruins, the 12-foot thick walls of the keep and tower can still be seen. Along with the castle, Launceston was also home to a powerful Augustinian priory, founded beside the river in 1136 and, although these buildings have gone, its chapel of ease, now **St Thomas' Church**, remains. This church boasts the largest font in Cornwall.

Elsewhere in the town, the streets around the castle are filled with handsome buildings including the impressive **Lawrence House** that was built in 1753 for a wealthy local lawyer. Given to the National Trust to help preserve the character of the street, the house is home to a **Museum**, which dedicates its numerous displays to the history of the area. To the west of the town and running through the beautiful Kensey Valley, the **Launceston Steam Railway** takes visitors on a nostalgic and scenic journey back in time. Travelling in either open or closed carriages, passengers can enjoy a round trip along five miles of narrow-gauge track to Newmills and back. the locomotives used to haul the trains were built in the 1880s and 1890s by the famous Hunslet Engine Company of Leeds and once worked on the slate carrying lines high in the mountains of North Wales.

Launceston is also the start, or the finish, of the **Tamar Valley Discovery Trail**, a 30-mile footpath from here to Plymouth that takes in many of the villages scattered along the Cornwall-Devon border. Passing through old mining country, past market gardens and through ancient river ports, walkers of the trail will also see the wealth of bird, plant and wild life that the varying habitats along the way support. In 1995, the Tamar Valley was designated an Area of Outstanding Natural Beauty.

AROUND LAUNCESTON

GUNNISLAKE

10 miles SE of Launceston on the A390

Often referred to as the first village in Cornwall, it was here in the 1520s that Sir Piers Edgcumbe built the **New Bridge** over the River Tamar that continues to serve as one of the major gateways into the county. In fact, this 180-foot-long granite structure remained the lowest crossing of the river by road right up until the 1960s when the massive suspension bridge linking Saltash with Plymouth was opened. The 16th century bridge meant that this charming village also had an important strategic value and, during the Civil War, it was the centre of bitter fighting. During the 18th and 19th centuries the village came alive with mining. Though the mines have closed some of the mine buildings have been immortalised by Turner in his great painting, *Crossing the Brook*, that also captures Gunnislake's famous bridge. The River Tamar is tidal as far as the weir upstream near Newbridge and salmon fishermen continue to come to Gunnislake, as they have done since medieval times, to catch the fish as they travel up river to their spawning grounds.

CALSTOCK

12 miles SE of Launceston off the A390

Well known for its splendid views of the Tamar Valley, the origins of the village go back beyond the Romans. As well as being visited by Romans in search of tin, at the time of the Domesday Book the manor of Calstock was owned by Asgar the Saxon. The village was an important river port in the 19th century when vast quantities of tin, granite and copper ore were brought here for loading on to barges to be transported down the Tamar to the coast. In the countryside surrounding Calstock the remains of old mine workings, along with the spoil heaps, can still be seen along with the remains of the village's boat-building industry. The decline of Calstock as a port came with the construction of the huge **Railway Viaduct**, which carries the Tamar Valley Line southwards to Plymouth. Completed in 1908, this giant 12-arched viaduct, the first in the country to be constructed of concrete blocks, stands 120 feet above the river. Probably one of Britain's most picturesque branch lines, the **Tamar Valley Line** can still be taken down to the coast. Though the river has lost most of its commercial traffic, it is a starting point for Tamar River canoe expeditions.

Just to the southwest of the village lies one of the best preserved medieval estates in the West Country – **Cotehele House**. Mainly built between 1485 and 1624, this low granite fortified manor house was the principal home of the Edgcumbe family until the mid-16th century when they moved their main residence to Mount Edgcumbe. Along with its Great Tudor Hall, fabulous tapestries and period furniture, the house, which is now in the care of the National Trust, incorporates some charming features such as the secret spy-hole in the Great Hall and a tower clock with a bell but no face or hands. Surrounding the house are, firstly, the grounds, containing exotic and tender plants that thrive in the mild valley climate and beyond that the estate with its ancient network of pathways that allow exploration of the valley.

The River Tamar runs through the estate and close to an old cider house and mill is **Cotehele Quay**, a busy river port in Victorian times. The quay buildings now house an outstation of the National Maritime Museum, an art and craft gallery and a licensed tea room. The restored Tamar sailing barge *Shamrock* is moored alongside the museum.

CALLINGTON
9½ miles S of Launceston on the A388

Situated on the fertile land between the rivers Tamar and Lynher, Callington is now rich fruit growing country. During the 19th century, the landscape was very different as it was alive with frantic mining activity. The area's heritage, landscape and character are depicted on many of the walls of the town's buildings, thanks to the interesting and unusual **Mural Project**.

Overlooking the River Lynher, southwest of this old market town, lies **Cadsonbury Hillfort** – a massive Iron Age bank and ditch that are thought to be the remains of a local chief's home. To the northeast lies **Kit Hill**, now a country park, where a 19th century chimney stack built to serve one of the area's mines adds a further 80 feet to the hill's summit.

NORTH PETHERWIN
5 miles NW of Launceston off the B3254

Found above the River Ottery, this village is home to the **Tamar Otter Park**, a branch of the famous Otter Trust, dedicated to breeding young otters for release into the wild to prevent the species from becoming extinct in lowland England. Visitors can watch the otters playing in large natural enclosures, see them in their breeding dens, or holts, and watch the orphans in the rehabilitation centre. Also here are a dormouse conservation project, refreshment and gift shop, lakes with waterfowl and an area of woodland where fallow and Muntjac deer roam freely.

LOCATOR MAP

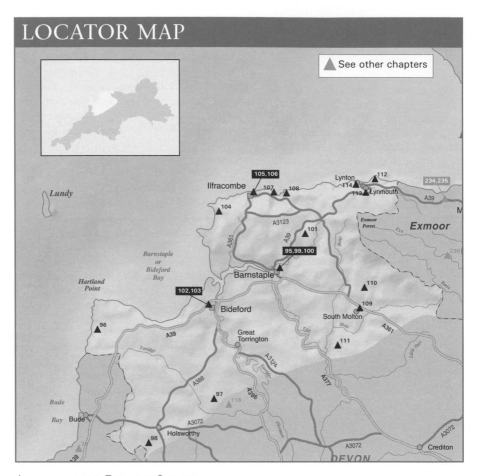

See other chapters

ADVERTISERS AND PLACES OF INTEREST

95	Brend Hotels	page 114
96	Docton Mill & Gardens, Lymebridge, Hartland	page 117
97	Cowslip Cottage, South Hay, Shebbear	page 119
98	Leworthy Farmhouse Bed & Breakfast, Pyworthy, Holsworthy	page 120
99	Jalapeno Peppers, Barnstaple	page 121
100	Fusions - Barnstaple's Delicatessen, Barnstaple	page 122
101	Arlington Court, Arlington, Barnstaple	page 123
102	Moody Dragons, Bideford	page 126
103	The Burton Art Gallery & Museum, Bideford	page 127
104	The Narracott Hotel, Woolacombe	page 130
105	Ilfracombe Aquarium, Ilfracombe	page 132
106	Chambercombe Manor, Ilfracombe	page 133
107	Watermouth Castle, Ilfracombe	page 135
108	Combe Martin Wildlife & Dinosaur Park, Combe Martin	page 136
109	Drewstone Farm, South Molton	page 137
110	Lambscombe Farm Cottages, North Molton, South Molton	page 138
111	The Old Rectory Cottages, Kings Nympton	page 140
112	Exmoor Sandpiper Inn, Countisbury, Lynton	page 142
113	Seaview Villa, Lynmouth	page 143
114	Gunns Art Gallery, Lynton	page 144

Devon is a county with an almost endless list of attractions for the visitor. The coasts, both north and south, offer fine sandy beaches, spectacular scenery and wonderful walks in the bracing air. Popular resorts, picturesque fishing ports and quiet little villages are dotted along the coastline, while inland there are unspoilt villages of thatched cottages, picturesque churches, traces of ancient civilisations and ancient industries, lovely gardens, more breathtaking views.....and Dartmoor. This bleak expanse of truly wild landscape with its dramatic tors has inspired many writers, notably Sir Arthur Conan Doyle, who made the moor even bleaker and wilder than it is in his novel *The Hound of the Baskervilles*.

Narrow Streets, Clovelly

The North Devon coast, from Hartland Point to Exmoor, is a glorious stretch of coastline offering spectacular coastal scenery and fine sandy beaches. Several of the popular holiday resorts along the coast were developed when interest increased in sea bathing and sea water therapies, made fashionable by George III at Weymouth and his son at Brighton. However, Westward Ho! was developed on the strength of the success of Charles Kingsley's famous novel of the same name inspired by the Devon countryside.

The South West Coast Path takes in many interesting, picturesque places along the coastline including the attractive towns of Bideford and Ilfracombe, and the village of Clovelly, a quaint place that tumbles down a steep hillside in a series of terraces. Also on the route is Barnstaple, one of the country's oldest boroughs, a place associated for many with the tale of Tarka. Returning to Devon after fighting in World War I, Henry Williamson rescued an orphan otter cub, and named it Tarka. The animal stayed with him until one day it became caught in a rabbit trap. As Williamson was releasing the terrified creature, Tarka slipped from his grasp and disappeared, never to be seen again. So inspired, Williamson wrote his

A Warm Welcome to the West

During your stay in the West Country you'll enjoy spectacular scenery and some of the prettiest towns and villages in England. Each outing brings new delights: visit traditional country markets, stroll along golden sands, indulge yourself with a traditional cream tea or walk ancient bridleways. Whatever you do and wherever you choose to stay, your visit to the West will remain with you – until you return next year!

Welcome to the Brend Hotels

For over twenty years our guests have been enjoying the warmest of welcomes. Owned and supervised by the Brend family, each of our establishments has its own unique character nurtured and developed over our many years of experience.

The Imperial Hotel, Barnstaple offers you 4 star luxury in the heart of the town, with its fine cuisine and superb service. Overlooking the River Taw and the ancient Long Bridge, it makes the perfect base for a luxurious holiday.

The Barnstaple Hotel is conveniently situated on the edge of the historic town of Barnstaple and close to the rugged beauty of the North Devon coastline. It is particularly popular for its health and leisure facilities, from indoor and outdoor heated pools to aromatherapy massage.

The Royal & Fortescue Hotel, Barnstaple was formerly a coaching inn patronized by King Edward VII. While it retains its original character it also boasts a stylish bar bistro offering a vast range of dishes.

The Park Hotel, Barnstaple is just a five minute walk from the bustling High Street yet its outstanding position next to the River Taw and Rock Park makes it a picturesque base from which to explore the North Devon countryside.

The Saunton Sands Hotel, Saunton boasts a stunning cliff top location that overlooks five miles of golden sand. Guests can enjoy exquisite dining in the hotel or at the stylish beachside restaurant, extensive leisure and sporting facilities, including links Golf Course and luxurious accommodation – everything that makes for a truly memorable stay.

Brend Hotels

Brend Hotel's Head Office and Central Reservations,
1 Park Villas, Taw Vale, Barnstaple, North Devon
EX32 8NJ Tel: (01271) 344496 Fax: (01271) 378558

The Royal Hotel, Bideford is situated at the end of the old bridge, adjacent to the 'Kathleen and May' - a magnificent 19th century sailing ship. Elegant surroundings, fine cuisine and the many attractions of Bideford, 'the little white town', make for a stay to remember.

The Carlyon Bay Hotel, St. Austell is set in 250 acres of landscaped grounds with breathtaking views of St. Austell Bay. The hotel's 18 hole Championship cliff-top golf course is spectacular, while non-golfers can make the most of the hotel's well-equipped leisure and sporting facilities.

The Victoria Hotel, Sidmouth is a grand hotel surrounded by five acres of landscaped gardens. This luxurious hotel provides every modern amenity whilst epitomizing the traditional values of personal attentive service, fine cuisine and comforts beyond compare. The great majority of rooms are south facing with exceptional sea and coastal views.

The Belmont Hotel, Sidmouth was once a Victorian summer residence and lies on the town's elegant sea front. Fine dining is further complemented by the accompaniment of our resident pianist making for a vintage holiday in the traditional style.

The Royal Duchy Hotel, Falmouth offers you 4 star luxury from its seafront location. Explore a wealth of local gardens such as The Eden Project, Trebah, Glendurgan and The Lost Gardens of Heligan or meander through the town's quaint streets and discover over 300 years of maritime heritage.

The Devon Hotel, Exeter, is characterised by Georgian grace. 'Carriages', the hotel's new brasserie and bar, serves a mouthwatering range of international dishes to savour before discovering the historic city's magnificent architecture and many big name stores.

Discover the true taste of the West Country from a Brend Hotel. We look forward to welcoming you soon.

Lundy Church, Lundy Island

novel, *Tarka the Otter*, basing it on his own experiences. The land between the River Torridge and Taw, to the south of Barnstaple, has become known as Tarka Country, as this was the land where his fictitious otter lived and roamed. Opened in 1992 by Prince Charles, the Tarka Trail, a figure of eight long distance foot path and cycle path, takes in many of the towns and villages mentioned in the book.

Further inland, the countryside is characterised by small, unspoilt villages of thatched cottages and lonely farmsteads. Apart from the period when the woollen trade flourished here in the Middle Ages, the economy of this beautiful area has never been particularly buoyant and so there are few grand houses or abbeys but there are some ancient and charming market towns. Crediton dates back to the 7th century and South Molton lies close to the foothills of Exmoor National Park. Designated as tranquil by the Council for the Protection of Rural England, this delightful countryside with its relaxed lifestyle has many visitors falling under its spell as they explore the narrow country lanes and the hidden river valleys.

HOLSWORTHY

This old market town lies just four miles from the Cornish border, serving a large area of rural Devon. Each Wednesday, it comes alive with its traditional street market, and in July the town plays host to the three-day long **St Peter's Fair**, an ancient event first held here in 1185. However, the **Pretty Maid Ceremony**, which opens the fair, is a somewhat curious custom that only dates back to 1841. At that time a wealthy Holsworthy merchant bequeathed a legacy to the town to provide a small payment each year to a local spinster who fitted the following description: she be under the age of 30, noted for her good looks, have a demure manner and regularly attend church. Despite the change in attitudes in the last 150 years or so, this is still a keenly fought, though very good-natured, competition. Holsworthy's most striking architectural features are the two Victorian viaducts that once carried the railway line through to Bude. Situated high above the southern outskirts of the town, they now form part of a footpath along the old track bed and it is possible to walk across them. Those making the climb will be rewarded with some stunning panoramic views. In the parish church is an organ, originally built by Renatus Hunt, in 1668, for All Saints' Church, Chelsea. By 1723, the organ was declared worn out by the London church. Nevertheless, it was purchased by the church in Bideford where it gave another 140 years of faithful service before, once again, being written off. A move to Holsworthy followed and the organ, in playing condition, has remained here ever since. Housed in an 18th century parsonage, the volunteer-run **Holsworthy Museum** gives visitors an insight into local history and traditions by various themed displays.

The countryside around the town is particularly popular with cyclists and there are three designated routes starting and finishing in Holsworthy. The town also lies on the 250-mile long cycle route, the **West Country Way**, opened in 1997, between Padstow in the west and Bath and Bristol to the east.

To the east of Holsworthy lies **Dunsland**, an ancient manor whose Tudor house was, after much restoration work by the National Trust in the 1960s, destroyed by fire. However, the outbuildings and parkland, landscaped in 1795, have survived. Those exploring the many footpaths of the estate, will find **Cadiho Well**, said to have sprung up on the site where Cadiho, the first Norman owner of the manor, was killed by his Anglo Saxon predecessor.

AROUND HOLSWORTHY

HARTLAND
14 miles N of Holsworthy on the B3248

A royal possession from the time of King Alfred until the Norman Conquest, this pleasant village of narrow streets and a small square was once larger and more important than Bideford. It was at its most prosperous in the 1700s, though it continued to be a busy centre right up to the 19th century. Hartland has some fine Georgian buildings that have survived from that period. The most striking building, however, is the parish **Church of St Nectan** to the west of the village centre. While the exterior, with its 128-foot tower, is impressive, it is the interior and the glorious 15th century, exquisitely carved screen that makes this church one of the most visited in the county. In the churchyard is the grave of Allen Lane, who revolutionised publishing in 1935 by his introduction of Penguin Books – paperback novels that were sold at sixpence (2.5p) each.

To the west of the village lies **Hartland Abbey**, founded in 1157 and given by Henry VIII, at the time of the dissolution in the 16th century, to William Abbott, Sergeant of the Royal wine cellars. Still in the same family today, the house was partly rebuilt in the mid-18th

Hartland Point

century in the Strawberry Hill Gothic style. In the 1860s, architect Sir George Gilbert Scott was commissioned to add the front hall and entrance. The abbey's owner at the time, Sir George Stucley, had recently visited, and admired, the Alhambra Palace in Spain and he asked Gilbert Scott to create something in that style. The result is the elegant Alhambra Corridor with its blue vaulted ceiling and white stencilled patterns. Housed in the abbey is a wonderful collection of paintings, porcelain and furniture, acquired by the family over generations and, in the former Servants' Hall, there is a unique exhibition of documents dating right back to 1160.

Further west lies **Hartland Quay**. Despite being exposed to the full force of the Atlantic's ferocious storms, it was a busy landing place until the sea finally overwhelmed the quay in 1893. Several of the buildings here, some of which date back to the 16th century, have been converted into a comfortable hotel while another is now a **Museum** with records of the many shipwrecks that have littered this jagged coastline.

Reached by winding country lanes, to the north of the quay, **Hartland Point** was called, on Ptolemy's map of Britain in Roman times, the 'Headland of Hercules' a very apt name as the headland's fearsome stretch of up-ended rock rises at right angles to the sea. One local legend suggests that Hercules actually landed here, defeated the English giants and then successfully governed the region. Another story

suggests that the headland was the site of the cell of the 6th century Welsh hermit, St Nectan. Those making their way out here will be rewarded with breathtaking views that also take in the lighthouse, built in 1874.

A couple of miles southwest of Hartland village, and only a short walk from the famous **Spekes Mill Mouth Coastal Waterfall**, are the wonderful gardens at **Docton Mill** (see panel below). Well-known for their magnolias, these sheltered gardens provide a colourful and peaceful haven throughout the year.

CLOVELLY
13½ miles N of Holsworthy off the A39

This unbelievably quaint and picturesque village, which tumbles down a steep hillside in terraced levels, is many people's idea of the typical Devonshire coastal village. The whitewashed cottages are bedecked with flowers right throughout the summer and from the little sheltered harbour, the enchanting

DOCTON MILL AND GARDENS

Lymebridge, near Hartland, Devon EX39 6EA
Tel: 01237 441369 website: www.doctonmill.co.uk

Created in 1980 the gardens at **Docton Mill** was designed and planted by Iris Pugh and it is to her that the gardens' famous magnolia collection is dedicated. However there are many more plants, trees and shrubs to see at this sheltered site that makes the most of the old mill buildings with its adjoining leat, head weir and tailrace. Traced back to Saxon times and having featured in the Domesday Book, Docton Mill gardens provide visitors with chance to see riverbanks of native ferns and wild flowers, some great oak trees and a mixture of shrubs and perennials in the old orchard. Visitors can also enjoy some light refreshment at the gardens before making the short walk down to the famous Speke's Mill Mouth coastal waterfall and beach.

view of this unique place is certainly worth a photograph or two. One of the reasons that Clovelly has remained so unspoilt right into the 21st century is that it has belonged to the Rous family since 1738 and they have ensured that it has remained free of such modern defacements as telegraph poles and other street furniture.

The only way down to the beach and the beautifully restored 14th century quay is on foot or by donkey. For those who cannot manage the climb back up the steep incline, there is a Land Rover service that runs from the Red Lion Hotel. This is rather limiting for the residents of Clovelly so, over the years, they have devised a transport system of their own and the village's weekly supplies are delivered by sledge.

During the summer there are regular boat trips from the quayside around this sheltered bay and it is also from here that the *Jessica Hettie* makes the daily trips out to Lundy Island and back.

Clovelly

This captivating village has some strong literary connections. Charles Kingsley lived and attended school here in the 1820s and the **Kingsley Exhibition** explores the novelist's links with the village. The **Fisherman's Cottage**, next door, provides an insight into what life was like in Clovelly at that time. The village's award-winning **Visitor Centre** covers the history of Clovelly and the surrounding area from as far back as 2000BC to the present day.

WOOLFARDISWORTHY

11 miles N of Holsworthy off the A39

The extraordinary name of this village (pronounced 'Woolsery') goes back to Saxon times, when the lands around this settlement were owned by Wulfheard who established a 'worthig', or homestead, here. Just to the north of the village is a popular family entertainment complex, the **Milky Way Adventure Park,** where both children and adults can try their hand at archery and laser target shooting in the massive indoor play area, visit the cuddly animals at Pets' Corner, see some fascinating birds of prey, watch sheep dogs train and ride on a miniature railway.

SHEBBEAR

7 miles NE of Holsworthy off the A388

This attractive village still displays its Saxon origins as it is set around a spacious square with a church at one end and an inn at the other. Lying in a hollow just outside St Michael's Church churchyard is a huge stone, weighing about a ton, known as the **Devil's Stone**. According to one local legend, the boulder was place here by the Devil who challenged the villagers to move it while threatening disaster if they could not. Therefore, every year on 5th November (a date set long before the Gunpowder Plot) the bell ringers leave the belfry of the church armed with sticks and crowbars and, once they have successfully turned the stone over, they return to the bell tower to signal their success with a peal of bells. Other stories suggest that the Devil lives beneath the stone and by turning it over the villagers ensure that he is kept down for another 12 months or that the stone was originally intended to be the foundation for the church at Henscott and the Devil moved it here.

SHEEPWASH

9 miles E of Holsworthy off the A3072

This community was devastated by fire in 1742 and the destruction was so great that for more than 10 years the village remained completely deserted. Slowly, however, the villagers returned and rebuilt their houses in stone. The area around the village square is a perfect example of a Devon village. Along one side is the famous Half Moon Inn, beloved by fishermen while, on another, the old church tower rises above the pink washed thatched cottages. Right at the centre of the square, and sheltered by cherry trees, stands the village's ancient pump. Just to the south of the village the minor road crosses the River Torridge by bridge but, until well into the 17th century, the only means of crossing the river at this point was by a series of stepping stones. One day, when the river was in full spate, a young man, attempting to return to Sheepwash, was swept off the stones and drowned. His father, John Tusbury, was grief-stricken but responded to the tragedy by

COWSLIP COTTAGE

South Barn Farm, South Hay, Shebbear, Devon EX21 5SR
Tel: 01409 281857 Fax: 01409 281442
e-mail: g.a.r.stone@btopenworld.com

Cowslip Cottage is an attractive single-storey barn conversion situated next to the main farmhouse a mile from the historic village of Shebbear. Recently extensively refurbished by owners Gill and Reg Stone, the cottage can sleep up to eight guests in three bedrooms, two with shower and toilet en suite, the third with shower, toilet and bath facilities. A cot can be supplied if required. The

daytime accommodation consists of a bright, spacious open-plan living room with a beautifully fitted kitchen, and adjoined to the side of the cottage is a separate utility room with a washing machine and tumble dryer.

The cottage boasts a wood log burner as well as full central heating, and the windows are fully double glazed, so the whole place is delightfully warm and comfortable throughout the year. It has its own garden area, and the views over the two-acre lake (stocked with tench and roach), the rolling Devon countryside and Dartmoor in the distance are truly memorable. The River Torridge, renowned for brown trout and the occasional salmon, runs through the grounds of the 60-acre South Barn Farm.

providing the money to build a bridge and sufficient funds for it to be maintained by the Bridgeland Trust, which he also established. Any surplus income from the Trust, he stipulated, should then be used to maintain the village's church and chapel. The Trust continues its good works today and as well as maintaining the bridge it also funds outings for the village children and pensioners.

NORTHLEW

10 miles SE of Holsworthy off the A3072

This pretty village of thatched cottages is dominated by its charming 15th century church on a hilltop overlooking the River Lew. Along with its Norman remains, the church has one particularly interesting stained glass window that features four saints. St Thomas, after whom the church is dedicated, is shown holding a model of the church. St Augustine, the first Archbishop of Canterbury, holds the priory gateway. St Joseph carries the Holy Grail and the staff that grew into the famous Glastonbury thorn tree. The fourth figure, a simply clad man in a brown habit, carrying a bishop's crozier and a spade, is St Brannock, who is credited with being the first man to cultivate the wild lands of this area by clearing the woodland and putting the land under the plough. He is, therefore, regarded as the patron saint of farmers.

CLAWTON

3 miles W of Holsworthy on the A388

Devon, like its neighbour Cornwall, is fortunate in having a mild climate and over the last 30 years or so a number of vineyards have been established in the county. Set in more than 78 acres of vines and orchards, **Clawford Vineyard**, in the valley of the River Claw, welcomes

Barnstaple Bridge

that still continues nearly 1,000 years later. There is a produce market twice a week but the **Pannier Market** is open every weekday and it is housed in a rather grandiose building of 1855 that resembles a large Victorian railway station. The market takes its name from the pannier baskets (two wicker baskets connected by a leather strap draped across the back of a donkey, pony or horse) that the farmers used to carry their goods to the market. Opposite lies **Butchers' Row**, a quaint line of Victorian shops with brightly coloured canopies, originally occupied exclusively by butchers.

visitors to sample its home grown wines and ciders. Autumn is a particularly good time to visit as that year's vintage can be seen being produced.

BARNSTAPLE

Claiming to be Britain's oldest borough, Barnstaple, at the head of the Taw estuary, was the administrative and commercial capital of this region at the time of the Domesday Book when it was recorded as one of four boroughs in Devon. At that time, Barnstaple had its own mint and a well-established market

Many of the town's buildings date from an earlier age. The **Church of St Peter and St Paul** was built in the early 14th century. After having its spire twisted by a lightning strike in 1810, the building suffered again at the heavy hands of Victorian restorers. Close by are the much more appealing 17th century **Horwood's Almshouses** and the charming 15th century **St Anne's Chapel** that served for many years as the town's Grammar School, although it was originally built as a bone house. During

FUSIONS - BARNSTAPLE'S DELICATESSEN

15 Butchers Row, Barnstaple, Devon EX31 1BW
Tel: 01271 379742

Butchers Row, a line of smart Victorian shops with colourful canopies, was originally occupied exclusively by butchers shops. That has now changed, and among the latest and best of the newer occupants is **Fusions - Barnstaple's Delicatessen**, the brainchild of James Davies and Charlie Davidson. Their aim is to make this the best delicatessen the area has ever known, the very best source of high-quality foods and a focus for anyone who likes to cook and take pleasure in what goes on the table. It caters for customers who

need to re-stock their kitchens; for those who have a special event or celebratory meal to prepare; and for anyone needing a quick lunch in town or a ready-to-eat meal to take home.

The stock covers an impressive range of beautiful food, from cooked meats and charcuterie to cheeses from near and far, delicious home-made pies and pasties and pâtés, olives and olive oils, pesto, home-made soups and pizzas and farmhouse bread, beans and pulses and rice, wholefoods and organic products, fresh herbs and all kinds of specialities both local and exotic. The choice changes constantly, and every trip to this outstanding delicatessen is an experience to savour.

the late 17th century John Gay, author of *The Beggar's Opera*, was a pupil here and the town has several other literary connections. William Shakespeare visited in 1605 and it was the sight of its narrow streets bustling with traders that inspired him to write *The Merchant of Venice*. The diarist Samuel Pepys married a 15-year-old Barnstaple girl in 1655. Another of the town's medieval structures is the impressive 16-arched bridge spanning the River Taw. The town lies at the furthest point downstream where it was possible to ford the river and the first bridge here was built in the late 13th century.

One of the most attractive buildings in the town is **Queen Anne's Walk**, a colonnaded arcade with some lavish ornamentation and a statue of Queen Anne on top of its central doorway. Opened in 1708, it was used by the Barnstaple wool merchants who accepted that any verbal bargain they made over

the Tome Stone would be legally binding. The building stands on the old town quay from where, in 1588, five ships set sail to join Drake's fleet against the Spanish Armada. The building is now home to the **Barnstaple Heritage Centre**, a wonderful place where more can be found out about this ancient town.

One of the town's most enduring industries has been pottery, made here continuously since the 13th century, and local Fremington red clay is still used. Another interesting museum has the unusual distinction of being housed in a former signal box. The **Lynton and Barnstaple Railway Museum** records the history of this narrow-gauge railway that ran between 1898 and 1935. Barnstaple is also the northern terminus of the **Tarka Line**, a wonderfully scenic 39-mile route that follows the gentle river valleys of the Rivers Yeo and Taw, where Tarka the otter had his home.

Although the railway is actually the main line route to Exeter, it was renamed in honour of one of the area's major visitor attractions.

Walkers can discover the countryside that inspired the novel by taking the **Tarka Trail** an unusual figure of eight long distance footpath of some 180 miles that crosses over at Barnstaple. Wandering through the delightful and varied Devon countryside, taking in coastline, wooded river valleys and rugged moorland, the trail follows in the footsteps of Henry Williamson's fictitious otter.

AROUND BARNSTAPLE

SHIRWELL

3 miles N of Barnstaple off the A39

The renowned yachtsman Sir Francis Chichester was born in the village, the son of its vicar, and is buried in the churchyard of St Peter.

MUDDIFORD

3½ miles N of Barnstaple on the B3230

Despite its rather unappealing name, Muddiford is an attractive village that got its name from the 'muddy ford' by which medieval travellers crossed the river to get here. Just to the southwest of Muddiford is the ancient village of **Marwood**, where the **Marwood Hill Gardens** comprise 18 acres of pastureland with three lakes surrounded by rare and unusual trees and shrubs – a collection started more than half a century ago. The lakes, home to ducks and multi-coloured carp, are linked by the largest bog garden in the West Country. Whatever the time of year, these gardens provide a continuous spectacle of colour from the spring flowers to the autumn leaves. The gardens are home to the national collections of Astilbe, Iris and Tulbaghia.

To the northeast of the village lies **Arlington Court** (see panel below), the

ARLINGTON COURT

Arlington, Nr Barnstaple, Devon EX31 4LP
Tel: 01271 850296 Fax: 01271 851108
website: www.nationaltrust.org.uk

Nestling in the thickly wooded valley of the River Yeo lies the 3,500 acre **Arlington Court** estate. At its centre stands Arlington Court, the intimate and intruiging Victorian home of Miss Rosalie Chichester. Crowded with treasures amassed from her travels, her collections include model ships, tapestry, pewter and shells. Arlington's stable block houses one of the best collections of 19th century horse-drawn vehicles in the country, which ranges

from a very grand State Chariot with highly ornamented harness, to the sombre plumed bier carrier, and offers carriage rides around the grounds. The 30 acre gardens are largely informal, featuring a beautiful Victorian garden complete with conservatory and ornamental pond leading to a partially restored walled garden which is slowly coming back to a productive vegetable area.

Miss Chichester was a keen conservationist and encouraged wildlife. Today the estate is home to deer, otters, heron, badgers and countless birds. Draped from the trees and shrubs are lichen that thrive in the moist air. The parkland is especially important for bats, providing flight lines from the house to their feeding areas. In the basement, from May to September, visitors can view the comings and goings of Devon's largest colony of Lesser Horseshoe bats via the newly installed 'batcam'.

family home of the Chichesters from 1534 until the last owner, Miss Rosalie Chichester, died in 1949.

During her lifetime Rosalie transformed the grounds of Arlington into something of a nature reserve. After building an eight-mile perimeter fence to protect the native wildlife, she introduced free grazing Shetland ponies and Jacob sheep that remain here still and red deer can also be seen grazing in the woods. Around the lake, created when the house was built, there are heron, teal, orchard and tufted duck. Another of Rosalie's eccentric interests was the rescuing of horse drawn carriages from destruction. The collection can be found housed in the old stable block where visitors can not only take carriage rides but also find refreshment and a gift shop. A network of footpaths criss-cross the estate and walkers can take in the gentle and secluded banks of the River Yeo or walk through the estate to local hamlets such as Lahore and Arlington Becket.

LANDKEY

2 miles SE of Barnstaple off the A361

Historians believe that the name of this village was derived from 'lan', the Celtic for church, and the saint to whom the building is dedicated, St Kea. According to legend, St Kea rowed over from Wales, with his personal cow on board, determined to convert the pagans of north Devon to Christianity. Unfortunately, his undoubted eloquence did not impress those he preached to and so they chopped of his head. Unperturbed, St Kea calmly retrieved his severed head and continued, with his head in his hand, to preach the Gospel for many years.

Just to the southwest lies **Bishop's Tawton**, another place whose name is linked with the Church. The village takes its name from the River Taw on which it sits and from the medieval Bishop's Palace that stood here up until the mid-16th century. While only a few fragments of the palace remain, the village does have one particularly bizarre building – a sociable three-seater outside lavatory that has been granted Grade II-listed status.

SWIMBRIDGE

4 miles SE of Barnstaple off the A361

For almost half a century, from 1833, this attractive village was the home of the Rev John Russell, who was the breeder of the first Jack Russell terriers as well as being known as the celebrated hunting parson. A larger than life character, Russell was an enthusiastic master of foxhounds. When his Bishop tried to stop him pursuing such an unseemly sport for a man of the cloth, Russell transferred the pack of hounds into his wife's name and continued to hunt on a regular basis. Still riding to hounds in his late 70s, Russell died in 1880 at the age of 87, and hundreds of people attended his funeral. Despite his love of hunting, Russell was a diligent parson, best remembered by his congregation for his short sermons. However, as his groom was standing outside the church with his horse saddled and ready to hunt, perhaps Russell had another reason for keeping his sermons brief!

The village itself has some elegant Georgian houses and a pub, renamed in 1962, after Swimbridge's most famous resident. Jack Russell societies from around the world frequently hold their meetings here. The mainly 15th century Church of St James has an unusual lead-covered spire and a wealth of ecclesiastical treasures.

GREAT TORRINGTON

10 miles SW of Barnstaple on the A386

This hilltop town was once home to a castle that was demolished as early as 1228. Its elevated site is now a bowling green that goes by the name of **Castle Hill**. On the opposite bank of the River Torridge and close to the bridge, stands a tiny 14th century church, originally built as a chapel for a leper hospital as its inmates were not allowed to cross the river and worship with the townsfolk. The present, spacious parish **Church of St Michael and All Angels** is one of only a few in the country, built during the days of the Commonwealth. It replaced an earlier building that was blown up by gunpowder. During the Civil War, the Parliamentarian General Fairfax captured Great Torrington in 1645, rounded up the Royalist prisoners and herded them into the church that they had been using as an arsenal. In the darkness, the 80 barrels of gunpowder stored there were somehow set alight. In the huge explosion that followed 200 men lost their lives, General Fairfax was nearly killed, and the church was demolished.

This ancient town continues to hold its **May Fair** as it has done each year since 1554. A May Queen is crowned, there is maypole dancing in the High Street and a banner proclaims that "Us be plazed to zee 'ee."

Great Torrington has several thriving industries including **Dartington Crystal**, now one of the West Country's leading tourist attractions. Visitors can see skilled craftsmen blowing and shaping the molten glass and the history of glass making, from the early days of the Egyptians to the present day, is explained. Although the business was only set up in the 1960s, Dartington Crystal is now exporting its beautifully designed handmade crystal all over the world.

Just to the south of Great Torrington and occupying a breathtaking location in the Torridge Valley is the Royal Horticultural Society Garden **Rosemoor**, a wonderful place that includes mature planting in Lady Anne Palmer's magnificent garden and arboretum. Along with the mass of plants there are trails for children, a shop, a plant centre and an award-winning Visitor Centre with a licensed restaurant.

To the north of Great Torrington lies **Weare Gifford** (pronounced 'Jifford'), an attractive village that claims to be the longest riverside village in England. It straggles for almost two miles along the bank of the River Torridge, a peaceful place where it appears, in many ways, time has stood still. The villagers have even refused to have full street lighting and so Weare Gifford has avoided the lamps that blemish many other pretty places.

Another attraction here is the old 15th century manor house, **Weare Gifford Hall**. It lost some of its outer walls during the Civil War but the splendid gatehouse, with its mighty doors and guardian lions, has survived. For centuries, the hall was the home of the Fortescue family and, in the nearby church, there is an interesting family tree with portraits of past Fortescues carved in stone.

BIDEFORD

8 miles SW of Barnstaple on the A386

An attractive town set beside the River Torridge estuary, the first bridge to be built across the estuary's shallow neck was constructed in around 1300, linking Bideford with its aptly named satellite village of East-the-Water. It was 670 feet long and constructed of massive oak lintels of varying length creating a series of irregular arches. It must have been very impressive for its time even if its appearance was a little odd. In 1460, when the bridge was rebuilt in stone, the curious dimensions were retained and, despite further widening in the 1920s, they are still visible today. The bridge is unusual in another manner as it is managed by an ancient corporation of trustees, known as 'feofees', whose income, derived from various properties in the town, is used to maintain the bridge as well as support local charities and good causes. The new high level bridge, opened a mile downstream in 1987, provides panoramic views of the town and has relieved its traffic congestion.

Bideford received its market charter from Henry III in 1272 and markets are still held here twice a week though, since 1883, they have been held in the splendid **Pannier Market**. A wonderful example of a Victorian covered market, all manner of goods are on offer here, besides the more traditional local produce.

Surprising as it might seem today, Bideford was once Britain's third busiest port. Many commodities passed through the dock, but the town specialised in tobacco from the North American colonies. For almost two centuries Bideford prospered on the back of the tobacco trade until the American War of Independence saw supplies cut to almost nothing.

Evidence of this golden age can still be seen around the town in the various opulent merchants' houses that have survived. The **Royal Hotel** in East-the-Water, a merchant's residence built in 1688, has fine plasterwork ceilings that are the most extravagant to be found in Devon. While staying at the Royal Hotel, Charles Kingsley wrote *Westwood Ho!*, the swashbuckling Elizabethan story based

around Bideford, which he described as a "little white town". His research for the book, which follows the adventures of Sir Amyas Leigh and the Spanish Armada, took Kingsley south to Kilkhampton church to see the monument to the seafaring Grenville family and then on to their mansions. Said to have only taken seven months to complete, the book is over a quarter of a million words long. There is a **Statue of Kingsley** on Bideford Quay at the foot of the narrow maze of lanes that formed the old seaport.

Close to the Quay is the **Burton Museum and Art Gallery** opened in 1994, and the collections here range from late 18th century harvest jugs and model ships made by French prisoners of the Napoleonic Wars to paintings by well known north Devon artists and an exhibition of quilts.

One excursion from Bideford that should not be missed is the day trip to **Lundy Island** on board the island vessel *MS Oldenburg*. This unique and unspoilt lump of granite rock, three miles long and half a mile wide, derives its name from the Norse 'lunde ey', meaning puffin island. These attractive birds are still in residence today along with many other species – over 400 have been spotted on Lundy. Undisturbed by cars, the island has a small village, complete with a church, a pub and a shop that sells the famous Lundy stamps. There are also the ruins of the 13th century castle.

Just a couple of miles north of Bideford is the small town of **Northam** that was, in 1069, the landing place for the three illegitimate sons of slain King Harold who came here from Ireland with an invasion force of over 60 ships. Their attempt to regain the throne was

THE BURTON ART GALLERY & MUSEUM

Kingsley Road, Bideford, Devon EX39 2QQ
Tel: 01237 471455 e-mail: burtonartgallery@torridge.gov.uk
Fax: 01237 473813 website: www.burtonartgallery.co.uk

Situated in Bideford's Victoria Park, close to the banks of the River Torridge and the 24-arch ancient Long Bridge, the **Burton Art Gallery & Museum** hosts a variety of national touring exhibitions as well as many by South West artists. Exhibitions in 2003 have included ceramics by David Leach, prints by the Society of Wood Engravers, and etchings by Whistler. Autumn exhibitions include lithographs by French satirist, Honore Daumier (1808-1879) and 'Blind Alphabet' by Art Sense. Craft artists find the gallery a useful showcase, with fine furniture, textiles, silk paintings, batiks, prints, stained glass, jewellery and ceramics, a unique collection of work from some of the best craft artists.

The Bideford Museum reflects the history, trades and industry of its past. Richard Grenville's portrait stands beside Elizabeth 1's Charter of 1573 obtained when he was Lord of the Manor; information

panels tell of the first Red Indian in England, of the Plague of 1646 and of the Bideford Witches, the last to be executed in England. Bone ship models made by Napoleonic prisoners of war, Victorian card cases and many fine examples of North Devon slipware for which Bideford is famous, and a coin hoard from the 1600s, are just part of the museum's treasures. The permanent collection of oils and watercolours includes work by Fisher, Clausen, E Aubrey Hunt, Sir Alfred Munnings, Sir John Lavery, Hubert Coop, William Shayer, as well as modern works by Leslie Worth, Judith Ackland, Bertram Prance, Allin Braund and Reginald Lloyd. Open Tuesday-Saturday, also Sunday afternoon. The Café du Parc serves refreshments and meals throughout the day. All areas are wheelchair accessible.

mercilessly put down just to the south of the town on a site that, to this day, is known as **Bloody Corner**.

A little further north again, though on the east bank of the River Torridge, are **Tapeley Park Gardens** – some 20 acres of gardens divided into four distinctly different themed areas. Each is home to a fascinating wealth of flowers, trees, shrubs and vegetables. They include the kitchen garden and the organic permaculture fruit and vegetable garden. The famous Italian terrace borders, first laid out in the 19th century, have been restored and visitors can also enjoy lakeside walks, buy plants from the garden shop and relax at the tearoom. Recent additional attractions include a granite labyrinth on a promontory overlooking the sea, created from the remains of an obelisk that was erected in 1855 to honour Archibald Cleveland, one of just three officers to survive the Charge of the Light Brigade. On a clear day Lundy Island can be seen from the park.

To the west of Bideford is **The Big Sheep**, a working farm that has become one of the West Country's wackiest tourist attractions. Along with sheep racing and duck trailing events, there are more conventional entertainments such as sheep-shearing and cheese-making demonstrations, while children can let off steam at the adventure playground.

WESTWARD HO!
8½ miles SW of Barnstaple on the B3236

When, in 1855, Charles Kingsley's novel of Elizabethan daring-do was published it caught the rising tide of Victorian patriotism brought on by the on-going war in the Crimea and *Westward Ho!* became a great success. So much so that a company was formed to develop this spectacular site, with its rocky cliffs and two miles of sandy beach, and so the resort was created. However, the early years were not without mishap as a powerful storm washed away the newly built pier and most of the houses. In 1874, when Rudyard Kipling came here as a pupil at the United Services College he described the place as "twelve bleak houses by the shore".

Now very much established as a bustling holiday resort, the village is also home to the unusual **Pot Walloping Festival** that takes place here every spring. Local people along with visitors join together to throw the pebbles, dislodged during the winter storms, back on to the famous ridge. Once they have finished, everyone retires to the pub where pots of a different kind get a walloping. Just to the north of the resort is the **Northam Burrows Country Park**, nearly 700 acres of land, rich in flora, fauna and migratory birds that was once a grazing ground for rabbits when they were a

Lundy Island

very common source of food.

APPLEDORE
6 miles SW of Barnstaple on the A386

This delightful old fishing village of narrow winding lanes and sturdy 18th and 19th century fishermen's cottages overlooks the Taw-Torridge estuary. It is still very much a fishing village today. Although some of the lanes are too narrow to take cars, it is not uncommon to see boats, hauled up from the harbour and parked between the old buildings. Appledore is, therefore, a very appropriate place to find the **North Devon Maritime Museum** in a former shipowner's residence. Containing a wealth of seafaring memorabilia, other historical aspects of the village and surrounding area can be discovered here. There is a photographic exhibition detailing the military exercises in the estuary that were part of the preparation for the D-day landings and a reconstruction of a Victorian kitchen.

From Appledore's harbour visitors can take a short ferry ride across the Torridge estuary to **Instow**, the home of the **North Devon Yacht Club**.

BRAUNTON
4¼ miles NW of Barnstaple on the A361

Braunton lays claim to being the largest village in Devon and it is certainly a sizeable community spreading along both banks of the River Caen. Its importance as a port in medieval times is reflected in the size of its 13th century church – a substantial building, dedicated to St Brannoc, a 6th century Celtic saint who is said to have sailed here from Wales in a stone coffin. He lies buried beneath the altar and around the church can be seen carvings that depict several of the saint's miracles, most of which concerned animals. One local story describes how he taught the people

to till the land and used wild deer to pull his plough. Another tells that, after someone had stolen his cow, killed it and cooked it, at St Brannoc's call, the cow rose from the cooking pot, reassembled itself and continued to supply the saint with milk for many more years. In several carvings there are pictures of a sow with piglets and these refer to the commonly held belief that, in a dream, St Brannoc was instructed to build a church where he saw a sow and her litter of seven piglets.

There is further evidence of Saxon occupation of this area in **Braunton Great Field**, just southwest of the village. It is one of the few remaining examples of a Saxon open field strip system still being actively farmed. The original 700 half-acre strips were separated by an unploughed landshare one foot wide. Although, down the centuries, many of the strips have changed hands and combined, there are still around 200 individual ones remaining.

Just a little further on lie the dunes of **Braunton Burrows** whose southernmost parts have been designated a nature reserve, noted for its fluctuating population of migrant birds as well as rare flowers and insects.

CROYDE
8 miles NW of Barnstaple on the B3231

This is a lovely little seaside village renowned for its excellent family-friendly beach. Just to the northwest of Croyde lies **Baggy Point**, a headland made of Devonian rock (so named because it was first identified in this county) and a popular nesting place for seabirds, including herring gull, fulmar, shag and cormorant; grey seals can often be seen from here. Running northwestwards from the cliffs is Baggy Leap, a shoal on which, in 1799, the *HMS Weazle* was driven during a gale

THE NARRACOTT HOTEL

Beach Road, Woolacombe,
Devon EX34 7BS
Tel: 01271 870418
Fax: 01271 780600
e-mail: terrywyld@btconnect.com
website: www.narracott.co.uk

The Narracott Hotel offers practical modern amenities for singles, couples and families on holiday along with spectacular views over the three-mile sweep of sandy beach that is Woolacombe Bay. The beach is only a five-minute walk from the hotel, and the best bedrooms, the Bay View Rooms, are those situated at the front, with private balconies to make the most of the natural beauty of the Woolacombe landscape and its beach. Village Rooms at the rear and side of the building, of equal standing to the Bay View Rooms, and Standard Rooms at the rear lack nothing in comfort but do not enjoy sea views. All rooms, whatever the category, have private bath or shower, and many have both. TV, radio, direct-dial telephone, beverage trays and wake-up and baby listening devices are standard (cots available on request), and all rooms are centrally

heated during the cooler months. Guests are entitled to free use of the heated indoor swimming pool, squash court, badminton, American pool table and table tennis, and other facilities offered by this well-run modern hotel include the use of sun beds for topping up the tan and a sauna for a leisurely steam. Evening is the time to relax and unwind, and at the Narracott guests can do that in style! There's cabaret and seasonal live entertainment on many evenings, and the hotel has two large dance floors that are a hard-to-resist temptation to get into the swing of things! To while away a quieter hour or two, the ocean view lounge is the place to be. Bookings can be made on a bed & breakfast or dinner, bed & breakfast basis, and discounts are offered for stays of three or more nights. The hotel restaurant (non-smoking) provides a selection of dishes for both breakfast and dinner, and a comprehensive wine list is available.

The stretch of golden sands at Woolacombe, which holds the coveted Blue Flag award for its cleanliness, is perhaps the finest in the region, and the National Trust land on both sides and the Downs are well worth exploring. Whether it's a coastal stroll, a ramble on nearby Exmoor or a wander through thatched villages or the market and harbour towns, the sights and delights of Devon are all within easy reach of the hotel.

Croyde Bay

hamlet with a few families trying to scratch a living from fishing. The craze for sea bathing, initiated by George III at Weymouth and endorsed by his son at Brighton, inspired the two families who owned much of the land around Woolacombe, the Fortescues and the Chichesters, to begin building the elegant Regency villas and houses that make this such a charming place today.

with the loss of all 106 souls on board. To the northeast of Croyde lies the village of **Georgeham**, where Henry Williamson settled in 1921 after his return from World War I. It was here that he wrote his famous novel published in 1928, *Tarka the Otter* – a tale of an otter that is hunted and finally killed by an otter hunt. Tarka lived in the land between the Taw and Torridge rivers and many of the little villages and settlements feature in the story. The writer lived a very simple life in a wooden hut that he built himself. For a while he farmed in Norfolk, but returned to Georgeham, where he died in 1947. He lies buried in Georgeham churchyard of St George.

The two families were considered by their friends to be embarking on a suicidally rash enterprise. During the first few years, only a trickle of well-to-do visitors in search of a novel and comparatively inexpensive resort found their way to Woolacombe. However news began to spread by word of mouth and slowly the trickle of visitors grew. Today holidaymakers flood to this beautiful beach that has qualified for the coveted EC yellow and blue flag.

Despite the pleasant surroundings of the beach, it is said to be haunted by the ghost of Sir William de Tracey, who lived at nearby Mortehoe. One of the four knights who murdered St Thomas à Becket, his ghost is said to attempt to spin a rope from the sand. Each time it seems that he might succeed a black dog appears with a ball of fire in its mouth and sets fire to the flimsy cord.

Mortehoe is the most northwesterly village in Devon and its name, meaning 'raggy stump', reflects the rugged character of the Morte peninsula. A short walk from the village leads up to the dramatic and treacherous coastline with exhilarating views across to Lundy Island. Much of this coastline, between

WOOLACOMBE
9½ miles NW of Barnstaple on the B3343

A favourite resort that lies between the two dramatic headlands of Baggy Point and Morte Point, Woolacombe has a wonderful stretch of golden sand, one of the finest in north Devon. There are rock pools for children and monster waves rolling in from the Atlantic for surfers. However, back in the early 19th century, Woolacombe was little more than a

Woolacombe Sands

Ilfracombe and Woolacombe is unspoilt and is in the ownership of the National Trust.

ILFRACOMBE
9½ miles NE of Barnstaple on the A361

Although Ilfracombe is the largest seaside resort on the North Devon coast today, up until 1800 it was just a small fishing town with a market, relying entirely on the sea for its livelihood and its principal means of communication. The entrance to the town's sheltered, natural harbour is guarded by **Lantern Hill**, a steep-sided conical rock on top of which stands the medieval **St Nicholas Chapel**, now restored with funds raised by the local Rotary Club. Although in the 14th century there were no lighthouses, the kind folk of Ilfracombe displayed a light in the chapel's projecting window on the seaward side of the building. When it became a house after the Reformation, the owners continued to show a lantern to help sailors.

As with so many resorts, Ilfracombe developed in direct response to the early 19th century craze for sea bathing and seawater therapies. The **Tunnel Baths**, with their extravagant Doric facade, were opened in 1836, by which time a number of elegant residential terraces had been built on the hillside to the south of the old town. The arrival of the railway, in 1874, brought even more visitors flocking to the town and most of the architecture dates from this time. At around the same time the harbour was enlarged to cope with the paddle steamers, bringing in holidaymakers from Bristol and south Wales. The harbour is still busy today with a regular service out to Lundy Island and

ILFRACOMBE AQUARIUM

Ilfracombe, Devon
Tel: 01271 864533
website: www.ilfracombeaquarium.co.uk

The Ilfracombe Aquarium is housed in the Old Lifeboat House, below St Nicholas' Chapel on Lantern Hill and next to Ilfracombe Harbour. The Aquarium which opened in July 2001 provides an all weather facility enabling visitors to share in the beauty. It houses an impressive species collection in carefully recreated natural habitats and displays both freshwater and marine fauna which are fascinating in both their appearance and behaviour. It is also essential that you visit the fun fish retail area and outdoor café where simple snacks and drinks are served. Open daily mid-March to January. Disabled access.

Ilfracombe Harbour

scenery and from the town westwards, much of this wonderful stretch of coast is now in the hands of the National Trust. The harbour is also home to **Ilfracombe Aquarium** (see panel opposite).

Ilfracombe Museum tells the story of the town and the surrounding area, and the Lundy Room gives visitors plenty of interesting background information on Lundy island. Next to the Museum, housed in the disused laundry of the now long forgotten Ilfracombe Hotel, is the town's **Landmark Theatre**, a superb multi-purpose theatre and arts centre with a café and a spacious display area.

Just to the east of Ilfracombe, at **Hele Bay**, lies a lovingly restored 16th century mill, **Old Corn Mill and Pottery**. The mill has been saved from dereliction and after extensive restoration is once again producing flour that can be purchased at the mill shop. The mill's owner, Robin Gray, is a potter and visitors can see him busy at his wheel; his unique pieces are for sale at the mill. A mile or so south, in

cruise boats exploring the coastline of Exmoor. The **South West Coast Path** provides walkers with some spectacular

CHAMBERCOMBE MANOR

Near Ilfracombe, Devon EX34 9RJ
Tel: 01271 862624

Although the manor here was mentioned in the Domesday Book, the present **Chambercombe Manor** was not built until the 12th century and it still retains much of its medieval charm and character today. When, exactly, it fell from being a manor house to a farmhouse is unknown but fortunately such features as its plaster frieze and barrel ceiling in the bedrooms can still be seen.

Displaying period furniture from Elizabethan times up to the Victorian era, this is a delightful house

that allows visitors to soak up the atmosphere of what was also a family home. Along with the Great Hall, there is the private chapel of the Champernon family, the manor's first owners, an old kitchen and the Coat of Arms bedroom that was once occupied by Lady Jane Grey and it is the Grey coat of arms, who were descendants of the Champernons, that is depicted above the fireplace. Meanwhile, outside there is a paved courtyard, with ornamental ponds, a delightful garden of lawns, shrubbery and herbaceous borders, and a water garden beyond which lie the extensive grounds that take in the peaceful, secluded wooded valley in which the manor house is situated.

South West Coast Path and Woody Bay

Distance:	6.0 miles (9.7 kilometres)
Typical time:	180 mins
Height gain:	200 metres
Map:	Outdoor Leisure 9
Walk:	www.walkingworld.com ID:309
Contributor:	Bryan Cath

Access Information:

From the Ilfracombe direction go towards Combe Martin on the A399, continuing through Combe Martin and on up the winding road until it eventually straightens out. After a while the first turning on your left comes up, signposted to Hunters Inn. Take this road and keep on it all the way to Hunters Inn. Park in the car park opposite the toilets. From other directions, pick up the A399 Ilfracombe to South Molton road, and Hunters Inn is signed off this road above Combe Martin.

Description:

This walk will take you along a section of the South West Coast Path that is often considered to be one of the most scenic sections of its whole 630 miles. It starts by following the old coaching road giving easy walking and amazing views. On reaching the aptly-named Woody Bay, clothed mainly in sessile oak, you return via the lower coast path, locally known as the 'goat path', being narrow and closer to the sea and cliffs. You pass by one of the highest waterfalls along this section of the coast, overlook a rock arch and generally experience some wonderful coastal scenery.

Features:

River, sea, pub, toilets, National Trust/NTS, wildlife, birds, flowers, great views.

Walk Directions:

❶ Having parked in the car park opposite the toilets and National Trust shop, walk back towards the Hunters Inn and take the road on the right of the inn, continuing ahead when the road turns right up the hill.

❷ Go through the facing gate and follow the sign to Woody Bay 2.75 miles, on the wider track ahead.

❸ This climb brings you above Heddon's Mouth, with glorious views over the valley.

❹ Follow this track all the way to Woody Bay, with wonderful coastal views, to reach the gate by a hairpin bend.

❺ Follow the road down, following the left-hand fork to the car park.

❻ Have a look at the National Trust information board on the area, then continue down the hill to the small road that goes hard back on the left down through the woods, signposted to Martinhoe Manor. Follow this down through the woods, past Wringapeak House to the hairpin bend and carry on straight ahead over the stile, signposted Coastpath to Hunters Inn.

❼ Follow the sign to Hunters Inn, up through the woods, with views on your right (leaves permitting) of Lee Abbey and the Valley of Rocks, with Foreland Point lighthouse flashing in the distance.

❽ Carry on and over the stile, now being wary of the drop on your right!

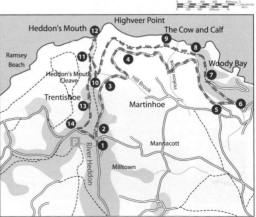

9 Soon you come to a high waterfall in a lovely valley. Carry on out to the point; a pause to look at the rock arch and surrounding scenery is most rewarding. Carry on up between the heather, around the next rocky point to more spectacular cliff scenery. Continue round the next two rocky points and down into the Heddon Valley.

10 When the path reaches the Heddon Valley path, turn hard right and walk down by the river to Heddon's Mouth.

11 Cross the bridge by the picnic area and continue down to reach the beach.

12 Having visited the beach and newly-restored limekiln, return to the picnic area by the bridge and continue across it, with the river on your left. In a while ignore the path going down to your left.

13 Pass through the gate and continue ahead, ignoring the signpost to Combe Martin up to the right, instead continuing along the level path.

14 On reaching the gate by the road, pass through and turn left to follow the small road over the bridge and on back to Hunters Inn. Be aware of cars, particularly on the narrow bends.

a secluded valley, is **Chambercombe Manor** (see panel on page 133), which was mentioned in the Domesday Book.

A couple of miles east of Ilfracombe, at the end of the beautiful Sterridge Valley, lies the picturesque coastal village of **Berrynarbor**, with its narrow streets, quaint cottages, 15th century manor house (later a school) and a tall-towered 12th century church. At the coast here is the pretty cove of Watermouth and the Victorian folly **Watermouth Castle** (see panel below).

COMBE MARTIN

9 miles NE of Barnstaple on the A399

Situated on the banks of the River Umber, Combe Martin is a popular seaside resort with a good sandy beach and, just a short walk away, some delightful secluded little bays. For children there is the added attraction of a large number of rock pools along Combe Martin Bay.

The village itself claims to have the longest main street in the country and,

WATERMOUTH CASTLE

Near Ilfracombe, Devon EX34 9SL
Tel: 01271 863879 Fax: 01271 865864
e-mail: enquiries@watermouthcastle.com
website: www.watermouthcastle.com

Watermouth Castle is a Victorian folly that has been transformed into a family theme park with attractions to suit all ages. In the castle's great hall, home to a collection of suits of armour, visitors can enjoy mechanical music demonstrations whilst, elsewhere in the castle, there are displays on Victorian life, antique pier machines and even a room devoted to model railways. Down in the depths of the dungeon labyrinths animated fairy tales come to life, there are craft shops from a bygone age but beware as this is also a place of witches, ghouls and phantoms!

Meanwhile, the castle grounds, too, have been transformed into a wonderful playground and here can be found the mystical water gardens with jumping fountains and a floating marble ball. In gnomeland, visitors can wander around the village and see the little people going about their daily business whilst, in adventure land, there is crazy water golf and a water ride. Finally there is the castle courtyard, where a tempting range of meals and snacks are available, along with a gift shop and, throughout the grounds, there are picnic areas.

at over two miles from end to end, it must certainly be in with a good chance. Along here is a wide selection of inns, cafés, restaurants and shops and also the **Combe Martin Museum**.

The village is also home to a remarkable architectural curiosity, **The Pack o' Cards Inn**, built in the early 18th century by Squire George Ley with the proceeds of a particularly lucrative evening at the card table. A grade II-listed building, it represents a pack of cards with four decks, or floors, 13 rooms and a total of 52 windows. The inside has not been forgotten either and there are many features that represent the cards in each suit.

On the southern outskirts of the village lies the **Combe Martin Wildlife and Dinosaur Park** (see panel below) where 250 species of animals, including a large and lively group of apes and monkeys, and some life-size animated

dinosaurs can be found lurking in the woods. Dinosaurs feature again in the museum and visitors can watch the daily sea lion shows, marvel at the falconry displays, handle some of the animals and ride the 'Earthquake ride'.

SOUTH MOLTON

This pleasant old market town, which is thankfully now bypassed by the main north Devon road, has been a focal point for the local agricultural industry as far back as Saxon times. In common with many towns throughout Devon, South Molton was also a centre for the wool trade in the late Middle Ages. The town centre has been overtaken by first Georgian and then Victorian buildings. There are still some buildings of note including the **Market Hall and Assembly Rooms**, the eccentric **Medical Hall** with its iron balcony and four Ionic

COMBE MARTIN WILDLIFE AND DINOSAUR PARK

Combe Martin, Devon EX34 0NG
Tel: 01271 882486 Fax: 01271 882486
e-mail: combemartinpark@hotmail.com
website: www.dinosaur-park.com

Set in natural parkland **Combe Martin Wildlife and Dinosaur Park** is home to a wide variety of animals but it

is, perhaps, the collection of life-size dinosaurs that draw most people to the park. Some of the models are animated including the UK's only full size animatronic T-Rex and a 'Spitting Dilophosaurus'. Set out in the parkland, this is a fantastic way to see these once great creatures. However, dinosaurs are just a small part of the park and there are 26 acres of sub-tropical gardens to explore with rare plants, cascading waterfalls and free flying exotic birds. The park is also home to Snow Leopards, Timber Wolves, Meerkats, Apes and Monkeys, Sealions, a Tropical Butterfly House and lots more, all in immaculately kept enclosures.

Other attractions are the Spectacular Light Show, Destination Mars and Earthquake Canyon, the most unique ride in the UK - experience a giant earthquake and survive! A superb day out for all the family, Combe Martin Wildlife and Dinosaur Park is full of surprises. Open March to November.

DREWSTONE FARM

South Molton, North Devon EX36 3EF
Tel/Fax: 01769 572337
e-mail: ruth_ley@drewstonefarm.fsnet.co.uk
website: www.devonself-catering.co.uk

Eric and Ruth Ley invite guests to enjoy the experience of family farm life on their 300-acre sheep and arable farm in the foothills of Exmoor, or just relax in the tranquil surroundings. **Woodland Hideaway** cottage is set overlooking a wooded valley at the end of a half mile private drive, away from the main farmstead. It has been furnished and fitted to provide comfortable, tasteful accommodation, with central heating and double glazing. The kitchen has all the expected up-to-date equipment, whilst the lounge opens directly on to the lawn. On the main farm the **Farmhouse Cottage** dates back to the 16th century and retains much old-world charm while providing modern amenities with nearby games room. **Drewstone Arches**, a superb barn conversion has its kitchen and lounge located upstairs to maximise the magnificent countryside scenery.

The Cottages all ETB 4 star, non smoking with 3 bedrooms, woodburners, enclosed lawns, garden furniture and ample parking provide a unique setting for the ideal get-away-from-it-all location, along with stunning views and delightful walks.

Exmoor lies two miles to the north, and the villages of North and South Molton are also nearby. To the west are some of the best beaches and surfing in the country.

columns, and the **Guildhall** of 1743 which overhangs the pavement in a series of arches.

Just on the southwestern outskirts of the town lies **Quince Honey Farm** where the mysterious process of honey making is explained in a series of displays and demonstrations.

AROUND SOUTH MOLTON

NORTH MOLTON

3 miles N of South Molton off the A361

Tucked away in foothills of Exmoor National Park, this once busy wool town was also a busy mining centre. Between the mid-16th century and the late 19th century copper and iron, extracted from the surrounding hills, was brought here before being transported down the River Mole to the sea at Barnstaple. Some of the mine buildings can still be found in and around the town while the remains of the old Mole Valley tramway are also still visible.

Further evidence of North Molton's prosperous past lies in its 15th century parish church, with its high clerestory and 100-foot high pinnacled tower, which seem rather grand for this remote community today. Also within the church is a clock that was purchased in 1564 for the then exorbitant price of £16 14s 4d. However, since it remained in working order for 370 years – its bells chimed for the last time in 1934 – it proved to be a very sound investment.

To the west of the church is the **Court Barton**, a fine 16th century house, where the biographer and critic Lytton Strachey stayed as part of a reading party in 1908. It would seem that the eminent writer greatly enjoyed his time in North Molton. He reported enthusiastically on the area's "mild tranquillities" and the way of life here that encompassed "a surplusage of beef and Devonshire cream".

LAMBSCOMBE FARM COTTAGES

Twitchen, North Molton, South Molton, Devon EX36 3JT
Tel: 01598 740558
e-mail: farenden4@aol.com website: www.lambscombefarm.co.uk

Set deep in unspoilt countryside on the southern edge of Exmoor, a
Grade II listed farmhouse and barns have been stylishly converted to
provide luxurious non-smoking self-catering accommodation in five
cottages sleeping from two to eight. **Lambscombe Farm Cottages** retain
many period features, giving each its own unique appeal, but also lack
nothing in comfort and amenities, with kitchens equipped to the highest modern standards and all
the expected extras in the lounges. Each cottage has a private garden, and shared amenities include a
recreation room, a playing field, a barbecue and an enclosed garden with children's play area. No pets.

WEST ANSTEY

8½ miles E of South Molton off the B3227

The Two Moors Way, the long distance
footpath that links Exmoor and
Dartmoor, passes a little to the east of
this tiny hamlet, situated just a mile or
so from the county border with
Somerset. Despite being so small, West
Anstey does have its own church,
boasting a fine Norman font.

The area around the settlement is one
of the emptiest in Devon – wonderful
open countryside, dotted with the
occasional farm or cluster of cottages.

To the northwest of West Anstey, and
in the parish of **Molland**, lies Great
Champson, the farm where, in the 18th
century, the Quartly family introduced
and developed their celebrated breed of
red North Devon cattle.

BISHOP'S NYMPTON

3 miles SE of South Molton off the A361

This village takes the 'Nympton' element
of its name from the River Yeo, known in
Saxon times and earlier, as the Nymet,
meaning the 'river at a holy place'.
King's Nympton, George Nympton and
several Nymets have the same origin. The
Bishop part of the name suggests that
this pleasant village of thatched cottages,
was once the home of a bishop's palace
but no evidence of any kind has yet been

found. However, Bishop's Nympton does
have some ecclesiastical connections as it
is home to what is considered to be one
of the most beautiful churches in Devon.
For many years this 15th century church
had a stained glass window, dating
from Tudor times and paid for by
Lady Pollard, the wife of Sir Lewis,
an eminent judge and one of the
village's leading residents.

According to a local story, while Sir
Lewis was away on business in London
the detailed designs for the church
window were entrusted to his wife. At
this time Lady Pollard had 21 children –
11 sons and 10 daughters - but in the
completed window there are 22
offspring. Sir Lewis presumed, correctly,
that his wife was expecting, as was usual
when he returned from London.
However, what is particularly odd about
the story is not that Lady Pollard
predicted the forthcoming child but that
she also predicted its sex. Sir Lewis is
believed to have told this story to
John Price, the author of *The Worthies
of Devon*.

CREDITON

17½ miles SE of South Molton on the A377

This sleepy market town was, in AD 680,
the birthplace of Wynfrith who went on
to become one of only a few Britons to
become saints. On becoming a monk,

Wynfrith adopted the name Boniface and rose swiftly through the ranks of the Benedictine Order. In 731, the Pope sent him to evangelise the Germans. Remarkably successful, Boniface converted several German states to Christianity and his reward was being created Archbishop of Mainz at the age of 71. Tragically, just three years later he and over 50 members of his party were ambushed and murdered while on their way to the great monastery at Fulda, in Hesse, that Boniface had founded. He was laid to rest there and greatly revered throughout all Germany. It was only a few years later that the Pope formally pronounced his sanctification.

However, it was nearly 1,200 years before the people of Crediton gave their most famous son any form of recognition and, finally, in 1897, an east window was installed in the town's cathedral-like **Church of the Holy Cross** that depicts scenes from his life. A few years later a statue of the saint was erected in the gardens to the west of the church. This church, which dates from the early 15th century, is one of only a handful of buildings that escaped the series of devastating fires that spread through medieval Crediton and of many other towns. As a result, the town's buildings are mainly 18th and 19th century. Another building to survive was the early 14th century **Lady Chapel**, home to the town's famous grammar school from the time it was granted a royal charter by Edward VI until 1859, when it moved to its present site at the west end of the High Street. The king also granted a royal charter to the church, stating that it be run by a board of governors. The room where they met, in the church's Chapter House, has a floor, cut from a single elm tree and, dating back over 700 years. It is, not surprisingly, quite uneven.

CHULMLEIGH
7½ miles SW of South Molton on the B3042

Another of this area's sleepy little market towns, Chulmleigh lies sprawled across the hills above the leafy valley of the Little Dart river. With its narrow, cobbled lanes, courtyards, quiet squares and thatched cob cottages, it is an attractive place to explore. A busy woollen trading centre in the Middle Ages, the town's prosperity from wool lasted longer than most other places as it lay on the old wagon route to Barnstaple. However, the completion of a turnpike road along the Taw valley in 1830 saw most of the trade diverted away from Chulmleigh. The opening, 25 years later, of the railway between Barnstaple and Exeter put the final nail in the coffin of Chulmleigh's era as a trading centre.

To the south of Chulmleigh lies **Eggesford Forest** where, in 1919, the newly formed Forestry Commission planted its first tree. This is commemorated by a stone unveiled by the Queen in 1956, which also marks the planting of over a million acres of trees by the Commission. There are two walks through the forest, each around a mile long, providing visitors with the opportunity to see the red deer that live among the trees. Near the commemorative stone are an information office, picnic site and car park.

NORTH TAWTON
15½ miles SW of South Molton off the A3072

Situated on the Tarka Trail, this once scattered community grew in medieval times on the wealth of the woollen industry. The decline of local textiles in the late 1700s dealt North Tawton a blow from which it has never recovered – the population today is less than in 1750. This small market town also suffered at

THE OLD RECTORY COTTAGES

Kings Nympton, North Devon EX37 9SS
Tel: 01769 580546 Fax: 01769 581519
e-mail: Krobinsontor@aol.com
website: www.northdevon.com/oldrectory

In the heart of Kings Nympton, with its Saxon church and pretty thatched dwellings, **The Old Rectory** provides year-round self-catering accommodation in four luxury, newly refurbished cottages. Converted from the original coach house and stables, they boast log fires, fully equipped kitchens, dishwashers, DVDs, stereos, indoor heated swimming pool and BBQ's, in fact everything that you will need for a romantic break or fun filled family holiday.

The cottages are set in four acres of wonderful gardens including a bluebell wood and duck ponds with views of Exmoor in the distance. The Old Rectory is a first-class base for touring the areas many attractions and experiencing one of the country's last areas of outstanding natural beauty.Pursuits such as walking, golf, fishing and shooting are in abundance locally and attractions such as Saunton Sands Golf Course, Rosemoor Gardens and North Devons spectacular beaches are a short drive away. Owner Karen Robinson is an experienced caterer and is happy to provide meals by arrangement in the comfort of your own cottage and should you prefer to eat out, the excellent local is just a minutes walk away.

the hands of several devastating fires that destroyed many of the town's older and more interesting buildings. **Broad Hall** dates back to the 15th century and is a private residence. During the time that this was an important borough it was governed by a portreeve, an official who was elected each year. The practice stopped relatively recently – at the end of the 19th century.

In a field close to the town lies **Bathe Pool**, a grassy hollow that is said to fill with water at times of national crises or when a prominent person is about to die. The pool has been reported to have filled at the time of the death of Nelson, Wellington and Edward VII and also just before the outbreak of World War I.

HATHERLEIGH

17½ miles SW of South Molton on the A386

This medieval market town, continues to hold a market and is popular with

fishermen trying their luck on the River Torridge and its tributary. Hatherleigh was owned by Tavistock Abbey from the 900s up until the dissolution in the 16th century. The picturesque, thatched George Hotel, originally the Abbot's courthouse, is believed to date from around 1450. The London Inn is also believed to date from the mid-15th century. A fire in 1840 destroyed much of Hatherleigh's old town centre. The town's 15th century church escaped the flames but, in 1990, hurricane winds caught its spindly tower and tossed it through the roof of the nave. Fortunately, the church was empty at the time.

A good place from which to begin an exploration of Hatherleigh is the **Hatherleigh Pottery**, a working pottery and textile studio where there are exhibits and displays detailing the life and countryside in and around this

1,000-year-old town. While the closure of the railway line between Okehampton and Bude, as part of the Beeching's cuts of 1966, took away a much valued local amenity, long stretches of the track bed, which passes by Hatherleigh, now provide attractive walking.

Just a couple of miles north of Hatherleigh is the pleasant little village of **Meeth**, whose Old English name means 'the meeting of the streams' and a small brook does indeed run into the River Torridge here. From the early 18th century, Meeth and the surrounding area was well known for its pottery clay and there are still some extensive clay works northwest of the village. However, walkers and cyclists will know Meeth better as the southern terminus of the **Tarka Trail** that runs northwards through Bideford and Barnstaple.

Lynmouth Harbour

LYNMOUTH

For centuries Lynmouth was a village scraping a living from the land and the sea and particularly noted for its catches of herring most of which were also cured here. Thankfully, just as the herring shoals were moving to new waters this part of the north Devon coast began to benefit from two great enthusiasms: romantic scenery and sea bathing. Coleridge and Wordsworth came here on walking tours in the 1790s and Shelley visited in 1812. Robert Southey, later to become the Poet Laureate, first used the phrase "English Switzerland" to describe the dramatic scenery that Gainsborough considered the "most delightful" for a landscape painter. However, by the mid-19th century the steep cliff between

Lynmouth and its neighbour along the coast, Lynton, was affecting the growing tourist trade. Bob Janes, a local engineer, designed the **Lynton-Lynmouth Cliff Railway**, which was financed by Sir George Newnes, the publisher and newspaper tycoon. Opened on Easter Monday 1890, this ingenious railway, which still runs today, rises some 450 feet in just 900 feet and is powered by water. Each of the two carriages has a huge water tank beneath it. The tank is filled at the top of the cliff to carry that carriage down to the bottom, taking the other carriage to the top. The tank is then emptied while the other carriage's tank is filled to bring them back to their original positions. The trip takes just 90 seconds and so good were Janes's designs for the braking and hydraulic systems that they have not been changed since the railway was built.

One of the most picturesque villages in Devon, Lynmouth lies at the confluence of the East and West Lyn Rivers. It has a tiny harbour surrounded by wooded hills, a curious Rhenish Tower on its pier and Mars Hill, an eye-catching row of thatched cottages. This lovely setting still draws artists and craftsmen. **Lynmouth Pottery** is not only a working pottery

EXMOOR SANDPIPER INN

Countisbury, Nr Lynton, Devon EX35 6NE
Tel: 01598 741263 Fax: 01598 741358
e-mail: info@exmoor-sandpiper.co.uk
website: www.exmoor-sandpiper.co.uk

High above Lynton and Lynmouth, the
Exmoor Sandpiper Inn offers a combination
of location, ambience and hospitality that is
very hard to beat. American Scott Herbst, who
runs the inn with his wife Louise and
daughter Lily, has been in the catering trade
all his working life, and knows exactly what
will win new customers and keep the old ones
coming back. The first strong point is the inn itself, built in the 13th century and sympathetically
added to in the 17th and 20th centuries.

Great black beams and rustic furniture set the tone in the public areas, where the feature fireplaces

include an original 13th century inglenook
which until recently was used for smoking
hams. The second is the welcome – the same
smiles for everyone, grown-ups, children, dogs,
even walkers with muddy boots. Once inside,
the bar and lounge areas have plenty of
comfortable sofas and chairs to sink into and
relax, and when the sun shines, the patio, with
stunning views of the coastline, really comes
into its own.

The third big attraction is the food, which
the owners take very seriously and which is a
major factor in the inn's popularity. Local fish,
meat and game are used widely in the dishes on
the all-day menus, which cater for most tastes
and all appetites. Some of the dishes are pub classics such as steak & ale pie or lasagne (meat or
vegetarian), while others have subtle variations from the usual, shown by Cajun chicken Caesar salad
or bangers & mash with red onion gravy. Plain grills are always in demand, and the daily specials list
tempts with the likes of sea bass with nut brown butter, crevettes with garlic mayonnaise or tenderloin
of pork with an apple and calvados cream sauce. The owners are very keen on introducing children to

good food and, as well as providing a kids' menu,
they are happy to split an adult dish between two
little gourmets, and their future plans include cooking
classes for kids. Wine is also taken very seriously at
the Exmoor Sandpiper, and the helpfully annotated
list is particularly strong in the New World, with lots
available by the glass.

This is place to relax and take one's time, and for
visitors staying overnight the inn comes up trumps
yet again with 16 comfortable en suite guest
bedrooms. These are let on a bed & breakfast basis,
with growing discounts for stays of longer than one
night. With established walks starting from the inn
and the South West Coast Path and Exmoor National
Park close by, this is a great base for a walking or
touring holiday.

but also a place where visitors can try their hand at throwing a pot on a potter's wheel. More hands-on experience is offered at the **Exmoor Brass Rubbing and Hobbycraft Centre**.

Lynmouth's setting beside its twin rivers is undeniably beautiful but it has also proved to be tragically vulnerable. On the night of 16th August 1952, a cloudburst over Exmoor deposited nine inches of rain onto an already soaked moorland. In the darkness the normally placid East and West Lyn Rivers became raging torrents and burst their banks, sweeping away trees and boulders in their wake. The debris-filled torrent smashed its way through the village and destroyed dozens of houses, leaving 34 people dead and many injured. That night saw many storms across southern England but none had the ferocity of the deluge that engulfed this pretty village. At the **Flood Memorial Hall** is an exhibition that recounts the events if that terrible night. Following the devastation, the village was rebuilt, along with its harbour and the **Rhenish Tower**, the folly at the end of the pier. This was not the first storm to hit Lynmouth. In 1899, the Lynmouth lifeboat was involved in a tale of epic endurance during another exceptional storm. A full-rigged ship, the *Forest Hill*, was in difficulties off Porlock but the storm was so violent it was impossible to launch the lifeboat at Lynmouth. Instead the crewmen dragged their three-and-a-half-ton boat, the *Louisa*, 13 miles across the moor and over Countisbury Hill, with a gradient of 1,000 feet in two miles. Once at Porlock Weir, the lifeboat was successfully launched and every crew member of the stricken ship was saved.

To the east of the village in a picturesque valley lies **Watersmeet House**, an old fishing lodge that has been a tea

---

SEAVIEW VILLA

6 Summerhouse Path, Lynmouth, Devon EX35 6ES
Tel: 01598 753460 Fax: 01598 753496
e-mail: reservations@seaviewvilla.co.uk
website: www.seaviewvilla.co.uk

Personal service and attention to detail are bywords at **Seaview Villa**, a beautiful Grade II listed building dating from 1721. Stephen Williams, design director, and Christopher Bissex, drama teacher, recently changed careers to run this superb little guest house, which has earned the top rating in its class from the AA. A great deal of care and thought has gone into the guest bedrooms, which offer

abundant luxury and comfort with the finest Egyptian cotton bedding and generous bath sheets; modern amenities of TV-video and CD-radio alarm are standard, and most of the rooms have en suite facilities.

Home-baked bread is a feature of breakfast, which offers the options of full English, lighter Continental style or vegetarian. An evening meal can be arranged with a little notice, and the owners are happy to make all the rooms available for a house party. Seaview Villa, which commands terrific views from its position tucked away from the bustle of the town, is an ideal base for total relaxation, for an active seaside holiday (great surfing), for discovering the scenic delights of coast and countryside or for enjoying the well-marked walks that start from the front door. Seaview is a non-smoking establishment.

garden since 1901 and from where several scenic walks begin. As well as providing refreshments, the house has a National Trust shop and information point.

Often mentioned in the same breath as Lynmouth, **Lynton**, just half a mile along the coast to the west and reached by the cliff railway, has a very different character. The younger of the two settlements, Lynton sits on top of the great cliff while Lynmouth lies far below. A bright and breezy village, of chiefly Victorian architecture, Lynton is home to the **Exmoor Museum** housed in a restored 16th century dwelling. Here an intriguing collection of tools and the bygone products of local craftsmen can be seen along with other exhibits that recount the area's history. To the west of Lynton is one of the most remarkable natural features in Devon, the **Valley of the Rocks**. When the poet Robert Southey visited here in 1800, he was most impressed by this natural gorge, which he described as "covered with huge stones" with "rock reeling upon rock." In *Lorna Doone*, RD Blackmore transforms the site into the Devil's Cheesewring where Jan Ridd visits Mother Meldrun who is sheltering under a lichen-covered rock. Coleridge was equally inspired by the valley, which he walked in the company of Wordsworth and his sister Dorothy. The result was his immortal poem *The Rime of the Ancient Mariner*.

AROUND LYNMOUTH

Doone Valley
4 miles E of Lynmouth off the A39

This scenic valley is a long enclosed sweep of green pasture and mature woodland. It was immortalised by RD Blackmore in his classic romantic novel,

---

Gunns Art Gallery

Burlington House, 11 Lee Road, Lynton, Devon EX35 6HW
Tel/Fax: 01598 753352
e-mail: art@gunnsgallery.co.uk
website: www.gunnsgallery.co.uk

After more than 20 years of teaching in Hertfordshire, Peter Shimwell escaped the rat race to glorious North Devon, where he met his partner Angela. His experience of antiques fairs and craft markets persuaded him that the time had come for a serious career change, and he duly acquired **Gunns Art Gallery**. The gallery is well known for showing a wide range of original work by award-winning artists, among them Charlotte Atkinson, Adam Barsby, Mick Cawston, Louise Fox, Govinder, John Horswell, Ged Mitchell, Richard Pargeter, Janet Rogers and Jonathan Shaw.

The gallery also stocks an impressive selection of prints dating from 1790 to the 1950s - advertising posters are particularly popular - and artists materials. The stock is always changing, and many of Peter's customers are very regular visitors. Gunns Art Gallery was started by George Gunn in 1893 in a building - originally a hotel - that was constructed by the Jones brothers, who were also responsible for Lynton's famous Cliff Railway. Peter totally renovated the building when he took over, and above the three floors of display space he has created two comfortable holiday apartments.

Valley of the Rocks

Lorna Doone. The now demolished medieval farm known as Hoccombe Combe is thought to have been the home of a wild and unruly Exmoor family whose real-life exploits provided the inspiration for the story. The beautiful little 15th century church to the east, at **Oare**, is thought to be the setting of the heroine's dramatic, interrupted wedding. Inside the church, where RD Blackmore's grandfather was once rector, there is a fine set of 19th century box pews and an unusual piscina shaped like a man's head.

To the north, on the coast at the Devon-Somerset border, is **County Gate**, one of several dramatic viewpoints along this spectacular stretch of coastline. Here, the great whale-backed hills of Exmoor plunge down to the sea and there are breathtaking views across the Bristol Channel to South Wales. This headland is also home to one of the few Roman remains on Exmoor, a lookout station for observing cross-channel raiding parties.

PARRACOMBE
5 miles SW of Lynmouth off the A39

The village's redundant **Church of St Petroc**, noted for its marvellous unspoilt interior, owes its survival to John Ruskin, who led protests against its demolition in 1879 after another church had been built lower down the hill. Today's visitors can marvel at the unique gated screen between the chancel and the nave that bears a huge tympanum painted with the royal arms, the Lord's Prayer, the Creed and the Ten Commandments. Close by is one of the most spectacular wooded valleys on Exmoor, **Heddon Valley**, offering visitors beautiful coastal and woodland walks. Owned by the National Trust, there is an information centre and a gift shop that also sells refreshments in the valley.

CHALLACOMBE
6 miles SW of Lynmouth on the B3358

Famous for its ancient inn, The Black Venus, Challacombe lies just inside Exmoor National Park, a mile and a half from the **Edgerley Stone**, which marks the border between Devon and Somerset. There has been a settlement here for centuries and it was the ancient Britons who gave the village its name, though experts cannot agree whether the name means 'cold valley' or 'calves' valley'. Either interpretation would be valid as the wind is never still here and beef cattle are raised on the surrounding moorland.

LOCATOR MAP

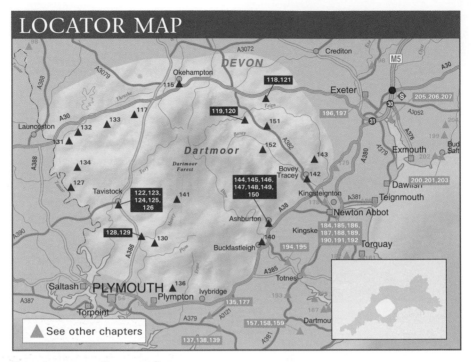

ADVERTISERS AND PLACES OF INTEREST

115 Upcott House, Okehampton — page 148
116 Buckland House, Buckland Filleigh — page 149
117 White Hart Inn, Bridestowe — page 150
118 Netherton Vine Cottages, Drewsteignton — page 151
119 Mill End Hotel, Chagford — page 152
120 Cyprians Cot, Chagford — page 152
121 Castle Drogo, Drewsteignton, Exeter — page 153
122 Browns Hotel & Wine Bar, Tavistock — page 156
123 Randell Cox Floral Design, Tavistock — page 157
124 No. 13, Tavistock — page 158
125 Encore Contemporary Homestyle, Tavistock — page 158
126 Mount Tavy Cottage, Tavistock — page 159
127 Lamerhooe Lodge, Horsebridge — page 160
128 Buckland Abbey, Yelverton — page 161
129 Harrabeer Country Hotel, Yelverton — page 162
130 Callisham Farm, Meavy, Yelverton — page 162
131 Tinhay Mill, Tinhay, Lifton — page 164
132 Dingles Steam Village, Milford, Lifton — page 165
133 The Harris Arms, Lewdown — page 165
134 Endsleigh Gardens Nursery, Milton Abbots, Tavistock — page 166

135 Goutsford, Ermington, Ivybridge — page 166
136 The Dartmoor Wildlife Park, Sparkwell — page 167
137 Wild Goose Antiques, Modbury — page 168
138 Ringrose Gallery, Modbury — page 168
139 Arwyn Jones Ceramics, Modbury — page 169
140 Buckfast Butterflies & Dartmoor Otter Sanctuary, Buckfastleigh — page 170
141 The Railway Inn, Princetown — page 171
142 The Devon Guild of Craftsmen, Bovey Tracey — page 173
143 Frost Farm, Hennock, Bovey Tracey — page 174
144 Tessdesigns, Ashburton — page 175
145 Foxgloves, Ashburton — page 175
146 Holne Chase Hotel, Ashburton — page 176
147 Roborough House, Ashburton — page 177
148 The Shambles, Ashburton — page 177
149 The Ashburton Delicatessen, Ashburton — page 178
150 Gages Mill, Ashburton — page 178
151 Great Sloncombe Farm, Moretonhampstead — page 182
152 Becky Falls Woodland Park, Menaton — page 183

IN AND AROUND DARTMOOR 4

High, bleak and wild, Dartmoor is southern England's only true wilderness and it is easy for walkers to lose their way in the rolling granite uplands, especially when the mists descend unexpectedly. It covers an area of some 368 square miles and rises to a height of more than 2,000 feet. Thousands of years of erosion have reduced the moorland's peaks, believed to rise at one time to 15,000 feet above sea level, into a plateau of whale-backed granite ridges. The highest and most dramatic area of the moor lies just below the ancient town of Okehampton where High Willhays and Yes Tor rise to a height of 2,038 feet and 2,029 feet respectively. The tors are Dartmoor's most characteristic feature and these great chunks of

Scorhill Stone Circle, Dartmoor

granite have withstood the effects of the wind, rain and ice better than the less resistant rocks which once surrounded them. This area, too, is rich in prehistoric remains. The moorland is littered with stone circles, menhirs, burial chambers and single, double or even triple rows of stones including a row of 150 stones on Stall Moor that is believed to be the longest prehistoric stone row in Europe.

In medieval times, the moorland was the scene of much commercial activity as tin has been mined here since at least the 12th century. There is still evidence of mining on the moors and Devon has four stannary towns, where the metal was brought to be weighed and assayed. Later, the land here was exploited for lead, copper, iron and even arsenic. Today, Dartmoor's most famous, or infamous, building is its prison, right in the middle of the bleak moorland at Princetown. Originally built by French prisoners of war from granite quarried from the moor, it is a building as inhospitable as the countryside that surrounds it.

It is also famed for its Dartmoor ponies that have roamed here freely since at least the 10th century. Sir Arthur Conan Doyle made the moorland even bleaker and wilder than it is in his mysterious and spine-chilling novel, *The Hound of the Baskervilles.* This famous Sherlock Holmes tale was inspired by stories told to Conan Doyle by his guide, Harry Baskerville. Though he took the liberty of changing some of its geography, the novel has brought many visitors to Dartmoor.

Surrounding the National Park there are the charming and delightful towns of Okehampton, Tavistock, Ivybridge and Bovey Tracey, that have served the needs of those who lived and worked on the moors for centuries. In the less harsh landscape of the eastern area of Dartmoor lies Widecombe a wonderful, scenic village that is home to the famous fair.

OKEHAMPTON

The location of this ancient town, between the puckered green hills of north Devon that roll away to the coast and the wild expanse of Dartmoor to the south, has shaped its history. Dartmoor's great peaks, **High Willhays** and **Yes Tor**, rising to over 2,000 feet are, officially, mountains. However this is quite low compared with their original height.

Geologists believe that, at one time, the surfaces of Dartmoor rose to over 15,000 feet above sea level. After millions of years of erosion these surfaces have been reduced to a plateau of whale-backed granite ridges, strewn with fragments of surface granite, or moorstone. It was this 'ready-to-use' stone that made Dartmoor one of the most populous areas of prehistoric Britain. The early settlers used the easily quarried granite to build their stone rows, circles and burial chambers.

Upcott House

Upcott Hill, Okehampton, Devon EX20 1SQ
Tel: 01837 53743
e-mail: info@upcotthouse.com
website: www.upcotthouse.com

Half a mile from Okehampton, on the Hatherleigh road, **Upcott House** is a quiet, civilised holiday retreat in woodland looking out across the Okement Valley to Dartmoor. In this beautiful setting Kay and John Bickley offer a real family atmosphere and comfortable bed & breakfast accommodation in well-appointed double rooms, all with TV, tea-makers, central heating and vanity units and some with en suite facilities. Breakfast is served in the rooms or in the dining room, and packed lunches and evening meals are available with notice.

The house was built in 1885 as a gentleman's country residence, but for most of its life, until 1965, it was a boys' school. It stands in its own attractive grounds with seats for relaxing in the fresh country air and various things to keep the children happy. It's just a gentle stroll to Okehampton, where the attractions include the Museum of Dartmoor Life and the Dartmoor Park Visitor Centre. Other gentle strolls are provided by the numerous established walks that start from hereabouts, while those looking for something more strenuous will take their packed lunch and head for High Willhays and Yes Tor, Dartmoor's great peaks.

Stone was also used to build their distinctive hut circles of which there are many remains scattered across the moor today.

From Celtic times Okehampton has occupied an important position on the main route to and from Cornwall. Situated on the top of a wooden hill, and dominating the surrounding valley of the River Okement, are the remains of **Okehampton Castle**. The largest medieval castle in Devon, these romantic ruins are still impressive, despite having been dismantled on the orders of Henry VIII after the owner, the Earl of Devon, had been found guilty of treason. The castle is in the custodianship of English Heritage.

Housed in an ancient mill with its now restored water wheel outside, is the **Museum of Dartmoor Life**. This is an ideal place to begin any exploration of the town and learn how, down the centuries, people lived and worked in the area. In the surrounding courtyard are the Tourist Information Centre, the craft and gift shops and a tearoom.

Among the town's buildings of note are the 15th century **Chapel of Ease** and the **Town Hall**, a striking three-storey building dated 1685, originally built as a private resident but converted to its current use in the 1820s. There is also an interesting Victorian arcade in the town reminiscent of the Burlington Arcade, London. The beautifully restored Okehampton Station lies at the centre of the Dartmoor Railway, which climbs into the National Park and terminates at Meldon Viaduct.

Many walks into the northern reaches of Dartmoor begin here. Those wishing to travel further afield, will find several excellent riding stables that take the horses out along a network of quiet lanes and bridleways.

BUCKLAND HOUSE

Buckland Filleigh, Beaworthy, Devon EX21 5JD
Tel: 01409 281645
e-mail: enquiries@bucklandhouse.co.uk
website: www.bucklandhouse.co.uk

On a site going back to the time of William the Conqueror, **Buckland House** is a magnificent Grade II* mansion standing proudly in unspoilt countryside. It offers the most splendid self-catering accommodation for families or groups of friends, and though grand, it has a warm, welcoming and very relaxing atmosphere. Among the expanse of day rooms are a two-storey gallery ballroom with a grand piano, a huge dining room, a snooker room with a full-size table, a fully equipped kitchen, a Tudor sitting room and library, a laundry room and large children's play room.

On the first floor, reached by an imposing staircase, there are 15 bedrooms and nine bathrooms; three of the rooms have four-poster beds, and five of the bathrooms contain splendid Victorian ball and claw baths. The park around the house boasts fine specimen trees, a croquet lawn, a lake with a rowing boat and an outdoor swimming pool; there are lovely walks through the 250 acres of private

woodland, and the village church lies within the grounds. Pony and trap rides can be arranged through the owners, who live next door in the coach house, and other facilities available include babysitting, skeet shooting and a full catering service.

WHITE HART INN

Bridestowe, Devon EX20 4EL
Tel/Fax: 01837 861318

The White Hart Inn is a 16th century Devon longhouse situated in a pretty village just down the road from Okehampton. The immaculate white-painted frontage is adorned with flowers, with picnic benches on a little lawned area, while inside all is quaint and traditional, with beams and panelling, carpets, rustic furniture, open fires and a feature stone bar. Partners Kathy and Anita serve freshly cooked dishes, from light snacks to full meals, and recently refurbished en suite bedrooms provide quiet, comfortable bed & breakfast accommodation for guests staying overnight.

AROUND OKEHAMPTON

STICKLEPATH

3½ miles SE of Okehampton off the A30

This little village on the very edge of Dartmoor and on the banks of the River Taw is home to one of the most interesting industrial and archaeological remains in Devon. **Finch Foundry** was built in the 19th century as a water-powered forge that produced a range of agricultural and mining hand tools between 1814 and 1960. Its three water wheels still drive the huge tilt hammer and grindstone and there are regular demonstrations showing just how the foundrymen fashioned a wide range of implements. Now owned by the National Trust, this living museum of water power also has a shop and a café.

Just a short distance up river lies the village of **Belstone**, a picturesque scene with its thatched cottages, 13th century church and a triangular green complete with stocks and a stone commemorating the coronation of King George V. The Post Office, once housed in a former chapel, is now located in the village hall. From the village a footpath leads up to the ancient standing stone circle known as the **Nine Stones**, although there are actually well over a dozen of them. A local legend tells that these stones, found

under Belstone Tor, were formed when some maidens were discovered dancing on the Sabbath and were turned to stone as a punishment. However, the stones were in place long before Christianity reached England. Another claim, that the mysterious stones change position at noon, is equally unlikely! Another path leads south to a spot on the northern edge of Dartmoor where the ashes of the Poet Laureate Ted Hughes are scattered and where a granite stone was placed to his memory.

Just to the southeast of Sticklepath lies **South Zeal**, another village glad of the road building of the 1970s that eventually saw it bypassed. The village sits on either side of the old main route between Exeter and Launceston. Although called a major road right up until 1975, it is little more than a winding country lane. On a little oasis in the middle of the village's broad main street stands a simple medieval market cross along with St Mary's Chapel, rebuilt in 1713. To the south of the village, are the remains of a short-lived copper mine that provided the inhabitants of South Zeal with much needed work between 1901 and 1909.

A little further on again, and just south of the village of **Whiddon Down**, stands the **Spinster Rock**, the best surviving chamber tomb in Cornwall.

According to local legend, three spinsters erected the dolmen early one morning – an impressive feat as the capstone, supported by just three uprights seven feet high, weighs 16 tons!

For lovers of solitude, this memorable countryside was effectively used by Sir Arthur Conan Doyle in *The Hound of the Baskervilles*. Recalling the villain's fate, walkers should beware of the notorious 'feather beds' – deep bogs signalled by a quaking cover of brilliant green moss.

DREWSTEIGNTON
9½ miles SE of Okehampton off the A30

A place of thatched cottages grouped, along with its medieval church, around a village square, Drewsteignton is another much photographed Devonshire village. This appealing village stands on a ridge overlooking the River Teign and the well-known beauty spot **Fingle Bridge**, a 400-year-old structure over the river. From

Castle Drogo

NETHERTON VINE COTTAGES

Drewsteignton, Dartmoor, Devon TQ13 8QY
Tel/Fax: 01647 281602

Netherton Vine Cottages comprises two delightful self-catering properties close to the village of Drewsteignton within Dartmoor National Park. Michaelmas has four bedrooms, two bath/shower rooms, a comfortable sitting room with a woodburner in a granite inglenook fireplace, and a large well equipped farmhouse kitchen/dining room. Antique furniture and original beams are notable features, and the cottage overlooks its own private garden with a lawn, herbaceous borders and a terrace for alfresco dining. Adjoining Michaelmas, the enchanting Gardeners is furnished and equipped to the same high standard, with two bedrooms, bath/shower room, charming sitting room (inglenook woodburner), kitchen and private walled garden.

Both cottages have oil-fired central heating, TVs, video, CD player, radio and telephone, and shared amenities include a formal rose garden, a croquet lawn, boules pitch, one acre paddock with a pony and rare-breed hens. Owners Angela and Anthony Thomas live next to the cottages and are always ready with advice or help whilst keeping a low profile. Much of the land around the cottages belongs to the National Trust's Castle Drogo estate and provides excellent year round walking. Fishing, riding and golf are all available nearby. Well behaved dogs welcome. **ETC 5 Star.**

MILL END HOTEL

Dartmoor National Park, Chagford,
Devon TQ13 8JN
Tel: 01647 432282 Fax: 01647 433106
website: www.millendhotel.com

Situated in Dartmoor National Park, with
the River Teign flowing through the
beautiful, established gardens, the **Mill
End Hotel** is a charming small hotel
offering guests the very best in traditional
English hospitality. Mill End dates from
the 18th century, when it was built as a
flour mill. Today, owner Keith Green has
created the perfect environment for a
quiet and luxurious holiday. The
bedrooms are bright and comfortable; ground-floor rooms have stone-flagged patios with tables and
chairs overlooking the lawn (a lovely spot for cream tea), while upstairs rooms enjoy delightful views
of the Devon countryside.

Guests will find plenty of cosy corners for curling up with a good book, and the whole house is
filled with little treasures assembled by generations of owners. The award-winning restaurant is friendly
and unpretentious, with the finest local produce in abundance, including free-range eggs, home-
cured gravad lax, wild boar, fresh fish from Brixham and Looe, and of course clotted cream. The fine
food is complemented by an outstanding wine list. The hotel is a paradise for walkers - it lies on the
Two Moors Way - and anglers, with 600 yards of private salmon and trout fishing, eight miles of game
fishing and still water fishing on local lakes.

CYPRIAN'S COT

47 New Street, Chagford, Devon TQ13 8BB
Tel: 01647 432256
e-mail: shelagh-weeden@lineone.net

Shelagh Weeden makes her Bed & Breakfast guests feel
really welcome at **Cyprian's Cot**, an early 16th century
Grade II listed building of great charm and character.
The whole place has an inviting, home-from-home
feel, and the bedrooms, prettily furnished with
country cottons, combine old features with the
amenity of a private bathroom (in the double room)
or an en suite shower (in the twin). Guests can relax and plan their days or watch television in the
lounge, where on cooler evenings a log fire is lit in the large inglenook fireplace.

An original oak screen separates the lounge from
the oak-panelled dining room, where guests start the
day with a breakfast choice that makes good use of
local free-range produce. The cottage is conveniently
located close to the centre of Chagford, but the
countryside is also close by - the garden leads straight
on to fields, and the views over the Moor are
particularly stunning in the setting sun. Chagford has
its own attractions, including interesting shops and a
very fine restaurant. It's a popular centre for country
lovers, and walkers are most welcome at Cyprian's Cot
- maps and drying facilities are available.

here there are circular walks as well as footpaths up and down the river. One of the most scenic is the **Hunters' Path** that climbs up through an oak wood, to well above the tree line, from where there are fabulous views out over northern Dartmoor.

To the south can be found **Prestonbury Castle** and **Cranbrook Castle**, not castles but Iron Age hill forts, while, to the southwest, lies **Castle Drogo**, a granite structure that looks every inch a medieval castle although it is not. Situated high above the River Teign and with commanding views of Dartmoor, the castle was built, between 1910 and 1930, for the self-made millionaire Julius Drewe (see panel).

CHAGFORD

8½ miles SE of Okehampton on the B3192

This ancient settlement, beautifully situated between the pleasant wooded valley of the North Teign River and the stark expanses of the high moor, was also one of Devon's four stannary towns. Nothing remains in the town from that era although careful exploration of the surrounding countryside will reveal some scant evidence of mining activity. In the centre of the town stands the former **Market House**, a charming octagonal building erected in 1862, while, around the square, there are some old style family shops offering interesting shopping with plenty of atmosphere.

In the town's chiefly 15th century Church of St Michael there is an elaborate monument to Sir John

CASTLE DROGO

Drewsteignton,
near Exeter EX6 6PB
Tel: 01647 433306
Fax: 01647 433186

Castle Drogo (National Trust) is spectacularly sited on a rocky outcrop with commanding views out over Dartmoor and the Teign gorge. It was built for Sir Julius Drewe, a self made millionaire, on land once owned by his Norman ancestor, Drogo de Teigne. Surrounding this 20th century dream country home, lies an equally impressive garden – the highest in the Trust. The square shape of the castle and the large rotund croquet lawn exemplifies the simple ethos of the architect, Lutyens, of "circles and squares". From spring bulbs in the formal garden, the rhododendron garden, the stunning herbaceous borders, the rose garden and the winter garden there is colour and interest here all year round.

Wyddon who died in 1575. The building is best known as the scene of the tragic death of one of his descendants in October 1641. Mary Whiddon was shot at the altar by a jealous lover as she was being married. This incident is thought to have inspired RD Blackmore to write *Lorna Doone*. Her tombstone bears the inscription "Behold a Matron yet a Maid." The ghost of Mary is believed to haunt Whiddon Park Guest House. In 1971, early on the morning of a wedding reception that was to take place there later that day, a young woman dressed in black is reported to have appeared before one of the guests.

Between 1854 and 1895 the town was the home of James Perrot, the famous Dartmoor guide, who noted that as late as 1830 some of the farms in this area had no wheeled vehicles. On the other hand, Perrot lived to see the town install electric street lighting in 1891 making it one of the first communities west of London to possess such a modern innovation. It was also Perrot who began the curious practice of letterbox stamp collecting and he installed the first

Gidleigh

Today, it is like an oasis, with its beech trees contrasting with the surrounding bleak moorland. The village is, perhaps, best known for its **Clapper Bridge**, probably dating from the 13th century and the best preserved example of its kind in Devon. Spanning the East Dart River, a few yards down stream from the road bridge, the clapper bridge is a wonderful example of medieval minimalist construction with just three huge slabs of granite laid across solid stone piers. Not wide enough for wheeled vehicles, the bridge would have been used by walkers and packhorses following the post road from Exeter into Cornwall. From here there are many pleasant walks up the East Dart River although anyone wishing to cross the river during the walk should note that, after heavy rain, this may not always be possible.

letterbox at **Cranmere Pool**, near the heart of the moor, so that his Victorian clients could send a postcard home, stamped to show where they had been. Today, there are hundreds of letterboxes scattered all over Dartmoor.

To the west of the town a pleasant country lane leads upstream from Chagford Bridge and through the wooded valley of the North Teign to the **Holed Stone**. It is said, by local people, that anyone climbing through the large round cavity in the centre of the stone will be cured of a whole host of afflictions, ranging from rheumatism to infertility. The land to the south of Chagford rises abruptly towards **Kestor Rock** and **Shovel Down**, the sites of two impressive Bronze Age settlements, while, further on, at the point where the parishes of Chagford and Gidleigh end, is the beginning of the land belonging to the Duchy of Cornwall.

POSTBRIDGE

11 miles SE of Okehampton on the B3212

The wealth of Bronze Age remains that litter the area around Postbridge suggests that, in prehistoric times, this was one of the main meeting places on Dartmoor.

To the west of Postbridge are the ruins of **Powder Mills**, a 19th century gunpowder factory. The abundance of space here was about the only safety feature at the factory and the batches of powder were tested by firing a proving mortar that can still be seen near the cottages. A little further on lies a low tor, **Crockern Tor**, that was, between 1474 and 1703, the meeting place of the Stannary Court, the administrative body of the Dartmoor miners, and to which each of the four stannaries in Devon sent 24 representatives.

To the northeast lies **Warren House Inn**, which claims to be the third highest tavern in England. The inn used to stand on the other side of the road but, in 1845, a fire destroyed that building. According to tradition, when the inn

Clapper Bridge, Postbridge

was rebuilt, the landlord carried some still-smouldering turf across the road to the hearth of his new hostelry and the fire he started then has been burning ever since. A pleasant sight even in summer as it can be cold on the high moor, the fires must have been even more welcome in the winter of 1963 when Warren House Inn was cut off by heavy 20-foot deep snow drifts for almost three months and supplies had to be flown in by helicopter. Naturally this remote inn has many good tales linked with it and one, in particular, tells of a traveller who stayed here one winter's night. On retiring to his room he opened by chance a large chest and discovered a dead body hidden within. "Why!", exclaimed the landlord when he was confronted with the deceased, "'tis only feyther! 'Twas too cold to take 'un to the burying so mother salted 'un down!"

LYDFORD

8 miles SW of Okehampton off the A386

Though it may be hard to believe today, in Saxon times, Lydford was one of just four royal boroughs in Devon, along with Exeter, Barnstaple and Totnes. What made Lydford so important was its strategic position on the River Lyd. In the 11th century, the Normans built a fortification here that was superseded just a hundred years later by the present **Lydford Castle**. This austere stone fortress, now in the hands of English Heritage, served for decades as a court and prison for the independent tin miners of Dartmoor. The justice meted out from here was notoriously arbitrary. In the 17th century, William Browne of Tavistock observed:

> *I oft have heard of Lydford law,*
> *How in the morn they hang and draw*
> *And sit in judgement after.*

The expression 'Lydford Law' still implies rough and swift justice when a summary trial is held after the sentence has already been carried out.

Encompassing the whole of the Forest of Dartmoor, Lydford parish is the largest, by area, in England. For many centuries, the dead have been brought down from the moor along the ancient Lych Way for burial at the town's St Petroc's Church.

To the southwest of the village, the valley of the River Lyd suddenly narrows to form the mile and a half long **Lydford Gorge**, one of Dartmoor's most spectacular natural features. There is a circular walk around the gorge that begins high up before passing through the enchanting riverside scenes and past the thrilling **Devil's Cauldron**. However the walk can be arduous and stout

BROWNS HOTEL, WINE BAR & BRASSERIE

80 West Street, Tavistock, Devon PL19 8AQ
Tel: 01822 618686 Fax: 01822 618646
e-mail: enquiries@brownsdevon.co.uk
website: www.brownsdevon.co.uk

"At last, affordable chic in the West." This was the verdict of a couple after a stay at **Browns**, a boutique town house hotel right in the centre of the ancient market town of Tavistock. Built as a coaching inn in the 17th century, it has been beautifully restored, retaining period features such as slate flagstones and massive beams. The only four-star hotel in the region, Browns combines English elegance with the feel of contemporary Europe, offering the highest standards of comfort, hospitality and service to business and leisure

visitors as well as the many local residents who have taken the hotel to their hearts. The 20 guest bedrooms, among them a family room and a four-poster room, are all en suite, with TV including video and satellite channels, telephone with data ports, and an electronic safe. Tea and coffee making facilities are also included, along with a complimentary newspaper delivered to the room each day.

Under a glass panel in the airy conservatory, water is drawn from a well as it has been for many centuries. The wine bar is a perfect place to relax, with comfortable sofas and roaring log fires in winter, while the court-yard provides an ideal spot for taking the sun.

Browns has an enviable reputation for the standard of its cuisine, which is not surprising, as the head chef is the highly talented and very experienced John McGeever, an original member and past chairman of the Master Chefs of Great Britain. John sets great store by locally grown and reared produce, and in the stylish Brasserie food is served all day, from

morning coffee with cakes and pastries to a light or full lunch, afternoon tea and the full evening à la carte menus. These include organic and vegetarian dishes and the renowned Sunday roast, and the fine food is complemented by an extensive selection of wines available by bottle or glass. Children are welcome in the Brasserie, and smaller portions can be ordered for them.

A modern gym is among the amenities on site, and a saline luxury swimming pool is being installed during 2004; golf, riding and fishing are among the many activities available locally.

White Lady Waterfall, Lydford

were the only places licensed to weigh and stamp the metal extracted from the moor. For most of its recorded history, Tavistock has had only two owners: Tavistock Abbey and the Russell family. The Benedictine abbey was founded here, beside the River Tavy, in around 974 close to a Saxon stockade, or stoc, now incorporated into the town's name. A wealthy establishment, the town grew up around the abbey and, following the discovery of tin on the nearby moors in the 12th century, both flourished. However, in the 16th century, Henry VIII closed the abbey and sold its buildings and considerable estate to John Russell, whose family, as earls and dukes of Bedford, owned most of the town until 1911.

The present town is, essentially, a creation of the Russell family who, after destroying most of the abbey buildings, created a completely new town plan. Later, in the 1840s, Francis, the 7th Duke, used some of the family's profits from their copper mines to build the imposing **Guildhall** and several other

footwear should always be worn. Back in the 17th century, the then remote Lydford Gorge provided a secure refuge for a band of brigands who called themselves the Gubbinses. Their leader, Roger Rowle, was dubbed the 'Robin Hood of the West' and adventures based upon his exploits are recounted in Charles Kingsley's novel, *Westward Ho!*

TAVISTOCK

This handsome old town is one of Devon's four stannary towns (a name that come from the Latin word for tin – stannum). These towns (the others are Ashburton, Chagford and Plympton)

No.13

13 Duke Street, Tavistock, Devon PL19 0BA
Tel: 01822 618188

No 13 is a well established Ladies Boutique opened by Annette Pettifer in 1995, situated in the centre of town in an attractive

greystone listed building. The high quality contemporary clothes that Annette personally selects have a sophisticated elegance which attract women of all ages and lifestyles.

The array of well regarded designer labels includes Lamberto Losani, Isekiko, Rene Lezard, Annette Gortz, Sonja Marohn, Joyce Ridings and Paul Costelloe. Shoes by Luc Berjen and a selection of jewellery by Barbara Easton. The success of No 13 depends not only on the product range but the friendly service that has been its hallmark from the start. Open 10am to 5pm Monday to Saturday.

ENCORE CONTEMPORARY HOMESTYLE

16 Duke Street, Tavistock, Devon PL19 0BA
Tel: 01822 618864
website: www.encore-tavistock.co.uk

Part of the historic Pannier Market on the main street of the handsome old stannary town of Tavistock, **Encore Contemporary Homestyle** is a retail shop that puts the emphasis firmly on quality. The modern interior of this stand-alone shop covers two floors of contemporary homestyle living, with many items suitable for personal purchases or as a really special gift to celebrate a wedding, birthday or other occasion - and the perfect gift is complemented by appropriate cards and a gift wrap service.

Partners Barbara Penfold and Barry Wright, who moved to Cornwall from retail premises in Essex

five years ago, have worked very hard to get the right balance of products, and they pride themselves on stocking items which offer a combination of top quality, top design and very reasonable prices. Among the main products they deal in are Bridgewater China, Burleigh China, Cath Kidston soft furnishings, distressed furniture, dressers, chests, bedroom furniture, classic table lamps and candles, baskets, teapots and much, much more. Items are carefully sourced from the UK and many European countries, including France, Greece, Denmark and Sweden. A mail order is available at Encore, which is open from 9am to 5pm Monday to Saturday.

civic buildings. He also remodelled the Bedford Hotel and constructed a model estate of artisan's cottages on the western side of the town. A statue of the duke stands in Bedford Square while, at the western entrance to Tavistock, there is a statue of Sir Francis Drake who is believed to have been born at nearby Crowndale.

Although little of the abbey remains today, the town's medieval parish church, built to serve the town's common folk, still stands. An especially good monument to Sir John Glanville can be found in the Lady Chapel while there is some superb William Morris glass in the northeast window. However, one of the abbey's legacies is the annual three day fair, granted its charter in 1105. It has evolved into the **Goose Fair**, a marvellous traditional street fair held in October. Tavistock was also permitted to hold a weekly market which, 900 years later, still takes place every Friday in the **Pannier Market**, a building that was another gift to the town from the 7th Duke. Virtually unaltered since it was built in the 1850s, the market building is considered to be one of the finest in the southwest.

Beside Drake's statue is the **Fitzford Gate**, the original gatehouse of a private residence that no longer exists. According to local stories, several times a year the ghost of Lady Howard rides through the gates in a coach of bones, drawn by headless horses and preceded by a fierce hound with only one, central eye. This gruesome procession journeys to Okehampton church where Lady Howard descends, picks a blade of grass from the churchyard and, clutching it to her chest, returns to Fitzford Gate. Born in 1536, Lady Howard was twice widowed before she was 16 years old and is said to have murdered all her four husbands. However, this is not entirely true as her fourth husband outlived her.

Also on the western side of Tavistock can be found the beginning of the **Tavistock-Morwellham Canal**, built in the early 19th century. At this time the town and surrounding area was experiencing a copper boom and the moving force behind the canal was a young mining engineer, the manager of the Wheal Friendship mine, John Taylor. Started in 1803, the canal was designed to follow the contours of the land as far as Morwell Down, through which a tunnel over a mile long would carry the water to Morwellham.

The tunnel took 14 years to complete, long after other sections of the canal had been finished, and, by 1872, the canal had closed as it could no longer compete with the railways that arrived in Tavistock in 1859.

MOUNT TAVY COTTAGE

Tavistock, Devon PL19 9JL
Tel: 01822 614253
e-mail: graham@mounttavy.fsnet.co.uk
website: www.mounttavy.freeserve.co.uk

Graham and Joanna Moule offer a choice of holiday accommodation in delightful countryside close to Tavistock on the edge of Dartmoor yet only one hours' drive from the Cornish Coast and Eden. **Mount Tavy Cottage** is a 250-year-old gardener's cottage set in grounds of 10 acres and offering bed & breakfast accommodation (with the option of an evening meal by arrangement). The Pump House, for two or three, is a charming lodge-style self-catering cottage beside a lake, and the Wood Shed, sleeping up to six, is an ideal base for those who enjoy walking, cycling, riding, fishing or golf.

LAMERHOOE LODGE

Townlake, Horsebridge, Tavistock, Devon PL19 8PG
Tel: 01822 833715
e-mail: stay@lamerhooe.co.uk
website: www.lamerhooe.co.uk

Lamerhooe Lodge is the family home of William and
Anne May Somerville, who offer warm hospitality and a
delightful holiday base in two comfortably furnished
twin bedrooms. The lodge, which was built as a fishing
lodge by a pupil of Lutyens, enjoys a very peaceful
location and lovely views over the River Tamar, which forms the natural boundary between Devon
and Cornwall. Its gardens include a large kitchen garden which supplies most of the fresh vegetables
used by Anne, who is a professional cook. Regret no children.

AROUND TAVISTOCK

BRENT TOR
4½ miles N of Tavistock off the A386

Brent Tor, a 1,100 foot volcanic plug that
rears up from the surrounding
countryside is one of the most striking
sights in the whole of Dartmoor. The
Church of St Michael of the Rocks
stands on the top of it. The fourth
smallest complete church in England, St
Michael's is only 15 feet wide and 37 feet
long and has walls only 10 feet high but
three feet thick. Constructed of stone
that was quarried from the rock beneath,
the church is surrounded by a steep
churchyard that contains a surprising
number of graves considering its
precarious and seemingly soil-less
position. Sometimes lost in cloud, the
scramble to the summit of Brent Tor is
rewarded, on a clear day, with
magnificent views of Dartmoor, Bodmin
Moor and the sea at Plymouth Sound.

LEWDOWN
8 miles N of Tavistock off the A30

The completion of the bypass in the
early 1990s takes the main road between
Exeter and Launceston away from the
centre of this village, making Lewdown

a much quieter and more enjoyable
place to visit. The village also lies within
the parish of Lewtrenchard, whose
rector for 43 years, between 1881 and
1924, was Rev Sabine Baring-Gould. Best
known as the composer of the hymn,
Onward, Christian Soldiers, Baring-Gould
was also a prolific writer. He regularly
produced two or three books a year –
novels, historical works such as *Curious
Myths of the Middle Ages*, and books on
Devon legends and folklore. Despite his
parish work and his busy writing
schedules, Baring-Gould found time to
restore St Peter's Church. His most
remarkable success was the creation of a
replica of a medieval screen that his
grandfather, also a rector here,
had destroyed.

The reverend gentleman scandalised
Victorian society by marrying a
Lancashire mill girl but it proved to be a
happy and romantic union and they
had a large family. One local story tells
how, one day, emerging from his study,
the rector saw a little girl coming down
the stairs. "You look nice, my dear, in
your pretty frock," he said. Vaguely
remembering that there was a children's
party taking place at the rectory, he
asked, "Whose little girl are you?".
"Yours, papa," she answered and then
burst into tears.

MARY TAVY

3 miles NE of Tavistock on the A386

The twin villages of Mary Tavy and **Peter Tavy** lie on opposite banks of the River Tavy and each takes its name from the saint of its parish church. Roughly twice the size of its east bank twin, Mary Tavy stands in the heart of Dartmoor's former mining area. Just to the north of the village, lies a survivor from those days. **Wheal Betsy**, a restored pumping engine house, was once part of the Prince Arthur Consols mine that produced lead, silver and zinc. In the village, the grave of William Crossing, the historian of the moor whose magisterial guide first published in the early 1900s is still in print, can be found in the churchyard. Crossing moved to Peter Tavy in 1909 and described it as "a quiet little place, with a church embosomed by trees, a chapel, a school and a small inn". Inside the impressive medieval church there is a poignant memorial to the five daughters of a 17th century rector, the oldest of whom was less than a year when she died.

YELVERTON

5 miles SE of Tavistock on the B3212

An attractive small town on the very edge of Dartmoor, from Yelverton there are superb views northwards across the Walkham Valley to Brent Tor and its summit church. The town, itself, is quite flat and its broad main street is lined with a wide verge, which has caused it to be described as 'rather like a thriving racecourse.' In prehistoric times, the area around the town was quite heavily populated and there are a large number of stone circles and rows, hut and cairn circles and burial chambers to be found here. According to a local story, Yelverton is one of a very few old towns to have been renamed by a railway company. Originally called 'Ella's ford town', or Elfordtown, when the Great

BUCKLAND ABBEY

Yelverton, Devon PL20 6EY
Tel: 01822 853607

Buckland's peaceful setting belies its exiting past as the home of Sir Francis Drake. Exhibitions reveal the secrets of medieval and monastic life, the Dissolution and the Armada. See Drake's Drum, the beautiful plasterwork of the Great Hall and the fascinating kitchen. A plasterwork ceiling has recently been sculpted in the Drake Chamber.

Visit the box hedged herb garden, the Elizabethan garden, the massive Great Barn and estate walks. The three galleries have been re-designed with an exciting introductory film and computer interactives. Presented in association with the city of Plymouth Museum.

THE HARRABEER COUNTRY HOUSE HOTEL

Harrowbeer Lane, Yelverton, Devon PL20 6EA
Tel: 01822 853302
e-mail: reception@harrabeer.co.uk
website: www.harrabeer.co.uk

The **Harrabeer Country House Hotel** is a small and very
friendly family run hotel run by Michael and Amanda
Willats - it was a top 20 finalist for the prestigious AA
Landlady of the Year Award for 2002. The handsome old
Devon longhouse has six comfortable guest bedrooms,
all with en suite or private facilities, a gracious sitting room, a bar and an attractive restaurant where
an excellent breakfast is served (also evening meals by arrangement). A pretty, secluded garden provides
a delightful retreat when the sun shines. The owners also offer accommodation in two self-catering
suites in a recently converted barn.

CALLISHAM FARM

Meavy, Yelverton, Devon PL20 6PS
Tel/Fax: 01822 853901
e-mail: wills@callishamfarm.fsnet.co.uk
website: www.callishamfarm.fsnet.co.uk

Esme Wills and her family provide a warm Devonshire
welcome all year round at **Callisham Farm**, which is
located near the village of Meavy in the Dartmoor
National Park. Their traditional, homely farm offers
peace and tranquillity amid pretty woodland and
babbling brooks, and the surrounding countryside
provides delightful walks. The handsome old granite
and stone farmhouse has three guest bedrooms, all facing south, with a lovely view to open fields and

Callisham Tor; they all have en suite facilities, TV and
beverage trays.

The guests' lounge is particularly warm and cosy, with
a large woodburning stove in an inglenook fireplace, and
a hearty English breakfast is served in the light, airy,
'proper countrified' breakfast room - vegetarian and special
diets can be catered for on request. Meavy, with its
picturesque village green, 12th century church and 800-
year-old inn, is a short stroll across the fields, and Tavistock
and Plymouth are an easy drive away. The farm is an ideal
centre not just for walking and touring but also for cycling,
riding, fishing and golf.

Western Railway opened its station here,
in 1859, the company's officials
transcribed the local pronunciation of
Elfordtown as Yelverton.

BUCKLAND MONACHORUM

4 miles S of Tavistock off the A386

Tucked away in a secluded valley above
the River Tavy, **Buckland Abbey** (see

panel on page 161) was originally
founded in 1278 by Amicia, Countess of
Devon, and though small it became an
influential Cistercian monastery.
However, it is better known as the last
home of Sir Francis Drake. He purchased
the former Abbey in 1581 from his rival,
Sir Richard Grenville, who had
remodelled the ecclesiastical buildings

into a house in the 1570s. The two men were not friends, so Drake bought the property anonymously and Sir Richard is said to have been mortified on hearing that Drake had acquired the imposing old building. Buckland Abbey remained in the Drake family until 1946, when it was bought by Captain Arthur Rodd who presented it to the National Trust. Along with the handcrafted plasterwork ceiling in the Drake Chamber there is an exhibition here charting 700 years of history at the abbey. Of the many exhibits at the abbey, Drake's Drum takes pride of place; according to legend, the drum will sound whenever England is in peril. The drum was brought back to England by Drake's brother, Thomas, who was with the great seafarer when he died - rather unheroically of dysentery - on the Spanish Main in 1596. Elsewhere at the abbey visitors can see a magnificent monastic barn, a craft workshop and a herb garden while there is a network of delightful footpaths through the estate.

Back in the village, on the site of the medieval vicarage, is **The Garden House**, surrounded by a delightful garden, created, after World War II, by Lionel Fortescue, a retired schoolmaster.

To the southwest of Buckland Monachorum, and set back from the River Tamar, is **Bere Alston**, for centuries a thriving little port from where the products of Dartmoor's tin mines were transported around the world. All that commercial activity has long since gone but the river here is still busy with the to-ings and fro-ings of sleek pleasure craft. Just a few miles upstream from Bere Alston is one of the county's most popular visitor attractions, **Morwellham Quay**. Just 25 years ago, it was a ghost town with the Tamar valley breezes whistling through its abandoned buildings. Now restored, this historic site faithfully recreates the

busy atmosphere of the 1850s when half the world's copper came through this tiny harbour. Visitors can journey through the mines on a riverside tramway, and another highlight is the restored Tamar ketch *Garlandstone*. Although Morwellham lies some 20 miles upstream from Plymouth, the Tamar river at this point was deep enough for 300-ton ships to load up with the precious minerals. Once known as the Devon Klondyke, Morwellham suffered a catastrophic decline when cheaper sources of copper were discovered in South America.

The quayside inn, too, has been restored and it was here that the dockside labourers used to meet for ale, food and the latest news of the ships that sailed from Morwellham. In those days, the news was chalked up on a blackboard and it still is. Though out of date, the stories nonetheless remain intriguing.

GULWORTHY
2 miles SW of Tavistock on the A390

This little village lies at the heart of an area that, in the mid 1880s, had a world wide reputation. A quarter of the world's supply of copper was extracted from this part of Devon and, more alarmingly, so was half of the world's requirements for arsenic. Mining for copper in this area has long been abandoned, due to the discovery of cheaper sources around the world, particularly in South America. Gulworthy's arsenic has also gone out of fashion as an agent of murder.

LIFTON
9 miles NW of Tavistock on the A30

Situated on the banks of the River Lyd, Lifton was, in medieval times, an important centre of the wool trade. Dartmoor sheep tend to have rather coarse fleeces, due to the cold pastureland so the weavers of Lifton

TINHAY MILL

Tinhay, Lifton, Devon PL16 0AJ
Tel/Fax: 01566 784201
e-mail: tinhay.mill@talk21.com
web: www.tinhaymillrestaurant.co.uk

Nestling in a valley close to where the River Lyd meets the River Thrushel, **Tinhay Mill** is a restaurant with rooms with a very special appeal. The house dates from the 15th century, and the beamed ceilings, the open fireplaces and the numerous nooks and crannies create a lovely traditional ambience that keeps guests returning again and again. The old-world look is far from being the sole attraction, however, as Tinhay Mill is establishing a reputation as one of the very best eating places in the region. The hosts at the Mill are Paul and Margaret Wilson, who started the business in July 1997 and have never looked back.

Margaret's three-course dinner menu sets great store by local produce, organic wherever possible, and making a final choice from the five or six options for each course is not easy! A typical meal might start with a warm salad of local scallops or a fresh summer vegetable kebab with a dressing of fresh herbs and Devonshire blue cheese; continue with roast sea bass with a bay leaf and lemon grass cream sauce or classic rack of lamb; and end with rice pudding flavoured with gin (Plymouth, of course!) or almond cream terrine served with a brandy snap filled with a pear and champagne sorbet.

Tinhay Mill recently received the Bronze award from Taste of the West for Restaurant/Hotel in Devon 2003, given for best use of local produce in the menus with traceability of origin. Over 640 restaurants/hotels took part by invitation, so this award really was a feather in the Tinhay cap. Margaret, has written three books on West Country recipes. Tinhay Mill is not just an outstanding choice for a meal, it's also a delightful place for bed & breakfast, either for dinner guests who want to stay over or for tourists and holidaymakers looking for a base. The bedrooms - twins or doubles - are elegant, spacious and very comfortable, with en suite shower rooms, TV, clock radio, hairdryer and other extra touches that contribute to a thoroughly enjoyable stay. The breakfasts are just as memorable as the dinners, so overnight guests have the best possible start to the day. The Mill operates a non-smoking policy throughout. No children or pets. Places to visit in the area include many National Trust properties nearby, Dartmoor National Park (10 minute drive) and Eden Project (45 minute drive).

DINGLES STEAM VILLAGE

Milford, Lifton, Devon PL16 0AT
Tel: 01566 783425 website: www.dinglesteam.co.uk

Opened in 1995 by steam enthusiast, Fred Dibnah, **Dingles Steam Village** makes Britain's industrial heritage come alive and here visitors can see one of the best working steam collections in the country. In this beautiful rural location, this Steam Village is home to a wide range of working traction engines, steam rollers, fairground attractions and vintage machinery that, when steamed up and working, are even more fascinating to look at then when they are 'resting'. Meanwhile, the village also has an excellent café, play areas for children, a gift shop, riverside walks and a collection of vintage road signs.

petitioned Henry VII, "by reason of the grossness and stubbornness of their district" to allow them to mix as much lambs' wool and flock with their wool "as may be required to work it". Just to the east of Lifton lies **Dingles Steam Village** (see panel above), where visitors can see a whole host of traction engines as well as enjoy delicious homemade meals from Mrs Dingles' kitchen.

THE HARRIS ARMS

Portgate, nr Lifton, Devon EX20 4PZ
Tel: 01566 783331 Fax: 01566 783359
e-mail: harrisarms@whiteman.powernet.co.uk
website: www.theharrisarms.com

What started life in the 16th century as a "Road House" selling ale to travellers has become one of the most popular destination eating venues in the region. The reputation of **The Harris Arms**, which lies on the old A30 between Lifton and Lewdown in the parish of Stowford, has become even greater since the arrival of licensees Andy and Rowena Whiteman, whose knowledge of superb food and excellent wines has been gleaned from years of searching for their "ultimate food and wine experience" and time spent living in New Zealand, Ireland, France, Italy and Spain. Both Andy and Rowena are trained wine makers. Their wine list is eclectic and full of interest, with many wines sourced from small producers, and priced fairly. They are also experienced in the restaurant business, and with head chef Tim Treseder they are building on the Inn's established reputation as the eating-place of choice for discerning diners from the triangle of towns of Launceston, Okehampton and Tavistock. Local seasonal produce features prominently on the menus, and food is served lunchtime and evening every day except Tuesday, when the inn is closed.

This is great fishing country, and among the many other attractions in the vicinity are Lydford Gorge, one of Dartmoor's most spectacular natural features, and Dingles Steam Village with one of the best collections of steam-powered vehicles in the country. The Inn is located less than 5 minutes from the A30 duel carriageway - at the Broadwoodwidger/Dingles Steam Village exit near Launceston - follow the signs for Lifton then Portgate.

ENDSLEIGH GARDENS NURSERY

Milton Abbot, Tavistock, Devon PL19 0PG
Tel: 01822 870235 Fax: 01822 870513
website: www.endsleigh-gardens.com

Endsleigh Gardens Nursery occupies the Victorian walled garden of the Duke of Bedford's former estate at Endsleigh, which is located in the woods above the River Tamar. In this idyllic sunny setting, the nursery was
established 40 years ago by Morris Taylor, who

had been the Duke's head gardener for many years. Today, the nursery is run by Morris's son Michael, who employs all the traditional skills learned from his father as well as modern techniques such as a very effective new system of biological pest control.

Michael is a skilled grafter, and, helped by his wife and a staff of five, he produces a range of trees and shrubs not easily found elsewhere. Japanese maples, cornus, flowering cherries and wisteria are among the nursery's specialities, and they also produce a fine variety of roses and an interesting range of old apple and cherry trees rescued from orchards and gardens in the Tamar Valley area - among the apples are Pig's Nose, Slack-ma-Girdle and Plympton Pippin. As a retail nursery, Endsleigh is able to offer a much wider selection of trees, shrubs and plants than the average garden centre, and customers really are spoiled for choice. Opening hours are 8am to 5pm (Sunday from 10am). A mail order service is available.

IVYBRIDGE

Situated in the beautiful valley of the River Erme, the original bridge here was just wide enough to allow a single packhorse across. The more recent 13th century bridge, that is still used, is also very narrow. The other crossing here is the impressive viaduct that carries the railway across the valley. Originally constructed in the mid-19th century to Brunel's designs in wood, the viaduct was rebuilt in stone in 1895. The town grew rapidly in the 1860s when a quality papermaking mill was established here making use of the water from the river. Ivybridge has continued to grow and is now a commuter town for Plymouth.

This is a town known to many serious walkers as the southern starting point of

GOUTSFORD

Ermington, Ivybridge, Devon PL21 9NY
Tel: 01548 831299 e-mail: carolfarrand@tiscali.co.uk
Fax: 01752 601728 website: www.smoothhound.co.uk

Once an estate worker's cottage and barns, **Goutsford** is situated in woodland in the lovely South Devon countryside. The Farrand family and Rosie the cat are the most welcoming of hosts, and three light, bright, spacious bedrooms provide very comfortable, characterful bed & breakfast accommodation. The rooms all have their own large bathroom,(shower and bath) with books, TV, radio and tea/coffee available. A super breakfast starts the day, and guests can return from a day in the open air to a delicious cream tea in the garden. Children over 10 are welcome; no smoking in the house.

the **Two Moors Way**, the 103-mile long footpath that crosses both Dartmoor and Exmoor before finishing at Lynmouth on the north coast. The trek from here begins with a stiff 1,000-foot climb up Butterdon Hill, just outside Ivybridge.

A few miles northwest of Ivybridge is the **Dartmoor Wildlife Park** (see panel), where more than a thousand wild creatures live in around 30 acres of beautiful Devon countryside. The park is also the home of the **West Country Falconry Centre**. This has a large static display as well as regular flying displays when visitors can see the eagles, peregrines, buzzards and many other birds of prey being put through their paces.

THE DARTMOOR WILDLIFE PARK

Sparkwell, Devon PL7 5DG
Tel: 01752 837645
website: www.come.to/dartmoorwildlife

Only five minutes drive from the A38 Devon Expressway, the **Dartmoor Wildlife Park** has been a favourite family attraction for over 35 years, set in 30 acres of beautiful Devon countryside.

The park holds the largest collection of Big Cats in the south west and other carnivores include wolves, bears, foxes and small cats such as the caracal, lynx and pumas. The Wildlife Park is now the headquarters of the British Big Cat Society and there is a Talk, Touch and Learn all-weather facility.

The West Country Falconry Centre is a large collection of birds of prey; there are twice daily flying displays from Easter to the end of October (Fridays excepted) and if you have ever fancied yourself as a falconer there are Falconry Courses available too. The birds on display include eagles, peregrimes, owls, buzzards, kestrels and many others. Daily events include the Close Encounters Talks at 2pm and the Big Cat Feeding at 3.30pm. There is also a restaurant, bar and gift shop with a good range of souvenirs. Don't miss the Annual Classic and Vintage Car and Bike Rally which is held on the second Sunday in September.

AROUND IVYBRIDGE

MODBURY
3 miles S of Ivybridge on the A379

Three steep streets make up the greater part of this town, which boasts a number of handsome 18th century houses and the impressive St George's Church (mainly 13th and 14th century). The most influential family during Tudor times were the Champernownes, and the children of Katherine Champernowne included Aidrian Gilbert, who discovered the North West Passage, and Sir Humphrey Gilbert, who claimed St John's, Newfoundland, for Queen Elizabeth I in 1583. The colonists who accompanied Sir Humphrey were unwilling to stay, so they set out to

WILD GOOSE ANTIQUES

34 Church Street, Modbury,
South Devon PL21 0QR
Tel: 01548 830715
e-mail: wildgoose@kfreeman0.fsnet.co.uk
website: www.btinternet.com/
~wildgooseantiques/

The husband and wife team of Ty and Kay Freeman pride themselves on the friendly, personal service that brings customers back time after time to **Wild Goose Antiques**. They always have a good stock of old pine furniture, they can supply reproduction pine (or oak) original designs from a single chair to a full restaurant refit, and they offer a pine stripping service.

Pine is a speciality, but there's much more to be seen at Wild Goose Antiques, including brass and iron bedsteads, cast-iron fireplaces and a wide range of decorative items large and small, including 'kitchenalia', bed linen, all sorts of lighting and lamps, unusual bronzes and sculptures and garden statuary. Wild Goose is located on the main A379 Plymouth-Kingsbridge road between the Exeter Inn and Bistro 35. Browsers are always very welcome, and the owners invite visitors to "Come and have a Gander!"

RINGROSE GALLERY

Unit 2, Modbury Court, Modbury, Devon PL21 0QR
Tel: 01548 831503

Behind an attractive little shopfront set slightly back off the main street, the **Ringrose Gallery** has been developed by Sarah Ringrose to display and sell a selection of delightful and

unusual things to enhance the home or to provide a beautiful gift.

Artist and printmaker Sarah has exhibited at Country Living shows for many years and opened the gallery and workshop in 2002. She sells her own work and that of other professional artists and designer-makers, and

the range of contemporary work covers many media, including original paintings and etchings, limited edition prints, photography, embroidery, sculpture, jewellery, ceramics, glassware and metalware. Sarah has a professional but admirably relaxed approach to life, and it's always a pleasure to visit her gallery and to take time to find just the right gift for any occasion.

ARWYN JONES CERAMICS

2 Galpin Street, Modbury, South Devon PL21 0QA
Tel: 01548 831330
e-mail: arwyn.jones@freeispshares.co.uk

Arwyn Jones graduated with a degree in Ceramics from Loughborough College of Art and Design in 1995 and, after opening his first workshop and gallery in 1998, he moved to Modbury in 2001. Arwyn works in what may be considered a 'traditional' way, using the wheel to create oven and table ware in sound, functional forms. His main inspiration comes from the utilitarian wares of Spain and Portugal and the deep and subtle glaze finishes seen in the Far East. Consequently, his work has a simplicity that comes primarily from function, combined with an elegance that is clearly derived from the Orient; the resulting wares combine

style with practicality and durability, and every piece is a delight to use. The catalogue runs to some 50 items: bowls, oval and square dishes, vegetable and casserole dishes, jugs, plates, cups and saucers, teapots and storage jars are all available in a variety of sizes, and small items and accessories include egg cups, ramekins, mustard pots, marmalade jars, tea caddies and cutlery drainers.

The shop is open from 10am to 5pm Monday to Saturday and visitors are welcome to browse and to watch Arwyn at the wheel creating his beautiful pieces.

return to England. Sir Humphrey, who had rather eccentrically chosen to sail in the tiny (10-ton) *Squirrel*, was drowned when she went down in a storm.

DARTMEET

11 miles NE of Ivybridge on the B3357

Dartmeet is the famous beauty spot where the East and West Dart rivers meet. At their junction, the remains of an ancient **Clapper Bridge** can be seen just upstream from the more modern road bridge. Rising in the boggy plateau of north Dartmoor, the River Dart and its tributaries drain a huge area of the moor. Then the river runs for some 46 miles before entering the sea at Dartmouth.

In the days when the tin mines were working, this area was extremely isolated; it lacked even a burial ground of its own and the local people had to carry the dead over the moor to be buried at either Widecombe or Lydford. To the east

of Dartmeet, and hidden among bracken and gorse, is the **Coffin Stone**, a large boulder on which it was customary for the bearers to rest the body while making the moorland crossing. A cross and the deceased's initials were carved into the stone while the bearers had some liquid refreshment and got back their breath before continuing on their journey.

BUCKFASTLEIGH

9 miles NE of Ivybridge on the B3380

A former wool town on the banks of the River Mardle. Several old mills can still be seen here, while the large houses of the mill owners lie on the outskirts of the town. A unique insight into the lives of local folk is provided in an old village inn that has been restored and reopened as the **Valiant Soldier Museum and Heritage Centre**. Buckfastleigh is also the western terminus and headquarters of the **South Devon Railway**, formerly

South Devon Railway

Dartmoor Otter Sanctuary (see panel below) where the exotic butterflies can be seen in a specially designed tropical rain forest environment. The otters can be watched from the underwater viewing area. A couple of miles south of Buckfastleigh lies **Pennywell**, a spacious all weather family attraction that offers a wide range of amusements and activities, including go kart riding and numerous hands-on activities. On selected dates during the season Pennywell and the sanctuary are linked by a vintage bus service that also calls at **Buckfast Abbey**.

called the Primrose Line, whose steam trains continue to make the seven mile journey through the valley of the River Dart to Totnes. The Dart is fast flowing here and, as well as being a salmon river, its banks are home to herons, swans, kingfishers, badgers and foxes.

Another popular attraction close to the town is the **Buckfast Butterflies and**

Another mile or so further south lies the village of **Dean Prior** whose vicar, between 1630 and 1674, was the poet and staunch royalist, Robert Herrick. Best known for the line "Gather ye rosebuds while ye may" from the opening of *To the Virgins, to make Much of Time* and for *Cherry Ripe*, Herrick was expelled from here during the time of the Commonwealth but returned to

---

BUCKFAST BUTTERFLIES AND DARTMOOR OTTER SANCTUARY

Buckfastleigh, Devon TQ11 0DZ
Tel: 01364 642916 e-mail: info@ottersandbutterflies.co.uk
website: www.ottersandbutterflies.co.uk

The tropical landscaped gardens at **Buckfast Butterflies and Dartmoor Otter Sanctuary** are home to a wide variety of exotic butterflies from around the world that live, breed and fly freely here along with small birds and other tropical creatures such as terrapins and leaf cutting ants. Meanwhile, in specially designed outside landscape, three species of otter, including the native British otter, can be seen both on land and in the water. The otters, some of whom have been rescued and some that have

been bred here, are fed three times a day and both they and the butterflies provide plenty of opportunity for budding wildlife photographers to hone their skills.

Dean Prior on the Restoration of the king in 1662. He apparently found rural Devon life dull and preferred London where he had a mistress 27 years his junior. Perhaps to brighten up the monotony of his Devonshire existence, Herrick kept a pet pig that he took for walks and trained to drink beer from a tankard. Herrick died in 1674 and was buried in the churchyard, where a simple stone marks his assumed last resting place.

SOUTH BRENT
4½ miles NE of Ivybridge off the B3213

Standing on the southern edge of Dartmoor, this sizeable village was once an important centre for woollen production and, alongside the River Avon, there are some attractive old textile mill buildings. In the Victorian era one of these mills was managed by William Crossing, whose famous *Crossing's Guide to Dartmoor* provides a fascinating picture of life on the moorland in the late 19th century. In the days of stagecoach travel, South Brent was a lively place with two posting houses that served the competing coaches. It was said that four horses could be changed here in 45 seconds and a four-course meal served in 20 minutes!

CORNWOOD
3 miles NW of Ivybridge off the A38

A pleasant village on the River Yealm, this is a good base from which to search for the many Bronze Age and industrial remains scattered across the moorland. One of the most remarkable sights on Dartmoor is the double line of stones that were set up on Stall Moor during the Bronze Age. One of the lines is almost 550 yards long while the other begins with a stone circle, crosses the River Erme and finally ends at a burial chamber some two miles from where it started.

PRINCETOWN
11½ miles NW of Ivybridge on the B3212

Situated at the heart of the Dartmoor, some 1,400 feet above sea level, Princetown is an isolated and bleak settlement surrounded by some spectacular scenery. It is notorious for its atrocious weather. The average annual rainfall of between 80 to 100 inches is more than three times that of Exeter only 20 miles away. It is also famous as being the home of one of the country's best-known and most forbidding prisons – **Dartmoor Prison**. That a settlement should have grown up here at all is amazing and Princetown was the

THE RAILWAY INN & THE CARRIAGE RESTAURANT

Two Bridges Road, Princetown, Yelverton, Devon PL20 6QT
Tel: 01822 890232

Originally the alighting point for the horse-drawn tramway that ran from Plymouth, **The Railway Inn** has a 200-year history of hospitality. The inn supplies a range of excellent home-cooked food ranging from the standard bar menu to the full a la carte menus served in **The Carriage Restaurant**. Visitors can enjoy a variety of real ales, beers, lagers, wines and spirits by an open log fire in the bar. The inn has 2 bars, a non-smoking restaurant, a pool room, skittle alley and beer garden. For overnight guests the inn has five comfortable bedrooms, making it an ideal base for exploring beautiful Dartmoor. Children and dogs are welcome.

Haytor Rocks, Dartmoor

brainchild of Sir Thomas Tyrwhitt, the owner of the local granite quarry. He proposed that a special prison be built here to house the thousands of French troops captured during the Napoleonic Wars, who were becoming too numerous and unruly for the prison ships occupying Plymouth Sound. Completed in 1809, the prison was built by the prisoners themselves using granite from Tyrwhitt's quarry. Paid at a rate of sixpence a day, the prisoners also built the main east-west road across the moor (still used today) and the famous Devonport leat, which supplied water to the dockyard.

When it opened the prison held as many as 9,000 French and, later, American inmates but by 1816, with the cessation of hostilities, the prison became redundant and was closed. The settlement that had grown up around the prison and the quarry virtually collapsed as a result. Fortunately, in 1823 the quarries were re-opened when granite was need for the construction of the horse drawn Dartmoor Railway, another of Sir Thomas's initiatives. The prison was eventually re-opened in 1850 for long-serving convicts (who had

previously been deported) and since then it has been considerably enlarged and upgraded; it currently houses around 250 guests of Her Majesty.

Elsewhere in the town is the church of St Mary in whose churchyard stands a tall granite cross in memory of all those prisoners whose bodies lie in unmarked graves. The mortality rate of the inmates in the early 19th century was 50 per cent. Since the beginning of the 20th century, prisoners' graves have been marked, just with their initials and date of their death, and the lines of small stones are a gloomy and depressing sight.

Princetown is home to the National Park's **High Moorland Visitors' Centre**, which contains some excellent and informative displays about the moor and a wide-ranging stock of books, maps and leaflets. The centre is housed in the former Duchy Hotel where Sir Arthur Conan Doyle stayed while researching his novel *The Hound of the Baskervilles*, published in 1902. Having 'killed' his pipe-smoking sleuth in a previous novel, Sir Arthur was touring Devon when he stumbled upon the stories of a spectral hound that haunted the moorland. The local tales were based upon Squire Cabell of Brook, near Buckfastleigh, a man so evil that, when he died in 1677, a pack of fire-breathing hounds were said to have emerged from the moor to carry his soul down to Hell. Sir Arthur returned to his home in Surrey, where he wrote the book. He took a considerable risk in reviving Sherlock Holmes and exaggerating many of the features of Dartmoor, making it even larger and even wilder than in reality, turning Grimspound into Grimpen Mire, and moving the location of Princetown.

BOVEY TRACEY

This ancient market town takes its name from the River Bovey, on which it stands, and the de Tracey family who were granted the manor here by William the Conqueror. The best-known member of the family was Sir William de Tracey who was one of the four knights who murdered Thomas à Becket at Canterbury Cathedral in 1170. Just six years after the death of the archbishop, the church here was re-dedicated to include the name St Thomas of Canterbury but it remains unproven that Sir William rebuilt the

church in remorse for his crime.

Unlike many Devon towns and villages, Bovey Tracey has never suffered a major fire, although the church was destroyed by fire in medieval times and the present building dates from the 15th century. This is fortunate since, until recent times, the fire-fighting facilities in Bovey Tracey were very limited. As late as 1920 the town had a fire engine but no horses to pull it; it was manned by five volunteers. In that year, the parish council issued a notice advising "all or any persons requiring the Fire Brigade with Engine must take the responsibility of sending a Pair of Horses for the purpose of conveying the Engine to and from the Scene of the Fire".

Although a small town, Bovey Tracey has a remarkably wide selection of shops as well as the **Riverside Mill** (see below),

THE DEVON GUILD OF CRAFTSMEN

Riverside Mill, Bovey Tracey, Devon TQ13 9AF
Tel: 01626 832223 Fax: 01626 834220
e-mail: devonguild@crafts.org.uk
website: www.crafts.org.uk

The Devon Guild of Craftsmen is the leading contemporary craft organisation in the South West. The Guild's home, situated on the fringes of Dartmoor, is the Riverside Mill, a 19th century Grade II listed building on the River Bovey in the centre of Bovey Tracey. It houses one of the largest craft shops in the country, an acclaimed café and a gallery that hosts six major exhibitions each year.

The gallery is a showcase for makers, artists and designer-craftsmen of national and international repute, and

the craft shop sells the work of over 240 makers from throughout the South West, from jewellers, textile makers and ceramicists to furniture makers, sculptors and metalworkers. In the first half of 2004, the Mill will undergo a major refurbishment that will create the largest contemporary craft venue in the South West, with a new gallery space, extended craft shop and a rooftop café with a lift to the first floor. The Mill will remain open during the work at its usual hours - 10am to 5.30pm 7 days a week. Admission is free to all the facilities, and there's ample adjacent parking. Full details of all the exhibitions, events and workshops can be found on the website or by requesting the annual events brochure.

FROST FARM

Hennock, Bovey Tracey, South Devon TQ13 9PP
Tel/Fax: 01626 833266
e-mail: Linda@frostfarm.co.uk
website: www.frostfarm.co.uk

In a beautiful valley location two miles from Bovey
Tracey, with easy access to Dartmoor and the coast,
Frost Farm is an ideal holiday base for either touring
or relaxing. The 17th century Grade II listed building,
full of character and charm, has three spacious non-
smoking guest bedrooms with country furnishings,
pinewood beds, comfortable sofas, central heating and TVs. One of the rooms is on the ground floor,
making it suitable for less mobile guests. Lettings are on a bed & breakfast basis, with a good country
farmhouse meal to start the day. Guests are free to relax in the garden or to stroll around the working
beef, cattle and crop farm, and Hennock village and Bovey Tracey are an easy walk away.

Owner Linda Harvey also offers self-catering facilities at nearby Stickwick Farm, where three
properties combine period charm with up-to-date amenities. The late-19th century Manor House can

accommodate 12 in comfort in 8 bedrooms, with
three bath/shower rooms, a roomy lounge, a fully
equipped farmhouse kitchen and a utility room.
The adjacent 17th century farmhouse (sleeps up
to seven) and the charming cottage, with
accommodation for up to five, share a games
room and barn and a garden with children's
activities and a barbecue and picnic area.

run by the Devon Guild of Craftsmen.
Here, there is a programme of changing
craft exhibitions and demonstrations, a
Museum of Craftsmanship, a study
centre and a shop. A footpath through
the town follows the track bed of the
former railway from Moretonhampstead
to Newton Abbot and takes in part of the
River Bovey.

Just to the north of Bovey Tracy lies
Parke, the former estate of the de Tracey
family. Left to the National Trust in 1974
after the death of the then owner, Major
Hole, it is now the headquarters of the
Dartmoor National Park Authority.

AROUND BOVEY TRACEY

ILSINGTON

2½ miles SW of Bovey Tracey off the B3387

Like so many towns and villages in and
around Dartmoor, Ilsington was once an

important centre of the wool industry. At
the heart of the village lies the church.
Entry to the churchyard is through an
unusual lych gate. The church has an
upper storey that once served as the
village schoolroom. The present
structure is actually a replica of the
original medieval gate that apparently
collapsed when someone slammed the
gate too enthusiastically. Inside are some
interesting medieval pew ends, carved
with distinctive poppy heads, thought to
be the only examples of their kind in
Devon. Nearby is the church house,
dating from the 1500s, now sub-divided
into residential dwellings known as **St
Michael's Cottages**.

This small village was the birthplace of
the Jacobean dramatist John Ford, whose
most successful play, *Tis Pity She's A
Whore*, written in 1633, is still
occasionally revived.

This large parish includes three of

Dartmoor's tors – Rippon, Saddle and Haytor Rocks. The latter is perhaps the most dramatic, rising to almost 1,500 feet and providing a popular challenge to rock climbers. In the early 19th century, the shallow valley just north of the village, beyond **Haytor Rocks**, was riddled with quarries, supplying granite for such well known buildings as London Bridge, the National Gallery and the British Museum.

ASHBURTON
6½ miles SW of Bovey Tracey off the A38

Surrounded by gentle hills, this appealing town, which has the River Ashburn flowing through its centre, has a history going back to long before the Norman Conquest. In AD 821, the town elected its first Portreeve, the Saxon equivalent of a mayor, and this traditional office continues today although its functions are now purely

TESSDESIGNS

6 East Street, Ashburton, Devon TQ13 7AA
Tel/Fax: 01364 654499
e-mail: tess@tessdesigns.co.uk website: www.tessdesigns.co.uk

Behind a bright, cheerful frontage, **Tessdesigns** is stocked with stylish home goods and accessories featuring some top designer names. The goods on display include linen and china from Cath Kidston, baskets and candles from Broste, Mexican silver from Tales of the Earth, vases and baskets from Parlane, jewellery from Carrie Elspeth, U:Kwenza, Big Metal, Heaven and Balloon Accessories, children's ranges, fabulous bags from Terre Rouge and the Special EFX range of gifts for men. Tess Coulson offers a mail order service. Open from 9.30am to 5.30pm Monday to Saturday.

FOXGLOVES

3 West Street, Ashburton, Devon TQ13 7DT
Tel/Fax: 01364 652645
e-mail: info@foxglovesonline.co.uk
website: www.foxglovesonline.co.uk

In the centre of the ancient stannary town of Ashburton, next to the Museum, **Foxgloves** is owned and run with great enthusiasm by Charmian and Keith Benwell, who left the Home Counties and opened the shop in the spring of 2000. Their dismay at the standardised options offered by national retail groups encouraged them to open a shop that was 'refreshingly different', an assessment heartily endorsed by their many regular customers. Buying direct from manufacturers and craftspeople, they offer a unique collection of home accessories, gifts and toys from local, British and European sources, all attractively displayed in the windows and in the light, bright interior of the Grade II listed building.

Everything on show is chosen for its style and originality, and the range offers something to suit all pockets. Home accessories include cushions, throws, table linen, table lamps (Lene Bjerre) and elegant taper candles from Denmark; trays and place settings (Mona Svard) from Sweden; table top accessories (from France); and pottery from Emma Bridgewater and Poland's Boleslawiec. Among the gifts are leather journals and pens from Rubinato, Bristol Blue Glass and toiletries from Camille Beckman, Durance and Soap of the Earth. The shop also stocks Jellycat soft toys, playmats and cushions and early learning toys. Opening hours are 9.30am to 5.30pm Monday to Saturday.

HOLNE CHASE HOTEL

Ashburton, Devon TQ13 7NS
Tel: 01364 631471 Fax: 01364 631453
e-mail: info@holne-chase.co.uk
website: www.holne-chase.co.uk

White's Directory of Devon, written in 1850, describes **Holne Chase** as enjoying 'a peculiarly secluded and romantic situation', and that description remains just as true today. This outstanding Victorian country house nestles serenely in a woodland clearing overlooking sloping lawns within Dartmoor National Park. It stands on the site of an 11th

century hunting lodge, and today is still very much a sporting retreat as well as a delightful refuge from the stresses and strains of everyday life. Sebastian and Philippa Hughes run the hotel like a private home with the loyal assistance of Batty the basset hound, who welcomes animal lovers and canine visitors to her domain.

The six handsomely converted suites in the old stables are ideally suited to guests keen to fish, ride, shoot or hike on the moors, and all the rooms in the main part of the hotel are recently refurbished with pretty English fabrics mirroring fresh flowers from the garden. The walled garden also provides fruit and vegetables for the hotel's kitchen, where the chef makes excellent use of top-quality local produce including seafood from Brixham and Looe and seasonal game. Holne Chase offers many amenities, among them a fine garden, a croquet lawn, a putting green, a helipad and fishing. Beauty treatments are available, for humans and dogs, as well as livery and stabling for guests who want to bring their own horses. Riding, golf and shooting can all be arranged nearby. Two meeting rooms can cater for up to 100, and the hotel is licensed for civil weddings and other celebrations and ceremonies.

To find Holne Chase from the M5 and A38 towards Plymouth take the second turning for Ashburton at Pear Tree Cross, following signs for Dartmeet. The hotel entrance is on the right, 300 metres after Holne Bridge. This is superb walking country, and within a short drive are some of the region's top attractions, including Dartmoor National Park, Buckfast Abbey and Dartington Hall. The owners also have another of Devon's most outstanding hotels, St Olaves in Exeter (see separate advertisement on page 229).

ceremonial. Each year, on the fourth Tuesday in November, officials gather to appoint not just their Portreeve but also the ale tasters, bread weighers, pig drovers and even a viewer of watercourses.

In medieval times, Ashburton's prosperity was based on tin. As one of Devon's stannary towns, it benefited from the trade generated by the Dartmoor tinners, who were obliged to come here to have their metal weighed and stamped and to pay duty. Later the cloth industry was the town's mainstay and several fulling mills along the banks of the river produced cloth that was exported as far afield as China by the East India Company.

The town is characterised by its many attractive houses and shops, with

ROBOROUGH HOUSE

85 East Street, Ashburton, Devon TQ13 7AL
Tel: 01364 654614 e-mail: roborough@btinternet.com
website: www.roboroughhouse.co.uk

Owner Fiona Daly provides the warmest of welcomes at her friendly bed & breakfast establishment in the ancient stannary town of Ashburton. Her restored listed period house has spacious twin and double letting bedrooms, one of them on the ground floor, all with en suite facilities, TV, radio alarm, refreshment tray and hairdryer; some rooms can accommodate an extra bed or cot to turn them into family rooms. A restaurant and licensed bar will be available from spring 2004. A lovely feature of Roborough House is its large 'wild' garden, which includes a Victorian knot garden and a lawn with children's play equipment.

THE SHAMBLES

24 North Street, Ashburton, Devon TQ13 7QD
Tel: 01364 653848

Five dealers with different specialised fields of expertise got together in 1987 to open **The Shambles** in a mid-18th century slate-hung town house. Paula Spendlove and Carole Keith ('The Girls'), Pat Chapman, Pam Paice and Morris Tucker have a common philosophy that everything for sale here must be unusual and it must be interesting, so a visit to their showrooms will always be rewarded with some original ideas for enhancing the home or finding a perfect gift for a special occasion.

The ever-changing stock includes furniture down the centuries, curtains and rugs, soft furnishings, chandeliers, pictures and etchings, jewellery, samplers, sewing boxes and sewing collectables, cutlery,

silverware, tureens and a fascinating collection of period and vintage decorative items. One of Pat Chapman's specialities is early Staffordshire ware, while octogenarian Morris is an expert on maritime artefacts and items relating to the culture of the Native Americans. The house is interesting in its own right, with original features such as a walk-in woodburning hearth, and the goods for sale are beautifully displayed in room sets that include full bedrooms and a dining table set for 12.

THE ASHBURTON DELICATESSEN

16 North Street, Ashburton, Devon TQ13 7QD
Tel/Fax: 01364 652277

Sarah Hayward, a talented and experienced chef, cooked on luxury private yachts for 15 years before weighing anchor in Ashburton in the summer of 2002. She took over the **Ashburton Delicatessen** and completely refurbished and renovated it while retaining its old-fashioned deli feel with old oak shelves and other original touches. Behind the cheerful green canopied frontage, the deli stocks an amazing range of goodies, from charcuterie and rotisserie chickens to ice creams from Salcombe Dairy, cheeses from the West Country and further afield, pickles and preserves and oils, and a selection of wines from local wineries and from the Old and New Worlds.

Sarah is always ready with help and advice for her customers, including letting them in on some of her recipe secrets. Ashburton is a very pleasant place for a leisurely stroll, with many attractive old houses and shops with distinctive slates and tiles; in the same street as the deli is one of the most interesting, the House of Cards, its tiles decorated with clubs, diamonds, hearts and spades. But for lovers of good food, *the* House in North Street is the House of Hayward - the Ashburton Delicatessen, open every day except Sunday.

GAGES MILL

Buckfastleigh Road, Ashburton, Devon TQ13 7JW
Tel/Fax: 01364 652391
e-mail: richards@gagesmill.co.uk
website: www.gagesmill.co.uk

Gages Mill is a carefully converted 14th century Grade II listed former wool mill on the edge of Dartmoor National Park, one mile from Ashburton on the road to Buckfastleigh. It is the home of Andrew and Linda Richards, who offer a warm welcome, excellent home cooking and bed & breakfast accommodation that has lots of old-world charm as well as all everything needed for a comfortably, relaxing break. Seven bedrooms have full en suite facilities, and all have central heating, tea-makers, radio-alarms and hairdryers. One of the rooms – a twin – is on the ground floor. Residents have the use of a large dining room/lounge with a corner bar, from which stone archways lead to a stone-walled sitting room with TV.

The house stands in an acre of beautiful grounds where guests can enjoy a game of croquet or take in the scenery in this lovely farming valley. The area affords many opportunities for walking, riding, and fishing, and the numerous attractions that Dartmoor has to offer include archaeological sites and ancient stone circles, National Trust houses and gardens, the South Dartmoor Steam Railway – and above all the spectacular natural beauty.

distinctive slate hung front elevations. Housed in the former home and workshop of a brushmaker, **Ashburton Museum** offers a fascinating insight into the history of this stannary town as well as the domestic and rural life of Dartmoor down the centuries. the collections include old farming implements, Victorian toys, a model of the old Market Hall and Native American artefacts donated by Paul Endicott, whose parents had left Ashburton for Oklahoma at the beginning of the 20th century.

WIDECOMBE IN THE MOOR
6 miles W of Bovey Tracey off the B3212

Enjoying a delightful setting in the valley of the East Webburn River, Widecombe in the Moor is a very pleasant village with a grand old church that has been dubbed the **Cathedral of the Moors**. Dedicated to St Pancras, the church was built with funds raised by the tin miners of the 14th century. Though enlarged during the next two centuries, its massive 120-foot granite tower with the backdrop of the high moorland, remains its most impressive feature. Inside the church a panel recalls the disastrous events of 21st October 1638, when a bolt of lightning struck the tower while the church was full of parishioners. Huge blocks of masonry were dislodged and fell onto the worshippers, killing four outright and leaving 60 badly injured. However, according to a local story, the events of that day were not unexpected as the Devil had been seen earlier spitting fire and riding an ebony stallion across the moors.

In addition to the church there are two other buildings in the village that are worthy of a mention. **Glebe House** is a handsome 16th century residence, now converted into a shop. **Church House**, originally a brewhouse, dating back to 1537, is now leased from the National Trust as the village hall. In between, the house was a schoolroom, a refuge for those travelling across the moor to attend church and an almshouse.

However, Widecombe is most famous for its jolly fair. Taking place in September, **Widdecombe Fair** is known the world over from the song that tells of the adventures of Uncle Tom Cobleigh, his friends and the old grey mare on their way to attend the fair. A succession of Tom Cobleighs have lived around Widecombe over the centuries but the song probably refers to a gentleman who died in 1794. An amorous bachelor, Uncle Tom Cobleigh had a mane of

Widecombe in the Moor

Haytor Ramble

Distance:	4.0 miles (6.4 kilometres)
Typical time:	180 mins
Height gain:	150 metres
Map:	Outdoor Leisure 28
Walk:	www.walkingworld.com ID:1589
Contributor:	Dennis Blackford

Access Information:

On the B3387 Bovey Tracey to Widdecombe road. About 300 metres past the Haytor Vale & Ilsington turning you will pass the bottom car park (tarmac but hot and crowded) where the toilets are. Ignore this car park and continue on for about 200 metres to the middle car park (grass) and park here. There should be buses from Bovey Tracey.

Description:

This circular walk starts at Haytor car park and after a visit to the scenic quarry with its lake heads out over the moor to a secret pool that most walkers are unaware of as it is invisible from a distance of a few tens of metres. From the pool we walk through a gorse and heather part of the moor to Smallacombe Rocks, passing the stone circle sites of ancient round houses. After looking around the rocks with their spectacular outlook we head back towards Haytor and turn onto a Granite Railway to visit a wilder quarry before heading down to Becka Brook (lovely place to picnic). From the stream we return to Haytor by a different route, climbing up over the Tor itself before returning to out starting point.

Additional Information:

Toilets at bottom car park. Ice cream vending van at bottom and top car parks. Park ranger and information at lower car park. This is wild, open moor so care and precautions should be taken. Strong walking boots or shoes, with good tread are strongly recommended. Conditions can change very quickly here so a wind and waterproof extra garment such as a cagoule is also recommended together with a map, compass, water and snack food. Even in mid-summer, it can get very cold on the moor. August and September are possibly the best time to see the gorse and heather in flower.

Features:

Hills or fells, river, toilets, wildlife, birds, flowers, great views, butterflies, industrial archaeology, moor.

Walk Directions:

1 Park in the middle car park which has a firm grass surface and is always far less crowded than the others. Looking across the road, you will see the unmistakable shape of Haytor which can be seen for tens of kilometres in most directions. Leave the car park by the lower of the two entrances and cross the road. After crossing the road, follow the fairly wide path bearing diagonally to the right away from the Tor.

2 After a few hundred metres, the path widens out and takes you directly to a wooden gate in a wire fence. Go through the gate into the scenic quarry, turn left on the hard dirt path.

3 After looking around the quarry, follow the path around the left hand edge of the lakes. Follow the path up and over the wooden stile. Continue on the distinct path across the moor for a few hundred metres towards the distant rocky outcrop.

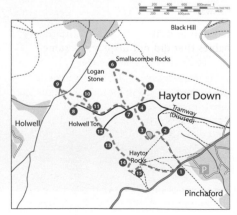

4 The path crosses the granite railway where you can still see the tracks carved from stone. In the distance you can see the outcrop of Smallacombe rocks. Do not take the path directly towards the rocks but look for the one diagonally to the right. Follow this path across the moorland (do not follow the railway).

5 A few hundred metres will suddenly bring you to the secret pool hidden down a fold in the moor. Walk round the left hand edge of the pool and follow the small path through the gorse and heather towards Smallacombe Rocks. As you approach the outcrop, down in the bracken on your left, there are circles of stones with a depression in the centre. These are the remains of ancient roundhouses.

6 After looking around the rocks and seeing the spectacular views over the valley, turn again towards Haytor and follow the wide path which is fairly clearly visible.

7 When you reach the railway again, turn right and follow it for about 50 metres until you reach the 'points' in the track. Follow the branch to the right. The track goes downhill for about 800 metres to a rugged quarry with a 'spoil heap' projecting over the valley.

8 Just before the track appears to end in a pile of rocks, look for a small path down to your right. The first part is a steep scramble down a rocky path (approx 5 metres) before it becomes a zig-zag path that heads for the trees at the bottom of the valley. Note: If you do not want to attempt this rough section of the walk, retrace your steps out of the quarry until you see the track up to your right and rejoin the walk at waymark 11.

9 There is another scramble down a rocky path (approx 6 metres drop) to the lovely Becka Brook which is a great place for a picnic in the shade of the trees and the music of the river. When you have finished here, retrace your steps up the scramble. When you again see the wide path you came down on, look for a smaller branch to your left and follow this path as it winds through the bracken and heather.

10 The path is not always very definite so aim for the 'big' tree to the left of the rocks. After passing the tree, bear right to pass on the left of the pile of rocks from the quarry. The track ascends here to rejoin the railway at the entrance of the quarry.

11 After reaching the railway, cross over and follow the wide track up hill, diagonally to your left.

12 This path will bring you out to the upper railway track. Turn left on it for about 10 metres then turn diagonally right up the side track towards the rocks.

13 After a few hundred metres, the path heads towards Haytor. Where the path appears to go down a little valley (centre of picture) go to the right of the rocks and continue on the path which will again head towards the Tor.

14 The path disappears in a boulder strewn grassy area. Head towards the massive rock to pass on its right.

15 Having passed the Tor, bear left around a smaller outcrop of rock to follow the wide track back to the car park. We hope that you enjoyed your visit to the moor.

---

red hair and he refused to maintain any babies that did not display the same characteristic.

From Widecombe, a country lane leads northwards to **Grimspound**, perhaps the most impressive of all Dartmoor's Bronze Age relics. A settlement occupied between 1800BC and 500BC, it is still possible to make out the positions of door lintels and stone sleeping shelves. Today, however, this bleak and moody landscape is best remembered as the one to which Sir Arthur Conan Doyle had his hero Sherlock Holmes send his accomplice Dr Watson while trying to solve the mystery of *The Hound of the Baskervilles*.

LUSTLEIGH
2½ miles NW of Bovey Tracey off the A382

One of Dartmoor's most popular and most photographed villages, Lustleigh has a ravishing assortment of 15th and 16th century thatched cottages, picturesquely grouped around the church. Appropriately for such a genuinely old-world village, Lustleigh keeps alive some of the time-honoured traditions of country life. May Day continues to be enthusiastically celebrated with a procession through the village, dancing around a maypole and the coronation of a May Queen. From the village there are some delightful walks through the wooded and steep-sided Bovey valley. Also close by is the **Becky Falls Woodland Park**, with its waterfalls, rugged landscape and attractions for all the family (see panel opposite). Here, too, is **Yarner Wood Nature Reserve**, home to pied flycatchers, wood warblers and redstarts.

MORETONHAMPSTEAD

6 miles NW of Bovey Tracey on the A382

Moreton, as this little town is known locally, has long claimed to be the 'Gateway to east Dartmoor', a role greatly enhanced by the opening of the

branch railway from Newton Abbot in 1866. It has since been a victim of the Beeching cuts of the 1960s. This is the gentler part of Dartmoor, where the landscape is one of woods and plantations and steep sided river valleys. Surrounded by fields, the tower of St Andrew's Church is a well-known skyline landmark. Built of Dartmoor granite in the early 15th century, this church overlooks the Sentry, or Sanctuary Field, an attractive public park. During the Napoleonic Wars there were, at one time, no fewer than 379 French officer prisoners of war living in the town, on parole from the military prison that had just been established at Princetown. In the churchyard are the headstones of two French officers dated 1810 and 1811. One of the many French officers detained here was General Rochambeau, a man who must have sorely tested the patience of the inhabitants. Every time

GREAT SLONCOMBE FARM

Moretonhampstead, Devon TQ13 8QF
Tel: 01647 440595
e-mail: hmerchant@sloncombe.freeserve.co.uk
website: www.greatsloncombe.co.uk

Trudie, Robert and Helen Merchant welcome guests throughout the year at **Great Sloncombe Farm**, a traditional Devon dairy farm set among meadows and woodland in glorious Dartmoor. The three letting bedrooms are in the wonderful 13th century granite and cob farmhouse, where oak timbers, granite fireplaces, sloping floors and crooked walls contribute to the delightful old-world charm. The traditionally furnished bedrooms - Barley, Clover and Cornflower - all have en suite shower rooms and views of the meadow, and the largest, Cornflower, has a pine four-poster and a separate dressing room.

The lounge with its beams and brasses is a perfect spot to relax, to plan the day's activities or to enjoy a book or a board game, and in the cosy dining room a farmhouse breakfast starts the day and generously served dinners cater for outdoor appetites. Beef, eggs and seasonal vegetables are home-produced, and wherever possible the rest of the ingredients are locally sourced. The family-run farm is a really delightful place for relaxing, for gentle country strolls in the countryside or for exploring this beautiful part of the world.

BECKY FALLS WOODLAND PARK

Manaton, near Newton Abbot, Devon TQ13 9UG
Tel: 01647 22159 Fax: 01647 221555
e-mail: beckyfalls@btconnect.com
website: www.beckyfalls-dartmoor.com

High on Dartmoor lies a hidden, peaceful valley that has been attracting visitors for over a century, **Becky Falls Woodland Park**, with its oak woodland, waterfalls and rugged landscape is as appealing today as it was then. However, along with the beauty of the waterfalls, visitors here can see and ride Dartmoor ponies, play with the rabbits, lambs and pygmy goats and watch the birds of prey and owls. There is a special nature trail for children, craft shops with demonstrations and a licensed café. The park is open throughout the season and, weather permitting, at weekends in the winter.

word came through of a French victory, he would don his full dress uniform and parade through the streets of the town.

One of the town's most interesting buildings is the row of **Almshouses** in Cross Street, built in 1637, with a striking arcade supported by sturdy granite columns. Just across the road is **Mearsdon Manor Galleries**, the oldest house in Moreton, dating back to the 14th century.

Just to the southwest of the town lies **North Bovey** that has often been described as one of the loveliest villages in Devon. Set beside the River Bovey, this unspoilt village of thatched cottages is grouped around a green with a 15th century church. The delightful, ancient inn, built in the 13th century, originally acted as a lodging house for the stonemasons working on the construction of the village church.

LOCATOR MAP

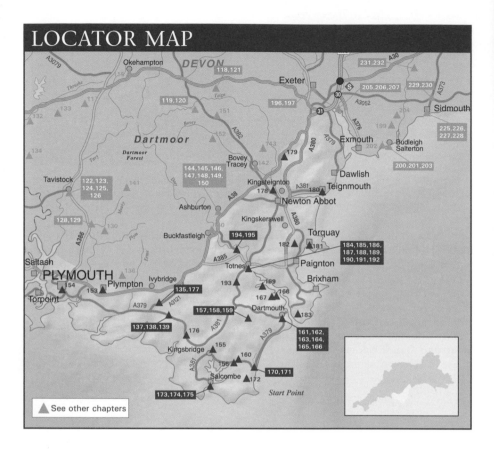

See other chapters

ADVERTISERS AND PLACES OF INTEREST

153 Plym Valley Railway, Plympton,   page 188
154 Plymouth Dome, Plymouth   page 189
155 The Busy Bee, Kingsbridge   page 192
156 The China Matching Service,
      Frogmore, Kingsbridge   page 193
157 The George Inn, Blackawton, Totnes   page 194
158 Woodside Cottage, Blackawton,
      Dartmouth   page 194
159 Hemborough Farm, Blackawton,
      Totnes   page 195
160 Cotmore Farm, Chillington,
      Kingsbridge   page 195
161 Ethera, Dartmouth   page 196
162 Dartmouth Museum, Dartmouth   page 197

163 Stewart Gallery & Studio, Dartmouth   page 197
164 Higher Bowden, Dartmouth   page 198
165 Uniek, Dartmouth   page 199
166 Greenswood Farm, Dartmouth   page 200
167 Fingals at Old Coombe Manor Farm,
      Dittisham, Dartmouth   page 200
168 Coombe Farm Gallery, Dittisham   page 201
169 North Barn, Cornworthy, Totnes   page 201
170 Torcross Apartment Hotel, Torcross,
      Kingsbridge   page 202
171 Sea Shanty Licensed Restaurant,
      Torcross, Kingsbridge   page 202
172 Higher Beeson House, Beeson,
      Kingsbridge   page 203

PLYMOUTH AND THE SOUTH HAMS 5

Plymouth Hoe

The largest centre of population in the southwest peninsula, Plymouth developed at the end of the 12th century when its potential as a military and commercial port was recognised. But it was not until the 16th century that it became the main base for the English navy, when Sir Francis Drake famously finished his game of bowls before leading the fleet from Plymouth against the Spanish Armada. The home of the Royal Naval College, Plymouth was heavily bombed during World War II, so much so that the city centre was rebuilt to the designs of Sir Patrick Abercrombie in the 1950s. Still an important commercial centre today, Plymouth boasts one of the county's great stately homes, Saltram House, which occupies a superb site overlooking the River Plym.

ADVERTISERS AND PLACES OF INTEREST

173 Maryknowle Cottage, Salcombe — page 204
174 Coves Quay Gallery, Salcombe — page 204
175 Blue, Salcombe — page 205
176 Court Barton Farm, Aveton Gifford — page 207
177 Plantation House Hotel, Ermington — page 208
178 Twelve Oaks Holiday Cottages, Teigngrace, Newton Abbot — page 209
179 Glen Cottage, Chudleigh — page 210
180 Turn of the Tide, Teignmouth — page 212
181 Bahamas Hotel, Torquay — page 213
182 The Pottery (Ann Saward), Cockington, Torquay — page 214
183 Nethway Farm Holiday Cottages, Kingswear, Dartmouth — page 216

184 The Conker Shoe Company, Totnes — page 218
185 The Old Forge at Totnes, Totnes — page 219
186 Esho Funi Interiors, Totnes — page 219
187 The Bear Shop, Totnes — page 220
188 PaperWorks, Totnes — page 220
189 The Totnes Wine Company, Totnes — page 220
190 Marshall Arts Gallery, Totnes — page 221
191 Fifth Element, Totnes — page 222
192 Kingsbridge Inn, Totnes — page 222
193 Pound Court Cottage, Harbertonford, Totnes — page 223
194 High Cross House, Dartington, Totnes — page 223
195 Sail & Oar, Dartington, Totnes — page 225

Torbay

To the east of Plymouth, as far as the River Dart and south of Dartmoor is the South Ham, an area well known for its mild climate, fertile soil and lush pasture. The rivers that drain Dartmoor and flow into the south coast cut right through the South Ham, acting, until relatively recent times, as a great barrier to communication and expansion. The only two towns are Totnes and Kingsbridge. The area is characterised by wonderfully picturesque ports and charming, sleepy villages, linked by narrow, winding country lanes.

West of the River Dart is a stretch of coastline called the English Riviera. This might seem pretentious but there are palm trees waving in the gentle breeze along the coast. As exotic plants and shrubs were brought back from far-off places by the ships arriving at the south Devon ports, some of the new plants found their way into local gardens. The first palm tree arrived here in 1820. It took well to the mild climate and hundreds more were planted along the seafronts of the newly fashionable resorts along the coast, most notably, Torquay. This elegant resort was used in the Roger Moore TV series *The Saint* as a substitute for Monte Carlo. Along with the resorts, popular seaside towns and pretty little ports along the

Bolt Tail, nr Kingsbridge

coast, this area is also the home of several grand and interesting houses. Oldway Mansion, the home of the sewing machine millionaire Isaac Singer, was exuberantly extended by his son Paris. Torre Abbey dates back to the 12th century.

PLYMOUTH

The most famous part of this historic city is undoubtedly **Plymouth Hoe** and this is also an excellent place to start any exploration with an historical event known to every schoolchild. On the Hoe, a park and promenade overlooking **Plymouth Sound**, on Friday 19th July 1588, Sir Francis Drake was playing bowls when he was told of the approach of the Spanish Armada. In true British fashion, Drake completed his game before boarding the *Golden Hind* and sailing off to intercept the Spanish ships. The

Sutton Harbour from the Royal Citadel

Hoe is still an open space from where there are superb views of the sea and the wooded headlands and here stands a statue of Drake looking proudly out to the horizon, striking a splendidly belligerent pose.

Just offshore, in the waters of the mouth of the River Tamar, lies **Drake's Island**, an English Alcatraz, known in medieval times as St Nicholas' Island. Its name was changed when Sir Francis Drake was appointed governor and he began to fortify the island. Drake's Island remained a military base until 1956 and it was also used as a prison for a few years during the late 17th century. Two miles from Plymouth Hoe is the remarkable **Plymouth Breakwater** with its lighthouse at one end. It protects the Sound from the prevailing southwesterly winds and was built by prisoners in the early 19th century. This massive mile-long construction required around four

million tons of limestone and its upper surface was finished with enormous dovetailed blocks of stone.

Fourteen miles out in the English Channel another lighthouse, the famous **Eddystone Lighthouse**, can be seen on a clear day. The present building is actually the fourth structure. The first, made of timber, was swept away during a storm in 1703. In the mid-18th century a more substantial stone lighthouse was built by John Smeaton. This stood for 120 years before the rocks on which it was built began to collapse. Dismantled and re-erected on Plymouth Hoe, **Smeaton's Tower** is now one of the city's most popular attractions. From the top there are excellent views of Millbay Docks, Plymouth's busy commercial port.

Plymouth's oldest quarter, the **Barbican** is today a lively area of restaurants, pubs and an innovative small theatre, but it was once the main trading area of the town where merchants exported wool and imported wine. Close by is **The Citadel**, a massive fortress, built as a defence against a seaborne invasion by Charles II. It remains a military base today but there are guided tours around the building during the summer. Near here is a reminder that Plymouth was the departure point for the Pilgrim Fathers who sailed off to a new life in Massachusetts. The **Mayflower Stone** stands at the point where they boarded their ship. Many other emigrants departed from the city with the result that there are now more than 40 communities named Plymouth scattered around the English-speaking world. Other significant events in Plymouth's history are also remembered at the stone: the sailing, in 1839, of the *Troy*, an early emigrant ship to New Zealand, and the return of the Tolpuddle martyrs who had been transported to Australia.

A number of other interesting buildings from Plymouth's past, which survived the devastating bombing raids of World War II, can be seen in the Barbican district: **Prysten House** dates from the 15th century; the **Elizabethan House** has a rich display of Elizabethan furniture and furnishings; and the **Merchant's House**, regarded as Devon's finest Jacobean building, is crammed with interesting objects relating to Plymouth's past. The city is also home to **Jacka's Bakery**, which claims to be the oldest commercial bakery in the country and is reputed to have supplied *The Mayflower* with ship's biscuits. This area is also home to the **National Marine Aquarium**, where state-of-the-art techniques allow visitors to travel through the oceans of the world to encounter brilliantly coloured fish, seahorses and even Caribbean sharks.

On the night of 21st March, 1941, the entire centre of Plymouth was razed to the ground during a bombing raid that used high explosives and incendiary bombs. More than a thousand people were killed and many more injured. After the war was over, the renowned town planner, Sir Patrick Abercrombie, was commissioned to design a new city centre. Although it was built in the 1950s when wartime restrictions on building materials were still having an effect, the centre has a period charm of its own. The new plan incorporated some excellent facilities such as a first-rate **Museum and Art Gallery**, the **Theatre Royal**, an **Arts Centre** and the **Pavilions** complex of concert hall, leisure pool and skating rink.

PLYM VALLEY RAILWAY

Marsh Mills Station, Coypool Road,
Plympton, near Plymouth, Devon PL7 4NW
Tel: 01752 330881
e-mail: plymvalrwy@btinternet.com
website: plymrail.co.uk

The object of the **Plym Valley Railway** is to relay and restore a short section of the former Great Western Railway branch line from Plymouth to Launceston via Tavistock and, in particular, the section that runs from Marsh Mills, Plympton to the local beauty spot of Plym Bridge, a distance of around a mile and a quarter. A series of heritage steam and diesel locomotives from the 1950s and 1960s operate the services that run on Sundays and there is also a buffet and souvenir shop at Marsh Mills.

PLYMOUTH DOME

Hoe Road, Plymouth, Devon PL1 2NZ
Tel: 01752 603300
e-mail: plymouthdome@plymouth.gov.uk
website: www.plymouthdome.info

No visit to Plymouth is complete without spending some time at **Plymouth Dome**, which stands on the city's scenic waterfront, The Hoe, just a short distance from the centre. Completed in 1989, it makes a fine introduction to the city, with a wide range of atmospheric attractions and interactive displays that explain the city from geographical and historical viewpoints. Visitors can hear about Drake, Cook, Raleigh and the Pilgrim Fathers; learn about the great engineers who used their skills to build lighthouses (including the neighbouring Smeaton's Tower); and to see how Plymouth rose from the ashes of the Blitz. The panoramic windows provide a wonderful view point overlooking the Sound, and text panels explain the various points of interest around the Bay. Among the many other attractions, the Climate Zone provides a hands-on link to the Met Office and illustrates how the oceans affect our world. The glass-roofed Dolphin Café is a pleasant spot to enjoy a cup of tea or coffee and a light snack, and the Dome's shop is full of gifts and souvenirs of the Dome and the city.

Smeaton's Tower, originally built 14 miles out to sea on the treacherous Eddystone Rocks, was moved to the Hoe in 1882 and has been one of Plymouth's most famous landmarks ever since.

AROUND PLYMOUTH

PLYMPTON

5 miles E of Plymouth on the B3416

Plympton is home to **Saltram House and Park**, a prestigious 18th century mansion surrounded by a large estate near the tidal creek of the Plym estuary. The house, which contains fine period furniture, china and pictures, was the home of the Parker family, who commissioned Robert Adam to create the magnificent state rooms in the 1790s. There are superb 18th century gardens complete with an orangery and, in the extensive estate, there is an amphitheatre that is a relic of the opulence of the Georgian era. One of Devon's grandest mansions, Saltram is now in the care of the National Trust and is home to a wide variety of birdlife and other wildlife.

Anyone who saw the film of Jane Austen's novel *Sense and Sensibility* will recognise the mansion as the location for Norland House. The **Plym Valley Railway** (see panel) runs from Marsh Mills, Plympton, to the local beauty spot of Plym Bridge.

PLYM BRIDGE

3½ miles NE of Plymouth off the 3432

To the north of the village lies the luxuriant oak woodlands of **Plym Bridge Woods** beside the River Plym. At their best during the spring, when the woods are carpeted with flowers, there are waymarked paths through the woods allowing visitors to appreciate the wealth of bird and animal life. In the 17th century, this was a less than peaceful place as tons of slate were quarried from the exposed rock; the woods are littered with fascinating industrial archaeological remains.

Wembury

Distance:	4.8 miles (7.6 kilometres)
Typical time:	120 mins
Height gain:	200 metres
Map:	Outdoor Leisure 20
Walk:	www.walkingworld.com ID:2072
Contributor:	Dave Pawley

Access Information:

From the Plymouth direction as you drive into Wembury you will pass the Odd Wheel pub on your right, a few yards along the road turn left and 100 yards on turn left again into Barton Close and at the end of the road are playing fields and a large car park. There are buses from Plymouth bus station to Wembury for those who wish to use public transport.

Description:

A walk with a bit of everything, footpaths through fields, views of Dartmoor at one point, the sea and the lovely river Yealm. It includes a section of the South West Coastal path and even the start of the Devon version of the Coast to Coast path. What more could you want, beach and a swim or surf, yes even that is on offer. The walk takes you from the large village of Wembury out across fields and roads to high above the river Yealm and a loop down to the very edge of the river and the ferry across it. From there up again to take the coastal path west along to Wembury Beach where there is a church, car park, toilets and a shop and the start of the coast to coast walk. The route is then up a splendid valley and along footpaths and a small amount of road walking to near Knighton before returning to the car park.

Additional Information:

The Great Mewstone Island was once inhabited, if only by a man sent there in isolation for six years as a punishment. There is an excellent signpost right by the beach which indicates just how long the SW coastal path is and the distance of the coast to coast path which runs from Wembury Beach up to Lynmouth in the North. At Waymark 10 the Crooked Wheel is well worth a visit and as with almost all pubs these days food is served. The Jazz is very good, every Thursday evening.

Features:

Hills or fells, river, sea, pub, toilets, play area, church, wildlife, birds, flowers, great views, food shop.

Walk Directions:

1 Leave the car park at Barton Close near the Odd Wheel public house and follow the track along at the rear of the tennis courts and descend slightly. After a couple of hundred metres you will pass houses to your left. Although the path continues ahead as a lane, there are stone steps to your right up through a hedge leading into a field.

2 Turn right and walk up the steps and follow the track across a field, through kissing gates and along the side of another field to emerge by a lovely small Manor house over a stile onto a road. Follow the road then rough track along south east. After about half a mile you will come to a gate with a house to the left hand side and just beyond the gate there are three tracks, one ahead, one to the left and the other to the right. This walk takes you along all three! First down to the river Yealm before returning back again the coastal path.

3 Go through the gate and just by the gatehouse turn left and follow the footpath which will loop you right down to the very edge of the very scenic River Yealm. As you descend the views unfold before you. Make your way down an increasingly steep path until you are just above river level where, during the summer months, the passenger ferry departs for the short hop to theother bank.

4 Continue along the loop, walking to the left of a lovely waterside house and then follow the track back steeply uphill until you reach the gate house /gate again. The main coastal path is off to your left.

5 Turn left though a gate and onto the coastal path which leads you along overlooking the mouth of the Yealm. Continue along parallel to the mouth of the river below and do not take the track leading inland at a junction. After about a mile you will pass a house on your right. Just beyond the house, turn left and follow the track which descends towards the sea and you will pass a church to your right. Descend to the Car park and at the far end make your way down to the beach, passing between a small shop and toilets.

6 Cross over a small bridge just above the beach. By the signpost turn inland from the coastal path and start the coast to coast walk, but not for long. Make your way up a valley. The track leads you up and over a stile to a road after several hundred yards. Turn left on the road and follow it down where you will see another sign guiding you right to continue up the valley.

7 Turn right onto the track which continues east up the valley. There are two parallel tracks, take the upper one, the lower bridlepath is very very muddy. The track eventually emerges over a stile and onto a road. Turn left and walk down the road for a hundred yards or more and you will see a sign pointing up by some renovated houses, showing Knighton and Train Road.

8 Follow the wide track up with a house to your left and right. Just beyond the second house take a narrow track which leads you steeply uphill, not the broader one which is to the left and right. You go up through trees, over a stile and into a field. Continue to walk up the field, heading north east. After passing through two fields you will see a footpath sign to your left. Ignore it and continue ahead. The field is cultivated and the footpath narrow as it levels out. You will reach a gap in the hedge, once a gate was there but not now.

9 Just beyond the wide gap in the hedge, the path turns slightly right to lead you diagonally across a field as it descends. Again the track is narrow through the cultivated field. At the far corner there is a stile leading out to a narrow lane. Turn right and follow the road which leads you downhill then directly up to the Crooked Wheel Pub.

10 Just beyond the Crooked Wheel Pub is the main road you travelled along to reach the car park. Turn right onto the road and a few yards along there is narrow pedestrian only track off to your left which leads you up by a school to your left and directly back into Barton Close and the car park.

TAMERTON FOLIOT
4 miles N of Plymouth on the B3373

This village, which overlooks a large creek running into the River Tamar, was the birthplace of Gilbert Foliot, who was the Bishop of London for 25 years between 1153 and 1188. He was an arch adversary of Thomas à Becket, who had Foliot excommunicated, although this punishment was later overturned by the Pope.

NEWTON FERRERS
6 miles SE of Plymouth on the B3186

One part of this picturesque fishing village lies beside the River Yealm while the rest sits alongside a large creek that dries up at low tide making it possible to walk across to Noss Mayo on the southern bank. A quaint and scenic place much loved by artists, Newton Ferrers is also one of the most popular yachting centres on the south coast.

Just to the west lies **Wembury** whose clifftop church stands out as a dramatic landmark. From the clifftop path there are some superb views out over the Yealm estuary and Plymouth Sound. From here, too, can be see the **Great Mew Stone**, a tiny islet that lies about a mile offshore out in Wembury Bay. This lonely spot was inhabited until the 1830s when its last residents, the part-time smuggler Sam Wakeham and his family, gave up the struggle to make a living here. The Mew Stone is now the home of seabirds and is, occasionally, used by the *HMS Cambridge* gunnery school (occasions that are surely not very popular with the birds). On the beach near the estuary is a former mill house, **The Old Mill**, now a café owned by the National Trust.

Turnchapel
1 mile SE of Plymouth off the A379

Strung out along the waterside and with superb views across Cattewater to Plymouth, this village, with its pubs, church and waterfront, was declared a Conservation Area in 1977. From the nearby Mountbatten Peninsula there are excellent views to Plymouth Hoe and Drake's Island. It was at RAF Mountbatten that Lawrence of Arabia served as a humble aircraftman for several years.

A short distance to the south is a stretch of coastline that is known as **Abraham's Garden**. A local story tells that, during the dreadful plague of 1665, a number of Spanish slaves were buried here and, in their memory, the shrubbery always remains green, even in winter.

KINGSBRIDGE

A pretty town, at the head of the Kingsbridge estuary, Kingsbridge's name

The Busy Bee

6 Fore Street, Kingsbridge, Devon TQ7 1NY
Tel: 01548 857028
e-mail: busybee.kingsbridge@virgin.net
website: www.bbkb.com

Located in the centre of Kingsbridge, **The Busy Bee** is a very aptly named shop that has been built up over the years and is owned and personally run by Sarah McGrath.

The boldly painted black and yellow exterior is hard to miss, and, once inside, customers will find that Sarah stocks just about everything any budding craft enthusiast could want. From brightly coloured fabrics, embroidery threads, tapestry wools, and knitting yarns through to Winsor & Newton paints. Beads, pipe cleaners, pompoms and bells, fabric, silk and glass paints are also available.

This Aladdin's Cave is sure to be an inspiration to artists and craft workers alike. Sarah has also recently started stocking Dolls Houses, furniture and accessories. There is also a Mail Order Service and a website, which is growing all the time.

reflects the fact that there has been a bridge here since the 10th century. However, the **Kingsbridge Estuary** is not strictly speaking an estuary as no river runs into it. This broad expanse of water is a ria, or drowned valley, providing an attractive setting for the town and its quayside. The narrow alleys bear descriptive names such as Squeezebelly Passage. **The Shambles**, an Elizabethan market arcade whose late 18th century upper floor is supported on six sturdy granite pillars, is a reminder that this was once an important market town serving the surrounding towns and villages. Kingsbridge's rather modest Victorian town hall has an unusual onion-shaped clock tower that adds a touch of glamour to the building.

For anyone looking to learn more about this area of Devon, a visit to the **Cookworthy Museum of Rural Life** is a must. Housed in the former Grammar School founded in 1670, the museum is named after William Cookworthy, who was born in the town in 1703. Working as an apothecary in Plymouth, Cookworthy came across traders from the Far East who brought back fine porcelain from China. The English pottery makers who were failing to produce such delicate china were in despair. However, Cookworthy identified the basic ingredient of the Chinese porcelain as kaolin, huge deposits of which lay in the hills just to the north of Plymouth. Ever since, the more common name for kaolin has been china clay.

AROUND KINGSBRIDGE

CAPTON
8½ miles NE of Kingsbridge off the A3122

Tucked away in the hills to the northwest of Dartmouth and well hidden

THE CHINA MATCHING SERVICE

Fern Lea, Frogmore, Kingsbridge, South Devon TQ7 2NZ
Tel: 01548 531372
e-mail: enquiries@chinamatchingservice.co.uk
website: www.chinamatchingservice.co.uk

The **China Matching Service** is a boon to anyone who has ever been searching for a replacement dinner plate or additional pieces for a tea or dinner service that is no longer in production. Miriam Clark has been providing this invaluable assistance for more than 20 years, trying (with great success) to find and supply those missing items for services produced from the 1960s onwards and now discontinued, with patterns in makes such as Royal Doulton, Royal Albert, Wedgwood, Denby, Midwinter and Meakin. It is generally a mail-order service, with enquiries received by letter, telephone and increasingly by the e-mail.

Orders can be despatched worldwide, and China Matching can even offer a gift-wrapping service if anyone would like to purchase a surprise gift to be delivered direct to the recipient. If a pattern is not immediately available the customer's requirements are kept on a register and a search will be made to try to locate any pieces. Mrs Clark lives in a beautiful holiday area, and many a visitor has dropped in with a broken piece to enable her to see the pattern required. The service is both personal and very useful, and the return customers and the many letters of thanks are testimony to its efficiency.

THE GEORGE INN

Blackawton, Nr Totnes, South Devon TQ9 7BG
Tel: 01803 712342
e-mail: george@thegeorgeinn.biz
website: www.greatbeer.co.uk/devgein

Local residents and visitors to the West Country are united in their praise of the **George Inn**, where the welcome from licensees Vic and Ruth Hall, the beer, the good wholesome food and the accommodation have all won many friends. The main bar is partly timbered, and the lounge at the end enjoys nice views across the fields, views shared by the pleasant little beer garden. This super free house offers a fine selection of draught and bottle beers, and a fine variety of home-cooked dishes catering for all appetites is available lunchtime and evening. The extensive menu is supplemented by seasonal and local dishes on the daily specials board in the

bar lounge; particular favourites include the fish and seafood specials and pub classics such as liver & bacon and meat pies.

The George also caters well for overnight guests with comfortable bed & breakfast accommodation in an en suite twin room, two doubles and a family room. Very much the social hub of the lovely village of Blackawton, this outstanding inn is a great base for country walks, and it's only a short drive to Dartmouth and the smaller coastal towns of Slapton, Strete and Stoke Fleming.

WOODSIDE COTTAGE

Blackawton, Nr Dartmouth, Devon TQ9 7BL
Tel: 01803 712375
e-mail: stay@woodsidedartmouth.co.uk
website: www.woodsidedartmouth.co.uk

Originally the gamekeeper's lodge for the Oldstone Estate, 18th century **Woodside Cottage** has been transformed into a comfortable and attractive home of great charm and an ideal spot for a break from city routine. Owners Tim and Sally Adams provide a warm welcome, starting with tea and home-made cake, that sets the tone of this civilised place set in idyllic surroundings near the ancient village of Blackawton and a short drive from Dartmouth. Each of the three centrally heated guest bedrooms has its own individual style, with pastel decor and carefully co-ordinated furnishings in keeping with the character

of the cottage; all have integral bath or shower rooms and share the same lovely views.

Delicious breakfasts using the very best local produce are served in the old beamed dining room, and the owners will gladly cater for special diets and prepare packed lunches. Guests are welcome to make use of the sitting room with its library and log fire, the conservatory and the grounds, where Tim and Sally have created a new woodland garden and have undertaken imaginative mixed planting within the fine old drystone terraces. No smoking, pets or children.

HEMBOROUGH FARM

Blackawton, Nr Totnes, Devon TQ9 7DF
Tel/Fax: 01803 712398

In a beautiful rural setting, with uninterrupted views across open countryside, **Hemborough Farm** is a perfect choice for a break from city life. Light, airy en suite bedrooms in the lovely old stone farmhouse have central heating, TV and tea/coffee makers, and one of the rooms is ideal for families. Owner Ruth Rowden sees that guests start the day well with a full English breakfast and can provide packed lunches with a little notice – ideal for guests setting out from this working farm to enjoy a day exploring the many scenic and historic delights of the region. No pets.

COTMORE FARM

Chillington, Nr Kingsbridge, Devon TQ7 2LR
Tel: 01548 580374

Cotmore Farm, enjoys a sheltered south-facing location among rolling hills and hedge-lined fields, approximately one mile from the sea and the South West coast path. The self-catering accommodation is in the Old Stables, where there is an en suite double bedroom, lounge and compact kitchen. French windows in all the rooms open onto a private garden with distant views to the sea. Dogs are welcome.

off the beaten track, Capton is a quaint little place. Excavations on a nearby hilltop in the 1980s revealed the remains of a Neolithic chambered tomb along with a number of artefacts dating from Palaeolithic to medieval times.

DARTMOUTH

9 miles NE of Kingsbridge on the A379

One of England's principal ports for centuries, it was at Dartmouth, in the 12th century, that crusaders on both the second and third crusades mustered before sailing. Here, too, in the shelter of the harbour, Queen Elizabeth's men o' war lay in wait to see off stragglers from the Spanish Armada. Millions of casks of French and Spanish wine have been offloaded on to Dartmouth's narrow quays. In 1620, *The Mayflower* put in here for repair before sailing for Plymouth and then the New World. However, it was Alfred the Great who developed Dartmouth as a strategic

Dartmouth Waterfront

Dartmouth Castle

In 1373, Geoffrey Chaucer, as Inspector of Customs, visited the town. He is believed to have modelled the Shipman in his famous *Canterbury Tales* on the then Mayor of Dartmouth, John Hawley. An enterprising merchant and seafarer, Hawley was responsible for building the first **Dartmouth Castle**, the dramatically sited fortress that guards the entrance to the Dart estuary. The present building was erected by Edward IV after the War of the Roses. Along with the castle, the town had another defence against invasion. In times of danger, a heavy chain was strung across the harbour to Kingswear Castle on the opposite bank. There is an impressive monumental brass to Hawley and his

base and the town has a long connection with the Royal Navy, the oldest of the British services. Dartmouth's famous and historic quayside has also been used by many television and film companies as a location. *The Onedin Line* and *Sense and Sensibility* were filmed here.

ETHERA

4 Union Street, Dartmouth,
Devon TQ6 9DP
Tel: 01803 839333
Fax: 01803 833356
e-mail: pipmita@aol.com
website: www.etherajewellery.com

The beautiful town of Dartmouth is an appropriate setting for **Ethera**, a family business of three designers who create fine precious and costume jewellery. The emphasis is on quality, enchantment, fantasy and fun, and the artists, working in gold, silver or costume materials, take their inspiration from the Art Nouveau era, the Pre-Raphaelites, the Faerie Realm and the stunning English countryside.

Anyone looking for a really special gift can view the full collections at the Dartmouth shop, where the costume sets have romantic names such as Moonlight Snowfall, the Faerie Queen, Butterfly Kisses and the Firebird. Pip & The Weasel's World, in silver, is a fun range of animals and other creatures, while the Secret Garden, also in silver, is a delicate, flower-filled and very feminine range. The designs in gold make up a varied collection of jewellery set with precious, semi-precious and coloured cubic zirconium that moves away from the traditional and dares to be different. The designers can also undertake individual commissions and are happy to discuss design queries in person, by telephone or by e-mail.

two wives in the Church of St Saviour, a part 14th century building down by the quayside against whose walls ships used to tie up before the New Quay was built in the 16th century. Here, too, lies the **Custom House**, a handsome 18th century building with elaborate plasterwork ceilings.

Housed in another of the town's old buildings, the timber-framed **Butterwalk** dating from 1640, is the **Dartmouth Museum** (see panel), where the working steam pumping engine built by Thomas Newcomen is one of the many interesting exhibits. Born in Dartmouth in 1663, Newcomen designed and built, at his ironmongery business, an atmospheric steam engine to pump water out of

DARTMOUTH MUSEUM

The Butterwalk, Duke Street, Dartmouth, Devon TQ6 9PZ
Tel: 01803 832923
e-mail: dartmouth@devonmuseums.net
website: www.devonmuseums.net/dartmouth

People come to Dartmouth today to enjoy the splendour of her scenery, but mariners have been visiting the Dart for centuries because of its sheltered deep water. The Museum

has a strong nautical theme with a large collection of models illustrating the development of ships from early dugouts to 20th century liners and naval craft, and a large collection of photographs and documents maps the history of the ancient town. The Museum is housed in a spectacular Grade I listed building with carved ceilings and wall panels both inside and out.

STEWART GALLERY & STUDIO

3 The Old Market, Dartmouth, Devon TQ6 9QE
Tel: 01803 839555
e-mail: james@stewartgallery.co.uk
website: www.stewartgallery.co.uk

A stone arch provides an attractive entrance to **Stewart Gallery**, which is located in Dartmouth's historic old market square. Unlike many galleries, this is also very much a working studio, which means that visitors have the opportunity not only to browse through the artwork on display but also to see an artist at work in his studio.

That artist is the owner James Stewart, whose work is well known not only locally but much further afield. His work can be found in selective venues throughout the UK, London's West End and New York where he is particuarily in demand.

He is best known for his bird's eye view paintings, but he is a versatile artist, as can be seen by the works on display in the gallery. The wall space is shared with several other talented artists, the majority of whose work is in oils or acrylic. The subject matter varies from traditional landscapes and seascapes to portraits, still life studies and abstracts, and apart from the original works the Gallery has a selection of prints and cards. Everything in the Stewart Gallery is for sale, and James has also undertaken commissions including advertising, album cover designs and private portraits.

HIGHER BOWDEN

Near Dartmouth, Devon TQ6 0LH
Tel: 01803 770745 Fax: 01803 770262
e-mail: cottages@higherbowden.com
website: www.higherbowden.com

Guests at **Higher Bowden** enjoy freedom, comfort and beautiful surroundings in 13 self-catering holiday cottages of distinction set in 6.5 acres of landscaped grounds. Developed from the buildings of two adjacent 17th century farms, they nestle on a south-facing hillside in the picturesque South Devon countryside. The cottages, which sleep from two to eight guests, combine character with modern amenity, all having direct-dial telephone, 13-channel TV, video and radio. Electric heaters, night storage heaters and log-burning stoves in inglenook fireplaces keep things cosy in even the chilliest weather, and the fitted pine kitchens include fridge-freezer, microwave, dishwasher and washer-drier as well as a full range of other equipment. Beds are new, large and very comfortable, and each cottage, apart from the snug one-bedroom Little Bowden has at least two bathrooms and at least one power shower.

Each cottage has its own outside sitting area (many have private terraces) with barbecues and furniture provided. Leisure facilities on the premises include an indoor swimming pool, sauna, mini-gym, snooker room, games room with pool, darts, table tennis and table football, putting green and a floodlit artificial grass tennis court. Higher Bowden also provides exceptional facilities for families with young children, and the toddlers' playroom, two well-equipped playgrounds and a trampoline will keep the little ones amused and exercised for hours. A cot or high chair can be provided for any of the cottages, and baby-sitting is available by appointment. Bed linen and bathroom and kitchen tea towels are provided, along with a basket of logs for the fire and two pints of milk for guests' arrival.

This is very much a family business, and Directors Peter and Lin Horne are always on hand to solve any little problems and to give advice on what to see and do in the vicinity. Some guests will see very little reason to leave the premises except for food and drink, for apart from all the leisure facilities the landscaped ground provide a beech walk, a nature walk looking down on the valley below and easy strolls through the shrubbery with seats to pause and take in the lovely peaceful views.

The hillside on which the cottages stand runs down to the Blackpool Valley, and the award-winning beach at Blackpool Sands is only a mile away. Dartmouth is within a 15-minute drive, and all the numerous attractions of South Devon are easily accessible.

River Dart, Dartmouth

famous building is undoubtedly its **Britannia Royal Naval College**, a sprawling red and white building, constructed between 1899 and 1905, which dominates the northern part of the town. The **Britannia Museum** tells the history of the College. The harbour here is busy with naval vessels, pleasure boats and ferries, and it is particularly colourful during the June **Carnival** and the **Dartmouth Regatta** in late August.

coal mines. However, the engine wasted a lot of the energy it produced and it was years later, while he was repairing an old Newcomen engine, that James Watt became interested in designing a more efficient machine.

Another curious building in Dartmouth is its railway station, which must be one of the few in the world that has never seen a train. It was built by the Great Western Railway as the terminus of their line from Torbay, and passengers were ferried across the water from Kingswear where the railway line actually ended. Dartmouth's most

One of the loveliest rivers in England, the River Dart rises in the great central bogs of Dartmoor and flows for some 46 miles before entering the sea at Dartmouth. Called the 'English Rhine' by Queen Victoria, the Dart, along with its tributaries, drains much of the moorland. Much of the coastline around the Dart estuary and southwards around Start Bay is now in the care of the National Trust. As well as providing a valuable nesting area for seabirds, the area also contains some ancient oak woodland and the remains of lime kilns.

GREENSWOOD FARM

Dartmouth, South Devon TQ6 0LY
Tel/Fax: 01803 712100
e-mail: stay@greenswooddartmouth.co.uk
website: www.greenswooddartmouth.co.uk

An idyllic setting, a warm welcome, genuine hospitality, comfortable accommodation and life conducted at a gentle, civilised pace - all this and more is offered by Helen and Roger Baron at **Greenswood Farm**. The heart of this small working farm is a 15th century Devon longhouse, and the three guest bedrooms combine the character of exposed timbers with en suite facilities and modern amenities. A full English breakfast, with local produce and eggs from the farm's own hens, is served in the beamed dining room, and vegetarian and special diets can be catered for; evening meals are sometimes available by prior arrangement.

The sitting room with its inglenook fireplace is a perfect spot to relax, and guests are free to roam in the large, beautifully landscaped gardens, whose attractions include three ponds. There is also a delightful walk from the garden across the field towards the wood. The farm lies in its own secluded valley off the A3122 not far from Dartmouth Golf Club. Dartmouth is only four miles away, and even closer is the South West Coast Path, leading to sheltered beaches and nature reserves and providing magnificent clifftop walks and stunning vistas. Greenswood Farm has a strict no smoking policy. No children under 12.

FINGALS AT OLD COOMBE MANOR FARM

Coombe, Dittisham, Nr Dartmouth, Devon TQ6 0JA
Tel: 01803 722398   Fax: 01803 722401
e-mail: Richard@fingals.co.uk
website: www.fingals.co.uk

Richard Johnston's first Fingals was a busy restaurant in London's Fulham Road, and when he fell in love with a dilapidated Devon farmhouse, bought it and revived it, he gave it the same name. Tucked away in an enchanting secluded valley close to the River Dart, **Fingals at Old Coombe Manor Farm** opened with a single guest bedroom in 1981; it now has 10, including this stream side folly in the garden, all with en suite facilities and each with its own individual charm and personality. The whole place generates a feeling of warmth and well-being, and the sitting room, with oak beams, wood panelling, antique carpets and an

inglenook, is a perfect spot to relax, meet other guests or plan the day's activities.

Meals are served at a long table in the panelled dining room, and children can share in the family dinner or tuck into an earlier high tea. An oak-framed barn next to the main building provides a perfect self-catering base for a family of four, and further self-catering accommodation, for up to five guests, is in the Mill House, a splendidly converted old grain mill. All guests are free to use the hotel's facilities, which include a heated pool, jacuzzi, sauna, grass tennis court, croquet, table tennis and snooker.

COOMBE FARM GALLERY

Dittisham, Nr Dartmouth, South Devon TQ6 0JA
Tel: 01803 722352 Fax: 01803 722275
e-mail: mark@coombegallery.com
website: www.coombegallery.com

One mile from the picturesque village of Dittisham, **Coombe Farm Gallery** proudly displays some of the finest artists and makers currently working in the South West. Exhibits include paintings, ceramics, jewellery, glass and turned wood. The Gallery is open all year round from 10am to 5pm Monday to Saturday, Sunday by appointment. Coombe Farm Gallery has played an active role in promoting new West Country talent alongside internationally acclaimed artists. Works can be viewed and purchased at the Gallery and also on the website.

NORTH BARN

Whitestone Farm, Cornworthy, near Totnes, Devon TQ9 7HS
Tel: 01803 722384/865084

Found at the end of a private road and on the banks of the River Dart, **North Barn** has one of the most peaceful and spectacular locations of any holiday cottage. Once a derelict farm building, the barn has been imaginatively renovated and converted by owners Jilly and Peter Sutton to provide excellent holiday accommodation, ideal for two but with additional sofa beds. Whilst Peter has used all his professional skills as an architect to make the very best of this interesting old building and the wonderful location, Jilly, a highly regarded sculptor, has provided much of the flair and style to this unusual property. Fully equipped throughout, the most outstanding feature has to be the wonderful views from the barn's deck.

STOKE FLEMING

8½ miles NE of Kingsbridge on the A379

One of the most delightful villages in the South Hams, Stoke Fleming is perched high on the cliffs overlooking Start Bay and its prominent church has served as a landmark for mariners for centuries. Less than a mile from the village, a broad crescent of safe sandy beach overhung by Monterey pines is misleadingly named **Blackpool Sands**.

SLAPTON

5½ miles E of Kingsbridge off the A379

To the south of the village lies a remarkable sand and shingle bank separating the saltwater of Start Bay from **Slapton Ley**, Devon's largest natural freshwater lake, fed by three small rivers. The shallow lake and the land surrounding it is a fascinating Site of Special Scientific Interest. It is also a Nature Reserve where large numbers of freshwater fish, insects, water-loving plants and native and migrating birds thrive.

Usually, the stretch of sand and shingle beach at Slapton is a peaceful place whose vast expanse seldom gets crowded. But, in the lead up to the D-Day landings of World War II, it was a very different scene as rehearsals for the invasion were carried out here. As live ammunition was used, the 3,000 people living in the area were evacuated and the village was deserted save for the rats that roamed the streets. The events of those dark days are recorded in Leslie Thomas's novel *The Magic Army*. A tall stone obelisk, unveiled in 1954, commemorates the activities that took place here and the part that the people of the area played in the preparations for the invasion.

TORCROSS APARTMENT HOTEL

Torcross, Nr Kingsbridge, South Devon TQ7 2TQ
Tel: 01548 580206 Fax: 01548 580996
e-mail: enquiries@torcross.com
website: www.torcross.com

In a superb setting right by the water's edge, **Torcross Apartment Hotel** is an ideal base for a family holiday by the sea. The handsome late-Victorian building, painted a very cheerful sky blue, has been splendidly converted and modernised to provide a variety of self-catering apartments spread over its three floors. The apartments are furnished to a very high standard and are kept in excellent order. All are comfortably furnished and fully equipped for an independent, go-as-you-please holiday, with a full-size cooker, microwave oven, fridge, TV, central heating and fitted carpets; all have their own external or internal entrances. Options range from Beachside chalet

apartments for two, with patio doors opening on to a terrace, to Coastview apartments sleeping up to seven, some rooms intercommunicate – perfect for a large family or a group of friends – and a lift is available for elderly or disabled guests. Shared amenities in the building include a bar, a restaurant and three children's play areas.

Bookings are usually taken by the week, but outside the peak season short-break specials are available, running from Monday afternoon to Friday morning or Friday afternoon to Monday morning.

SEA SHANTY LICENSED RESTAURANT

Torcross, Nr Kingsbridge, South Devon TQ7 2TQ
Tel: 01548 580747

'Quality Food at Sensible Prices' is the proud motto of the **Sea Shanty Licensed Restaurant**, which has been run in fine style by Les Irons for the past six years. His stone-built restaurant a few steps from the beach is open from early in the morning right through to the evening in season, and the day starts with a choice for breakfasts. Other offerings range from ice creams to daytime snacks and a children's menu, and the Sea Shanty also provides an extensive

takeaway service. Family and party bookings are welcome, and the restaurant is a popular choice for private parties and functions; themed menus include traditional, fish and vegetarian.

Torcross came into prominence as one of the allied landing training areas in the Second World War. A Sherman tank that took part in the preparations was recovered from the sea in 1984 and now stands on display in the car park. Torcross is now a delightful holiday village with excellent family amenities and a happy, relaxed atmosphere typified by the staff and the customers at the Sea Shanty.

Further down the coast, at **Torcross**, a Sherman tank that took part in the preparations for D-Day was recovered from the sea in 1984. On display in the car park beside the tank are memorial tablets to the men who died during the exercise when an enemy E-boat attacked the landing forces and more than 600 Allied servicemen were killed.

BEESANDS
6 miles SE of Kingsbridge off the A379

Easy to reach on foot by taking the coastal path from Torcross, the journey by road to Beesands is a long one through a series of narrow country lanes. This tiny hamlet with just a single row of old cottages was a busy fishing village as recently as the 1920s, when boats laden with lobster, crab and mullet were drawn up the beach almost to the cottages themselves.

From here the **South West Coast Path** continues following the coastline to the ruined village of Hallsands, which was almost completely demolished by a violent storm in January 1917. Further south, at **Start Point**, is a lighthouse built in 1836 that is open to visitors during daylight hours.

CHIVELSTONE
5 miles SE of Kingsbridge off the A379

One of the county's most hidden places, Chivelstone is an unassuming village tucked away in a maze of country lanes and surrounded by a tranquil, rural landscape. This appealing village is the home of the only church in England that is dedicated to the 4th century Pope, St Sylvester. Historically, Sylvester is a mysterious figure but an old story claims that his saintly ministrations cured the Roman emperor, Constantine, of leprosy. Chivelstone church was built in the 15th century at a time where this disfiguring

---

HIGHER BEESON HOUSE

Beeson, Nr Kingsbridge, Devon TQ7 2HW
Tel: 01548 580623
e-mail: higher-beeson@virgin.net
website: www.higher-beeson.co.uk

Charles Rogers is the third generation of his family to live and work at **Higher Beeson House** and the first to open the property to paying guests. Charles and his wife Lynda have masterminded the conversion of the old stables into three very roomy and luxurious letting bedrooms. On the ground floor is a four-poster room, while upstairs are a double room and a family room with a double bed and bunk beds; all have spa baths, seating areas, TV and video, hairdryer and tea/coffee-making facilities. Shared amenities comprise a large fridge, a drying room and a cycle store.

Lynda loves hospitality, cooking and gardening, all of which soon becomes very apparent to guests! Her Aga-cooked breakfast, served across the courtyard in the family home, makes a memorable start to the day, and the gardens, developed from scratch from unused, unmanageable land, are truly spectacular, with woods, a pond with Muscovy ducks and a variety of unusual plants that flourish in the mild climate. This is excellent walking country, with paths leading to the South West Coast Path, and the beach is less than a mile away in the fishing village of Beesands.

MARYKNOWLE COTTAGE

Salcombe, Devon TQ7 3DB
Tel: 01548 842464
e-mail: maggie.hartley@virgin.net
website: www.maggie.hartley@virgin.net

Nestling in a beautiful secluded valley, **Maryknowle Cottage** is a lovely old stone apple barn recently converted to provide self-catering accommodation for six to eight people. On the ground floor are an en suite bedroom, a family bathroom, fully equipped kitchen/dining room and utility room with washer, dryer and freezer. Stairs lead from the dining area to the two upstairs bedrooms and a sitting room with TV and video. Features of the upstairs floor are the attractive exposed original timbers and the impressive 'cathedral' ceiling.

The accommodation offered by owner Mrs Hartley is very flexible, with some beds being either doubles or two singles, and a sofa in the sitting room converts to a bed. One of the upstairs rooms has a ladder leading up to a sleeping platform with a bed for two - but not sleepwalkers! There are gardens front and rear, and footpaths lead from the cottage to Salcombe (one mile), North Sands and Malborough. The cottage is part of Maryknowle Farm and is approached by a private lane: from Kingsbridge take the A381 Salcombe road. About a mile beyond Malborough, the lane signposted Maryknowle is marked on the right.

COVES QUAY GALLERY

6 Coves Quay, Thorning Street, Salcombe, Devon TQ8 8DW
Tel: 01548 842666 Fax: 01548 843568
e-mail: gallery@covesquay.co.uk
website: www.covesquay.co.uk

Located on a quiet quay in the beautiful town of Salcombe, **Coves Quay Gallery** has gained an enviable local and international reputation for showing and selling high-quality contemporary art from both up and coming and established West Country artists. Specialising in paintings, drawings, engravings, sculpture and ceramics, the constantly changing displays offer visitors an opportunity to view the work of artists rarely seen outside Devon and Cornwall. Guided by gallery director Mandy de

Looking out to Sea, Oil - John Brenton

Haan, assistant Judith Newman and artistic consultant Bobbi Fulcher-Smith, the gallery has built a creative network for artists through interior designers, corporate hire and private commissions.

Artists whose work can be seen in the Gallery include Lucy Pratt, Gary Long, June Arnold, John Brenton, Sue Lewington,, Michael Hill, penny McBreen, Nigel Hallard, Joy Nunn, David Rust, Bobbi Fulcher-Smith, Ernie and Gahan Oliver, Nigel Legge, Jenny Wright, Jenny Phillips, Eric Saxby, Tom Gange, Eric Ward, Charlie Baird, Robert Jones and CJ van Dop. Coves Quay Gallery is open daily throughout the year or by private appointment.

Day Sailing, Oil - Gary Long

disease was still common in England. Perhaps by dedicating their church to St Sylvester the villagers thought to protect themselves from a disease that meant total social exclusion for its victims.

SALCOMBE
3½ miles S of Kingsbridge on the A381

Standing at the mouth of the Kingsbridge 'estuary', this delightful town enjoys one of

Salcombe

the most beautiful natural settings in the country. Sheltered from the prevailing west winds by steep hills, the town basks in one of the mildest micro-climates in England. Like many other small ports along the southwest coast, Salcombe developed its own special area of trading. While Dartmouth specialised in French and Spanish wine, clipper ships brought the first fruits of the West Indies' pineapple harvest and oranges from the Azores to Salcombe. Although all that traffic has now ceased, the harbour throngs with pleasure craft and the small fishing fleet operates from **Batson Creek**, a picturesque location where the fish quay is piled high with lobster creels.

To the south of the town lies **Overbecks Museum and Garden**, a charming Edwardian house built in 1913 for Captain George Vereker. After his death, it was bought by the research chemist, Otto Overbeck, who lived here between 1918 and 1937. Now in the care of the National Trust, the house holds Otto Overbeck's wide ranging collection, including late-19th century photographs of the area, local shipbuilding tools, model boats, toys and much more. The beautiful, sheltered garden, with views out over Salcombe estuary, is planted with many rare trees, shrubs and plants, giving it a Mediterranean feel.

Much of the coastline around Salcombe, both east and west, is owned by the National Trust. A network of footpaths and the **South Devon Way** bring walkers to this beautiful stretch of

---

coastline, where there are also some interesting archaeological sites. Out towards **Prawle Point**, the southernmost tip of Devon, there is a circular stone lookout hut, ancient field boundaries and defensive earthworks. Birdwatchers here might be lucky enough to see cirl buntings, grasshopper and wood warblers, wryneck, yellow wagtail or other rare warblers, flycatchers or raptors. To the west, the rugged coastline has a long maritime history as well as being an area rich in both flora and fauna. Just inland, situated between Salcombe and Hope, is the pretty village of **Malborough**, whose lofty 15th century church spire is a well-known local landmark.

Salcombe Castle

HOPE COVE

5 miles SW of Kingsbridge off the A381

There are two Hopes here: the more modern Outer Hope and Inner Hope, one of the most photographed villages in the country. A picturesque huddle of thatched cottages around a tiny cobbled square, Inner Hope was once a thriving pilchard fishing village and, today, a few fishermen still land lobster and crab here.

BANTHAM

4½ miles W of Kingsbridge off the A379

This small village was once a centre of early tin trading between the ancient Britons and the Gauls. By the 8th century, Saxons were farming here. The sea has also provided a major source of income for the village and, during the boom years of the pilchard fishing industry, a fleet of fishing boats landed their catches here. Bantham continued to be a busy little port until the early 20th century with sailing barges bringing coal and building stone for the surrounding area.

BIGBURY ON SEA

5½ miles W of Kingsbridge on the B3392

Just off the shore of this popular family resort is

Bolt Tail, nr Hope

Burgh Island, Bigbury on Sea

Archibald Nettlefold. The extravagant Art Deco hotel that he built attracted many visitors including Noël Coward, the Duke of Windsor and Mrs Wallis Simpson and Agatha Christie. The Queen of Crime used the island as the setting for two of her novels: *And Then There Were None* and *Evil Under The Sun*.

AVETON GIFFORD

3 miles NW of Kingsbridge on the A379

Burgh Island, which is an island only at high tide. When the tide recedes, it can be reached by walking across the sandbank or by taking an exciting ride on the Sea Tractor. The whole of this 28-acre island, complete with its 14th century Pilchard Inn, was bought in 1929 by the eccentric millionaire

This pleasant village (whose name is pronounced 'Awton Jiffard') had one of the oldest churches in Devon until 1943 when it was almost completely destroyed by a German bomb. There are few buildings in this tiny village and certainly there are none as grand as those designed by Aveton Gifford's most

COURT BARTON FARM

Aveton Gifford, Nr Kingsbridge, South Devon TQ7 4LE
Tel: 01548 550312 Fax: 01548 559165
e-mail: info@courtbarton.freeserve.co.uk

There's a delightful family atmosphere at **Court Barton Farm**, which is the home of Jeremy and Jackie Harmer and their children Oliver and Rosie. The heart of the farm is a 16th century stone farmhouse where they offer bed & breakfast accommodation in three beautifully furnished en suite bedrooms with TV/video, tea/coffee-making facilities and thoughtful touches like fluffy dressing gowns. Behind the farmhouse, a 100-year-old stone barn has been stylishly converted into three luxury holiday cottages - the Old Stables, the Dairy and the Grain Store.

All the cottages have two bedrooms on the ground floor, ample lounge and dining space and

comprehensively equipped kitchens with oven, hob, microwave, dishwasher, washing machine and dryer. Oil-fired central heating keeps things cosy, and logs are supplied for the log burning stoves. There's ample parking space for each cottage, and front and rear patios with garden furniture and barbecue equipment. The family keep ponies, ducks, chickens and guinea pigs, and guests are free to roam in the eight acres of grounds with gardens, fields, paddocks and a duck pond. Footpaths and bridle paths are all around, Kingsbridge is only four miles away, and it's just four miles to the lovely Bantham Beach.

PLANTATION HOUSE HOTEL

Totnes Road, Ermington, Devon PL21 9NS
Tel: 01548 831100
e-mail: alancoby@aol.com
website: www.plantationhousehotel.com

An 18th century rectory just 2 miles from the A38 has established itself as one of the very best eating places in the region as well as a comfortable, welcoming hotel. Matisse Restaurant, whose walls are adorned with the vibrant colours of the eponymous artist, is served by a kitchen team of outstanding talent. Knowledgeable serving staff and a splendid wine list add to the memorable experience. Dinner at Matisse features local fish and seafood, duck and beef, and the lighter lunch menu tempts with such delights as crab bisque and a cheese soufflé made with local Vulscombe goat's cheese. Regular events include wine evenings (five courses with a different wine for each) and seven-course Club evenings.

The 12 spacious, stylishly furnished bedrooms, some with access for disabled guests, offer full en suite facilities, room service, tea/coffee makers, television and telephone with internet access. Breakfast is served in Matisse or out in the courtyard in the summer months, with a Continental breakfast available from room service. The Plantation Room is ideal for relaxing with the morning papers, chatting with friends over coffee or just sitting back and enjoying the views from the terrace; the Bar is open all day for tea, coffee and drinks.

famous son, Robert Macey. Born here in 1790, Macey first learnt his father's trade of stone masonry before training as an architect. He then walked all the way to London, where he successfully established himself and was responsible for designing many hospitals, factories, churches and theatres including, most notably, the Adelphi and the Haymarket Theatres.

To the east of Aveton Gifford lies the village of **Loddiswell** that, after the Norman Conquest, became part of the estate of Judhel of Totnes who had an insatiable appetite for salmon. Instead of rent, Judhel insisted that his tenants should provide him with a certain number of salmon and Loddiswell's contribution was a set of 30 salmon a year. The benign climate of the region has encouraged several wine-growers to plant vineyards in the area and the first vines at the **Loddiswell Vineyard** were planted in 1977.

NEWTON ABBOT

This ancient market town on the southern bank of the River Teign was the place where, in 1688, William, Prince of Orange, the 'glorious defender of the Protestant religion', was proclaimed King William III. This Glorious Revolution took place in front of the town's St Leonard's Church, of which only the tower remains today. The new king had landed earlier at nearby Brixham, and while in the town, on his way to London, he stayed at the handsome Jacobean manor house, **Forde House**, which is now used as council offices.

The whole character of this attractive town changed in the 1850s when the Great Western Railway made it their centre of locomotive and carriage repair works as well as the junction for the Moretonhampstead and Torbay branch lines. Tidy terraces of artisans' houses

Twelve Oaks Holiday Cottages

Twelve Oaks Farm, Teigngrace, Newton Abbot,
Devon TQ12 6QT   Tel: 01626 352769
website: www.twelveoaksfarm.co.uk

Twelve Oaks Holiday Cottages are located on a 250-acre
working farm specialising in Charolais beef cattle. The Gale
family have converted farm buildings into two very roomy
and comfortable adjacent holiday homes, Acorns and Oak
Leaves. Each has two bedrooms, two bathrooms and an
open-plan living room with dining and kitchen areas - pine kitchen units in Acorns, oak units in Oak
Leaves. They also have their own patio areas, and there's a heated swimming pool. The farm stands on
the edge of the village of Teigngrace bordered by the River Teign.

were built along the steep hillsides in the southern areas of Newton Abbot while, to the north are the Italianate villas of the well-to-do. To the south of town is a delightful attraction in the shape of the **Hedgehog Hospital** at Prickly Hill Farm - where else?

On the northern outskirts of the town lies **Newton Abbot Racecourse**, where National Hunt racing takes place from the autumn through to the spring. For the rest of the year, greyhound races, stock car races and country fairs are held.

To the west is a small medieval manor house, **Bradley**, surrounded by woodland and meadows. Incorporating parts of an earlier building, the 15th century hall house contains painted Tudor decoration and carving and some superb 17th century plasterwork. It is a wonderful example of domestic architecture. The house was given to the National Trust in 1938 by the then owner, Mrs AH Woolner, and her family continue to live here and manage the property.

AROUND NEWTON ABBOT

Chudleigh
5½ miles N of Newton Abbot off the A38

Once on the main road between Exeter and Plymouth, the construction of a

bypass in the 1960s significantly reduced the almost unbearable levels of traffic that were particularly heavy through the town during the summer season. It was here, at a coaching house, that William of Orange stayed on his journey to London and addressed the people of Chudleigh from one of the inn's upstairs windows. The Dutchman's English was so bad that his audience was unable to understand what he was saying though they clapped and cheered him all the same. Another royal visitor was Madame Royale, daughter of Louis XIV and Marie Antoinette, who sought shelter in the town after her parents were executed.

Clifford Street is named after Sir Thomas Clifford, Lord Treasurer to Charles II and a member of the king's notorious Cabal, his secretive inner cabinet. As was common at that time, Sir Thomas used his official position to amass a huge fortune. This was later put to good use by his grandson who employed Robert Adams and Capability Brown to design **Ugbrooke House and Park** to the south of the town. Dating from the mid-18th century and replacing an early Tudor manor house, Ugbrooke House is named after the Ug Brook that flows through the estate and that was dammed to create three lakes in the beautifully landscaped grounds. In the 1930s the 11th Lord Clifford left the

GLEN COTTAGE

Rock Road, Chudleigh, Devon TQ13
Tel/Fax: 01626 852209

For the past 20 years Jill Shears has been offering bed & breakfast accommodation at **Glen Cottage**, and many of her guests return year after year to enjoy her hospitality, the quiet seclusion and the lovely surrounding countryside. The substantial thatched dwelling started life as a counting house for the local quarry and is of a most unusual design, reaching up four storeys. Old beams and stonework are in evidence throughout, and the bedrooms - twins, doubles and a family room - combine comfort and character.

Guests have the use of a lounge with TV, and a full English breakfast is served in a bright dining room (optional evening meal by arrangement) that looks out on to Chudleigh Rock, where there are rocks, caves and waterfalls to explore and a varied wildlife to watch. Glen Cottage stands in four delightful acres of lovely woodland garden that is home to otters and many species of birds. Sporting guests will find riding and fishing facilities nearby, and the ancient wool town of Chudleigh is also well worth exploring with its shops and eating places and its thriving craft centre.

estate as he could not afford to live there. During World War II, Ugbrooke was used as a school for evacuated children and a hostel for Poles, while in the 1950s some of the ground floor rooms were used to store grain. Today, the house has been beautifully restored by the present Lord and Lady Clifford and is noted for its collections of paintings, dolls, military uniforms and furniture.

KENTON

10 miles NE of Newton Abbot on the A379

Founded in Saxon times, this picturesque village is famed for its glorious 14th century church whose tower, standing over 100 feet tall, is decorated with a wonderful assortment of ornate carvings. But it is **Powderham Castle**, to the east of the village, which brings people to this particularly part of Devon. Set in one of the finest deer parks in Devon beside the River Exe, the castle has been

the home of the Courtney family, the earls of Devon, since 1390, although the present building dates mostly from the 18th century. Along with the breathtaking grand staircase and impressive marble hall, the castle is home to many family portraits, including some by the Devon- born painter Sir Joshua Reynolds, and a longcase clock by Stumbels of Totnes that plays a tune at 4, 8 and 12 o'clock.

DAWLISH

7½ miles NE of Newton Abbot on the A379

Up until the beginning of the 19th century, Dawlish was a small settlement along the banks of the River Daw. Around a mile inland, it was protected from seaborne raiders. As early as 1803, Regency villas were being built along the Strand as the village was developed into a pretty seaside resort. Right from those early days, Dawlish attracted many distinguished visitors, particularly writers and poets including Jane Austen, John Keats and Charles Dickens, who, in his novel of the same name, had Nicholas Nickleby born at a farm near the town. By the time that Brunel's Great Western Railway arrived here in 1846, the town was already well known as a fashionable resort. The safe beach is now separated from the rest of the town by the railway line. This is much more appealing than it sounds as the line keeps traffic away from the beach. The arches of the viaduct carrying the track have attractively weathered over the years and provide a formal entrance to the beach. Displays at **Dawlish Museum** include collections of china, prints, toys and dolls, industrial tools and early surgical instruments, the last donated by a retired local doctor. The town's Victorian station is another interesting visitor attraction. The River Daw still flows through Dawlish though it has been beautified by early improvers who landscaped the stream into a series of shallow waterfalls and surrounded it with attractive gardens.

To the northeast of the town is **Dawlish Warren**, a sand spit that almost blocks the mouth of the River Exe. As well as the golf course, this is a Nature Reserve that is home to more than 450 species of flowering plant including the Jersey Lily, which is not found elsewhere on mainland Britain.

Further north again, at **Starcross**, the last surviving relics of Brunel's **Atmospheric Railway** can be seen. The engineer had intended that the railway between Exeter and Totnes should be powered by a revolutionary new system incorporating a third rail. This would be a long vacuum chamber, which would draw the carriages along by air pressure. His visionary plan also involved the building of ten great Italianate engine houses at three-mile intervals along the line. Unfortunately the project failed, partly due to a lack of finance and partly due to the effects of rain, salt and hungry rats on the leather seals of the vacuum pipes. However, at the exhibition at Starcross there is a working model of the 'new' railway system using vacuum cleaners as the engine houses. It takes volunteers up and down a track to show the viability of such a system. Despite having to fall back on more conventional methods of pulling his carriages, the track that Brunel laid between Exeter and Totnes is one of the most scenic in the country.

TEIGNMOUTH
5½ miles NE of Newton Abbot on the A379

There are two distinct sides to this town – the popular holiday resort and the working port – and these two parts seldom meet. On the coastal side of Teignmouth is the seaside resort, with its two-mile long sandy beach, promenade and pier, which draws many visitors throughout the year. The fine Regency and Georgian residential buildings add a touch of elegance while also of note are the **Church of St James**, with its striking octagonal tower of 1820, and the former **Assembly Rooms**, a colonnaded building housing the Riviera Camera. However, the rather fetching 25-foot-high lighthouse serves no real purpose at all.

On the northern bank of the River Teign, the working port is reached by a narrow channel with currents so fast and powerful that boats can only enter the harbour with a Trinity House pilot on board. **The Quay** was built in 1821 from granite taken from the quarries at Haytor Down. This durable stone was used throughout the country but most notably at the British Museum, London. Destroyed by the French in 1690, Teignmouth was once again in the front

TURN OF THE TIDE

7 The Triangle, Teignmouth, Devon TQ14 8AU
Tel: 01626 777455
e-mail: sal@andersons5.fsnet.co.uk
web: www.turnofthetide.net

In a pedestrian area very close to the seafront, **Turn of the Tide** is a bright modern gallery owned and run by James Joyce and Sally Anderson. Since opening

in October 2000, it has built up a fine reputation for the high quality of the artists it showcases. Visitors can spend many a happy hour browsing and choosing from the ever-changing displays of paintings, prints, cards, ceramics, jewellery, glass, stained glass, woodcarvings and sculptures produced by some of the finest contemporary artists in Devon and Cornwall. These include paintings by Robert Jones, Michael Praed, Caroline Atkinson and Sally Anderson; Glass by Lesley and Norman Stuart Clarke; Pots and ceramics by Louise Thorn, Carol Scott and Adrian Brough; Jewellery by C.J VanDop, Esther Filcher, Heather Mills, Hilary Bravo and many others.

Turn of the Tide is another good reason to visit the popular holiday resort and working port of Teignmouth with its long sandy beaches, promenade and pier, its natural harbour- where you can watch the fishing boats come and go- and its delightful Regency and Georgian houses.

line when, during the World War II, 75 people were killed in German bombing raids.

On the opposite bank of the Teign estuary lies **Shaldon**. From the Marine Parade here, there are excellent views of the busy traffic sailing up and down the river. There are also several attractive Regency houses that are a reminder of the times when affluent Londoners, unable to holiday in a Napoleon-dominated Europe, began to discover the delights of England's south coast. Just north of the town lies the **Shaldon Wildlife Trust's** breeding centre for rare small mammals, reptiles and exotic birds.

TORQUAY

6 miles SE of Newton Abbot on the A3022

Torquay's oldest building is **Torre Abbey**, founded in 1195 and largely remodelled as a Georgian mansion by the Cary family in the first half of the 18th century. Within the grounds of the house are some abbey remains and the religious house's medieval tithe barn, called the **Spanish Barn** after nearly 400 prisoners from the Spanish Armada were detained here in 1588. Sold to Torbay Council in the 1930s, the house and gardens are open to the public and the principal reception rooms house a collection of paintings, silver, porcelain and glass.

During the 19th century, Torquay became a genteel resort, with some imposing hotels. Like Rome, spread across seven hills, it became known as 'The English Naples'. The undisputed premier resort of southwest England, Torquay enjoyed royal patronage. Edward VII came here on the royal yacht *Britannia*, which anchored in the bay, and each evening he would discreetly travel to the Imperial Hotel to his waiting mistress, Lily Langtree.

Coastline at Babbacombe, nr Torquay

Still a very popular and elegant resort, Torquay is best known as being the birthplace, in 1890, of Agatha Mary Clarissa Miller (later Agatha Christie). She lived here until after her first failed marriage in 1914. Agatha came back here in 1916 while her second husband Colonel Archie Christie was on active service in World War I and it was while here that she began her first crime novel. However, it was not until 1926 and the publication of *The Murder of Roger Ackroyd* that Agatha found fame as a writer. Her disappearance a few months later in Harrogate and a nervous breakdown followed but she went on to marry again. In 1938, she moved to the country house Greenway that overlooks the River Dart. One of the town's most popular attractions can be found in the Abbot's Tower at Torre Abbey which houses the **Agatha Christie Memorial Room** where a wonderfully personal collection of her memorabilia, donated by her daughter, is on display. Along with her 1937 Remington typewriter, on which she wrote all her novels, short stories and plays, the rooms contains manuscripts, letters and a photograph taken in 1973 on the occasion of the 21st anniversary of her play *The Mousetrap*, still running in London today.

At the **Torquay Museum**, an exhibition of photographs records the life of Dame Agatha Christie as well as providing a pictorial record of Torquay over the last 150 years. Amongst the museum's treasures are many items discovered at **Kents Cavern**, a complex of caves that were first excavated in the 1820s and from where an amazing collection of animals bones (all that remains of mammoths, sabre-toothed tigers, grizzly bears, bison and cave lions) were extracted. It was believed the caves were the homes of cave dwellers some 30,000 years ago. This makes them the oldest known residences in Europe.

Just to the north of the centre of Torquay is **Babbacombe Model Village** created by Tom Dobbins. As well as over

THE POTTERY (ANN SAWARD)

Cockington Court, Cockington, Torquay, Devon TQ2 6XA
Tel: 01803 607773
e-mail: annsaward_thepottery@yahoo.co.uk

Ann Saward has been producing hand-thrown high-fired stoneware pottery since 1978, and after 21 years of selling by way of exhibition and gallery outlets she and her husband David set up a new pottery at Cockington. Largely self-taught, with the freedom to develop her own style and ideas, she produces an extensive range of wheel-thrown stoneware, from large candlesticks and unique table lamps to a wide variety of items for the home, kitchen and table including distinctive bowls and dishes. Basic glazes in ivory and rich blues and greens are enhanced with brushed-on oxides that give a subtle selection of colours to suit the most individual of decors.

Each piece is a signed original, and all the pottery is ovenproof and dishwasher and microwave safe. David's role is primarily that of technician and providing essential back-up, but he also enjoys producing his own special slab-built dishes. Visitors can browse at leisure among the attractive sales displays and also watch the many and varied processes involved in making the pots. 65 countries are represented in the visitors' book, and a shipping service is available. The Pottery is located in the original Tudor kitchen of Cockington Court, which stands in a 450-acre Country Park with woodland walks, an arboretum, rose garden and organic kitchen garden.

400 beautifully crafted models, many with amusing names such as Shortback and Sydes (the barbers), Walter Wall (carpets) and Jim Nastick (health farm),the village also has delightful gardens, with 500 types of dwarf conifers, a model railway and an ornamental lake.

Just a mile or so west of the resort is the pretty rural village of **Cockington**, an idyllic place of thatched cottages whose village pub, the Drum Inn, was designed by Sir Edward Lutyens and first opened in 1930. A short walk from here is **Cockington Court**, a part Tudor manor house that was, for almost 300 years, the home of the Mallock family but is now a Craft Centre and Gallery. In the 1930s a trust was formed to preserve the village and this has been wonderfully successful over the years.

Paignton, Brixham and Torquay form **Torbay**, the most extensive conurbation

in Devon, strung out along the sweep of Tor Bay. Superb beaches and a wealth of leisure activities have made this the county's busiest resort area. Paignton prides itself on being an unbeatable family resort, while Brixham is an enchanting fishing town where life still revolves around its busy harbour.

PAIGNTON

7 miles SE of Torquay on the A379

In the early Victorian era this was a little farming village, noted for its cider. The village's two superb sandy beaches and the development of Torquay saw Paignton become a resort, complete with pier and promenade, which still appeals today, particularly to families. One of the main attractions here **Paignton Zoo**, set in beautiful botanic gardens and home to some 300 species of animals from around the world, is dedicated to protecting and conserving endangered species. Asiatic lions and Sumatran tigers are seen in their own forest habitat and the orang-utans and gorillas roam freely on large outdoor islands. A journey around the zoo can be taken on the Jungle Express miniature railway offering good views of these and the many other animals.

A train journey of a different kind can be enjoyed on the **Paignton and Dartmouth Steam Railway**,

Paignton Harbour

following the coastline along the bottom of Tor Bay before travelling through the wooded slopes that border the Dart estuary to Kingswear. Here passengers alight and catch a ferry to Dartmouth. The locomotives and carriages all bear the chocolate and gold livery of Brunel's Great Western Railway and, on certain services, passengers can dine in luxurious Pullman style on the Riviera Belle Dining Train.

Situated just south of the centre of the town, on Goodrington Sands, is **Quaywest**, which claims to be Britain's "biggest, best, wildest and wettest waterpark". Along with its hairy water slides, there are numerous other amusements such as go-karts, bumper boats and crazy golf as well as bars, restaurants and cafés.

The town's most interesting building is undoubtedly **Oldway Mansion**, built in 1874 for Isaac Singer, the millionaire sewing machine manufacturer. Unfortunately, Isaac died just a year after the mansion was completed and it was his son, Paris, who gave the house its exuberant form. The south side mimics a music pavilion found in the grounds of Versailles and a hallway is modelled on Versailles' Hall of Mirrors. In the sumptuous ballroom Paris's mistress,

Isadora Duncan, would display the new method of dancing that she had created based on the dances of classical mythology. Sold to Paignton's Borough Council in 1946, the mansion is now a Civic Centre, but many of the rooms and the grounds are open to the public.

BRIXHAM

10½ miles SE of Newton Abbot on the A3022

The most southerly of the three towns that make up the great Torbay conurbation, Brixham was, in the 18th century, the most profitable fishing port in Britain. Fishing is still the most important activity in this little town although the fishing fleet has to pick its way through flotillas of yachts and tour boats. On the quay, the stalls sell the boats' daily catch, fresh from the sea, and around the harbour, in the maze of narrow streets, is a host of small shops, restaurants, tearooms and galleries.

William, Prince of Orange, landed here in 1688 to claim the British throne as William III. And in 1815 the ship *Bellerophon* anchored in the bay providing Napoleon with his closest view of England before he was transferred to the *Northumberland* for his journey to his final exile on St Helena. Brixham has one more claim to fame: the vicar of All

Brixham

colonies of seabirds such as fulmars, kittiwakes and guillemots nest on the cliffsides.

This headland is also associated with one of the many flying saucer sightings that have occurred around the world. In April 1967, a mysterious object was reported hovering for about an hour just a couple of thousand feet over ahead. Described as a huge, dome-shaped object with a door on one side, the UFO eventually gained height rapidly and disappeared.

Saints' Church, Henry Francis Lyte, composed one of England's best loved hymns – *Abide with Me* – during his last illness in 1847.

At only 15 feet high, Brixham's lighthouse has been called the "highest and lowest lighthouse in Britain" because it stands at the top of the 200-foot cliffs at the most easterly point of **Berry Head**. The lighthouse lies within **Berry Head Country Park**, noted for its incredible views. From here, on a clear day, Portland Bill can be seen 46 miles away. The park is home to rare plants, such as the white rock-rose, while

KINGSWEAR
13 miles SE of Newton Abbot on the B3205

Situated on the steeply rising east bank of the River Dart, Kingswear has panoramic views of Dartmouth stretching out across the hillside on the opposite riverbank. Kingswear is also the terminus of the Paignton and Dartmouth Steam Railway and passengers alight here to catch a ferry over the water to Dartmouth. There is a car ferry, too.

Above the town stand the impressive remains of **Kingswear Castle**, built as a

NETHWAY FARM HOLIDAY COTTAGES

Broad Street, Kingswear, Nr Dartmouth, South Devon TQ6 0EE
Tel: 01803 752477

In a secluded rural setting on a working farm, **Nethway Farm Holiday Cottages** occupy a charming group of stone barns, skilfully converted using traditional materials. Sleeping from four to six, they are all comfortably and tastefully furnished and comprehensively equipped for self-catering. Shared amenities include a landscaped garden, an indoor pool and sauna, indoor and outdoor play areas and a fishing lake, and young guests can help fed the farm animals. The sea is only a mile away, and the coast and countryside provide wonderful walks and plenty of activities.

twin to Dartmouth Castle to guard the entrance into the Dart estuary. It was between these two castles that a huge iron chain was strung when there was thought to be an added threat of invasion.

To the northeast of the town lies **Coleton Fishacre House and Garden**, a wonderful house designed in the 1920s for Rupert and Lady Dorothy D'Oyle Carte (of Gilbert & Sullivan fame) who went on create the magnificent coastal garden that basks in the mild climate of south Devon. With a wonderful array of exotic and rare plants, these gardens contain formal arrangements, wooded areas with wild flowers and water features.

GALMPTON
9½ miles SE of Newton Abbot off the A3022

Dame Agatha Christie moved here to the eastern banks of the River Dart for the last 30 years of her life. Her house and estate, **Greenway**, is still lived in by her daughter. While the house is not open to the public, the gardens are occasionally open in aid of the National Gardens Scheme.

COMPTON
4 miles S of Newton Abbot off the A380

This village is home to **Compton Castle**, a wonderful fortified manor house built between the 14th and the 16th centuries and home to the Gilbert family for almost all of the last 600 years. A half-brother to Sir Walter Raleigh, Sir Humphrey Gilbert was a coloniser of Newfoundland in the 16th century (see under Modbury). It was shortly before this that the manor house was fortified during the reign of Henry VIII. Restored in the 20th century, Compton remains a rare example of a late medieval manor house. It is still occupied by the Gilbert

family although now owned by the National Trust.

BERRY POMEROY
6½ miles S of Newton Abbot off the A381

Arriving with William the Conqueror in 1066, the de la Pomerais family came to this village and held lands here for almost 500 years. In the early 14th century, the dynasty built **Berry Pomeroy Castle** on a wooded promontory above Gatcombe Brook and the remains can still be seen there today. In 1548, the Pomeroys, as they had become known, sold the estate to Sir Edward Seymour, the brother of Jane who had been the third wife of Henry VIII. He built a mansion within the medieval castle but this, too, is now a shell. The castle is still owned by a descendant of Sir Edward, the Duke of Somerset, and is administered by English Heritage.

Several local legends revolve around the castle and the ancient Pomeroy family who lived here. It is said that for their part in the religious rebellion in 1549, Edward VI ordered that their castle's fortifications be greatly reduced. The Pomeroy family would not obey the order and, when troops arrived to enforce the king's decree, two brothers rode over the castle's ramparts to their death. Another story concerns two Pomeroy sisters, Eleanor and Margaret, who were in love with the same man. Eleanor, jealous of her beautiful sister, imprisoned Margaret and starved her to death. Margaret's ghost is said to haunt the castle ruins.

TOTNES
7½ miles SW of Newton Abbot on the A385

Claiming to be the second oldest borough in England, Totnes sent its first member of Parliament to London in

THE CONKER SHOE COMPANY

28 High Street, Totnes, Devon TQ9 5RY
Tel: 01803 862490 Fax: 01803 866457
e-mail: info@conkershoes.com
website: www.conkershoes.com

The Conker Shoe Company recently completed 25 years of shoemaking excellence, building and maintaining an enviable reputation for quality and customer service. The Company's light, spacious shop is situated a short walk up from the East Gate Arch in the

heart of old Totnes, and

it is here that partners Guy Metcalfe and Prem Ash run the production as well as the sales.

Originally serving a niche market with bright and multi-coloured shoes, the majority of the 4,000 pairs of shoes and boots made each year are now being ordered in supple blacks and browns, rich burgundy, dark green or navy. As Conkers became synonymous with quality, comfort and good service the customer base extended to whole families.

Shoe sizes range from small child size 5 to adult size 13. Four standard widths can be bought off the shelf, though a large part of the workload involves slightly modified fittings. The friendly and efficient service at Conkers means that customers are treated as individuals, each with his or her own fitting needs. A modified fit, to accommodate longer toes, small bunions, higher insteps etc, costs only a few pounds more than a standard fit, and, as the records show, most customers re-order over and over again.

For customers not able to visit the shop in person, the company offers a mail order purchasing service through the catalogue or by e-mail. The beautifully produced catalogue contains the full range illustrated and even has instructions showing customers how to submit their own foot drawings. It also cites satisfied customers as comparing their Conkers to

such cherished possessions as a Gibson guitar, a Waterman pen or a Zippo lighter – praise indeed! Besides the shoes, the shop also carries a wide range of designer clothing,

leather goods (cases, handbags, purses, belts) and everything needed to keep Conkers looking good.

Through the glass doors at the back of the shop customers can see the dedicated Conker team hard at work making the shoes; the 19th century workshop is thought to stand on the site of an earlier theatre.

THE OLD FORGE AT TOTNES

Seymour Place, Totnes, Devon TQ9 5AY
Tel: 01803 862174 e-mail: enq@oldforgetotnes.com
Fax: 01803 865385 website: www.oldforgetotnes.com

A warm welcome awaits visitors to **The Old Forge at Totnes**, where cosy, cottage-style bedrooms provide bed & breakfast accommodation that is both comfortable and full of character. All rooms have en suite or private facilities, TV, telephone, beverage trays and many thoughtful extras. A cottage suite is suitable for up to six people, and the Courtroom suite has the unusual amenity of private roof garden. The Old Forge, which dates back 600 years, has a residents' lounge, a conservatory and a delightful walled garden, and the day starts with an excellent breakfast.

1295 and, in 1359, it elected the first of its nearly 650 mayors. However, according to local legends and the fanciful *History of the Kings of Britain,* written by the 12th century chronicler Geoffrey of Monmouth, Totnes has a much older heritage. It is said to have been founded by a Trojan named Brutus in around 1200 BC. Brutus, the grandfather of Aeneas, the hero of Virgil's epic poem *The Aeneid*, supposedly sailed up the River Dart and decided to found the first town in this new country. The name Britain is also supposed to come from his name. The **Brutus Stone**, in the pavement of the town's main shopping street, commemorates this event

However, the first recorded evidence of a settlement set high on the hill above the highest navigable point on the River Dart was made in the mid-10th century

ESHO FUNI INTERIORS

Warlands, Totnes, Devon TQ9 5EL
Tel: 01803 862010

Tucked away just off the main street of Totnes, **Esho Funi Interiors** is a shop full of interest, a wonderful little bazaar of a place with a stock of beautiful and unusual goods and gifts gathered from all over the world. Behind the pretty facade, painted white with red for the sign and woodwork and adorned by flower displays, the shop is the reflection of the style and flair of owner Suzanne Sayer, Her eye for design, so splendidly illustrated and widely admired in her own home, inspired her to open a shop filled with the fabrics and colours that she loves, and Esho Funi is the result. Her serene outlook on life is very evident in the look and the ambience of the shop, and even in its very name, which translates as 'our inner being outwardly reflected'. Anyone looking for something that's both beautiful and a little out of the ordinary will certainly find it among the furniture and fabrics, the lamps and mirrors, the silver jewellery and glassware, the pictures and prints, the bags, the cushions and the lovely bejewelled bedspreads.

Suzanne has plans to open a shop with her son in London's Portobello Road.

THE BEAR SHOP

94 High Street, The Narrows, Totnes, Devon TQ9 5SN
Tel: 01803 866868 Fax: 01803 866086
e-mail: bear.shop@tinyworld.co.uk
website: www.bear-shop.co,uk

Never having quite recovered from the loss of his childhood teddy bear companions, James Sturges opened **The Bear Shop** in Totnes in 1992. The initial stock comprised about 200 bears, but by 1999 expansion necessitated a move to larger premises and now there are upwards of 1,000

teddies in residence. The Bear Shop is also a Steiff Shop within a shop, as the aristocratic Steiff bears are very much the speciality.

The shop carries a wide range of regular and limited Steiff items both current and from past years and are ready with help and advice for anyone looking for a particular Steiff bear. James and his wife Norissa also stock teddy Hermann, Hermann Spielwaren, Merrythought, Deans, Boyds and Gund – all the elite of Teddyworld, as well as the very popular Artist bears and the occasional old bear, though good old bears are almost becoming an endangered species. The highlight of the year at The Bear Shop is the main Steiff Event, where a good time is had by all in the shop and in a local hostelry.

PAPERWORKS

63 High Street, Totnes, Devon TQ9 5PB
Tel: 01803 867009 Fax: 01803 866515
e-mail: shop@paperworkstotnes.com

Unusual and hand-made paper and stationery is the stock in trade of **PaperWorks**, owned and run by partners Heidrun and David Guest. It is a paradise for lovers of paper and original design, with an amazing range of papers for all kinds of art, craft and decorative use. This unique and fascinating High Street shop, fronted by Heidrun's colourful and often witty window displays, also sells greetings cards, gift wrap and decorated stationery as well as a wide selection of paper-related gifts and craft materials. A place made for browsing and enjoying the wealth of colour and visual stimulation on offer.

THE TOTNES WINE COMPANY

36 High Street, Totnes, Devon TQ9 5RY
Tel: 01803 866357 website: www.totneswine.co.uk

On the main street of town, **Totnes Wine Company** is a private wine merchant owned by the Pound family and managed by the very experienced Nigel Pound. Totnes Wine specialises in small wine estates from throughout the wine-producing world; most of the wines are exclusive to the company in the South West and for many they are the sole UK stockist. Quality and reliability have long been the hallmarks of the Totnes Wine Company, and the enthusiastic team is always ready with expert advice. Tastings, tutorials and wine events are held on a regular basis, and the company has a nationwide delivery service.

when King Edgar established a mint here. There was already a Saxon castle here but the impressive remains of **Totnes Castle** are of the once imposing Norman fortification that towered over the town and that is generally recognised to be the best preserved motte and bailey castle in Devon. Along with the castle, a substantial proportion of the town's medieval walls still remain and the superb **East Gate**, which straddles the main street, has been meticulously restored after being damaged by a fire in 1990. Close by is the charming **Guildhall** of 1553 that, today, houses both the town's council chamber and the now redundant town gaol.

Almost directly across the street is another magnificent Elizabethan building, constructed in 1585 for Nicholas Bell who had made his fortune from the local pilchard fishing industry. On his death, his wife Anne married Sir Thomas Bodley and it was the profit from the pilchards that funded the world famous Bodleian Library at Oxford University. However, Totnes' Elizabethan heritage really comes alive during the summer when, on Tuesday mornings, the people dress up in Elizabethan white ruffs and velvet gowns for a charity market that has, over the years, raised thousands of pounds for charity.

For centuries, Totnes was a busy river port and, down by the elegant stone structure of Totnes Bridge, the quayside was lined with warehouses. Some of these survive today, converted into desirable flats and town houses. Nearby, on the Plains, stands a granite obelisk to the famous explorer William Wills, a Totnes man who died from starvation while attempting to recross the Australian desert with Robert Burke in 1861.

The town had a booming cloth industry, once second only in

MARSHALL ARTS GALLERY

3 Warland, Totnes, Devon TQ9 5EL
Tel: 01803 863533
e-mail: annette@marshallartsgallery.co.uk
website: www.marshallartsgallery.co.uk

The spacious **Marshall Arts Gallery** is a breath of fresh air, an oasis of calm just off the bustling main street of Totnes. It offers a wide variety of carefully chosen contemporary art and craft from around Britain. Collections include ceramics both functional and sculptural, jewellery, wood, metalwork, textiles, glass, automata, paintings and original prints. These are complemented by a selection of inexpensive and stylish gifts, housewares and stationery. Owners Annette Vaitkus and Kevin Bunclark are assiduous in choosing work for the gallery, picking items for their individuality, quality and good design.

The result is a delightfully eclectic collection featuring some of the country's most talented artists and designer-makers. The overall look is harmonious, stylish and slightly whimsical; many of the pieces are gently humorous, and there is a subtle nautical theme to much of the work. Prices range from a few pounds to a few thousand. Special exhibitions are held twice a year, giving a fresh look to the gallery and introducing new work. Opening hours are 10am to 5.30pm Monday to Saturday. Marshall Arts Gallery is at the lower end of Totnes, near the river and one street back from The Plains. There's plenty of parking nearby.

FIFTH ELEMENT

3 Civic Hall Shops, Market Square, Totnes, Devon TQ9 5SF
Tel/Fax: 01803 840740   website: www.fifthelementdiamonds.co.uk

Working from **Fifth Element**, his studio in the middle of historic Totnes, Trevor Forrester produces beautiful jewellery that reflects his passion for history, travel and native art, and also remains true to his roots of contemporary design. He is equally at home working with silver as gold and platinum, often mixing various metal colours within a single piece along with hand-picked stones sourced from all over the world for their beauty and quality. At Fifth Element all jewellery work can be carried out - design, making, alterations, repairs and remodelling - and Trevor is always happy to welcome visitors and discuss their dream jewellery.

importance to Exeter. The 15th century parish Church of St Mary is one of the reminders of those prosperous days. Today, the town has become something of a natural health capital and in 1989 the first Natural Health Centre in Britain was established here. This has led many other alternative therapy practitioners to come here, from acupuncturists to chiropractors and reflexologists.

   Totnes Museum provides an overall view of the history of Totnes and the surrounding area. It is housed in another of the town's attractive Elizabethan buildings, whose upper floors overhang the street. Among the many local exhibits is one that honours one of the town's most famous sons, Charles Babbage (1791-1871), whose analytical machine was the forerunner of the modern computer. Displays here record his doomed, but inspirational, struggle

KINGSBRIDGE INN

9 Leechwell Street, Totnes, Devon TQ9 5SY
Tel: 01803 863324

At the top of the town, on the old road to Kingsbridge, the **Kingsbridge Inn** has a long tradition of providing a warm welcome, excellent food and a good drop of ale. That tradition continues and flourishes under landlady Pauline Kennedy and her staff, including chef Marie Hearse. The bar has a super old world look, with old beams everywhere (mind your head!), a slatted wood bar counter, old brass lamps, and open fire and lots of cosy corners.

   Five real ales provide a great choice for connoisseurs, and Marie's menus cater for all tastes and appetites with

pub classics alongside more exotic offerings such as Thai-style fish cakes or boeuf bourguignon. Sunday lunchtime brings traditional roasts with all the trimmings, and there's live music on Sunday evening. The inn has a very interesting history and was once the haunt of liquor smugglers. An old pump in the inn used to draw water from the nearby wells that give the road its name; the waters were said to have special healing powers, but the regulars no doubt make the same claim for the real ales!

POUND COURT COTTAGE

Old Road, Harbertonford, Nr Totnes,
Devon TQ9 7TA
Tel: 01803 732441
e-mail: poundcourtcottage@tiscali.co.uk
website: www.poundcourtcottage.co.uk

Mike and Linda Allen offer comfortable and characterful guest accommodation at **Pound Court Cottage**, a substantial building in the village centre. The setting, at the point where the Harbourne river meets the Harberton stream, is delightfully fresh and green, a perfect spot to take a break from the hustle and bustle of city life. The three bedrooms all have en suite facilities, TV, tea-makers and hairdryers, and ample off-road parking is available.

The tariff is quoted on a room only basis, or with a small supplement for breakfast. This is served in the Wine Bar, which is part of the same building. **Pound's Wine Bar** – small, cosy and atmospheric – features sturdy 200-year-old walls and fireplaces, and the stylish colours and decor combine to make a pleasant and relaxing setting; when the sun shines, the terrace by a little weir and an old bridge by the village green is the place to be. The bar is stocked with a wide selection of well-chosen, well-priced wines along with port, sherry, bottled ales and lagers and a small range of bistro style food.

to perfect a calculator using only mechanical rather than electronic means.

DARTINGTON

7 miles SW of Newton Abbot on the A384

In 1925, Leonard and Dorothy Elmhirst purchased **Dartington Hall** and its surrounding estate, which had been left to decay for some time. The hall had originally been built in the 1390s by John Holand, Earl of Exeter and, as well as the Great Hall having lost its roof, several of the buildings around the two large quadrangles were being used as stables, cow sheds and hay lofts.

The Elmhirsts were idealists and since Dorothy (née

HIGH CROSS HOUSE

Dartington Hall, Totnes,
Devon TQ9 6ED
Tel: 01803 864114
Fax: 01803 867057

A blue and white house that was built in 1932on the Dartington Hall estate, **High Cross House** is a wonderful example of a modernist house and it was originally a house for the headmaster of the progressive school that Leonard and Dorothy Elmhirst established on the estate. Although the school is now closed, the ideals of rearing children within a cultural community are remembered here. The house is now home to the Dartington Hall Trust Archive and Collection. On display here are paintings and ceramics by leading artists and craftsmen of the first half of the 20th century.

The principal rooms of the house have remained unchanged since Leonard and Dorothy's day and the period pieces of furniture include the original sofas and tubular steel chairs. There is a display of photographs and text from archive documents that chart the first 15 years of the estate after 1925 when the experiment in education began and a range of industries were established.

Dartington

Distance:	4.8 miles (7.5 kilometres)
Typical time:	120 mins
Height gain:	65 metres
Map:	Explorer 110
Walk:	www.walkingworld.com ID:1782
Contributor:	Dennis Blackford

Access Information:

By car take the A385 from Totnes to Shinners Bridge, turn right at the roundabout for about 100 metres and the Cider Press is clearly marked on your right. Park in the upper 'overflow' car park in the summer or main car parks in winter.

Description:

Starting from the Cider Press Craft Centre we walk along a quiet country lane in the Dartington Hall Estate to the gardens of the hall. After an optional look around the hall itself we travel down the long, tree lined main drive of the hall with extensive views over the River Dart to the ancient Water Meadow. There is an optional detour along the river bank to the historic town of Totnes with its castle and museum. We return back along the river bank to the water meadow where we follow its side to a woodland track back to the Cider Press.

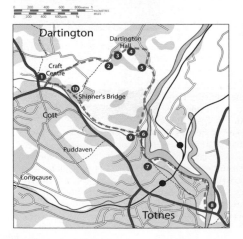

Additional Information:

Refreshments and toilets at the Cider Press, Dartington Hall and Totnes. The walking is generally good with wide tracks and country roads so is very pushchair friendly.

Features:

River, pub, toilets, museum, church, castle, wildlife, birds, flowers, great views, butterflies, cafe, gift shop, food shop, industrial archaeology, public transport, restaurant, tea shop, woodland.

Walk Directions:

1 From the car parks - leave at the far end and turn left up the path. Cross the road and walk up the lane past the overflow car parks. Follow the country lane to the junction with the access road to Dartington Hall. Turn right along the tarmac footpath on the right hand side of the road.

2 Where the footpath ends at a large white signpost, go to the right and through the gate into the gardens of Dartington Hall.

3 Follow the wide drive down through the gardens or detour through any of the woodland paths to the left. Near the end of the drive, look for the wide, paved path on the right leading down to the swan fountain. Follow this path to the end. Turn left along the hedged pavement and then right, through the hedge and along the terrace in front of the buildings. Note: the grass area used to be used for jousting tournaments.

4 At the end of the terrace, go up the first flight of steps, then turn right down another flight to the grass. Note; If you wish to look around the buildings or visit the toilets, continue up the steps turning left at the top for 100 metres then left past the restaurant into the quadrangle. Go out through the arched gateway and turn left on the road, then left again along the wide path to pass the tranquil Zen Mediation garden. Go on through the church yard to rejoin the terrace again.

5 At the bottom of the steps, turn left along the lawn and walk down to its end. Go through the gate at the bottom of the field and turn right onto the tree lined drive following it down to the gate house.

6 Pass the gatehouse and through the gates to turn left onto the river walk. Follow along the bank of the river. Note; The meadow seen just before the gatehouse is the water meadow

and will be the way back to the Cider Press for those who wish to shorten the walk - missing out the river walk and Totnes.

7 Just past the weir, cross the wooden bridge to follow along the bank of the river. Note; The wide path passing the bridge brings the walker a little outside the top of Totnes.

8 The river path ends at Brutus Bridge. Go up the steps to the bridge and turn right into the town.

9 After visiting the town, return along the river, past the gatehouse to the Water Meadow mentioned in waymark 6 and follow the cycle path along the right hand side of it.

10 When you see the water mill - either take the wide path along the side of the road, or go up the steps on the woodland path. They join a few hundred metres further along and after passing some old lime kilns, you return to the Cider Press Centre.

Whitney) was one of the richest American women of her time, they possessed the financial resources to put their ideals into practice. They restored the Hall, opened a progressive school and set about reviving the local rural economy. Many artists came to work and teach on the estate. The Irish playwright Sean O'Casey left London and moved close to Dartington so that his children could attend the school within the cultural community that the couple had also created. His son Breon O'Casey,

jeweller and abstract painter, went on to join the St Ives colony of artists and now lives near Penzance.

The Headmaster's house, **High Cross House** (see panel on page 223), is now the home of The Dartington Hall Trust Archive and Collection which is open to the public May to October, Tuesday to Friday 2pm - 4.30pm. Dartington Hall itself caters for business conferences, diners and overnight guests, and the beautiful gardens can be viewed for a small donation.

SAIL & OAR

Unit 12, Brook House, Dartington, Totnes, Devon TQ9 6DJ
Tel: 01803 866 680   Fax: 01803 863 878
e-mail: boatbuilder@sailoar.co.uk
website: www.sailoar.co.uk

Julian Burn, taught Languages for 20 years before starting **Sail & Oar** in 1988 in order to to build and restore **wooden boats** to **superlative standards**. Consulting closely with the buyer, Julian builds any design up to 26 feet (8 metres), recently, a superb 13 foot rowing boat (pictured right) to a traditional elegant, fine-lined design. With modern low maintenance clinker construction, she is beautifully fitted out in teak and stainless steel.

In 1992 he expanded to use his teaching skills in *Build-a-Boat* courses and *Advice Line*. *Build-a-Boat* courses are by arrangement

to suit the 'student'. They receive constant guidance while building the hull in

Sail & Oar's workshop, then takes it home to fit out, with free *AdviceLine* help. *AdviceLine* is a telephone service to enable customers to undertake entirely at home a project like building or repairing a boat. A recent *Build-a-Boat* 'student' undertook his first boat - a magnificent clinker dinghy (pictured left) suitable for five people to sail, but easy to manage for one person only. He spent, he said, **"the happiest nine months of my life."**

LOCATOR MAP

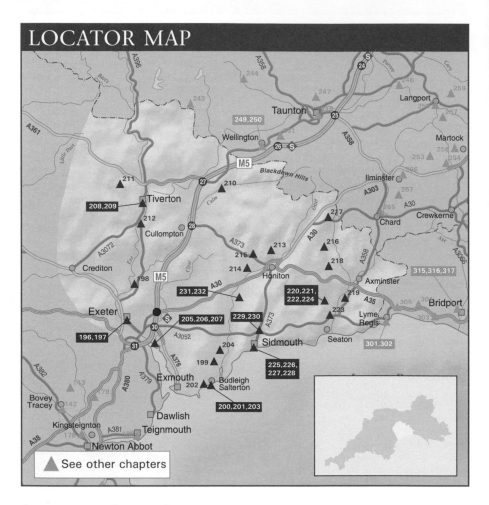

ADVERTISERS AND PLACES OF INTEREST

196 St Olaves Hotel, Exeter   page 229

197 Exeter's Underground Passages, Exeter   page 230

198 Bussells Farm Holiday Cottages, Stoke Canon, Exeter   page 232

199 Bicton Park Botanical Gardens, East Budleigh, Budleigh Salterton   page 233

200 The Brook Gallery, Budleigh Salterton   page 234

201 Days of Grace, Budleigh Salterton   page 234

202 Tidwell Manor, Knowle, Budleigh Salterton   page 235

203 Budleigh Salterton Riding School & Holiday Cottages, Budleigh Salterton   page 236

204 Lufflands, Yettington, Budleigh Salterton   page 236

205 Reka Dom, Topsham, Exeter   page 238

206 Place Settings, Topsham, Exeter   page 238

207 The Galley Restaurant with Cabins, Topsham, Exeter   page 239

208 Tiverton Castle, Tiverton   page 240

209 John Neusinger   page 241

210 Country Antiques & Interiors, Uffculme   page 242

211 The Rose & Crown, Calverleigh, Tiverton   page 242

212 Bickleigh Mill, Bickleigh, Tiverton   page 244

EXETER AND EAST DEVON 6

This is a beautiful and often overlooked part of Devon, as many pass through here on the motorway for destinations further southwest. However, this area has plenty to offer: interesting market towns, pretty villages, elegant resorts,

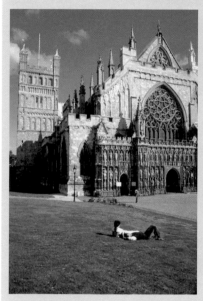

spectacular coastline, ancient history and, of course, the county town – the city of Exeter. A Roman stronghold that had also been the home of a Celtic tribe, Exeter became a major ecclesiastical centre in the 7th century when an abbey was founded here. The Normans constructed the magnificent St Peter's Cathedral and, today, it remains one of the best examples of the Decorated style of church architecture. This area's most famous son is undoubtedly Sir Walter Raleigh, who was born at Hayes Barton, Yettington near Exeter, in 1552. He apparently never lost his soft Devon burr, a regional accent, then considered uncouth by 16th century London society. He was much mocked for this by his enemies at the court of Queen Elizabeth.

Further up the River Exe is Tiverton, a town built on the prosperity that it gained from the woollen trade. Here, at the

Exeter Cathedral

ADVERTISERS AND PLACES OF INTEREST

213 Ellishayes Farmhouse, Combe Raleigh page 246
214 Deer Park Country House Hotel,
    Buckerell, Honiton   page 247
215 Ridgeway Farm B&B, Awliscombe   page 247
216 Corrymoor Mohair Socks, Stockland   page 248
217 The Belfry Country Hotel, Yarcombe   page 248
218 Burrow Farm Gardens, Dalwood,
    Axminster   page 249
219 Kate's Farm, Musbury, Axminster   page 250
220 The Tannery Shop, Colyton   page 251
221 The Garden Shop, Colyton   page 251
222 The Old Bakehouse, Colyton   page 252

223 Horriford Farm, Colyford, Colyton   page 253
224 Hardy's Hill Bed & Breakfast, Colyton page 253
225 Norman Lockyer Observatory,
    Sidmouth   page 254
226 Sidmouth Trawlers, Sidmouth   page 255
227 The Royal Glen Hotel, Sidmouth   page 256
228 Cheriton Guest House, Sidmouth   page 257
229 Core House Cottages, Sidford,
    Sidmouth   page 258
230 The Salty Monk, Sidford, Sidmouth   page 258
231 Fluxton Farm, Ottery St Mary   page 259
232 Cadhay Manor, Ottery St Mary   page 260

town's Old Blundell's School, RD Blackmore received his education and he used the school as the setting for the first chapter of his famous novel *Lorna Doone*. While Tiverton was built on wool, Axminster has become synonymous with carpets. Using a technique developed by a local weaver, Thomas Whitty,

Exeter Quayside Museum

these luxurious and highly desirable carpets grace floors around the world and also the floor of the town's St Mary's Church. Finally, there is Honiton where, from Elizabethan times, a large proportion of the town's population, even children, were involved in hand-made lace. Queen Victoria insisted on Honiton lace for her wedding dress, reviving interest in it during the 19th century and the lace continues to be made here, though on a smaller scale.

Beech at Beer

East Devon has a Heritage Coastline that can be explored and walked, by taking the South West Coast Path. Apart from a wealth of bird, plant and wildlife, this stretch of coast is known for its genteel and elegant resorts, once the holiday preserve of the well-to-do, looking for British alternatives to a Napoleon dominated Europe. Old fishing villages such as Budleigh Salterton and Exmouth were thus saved from obscurity. Sidmouth, visited by Jane Austen and James Makepeace Thackeray, was really put on the map when the Duke of Kent moved here in 1819, with his daughter Princess Victoria (later Queen Victoria).

EXETER

A lively and thriving city
with a majestic cathedral,
many fine old buildings and
a wealth of excellent
museums, Exeter's history
goes back over 2,000 years to
before the time of the Roman
invasion. At this time the
city's main street was already
in place as it formed part of
an ancient trackway that
crossed the West Country. It
was these inhabitants, the
Celtic tribe of the Dumnonii,
who gave the river the name Eisca,
meaning 'a river abounding in fish'.
Around 200 years later the Romans,
naming the settlement Isca, made this
their southwestern stronghold and
surrounded it with a massive defensive
wall. Although most of the wall has

Exeter Cathedral Grounds

gone, a spectacular **Roman Bath House**
was uncovered in the Cathedral Close
in the 1970s.

After the Romans withdrew from the
country, the city became a major
ecclesiastical centre and, in AD 670, King
Cenwealh founded an abbey on a site

St Olaves Hotel

Mary Arches Street, Exeter, Devon EX4 3AZ
Tel: 01392 217736 Fax: 01392 413054
e-mail: info@olaves.co.uk website: www.olaves.co.uk

Just 400 yards from Exeter Cathedral, **St Olaves Hotel** is an
oasis of calm in the heart of the city, a stylish Georgian town
house with the valuable asset of a private walled garden.
Down the years it has built up a well-deserved reputation for
its welcoming home-from-home atmosphere, its high
standards of comfort and service and its fine dining. Owners
Sebastian and Philippa Hughes have recently carried out a
compete refurbishment, creating a new dining room, drawing room and bar while retaining all the
best period features, including the stunning spiral staircase. Sporting prints adorn the drawing room,
while upstairs there's a fresh country feel in the 15 prettily decorated and well-furnished en suite

bedrooms, which include two suites. All the rooms have
central heating, TV, radio, telephone, fax/modem socket
and tea/coffee makers.

The chef seeks out the best West Country produce for
his frequently changing menus, which combine traditional
and contemporary influences. Light lunches and afternoon
teas are served either in the conservatory or in the walled
garden, and private dining rooms are available for special
occasions (the hotel is licensed for civil wedding
ceremonies). The owners also run the Holne Chase Hotel
near Ashburton - see separate advertisement on page 176.

where the cathedral now stands. Viking raiders in the 9th century ransacked and occupied Exeter twice before being seen off by King Alfred. Some 20 years after the Battle of Hastings, William the Conqueror took control of Exeter but only after a siege that lasted 18 days. He immediately ordered the construction of **Rougemont Castle**, the gatehouse and tower of which can still be seen at the top of Castle Street. Work was also started on the construction of **St Peter's Cathedral**, a massive building project that was not completed until 1206. Just 50 years later, all but the cathedral's two massive towers were demolished and work began on the present building. A wonderful example of the Decorated style, the 300-foot nave has stone piers rising some 60 feet then fanning out into sweeping arches. Equally impressive is the west front, where a staggering display of over 60 sculptures, carved between 1327 and 1369, can be seen. They depict a curious mix of Biblical characters, soldiers, priests and Saxon and Norman kings. Another strange carving can be found beneath the misericord seats in the choir stalls where, amongst other carvings, there is one of an elephant. However, as the carver had no model to work from he has given the animal tusks that look like clubs and rather eccentric feet. It has been suggested that the carving was based on the first elephant to come to Britain as a gift to the Henry III in 1253. The carver had probably heard stories of the creature and made up the rest.

In 1941 much of the old part of the city was destroyed by a German air raid and, although the cathedral survived, it was badly damaged. When restoration work began in 1943, a collection of wax models was discovered hidden in a cavity. Including representations of

EXETER'S UNDERGROUND PASSAGES

Romangate Passage, Off High Street, Exeter, Devon EX4 3PZ
Tel: 01392 665887

Dating from the 14th century, **Exeter's Underground Passages** are a unique attraction – the only one of its kind open to the public in Britain. On guided tours beneath the streets of Exeter and through displays and a video, visitors can discover how water was brought into Exeter. During school holidays, throughout the year, there are special activities from quizzes to treasure hunts. Information about opening times can be obtained from Exeter Tourist Information Centre.

human and animal limbs, the complete figure of a woman and a horse's head, they are thought to have been brought here by pilgrims who would place their wax models on the tomb of Bishop Edmund Lacy. By placing a model of an injured or withered limb on the tomb the pilgrims believed that they would be cured of their affliction.

The magnificence of the cathedral means that the city's other ecclesiastical buildings tend to be overlooked but it is well worth seeking out **St Nicholas' Priory**, a charming little Norman priory, now a small **Museum** where visitors can see the original Prior's cells, the 15th century kitchens and the imposing central hall with its vaulted ceiling and sturdy Norman pillars. The **Church of St Mary Steps** contains the ancient

Exeter Historic Quayside

'Matthew the Miller' tower clock named after a medieval miller well known for his punctuality.

In the High Street stands the remarkable **Guildhall**. Used as a town hall ever since it was built in 1330, it is one of the oldest municipal buildings in the country. However, the foundations of the building are even older. The present hall was constructed on the site of a building, erected by either the Saxons or the Normans. The hall was remodelled in Elizabethan times, when the arched front and the five large windows in the Mayor's Parlour were added. Another fine medieval building is the **Tucker's Hall** that was built in 1471 for the Company of Weavers, Fullers and Shearmen. Home to some superb carved panelling and a collection of rare silver, a giant pair of fulling shears that are nearly four feet long can also be seen.

As well as being an ecclesiastical centre, Exeter was also an important port and this is reflected in its dignified **Custom House** built in 1681. It now forms the centrepiece of the **Exeter Historic Quayside**, where the old warehouses have been converted into a fascinating complex of craft shops and

cafés. Here, too, can be found the **Seahorse Nature Aquarium**, which is solely dedicated to these small and beautiful creatures. Although Exeter is linked to the sea by the River Exe, the 13th century Countess of Devon, with a grudge against the city, built a weir across the river so that boats could sail no further upstream than Topsham. Some 300 years passed before action was taken by the city and the world's first ship canal was constructed to bypass the weir. Originally only three feet deep, this was changed to 14 feet over the years and the **Exeter Ship Canal** continued to be used until the 1970s. However, the M5 motorway, which crosses the canal on a fixed height bridge too low to allow big ships to pass, finally achieved what the Countess of Devon began so many centuries ago. There are scenic riverside walks along the banks of the River Exe and a ferry cross the river from the city's old quayside to the **Piazza Terracina**, an exhibition that explores over 500 years of trading through the port of Exeter. The museum also contains an extraordinary collection of boats, including a reed boat from Lake Titicaca and an Arab dhow.

There are other excellent museums in Exeter including the **Royal Albert Memorial Museum** with its displays of local history, archaeology and paintings and the **Devonshire Regiment Museum**. Close to the remains of the castle, the **Rougemont House Museum** is home to a copious collection of costumes and lace. The **Underground Passages** (see panel opposite), constructed in the 14th and 15th centuries, are a maze of subterranean passages originally built to bring water to the city from springs beyond the city walls.

Exeter University campus is set on a hill overlooking the city, and the grounds, laid out by Robert Veitch in the 1860s, offer superb views of the tors of Dartmoor. The landscape boasts many rare trees and shrubs, and the University has followed Veitch's example by creating many new plantings, including areas devoted entirely to Australasian plants. **Exeter University Sculpture Walk** comprises more than 20 sculptures, including works by Barbara Hepworth and Henry Moore, set out both in the splendid grounds and within the university buildings.

To the southwest of the city lies the **Devon and Exeter Racecourse**, one of the most scenic in the country and one that is considered to be Britain's favourite holiday course.

AROUND EXETER

BROADCLYST
5½ miles NE of Exeter off the B3181

Just to the north of the village and set within the fertile lands between the Rivers Clyst and Culm, lies the large estate of **Killerton**, centred around the grand 18th century mansion house that was the home of the Acland family. Furnished as a comfortable family home, the house contains a renowned costume collection and a Victorian laundry. While the house provides some interest it is the marvellous grounds laid out by John Veitch in the 1770s that make a visit here special. Veitch introduced many rare trees to the arboretum along with rhododendrons, magnolias and herbaceous borders, and in the parkland are several interesting structures including a 19th century chapel and the

---

BUSSELLS FARM HOLIDAY COTTAGES

Huxham, Stoke Canon, Nr Exeter, Devon EX5 4EN
Tel: 01392 841238
website: www.bussellsfarm.co.uk

Lucy and Andy Hines welcome guests to **Bussells Farm Holiday Cottages**, which nestle in a green and peaceful valley that runs from Tiverton to Exeter. Set around a pedestrian courtyard, the seven light, spacious cottages have been stylishly converted from 19th century stone barns. Six of the cottages have three bedrooms, and the biggest - Kingfisher - has four.

They are all comfortably furnished and very well equipped; each has a separate lounge with TV, and a kitchen/dining room fitted to the highest standards. All the bedrooms have fitted wardrobes, and each cottage has a bath, shower and central heating. Amenities include a heated outdoor pool, a

games room and a children's adventure playground. Guests have access to 30 acres of farmland, stables and lakes; Bussells is a popular choice for fishing holidays, and the lakes provide first-class coarse fishing, being amply stocked with carp, bream, roach, pike and tench. The local lanes and bridle paths provide excellent walking or cycling (bikes can be hired). Dartmoor and many good beaches are within an easy drive, and the city of Exeter is only 15 minutes away. Even closer are Bickleigh, with its mill and little railway, and the National Trust's Killerton, where among the highlights are a notable costume collection and splendid gardens. Dogs welcome. ETC 4Star.

Dolbury Iron Age hill fort. Here, too, can be found **Marker's Cottage** dating from the 15th century and containing 16th century paintings, and **Forest Cottage**, originally a gamekeeper's cottage. Circular walks around the grounds and estate provide ample opportunity to discover the wealth of plant, animal and birdlife that thrives in this large estate.

YETTINGTON
9½ miles SE of Exeter off the B3178

Just to the south of the village is **Hayes Barton**, a wonderful E-shaped Tudor house that was, in 1552, the birthplace of Sir Walter Raleigh. The family's pew, carved with their coat of arms, can still be seen in All Saints' Church, along with a series of more than 50 16th century bench-ends that were carved by local craftsmen into weird and imaginative depictions of their various trades.

To the northwest of the village is the famous **Woodbury Common**, a viewing point that is over 560 feet high, from where there are spectacular views across the Exe estuary to Dartmoor and along the south Devon coast.

OTTERTON
11½ miles SE of Exeter off the B3178

A charming mix of traditional cob and thatched cottages mingling with buildings constructed in the area's distinctive red sandstone, this delightful village lies on the banks of the River Otter. The Domesday Book recorded that there was a mill here beside the river and this almost certainly stood at the same site as the present **Otterton Mill**. A handsome, part-medieval building, the mill was restored to working order by Desna Greenhow in the 1970s and visitors can now buy packs of flour ground by the same methods that were in use long before the Norman Conquest.

BICTON PARK BOTANICAL GARDENS

East Budleigh, near Budleigh Salterton,
Devon EX9 7BJ
Tel: 01395 568465 Fax: 01395 568374
e-mail: info@bictongardens.co.uk
website: www.bictongardens.co.uk

Set in the picturesque Otter Valley, near the coastal town of Budleigh Salterton, **Bicton Park Botanical Gardens** span three centuries of horticultural history. The 63-acre park's oldest ornamental area is the Italian Garden that was created in the axial style of the Versailles landscaper, André le Notre in around 1735 by Henry Rolle, the park's owner. By that time, formal garden design was becoming unfashionable in England and this might explain why the garden was located out of view of the house.

However, today, the full grandeur of the Italian Garden can be seen from the spacious restaurant, that is housed in the classically styled Orangery that was built at the beginning of the 19th century. Bicton's high-domed Palm House, one of the world's most beautiful garden buildings, was the first of many developments made here between 1820 and 1850 whilst others include the important collection of conifers in the Pinetum that is now the subject of a rare species conservation project. The gardens also contain St Mary's Church, where Queen Victoria once worshipped, and the exotic Hermitage that was built in 1839 by Lady Louise Rolle as a summerhouse. A large museum reflects changes in agricultural, and rural life generally, over the past 200 years. These Grade I listed gardens, which are open all year, also feature a narrow-gauge railway that meanders through the gardens, a gift shop, a garden centre and children's indoor and outdoor play areas.

THE BROOK GALLERY

Fore Street, Budleigh Salterton, Devon EX9 6NH
Tel/Fax: 01395 443003
e-mail: rhennah@aol.com
website: www.brookgallery.co.uk

Fiona and Roger Hennah provided yet another reason to visit the lovely old town of Budleigh Salterton when they opened **The Brook Gallery** in 1997. It takes its name from the brook that runs opposite, and fresh flowers add to the charm of the setting in a particularly attractive part of town overlooking the sea. The gallery has enjoyed six years of continuous growth, and the light, spacious surroundings show the displays to the very best effect. The main focus is on original prints, etchings, lithographs, screenprints, wood engravings and linocuts, all representing excellent value compared with major city galleries.

The pictures range from rare collectable master prints to works by Royal Academicians and artists both local and international who are in the process of establishing or enhancing their reputations. The list of featured artists includes many world famous names, among them Norman Ackroyd, Marc Chagall, Salvador Dali, Dame Elisabeth Frink, Sir Terry Frost, Edvard Munch, David Hockney, Paul Hogarth, Dame Laura Knight, Henri Matisse, Anita Klein, Joan Miro, Henry Moore, Pablo Picasso, John Piper and Augustus John. The Brook Gallery is open from 10.30am to 4.30pm Tuesday to Saturday or by appointment.

DAYS OF GRACE

15 Fore Street, Budleigh Salterton,
Devon EX9 6NH
Tel: 01395 443730
e-mail: lduriez@onetel.com

Long known in the area for her passion for antique lace and vintage clothing, costume collector Linda Duriez has extended her range at **Days of Grace** to include rare treasures - old and new - for the home, from furniture, quilts, household linen, pretty china, enamelware and jewellery to a back room filled with antique lace and silk bridal wear from Victorian times through to the 1950s. Goods spill out on to the courtyard in front of the shop, which is reached across a little bridge among the daisies. The blue and white striped awning gives the place a distinctly French look and feel, as do the lovely cushions and throws, the odd French day bed and metal chair - even the soap comes from France.

Outside, visitors can sit on the bench and drink in the atmosphere or enjoy refreshments at the delightful café next door with its outside seats - all part of the experience and guaranteed to make a visit to the aptly named Days of Grace even more enjoyable. This unique shop, the first port of call for many collectors and dealers from all over the South, should be on the itinerary of every visitor to Budleigh Salterton.

The mill is also home to a craft centre, shop and restaurant. Close to the village church stands a manor house, built in the 11th century as a small priory belonging to Mont St Michel in Normandy. Today, it is divided into private apartments.

Another interesting feature of the village is the little stream that runs down Fore Street. At the bottom of the hill it joins with the River Otter and from this point there is an attractive walk down the river to Budleigh Salterton. Centuries ago this was a busy waterway with many different cargoes, particularly salt, being carried in and out of the Otter estuary. Today the estuary and its banks are a nature reserve rich in birdlife.

Just to the north of the village is **Bicton Park Botanical Gardens** (see panel on page 233) laid out in the 18th century by Henry Rolle to plans by André le Notre, the designer of Versailles.

BUDLEIGH SALTERTON

11½ miles SE of Exeter on the B3178

The name of this pleasant and refined town is derived from the salt pans that lay at the mouth of the River Otter and that brought great prosperity to Budleigh Salterton in the Middle Ages. The little port here was busy with ships loading up with salt and wool but, by the mid-15th century, the estuary had silted up and the salt pans were flooded. A long period of obscurity then followed until, in the 19th century, the town started to develop as a holiday resort for Victorians 'of the better sort', who approved of the two-mile-long beach, composed of pink shingle rather than sand. At that time, sand was thought to attract rowdy holidaymakers! The steeply shelved beach was another deterrent and this is still a place for paddling rather than swimming. Today, the town retains much

TIDWELL MANOR

Knowle, Budleigh Salterton, Devon EX9 7AG
Tel/Fax: 01395 442444
e-mail: CVHolt2@aol.com
website: www.devon-online/tidwell

Set in grounds of about two acres **Tidwell Manor,** a beautiful Georgian country house, nestles in an Area of Outstanding Natural Beauty and close to the Jurassic coast. Ideally situated for those looking for peace and quiet in an area steeped in history yet close to the city of Exeter and all its hustle and bustle.

Offering all the elegance of a bygone era, each room is individually furnished with en suite facilities. **Tidwell Manor** offers personalised service, tailor made to your requirements and includes accommodation, celebrations, conferencing and weddings.

Budleigh Salterton Riding School & Holiday Cottages

Dalditch Lane, Budleigh Salterton, Devon EX9 7AS
Tel: 01395 442035 Fax: 01395 446321
website: www.devonriding.co.uk e-mail: chrissy@devonriding.co.uk

Set in an Area of Outstanding Natural Beauty on the edge of the unique heathland of Woodbury Common, Budleigh Salterton Riding School and the adjacent beautifully appointed Budleigh Holiday Cottages, offer an excellent location for year round activities and an ideal setting for a relaxing holiday.

Catering for all ages and abilities, lessons at the riding school can be tailored to all needs on an individual or group basis, and are held in 2 large all weather ménages with jumping facilities.

The location in the countryside with stunning coastal views is ideal for country rides which can be booked for 1, 2 or 3 hours.

Among the special activities which make BSRS so outstanding are children's parties, yearly camps, seasonal shows and pub rides, Non-riders can spectate from the comfort of the office warmed in winter by an open log fire.

Budleigh Holiday Cottages offer self-catering accommodation throughout the year with a shared heated swimming pool in summer months. Just 2 miles from Budleigh's famous pebble beach and 3 miles from Exmouth's extensive sandy beaches - the cottages offer an immense variety of facilities whatever your interests all within a few miles.

If you're interested in sport there's sailing and windsurfing at Exmouth beach, fishing along the river Otter and within walking distance at the reservoir, and sea fishing at Beer and Budleigh Salterton.

Golfers have a choice of 2 of the finest courses in the South West, East Devon and Woodbury Park—both within 2 miles. There is endless walking including the South West Coast path along the World Heritage Jurassic Coastline and thousands of acres of heathland with coastal views on the doorstep, or woodlands, bridleways and lakes. The cathedral city of Exeter is just 11 miles and Dartmoor is within a half hour drive.

LUFFLANDS

Yettington, Nr Budleigh Salterton,
Devon EX9 7BD
Tel: 01395 568422
Fax: 01395 568810
e-mail: stay@lufflands.co.uk
website: www.lufflands.co.uk

Brenda and Colin Goode offer a warm and friendly welcome and a choice of cosy, comfortable bed and breakfast accommodation at **Lufflands**, a 17th century former farmhouse situated in an area of outstanding natural beauty. The accommodation comprises of an en-suite family room (double and two singles), an en-suite double and a single with a private bathroom. All rooms are tastefully decorated, very well-equipped and have tea/coffee making facilities. A traditional breakfast is freshly cooked to order or a vegetarian option is available. In the evening guests can relax and watch TV in the separate lounge/dining room with its inglenok fire place or enjoy the last rays of sunshine in the large secluded garden.

Brenda and Colin also offer self-catering accommodation in two cottages. Barn Cottage sleeps up to six in three bedrooms and Cider Cottage sleeps five in two bedrooms and has wheelchair access. Lufflands is an ideal base for a traditional beach holiday or for touring Dartmoor, Exmoor and the East Devon Jurrassic Coast. There are many places of interest in the area and activities to suit all ages and tastes whether it be walking, birdwatching, horse riding, golf or sailing.

of its respectable Victorian middle class gentility with trim villas, a broad promenade and a spotlessly clean beach flanked by 500 feet high red sandstone cliffs.

One famous Victorian visitor to Budleigh Salterton was the celebrated artist Sir John Everett Millais, who stayed here during the summer of 1870 in a curiously-shaped house known as **The Octagon**. It was beside the town's beach that he painted his most famous picture, *The Boyhood of Raleigh*, using his two sons and a local ferryman as models.

Found on the town's seafront is **Fairlynch Museum**, one of the very few thatched museums in the country, which houses numerous collections covering all aspects of life through the ages in the lower Otter Valley.

EXMOUTH
9 miles SE of Exeter on the A376

A small fishing village until the early 18th century, Exmouth, as its name suggests, lies at the mouth of the River Exe. It was its position, its splendid beach and glorious surrounding coastal scenery that led the village to become one of the earliest seaside resorts in Devon. Dubbed 'The Bath of the West', this was a place developed for the very top echelons of society. Lady Byron and Lady Nelson came here and stayed at lodgings in The Beacon, an elegant Georgian terrace overlooking the Madeira Walk and Esplanade. However, this early success hit a setback in the mid-19th century when Isambard Brunel routed his Great Western Railway down the other side of the Exe estuary. It was not until a branch line reached the resort in 1861 that business began to pick up again. During the summer, a passenger ferry crosses the river from here to Starcross. However, this is not just a popular seaside resort and the Exmouth

Docks are still busy with commerce.

From Exmouth, the **East Devon Way**, signposted by a foxglove, is a middle distance footpath of 40 miles that travels through the county to Lyme Regis just over the border in Dorset. Four other circular paths link in with the East Devon Way providing other options for walkers to enjoy and explore the quieter and more remote areas away from the coast.

On the northern outskirts of the town is one of the most unusual houses in Britain – **A La Ronde** – a unique 16-sided house, built in the late 18th century on the instructions of two spinster cousins. Jane Parminter, the daughter of a wealthy Barnstaple wine merchant, and her cousin, Mary Parminter, travelled widely through Europe on Grand Tours in the 1780s and 1790s, and it was the basilica of the San Vitale at Ravenna that inspired the designs for the house. The cousins lived here in magnificent feminist seclusion, forbidding the presence of any man in their house or in its 15 acres of grounds. What, therefore, no gentleman saw during the lifetime of the women, was the wonderfully decorated inside that the cousins created. These fabulous interiors, common in Regency times, are rare today. Due to their delicacy the feather frieze and shell-encrusted gallery can be seen only via closed circuit television in this National Trust property. Throughout the house the vast collection of pieces that the ladies brought back from their extensive travels is on display.

TOPSHAM
4 miles SE of Exeter off the A376

This delightful old town of narrow streets, lined with 17th and 18th century merchants' houses, many of which are built in the Dutch style with curved gable ends, has been declared a

REKA DOM

43 The Strand, Topsham, Exeter, Devon EX3 0AY
Tel/Fax: 01392 873385
e-mail: beautifulhouse@hotmail.com
website: www.rekadom.co.uk

Richard and Marlene Gardner extend a cordial invitation to stay at **Reka Dom**, a 17th century merchant's house with many interesting architectural features. Facing south, the three beautifully appointed bedrooms enjoy views over the Exe estuary towards Exmouth and the wooded Haldon Hills. *Estuary View* is a large twin-bedded room with private bathroom; *The Woodbury Suite* and *The Tower* both have a double bedroom, a small kitchen and bathroom/toilet, and in addition *The Tower* has a sitting room which, as one of the highest points in Topsham, commands truly outstanding panoramic views.

All rooms have a fridge, TV, video (free video library), easy chairs, tea/coffee-makers and a generous supply of home-made biscuits. A famously sumptuous breakfast is served in the Blue Room, where a log fire crackles in the winter months; vegetarian and special diets can be catered for. Rooms can be booked on a bed and breakfast or half-board basis; home-cooked three-course dinners feature the pick of local produce, and special occasion dinners for large numbers can also be arranged. Pets are welcome by prior arrangement at Reka Dom, which is strictly a non-smoking establishment.

PLACE SETTINGS

62 Fore Street, Topsham, Nr Exeter,
Devon EX3 0HL
Tel: 01392 876563

Behind an inviting cream-and-blue-painted frontage on the main street of Topsham, **Place Settings** is stocked with an impressive range of lovely gift ideas and items to enhance the home. Everything on the tables, shelves and racks in the bright, spotless display space is a delight, and inveterate browsers will have a fine time looking round the shop before deciding on their purchases.

Frames and pictures, calendars and diaries, pottery by Bridgewater, Nicholas Mosse and Burleigh, aromatics by Arran and Crabtree & Evelyn, table settings, linen goods, lavender boxes, quilts and throws, cushions, nightware, books on homes, health and lifestyle........ these are just some of what Place Settings has to offer, and a special gift becomes even more special when presented gift wrapped using the special gift wrapping service. Across the road, and in the same ownership, Play Settings sells high-quality toys, many of them made of wood, and a selection of very tempting Belgian chocolates.

THE GALLEY RESTAURANT WITH CABINS

41 Fore Street, Topsham, Exeter,
Devon EX3 0HU
Tel/Fax: 01392 876078
e-mail: fish@galleyrestaurant.co.uk
website: www.galleyrestaurant.co.uk

The Galley Restaurant with Cabins fulfils a dual role as a great place to eat and an equally attractive place to stay. The business of owners Mark Wright and chef Paul Da-Costa-Greaves is all about dreams and stories, adding depth and interest into people's lives in an ever changing world. The food reflects a slight contemporary twist and unique style being exotic and healthy with a little added touch of elegance. The Galley says "Cooking is an art, consisting of opposing elements (yin & yang) you might say! It is here we best offer our services. Welcome to the uplifting experience of The Galley."

The Galley is ideal for the business, romantic or city break user, and the overnight accommodation comprises double or twin rooms in nautical cabins rating five diamonds from ETC/RAC/AA. With panoramic river views or old-world features of exposed beams, slate flooring and open log fires, the cabins (all non-smoking) have private bath or shower, cable TV, telephones with internet connection, minibars and hot and cold beverage facilities. The tariff includes a continental breakfast. Private parking is available.

conservation area. Originally a port that developed in the Middle Ages, this had also been a port in Roman times. Thankfully, it was untouched by bombs during World War II despite being so close to the major target of Exeter. There are stunning views out across the Exe estuary with its extensive reed beds, salt marshes and mud banks, providing an important winter feeding ground and summer breeding area for birds from all over the world. The estuary is also home to the largest winter flocks of avocets in the county. There are walks along the banks of the estuary that lead right from Exeter to the coast at Exmouth.

TIVERTON

Originally known as Twyfyrde, or two fords, it is here that the River Lowman joins the River Exe. Tiverton is the only town of any size in the Exe valley and a strategic point on the river. In 1106, Henry I ordered the building of **Tiverton Castle** (see panel on page 240), around which the town began to develop and grow. Rebuilt and expanded over the years, the castle was besieged during the Civil War by the Parliamentarian General Fairfax who successfully took the stronghold in 1645. Later it was decreed that the castle should be destroyed beyond any use as a fortress and Cromwell's troops carried these instructions out to the letter leaving a mutilated but substantial structure with no defences.

Tiverton's prosperity was built on the woollen trade and from the late 15th century through to the trade's peak in 18th century, prosperous wool merchants put their wealth to good use. In the early 17th century, George Slee built himself a superb Jacobean mansion, the **Great House**. In his will he bequeathed £500, a huge sum of money at that time, to establish the **Slee Almshouses**, which were duly built right next door to Slee's residence. Later almshouses, founded by John Waldron and John Greenway, are still in use. As well as funding houses for the poor and needy, Greenway devoted another sizeable proportion of his fortune to the restoration of St Peter's Church.

Another wealthy merchant, Peter Blundell, chose a different avenue for his benefaction and endowed Tiverton with a school. It was in the **Old Blundell's School** building of 1604 that the author RD Blackmore received his education. He later used the school as the setting for the first chapter of his novel *Lorna Doone*. Now a highly regarded public school, Blundell's moved, in 1880, from its original position beside Lowman Bridge to its present location on the edge of the town. **Tiverton Museum of Mid-Devon Life** concentrates on the social history of Tiverton and has a wealth of displays in its 15 galleries.

On the southeastern outskirts of the town is a quay that marks the western end of the **Great Western Canal**. This was a branch of a rather grand scheme that proposed the building of a canal

TIVERTON CASTLE

Tiverton, Devon EX16 6RP
Tel: 01884 253200 Fax: 01884 254200
e-mail: tiverton.castle@ukf.net website: www.tivertoncastle.com

Few buildings evoke such an immediate feeling of history as **Tiverton Castle**, originally built in 1106 by Richard de Redvers on the orders of Henry I. The de Redvers were the first earls of Devon and, when the line died out in 1293, they were succeeded as earls by the Courtenays, who rebuilt and enlarged the castle and regarded it as their "head and chief mansion." In 1495, Princess

Katherine Plantagenet married William Courtenay, who became Earl of Devon. She died in 1527 and was buried in St Peter's Church next door. Unfortunately for the Courtenay family, this royal marriage led to their eventual downfall in that turbulent age and the senior line died out in 1556 and the castle subsequently had various owners down the ages. During the English Civil War the castle was besieged by Fairfax in 1645 and fell to him due to a lucky shot hitting a drawbridge chain. There is a fine collection of Civil War arms and armour, some pieces of which can be tried on. Nowadays, the castle is a peaceful, private house and the buildings, furnishings and exhibits reflect the castle's colourful history and development. With continuing conservation in the castle and beautiful walled gardens there is always something new and interesting to see. The castle is open from Easter to the end of September.

from Taunton to Topsham to link the Bristol and English Channels. Work began on the Tiverton to Lowdwells section in 1810 and it was finished just four years later. However, no more work was carried out for a further 13 years. Plans for the rest of the scheme were dropped and, although the Tiverton to Lowdwells section was used, it was never profitable and finally closed in 1869. Never allowed to deteriorate completely, the section has recently been re-opened as a country park with charming rural canalside walks.

A few miles north of Tiverton, up the Exe Valley, lies **Knightshayes Court** a striking Victorian Gothic house designed by William Burges in 1869. It remains a rare survivor of his work. The grand and

JOHN NEUSINGER

e-mail: mail@sheepshapefurniture.co.uk
website: www.sheepshapefurniture.co.uk

John Neusinger is a highly skilled furniture maker and a member of the Devon Guild of Craftsmen. He sells some of his work through shops and galleries, and also designs and makes commissioned orders to the individual requirements of his clients. Using a variety of English and foreign timbers, his pieces range from the traditional to the unorthodox. The

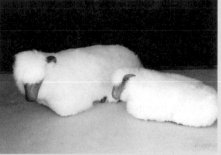

former are illustrated by a kitchen working table in English oak; a TV, video and music centre cabinet in English cherry; a fully fitted office in ash, with filing cabinets, cupboards and a double-side computer desk; oak chairs with rush seating and various tables and dressers. Among the less usual items are beautiful carved wooden feathers and his famous sheepshape furniture, for sitting on, leaning on or resting your feet. For more details of his work or to discuss a specific project visit Johns website at **www.sheepshapefurniture.co.uk** or e-mail him at **mail@sheepshapefurniture.co.uk**.

opulent interiors, blending medieval romanticism with lavish Victorian decoration, became too much for the owner, Sir John Heathcoat-Amory, the lace manufacturer. So he sacked Burges and employed the less imaginative but competent John Diblee Crace. Covered over during the time of the backlash against the High Victorian style, the rooms have been returned to their original grandeur by the National Trust, who were given the building by the builder's son in 1973. The house is surrounded by extensive grounds that include a water-lily pond, topiary and some rare shrubs.

Knightshayes Court

AROUND TIVERTON

BAMPTON

6 miles N of Tiverton on the B3227

An important centre of the wool trade during the Middle Ages, the village is now best known for its annual **Exmoor Pony Sale**, which takes place in late October. Apart from those few days in the autumn, Bampton remains a wonderfully quiet and

COUNTRY ANTIQUES & INTERIORS

The Old Brewery, High Street, Uffculme, Devon EX15 3AB
Tel/Fax: 01884 841770 Mobile: 07768 328433
e-mail: mike@englishcountryantiques.co.uk
website: www.englishcountryantiques.co.uk

Country Antiques & Interiors was formed in 1994, built on the success of English Country Antiques, which has been exporting antiques to the USA for the last 20 years. Housed in The Old Brewery (c.1858) in the main street of Uffculme is a connoisseur's selection of mostly 19th and early 20th century country and decorative furniture and items from England, Europe and further afield, both in showroom condition and for restoration.

The ever-changing stock typically ranges from a 10-foot pine farmhouse table to a 19th century lustre cup and saucer and includes old pine and specially designed pieces of furniture; repainted old

pine, oak, mahogany, fruitwood, bentwood, bamboo and upholstered pieces; lighting, brassware, metalware and wooden items; architectural conversions; mirrors of many types; garden items including tables, benches, planters and paraphernalia; marble pieces; old sailing pond yachts and nautical items. Among the smaller collectables are china, glass, metalware, silver plate, wooden items, leather, textiles, stoneware, earthenware and much more besides. Owner Michael Mead is pleased to welcome visitors to Country Antiques & Interiors, which is only five minutes from J27 of the M5 - but phone before setting out, as opening times can vary.

THE ROSE & CROWN

Calverleigh, nr Tiverton, Devon EX16 8BA
Tel: 01884 256301 Fax: 01884 251837

For well over 200 years the picturesque **Rose & Crown** has offered its customers a warm welcome, and the tradition of hospitality is being carried on in fine style by Alec and Pam Roud and their son Nick. The wide range of real ales and freshly cooked food available would have been beyond belief to the inn's original farming customers, but the family still give a time-honoured welcome to their 'regulars' and to their many visitors from further afield. The reasonably priced menu, served every lunchtime and evening in the bar and non-smoking restaurant, runs to more then 60 choices, from light snacks to hearty,

mouthwatering house specials, and head chef Mrs Roud sets great store by the finest and freshest local produce. Among the specialities are Pork Valentine with cream, farmhouse cider and apples, Mendip chicken casserole (promoted on TV's *Countdown*!), traditional Sunday lunches and delicious vegetarian main courses such as hazelnut and mushroom pie.

The high standard of food has earned the Rose & Crown national recognition as runners-up in the British Food Pub of the Year competition. The inn lies two miles west of Tiverton on the old Rackenford road.

tranquil place with some handsome Georgian cottages and houses set beside a tributary of the River Exe, the River Batherm. To the north of the village, the site of Bampton's castle is marked by a tree-crowned motte. A memorial in Bampton's parish church records, rather unsympathetically, the strange death of the parish clerk's son in 1776, apparently killed by a falling icicle:

Bless my I I I I I I [eyes],
Here he lies,
In a sad pickle,
Killed by an icicle.

UFFCULME

7 miles E of Tiverton on the B3440

An important centre of the woollen trade in medieval times, profits from this booming business helped to build the impressive parish church of St Mary in the mid-15th century. It houses a splendid rood screen believed to be the longest in Devon. To the west of this charming village's centre lies one of the few remaining reminders of Devon's once flourishing textile trade, **Coldharbour Mill**. It closed in 1981 and is now home to a working wool museum. Here visitors can see the whole process of woollen and worsted manufacturing, wander around the reconstructed rooms, workshops and cottages, relax in the restaurant and browse through the gift shop.

A little further upstream from Uffculme is **Culmstock**, a place of particular interest to lovers of the novel *Lorna Doone*. The author, RD Blackmore, lived here as a boy while his father was the village's vicar. One of Blackmore's playmates at Culmstock was Frederick Temple and, when they were old enough, the two friends went to Old Blundell's School in Tiverton, where they shared lodgings. Later, Blackmore was to

become one of the most successful authors of his day while Temple entered the church and, after rising to be the headmaster of Rugby School, reached the pinnacle of his profession when he became Archbishop of Canterbury.

In the heart of the village stands the church where Blackmore's father was vicar and growing from the top of the building's tower is a famous yew tree that has been surviving in this precarious position for over 200 years. Despite the fact that the only nourishment for the tree is the building's mortar, the tree's trunk has a girth of 18 inches. It is believed that the seed was probably carried up here in mortar used by a workman who came to repair the tower after the spire had been demolished in 1776.

BICKLEIGH

3 miles SW of Tiverton off the A396

This village, in the Exe valley, a charming place of thatched cottages and lovingly tended gardens in a beautiful riverside setting is, not surprisingly, one of Devon's most photographed villages. However, the village does not draw people just because of its beauty. It is also home to two of the area's most popular attractions. **Bickleigh Mill** (see panel on page 244) has been converted into a craft centre and a farm stocked with rare breeds while, across the river, **Bickleigh Castle**, a moated and fortified manor house with an impressive gatehouse, dates from the late 14th century. The interior houses some excellent Tudor furniture, including a massive four-poster bed, some fine oil paintings and an armoury from the Civil War. The castle is open throughout the season. Close to the castle is an even older chapel dating from the 11th century. Nearby, there is a 17th century farmhouse that retains its oak beams,

BICKLEIGH MILL

Bickleigh, Tiverton, Devon EX16 8RG
Tel: 01884 855419 Fax: 01884 855416
e-mail: general@bickleighmill.freeserve.co.uk
website: www.bickleighmill.com

An old mill building has been restored and renovated to become the centre of mid-Devon's largest rural shopping, eating, crafts and recreation complex. The Gift Shops at **Bickleigh Mill** are a treasure trove of gifts to

suit all pockets and delight all ages, while the Farm Shop tempts with a mouthwatering selection of locally produced food, including Devon clotted cream and clover honey. The Gallery is a showcase for original works of art from local artists and prints, and in the Pottery the Mill produces its own hand-painted pottery on the premises. One of the most popular attractions of Bickleigh Mill is the Restaurant & Café, where locally produced ingredients are the basis of a menu that offers the best of trad-

itional Devon country fare (apple tart with clotted cream is an all-time favourite). In the beautiful Dining Room antiques, soft lighting, exposed stone walls and a roaring winter fire create a warm, comfortable ambience, and large windows command glorious views over the grounds. Snacks and refreshments are also served in the Café Bar, and in the summer the cool and shady waterside tea gardens are the perfect spot for lunch, snacks and a traditional English afternoon tea. The Mill's extensive grounds include fishing ponds, picnic areas and lovely woodland walks.

Bickleigh Mill is what brings thousands of visitors to this traditional Devonshire village, but Bickleigh has an abundance of attractions for the visitor, including the Railway centre in the old station, and the unique five-arched bridge over the River Exe - reputed to have been the inspiration for the Simon and Garfunkel song *Bridge Over Troubled Water*.

River Exe at Bickleigh

large inglenook fireplaces and ancient bread oven.

The Exe Valley, which runs north of Exeter, passes through the heart of what is known as 'Red Devon' because of the distinctive colour of its soil derived from the red Permian rocks underneath. Unlike most of Devon's countryside, this is fertile, easily worked land and has been a prime agricultural area for centuries. For some reason, however, the land is particularly favourable for the growing of swedes, to which it gives a much sought-after flavour and appearance.

CADBURY
5½ miles SW of Tiverton off the A3072

Anyone coming to this delightful hamlet in the hopes of discovering a castle made of chocolate will be disappointed to learn that **Cadbury Castle** is not made of confectionery nor is it really a castle. Built high on a hilltop, about 700 feet above sea level, Cadbury Castle is actually an Iron Age hillfort and it is claimed that the views from here are the most extensive in Devon. On a good, clear day the landscapes of Dartmoor and Exmoor are in full view and, further away, the Quantocks and Bodmin Moor can also be seen.

Just to the east of Cadbury stands **Fursdon House**, which has been the home of the Fursdon family since the mid 13th century. Among the fascinating memorabilia on display, which includes old scrapbooks and some excellent 18th century costumes and textiles, is a letter written by Charles I during the Civil War. The exterior of the building shows a range of differing architectural styles reflecting the length of time that this family has lived here.

HONITON

The unofficial capital of east Devon, Honiton is a delightful little town in the valley of the River Otter which is often called the 'Gateway to the far Southwest'. Once a major stopping place on the great Roman road, Fosse Way, that ran from Lincoln to Exeter, Honiton's position on the main road into Devon and Cornwall has brought it prosperity over the centuries. Fortunately the construction of a bypass in the 1970s, carrying the main road around the town, has preserved the character and charm of this attractive market town that was under threat from major traffic congestion.

As it is surrounded by sheep pastures, it is not surprising that Honiton was the first town in Devon to manufacture serge cloth. However the town has become far better known for a much more delicate fabric, Honiton Lace, which is still much sought after today. Lace-making was first introduced to east Devon by Flemish immigrants who arrived here during the early days of the reign of Elizabeth I. It was not long before anyone who could afford this extravagant material was displaying it on their collars and cuffs as a symbol of wealth and status. Demand grew and, by the end of the 17th century, over 5,000 people were employed in the industry. Most were working from home, making fine bone lace by hand. Such was the pressure to produce more and more lace that children as young as five were being sent to lace schools, where they would receive a very basic education in reading, writing and arithmetic but a much more intensive education in the highly skilled art of lace-making.

The arrival of machine-made lace in the late 18th century almost wiped out the industry in Honiton. But when Queen Victorian insisted on wearing hand-made Honiton lace on her wedding day, she established a new fashion for the lace that was to persist throughout the 19th century. The lace is still made here today, but on a much smaller scale. It can be bought from local shops and can be seen in **Allhallows Museum**, which houses a unique collection of traditional lace and puts on demonstrations of lace-making. The museum is housed in a part 15th century building that served as a school for over 300 years and is one of the few buildings to survive a series of fires that devastated the town in the mid-18th century. The gracious Georgian residences built following the fires have given the town the pleasant and unhurried atmosphere of a prosperous 18th century coaching town.

Another building to escape the ravages of the fires was **Marwood House** in the High Street, built in 1619 by the second son of Thomas Marwood, one of Queen Elizabeth's many physicians. Thomas achieved great celebrity when he

---

ELLISHAYES FARMHOUSE

Combe Raleigh, Honiton, Devon EX14 4UQ
Tel: 01404 47365
website: www.ellishayesfarm.co.uk

Lorraine and Graham Brooker welcome guests into the friendly, relaxed atmosphere of their delightful Grade II listed farmhouse. **Ellishayes**, which overlooks a beautiful Devonshire valley, has three letting bedrooms - two family rooms and one double, all furnished to a very high standard and all with en suite facilities, TV and tea/coffee-makers. A traditional full English

farmhouse breakfast starts the day, and packed lunches and evening meals are available on request.

A separate function room can be used for family get-togethers, small wedding parties and even

ballroom dancing - for which the owners can provide a catering service. Ellishayes is tucked away peacefully down its own private drive a short distance from the main A30 near Honiton. Wildlife abounds in the locality, and the farmhouse is an ideal base for walking, cycling, fishing and riding. The Blackdown Hills, in a designated Area of Outstanding Natural Beauty, is close by, and Honiton, Exeter and the delights of the South Devon coast are all easily reached. Ellishayes is open all year round.

managed to cure the Earl of Essex after all other physicians had failed. For this he received his Devonshire estate. He was equally successful at maintaining his own health as he lived to the age of 105 – an extraordinary feat today but even more remarkable then.

On the western side of the town is **St Margaret's Hospital**, founded in the Middle Ages as a refuge for lepers, who were isolated from the rest of the townsfolk. In the 16th century, this attractive thatched building was converted into almshouses. Although Honiton does not have a true castle, there is an early 19th century castellated toll house, known as **Copper Castle**, on the eastern side of Honiton while further east again, on Honiton Hill, is the massive folly of the **Bishop's Tower** that was built in 1842 and formed part of Bishop Edward Copplestone's house.

AROUND HONITON

DALWOOD
5½ miles E of Honiton off the A35

Despite clearly being within the county of Devon, by some administrative quirk, until 1842 this little village was actually part of Dorset. Dalwood's other claim to fame is as the home of **Loughwood Meeting House**, one of the oldest surviving Baptist chapels in the country. It was built in the 1650s by this persecuted community from Kilmington, who risked imprisonment or transportation if they were discovered practising their faith. A simple little building with a quaint thatched roof and a whitewashed interior, the chapel was hidden by dense woodland. Used until 1833, it was left deserted for years before being purchased and restored by the

DEER PARK COUNTRY HOUSE HOTEL

Buckerell, Honiton, Devon EX14 3PG
Tel: 01404 41266 e-mail: admin@deerparkcountryhotel.com
Fax: 01404 46598 website: www.deerparkcountryhotel.com

Deer Park Country House Hotel is a charming Georgian mansion set at the end of a long drive in glorious Devon countryside. The friendly welcome from Stephen and Anne Noar is second to none, and the bedrooms offer a fine combination of peace, comfort and traditional elegance. Anne's cooking, using the finest local ingredients as much as possible, is complemented by well-chosen wines, and guests can enjoy excellent trout fishing on the River Otter, which flows through the grounds, or gentle strolls along its banks. The hotel has a croquet lawn, squash and tennis courts and a heated swimming pool.

RIDGEWAY FARM B&B

Awliscombe, Honiton, Devon EX14 3PY
Tel: 01404 841331 Fax: 01404 841119
e-mail: jessica@ridgewayfarm.co.uk
website: www.smoothhound.com/ridgewayfarm

Set in an area of peace, tranquillity and Outstanding Natural Beauty, **Ridgeway Farm**, which has an AA four Diamond rating, is a traditional 18th century farmhouse offering cosy, comfortable bed and breakfast accommodation. The two guest bedrooms have en suite facilities, television, tea trays and central heating, and there's also a television in the guest lounge. Evening meals can be provided by arrangement. The farm, which is owned and run by Jessica Colson, is located on the outskirts of Awliscombe, three miles from Honiton and easily accessible from the A30 or M5 (J28).

CORRYMOOR MOHAIR SOCKS

Corrymoor Farm, Stockland, Honiton, Devon EX14 9DY
Tel/Fax: 01404 861245
e-mail: socks@corrymoor.com website: www.corrymoor.com

The Corrymoor flock of pedigree Angora goats was established in 1986 and the Whitley family started producing **Corrymoor Mohair Socks** in 1993. Careful selection has produced large, deep-bodied goats of good temperament with fine, lustrous fleeces free from the short, thick fibres (known as kemp) which can make poor-quality mohair itchy. The goats are shorn twice a year, after which the fleeces are graded and the 'raw' mohair washed, combed and spun then knitted and dyed to produce the finished goods. A special sort of nylon is added during the process to give the elasticity that is lacking in the mohair - the mix varies from 55% mohair/45% nylon to 68%/32% for the heavier duty socks and 90%/10% for the snug bedsocks.

Corrymoor socks are available in eight styles, four sizes and more than a dozen colours, and the

hundreds of testimonials from satisfied customers are a tribute to the qualities of the Corrymoor product: they don't smell, they don't shrink and they are kind to sensitive skins. The business now boasts a customer list of more than 20,000 and a thriving mail order service; it exports to more than 20 countries. On their organically run 128-acre farm in the rolling hills of East Devon the Whitleys - Stephen, Jenny and their children Kirsten, Lucy and Alice - also raise cattle and sheep.

THE BELFRY COUNTRY HOTEL

Yarcombe, Nr Honiton, Devon EX14 9BD
Tel: 01404 861234 Fax: 01404 861579
website: www.thebelfrycountryhotel.com

The Belfry Country Hotel is a wonderful place to unwind and relax. The Grade II listed building is a former village school situated in picturesque Yarcombe. The resident owners, Katie and Paul Blake, and their cats, extend a genuinely warm welcome creating an atmosphere of friendliness and peaceful relaxation. Fine food predominates and guests may begin the day with anything from a slice of toast to a whole side of smoked haddock, full English breakfast or the chef's winter special of oatmeal brulée. Dinner guests choose in advance from the superb menu and their meal is freshly prepared from the finest local ingredients. The Belfry is fast gaining a reputation with residents and locals alike, for fine dining and a splendid wine list.

With only six, individually styled luxury en-suite bedrooms The Belfry provides a high standard of accommodation blending traditional features with modern comforts. With guest comfort very much in mind there are thoughtful touches including freshly baked goods, mineral water, luxury bathrobes, top quality towels and linens and CD players in every room. Guests can relax in the lounge with the day's papers or a book from the owner's extensive collection.

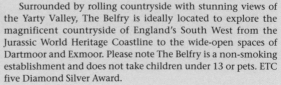

Surrounded by rolling countryside with stunning views of the Yarty Valley, The Belfry is ideally located to explore the magnificent countryside of England's South West from the Jurassic World Heritage Coastline to the wide-open spaces of Dartmoor and Exmoor. Please note The Belfry is a non-smoking establishment and does not take children under 13 or pets. ETC five Diamond Silver Award.

National Trust in 1969.

A couple of miles south of Dalwood is another National Trust property, **Shute Barton**, an exceptional example of a medieval unfortified manor house dating from around the late 14th century. Originally built in 1380 by Sir William Bonville, it was enlarged in the late 15th century by the then owners, the Grey family. They went on to lose the estate in 1554, when Henry Grey, Duke of Suffolk was beheaded for trying to put his daughter, Lady Jane Grey, on the throne of England. Although only parts of the original building have survived the centuries, they include some remarkably impressive features such as the Great Hall with its massive beamed ceiling and the ancient kitchen with its huge range, which was capable of roasting a whole ox. The last private owners of Shute Barton were the Pole family, who lived here between 1780 and 1959. This local dynasty is commemorated by some grand monuments in the Church of St Michael. Among them is the overbearing memorial to Sir William Pole that depicts the Master of the Household to Queen Anne standing on a pedestal dressed in full regalia.

Close by are the **Burrow Farm Gardens** (see panel above), beautifully landscaped gardens that provide a peaceful place for a relaxing afternoon's outing as well as plenty of interest for keen gardeners.

BURROW FARM GARDENS

Dalwood, near Axminster, Devon EX13 7ET
Tel: 01404 831285
website: www.burrowfarmgardens.co.uk

The beautifully landscaped seven-acre gardens of **Burrow Farm Gardens** were created over the last 40 years by Mary Benger and they will appeal to both plantsmen and those seeking a relaxing walk around a tranquil landscape that also offers extensive views. The gardens include a fascinating woodland garden created in an ancient Roman clay pit and the most recent addition – Millennium mill garden. Sweeping lawns lead between island beds of unusual shrubs and herbaceous plants down to the lake whilst the pergola walk features old roses and herbaceous plants. The terrace and courtyard gardens are colour themed and they specialise in later summer flowering plants. Burrow Farm Gardens has been awarded star status in the Good Gardens Guide.

AXMINSTER
9 miles E of Honiton on the A358

This little town grew up at the junction of two important Roman roads, the Fosse and the Icknield Ways. During the Middle Ages, it was an important religious centre with a Minster, standing beside the River Axe, from which the town takes its name. Now a ruin, Newnham Abbey was founded in 1247 by Reginald de Mohun. However, it is as a centre for the manufacture of carpets that the town is famous, in particular, luxuriously woven carpets that still bear the town's name. While wandering around London's Cheapside market in the mid-18th century, Thomas Whitty, an Axminster born weaver, saw huge Turkish carpets, up to 12 yards long and eight yards wide. He hurried back to Axminster to puzzle out how to produce a seamless piece of carpet of that size. After many months, Thomas had solved the puzzle and, on Midsummer's Day in 1755, he revealed the first of his luxurious carpets to the world. So much time and labour went into the making of just one of Thomas's Axminster carpets that the completion of each carpet was celebrated by a procession to St Mary's Church, where a peal of bells would be rung. The high cost of the carpets and the fine workmanship made them highly desirable items. One distinguished purchaser of an Axminster carpet was, ironically, the Sultan of Turkey who, in 1800, paid the colossal sum of £1,000 for a particularly fine specimen. But the extraordinarily high labour costs involved in producing the exquisite hand-tufted carpets crippled Whitty's company and, in 1835, the looms were sold to another carpet factory at Wilton.

Carpets are still manufactured here using the latest computerised looms and the factory welcomes visitors, while the **Axminster Museum** dedicates some of its exhibition space to the industry that made this modest town a household name around the world. Axminster is the home of what must be one of the most comfortable and luxurious churches in the country. Situated adjacent to Whitty's old factory, St Mary's Church finally, after pealing its bells in celebration for many completed carpets,

got its own and, inside, the pews are set back so that visitors and the congregation can admire the Axminster carpet in all its magnificence.

SEATON
8½ miles SE of Honiton on the B3172

Situated at the mouth of the River Axe, Seaton was once a busy port. By the 16th century, the Axe estuary had filled up with stone and pebbles and there was no further development of any note until the 19th century. With its red cliffs on one side and white on the other, Seaton expanded during the Victorian era as wealthy families, looking for sea air, came and built their villas. One of the first concrete bridges in the world was erected over the River Axe in 1877. The attractive appearance of this little seaside town is enhanced by its well maintained gardens and public parks. While the western area has a quiet and retiring ambience, the eastern part of the town is livelier.

The railway line that brought many of the Victorians here over 100 years ago has been replaced by the narrow-gauge **Seaton Tramway**. It provides a rather different way in which to discover the Axe Valley, as the colourful open-topped tramcars (also some fully-enclosed single-deckers) trundle through an area

---

KATE'S FARM

Lower Bruckland Farm, Musbury, Axminster,
Devon EX13 8ST
Tel: 01297 552861

Kate's Farm is a Grade II listed 16th century Devon longhouse and working organic farm in a secluded valley in a designated Area of Outstanding Natural Beauty. Owner Kate Satterley has two letting bedrooms - a double room and a family room with a double and two bunk beds - for bed and breakfast accommodation. A full English breakfast is served in the lounge, which has original flagstones, beams, an inglenook fireplace and a bread oven. The farm, which has two large trout lakes, is an ideal base for exploring both the coast and the countryside.

famous for its birdlife. Really dedicated tram fans, after a short lesson, are even permitted to take over the driver's controls.

COLYTON
8 miles SE of Honiton on the B3161

The tramway that starts at Seaton runs by way of Colyford to this ancient little town of narrow winding streets and interesting stone houses. Throughout its long history, Colyton has been an important agricultural and commercial centre with its own corn mill, tannery, sawmill and iron foundry. Many of the town's older buildings, such as the 16th century vicarage, are grouped around its part Norman church, which has a very unusual lantern tower. Here, too, is the Old Church House, a part medieval building, enlarged in 1612 and used as a

Beach at Beer

THE TANNERY SHOP

Tannery Yard, King Street, Colyton, Devon EX24 6PD
Tel: 01297 552221
website: www.thetanneryshop.com
The Tannery Shop sells a selection of top-quality items made from leather produced by the centuries-old traditional oak-bark process at the Tannery which is located in the same courtyard. The stock also includes other superb leather goods and gifts from around the world, including hats from South Africa, handbags from France and Canada, purses from Denmark, belts, leads, wallets, slippers and sheepskin rugs. The shop is open from 10am to 5pm Monday to Saturday.

THE GARDEN SHOP

Tannery Yard, King Street, Colyton, Devon EX24 6PD
Tel: 01297 551113
website: www.the-gardenshop.co.uk

The Garden Shop is a small, family run garden and plant centre specialising in choice and unusual items for indoors and outdoors. Superb

plants, pots and containers of all kinds, a great selection of cards, artificial flowers, gifts and a lot more besides, and, as agents for Scott's gazebos, you will find examples of their fine garden buildings. Open 9am-5.30pm Mon-Sat with easy parking.

THE OLD BAKEHOUSE

Lower Church Street, Colyton,
Devon EX24 6ND
Tel/Fax: 01297 552518
e-mail: mail@uk-westcountry.co.uk
website: www.theoldbakehousebandb.co.uk

The Old Bakehouse is a Grade II listed 400-year-old building tastefully restored by owners Frances and Paul to incorporate comfortable guest accommodation and a delightful bistro-style restaurant. The **bed and breakfast** accommodation comprises double, twin and family en-suite rooms and cots and high chairs can be made available; guests have the use of a fridge, tumble dryer and iron.

The bedrooms are all non-smoking, but guests can smoke in the lounge. Evening meals can be taken during Bistro opening times, and special diets can be catered for with notice.

Discount rates are offered for stays of four to seven or seven to ten nights. The Old Bakehouse, which is open all year round, is an ideal base from which to explore the beautiful countryside and the Jurassic Coast - designated a World Heritage Site.

Colyton is also well worth taking time to discover, and is perfectly placed for walkers on the East Devon Way and cyclists on the Wessex Way Cycle Path. A treat not to be missed is the 25-minute tram ride through the lovely Axe Valley from Colyton to the terminus close to the beach at Seaton.

The **Bistro** is Colyton's quality restaurant, and comprises non-smoking dining rooms, a comfortable guest lounge and a delightful tea garden. The meals are all freshly cooked to order, using fresh local produce whenever possible. Vegetarian, vegan, gluten-free and other special diets can be caterd for with a little notice. The Bistro is open daily for lunch and dinner and is available for functions, private parties and other group bookings. For restaurant bookings please contact Sally or Steve on 07965900351.

HORRIFORD FARM

Colyford, Colyton, Devon EX24 6HW
Tel/Fax: 01297 552316
e-mail: horriford@datacottage.com
website: www.datacottage.com/horriford

'East Devon's Best Kept Secret', **Horriford Farm** is a 16th century character farmhouse run by Val and Colin Pady as a guest house. En suite guest bedrooms combine original features with up to date amenities. Horriford is a working farm where guests can enjoy excellent home cooking, local walks, including the South West Coast Path, and coarse fishing.

grammar school until 1928.

From Seaton, eastwards, the **South West Coast Path** follows the coastline uninterruptedly all the way to Lyme Regis in Dorset. Considered by naturalists as the last and largest wilderness on the southern coast of England, this area of unstable cliffs, wood and scrub is a haven for wildlife.

To the west of Seaton, and set between the high white chalk cliffs of Beer Head and Seaton Hole, is the picturesque old fishing village of **Beer**, best known for the superb white freestone that has been quarried here since Roman times. Much prized for carving, the results can be seen in churches all over Devon as well as in the Tower of London and Westminster Abbey. Not surprisingly the man-made caves at Beer Quarry, where the stone was extracted, became the haunt of smugglers; among those using the quarry

HARDY'S HILL BED & BREAKFAST

Southleigh Road, Colyton, Devon EX24 6RU
Tel: 01297 553739
e-mail: jennie.moon@talk21.com
website: www.hardyshill.co.uk

Located down a quiet lane a mile south of Colyton, **Hardy's Hill** is a peaceful, delightful base for a walking or touring holiday. The accommodation offered by owner Jennie Moon comprises an 18th century cottage and a

self-contained studio, both combining attractive period features with modern comfort. The cottage has a twin bedroom with vanity unit and a private bathroom, while the studio has a double and a single bedroom with shower, washing facilities, and a kitchen and sitting room, overlooking the Coly Valley.

The cottage and the studio both have TV, radio and tea/coffee trays with a kettle and a supply of biscuits. Breakfast is served in the cottage dining room. Perched on a hillside, Hardy's Hill enjoys terrific views over fields that lead down to the River Coly. Colyton is just minutes away, and the area is a delight to explore, with abundant scenic walks that take in both countryside and coast. Hardy's Hill, which is open for most of the year, is a non-smoking establishment for adults; pets can be accommodated by arrangement. There's ample parking space, secure storage for bicycles and room to store muddy walking boots.

to hide themselves and their contraband was the notorious Jack Rattenbury, a native of Beer who published his *Memoirs of a Smuggler* in 1837.

BRANSCOMBE

8 miles SE of Honiton off the A3052

This scattered village of farmhouses and cottages lies on one of the most spectacular stretches of Heritage Coast in east Devon. It is a vista of flat-topped hills, deep valleys leading down to the sea, shingle beaches, hedge-lined country lanes and thatched cottages. The **South West Coast Path** follows the coastline through this delightful landscape, which is a haven for rare plants and butterflies.

Branscombe is home to what was, before it closed in 1987, the last traditional working bakery in Devon.

Branscombe Church

Now in the hands of the National Trust, the stone-built and thatched **Old Bakery** is a tearoom although in the baking room the old baking equipment has been preserved. Next door is the restored water-powered **Manor Mill** that provided the flour for the bakery while at the **Forge** a blacksmith continues to create ironwork items and implements that can be purchased here. The bakery, the mill and forge are owned by the National Trust.

SIDMOUTH

8 miles S of Honiton off the A3052

As with many resorts on the south coast, Sidmouth benefited greatly from Napoleon's conquest of Europe, which denied the leisured classes of the late 18th and early 19th century access to their favourite

NORMAN LOCKYER OBSERVATORY

Sidmouth, Devon EX10 0YQ
Tel: 01395 512096

There are few public access observatories in Britain; the **Norman Lockyer Observatory** has a planetarium and large telescopes, including those used to discover helium and establish the sciences of astrophysics. Lockyer's achievements include the establishment of meteorology, astro-archaeology, the science journal, Nature, the Science Museum and government departments for Science and Education. The radio station commemorates the contribution of Sir Ambrose Fleming, a local hero, to the invention of the radio valve. Programme of public events available from local tourist offices and libraries, or contact The Observatory Secretary or phone 01395 512096 for party bookings.

SIDMOUTH TRAWLERS

Fisherman's Yard, The Ham,
Port Royal, Sidmouth, Devon
Tel: 01395 512714

Tucked away in Fisherman's Yard at the far eastern end of the Esplanade is **Sidmouth Trawlers**, a fishmonger well known in the area for the excellent quality of its locally caught fish and shellfish. Established in the 1960s by Stan Bagwell, from a long line of fishermen, this family-run business maintains the highest standards in endeavouring to provide for all lovers of seafood a large variety of fish and shellfish sourced from local fishermen.

The family takes great pride in the various national craftsmanship awards they have won over the years, and filleting and preparation is all part of the service. No one coming to Sidmouth should miss the opportunity to visit this superb fishmonger's. Insulated packaging is available to take home a selection of the freshest seafood - from brill, Dover sole, mackerel and scallops to freshly cooked lobster and crab - to be found anywhere in the country. A ready-to-eat service is also available for whelks, cockles, mussels, prawns and crabmeat, and generously filled sandwiches are made to order.

resorts on the Continent. So they began to hunt around England for alternatives places for entertainment and diversion. At the same time, sea bathing had become fashionable, so these years were a boom time for the south coast helped by its good links with London and its mild climate. Many poverty-stricken fishing villages, such as Sidmouth, were saved from complete obscurity and possible desertion.

The village's spectacular position at the mouth of the River Sid, with its dramatic red cliffs and broad pebbly beach, assured its popularity with the newcomers and a grand Esplanade was constructed lined with handsome Georgian houses. During the first two decades of the 19th century, Sidmouth's popularity doubled as the aristocratic and well-to-do built substantial 'cottages' and villas in and around the town. Many of these have been converted into impressive hotels.

One of the town's early visitors was Jane Austen, who came here on holiday in 1801 and, according to Austen family tradition, fell in love with a clergyman whom she would have married if he had not mysteriously died or disappeared. Later, in the 1830s, William Makepeace Thackeray visited and the town featured as Baymouth in his semi-autobiographical work *Pendennis* (published in 1848). During the Edwardian age, Beatrix Potter was a visitor on several occasions. However, while these notable visitors certainly added respectability, one visitor helped make Sidmouth's name more than anyone else. In 1819, in order to escape his creditors, the Duke of Kent moved to Sidmouth. His house is now the Royal Glen Hotel. It was here that his young daughter, who went on to become Queen Victoria, saw the sea for the first time. In an attempt to evade his creditors, the Duke had his mail directed to Salisbury

THE ROYAL GLEN HOTEL

Glen Road, Sidmouth, Devon EX10 8RW
Tel: 01395 513221/513456 Fax: 01395 514922
e-mail: info@royalglenhotel.co.uk
website: www.royalglenhotel.co.uk

The Royal Glen is a historic Grade I listed building that has been welcoming guests for more than 100 years. Throughout that time it has been run by the same family and is now in the safe hands of Orson and Jean Crane, their daughters Hilary Caldwell and Vivienne Bess, and their loyal staff. But the building has a history going back far beyond its days as a hotel. Before it became the Royal Glen, the building was

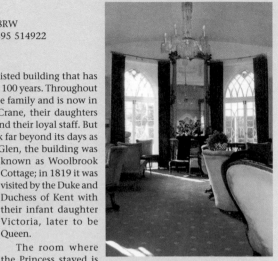

known as Woolbrook Cottage; in 1819 it was visited by the Duke and Duchess of Kent with their infant daughter Victoria, later to be Queen.

The room where the Princess stayed is now one of the hotel's 32 very comfortable bedrooms, each of which has its own individual appeal, differing in shape, size and furnishings. All the bedrooms have private bath or shower, TV, radio-alarm clock, telephone and tea-making facilities. The unique oval Drawing Room is a perfect place to relax after a meal, and when the weather is kind the veranda in the secluded garden is a pleasant spot to enjoy a drink. In Victoria's Restaurant, a tempting table d'hote menu makes excellent use of prime local produce in dishes that offer both traditional and inventive contemporary cuisine. Other eating options include bar snacks (available Monday to Saturday), traditional Sunday lunches, packed lunches and children's high teas.

The Drawing Room, restaurant and TV lounge are non-smoking areas, and smoking is also discouraged in the bedrooms. The hotel's indoor swimming pool - warm in the cooler months and cool in the height of summer - is a great place for working up an appetite or enjoying a relaxing float, while guests wanting an invigorating dip in the sea have only yards to walk. The Royal Glen has a putting green, while for full-scale golf there are three courses within ten miles of Sidmouth. Many other sporting activities are available in an around the town, but Sidmouth is also a perfect spot for unwinding and strolling.

and, each week, he would ride over to collect his letters. Though he had desperate financial worries, the Duke could not contain his delight in his young daughter. He would push the Princess in a carriage up and down the mile-long Esplanade, stopping passers-by to tell them to look carefully at his little girl, "for one day she will be your Queen." Some 50 years later, Queen Victoria presented a stained glass window to Sidmouth parish church in memory of her father.

A stroll around the town reveals a wealth of attractive Georgian and early Victorian buildings; surprisingly for a town of this size, Sidmouth has nearly 500 listed buildings.

Sidmouth Museum, near the seafront, is certainly worth visiting as it provides a very vivid presentation of the Victorian resort along with an interesting collection of local prints, a costume gallery and a display of lace. One of the most striking exhibits here is the *Long Picture* by Hubert Cornish. It is some eight feet long and depicts the whole of Sidmouth's seafront as it was in 1814. In 1912, Sir Joseph Lockyer founded the **Norman Lockyer Observatory** for astronomical and meteorological research (see panel on page 254).

Demure though it remains, Sidmouth undergoes a transformation in the first week of August each year when it plays host to the International Folklore, Dance and Song Festival, a cosmopolitan event that attracts a remarkable variety of Morris dancers, folk singers and even clog dancers from around the world.

The River Sid is one of England's shortest rivers, rising to the east of

CHERITON GUEST HOUSE

Vicarage Road, Sidmouth, Devon EX10 8UQ
Tel/Fax: 01395 513810
website: www.smoothhound.co.uk/hotels/cheritong.html

In their handsome town house backing on to the River Sid, Jane and Rob Speers welcome guests to a relaxing, stress-free break from the daily grind. The en suite bedrooms at **Cheriton Guest House** are warm and comfortable, and guests have the use of a very pleasant lounge. A good breakfast starts the day, and packed lunches and evening meals are available by arrangement. The front of the house is a blaze of colour from seasonal flowers and plants, but the real gem is a lovely secluded rear garden that has several times been a winner in the annual Sidmouth in Bloom contest.

It's an easy walk to the seafront, either by way of the town centre

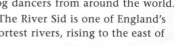

or along the River Sid (which at a mere four miles long is one of the shortest in the country). Cheriton Guest House, which is open all year round, is a non-smoking establishment. Jane Austen, William Makepeace Thackeray, Beatrix Potter and the infant Princess Victoria all graced Sidmouth with visits, and today it remains a very pleasant spot with its cliffs, its broad beach, its grand esplanade and its dignified Georgian houses.....and Cheriton Guest House is an ideal base from which to enjoy it all.

CORE HOUSE COTTAGES

Burscombe Lane, Sidford, Sidmouth, Devon EX10 0QA
Tel: 01395 512255
e-mail: burscombe@aol.com
website: www.corehousecottages

Core House, an 1820s building that was once a school, is
now a private residence where resident proprietor Susan
Pratt offers bed and breakfast accommodation in double
or twin rooms, all with en suite or private facilities. Guests
have the use of a television lounge, a pleasant patio and
attractive gardens. Within the eight acres of grounds in
which the house stands are **Core House Cottages**, three
luxury cottages and a garden apartment, all overlooking the beautiful valley of the River Sid.

Dairy Cottage has two bedrooms sleeping four
guests; Bell Cottage and the adjoining Oak Cottage
each have two bedrooms, and Bell also has an
additional bed settee; the Garden Apartment has one
bedroom and a bed settee in the lounge. All these
properties have been totally renovated, providing
everything needed for a self-catering holiday while
retaining many attractive original features. They all
have outside areas with garden furniture and barbecue
equipment. No smoking inside. Core House is located
half a mile up from the A3052; Sidmouth and the sea
are a five-minute drive away.

THE SALTY MONK

Church Street, Sidford, Sidmouth, Devon EX10 9QP
Tel: 01395 513174 Fax: 01395 577232
e-mail: enquirys@saltymonk.co.uk
website: www.saltymonk.co.uk

The Salty Monk is a delightful restaurant with rooms
housed in a 16th century building that was originally
used by Benedictine monks on their way to trade salt
at Exeter Cathedral. Since 1999 it has been owned and
run by Annette and Andy Witheridge, who with their
staff regale their guests with friendly hospitality,
personal service, comfortable accommodation and meals to remember. The individually decorated
bedrooms are full of the thoughtful extras that make a stay really special, from big fluffy bath sheets
and robes to magazines, home-made biscuits and chilled bottled water. Some rooms have a hydrotherapy
spa or hydro massage shower, and the suite boasts a king-
sized water bed and spa bath.

The owners both cut their culinary teeth in some of the
country's finest restaurants, and in the light, airy restaurant
overlooking the beautiful gardens they serve contemporary
English cuisine using top-quality ingredients supplied
wherever possible from the West Country. The sea is only
two miles distant at the Regency town of Sidmouth, and
other local attractions include several National Trust
properties, golf courses, gardens, antiques centres and the
famous Donkey Sanctuary.

Ottery St Mary and flowing through a narrow valley for just four miles before meeting the sea. The village of Sidford is best known for its packhorse bridge, dating from the 12th century. Further up the river lies **Sidbury**, whose church boasts a Powder Room. This was built as a storage room for gunpowder during the Napoleonic wars when the military thought that a French invasion was imminent. Above the village stands **Sidbury Castle**, not a conventional castle at all but the site of an Iron Age hillfort. From here there are panoramic views of the coastline from Portland Bill to Berry Head.

HARPFORD
7½ miles SW of Honiton off the A3052

Situated on the east bank of the River Otter, in the churchyard of Harpford's 13th century church, is a memorial cross to the Rev Augustus Toplady who was vicar here for a few years in the mid 18th century. It was this vicar who, in 1775, wrote the hymn *Rock of Ages*, which has proved, for more than 200 years, to be enduringly popular.

A couple of miles west of the village is **Aylesbeare Common**, an RSPB sanctuary, one of the best stretches of

heathland in the area and home to a variety of birds, including the Dartford warbler, stonechats and nightjars.

OTTERY ST MARY
5 miles SW of Honiton on the B3177

This small town is justly proud of its magnificent 14th century **Church of St Mary**, looking part cathedral and part Oxford college. These comparisons are justified, as when Bishop Grandisson commissioned the building in 1337, he stipulated that it should be modelled on his own cathedral in Exeter. He also wanted it to be a centre of learning and so accommodation for 40 scholars was provided. The striking exterior is mirrored by the beautiful interior and there are several medieval treasures including a 14th century astronomical clock, showing the moon and planets, that still functions with its original machinery.

The vicar here during the mid-18th century was John Coleridge, whose tenth child, Samuel Taylor, born in 1772, went on to become a celebrated poet. The family home was close to the church but, after his father died in 1781, Coleridge was sent away from Ottery to school. A bronze plaque in the churchyard wall

FLUXTON FARM

Ottery St Mary, Devon EX11 1RJ
Tel: 01404 812818 Fax: 01404 814843

The heart of **Fluxton Farm** is a delightful 16th century traditional Devon longhouse just south of Ottery St Mary and only four miles from the sea. Owner Ann Forth offers characterful bed and breakfast accommodation in 10 bedrooms, all but one with en suite facilities and most enjoying views across the beautiful Otter Valley. A full English breakfast is served in the beamed dining room, and guests have the use of two charming sitting rooms and a large lawned garden with a trout stream. The owners keep chickens, ducks, geese and lots of rescued cats.

CADHAY MANOR

Ottery St Mary, Devon EX11 1QT
Tel/Fax: 01404 812432

"John Haydon, esquire, sometime bencher of Lincoln's Inn, builded at Cadhay a fair new house and enlarged his demenses". So wrote Risdon in his book of Devon published in 1620. Much of the present house was built around 1550 and it remains in all essentials unchanged. Approached by an avenue of limes, Cadhay stands in a magnificent garden and looks out over the original medieval fish-ponds which may have been used by the Warden and Canons of the lovely Collegiate Church of St Mary of Ottery a mile away.

When John Haydon built his impressive mansion, he retained the Great Hall of an earlier building on the site and its fine timber roof, built between 1420-1470, which is still in place. In the early 1600s Haydon's great nephew, Robert Haydon, added an Elizabethan Long Gallery, forming a unique and attractive courtyard. It's known as the Court of Sovereigns because of the statues of Henry VIII, Edward VI, Mary and Elizabeth I which stand over the doors. Robert Haydon married Joan, eldest daughter of Sir Amias Poulett, and interestingly the present owners of Cadhay, the William-Poulett family, are descended from Sir Amias. Cadhay and its gardens are open to the public on the spring and late autumn bank holiday Sunday and Monday, then each Tuesday, Wednesday and Thursday during July and August.

honours Ottery's most famous son, showing his profile menaced by the albatross that features in his best known poem, *The Ancient Mariner*.

This is a delightful town with some fine Georgian buildings among which can be found a Georgian serge factory by the riverside, a dignified example of early industrial architecture. Here, too, is the **Tumbling Weir**, constructed in 1790, when the river was harnessed to provide power to the factory and the adjacent corn and grist mill. An especially interesting time to visit Ottery is on the

Saturday closest to 5th November when the town's Guy Fawkes celebrations include a time-honoured, and rather alarming, tradition of rolling barrels of flaming tar through the narrow streets.

A mile to the northwest of the town lies **Cadhay**, a beautiful Tudor manor house built in 1550 for the successful lawyer, John Haydon (see panel). Close by is **Escot Park and Gardens** where visitors can see an arboretum and rose garden along with a collection of wildlife that includes wild boar, pot-bellied pigs, otters and birds of prey.

DUNKESWELL
4½ miles NW of Honiton off the A30

Lying in the heart of the Blackdown Plateau, this little village has an unusual claim to fame. The 900-year-old Norman font in the Church of St Nicholas has carved on it a crude depiction of an elephant that is probably the earliest representation of this animal in England. The stonemason had almost certainly never seen an elephant in the flesh, but he made as good a job of it as of his satirical carvings of a bishop and a doctor. The font was originally located at **Dunkeswell Abbey**, a Cistercian foundation of which only the 15th century gatehouse survives. To the west of the village lies **Dunkeswell Memorial Museum**, standing on the site of the only American Navy air base commissioned on British soil during World War II. It is dedicated to the veterans of the US Fleet Air Wing 7 and RAF personnel who served at the base.

LOCATOR MAP

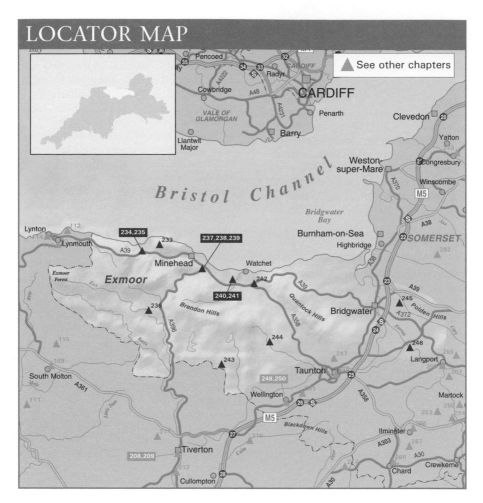

See other chapters

ADVERTISERS AND PLACES OF INTEREST

233 Hindon Organic Farm, Selworthy,
   Minehead   page 266

234 Hartshanger Holidays, Porlock   page 267

235 Porlock Antiques, Porlock   page 267

236 Karslake House Hotel, Winsford,
   Exmoor   page 268

237 The Linen Press, Dunster   page 269

238 The Crooked Window Gallery,
   Dunster   page 270

239 Moonlight, Dunster   page 270

240 Small World of Toys and Hobbies,
   Washford, Watchet   page 272

241 Earthcentric, Washford, Watchet   page 273

242 Ceramics by Martin Pettinger,
   Williton, Taunton   page 274

243 The Manor Mill, Waterrow, Taunton   page 278

244 Gaulden Manor Gardens & House,
   Tolland, Taunton   page 279

245 Chedzoy Farm Shop, Chedzoy   page 280

246 Trevor J Cottell, Burrow Wall   page 280

EXMOOR AND QUANTOCK HILLS 7

The high moorland plateau of Exmoor National Park straddles Somerset and Devon, 70 per cent of the land being in the former. It borders the Bristol Channel coast and is sometimes seen as Dartmoor's poor relation, but this is an area with a character all its own, a wonderful blend of moor and heath, swift flowing streams, deep wooded valleys and the high coastal cliffs. Many of the settlements here are ancient, dating back to well before the Norman Conquest. Throughout the National Park there are relics from the Bronze and Iron Ages such as hut circles, standing stones and barrows. This is also the land of the wild Exmoor pony and herds of red deer, matched by the wealth of bird and plant life. The moor is criss-crossed by a network of paths and bridleways providing superb opportunities for discovering the hidden delights of this glorious area on foot or on horseback.

Romantic Exmoor has become inextricably linked with RD Blackmore and his novel *Lorna Doone*, published in 1869. Although the story was written from childhood memories of Exmoor while Blackmore was in London, many of the descriptions correspond unmistakably to places in the area. Oare Church is the setting

Bridge over the River Barle, Exmoor

for Carver Doone's attempted murder, John Ridd goes to Porlock for gunpowder and lead and Watchet is the scene of Lorna's kidnap.

Minehead is a popular place today, but anyone visiting the holiday village, originally created by Billy Butlin in 1962, will find it hard to believe that the town was once a busy Celtic port. Pretty little Watchet has been a port since Saxon times and its harbour is still of significance today.

Once a major port to rival Bristol, Bridgwater's docks succumbed to the silting up of the River Parrett. However, this particular cloud had a silver lining, as the mud, when baked, was a very effective scourer and it was used up until the early 20th century to clean stone. To the west of Bridgwater lie the Quantock Hills, an Area of Outstanding Natural Beauty that extends from just outside Taunton to the coast at Quantoxhead. Rich with Neolithic and Bronze Age remains as well as plant and wildlife, the southern hills provide some of the most fertile agricultural land in Somerset.

On the eastern slopes of the Quantocks is the village of Nether Stowey, which has a strong literary connection. In the late 18th century Samuel Taylor Coleridge moved into a cottage in the village with his wife and son. In the short time that the family was here, Coleridge wrote many of this best-known works, including *The Rime of the Ancient Mariner* and *Kubla Khan*. He also spent much time walking along the north Somerset coast and through the countryside of the Quantocks and Exmoor with William Wordsworth.

While this northern region of Somerset has been the inspiration for many writers and artists down the years, the coastline also has a monument to the ingenuity of the 20th century. A few miles to the north of Nether Stowey, are the two nuclear power stations at Hinkley Point. Not a place on everyone's holiday itinerary, the power stations' visitor centre has some innovative and imaginative exhibitions on both nuclear power and the wildlife of the planet. Many people may prefer to visit the surrounding nature reserve with its rich flora and fauna.

MINEHEAD

Despite sounding like a product of the industrial age, Minehead is a popular seaside town, lying at the foot of the wooded promontory known as **North Hill**. It is one of the oldest settlements in Somerset. A busy Bristol Channel port since the time of the Celts, the old harbour lies in the lee of North Hill, making it one of the safest landing places in the West Country. At one time, ships arrived here with wool and livestock from Ireland, crops from the plantations of Virginia, coal from the South Wales valleys and day trippers from Cardiff and Bristol. The merchants and paddle steamers have gone and nowadays the harbour is the peaceful haunt of sailing dinghies and pleasure craft.

There is a good view of the old port from the **North Hill Nature Reserve** and a three-mile-walk starting near the

lifeboat station on the harbour side is an excellent way to explore this area of Minehead and its surroundings. The 14th century parish Church of St Michael stands in a prominent position below North Hill. For centuries, a light was kept burning in its tower to help guide ships into the harbour. Inside, the church contains a number of unusual features, including a rare medieval prayer book, or missal, which once belonged to Richard Fitzjames, a local vicar who went on to become Bishop of London in 1506.

The decline of Minehead as a port was offset by its gradual expansion as a seaside resort and the town went to great lengths to attract a suitably respectable clientele. So much so, in fact, that there was a local bylaw in force until 1890 that forbad anyone over 10 years of age from swimming in the sea "except from a bathing machine, tent or other effective screen". The arrival of the railway in

1874 failed to trigger the rapid expansion experienced by some other seaside resorts. Nevertheless, during World War I, Minehead was able to provide an escape from the ravages of war at timeless establishments like the Strand Hotel, where guests were entertained by such stars as Anna Pavolva and Gladys Cooper. Changes to Minehead over the years have been gradual but the most momentous change came in 1962 when Billy Butlin opened a holiday camp at the eastern end of the esplanade. Now updated and renamed **Somerwest World**, this popular attraction has done much to transform present-day Minehead into an all round family resort. The town is also the terminus of the **West Somerset Railway**, the privately owned steam railway that runs for 20 miles between the resort and Bishop's Lydeard, just northwest of Taunton.

AROUND MINEHEAD

PORLOCK WEIR
9 miles W of Minehead off the A39

Today this hamlet has a small tide-affected harbour full of pleasure craft but Porlock Weir was once an important seaport. The Danes sacked it on a number of occasions in the 10th century. In 1052, Harold, the future king of England, landed here from Ireland to begin a short-lived career that ended at the Battle of Hastings in 1066. A pleasant and picturesque place, Porlock Weir offers a number of interesting attractions, including a

working blacksmith's forge and a glass studio where visitors can see lead crystal being made in the traditional manner. A short distance offshore a **Submerged Forest**, a relic of the Ice Age, can be seen at low tide.

From Porlock Weir an attractive one and a half mile walk leads up through walnut and oak to **Culbone Church**, arguably the smallest church in regular use in England, and certainly one of the most picturesque. A true hidden treasure, measuring only 33 feet by 14 feet, this superb part-Norman building is set in a wooded combe that once supported a small charcoal burning community and was at other times home to French prisoners and lepers.

PORLOCK
8 miles W of Minehead off the A39

An ancient settlement once frequented by Saxon kings, in recent decades Porlock has become a popular riding and holiday centre. The village is filled with lovely old buildings, most notably the 15th century **Dovery Manor** with its striking traceried hall window and the largely 13th century parish church that lost the top section of its spire during a

Views near Porlock

HINDON ORGANIC FARM

Hindon Farm, Nr Selworthy, Minehead, Somerset TA24 8SH
Tel/Fax: 01643 705244
e-mail: info@hindonfarm.co.uk website: www.hindonfarm.co.uk

Hindon Organic Farm is a working farm offering Exmoor Organic Hill Farm meat produce and accommodation. Winners of the *Organic Producers of the Year Award*, recommended by *Which* and *Rick Stein Food Heroes*, they are also award winners for their commitment to green principles. Ducks dabble in the stream, peacocks parade and donkeys dawdle - idyllic. Visit the Farm Shop or stay, relax and unwind.

Roger and Penny Webber are proud to be organically farming with care and conservation, and are the third generation of this family on this 500-acre organic stock farm. The secluded farm is located in a valley three miles from Minehead, the Gateway to Exmoor, for pubs, beach and steam railway, and one mile from the thatched village of Selworthy for 'scrummy' cream teas. The farm is situated on the National Trust Holnicote Estate. Dunster Castle is five miles away, and within the Exmoor National Park. Guests can enjoy the wonderful walks from the door. Either wander the waymarked farm trail with spotty pigs, cattle and sheep in the fields, as well as

bluebells, primroses, badgers, hare and red deer, or walk further on up to the heather moor using the South West coast path - an area where Coleridge wrote *The Ancint Mariner*. There are glorious views over the sea, down to the bay at Porlock and beyond to Lynton. There is a shorter walk to the picnic wood with nothing but bird song to disturb you. Maybe just sit in peace in the garden, or read a book by the fire enjoying some of the goodies from the Farm Shop. Information, leaflets and maps on horse riding, mountain biking, water sports, country fairs, flower shows, Exmoor Food Festival and many other local attractions are also available.

Quality accommodation is provided either in the form of bed and breakfast in the 18th century farmhouse or self-catering in a 100 year old traditional farm cottage. Both offer charm and comfort with crisp white cotton sheets, wood floors, fresh flowers, log fires, local paintings and original features. Also available to both self-catering and bed and breakfast guests is the all organic breakfast - freshly squeezed orange juice, fresh baked crusty bread hot from the Aga - delicious with honey on the comb or maybe Penny's own plum jam - as well as local yogurt, butter and milk. Luxury muesli, prunes or fresh fruit is followed by a lovely brown egg from one of the farm chickens and Roger's homemade grilled crispy bacon and country pork sausages - provided by their own Gloucester Old Spot pigs - all served with tomatoes and mushrooms. You can certainly taste the difference with fresh own organic and local produce. The four star cottage is equipped to a high standard and self-catering guests are provided on arrival with a complimentary welcome hamper filled with organic and local produce, and for special occasions a bottle of organic bubbly.

Hindon Organic Farm Shop is open both to the public and to guests. Select from the farm's own organic meat produce; Aberdeen Angus beef, pork, bacon, ham, sausages or lamb, all organically reared on the farm and cut, packed and labelled on site. Also available is other organic and local produce, including chutneys, dry goods, vegatables and dairy products. Chill boxes to take home make great presents too. Mail order is available nationwide.

HARTSHANGER HOLIDAYS

Toll Road, Porlock, Somerset TA24 8JH
Tel/Fax: 01643 862700 e-mail: hartshanger@lineone.net
website: www.hartshanger.com

Hartshanger is an Edwardian gentleman's residence set
above the village of Porlock in the heart of Exmoor
National Park. It is the home of Alanna Edward and her
family, who offer beautiful self-catering accommodation
in two flats, one with two bedrooms in the main house,
the other with three bedrooms in the converted stable block. Both have fully equipped kitchens and
comfortable sitting rooms, and guests can roam in the grounds, enjoy the views or take a little exercise
on the all-weather tennis court.

PORLOCK ANTIQUES & GALLERY LTD

High Street, Porlock, Somerset TA24 8PU
Tel: 01643 862226 Fax: 01643 863461
e-mail: porlockantiques@aol.com

In a village of lovely old buildings and interesting shops, one of the
most interesting is Sara Goodson's **Porlock Antiques & Gallery Ltd.**
This unusual shop sells an eclectic mix of goods that run from antique
furniture to Persian carpets and rugs, English glassware, Italian table
china, lamps of all kinds and handmade stained glass, mirrors, candles and candlesticks. There are
desk accessories and games from Thuya Wood, blankets and throws from Sweden, photo frames,
gorgeous handbags, scarves and purses....the list goes on, and since the stock changes constantly,
every visit brings new ideas for special treats or unique gifts.

---

thunderstorm in the 17th century.
Porlock has the feel of a community at
the end of the world as it lies at the foot
of **Porlock Hill**, a notorious incline
where the road rises 1,350 feet in less
than three miles, with a gradient of 1 in
4 in places.

SELWORTHY
3 miles W of Minehead off the A39

This picturesque and much
photographed village is situated on the
side of a wooded hill. Just to the
northwest lies **Selworthy Beacon**, one of
the highest points on the vast **Holnicote
Estate**. Covering some 12,500 acres of
Exmoor National Park, it includes a four-
mile stretch of coastline between
Minehead and Porlock Weir. There are
few estates in the country that offer such
a variety of landscape. There are north-
facing cliffs along the coast, traditional

villages and hamlets of cottages and
farms and the **Horner and Dunkery
National Nature Reserve** where
Dunkery Beacon, the highest point on
Exmoor, rises to 1,700 feet. Virtually the
full length of the River Horner lies
within the estate, from its source on the
high moorland to the sea at Bossington
Beach, one of the best examples of a
shingle storm beach in the country. The
whole area is noted for its diversity of
wildlife and the many rare plant species
to be found.

This National Trust-owned estate has
over 100 miles of footpaths through
fields, moors and villages for walkers to
enjoy while the South West Coast Path
curves inland at Hurlstone Point to avoid
landslips in the soft Foreland sandstone.
Among the settlements in the estate is
this village of Selworthy created by Sir
Thomas Dyke-Acland to house his estate

Packhorse Bridge, Allerford

imaginatively presented displays is a Victorian kitchen, a laundry and dairy, and an old school room complete with desks, books and children's toys.

Winsford

7 miles S of Minehead off the A396

One of the prettiest villages in Exmoor, with picturesque cottages, a ford and no fewer than seven bridges, including an old packhorse bridge. On a rise to the west of the village stands the medieval church with a handsome tall tower that dominates both the village and the surrounding area. It may seem surprising that such an idyllic spot should have been the birthplace of the

workers. West of this model village is another estate village, **Allerford,** which has an elegant twin-arched **Packhorse Bridge**. In Allerford's old school is a **Museum** dedicated to the rural life of West Somerset. Among its many

Karslake House Hotel

Winsford, Exmoor, Somerset TA24 7JE
Tel: 01643 851242
e-mail: enquiries@karslakehouse.co.uk
website: www.karslakehouse.co.uk

Well situated for discovering the delights of Exmoor and the North and South Devon coasts, **Karslake House Hotel** enjoys a quiet, picturesque setting tucked away among wooded hills. Dating from the 15th century, the former malthouse is the home of Nick and Juliette Mountford, who offer very comfortable and homely guest accommodation in six individually decorated bedrooms with charming personal touches such as fresh flowers. All the rooms are centrally heated, with television, hair dryer, tea/coffee making facilities, mineral water and toiletries.

There's a good choice for breakfast, and guests can relax with complimentary afternoon tea and homemade biscuits in the lounge or out in the garden. Guests opting for an evening meal in the restaurant will enjoy local produce freshly cooked to order and complemented by a comprehensive selection of wines. Pre-dinner drinks and after-dinner coffee are served in the cosy sitting room, and the hotel has a well-stocked bar. Many activities, including riding, fishing and shooting, can be arranged, and the owners are ready with advice on the best ways to explore beautiful Exmoor.

firebrand Ernest Bevin, founder of the Transport & General Workers Union, World War II statesman and Foreign Secretary in the postwar Labour government.

DUNSTER

2 miles SE of Minehead on the A396

Although Dunster is one of the most popular of Exmoor's villages, this ancient settlement is also one of the least typical as it lies in the fertile valley of the River Avill. No visitor will be surprised to learn that this landscape inspired Mrs Alexander to compose the hymn *All Things Bright and Beautiful*. The village is dominated by **Dunster Castle** standing outside the village on the top of the wooded Conygar Hill. Founded by William de Mohun on this natural promontory above the River Avill, just a few years before the Domesday Book was compiled in 1089, the castle passed into the hands of the Luttrell family in 1379. It remained in that family until it was given to the National Trust in 1976 by Lt Col GWF Luttrell. The medieval castle was remodelled in 1617 by William Arnold. During the English Civil War, Dunster Castle was one of the last Royalist strongholds in the West Country to fall and here the garrison only surrendered after a siege lasting 160 days. While several Jacobean interiors have survived, the castle underwent some major alterations during the latter part of the 17th century. Some of the finest features date from that period, in particular the superb plasterwork in the dining room and the magnificent balustraded main staircase with its delicately carved flora and fauna. However, the overall medieval character of the exterior of the present day castle is due to restoration work undertaken by Anthony Salvin in the 1860s, when the

THE LINEN PRESS

22 Church Street, Dunster, Somerset TA24 6SH
Tel: 01643 821802 Fax: 01643 821713
e-mail: anneslinenpress@aol.com

Anne Fisher started dealing in antique linen in 1990 and in 1999 she opened **The Linen Press** in a fine old building next to Dunster's impressive parish church. She sells a wide range of linen, both old and new, to a growing list of customers at home and overseas, as well as other textile products and hand-painted and distressed furniture imported from Denmark.

The old linens are mostly bought privately from people disposing of unwanted family items, which Anne launders, starches and presses for display in the shop, either on pulley rails up high or on towel rails at floor level.

The stock also includes lots of old French monogrammed linen sheets, napkins and other bits and pieces, while the new items range from lavender bags to white cotton bedding and super kingsize bedspreads. The shop itself was, for over 100 years, the town's main general store, and older customers contrast today's smell of lavender with the bacon and paraffin smells of yesteryear. All the shop fittings are rescued items from old draper's shops, and on the floor is a deep-pile carpet in Black Watch tartan. The Linen Press is always a hive of industry, with Anne and her helpers busy ironing linens, or making lavender or rose-filled bags, large laundry bags or Liberty fabric-covered coat-hangers.

THE CROOKED WINDOW GALLERY

7 High Street, Dunster, Somerset TA24 6SF
Tel: 01643 821606 or 01643 821989
website: www.thecrookedwindow.com
e-mail: info@thecrookedwindow.com

Opening times: Mon-Sat 10.30am - 5.30pm
Other times by appointment

The Crooked Window Gallery is situated in Dunster's picturesque High Street and is so named because the movement in its timber framed construction has caused one of the shops bay windows to become distorted and bowed.

The building dates from the 15th century and is unusual for its decorative plasterwork, or 'pargeting', a feature quite untypical of this area. The Gallery is owned and run by Robert and Margaret Ricketts.

Robert buys, sells, collects and lectures on Antiques. You might be surprised to find an impressive collection of fine Georgian furniture and ancient Chinese ceramics- not normally seen outside London. Margaret is an artist specialising in intricately detailed oil paintings of animals- especially horses, and landscapes. She also sculpts in clay producing original ceramics and iron-resin castings. Within the atmospheric interior you will find an exciting range of jewellery in gold and silver, precious and semi-precious stones. There are quality crafts from other artists as well as interesting and unusual antique items and antique jewellery- all eminently suitable as gifts.

MOONLIGHT

29 High Street, Dunster, Somerset TA24 6SF
Tel: 01643 821252 or 01643 821477   e-mail: moonlight_dunster@freenet.co.uk

Opening times: Tues-Sat 10.30am - 5pm, Sunday 2pm - 5pm
Other times by appointment. Please telephone.

Overlooking Dunster's Yarn Market, across the street from the Luttrell Arms, sits a beautiful shop full of delights for the discerning collector of period lights. **Moonlight** sparkles with light from over 60 period lights and chandeliers, from the UK and abroad, including Victorian, Edwardian, Art Nouveau and Art Deco chandeliers, wall lights, ceiling lights and table lamps. Many more are held in stock to

meet customers' needs. Proprietor Chris Dietrich, who relocated to Dunster from London five years ago, has been in the lighting business for over 12 years and provides a personal service, including sourcing lights and providing advice. All lights are renovated and fully rewired in-house and a full renovation service is available for customers' own lights. Alongside the range of lights is a wide range of antique glass, porcelain, jewellery, small furniture and collectables from several local dealers ensuring that a visit to 'Moonlight' will enthral any visitor to Dunster.

Dunster Village and Castle

castle was transformed into a comfortable and opulent country mansion. The steeply terraced gardens with their striking collection of rare shrubs and subtropical plants were also laid out around this time and the castle and gardens are surrounded by a 28-acre deer park through which there are several footpaths.

The parkland of Dunster Castle is also home to another National Trust property, **Dunster Working Watermill**, built in the 18th century on the site of a pre-Norman mill. Now restored to working order, the mill, which is run as a private business, has a shop selling mill flour, muesli and mill souvenirs and a tearoom by the riverside.

Remnants of the ancient feudal settlement that grew up in the shelter of the castle can still be seen in the village today, particularly in the wide main street. At the north end of the main street lies a small octagonal building, which is the former **Yarn Market**. This was erected by the Luttrells in the early 17th century when the village was an important cloth trading centre. Such was Dunster's influence in this trade that a type of woollen cloth, renowned for its quality

and strength, bears the village's name. The nearby **Luttrell Arms**, converted from a private residence into an inn in the mid 17th century, is more than 100 years older. Distinguished by its fine 15th century porch, the inn is one of the few places in the country where the once common custom of burning the ashen faggot is still observed. On Christmas Eve, the faggot, a bundle of 12 ash branches bound with green ash bands, is burnt in the inn's great fireplace and, as each band burns through, another round of hot punch is ordered from the bar. While the ash is burning, the company sings the ancient Dunster Carol and when the faggot is finally consumed a charred remnant is taken from the embers ready to light the following year's fire.

The inn once belonged to Cleeve Abbey while the village's principal religious house, **Dunster Priory**, was an outpost of Bath Abbey. Now largely demolished, the only parts of the priory to survive are the splendid priory church and an unusual 12th century dovecote that can be seen in a nearby garden. It still contains the revolving ladder once used to reach the roosting birds. The priory church, rebuilt by the monks in a rose pink sandstone as early as 1100, is one of the most impressive of Somerset's parish churches. The church tower was added in the 15th century but its most outstanding feature is undoubtedly the fan-vaulted rood screen that extends across the nave and aisles. On the southern edge of the village, the ancient **Gallox Bridge**, a medieval packhorse bridge, spans the River Avill.

CARHAMPTON
3 miles SE of Minehead on the A39

A small inland village that was the site of a Viking victory in the 9th century. Carhampton's original village church was named after St Carantoc, an early Celtic missionary from across the Bristol Channel. He is reputed to have chosen this site for his ministry by throwing his stone altar overboard and following it to the shore. The present church building, though much restored, contains a remarkable 15th century painted screen that extends across the entire church. The old inn, near the churchyard lych gate, has the date 1638 set into its cobbled floor in sheep's knuckle bones.

Each January, the residents of Carhampton re-enact the ancient custom of wassailing the apple trees. A toast is made to the most productive apple tree in the district and cider is poured on to its trunk in a charming ceremony that probably has pagan origins. Local folklore tells of a mysterious woman from the village, Madam Carne, who died in 1612 having done away with three husbands. According to legend, her ghost returned home after her funeral to prepare breakfast for the mourners.

WASHFORD
6 miles SE of Minehead on the A39

This village is spread out across Vallis Florida, the flowery valley dedicated to 'Our Blessed Lady of the Cliff'. Washford is dominated by **Cleeve Abbey**, the only monastery in Somerset that belonged to the austere Cistercian order founded in 1198 by the Earl of Lincoln. This abbey is fortunate in that it was not allowed to fall into disrepair after the Dissolution of the Monasteries in 1539 like many great monastic houses. The cloister buildings at Cleeve were put to domestic use and

EARTHCENTRIC

Unit 8, Washford Mill, Washford, Watchet,
Somerset TA23 0JY
Tel: 01984 641510

One of many speciality outlets in the beautifully restored 16th century Washford Mill, **Earthcentric** is owned and run by Connie Maltman, who came here from London in the summer of 2002. Celtic arts and crafts are the theme of many of the unusual items on display, which include scented candles, aromatherapy products, crystals, locally-made bronzes, pewter ware, jewellery and a unique range of clothing. The relaxed atmosphere, with lovely smells and soothing background music, makes it a delight to browse here at leisure for an unusual gift.

they are now among the most complete in the country. Although the cruciform abbey church has been reduced to its foundations, the refectory, chapter house, monks' common room, dormitory and cloisters remain. Most impressive of all is the great hall, a magnificent building with tall windows, a wagon roof decorated with busts of crowned angels and medieval murals, and a unique set of floor tiles with heraldic symbols. The curved dormitory staircase has particularly fine archways and mullion windows, while the combined gatehouse and almonry, the last building to be constructed before the Dissolution, makes an imposing entrance to the abbey precinct. A short distance northeast of the village lies a more recent attraction, **Tropiquaria**. This wildlife park features tropical animals. There is an aquarium here as well as an aviary and visitors are offered the chance to stroke snakes, tickle tarantulas and in many other ways get in touch with their wilder side. Nearby Washford Mill is a three-storey complex that comprises a garden centre, craft units and a café-restaurant.

A couple of miles to the east of Washford lies the large village of **Williton**, once a Saxon royal estate and now on the busy holiday route to Minehead and the west. During the 12th century the manor was the home of Sir Reginald FitzUrse, one of the knights who murdered Thomas à Becket. To atone for his terrible crime, Sir Reginald gave half the manor to the Knights Templar. The other half of the manor remained in the FitzUrse family until the death of Sir Ralph, in 1350, whereupon it was divided between his daughters. The village today is the home of the diesel locomotive workshops of the West Somerset Railway and the **Bakelite Museum**, a fascinating place providing a nostalgic look at the 'pioneer of plastics'.

Just to the southeast of Williton lies the small but historic village of **Sampford Brett**, which was recorded in the Domesday Book. Its name is derived from the sandy ford that crossed Doniford stream close to the village and the local de Brett family. It was Sir Adam de Brett who obtained the village's first charter to hold a market (in 1306) and, today, Sampford Brett remains a lovely and unspoilt place.

WATCHET
6½ miles SE of Minehead on the B3191

Established as a port long before the Norman Conquest, in the 6th century, St Decuman is said to have landed here from Wales with a cow that he brought along to provide sustenance. The town's name is derived from the Welsh for 'under the hill'. Charles I was once described as wearing a waistcoat of Watchet blue, possibly taken from the very distinctive colour of the cliffs here that were worked for their alabaster. By the 10th century the Saxon port and settlement here was important enough to have been sacked by the Vikings on at least three separate occasions and Watchet today is the only port of any significance in Somerset. During the mid-19th century thousands of tons of iron ore from the Brendon Hills were being exported through the docks each year. Unlike many similar sized ports that fell into disuse following the arrival of the railway, Watchet docks continue to export goods principally bound for the Iberian Peninsula. It was from Watchet that Coleridge's imaginary crew set sail in *The Rime of the Ancient Mariner*, the epic poem written while the poet was staying at nearby Nether Stowey.

The scale of Watchet's parish church reflects the town's long-standing importance and prosperity. It is set well back from the town centre and contains several fine tombs belonging to the Wyndham family, the local lords of the manor who did much to develop the potential of the port. There is a local story that suggests that one 16th century member of the family, Florence Wyndham, had to be buried twice. The day after her first funeral the church

sexton went down into church vaults secretly to remove a ring from her finger. When the coffin was opened, the old woman suddenly awoke. In recent years, the town has become something of a coastal resort and one of its attractions is the small **Museum** dedicated to local maritime history.

EXMOOR NATIONAL PARK

The characteristic heartland of the **Exmoor National Park** is a high, treeless plateau of hard-wearing Devonian shale carved into a series of steep-sided valleys by the prolonged action of the moor's many fast-flowing streams. Whereas the upland vegetation is mostly heather, gorse and bracken, the more sheltered valleys are carpeted with grassy meadows and pockets of woodland. The deep wooded combes provide shelter for herds of shy red deer, which roam at will, but are seldom seen. Easier to spot are the hardy Exmoor ponies, now almost all cross-breeds, which often congregate at roadside parking areas where there can be rich pickings from holidaymakers.

Exmoor is crisscrossed by a network of paths and bridleways, which provide superb opportunities for walking and pony-trekking. Many follow the routes of the ancient ridgeways across the high

Tarr Steps, Exmoor

moor and pass close to the numerous hut circles, standing stones, barrows and other Bronze and Iron Age remains which litter the landscape. Among the finest examples are the stone circle on **Porlock Hill**, **Alderman's Barrow** north of Exford, and the delightfully named **Cow Castle** near Simonsbath. The remarkable medieval packhorse bridge known as **Tarr Steps** lies to the north of the village of Hawkridge, near Dulverton. A superb example of a West Country clapper bridge, it is composed of massive flat stones placed across solidly-built dry stone uprights. The Roman relic known as the Caractacus Stone can be seen a couple of miles to the east, near Spire Cross.

DULVERTON

12 miles S of Minehead on the B3222

Situated in the wooded Barle Valley on the edge of Exmoor, Dulverton is a pretty little town where the headquarters of the national park can be found in an old converted workhouse. This was the town where, in RF Delderfield's novel *To Serve Them all My Days*, the main character David Powlett-Jones falls asleep at the station on his way to begin teaching at a public school on Exmoor. Delderfield had grown up on the edge of Exmoor and he used both Devon and Somerset as settings for his novels.

MONKSILVER

8 miles SE of Minehead on the B3188

This pretty village of charming old houses and thatched cottages has, in its churchyard, the graves of Elizabeth Conibeer and her two middle-aged daughters, Anne and Sarah, who were murdered in June 1775 in the nearby hamlet of **Woodford**. Their tombstone bears a message to the unidentified murderer:

Inhuman wretch, whoe'er thou art
That didst commit this horrid crime,
Repent before thou dost depart
To meet thy awful Judge Divine.

Just to the south of the village is a particularly handsome manor house, **Combe Sydenham Hall**, built in the middle of the reign of Elizabeth I by George Sydenham on the site of a monastic settlement. Above the entrance, there is a Latin inscription that translates as "This door of George's is always open except to ungrateful souls." This was also the home of Elizabeth Sydenham, George's daughter, who was to become the second wife of Sir Francis Drake. After becoming engaged, Sir Francis left his fiancée to go off looting for Spanish gold and Elizabeth grew so weary waiting for her betrothed to return that she resolved to marry another gentleman. According to local stories, she was on her way to the church, when a meteorite flew out of the sky and

Wimbleball Lake

Distance:	4.4 miles (7.0 kilometres)
Typical time:	105 mins
Height gain:	200 metres
Map:	Outdoor Leisure 9 Exmoor
Walk:	www.walkingworld.com ID:1346
Contributor:	Paul Edney

Access Information:

Pay and Display car park at the South West Lakes Trust site off the A396 Minehead to Tiverton Road.

Description:

The only road walking, a short section on a quiet lane is got out of the way at the start. Be sure to leave time for a refreshing pot of tea here after your walk but please note the seasonal opening times. You are soon off the road and gain an impressive view of Wimbleball dam as you round a corner. You can also now see Haddon Hill above you. Once through a short section of Haddon Wood and out on to the open heath the views all around but especially behind you over Wimbleball Lake are superb and get even better as you gain height. Take plenty of breaks to admire these views up to the triangulation point.

This is the highest part of the walk. The descent is gentle at first with the views over the lake on your left as you cross the heath. When you leave the heath and go downhill through the trees the going becomes steeper but nowhere is it uncomfortably so. This short section of woodland is quite open and gives a good opportunity for bird spotting. Through the trees and you are now almost at the lake and will stay in contact with it nearly all the way back to the car park.

Once over the dam the path stays close to the lakeside and heads back to the sailing club adjacent to the start. This path comprises a mixture of woodland and open grassland with an occasional wooden bench on which to sit

and look across the water before that pot of tea from the cafe in the car park.

Additional Information:

Tea shop, picnic tables, grass play area, toilets, phone and children's play area at the start. Toilets at the Haddon Hill car park just off route at waypoint 7.

Features:

Lake/loch, toilets, play area, birds, great views, cafe

Description:

① Leave the car park by the gate to the left of the tearoom back onto the road and turn left. At the sailing club sign, 200 metres up the road, keep straight on up the No Through Road.

② At the sharp left-hand bend take the track on the right past the farm buildings, through a gate and down a paved track.

③ At the Y junction go through the left-hand gate and down the concrete road towards the dam. When you reach the dam turn right across the dam wall. Once over the dam go right at the T-junction signed Bury '2½ miles'.

④ After about 150 metres, take the steep steps in a gap in the wall on the left signed 'Footpath to Haddon Hill'.

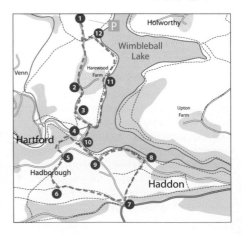

5 The path through the trees ends at a stile over a wire fence. Over the stile turn right on the wide gravel path for 10 metres then take the faint path on the left onto the heath land as shown in the picture. Head up the hill following the faint path. At times there are choices of paths but it does not really matter which ones you choose as long as you continue to head up, zig zagging towards the highest point in front of you where you will find the Hadborough triangulation point.

6 The triangulation point is set back beyond the main path, crossing in front of you, in a patch of heather and gorse bushes. Turn left here and follow the wide path gently down hill across the heath with superb views of Wimbleball Lake on your left.

7 Pass Haddon Hill car park and toilets on your right, keeping ahead on the main path until you reach the tarmacked road. Cross here onto the path shown in the picture. After only about 20 metres turn left at this faint cross-roads, heading to the left of the picture. The path heads down hill, initially alongside gorse bushes, narrow at first then opening up slightly when it starts going through sparse woodland. Cross the wider path when you

meet it and continue on the other side on the narrow path downhill though the trees.

8 Near the bottom of the hill, just above the lake, you meet the wide bridleway that runs between Bury and Upton. Turn left here signed 'Bridleway to Dam and Bury'.

9 The bridleway joins the road, the same one you crossed at the top of the hill, by these large boulders. Turn right here and take the road down the hill signed 'Wimbleball Dam and Bury'.

10 Turn right across the dam. At the far side of the dam turn right, over the stile and follow the grassy path above the lake.

11 The path goes through trees above the lake, across fields then over a little bridge. Ignore the gate for the farm on the left and follow the grassy path heading off to the right.

12 Keep following the grass path until you reach the sailing club that you pass on the left. At the gate above the sailing club turn left on the track ahead, past the children's play area on your right, up to the gate onto the main road which you passed at waypoint 2. Turn right here for the 200 metres back to the start.

---

smashed into the ground in front of her. Taking this as a sign that she should wait for Sir Francis she called off the wedding and, eventually, the couple were reunited. The meteorite, now known as 'Drake's Cannonball', is on display in the great hall; it is said to bring good luck to those who touch it. The 500-acre grounds around the hall have been designated a country park and they contain a working corn mill complete with waterwheel, a herb garden, a peacock house and a herd of fallow deer. The estate also incorporates a modern trout farm that stands on the site of a fully restored Tudor trout hatchery that dates from the end of the 16th century.

A mile or so to the west lies another ancient manor, **Nettlecombe Court**, once the home of the Raleigh family, relations of another great Elizabethan,

seafarer Sir Walter Raleigh. Later, the manor passed, by marriage, to the Cornish Trevelyan family and it is now a field studies centre open only by appointment.

To the southwest of the village are the **Brendon Hills**, the upland area within the Exmoor National Park from where, in the mid-19th century, iron ore was mined in significant quantities and then carried down a steep mineral railway to the coast for shipment to the furnaces of South Wales. At one time the Ebbw Vale Company employed almost 1,000 miners here and this strictly Nonconformist concern imposed a rigorous teetotal regime on its workers. Those wanting a drink had to walk across the moor all the way to Raleigh's Cross. The company also founded a miners' settlement with a temperance hotel and three chapels that became renowned for the achievements of its choir and fife and drum band. Those walking the slopes of the hills can still see sections of the old mineral railway and a two-mile stretch leading down to the coast at Watchet, which is now a pleasant footpath.

WIVELISCOMBE

13½ miles SE of Minehead on the B3227

This is an ancient and isolated village where the Romans once had a fort and a quantity of 3rd and 4th century coins have been uncovered in the area. Later, in medieval times, the local manor house was used as a summer residence of the bishops of Bath and Wells. The remains, including a striking 14th century archway, have now been incorporated into a group of cottages. During World War II, the church's crypt was used to store priceless historic documents and ecclesiastical treasures brought here from other parts of Somerset that were more at risk from aerial attack.

To the northeast of Wiveliscombe, close to the village of **Tolland**, is the delightful **Gaulden Manor** (see panel opposite), an estate that dates from the 12th century although the present house is largely 17th century. Gaulden Manor once belonged to the Turberville family whose name was borrowed by Thomas Hardy for use in his novel, *Tess of the D'Urbervilles* .

To the north and west of Wiveliscombe, below the Brendon Hills, are two reservoirs, **Wimbleball** and **Clatworthy**, which offer excellent facilities for picnickers, anglers and water sports enthusiasts.

BRIDGWATER

Situated at the lowest bridging point of the River Parrett in medieval times,

THE MANOR MILL

Waterrow, Nr Taunton, Somerset TA4 2AY
Tel/Fax: 01984 623317
e-mail: richard@themanormill.co.uk
website: www.themanormill.co.uk

Manor Mill nestles among the soft green hills of Somerset and occupies the south side of a wooded valley, beside the River Tone. This converted

water mill and its

neighbouring barns, which date back to the 17th century, have been sympathetically converted to provide a range of charming, comfortable and well-appointed self-catering accommodation with views over the river. Each cottage is equipped with linen and towels as well as a welcome pack of basic provisions upon arrival. Manor Mill has a heated swimming pool with access to a sun terrace, stone barbecue and children's play area. The extensive three and a half acres of grounds surrounding the mill are a haven of fields, water meadow and delightfully cultivated gardens.

Additional facilities include a utility room. A private dining Lodge for up to 20 guests, which is located in a secluded part of the grounds, is also available for hire for special occasions and private parties. Manor Mill is an excellent base for touring the West Country, with easy access to the glorious wilderness of Exmoor and the Quantock Hills as well as the coast of South Devon and North Somerset. Manor Mill offers a wonderful relaxing, peaceful atmosphere in a delightful rural location.

Bridgwater is an ancient inland port and industrial town. Despite having been fortified from before the Norman Conquest, the settlement that grew up around the castle remained little more than a village until an international trade in wool, wheat and other agricultural products began to develop in the late Middle Ages. Bridgwater grew and, at one time, it was the most important town on the coast between Bristol and Barnstaple. Although it is hard to believe now, it was the fifth busiest port in the country. The largely 14th century parish church, with its disproportionately large spire, is the only building to remain from that prosperous medieval era. The castle was dismantled after the English Civil War and the 13th century Franciscan friary and St John's Hospital disappeared long ago. Although the street layout here is still medieval, the buildings in the area between King Street and West Quay are some of the best examples of domestic Georgian architecture in the county.

Before the construction of a canal dock in the early 19th century, the ships arriving at Bridgwater used to tie up on both sides of the river below the town's medieval bridge and here, too, can be seen the last remnant of the castle, **The Water Gate**, on West Quay. After a long period of decline in the textile industry and as the river was beginning to silt up, Bridgwater underwent something of an industrial renaissance as new industries were established here during the early 19th century. The manufacture of Bridgwater glass, which had begun the previous century, continued to expand, and a canal terminus, complete with dock and warehouses, was built. The river mud that caused the decline of the town's port also proved to have hidden benefits, because when baked in oblong blocks it was found to be an excellent

GAULDEN MANOR GARDENS AND HOUSE

Tolland, Nr Taunton, Somerset
Tel: 01984 667213

Set in a beautiful valley between the Brendon and the Quantock hills is the historic **Gaulden Manor**, a medieval house parts of which are believed to date back to the 12th century. The house is famous for its plasterwork, the date of which can be assessed by the coats of arms on the overmantles and depict two families joined by marriage in 1639. Parties can view the interior of the house by appointment.

The house is surrounded by a series of gardens that include the rose garden, a well-stocked herb garden, a bog garden and a butterfly garden. Tucked away lies the Secret Garden planted with white shrubs and roses whilst beyond is the Monk's Fish Pond and island and a grassy walk with old shrub roses and geraniums leading back to the house. Not an overly neat garden, this is a place to explore with something new and different around each corner. Plants propagated from the garden are for sale.

scourer. As Bath Brick, it was used for nearly a century to clean grates and stone steps. The canal terminus, where the brickworks also stood, was finally closed in 1970 but has now been restored as a fascinating area of industrial archaeology.

Bridgwater's most famous son is the celebrated military leader, Robert Blake, who was born here in 1598. When in his 40s, Blake became an important officer in Cromwell's army and twice defended

Chedzoy Farm Shop

Westend Cottage, Chedzoy, Somerset TA7 8QR
Tel: 01278 425006
e-mail: kswarrington@aol.com

Keith and Sue started their business in a small way with homemade chutneys and preserves, and from those tasty beginnings came **Chedzoy Farm Shop**. Those high-quality award winning preserves are still one of the mainstays, made by hand in their kitchen in batches small enough to ensure the unmistakable and unbeatable homemade taste. The best

ingredients produce the best flavours, and no additives are used, so the farmshop's motto 'Tasting is Believing' is certainly fully justified. The owners also sell their produce at Somerset farmers' markets and can arrange tasting evenings.

The shop stocks many other foodstuffs, mostly made or sourced locally, including meat, game, poultry, eggs, dairy products, fruit and vegetables, homemade ready meals and baby food, cakes and breads, herbs and spices; local crafts are also on sale, notably artwork and willow baskets that are both handsome and practical. The owners keep a wide variety of domestic and farm animals that are guaranteed to keep visitors amused. The Battle of Sedgemoor took place at a spot between Chedzoy and Westonzoyland.

Trevor J Cottell

Westcott, Burrow Wall, Burrowbridge, Somerset TA7 0JQ
Tel: 01823 698127
e-mail: trevorjcottell@tiscali.co.uk
website: www.trevorjcottell.co.uk

Trevor J Cottell studied Furniture Design and Construction at the London College of Furniture and, in his 24 years as a maker, he has won great acclaim and numerous awards. A range of his unique, innovative and always interesting contemporary furniture is on display in his gallery, where the clean, simple decor and the delightful blue colour scheme bring out to best effect the lovely grains and shades of the pieces. Among the many woods he uses, oak is his favourite – he loves the figure, the colour and the texture - and his main aim is to combine beauty and utility in his furniture, in which the shapes and curves that appear in nature play an important part in the slender elegance of the finished product.

As well as his original designs, Trevor will design and make pieces to customers' orders. Many of his pieces, which include dining tables and chairs, rocking chairs, desks, stools, side tables, folding tables, book shelves, book stands, bookends, mirrors, letter racks and unusual boxes, are on display in his showroom, which is open from 10am to 5pm Friday and Saturday or by appointment.

Bridgwater Parish Church

Taunton against overwhelming Royalist odds. Just a decade later, he was given command of the British navy and went on to win a number of important battles against the Dutch and the Spanish. In so doing, he restored the nation's naval supremacy in Europe. The house in which he was born is now home to the **Admiral Blake Museum**, which contains a three-dimensional model of the Battle of Santa Cruz, one of Blake's most famous victories, along with a collection of his personal effects. However, Blake is not the only military leader to have stayed in Bridgwater as, during the late 17th century, the Duke of Monmouth stayed here before his disastrous defeat at the nearby Battle of Sedgemoor. The museum suitably illustrates this decisive battle in the duke's quest for the English throne. This is also a museum of local history and there is a large collection of

locally discovered artefacts on display that date from Neolithic times right up to the days of World War II.

AROUND BRIDGWATER

WESTONZOYLAND
3½ miles SE of Bridgwater on the A372

Just to the northwest of the village and on the southern bank of what is now the **King's Sedgemoor Drain** lies the site of the last battle to be fought on English soil. In July 1685, the well-equipped forces of James II heavily defeated the followers of the Duke of Monmouth in the bloody Battle of Sedgemoor. This brought an end to the ill-fated Pitchfork Rebellion that aimed to replace the Catholic King James with the Protestant Duke of Monmouth, the illegitimate son of Charles II. Around 700 of Monmouth's followers were killed on the battlefield while several hundred survivors were rounded up and taken to Westonzoyland churchyard, where many of them were hanged. The duke himself was taken to London where, ten days after the battle, he was executed on Tower Hill. However, it was during the infamous Judge Jeffrey's 'Bloody Assizes' that the greatest terror was inflicted on the surviving followers of the duke when well over 300 men were condemned to death and a further 600 were transported to the colonies. Today, a stark memorial marks the site of the lonely battlefield.

The village lies in the Somerset Levels and, in the 19th century, a steam-powered **Pumping Station** was built here to drain the water from the levels into the River Parrett. The oldest pumping station of its kind in the area, the engine on show here was in operation from 1861 until 1952. Now fully restored, it can be seen in steam at various times throughout the year. The station itself is a grade II listed building. Also on the site is a small forge, a tramway and a number of other exhibits from the steam age.

ENMORE
4 miles SW of Bridgwater off the A39

To the north of the village is the small redbrick country mansion of **Barford Park**, a delightfully proportioned Queen Anne house set in extensive grounds that incorporate a walled flower garden, a water garden and a large area of broadleaf woodland. The house, which contains some exceptionally fine examples of Queen Anne furniture, is still in daily family use and is open only by prior appointment.

To the west of Enmore the ground rises up into the **Quantock Hills**, an Area of Outstanding Natural Beauty that runs from near Taunton to the Bristol Channel at Quantoxhead. Rising to a high point of 1,260 feet at **Wills Neck**, this delightful area of open heath and scattered woodland supports one of the country's last remaining herds of wild red deer. The exposed hilltops are littered with Neolithic and Bronze Age remains, including around 100 burial mounds, many of which now resemble nothing more than a pile of stones. The richer soil in the south sustains arable farms and pockets of dense woodland and this varied landscape offers some magnificent walking with splendid views over the Bristol Channel, the Vale of Taunton Deane, the Brendon Hills and Exmoor. It was this glorious classical English landscape that the poets Wordsworth and Coleridge so admired while they were living in the area.

Southwest of Enmore in one of the loveliest areas on the southern Quantocks is **Fyne Court**, owned by the National Trust and housing the headquarters of the Somerset Wildlife

Trust and a visitor centre for the Quantocks. The main house here was built in the 17th century by the Crosse family. It was largely destroyed by fire in the 1890s and the only surviving parts are the library and music room that have been converted into the visitor centre. The grounds, which incorporate a walled garden, two ponds, an arboretum and a lake, have been designated a nature reserve. The most renowned occupant of the house was Andrew Cross, an early-19th century scientist who was a pioneer in the field of electrical energy. Known locally as the 'thunder and lightning man', one of Crosse's lightning conductors can still be seen on an oak tree in the grounds. Local stories tell how, during one of his electrical experiments, Crosse created tiny live insects. It was this claim that helped to inspire Mary Shelley to write her Gothic horror story, *Frankenstein*, in 1818.

BISHOP'S LYDEARD
9½ miles SW of Bridgwater off the A358

This large village is the southern terminus of the **West Somerset Railway**, the privately operated steam railway that runs to Minehead on the Bristol Channel coast. At nearly 20 miles it is the longest line of its kind in the country and it was formed when British Rail's 100-year-old branch between Taunton and Minehead closed in 1971. Running a summer service between Easter and the end of October, there are ten stations along the line and its special attractions include the first class Pullman dining car and the *Flockton Flyer*.

NETHER STOWEY
6½ miles NW of Bridgwater off the A39

This attractive village of 17th and 18th century stone cottages and houses is best known for its literary connections but Nether Stowey has a much longer history.

At one time, it was a small market town. A castle was built here in Norman times and the earthwork remains can be seen to the west of the village centre while its substantial manor house, **Stowey Court**, stands on the eastern side of the village. The construction of the manor house was begun by Lord Audley in 1497 shortly before he joined a protest against Henry VII's taxation policy. Sadly, he was not able to see the project through to completion as he was executed soon afterwards.

In 1797, a local tanner, Tom Poole, lent a dilapidated cottage at the end of his garden to his friend, Samuel Taylor Coleridge, who stayed here for three years with his wife and child. So began Nether Stowey's association with poets and writers. It was while here that Coleridge wrote most of his famous works, including *The Rime of the Ancient Mariner* and *Kubla Khan*. When not writing, he would go on long walks with his friend and near neighbour William Wordsworth, who had moved close to Nether Stowey from a house in Dorset at around the same time. Other visitors to the cottage included Charles Lamb. But it was not long before Coleridge's opium addiction and his rocky marriage began to take their toll. These were not the only problems for the poet as local suspicion was growing that he and Wordsworth were French spies. The home in which the Coleridges lived for three years is now **Coleridge Cottage**, a National Trust property where mementoes of the poet are on display.

A lane leads southwest from the village to the nearby village of **Over Stowey** and the starting point of the Forestry Commission's **Quantock Forest Trail**, a three-mile walk lined with specially planted native and imported trees. To the northwest of Nether Stowey lies the small privately owned manor house, **Dodington Hall**, which is occasionally open to visitors. A fine example of Tudor architecture, the great hall features a splendid oak room and a carved stone fireplace, while outside there are attractive semi-formal gardens.

EAST QUANTOXHEAD
11 miles W of Bridgwater off the A39

This is a picturesque village of thatched cottages with a mill and millpond and a handsome old manor house, **Court House**, standing on a rise overlooking the sea. The original owner's family bloodline can be traced back to the 11th century and the Domesday Book but, in the 13th century, the manor passed by marriage to the Luttrell family, who were also to become the owners of Dunster Castle. The manor house seen today dates from the 16th and 17th centuries and it was constructed by successive generations of the same family.

From the village there is a pleasant walk to the southeast, to **Kilve**, where the ruins of a medieval chantry, or college of priests, can be found. From here a track can be taken from the churchyard down to a boulder-strewn beach reputed to be a favourite haunt of glats – conger eels up to 10-feet long that lie in wait among the rocks near the shore. Once known as 'St Keyna's serpents', local people used to search for them using trained 'fish dogs'.

Further to the southeast lies the village of **Holford**, in the Quantocks, and a track from here leads up to the large Iron Age hill fortification known as **Dowsborough Fort**. Close by are also the dramatic viewpoints **Beacon Hill** and **Bicknoller Hill** and on the latter is another Iron Age relic, a livestock enclosure known as **Trendle Ring**. This is one of many archaeological sites in this area, which lies within the Quantock Hills Site of Special Scientific Interest.

LOCATOR MAP

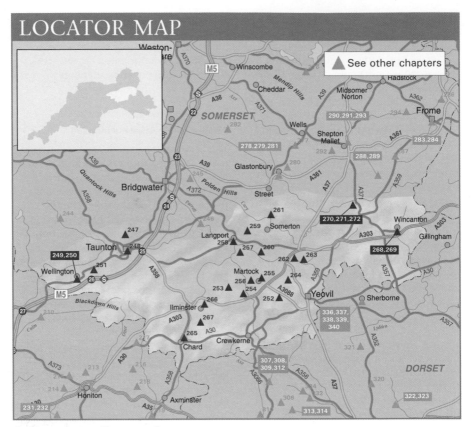

See other chapters

Weston-super-Mare

M5

Winscombe

Mendip Hills

Cheddar

Midsomer Norton

Hadstock

A370

A38

A39

A362

A371

SOMERSET

Frome

282

Wells

290,291,293

A361

283,284

Shepton Mallet

278,279,281

292

288,289

A39

Glastonbury

280

A361

A37

Bridgwater

A39

A372

Polden Hills

Street

A371

Wincanton

A303

261

Quantock Hills

A358

A38

245

248

259

Somerton

270,271,272

A303

Gillingham

247

Langport

258

257

260

A303

268,269

A357

A30

Taunton

248

25

262

263

A30

249,250

251

Martock

255

264

253

256

254

252

Yeovil

Sherborne

Wellington

26

266

Ilminster

267

265

A30

Crewkerne

336,337,
338,339,
340

M5

Blackdown Hills

A303

27

Chard

DORSET

Honiton

Axminster

307,308,
309,312

231,232

A35

322,323

313,314

A356

A3066

A37

ADVERTISERS AND PLACES OF INTEREST

247 Hestercombe Gardens,
   Cheddon Fitzpaine, Taunton   page 287

248 Jane Armour Trading, Taunton   page 288

249 Sunseed Wholefoods & Healthfoods,
   Wellington   page 290

250 C9, Wellington   page 290

251 Willowbrook Nursery & Garden Centre,
   West Buckland, Wellington   page 292

252 Montacute TV & Radio Museum,
   Montacute   page 294

253 Manor Farm, Shepton Beauchamp,
   Ilminster   page 296

254 One World, South Petherton   page 297

255 Michael Burton, Martock   page 298

256 Tom Clark Gallery, Hurst, Martock page 299

257 Muchelney Pottery (John Leach),
   Muchelney, Langport   page 300

258 Levelife, Langport   page 301

259 Pitney Farm Shop, Pitney, Langport page 302

260 The Devonshire Angel, Long Sutton,
   Langport   page 303

261 Monocot Nursery, Littleton,
   Somerton   page 304

262 Gilbert & Dale Antiques, Ilchester page 304

263 Fleet Air Arm Museum, Yeovilton,
   Ilchester   page 305

264 West Country Water Buffalo, Chilthorne
   Domer, Yeovil   page 306

265 Forde Abbey, Chard   page 307

266 The Meeting House Arts Centre,
   Ilminster   page 309

267 The Old Rectory, Cricket Malherbie,
   Ilminster   page 310

268 Ottery Antique Restorers, Wincanton page 311

269 The Cunning Artificer, Wincanton page 312

270 Needful Things, Castle Cary   page 313

271 Black & White, Castle Cary   page 314

272 Number One, Castle Cary   page 314

SOUTH SOMERSET 8

This region of Somerset is characterised by ancient Saxon towns and villages, willows that grow on the old marshlands of the Somerset Levels and warm honey-coloured building stone. Despite having been founded by the Saxon King Ine in the 8th century, Taunton did not finally become the county town until the 1930s. However this charming place, with its historic castle, old priory now the home of the county cricket team and its many old buildings dating back as far as Tudor times, is an excellent starting point to begin an exploration of the southern part of the county. To the north and east of the town lie the Somerset Levels, an area of marshland that, from medieval times onwards, has continued to be drained to provide rich and fertile farmland. Crossed by the Rivers Parrett, Isle and Cary, drainage ditches, known locally as rhines, have been constructed. Lined with rows of pollarded willows, these provide visitors with one of the regions most characteristic sights. For centuries the willows, or withies, have been cut and woven into baskets and, today, the basket-weaving industry that has been so important to southern and central Somerset is once again enjoying a revival.

Hestercombe House

Over the centuries, land rising above the wetlands has been settled. Two hills in particular were settled in ancient times and have given rise to local legends. Burrow Mump is said to have been the site of an ancient fortification belonging to King Alfred and it was at a nearby village, Althelney, that the king is said to have burnt the cakes. The Iron Age hill fort at Cadbury Castle is thought to have been the location of King Arthur's Camelot. Excavations have confirmed that there was indeed a fortification here from that period and the remote and romantic setting has enhanced this belief.

Yeovil, the only other large town in the area, dates back to the time of the Romans but, despite its age, it is a modern place perhaps best known as the home of Westland Helicopters. However, it is the area's ancient villages and old market towns, such as Norton Fitzwarren, Muchelney, Langport and

Ilminster, to name but a few, that provide the real source of interest here. Glorious old buildings, some dating back to the Norman era, can still be found but what makes these places so attractive is the honey-coloured limestone used in their construction. Known as hamstone, this was first quarried by the Romans from Ham Hill, just northwest of Yeovil and subsequent generations have continued to utilise this warm and flexible building material.

Fleet Air Arm Museum, Yeovilton

The rich farmland is littered with magnificent country and manor houses including the late medieval stone manor house of Lytes Cary, the Palladian Hatch Court and Montacute House, built in the late 16th century for Elizabeth I's Master of the Rolls. However, in this area the fine houses are often overshadowed by their gardens. There are some splendid examples here particularly those, such as Barrington Court, Hestercombe Gardens and Tintinhull House Gardens, that have been influenced by the early 20th century landscape gardener, Gertrude Jekyll.

TAUNTON

Despite a settlement being founded here by the Saxon King Ine in the 8th century, Taunton, the county town of Somerset, has only been its sole centre of administration since 1935. Before that date, both Ilchester and Somerton had been the county town. By Norman times the Saxon settlement had grown to have its own Augustinian monastery, a minster and a **Castle** – an extensive structure whose purpose had always been more as an administrative centre than as a military post. However, this did not prevent the castle from being the focus of two important sieges during the English Civil War. A few years later, the infamous Judge Jeffreys sentenced over 150 followers of the Duke of Monmouth

to death here during the Bloody Autumn Assizes. Even today, the judge's ghost is said to haunt the castle grounds on September nights.

The town's historic castle is now the home of the **Somerset County Museum**, a highly informative museum that contains a large collection of exhibits on the archaeology and natural and human history of the county. The **Somerset Military Museum** and some medieval almshouses are also to be found at the castle site. Another of the town's old building's is still making itself useful today. Somerset's County Cricket Ground occupies part of the priory grounds that once extended down to the river. A section of the old monastic gatehouse, known as the Priory Barn, can still be seen beside the cricket ground. Now

Vivary Park War Memorial

wool, and later silk, cloth-making centre during the Middle Ages. The profits earned by the medieval clothiers went into buildings. Here their wealth was used in the construction of two huge churches: St James' and St Mary's. The rest of the town centre is scattered with fine buildings including the timber-framed Tudor House in Fore Street. Taunton is still a thriving place with an important commercial centre, a weekly market and a busy light industrial sector that benefits from some excellent transport links with the rest of the country.

restored, this medieval stone building houses the fascinating **Somerset County Cricket Museum**.

Like many other West Country towns and villages, Taunton was a thriving

Today, the **Bridgwater and Taunton Canal** towpath has been reopened following an extensive restoration programme and it provides pleasant waterside walks along its 14 miles. A relative latecomer, the canal first opened in 1827 and it was designed to be part of an ambitious

HESTERCOMBE GARDENS

Cheddon Fitzpaine, near Taunton, Somerset TA2 8LG
Tel: 01823 413923 Fax: 01823 413747
e-mail: info@hestercombegardens.com
website: www.hestercombegardens.com

Lying southern slopes of the Quantocks, **Hestercombe Gardens** lie on an estate that goes back to Saxon times but, from the 14th to the late 19th centuries it was owned by one continuous family and it was Coplestone Warre Bampfylde who designed and laid out the

magnificent landscape garden in the mid-18th century. In 1872, the estate was acquired by the 1st Viscount Portman and it was his grandson, Hon Edward Portman who, in 1904, commissioned sir Edwin Lutyens to create a new formal garden that was planted by Gertrude Jekyll. Follies abound in this wonderful place and any walk around this 40-acre garden will include lakes, temples and magnificent views.

JANE ARMOUR TRADING

1a Bath Place, Taunton,
Somerset TA1 4ER
Tel: 01823 321939
Fax: 01823 256272
e-mail: info@janearmourtrading.co.uk
website: www.janearmourtrading.co.uk

A handsome old building in a shopping arcade in historic Bath Place is the setting for one of the most interesting card and gift shops in the county town of Somerset.

Jane Armour Trading was started in 1990 and moved to its current premises a year later. Since then, Jane Armour and her small, dedicated team have built up a loyal and strong following that stretches throughout Somerset, Dorset, Devon and beyond. This they have achieved by being firm believers in good customer relations, offering a high level of personal service and always priding themselves on their ability to help the customer to find exactly the right item.

The other reasons for the shop's success are the stock it has on display and the calm, comfortable and inviting environment that's just right for a spot of inspirational shopping. Many of the items on sale are just that little bit special, out of the ordinary, providing a choice not available elsewhere in town.

Greetings cards include the amusing variety (eg Simon Drew), photographic, contemporary and hand-made designs; there are ribbons galore and bags and gift wrap; hand-made paper in sheets and packs; notelets and envelopes; address books, albums and journals; wedding gifts, keepsakes and a growing range of accessories for the happy day; photo frames in metal or wood; glassware and Jelly Cat cuddly toys. All in all, a great place for browsing, and a sure source of a card or gift that's certain to delight.

During early 2004 Jane will be opening a second shop in Fore Street, right in the heart of the town centre, in which you will find even more of a selection of cards and gifts to choose from.

scheme to create a freight route between Exeter and Bristol to avoid the treacherous sea journey around the Cornwall peninsula. For many years, the canal was the principal means of importing coal and iron from South Wales to the inland towns of Somerset and of exporting their wool and agricultural produce to the rest of Britain.

Taunton's attractive **National Hunt Racecourse** lies on the opposite side of the motorway from the town and the combination of good facilities, excellent racing and glorious location make it one of the best country racecourses in Britain.

In the lanes to the north of Taunton lie the beautiful **Hestercombe Gardens** situated on the south-facing foothills of the Quantocks just north of the village of **Cheddon Fitzpaine** (see panel on page 287).

AROUND TAUNTON

Burrow Bridge
9 miles NE of Taunton on the A361

This village, on the River Parrett, is home to one of several pumping stations built in Victorian times to drain the Somerset Levels. The **Pumping Station** is open to the public occasionally throughout the year. Burrow Bridge is also the home of the **Somerset Levels Basket and Craft Centre**, a workshop and showroom stocked with handmade basket ware.

Rising dramatically from the surrounding wetlands is the conspicuous conical hill, **Burrow Mump**. Situated at a fording point on the River Parrett, this knoll has at its summit the picturesque remains of an unfinished chapel to St Michael begun in 1793 but for which funds ran out before its completion.

Burrow Mump is situated in the heart of the low lying area known as **King's Sedge Moor**, an attractive part of the Somerset Levels drained by the Rivers Cary and Parrett. A rich area of wetland, the moor is known for its characteristic pollarded willows, whose straight shoots, or withies, have been cultivated on a substantial scale ever since the taste for wicker developed during the 19th century. The traditional craft of basket-weaving is one of the Somerset's oldest commercial activities and it once employed thousands of people. Although the industry has been scaled down over the last 150 years, it is still alive and enjoying something of a revival.

The isolated Burrow Mump is reputed to be the site of an ancient fortification belonging to King Alfred, King of Wessex. He is said to have retreated here to escape from invading Vikings. It was during his time here that he is rumoured to have sought shelter in a hut in the nearby village of **Athelney**. While sitting at the peasant's hearth, absorbed in his own thoughts legend has it he burnt the cakes that the housewife had been baking. Not recognising the king, the peasant boxed his ears for ruining all her hard work. In the 19th century, a stone was placed on the site recalling that in gratitude for his hospitality, King Alfred founded a monastery on the Isle of Athelney.

Just to the west of Burrow Bridge, the **Bridgwater and Taunton Canal** winds its way through some of the most attractive countryside in the Somerset Levels. The restored locks, swing bridges, engine houses and rare paddle gearing equipment add further interest to this otherwise picturesque walk. The canal also offers a variety of recreational facilities including boating, fishing and canoeing while the canal banks are alive with both bird and animal life. **North**

SUNSEED
WHOLEFOODS & HEALTHFOODS

12 South Street, Wellington, Somerset TA21 8NS
Tel: 01823 662313
e-mail: info@sunseed.co.uk
website: www.sunseed.co.uk

The year 2004 sees the 25th anniversary of the opening of **Sunseed**, a specialist healthfood and wholefood store in one of the main shopping streets of Wellington. Throughout the years since 1979 it has built up a loyal customer base with its impressive range of products and the friendly, personal service. Along with herbs and spices, there's a wide variety of organic and non-GMO wholefoods including fresh organic fruit and vegetables. Here, also, customers will find a vast selection of vitamins, homeopathic and herbal remedies, aromatherapy oils and natural beauty products.

Tony Bourne, the shop's owner and his staff, offer personal service and advice backed by a touch-screen computer that acts as an encyclopaedic information station. The range of therapies available from fully trained professionals on a regular basis includes reflexology, homeopathy, remedial massage, aromatherapy, allergy testing and others. Customers who are unable to visit the shop in person can call or tap into Sunseed's services through the internet. A comprehensive mail order service is also available.

C9

4 Fore Street, Wellington, Somerset TA21 8AQ
Tel: 01823 667666 Fax: 01823 662222
e-mail: jillparr@btinternet.com

'Where Innovation Meets Tradition' is the motto of **C9**, whose full title is Cloud 9 (Worldwide Gifts) Ltd. This amazing shop is an Aladdin's Cave of gifts and collectables, gadgets and gizmos, toys and cards and wraps, combined with a traditional sweet shop and an internet café. The shop is well known locally and beyond for its range of Ty Beanies and other soft toys by Jellycat, Chubbleys and others. The mother-and-daughter team of Jill and Sam Parr are both involved with choosing

and buying the stock, which helps to ensure that all ages are catered for. They live up to their motto by keeping in touch with new trends but still ensuring that traditional tastes are never neglected.

The family has been at this present location since 2001, and the shop has been designed to make the very best use of the long, narrow interior with custom-built display areas. The colour scheme of dark blue and silver is a feature throughout, from the simple modern exterior to the bright display areas inside, and the owners and staff pride themselves on always presenting unusual and eyecatching window displays.

Newton, one of the pretty villages along the canal, is home to the small country manor of **Maunsel House** that is occasionally open to the public. At the canal's southern end, boats have access to the River Tone via **Firepool Lock** in the heart of Taunton.

LYNG

7 miles NE of Taunton on the A361

On a low rise above the wetlands, this pretty village was once, like many other villages in this region of Somerset, a centre of withy growing and basket-weaving. The original village church of St Bartholomew was the chapelry of the monastery that King Alfred founded at Athelney. Alfred's biographer described the village as being surrounded "by water and vast impassable peat bog".

HATCH BEAUCHAMP

5½ miles SE of Taunton on the A358

Hatch Beauchamp is a pleasant village that has managed to retain much of its rural atmosphere despite being on the major route between Ilminster and Taunton. Its name originates from *Hache*, a Saxon word meaning gateway and this refers to the ancient forest of Neroche whose boundary was just to the north and west. The suffix comes from the Norman family who owned the local manor and whose house stood on the land now occupied by one of the finest country houses in the area, **Hatch Court**. John Collins, a rich local clothier, commissioned the Axbridge architect, Thomas Prowse, to design the house. Built of attractive honey coloured limestone the resulting magnificent Palladian mansion was completed in 1755. Among its finest features are the hall with its cantilevered stone staircase, the curved orangery with its arched floor-to-ceiling windows and the semicircular china room with its elegant

display of rare porcelain and glass. There is also a fine collection of 17th and 18th century English and French furniture, 19th and 20th century paintings and a small military museum commemorating Britain's last privately raised regiment, the Princess Patricia's Canadian Light Infantry. The extensively restored grounds incorporate a walled kitchen garden, rose garden, arboretum and deer park.

To the west of the village are the remains of the ancient Forest of Neroche and it was close to the village of **Staple Fitzpaine** that Robert, Count of Mortain, a half-brother to William the Conqueror, converted an old Saxon fortress into a residential castle. By the late 13th century the castle was already in a very run down state and all that can be seen today of the old fortress is an immense ditch overshadowed by trees.

PITMINSTER

3 miles S of Taunton off the B3170

Recorded as Pipeminster in the Domesday Book, although there is no evidence of a minster ever having been built here, the village does have an old church containing 16th century monuments to the Colles family. Just to the north of Pitminster lies **Poundisford Park**, a small H-shaped Tudor mansion standing within a delightful, wooded deer park that once belonged to the bishops of Winchester. The house is renowned for its fine plasterwork ceilings and the grounds incorporate a formal garden laid out in the Tudor style.

WELLINGTON

6 miles SW of Taunton on the A38

This pleasant old market town was once an important producer of woven cloth and serge and it owes much of its prosperity to Quaker entrepreneurs and, later, the Fox banking family. Fox, Fowler and Co were the last private bank in England to issue notes and they only ceased in 1921 when they were taken over by Lloyds. The broad streets around the town centre are peppered with fine Georgian buildings, including the neoclassical **Town Hall**. At the eastern end of the town, the much altered church contains the ostentatious tomb of Sir John Popham, the judge who presided at the trial of Guy Fawkes.

To the south of the town stands the **Wellington Monument**, a 175-foot obelisk erected not long after the duke's great victory at Waterloo. The foundation stone was laid in 1817 by Lord Somerville but the monument was only completed in 1854. The duke himself visited the site and the town from which he took his title only once, in 1819.

NORTON FITZWARREN
2 miles NW of Taunton on the B3227

Large finds of Roman pottery have been excavated in and around this village, helping to confirm that Norton Fitzwarren was the Roman settlement of Theodunum. The village's name comes from the Saxon 'north tun' (meaning north farm) and the Norman family who were given the manor here after the Conquest. Norton Fitzwarren's antiquity and former importance gave rise to the old rhyme "When Taunton was a furzy down, Norton was a market town." Today, although the village has all but been consumed by its much larger neighbour, it has still managed to retain some of is individuality.

The land around Norton Fitzwarren is damp and fertile and, for hundreds of

WILLOWBROOK NURSERY & GARDEN CENTRE

West Buckland, Nr Wellington, Somerset TA21 9HX
Tel: 01823 461324

The Grabham family - Nigel, Carol and their son Stephen - provide a friendly, personal touch at the **Willowbrook Nursery and Garden Centre**, which stands at the foot of the Blackdown Hills on the main A38 between Wellington and Taunton. The centre first opened its doors in 1990, starting off as a nursery to serve the local area. It still grows a large proportion of the plants it sells, priding itself on the range and quality; they include a wide choice of award-winning shrubs, trees, roses, perennials, climbers, alpines and seasonal bedding plants.

The garden shop is stocked with everything that the novice or professional gardener should need from seeds and feeds to pots, tools, garden gifts, fencing, sheds, summerhouses and conservatories. The Pet Shop sells small animals and birds and

everything needed to keep them healthy and amused, and the pet area is home to rabbits, guinea pigs, chickens, ducks and a pot-bellied pig that the children adore. The Aquatic Centre features coldwater, marine and tropical fish and accessories, and Willowbrook also has a café/tea room and a lawned area with picnic benches.

years, cider apples have been grown here. Cider made here is now transported all over the world, but until the early 19th century, cider was a beverage very much confined to Somerset and the West Country. It was the Rev Thomas Cornish, a local clergyman, who first brought cider to the attention of the rest of the nation,when he produced a drink so appetizing that it found great favour with Queen Victoria. Close to one of the largest cider breweries in the area are the remains of an early Bronze Age bank and ditch enclosure, and artefacts excavated from here can be seen in the county museum in Taunton.

YEOVIL

Yeovil takes its name from the River Yeo, sometimes called the River Ivel. There was a Roman settlement here but the town really began to develop in the Middle Ages when a market was established that continues to be held every Friday. Yeovil's parish **Church of St John the Baptist** is the only significant medieval structure to survive as most of its other early buildings were destroyed by the series of fires that struck the town in the 17th century. A substantial building, with a solid-looking tower, the church dates from the late 14th century and has a surprisingly austere exterior given its exceptional number of windows. It has so many windows that it is sometimes referred to as the 'Lantern of the West'.

During the 18th century, Yeovil developed into a flourishing coaching centre due to its strategic position at the junction of several main routes. Industries such as glove-making, leather working, sailcloth making and cheese producing were established here. This rapid expansion was enhanced by the arrival of the railway in the mid 19th century. Then, in the 1890s, James Petter, a local ironmonger and pioneer of the internal combustion engine, founded a business that went on to become one of the largest manufacturers of diesel engines in Britain. Although production was eventually transferred to the Midlands, a subsidiary set up to produce aircraft during World War I has since evolved into a helicopter plant.

Today, Yeovil retains its geographical importance and is south Somerset's largest concentration of population. It is a thriving commercial, shopping, and market town best known perhaps as the home of Westland Helicopters. Situated in Wyndham House, the **Museum of South Somerset** documents the social and industrial history of the town and surrounding area, from prehistoric times to the present. Through a series of imaginative displays and exhibits the fascinating atmosphere of times past, from the days of the Romans to the agricultural and industrial revolutions, are brought to life.

AROUND YEOVIL

BALTONSBOROUGH
12 miles N of Yeovil off the A37

One of the 12 manors of Glastonbury Abbey, which lies just to the northwest, the lives of the people of the village were completely governed by the monks. The permission of the abbey had to be sought before a daughter could be married while on a man's death his chattels and beasts became the property of the abbey. St Dunstan is said to have been born here between 909 and 925 and the ancient flour mill in the village is thought to have been owned by Dunstan's father. Before entering Glastonbury Abbey,

Dunstan found favour at the court of King Athelstan but, once he had given up his worldly possessions, Dunstan followed an austere regime. By setting himself apart from the abbey's other novices, Dunstan soon rose through the ranks of the religious house to become abbot, whereupon he enforced the strict Benedictine code. The wealth of Glastonbury grew under Dunstan and he also encouraged pilgrims to make their way here to see the holy relics. Along with being a great cleric and an entrepreneur, Dunstan was also an

engineer. He was one of the first people to instigate the draining of the land in this area. From Glastonbury, Dunstan moved to Canterbury, where he was Archbishop up until his death.

BARWICK
1½ miles S of Yeovil off the A37

Pronounced 'barrik', this village is home to **Barwick Park**, an estate littered with bizarre follies, arranged at the four points of the compass. The eastern folly, known as **Jack the Treacle Eater**, is composed of a rickety stone arch topped

MONTACUTE TV AND RADIO MUSEUM

1 South Street, Montacute, Somerset TA15 6XD
Tel: 01935 823024
website: www.montacutemuseum.co.uk

The Montacute TV and Radio Museum found in the picturesque village of Montacute that has been used in the filming of Jane Austen's *Sense and Sensibility* has itself been featured on television, including Channel 4's *Collectors Lot* and the BBC's *Antiques Inspectors*. The museum has also made contributions to the BBC's *I Love the '70s* and *'80s* series. The vast collection here of fascinating memorabilia is guaranteed to bring back memories of classic TV and radio programmes through its superb multitude of items including toys, books and games. The collection also includes the automated puppets from the favourite 1970s children's cartoon *Top Cat*.

The television themes covered at the museum include other children's favourites such as *Sooty*, *The Magic Roundabout* and *Twizzle*; westerns such as *Wagon Train* and *Gun Law*; and science fiction featuring *Dr Who*, *Startrek* and Gerry Anderson's *Thunderbirds*. For quiz show fans there is *Double Your Money?*, comedy with *Sergeant Bilko* and everyone's favourite soap *Coronation Street*. There are over 500 radio exhibits ranging from vintage wirelesses of the 1920s to the colourful novelty transistors of today and for radio listeners there are *The Archers* and even the ventriloquist's doll from an early Archie Andrews show.

The museum was started from a collection of items belonging to Dennis Greenham who stated his own business in 1930 charging accumulators and subsequently went on to build up his own electrical business, which he still runs today in the neighbouring village of Norton-sub-Hamdon. The current

collector, Alan Hicken (Dennis's son-in-law), has substantially added to the collection over the years. In addition to the vast collection of television and radio memorabilia there is an extraordinary Alice in Wonderland collection, whilst the museum shop sells a vast range of television and radio related books and games. Meanwhile, whilst visitors are here they can enjoy a tasty meal or light snack along with homemade cakes and real West Country cream teas at the museum's tearooms and gardens. Bed and breakfast accommodation is also available and there are a number of village and woodland walks in the surrounding area.

by a curious turreted room. According to local stories, the folly is named after a foot messenger who ran back and forth between the estate and London on a diet of nothing more than bread and treacle. The estate also possesses a curious grotto and a handsome church with a Norman font and an unusual 17th century transeptal tower.

MONTACUTE

3½ miles W of Yeovil off the A3088

This charming village of golden Hamstone houses and cottages is also home to the magnificent Elizabethan mansion, **Montacute House**, built in the 1590s for Edward Phelips, Queen Elizabeth's Master of the Rolls by, probably, William Arnold, the architect of Wadham College, Oxford. There have been alterations made to the house over the centuries, most notably in the late 18th century, when the west front was remodelled by the fifth Edward Phelips. In the 19th century the fortunes of the Phelips family began to decline and, in the 1920s, following a succession of tenants, the house was put up for sale. A gift from Ernest Cook (the grandson of the travel agent Thomas Cook) enabled the National Trust to purchase this wonderful Elizabethan residence. Constructed of Hamstone, the house is adorned with characteristic open parapets, fluted columns, twisted pinnacles, oriel windows and carved statues. The long gallery, one of the grandest of its kind in Britain, houses a fine collection of Tudor and Jacobean portraits on permanent loan from London's National Portrait Gallery. Other noteworthy features include the stone and stained glass screen in the great hall and Lord Curzon's bath, an Edwardian addition concealed in a bedroom cupboard. An established story tells of how Curzon, a senior Tory

politician, waited at Montacute in 1923 for news that he was to be called to form a new government but the call never came. The house stands within a magnificent landscaped park that incorporates a walled formal garden, a fig walk, an orangery and a cedar lawn formally known as 'Pig's Wheaties's Orchard'.

Some 500 years before Montacute House was built, a controversial castle was erected on the nearby hill by Robert, Count of Mortain. The count's choice of site angered the Saxons as they believed the hill to be sacred as it is thought that King Alfred had buried a fragment of Christ's cross here. In 1068, they rose up and attacked the castle in one of many unsuccessful revolts against the Norman occupation. Ironically, a subsequent Count of Mortain was found guilty of treason and forced into donating all his lands in the area to a Cluniac priory on the site now occupied by Montacute village. The castle has long since disappeared, as has the monastery, with the exception of its fine 16th century gatehouse, now a private home, and a stone dovecote.

Montacute village is the home of the **TV and Radio Memorabilia Museum** (see panel opposite), where a vast collection of vintage radios, wireless receivers and television sets, from the 1920s through to the present day, is on display.

Found in the lanes to the southeast of Montacute and close to the village of **West Coker** is the magnificent **Brympton d'Evercy Manor House** dating from Norman times but with significant 16th and 17th century additions. The superb golden Hamstone south wing was built in Jacobean times to a design by Inigo Jones. Among the many fine internal features the manor house is home to the longest straight single span staircase in Britain and an unusual modern tapestry depicting an imaginary bird's eye view of the property during the 18th century. When viewed from a distance, the mansion house, the little estate church and the nearby dower house make a delightful lakeside grouping. In the church at **East Coker** were buried the ashes of the poet and playwright TS Eliot. This village, where his ancestors lived, is mentioned in *Four Quartets*, a poem written by Eliot.

BARRINGTON
10½ W of Yeovil off the B3168

To the east of the village is the beautiful National Trust owned **Barrington Court** famous for its enchanting garden influenced by the great 20th century garden architect Gertrude Jekyll. This estate originally belonged to the Daubeney family but it passed through several hands before becoming the property of William Clifton, a wealthy London merchant, who was responsible for building the house in the mid-16th century. In 1907, the by then dilapidated Barrington Court became the first country house to be purchased by the National Trust. It was restored in the 1920s by Col AA Lyle, to whom the Trust had let the property. The garden, too, was laid out during this time in a series of themed areas including an iris garden, a lily garden, a white garden and a fragrant rose garden. Gertrude Jekyll was brought in to advise on the initial planting and layout and the garden remains the finest example of her work in the Trust's care. There is also an exceptionally attractive kitchen garden with apple, pear and plum trees trained along the walls that, in season, produces fruit and vegetables for the licensed restaurant that can be found here.

Just to the southeast of the pretty

MANOR FARM

Shepton Beauchamp, Nr Ilminster, Somerset TA19 0LA
Tel: 01460 240221 Fax: 01460 240544

Over the past five years, Liz and Robert England have developed the outstanding business that is **Manor Farm**. The only pick-your-own establishment in this part of the county, it lives up triumphantly to its motto 'Where the Taste Counts', and anyone who experiences the taste will be very reluctant to visit a supermarket in future. Everything here has been grown and tended by the owners, who are justifiably proud that their involvement is complete from start to finish. The strawberries, often the cause of sore backs when bending, are thoughtfully grown at table-top

height, and the crops also include raspberries and other soft fruits,

broad and runner beans and pumpkins. In the summer, the surrounding fields are a splendid sight with their armies of man-height sunflowers, and Manor Farm has an unusual attraction in the shape of a maize maze cut in the form of three linked human figures – great fun for all the family, who can reward themselves after finding their way out with a feast of their pickings, perhaps washed down with a glass of the excellent local cider.

estate village of Barrington, the remains of a medieval open-strip field system can still be made out from the air around the village of **Shepton Beauchamp** while, to the north of Barrington, is the tranquil community of **Westport**. A peaceful settlement today, the village is a former inland port built at the height of the canal era by the Parrett Navigation Company for exporting wool and stone and importing coal and building materials.

Stoke sub Hamdon
5 miles NW of Yeovil off the A303

While the eastern part of this attractive village is home to a fine Norman church, in the western area of the village can be found the remains of a late medieval priory. **Stoke sub Hamdon Priory** was built in the 14th and 15th centuries for the priests of the now demolished chantry chapel of St Nicholas and the

remains here, which include an impressive great hall, are now in the hands of the National Trust.

South of the village lies the 400-foot **Ham Hill** (or Hamdon Hill), the source of the beautiful honey coloured stone used in so many of the surrounding villages. This solitary limestone outcrop rises abruptly from the Somerset plain and provides breathtaking views of the surrounding countryside. A substantial hill fort, built here during the Iron Age, was subsequently overrun by the invading Romans. The new occupants built their own fortification to guard their major route, the Fosse Way, and its important intersection with the road between Dorchester and the Bristol Channel at nearby Ilchester.

It was the Romans who discovered that the hill's soft, even-grained limestone made a flexible and highly attractive building material and they used it in the

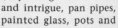

One World

17 James Street, South Petherton, Somerset TA13 5BS
Tel: 01460 241166

Drivers on the busy A303 will be well rewarded by making the short detour to the village of South Petherton and Nancy McMillan's delightful little gift shop. Behind its tiny bow-windowed frontage in a charming terrace of old buildings in local Hamstone, **One World** is filled with an amazing variety of gifts both practical and decorative, things to keep and treasure, to use about the house or to give as a really special present. Baskets are filled to overflowing with snuggly soft toys, there are cards galore and calendars and gift bags and wrapping paper, notebooks and paper napkins, photo frames, toys and games to amuse

and intrigue, pan pipes, painted glass, pots and bowls, decorative plaques to put on the wall and delicate mobiles to hang on the ceiling. Upstairs are three rooms filled with more goodies, including cushions and rugs, scarves and hats and wraps, candles and lamps and basketware in all shapes and sizes.

Nancy finds her stock all over the world, and on a blackboard outside the shop she chalks up some of the latest acquisitions - perhaps some beautiful, warm jackets from South America or some pretty jewellery. One World is open from 9am to 1pm and from 2.15pm to 5pm Monday to Saturday.

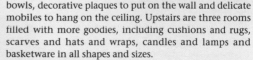

construction of their villas and temples. Later, the Saxons and then the Normans came to share this high opinion of Hamstone. By the time quarrying reached its height in the 17th century, a sizeable settlement had grown up within the confines of the Iron Age fort though, today, only a solitary inn remains. A war memorial to 44 local men who died during World War I stands on the summit of Ham Hill. Now designated a country park, the combination of the view, the old earthwork ramparts and the maze of overgrown quarry workings make this an attractive place for recreation and picnics.

MARTOCK

6 miles NW of Yeovil on the B3165

This attractive, small town is surrounded by rich arable land and the area has long been renowned for its prosperous land-owning farmers. Martock's long

established affluence is reflected in its impressive part 13th century parish church. A former abbey church that once belonged to the monks of Mont St Michel in Normandy, the church boasts one of the finest tie-beam roofs in Somerset and almost every part of it is covered in beautiful carvings.

The old part of Martock is blessed with an unusually large number of fine buildings and among these can be found the **Treasurer's House**, a small medieval house of two stories built in the late 13th century and now owned by the National Trust. Visitors can see the Great Hall, an interesting wall painting and the kitchen added to the building in the 15th century. Close by is the **Old Court House**, a parish building that served as the local grammar school for 200 years. To the west is Martock's 17th century Manor House, once the home of Edward Parker, who exposed the Gunpowder Plot

---

MICHAEL BURTON

Osborne Cottage, Martock, Somerset TA12 6JU
Tel: 01935 822362
e-mail: michaelburton_silver@hotmail.com
website: www.whoswhoingoldandsilver.com

Since graduating in 1973 in Silversmithing and Design, **Michael Burton** has been working to great acclaim with precious metals to produce a unique range of jewellery and other pieces which have been shown in exhibitions in the UK and around the world. His skills and specialist techniques have gained him many important commissions, including pieces for Queen Elizabeth II and the late Queen Elizabeth the Queen Mother, the Victoria & Albert Museum, the British Museum, the Worshipful Company of Goldsmiths, and Winchester and Westminster Cathedrals. He carves his work from the metals - silver, gold, platinum and copper - sometimes chasing out volumes and repoussing depths. He likes to combine

different metals and materials - perhaps titanium, gold, silver and mother of pearl, and his pieces range from minuscule pigs and other animals no more than 5mm high to carved and engraved jewellery, boxes, bowls and centrepieces. He is always happy to discuss commissioned works, and his workshop can be visited by appointment.

Exquisite craftsmanship came to Martock as long ago as the early 16th century, when the 128 carved oak panels in the roof of All Saints Church were completed.

TOM CLARK GALLERY

Hurst Barton, Hurst, Nr Martock,
Somerset TA12 6JU
Tel: 01935 822833 Fax: 01935 824455
website: www.tomclarkstonecarver.co.uk
e-mail: tom@tomclarkstonecarver.co.uk

Tom Clark, sculptor and stone carver, started carving in 1974 at Chichester where he did his apprenticeship.

Later he was involved in many large interesting restoration projects including St George's Chapel, Windsor, West Abbey, the National Gallery and Ely Cathedral. For the past few years he has been developing his own sculptural pieces inspired by travels in India and Egypt and by his great love of medieval art.

In the workshop alongside his 16th century Hamstone house he produces a wide variety of beautiful pieces in various types of limestone. These include bowls, birdbaths, classical images of lions and decorative elephants, architectural features, modern figures and heads. Also available reasonably priced limestone casts from his original carvings. As well as the stone carvings there will be various artists exhibiting paintings, drawings and photographs.

**Directions: very near the Somerset Guild of Craftsmen -
Home Gallery, Martock, 1 mile off the A303.**

---

after Guy Fawkes had warned him against attending Parliament on that fateful night.

A couple of miles to the east of Martock is another enchanting National Trust property, **Tintinhull House Garden**, set in the grounds of an early 17th century manor farm. Sadly not open to the public, the house overlooks an attractive triangular green that forms the nucleus of the sprawling village of **Tintinhull**. This is home to a number of other interesting buildings: a remodelled, part-medieval rectory, Tintinhull Court; the 17th century Dower House; and St Margaret's parish church, a rare rectangular single-cell church. Despite the age of the house, Tintinhull House Gardens were laid out as recently as the early 20th century in a series of distinctive areas, divided by walls and hedges, each with its own planting theme. There is a pool garden with a

delightful pond filled with lilies and irises, a kitchen garden and a sunken garden that is cleverly designed to give the impression it has many different levels.

To the west of Martock, near the charming hamlet of **East Lambrook**, is another beautiful garden that is well worth visiting. **Lambrook Manor Garden** was laid out for endangered species by the writer and horticulturist, Margery Fish, who lived at the medieval Hamstone manor house from 1937 until her death in 1969. Her exuberant planting and deliberate lack of formality created an atmosphere of romantic tranquillity that is maintained to this day. Now Grade I listed, the garden is also the home of the National Collection of the cranesbill species of geranium. The low-lying land to the north of East Lambrook is criss-crossed by a network of drainage ditches or rhines (pronounced reens) that eventually flow into the rivers Parrett, Isle and Yeo. Originally cut in the early 19th century, the ditches are often lined with double rows of pollarded willows, a sight that has come to characterise this part of Somerset. Despite having to be cleared every few years, the rhines provide a valuable natural habitat for a wide variety of bird, animal and plant life.

MUCHELNEY

9½ miles NW of Yeovil off the A372

This village's name means 'the Great Island' and it dates from the time when this settlement rose up above the surrounding marshland, long since drained to provide excellent arable farmland. Muchelney is also the location of an impressive part-ruined Benedictine monastery thought to have been founded by King Ine of Wessex in the 8th century. This claim was, in part,

confirmed when, in the 1950s, an archaeological dig unearthed an 8th century crypt. During medieval times **Muchelney Abbey** grew to emulate its great rival at Glastonbury. After the Dissolution in 1539, the buildings, dating mainly from the 15th and 16th centuries, gradually fell into disrepair. Much of its stone was removed to provide building material for the surrounding village. In spite of this, a substantial part of the original structure, including the south cloister and abbot's lodge, can still be seen today. The abbey is now under the custodianship of English Heritage.

Opposite the parish church, which its noted for is remarkable early 17th century illuminations, stands the **Priest's House**, a late-medieval hall house built by the abbey for the parish priest. Little has changed since the 17th century, when the building was divided, and the

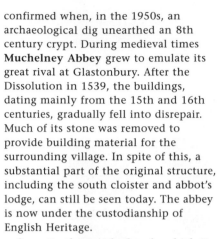

MUCHELNEY POTTERY (JOHN LEACH)

Muchelney, near Langport, Somerset TA10 0DW
Tel: 01458 250324
website: www.johnleachpottery.com

Just a mile south of the ancient village of Muchelney, John Leach, the eldest grandson of Bernard Leach, continues the family tradition at his own thatched-roofed **Muchelney Pottery**. Like his father, David Leach, and grandfather before him, John hand-throws his distinctive stoneware pots which are then fired, in age-old fashion, using a three-chambered wood fired kiln. The pots are practical, both microwave and dishwasher proof, and have a unique quality that comes from

their warmly toasted finishes and interior glazes. No two pots are ever

identical, further adding to their charm, and the range of tableware extends from jugs, casseroles and plates to bread crocks, chicken bricks and pasta pods. John's wife, Lizzie, manages the attractive Pottery Shop where a full range of the pots can be bought.

John's original signed designs, including his 'Black mood' pots, are on display and for sale in the newly-opened John Leach Gallery adjacent to the shop. Individual pots by Nick Rees and Mark Melbourne, the other two potters in the team at Muchelney, and work by invited artists and sculptors may also be bought in the Gallery. Tours of the workshop can be arranged and there are usually two public kiln openings a year. Visitors are also invited to walk around John's conservation pond and woodland, a County Wildlife Site, and home to a wealth of birds, plants and animals.

interesting features to see include the Gothic doorway, the beautiful tracery windows and a massive 15th century stone fireplace. The house now belongs to the National Trust and, though still a dwelling, it is opened on a limited basis.

Just to the west of the village, near **Drayton**, lies the privately-owned **Midelney Manor**, originally an island manor belonging to Muchelney Abbey. A handsome manor house with architectural features from the 16th, 17th and 18th centuries, this has been in the hands of the Trevilian family since the early 1500s. The estate incorporates a heronry, a series of delightful gardens, a unique 17th century falcon's mews and woodland walks.

LANGPORT

10½ miles NW of Yeovil on the A378

The old part of this former market town stands on a rise above an ancient ford across the River Parrett. A short distance downstream from this point, the river is joined by the Rivers Isle and Yeo. Defended by an earthwork rampart during Saxon times, by 930 Langport was an important commercial centre that minted its own coins. The only surviving part of the town's defences is the east gate incorporating a curious 'hanging' chapel that sits above the arch on an upper level. The tower of the church at nearby Huish Episcopi can be seen through the barrel vaulted gateway.

During the 18th and 19th centuries, Langport flourished as a banking centre and the local independent bank, Stuckey's, became known for its impressive branches, many of which can still be seen in the surrounding towns and villages although the bank has long since been taken over by NatWest. At the time of this amalgamation in 1909, Stuckey's had more notes in circulation

LEVELIFE

Beaufort House, Cheapside, Langport, Somerset TA10 9PW
Tel: 01458 252505
e-mail: info@levelife.freeserve.co.uk

Situated on the main street of the historic town of Langport, **Levelife** hosts a continuous programme of art and craft exhibitions from many of the leading artists in the area. The gallery and shop were opened in November 2002 by Paul

and Sam Dennis, who were inspired by the wealth of artistic talent in and around the Somerset Levels. With the support of the artists and of the customers, the first full year has been very encouraging, and the stunning and original window displays in the shop have become a talking point in the town and beyond.

Paul makes wood-fired stoneware pots glazed with materials such as wood ash and stone dusts, and other exhibits include paintings, prints and limited editions, glasswork, photography, willow sculpture, stone carving, textiles, basketry and woodturning. The approach of the proprietors is to let the pieces live in their own space, so the exhibition area is decorated in minimalist style. A new gallery recently opened on the first floor hosts shows by individual artists. Levelife is open from 10am to 5pm Tuesday to Saturday.

than any other bank in the country save for the Bank of England.

Throughout history, the **Langport Gap** has been the site of a number of important military encounters. Two of the most significant occurred over 1,000 years apart. In the 6th century, Geraint, King of the Dumnonii, was involved in a battle here while, in July 1645, the Parliamentarian victory at the Battle of Langport gave Cromwell's forces almost total control of the West Country during the English Civil War. More about life on the Somerset Levels and the Moors can be learnt at the **Langport and River Parrett Visitor Centre** through its series of hands-on exhibits and displays.

Just to the east, at **Huish Episcopi**, one of the finest examples in the country of a late medieval Somerset tower can be found at the village's church. At its most impressive in high summer when it can be viewed through the surrounding

greenery, this ornate structure is adorned with striking tracery, pinnacles and carvings. The church also has an elaborate Norman doorway, which still shows signs of the fire that destroyed much of the earlier building in the 13th century. A window in the south chapel was designed by Edward Burne-Jones, the 19th century Pre-Raphaelite.

The church at **Aller**, just northwest of Langport, was the scene of another historic event. It was here, in 878, that King Alfred converted Guthrum the Dane and his followers to Christianity following a battle on Salisbury Plain. The low wooded rise to the east of Aller is criss-crossed by a network of ancient country lanes,which pass through some pleasant hamlets and villages including **High Ham**, the home of the last thatched windmill in England. Dating from 1822, **Stembridge Tower Mill** (National Trust) continued to operate until 1910.

PITNEY FARM SHOP

Glebe Farm, Woodbirdshill Lane, Pitney, Nr
Langport, Somerset TA10 9AP
Tel/Fax: 01458 253002

Pitney Farm Shop is located at Glebe Farm, a family-run mixed organic farm of 100 acres situated nine miles south of Glastonbury. Mr and Mrs Wallrand rear sheep, beef cattle, pigs and free-range laying hens, all of them fed on an organic diet; organic vegetables are grown on the farm and picked daily. The farm received full organic status in March 2001 and is certified with the Soil Association. The farm shop was opened in May 2002 and provides a way for the owners to sell

their produce directly as well as offering other local and organic products that complement their own.

The beef, lamb and pork are available as individual joints or in larger cuts, all prepared by an excellent local butcher who comes regularly to the farm. The sows also produce dry-cured bacon, Italian-style cured meats, burgers and a variety of super sausages both familiar and more exotic, including pork & mixed herbs, spicy Tuscan, 'Bollywood Bangers' and the 'Pitney Porker' with pork, smoked gammon, chives and Dijon mustard. Other goods on sale in the shop include free-range eggs, farm-grown vegetables, local cheeses and preserves and superb pies and ice creams produced in Pitney.

THE DEVONSHIRE ANGEL

Long Sutton, Nr Langport, Somerset TA10 9LP
Tel: 01458 241271
e-mail: mail@devonshireangel.com
website: www.devonshireangel.com

The Devonshire Angel is a really delightful hostelry that started life in the 17th century as a hunting lodge. Located on an idyllic village green, its handsome stone exterior promises an abundance of old-world charm, but inside it's one surprise after another - bold, clean-cut lines, lots of natural wood, fresh flowers and plants everywhere, fantastic bedrooms, great modern

cooking and an unbeatable choice of beers - along with a great ambience created by Mark, his staff and his customers. The menu, devised and prepared by Sasha Matervich, changes every day and ranges from lunchtime toasted ciabattas and classics such as fishcakes or bangers & mash to evening dishes like goat's cheese and red onion tarte tatin or organic salmon with couscous, lime leaf, courgettes and candied baby peppers. Tapas dishes are served at the bar, where the amazing range of beers includes three real ales and probably more draught Belgian beers than anywhere in the country. The wide-ranging wine list includes six wines by the glass. A meeting room for up to 30 is available for business or private dining parties.

Exceptional overnight accommodation comprises 12 en suite rooms with Japanese-style king-size beds and wide-screen digital TV. Breakfast comes Continental style.

SOMERTON
9 miles NW of Yeovil on the B3151

At one time the capital of Somerset under the West Saxons, the settlement here grew up around an important crossroads. Expansion towards the end of the 13th century altered this old town's original layout creating the present open market place that is home to the distinctive **Market Cross** and town hall. Between 1278 and 1371, Somerton was the location of the county gaol and the meeting place of the shire courts as well as continuing to develop as a market town, reflected in the delightfully down-to-earth names of some of its streets such as Cow Square and Pig Street (now Broad Street).

Today, Somerton is a place of handsome old shops, inns and houses and its general atmosphere of mature prosperity is enhanced by the presence of a number of striking ancient buildings. These include the 17th century **Hext Almshouses** and the part 13th century church with its unusual transeptal south tower.

A couple of miles southeast of the town lies the charming manor house of **Lytes Cary Manor**, now in the care of the National Trust. This late medieval stone house was built by succeeding generations of the Lyte family, the best known member of which was Henry Lyte, the Elizabethan herbalist who dedicated his 1578 translation of Dodoen's *Cruydeboeck* to Queen Elizabeth "from my poore house at Lytescarie". After the family left the house in the 18th century it fell into disrepair but in 1907 it was purchased and restored by Sir Walter Jenner, son of the famous Victorian physician. Notable features

MONOCOT NURSERY

St Michaels, Littleton, Somerton, Somerset TA11 6NT
Tel: 01458 272356

In a pleasant little village that straddles the B3151 just north of Somerton, **Monocot Nursery** is the jointly-owned base of operations of two outstanding talents. Michael Salmon has for more than 50 years practised his trade of plantsman and nurseryman and has built up a reputation as one of the

leaders in his field. In three large greenhouses hundreds of bulbs and plants are grown. The Nursery issues three catalogues each year. Bulbs for autumn planting, bulbs for spring planting and a seed catalogue listing 300 - 400 species from plants in cultivation and from wild habitats.

Sharing the premises with the nursery is the **Pottery**, where Penny Guy, who for many years taught at Bristol, produces beautiful thrown stoneware, decorated plates, bowls, mugs and vases. A selection of

these can be seen attractively displayed in her workshop and gallery. The nursery and the pottery can be visited, but it's advisable to make a phone call to check opening times before setting out.

GILBERT AND DALE ANTIQUES

The Old Chapel, Church Street, Ilchester, Somerset BA22 8LW
Tel: 01935 840464 Fax: 01935 841599 e-mail: roy@roygilbert.com

Found in the heart of Ilchester, **Gilbert and Dale Antiques** specialises in French and English country furniture and accessories that, where necessary, have been sympathetically restored in the shop's own workshops. Owned and personally run by Joan Dale and Roy Gilbert, who has over 30 years experience in the business, the wonderful range of beautiful items to be found here varies from magnificent wardrobes and armoires, writing desks and occasional tables to intricate light fittings, brass and copper ware and porcelain. Lovingly polished to bring out the deep tones of the wood or the gleam of the metal, wandering around the spacious ground floor or the upstairs show room of Gilbert and Dale Antiques is a fascinating and enjoyable experience for anyone interested in the past.

The building, too, is unusual and was originally a Methodist chapel that was first opened in 1860.

Again, this has been well renovated to preserve the mullion windows with the original leaded glass whilst the addition of the floor to create the upstairs show room provides ample space to display the vast collection of pieces found here. To the rear of the display area is the antique shop's workshop, housed in what was once the schoolroom, and here skilled local craftsmen restore many of the pieces that Joan and Roy have collected. With one of the finest collections of 18th century French and English furniture in the area, and friendly expertise on hand as well, this is just the place for antique lovers to visit.

include a 14th century chapel and Tudor Great Hall. The present garden is an enchanting combination of formality and eccentricity. There is an open lawn lined with magnificent yew topiary, an orchard filled with quince, pear and apple trees and a network of enclosed paths that every now and then reveal a view of the house, a lily pond or a classical statue.

ILCHESTER

4½ miles NW of Yeovil on the A37

In Roman times, the settlement here stood at the point where the north-south route between Dorchester and the Bristol Channel crossed the Fosse Way. However, it was during the 13th century that Ilchester reached its peak as a centre of administration, agriculture and learning. Like its near neighbour Somerton, this was, for a time, the county town of Somerset. Three substantial gaols were built here, one of which remained in use until the 1840s. Another indication of this town's former status is the 13th century **Ilchester Mace**, England's oldest staff of office. Up until recently, the mace resided in the town hall but today a replica can be seen here, while the original mace is on display in the County Museum at Taunton.

The tiny **Ilchester Museum** is in the centre of the town, by the Market Cross, and here the story of the town from pre-Roman times to the 20th century is told through a series of exhibits that include a Roman coffin and skeleton. Ilchester was the birthplace, in around 1214, of the celebrated scholar, monk and scientist, Roger Bacon, who went on to predict the invention of the

FLEET AIR ARM MUSEUM

RNAS Yeovilton, near Ilchester, Somerset BA22 8HT
Tel: 01935 840565 Fax: 01935 842630
e-mail: info@fleetairarm.com website: www.fleetairarm.com
The Fleet Air Arm Museum is one of the world's largest aviation museums and visitors can come and experience the exciting development of Britain's Flying Navy through a succession of superb exhibits. However, this is much more than just a hanger full of vintage aircraft and the highly imaginative collection on display also tells the stories of the men and women of naval aviation.

For those wishing to know just what it is like on an aircraft carrier, visitors can be 'flown' aboard the museum's own carrier where they can tour its nerve centre and experience close at hand the thrills and noises of a working flight deck. Meanwhile, through the use of touch screen interactive displays, dramatic lighting and vivid sound, the history and atmosphere of many of the museum's exhibits can be explored further. And, for those who have always wanted to experience the adrenaline rush as a pilot successfully completes his challenging mission, the Merlin Experience has been specially designed to allow visitors to act out their long held flying fantasies. Along with a children's adventure playground, a large book and souvenir shop, restaurant, airfield viewing galleries and a picnic area, this museum has much to offer visitors of all ages and interests what ever the weather.

WEST COUNTRY WATER BUFFALO

Lower Oakley Farm, Chilthorne Domer, Nr Yeovil,
Somerset BA22 8RQ
Tel/Fax: 01935 840567

West Country Water Buffalo offer a healthy, succulent and tasty alternative to traditional beef, and at Lower Oakley Farm they are reared naturally in humane conditions in the Somerset countryside, fed solely on grass with no additives or concentrates. The UK Water Buffalo is of the gentle, placid Asian variety; it has not been altered or interbred and is the same today as it was 2,000 years ago. It should not to be confused with the

American bison or the African water buffalo - a much larger and more dangerous breed.

The meat from the Water Buffalo is 40% lower in cholesterol and 12% lower in fat than traditional beef, and is 10% richer in iron and other vital minerals. The animals are slaughtered locally and brought back to the butcher on the farm to hang for three weeks to allow the full flavour to develop. The meat is then vacuum packed and sold at the farm in the same form as conventional beef - fillet, sirloin, rump, T-bone, ribs, braising, flank, topside etc - as well as in burgers and plain or flavoured sausages. Chilthorne Domer lies a couple of miles northwest of Yeovil off the A37.

aeroplane, telescope and steam engine although he was eventually imprisoned for his outspoken ideas.

At **Yeovilton**, just to the east of this pleasant small town, is one of the world's leading aviation museums, the **Fleet Air Arm Museum** (see panel on page 305), one of the world's largest aviation museums, containing a unique collection of aircraft, of which around half are on permanent display.

CREWKERNE

A thriving agricultural centre during Saxon times, Crewkerne even had its own mint in the decades leading up to the Norman invasion. Evidence of this ancient former market town's importance and wealth can still be seen in the magnificence of its parish Church of St Bartholomew built using money

generated by the late medieval boom in the local wool industry. A building of minster-like proportions, this is one of the grandest of the many fine Perpendicular churches to be found in south Somerset. Unlike many other towns in Wessex, whose textile industries suffered an almost total decline in later years, Crewkerne was rejuvenated in the 18th century when the availability of locally grown flax led to an expansion in the manufacture of sailcloth and canvas webbing. Among the many thousands of sails made here were those for *HMS Victory*, Admiral Nelson's flagship at the Battle of Trafalgar. This resurgence was also boosted by the development of the London to Exeter stage coach route. This led to the rebuilding of Crewkerne with elegant Georgian buildings, many of which can still be seen. The main areas, around Church and Abbey Streets, have now been designated an Area of

Outstanding Architectural Interest.

To the west of Crewkerne lies the aptly named **Windwhistle Hill**, a high chalk-topped ridge from the top of which there are dramatic views on a clear day, southwards to Lyme Bay and northwards across the Somerset Levels to the mountains of South Wales. The town also lies close to the source of the River Parrett and from here the 50-mile **River Parrett Trail** follows the river through some of the country's most ecologically sensitive and fragile areas, the Somerset Levels and Moors. Old mills, splendid churches, attractive villages and ancient monuments as well as orchards, peaceful pastureland and traditional industries such as cider-making and basket-weaving can all be found along the route.

Just a couple of miles southwest of Crewkerne, close to the village of **Clapton**, are the varied and interesting **Clapton Court Gardens**. Among the many beautiful features of this 10 acre garden are the formal terraces, the rose garden, the rockery and a water garden. The grounds incorporate a large wooded area containing a massive ash tree that, at over 230 years old and 28 feet in girth, is believed to be the oldest and the largest in mainland Britain. There is also a fine metasequoia that is already over 80 feet tall although it was only planted in 1950, from a seed brought back from China.

FORDE ABBEY

Chard, Somerset TA20 4LU
Tel: 01460 220231 Fax: 01460 220296

Originally founded by Cistercian monks in the 12th century, **Forde Abbey** lay empty for over 100 years after the Dissolution of the Monasteries before its was sold to Edmund Prideaux, Oliver Cromwell's Attorney General in 1649.

The remains of the abbey were incorporated into the grand private house of the Prideaux family – the old chapter house became the family chapel – and later additions include the

magnificent 17th century plaster ceilings and the renowned Mortlake Tapestries that were brought over from Brussels by Charles I. Today, Forde Abbey is the home of the Roper family and it stands at the heart of this family run estate.

Along with the collection of tapestries, period furniture and paintings to see in the house, there is the refectory and dormitory that still survive from the time of the medieval monastery whilst the abbey is also home to the famous Eeles Pottery exhibition.

Meanwhile, the house is surrounded by wonderful gardens and they have been described by Alan Titchmarsh as "one of the greatest gardens in the West Country". There are sloping lawns, herbaceous borders, a bog garden, lakes and a working kitchen garden that supplies the abbey's restaurant with produce whilst rare and unusual plants are for sale at the Plant Centre. The estate is also known for its pedigree herd of cattle and the house, with its restaurant and tearoom, can be visited between April and October whilst the gardens and ground are open all year round.

AROUND CREWKERNE

HASELBURY PLUCKNETT
2 miles NE of Crewkerne on the A3066

This delightfully named and particularly pretty village has a large part-Norman church whose churchyard contains a series of unusual 'squeeze stones'. Just to the west of the village the lovely **Haslebury Bridge**, a medieval packhorse bridge, crosses the still young River Parrett.

TATWORTH
7½ miles SW of Crewkerne off the A358

To the northeast of this village lies a meadow watered by springs that rise on its borders. This meadow is the last remaining sign of 'common' land that was enclosed in 1819. Changes in the ownership of the land during the 1820s allowed too many farmers grazing rights on the land, and the meadow suffered from being over-stocked. Therefore, in 1832, the holders of those rights met and, calling their meeting 'Stowell Court', they auctioned off the meadow for one year and shared the proceeds. So an annual tradition was born and the Stowell Court still meets on the first Tuesday after April 6th every year. Although many more customs have been added over the years, the auction proceedings are unique. They begin when a tallow candle of precisely one inch in length is lit and they end with the last bid before the candle goes out. Today, Stowell Mead is managed as a Site of Special Scientific Interest and, as the land is not treated with fertilisers, pesticides or herbicides, it is home to many rare plants. There is no right of way across the land but it can be seen from the road.

A short distance to the southeast of Tatworth lies **Forde Abbey**, founded in the 12th century by Cistercian monks after they had made an unsuccessful attempt to found an abbey in Devon (see panel on page 307).

CRICKET ST THOMAS
4½ miles W of Crewkerne off the A30

This former estate village is home to the **Cricket St Thomas Wildlife and Leisure Park**, and formerly one of the country's least hidden places, Noel Edmonds' **Crinkley Bottom** theme park. Today, the attractions include stables, a children's adventure fort, wildlife world and a varied assortment of theme park crowd-pleasers designed to attract the young. Visitors to the park will find it hard to imagine that the central building, **Cricket House**, was once the family home of the great 18th century naval commander Admiral Sir Alexander Hood and, later, of the Bristol chocolate manufacturer, FJ Fry. The estate also incorporates the tiny St Thomas's Church with its impressive monument to Admiral Hood, who was later to become Viscount Bridport.

CHARD
7½ miles W of Crewkerne on the A30

The borough of Chard was first established in 1235 and, during the Middle Ages, it was a prosperous wool centre with its own mayor, or portreeve, and burgesses. However, few buildings date from before 1577, when a devastating fire raged through the town and left most of it as ashes. One building that did survive the destruction was the fine Perpendicular parish church. The town was rebuilt and, today, many of these 16th and 17th century buildings remain, including the courthouse and the old grammar school. Chard also has some striking Georgian and Victorian buildings. On the outskirts of the town the unusual round toll house, with its conical thatched roof, is a reminder of the days of stagecoaches and turnpike roads.

Chard has expanded rapidly since World War II; its population has more than doubled. Nevertheless the centre of this light industrial town still retains a pleasant village-like atmosphere that is most apparent in its broad main shopping street. At the western end of the town's High Street, housed in the attractive thatched Godworth House, is the award winning **Chard Museum**, which is an ideal place for visitors to find out more about this town's eventful past.

To the northwest of the town is a 200-year-old corn mill, **Hornsbury Mill**, whose impressive water wheel is still in working order. To the northeast, **Chard Reservoir Nature Reserve** is a conservation area that is an important habitat for wildlife. Kingfisher, great crested grebe and other rare species of birds have made their home in and around the lake. The nature reserve also has a two-mile circular footpath that takes in rustling reed beds, broadleaved woodland and open hay meadows.

A couple of miles west of Chard is **Wambrook**, a village that lies close to the Dorset-Somerset border. Visitors interested in animal welfare will be keen to visit the **Ferne Animal Sanctuary**. Originally founded in 1939 by the Duchess of Hamilton and Brandon while she was living at Berwick St John near Shaftesbury, the sanctuary moved to its present position in the valley of the River Yarty in 1975. This pleasant 51-acre site incorporates a nature trail, conservation area, dragonfly pools and picnic areas.

ILMINSTER

6 miles NW of Crewkerne off the B3168

This ancient ecclesiastical and agricultural centre, whose name means

THE MEETING HOUSE ARTS CENTRE

East Street, Ilminster, Somerset TA19 0AN
Tel: 01460 55783 Fax: 01460 54973
e-mail: info@themeetinghouse.org.uk
website: www.themeetinghouse.org.uk

'Art for All' is the philosophy behind the **Meeting House Arts Centre**, a charitable trust organisation situated in the old Unitarian Church in the historic town of Ilminster. The organisation is dedicated to the study and appreciation of the visual and performing arts, and the Arts Centre provides a convivial meeting place and a focal point for a wide variety of arts and community activities in what is largely a rural area.

The organisation works in partnership with the community, various charities, local schools and the South-west Somerset Arts Fraternity. The annual programme includes exhibitions of work by well-established known names, emerging artists and local

schoolchildren. Regular workshops include watercolour painting, textiles, stained glass and willow work. Musical events range from blues, folk and jazz to chamber music and light opera. The Colourists Art Club holds regular lectures and the Bridge Club play in the gallery every week. There is a craft market on the second Friday of each month. The craft shop sells a selection of unique local crafts, as well as artists' materials and, in the licensed café, visitors can enjoy excellent cakes and scones and interesting lunches, all accompanied by a great cup of coffee.

'minster on the River Isle', takes its name from the church founded here by the Saxon King Ine in the 8th century. By the time of the Domesday Book in 1089, the borough had grown and it was recorded as having a market and three mills. During the Middle Ages, it expanded into a thriving wool and lace-making town. This period of prosperity is reflected in the town's unusually large parish church, whose massive multi-pinnacled tower is modelled on that of Wells Cathedral. Any walk around the old part of Ilminster will reveal a number of delightful old buildings, many constructed in golden hamstone, including the chantry house, the old grammar school and a colonnaded market house.

On the outskirts of Ilminster is another lovely old building, the handsome part Tudor mansion, **Dillington House**, which is the former home of the Speke family. In the time of James II, John Speke was an officer in the Duke of Monmouth's ill-fated rebel army that landed at Lyme Regis in 1685. However, following the rebellion's disastrous defeat at the Battle of Sedgemoor, Speke was forced to flee abroad, leaving his brother, George, who had done no more than shake the duke's hand, to face the wrath of Judge Jeffreys. The infamous 'hanging' judge sentenced George to death, justifying his decision with the words "His family owes a life and he shall die for his brother."

Just to the southeast of Ilminster is the attractive village of **Dowlish Wake**, where, in the church, can be seen the tomb of another member of the Speke family, John Hanning Speke, the intrepid Victorian explorer who journeyed for over 2,500 miles through Africa to confirm that Lake Victoria was, indeed, the source of the River Nile. After his epic journey, Speke returned to England a hero but, tragically, on the very morning that he was due to report his findings to the British Geographical Association he accidentally shot himself while on a partridge shoot.

HINTON ST GEORGE
2 miles NW of Crewkerne off the A356

This pretty and unspoilt former estate village of hamstone houses and cottages was, for centuries, owned by the Poulett family and it is thanks to them that Hinton St George has been left virtually untouched. The Pouletts arrived here in the 15th century and the house that they rebuilt then, Hinton House, now forms the main structure of the present day mansion. Although this has now been converted into apartments, the

---

THE OLD RECTORY

Cricket Malherbie, Nr Ilminster, Somerset TA19 0PW
Tel: 01460 54364 Fax: 01460 57374
e-mail: info@malherbie.co.uk
website: www.malherbie.co.uk

The Old Rectory is a delightful, award-winning small country hotel in a tiny conservation hamlet two miles from Ilchester. In a pretty building with golden Hamstone walls and a thatched roof, Martin and Patricia Fry-Foley are welcoming hosts, and the house is full of warmth and character, from the flagstoned hall and oak-beamed sitting room to the five well-appointed en suite bedrooms overlooking the typical English country garden. Breakfast is served in the dining room with original paintings on its deep-blue walls, and a four-course evening meal is available with notice. No smoking. No children under 16.

building is still said to be haunted by the ghost of a young Poulett woman who died of a broken heart after her father shot dead the man with whom she was planning to elope.

Several ostentatious monuments to members of the Poulett family can be seen in the village's 15th century Church of St George. Another noteworthy building in Hinton St George is the so called Priory, a 16th century residence with a 14th century window at its eastern end, that is thought to have once belonged to Monkton Farleigh Priory in Wiltshire.

On the last Thursday in October, called 'Punkie Night', it is traditional for Hinton children to beg for candles to put inside their intricately fashioned turnip and pumpkin lanterns. It is considered very unlucky to refuse to give a child a candle as each lantern is thought to represent the spirit of a dead person who, unless illuminated, will rise up at Hallowe'en.

WINCANTON

This attractive old cloth-making town was also a bustling coaching town as it lies almost exactly half way between London and the long-established naval base at Plymouth. In the heyday of stagecoaches, up to 20 a day would stop here. At that time, the inns could provide lodging for scores of travellers and stabling for over 250 horses. The oldest part of the town stands on a draughty hillside above the River Cale. A surprising number of fine Georgian buildings, some of which were constructed to replace earlier buildings destroyed in a fire in 1747, can be found here.

Modern day Wincanton is a peaceful light industrial town whose best known attraction, **Wincanton National Hunt Racecourse**, harks back to the days when horses were the only form of transport. Horse racing began in the area in the

THE CUNNING ARTIFICER

41 High Street, Wincanton, Somerset BA9 9JU
Tel: 01963 824686 Fax: 01963 824671
e-mail: bernard@cunningartificer.demon.co.uk
website: www.artificer.co.uk

Bernard and Isobel Pearson started off in a small way as makers and sellers of ceramics in East Anglia. Over the years the business developed and expanded, and with the move to premises on the main street of Wincanton came the start of a long and triumphant association with Terry Pratchett, one of the world's most prolific and successful authors. The skills of Bernard and his team have transformed words into physical form, turning the architecture and places and people of Discworld into highly cherished limited editions, very involved in both design and construction. They are the finest Discworld creations produced anywhere, and Terry Pratchett has recognised the skills of Bernard by bestowing on him the sobriquet '**The Cunning Artificer**'.

The range runs from the imposing Guild Buildings to the Mighty Press, the Mighty Organ, Granny Weatherwax's Cottage, the Rincewind Marionette and smaller items such as plaques, portrait heads, door signs, coats of arms, jewellery and rings, books and prints, Ankh Morpork pennies - and, of course, the intriguing Thud board game. Since the editions are strictly limited (rarely more than 500), the brilliantly executed models have become sought-after collectors' items.

18th century and the racecourse moved to its present site to the north of the town centre in 1927. Wincanton is remembered as the course where the great Desert Orchid had his first race of each season during his dominance of steeplechasing in the 1980s. For golf enthusiasts, the racecourse incorporates a challenging nine-hole pay and play course, which is open throughout the year. Also worth visiting is the beautiful **Hadspen House Gardens** situated just to the northwest of the town.

AROUND WINCANTON

TEMPLECOMBE

4 miles S of Wincanton on the A357

To the east of the village is the unusual **Gartell Light Railway**, a rare 2-foot gauge line that runs for around a mile

through the beautiful countryside of Blackmore Vale on the trackbed of the Somerset and Dorset Railway, closed over 30 years ago. The trains run every 15 minutes from Common Line Station, which also has a visitor centre, refreshment room and shop. The nearby **Templecombe Railway Museum** houses a fascinating collection of artefacts, photographs and models that tell the story of the nearby station, once a busy junction where some 130 railwaymen worked.

SPARKFORD

6½ miles W of Wincanton on the A359

Transport of a different kind is remembered here at the **Haynes Motor Museum** thought to hold the largest collection of veteran, vintage and classic cars and motorbikes in the United Kingdom. This unique collection has over 200 exhibits and each one is driven or ridden at least once every six months around a specially constructed demonstration track.

Just to the southeast of the village lies **Cadbury Castle**, a massive Iron Age hill fort believed by some to be the location of King Arthur's legendary Camelot. First occupied over 5,000 years ago, the Romans are reputed to have carried out a massacre here in around AD 70 when they put down a revolt by the ancient Britons. A major excavation in the 1960s uncovered a wealth of Roman and pre-Roman remains on the site as well as confirming that there was certainly a 6th century fortification on the hilltop. This particular discovery ties the castle in with King Arthur who, at around that time, was spearheading the Celtic British resistance against the advancing Saxons. If Cadbury Castle had been Arthur's Camelot, it would have been a timber fortification rather than the turreted stone structure of the storybooks.

This easily defended hilltop was again fortified during the reign of Ethelred the Unready in the early 11th century. The poorly-advised king established a mint here in around 1000. Most of the coinage from Cadbury was used to buy off the invading Danes in an act of appeasement that led to the term Danegeld. As a consequence, most of the surviving coins from the Cadbury mint are now to be found in the museums of Scandinavia.

The mile-long walk around Cadbury Castle's massive earthwork ramparts demonstrates the site's effectiveness as a defensive position. This allowed those at the castle to see enemy's troop movements in days gone by and it now provides spectacular panoramic views for today's visitors.

CASTLE CARY

4½ miles NW of Wincanton on the B3152

Once the site of an impressive Norman

NEEDFUL THINGS

High Street, Castle Cary, Somerset BA7 7AN
Tel: 01963 351352 Fax: 01963 350353
e-mail: needfulthings@nascr.net

Needful Things is a delightful double-fronted shop on the main street of an equally delightful little Somerset town. Home accessories and soft furnishings are the main stock in trade, with everything to grace and enhance a home, from beautiful furniture to exquisite fabrics and materials. The range is impressive, and customers can either choose from the displays or have

something made to their own requirements from the pattern books.

The finishing touches are all there, too, from flowers to lighting and pictures, wall mountings and window hangings, and the cards and wrapping paper make a special gift even more special; there's also a small, select range of tastefully chosen ladies' clothing. A wonderland at Christmas, when every inch of space is filled with festive treasures, Needful Things is a joy at any time of the year, with its fabrics and colours and alluring aromas, and the charming owners John and Alison Lawrence put the seal on the pleasure of a visit.

BLACK & WHITE

Fore Street, Castle Cary, Somerset BA7 7BG
Tel: 01963 359190
e-mail: black.white@amserve.com

Owner Jane Milward runs **Black & White**, a charming
lifestyle shop in the centre of Castle Cary. The frontage
is indeed painted black and white, but once inside
colour takes over, with something cheerful and vibrant
to take the eye at every turn. The concept started with
leather goods, from bags to sofas, and those are still
very much in evidence, but there's now much more,
from funky clothes and boots to jaunty jewellery,
unusual lighting and contemporary artwork - even a selection of collars that any well-dressed dog
would be proud to wear.

castle of which nothing can be seen
today, this lovely little town has an
atmosphere of mature rural calm as well
as some interesting old buildings. There
is a handsome 18th century post office, a
tiny lock-up gaol called the **Round
House** dating from the 1770s and a
splendid Market House with a
magnificent 17th century colonnade.

Largely constructed in 1855, the Market
House is now the home of the **Castle
Cary District Museum**. However,
perhaps the most interesting site here is
the town's **War Memorial**, which stands
in the middle of a pond said to be part of
the old castle moat and where, in days
gone by, scolds and witches received
their usual punishment of a ducking.

NUMBER ONE

High Street, Castle Cary, Somerset BA7 7AN
Tel: 01963 351259

Proprietor Jilly Haigh-Lumby has worked long and
hard to create **Number One**, and the result of her
efforts is an absolute gem of a shop selling a wide
range of goods hand-picked by Jilly herself. The shop
comprises three distinct sections, so browsers should
allow plenty of
time. At the front is
a wide variety of
cards and contemporary gifts to suit all pockets and all occasions.
This area leads through to the home section, where dressers and
display cases are filled with pots and pans and other kitchenware
both traditional and contemporary, some of it bold and bright and
cheerful, some more muted and sophisticated.

At the back of the premises is the ladies' clothing section, where a
varied collection of very wearable garments is displayed in a gracious,
peaceful setting that shows to best effect the gorgeous fabrics and
textures. The clothes are complemented by a well-chosen selection
of shoes, bags, jewellery and other accessories, and Jilly's unerring
eye for style and quality ensure that everything is in the best of taste.
Castle Cary is a lovely little town, with plenty to see and do, and
Number One is a worthy addition to the list of attractions.

BRUTON

4½ miles NW of Wincanton on the A359

This remarkably well-preserved former clothing and ecclesiastical centre, beside the River Brue, is more like a small town than a village. The priory was first established here in the 11th century and although much of this has now gone the former priory church is now the parish church. The Church of St Mary has a rare second tower built over the north porch in the late 14th century. The light and spacious interior is well worth a visit as it contains a number of memorials to the Berkeley family, the local lords of the manor who also owned the land on which London's Berkeley Square now stands.

Across the river from the church is the **Patwell Pump**, a curious square structure that was the parish's communal water pump that remained in use until well into the 20th century. Further downstream a 15th century packhorse bridge can be seen near the site of the famous part 16th century King's School. However, **The Dovecote**, arguably Bruton's most distinctive building, can be seen on the crest of a hill to the south of the bridge. Built in the 15th century, it is thought to have doubled as a watchtower.

LOCATOR MAP

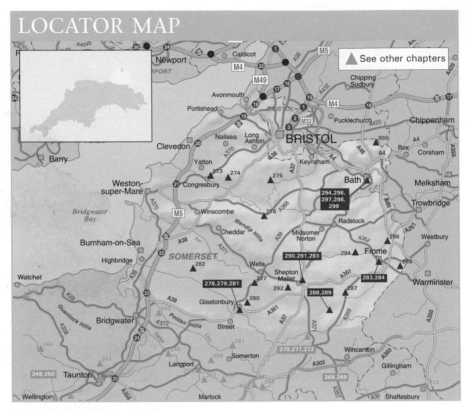

ADVERTISERS AND PLACES OF INTEREST

273 Church House Designs, Congresbury   page 321
274 Barleywood Crafts, Wrington   page 321
275 Willow, Chew Magna   page 322
276 West Harptree Nursery,
   West Harptree, Bath   page 322
277 Potting Shed Holidays, Coxley, Wells   page 329
278 Somerset Rural Life Museum,
   Glastonbury   page 331
279 Glastonbury Abbey, Glastonbury   page 332
280 Middlewick Holiday Cottages,
   Glastonbury   page 332
281 Heartfelt Trading, Glastonbury   page 333
282 The Sexey's Arms, Blackford   page 335
283 Enigma Contemporary Arts & Crafts,
   Frome   page 336
284 The Golden Goose, Frome   page 336
285 Tulsi, Temple, Corsley   page 338
286 Pickford House, Beckington, Bath   page 338
287 Christine-Ann Richards, Wanstrow   page 339

288 Sally Pollitzer, Batcombe   page 340
289 Valley View Farm Bed & Breakfast,
   Batcombe, Shepton Mallet   page 341
290 Bowlish House Hotel & Restaurant,
   Shepton Mallet   page 341
291 Monet, Shepton Mallet   page 342
292 Knowle Farm Cottages, West Compton,
   Shepton Mallet   page 343
293 East Somerset Railway,
   Shepton Mallet   page 343
294 The Talbot Inn, Mells, Frome   page 344
295 The Windsor Hotel, Bath   page 346
296 The Bath Sweet Shop, Bath   page 347
297 Loch Fyne Restaurant & Milsoms Hotel,
   Bath   page 348
298 The British Hatter, Bath   page 349
299 Bath Paradise House Hotel, Bath   page 350
300 Nailey Cottages, St Catherine's Valley,
   Bath   page 352

Elegant cities such as Bath, charming old market towns, the glorious countryside of the Mendip Hills, connections with the legends of King Arthur and coastal resorts like Weston-super-Mare are all part of the charm of this northeastern region of Somerset. Running from Weston-super-Mare to Frome, the limestone Mendip Hills cut across this area in a spectacular fashion. Although at their highest point they only reach just over 1,000 feet, they provide some magnificent panoramic views out across the flat lands of the Somerset Levels and over the Bristol Channel to South Wales. A wealth of prehistoric remains have been found here but two of the hills most popular and famous attractions are both natural – Cheddar Gorge and the caves at Wookey Hole. With cliffs over 400 feet high on either side of the road that runs through the

Mendip Hills in Winter

bottom of the gorge this is, indeed, a spectacular sight while the caves at Wookey Hole, from which the River Axe emerges, are famous for their echos and for their fantastic stalagmite and stalactite formations.

The Mendips are also the home of the smallest city in England, Wells, where a cathedral was founded, in the 12th century, on the site of a Saxon church. Wells is dominated by its cathedral, a magnificent building that contains a wonderful 14th century Astronomical Clock. It is also a busy market centre for the small towns and villages of this rural area of Somerset. Just to the southeast is an ecclesiastical centre that is not only older but far better known than Wells. Glastonbury, with an Abbey said to have been founded by Joseph of Arimathea in AD 60, is the earliest seat of Christianity in the British Isles. It is also believed to have been the last resting place of King Arthur and Queen Guinevere. Whether true or not, it is indisputable that in the Middle Ages this was a place of great importance: not only did the

Glastonbury Abbey

abbey's powers of influence stretch far and wide but it was considered such an eminent place of learning that scholars travelled here from all over Europe. Even more ancient than the abbey is the conical tor just outside the town that since prehistoric times has been considered a place of mystery and great spiritual power.

To the north of the Mendips lies the city of Bath, which in the 18th century became the most fashionable spa town in the country. Some 1,600 years earlier, it was equally fashionable among the Romans. Close by is the West Country's largest city, Bristol, which, despite its modern appearance, dates back to Saxon times, when a settlement was founded here at the strategically important bridging point of the Avon gorge. The gorge is now spanned by one of the city's most famous constructions, the Clifton Suspension Bridge, which was finally completed after the death of its designer Isambard Kingdom Brunel. However, it is as a port and a shipbuilding centre that Bristol is best known and, down by the old wharf, can be seen another of Brunel's masterpieces, the *SS Great Britain*, the first iron-hulled passenger liner, launched in 1843.

CHEDDAR

This sprawling village is best known for its dramatic limestone gorge, **Cheddar Gorge**, which is one of the most famous and most often visited of Britain's many natural attractions. It is characterised by its high vertical cliffs, from which there are outstanding views out over the Somerset Levels, the Quantock Hills and, on a clear day, across the Bristol Channel to South Wales. The National Trust owns most of the land around this magnificent ravine, which is a Site of Special Scientific Interest. Numerous rare plants grow here and it is also a haven for butterflies. A circular walk

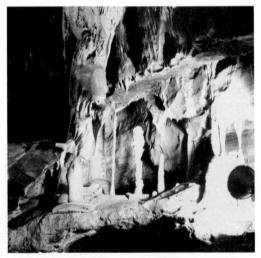

Cox's Cave, Cheddar

Cheddar Gorge

evidence of early human occupation of the caves, including flint and bone tools dating from the last Ice Age and artefacts from the Iron Age and the Roman occupation of Britain.

The term 'Cheddar Cheese' refers to a recipe that was developed in the mid-19th century by Joseph Harding, a farmer and pioneer food scientist from near Bath who made the first scientific investigation into cheese-making. As the name refers to a recipe and not a place, the cheese can be made anywhere in the world. However, north Somerset is dotted with cheese manufacturers of various sizes, from single farmhouses to large scale dairies, all making Cheddar cheese. A number of these places supplement their income by offering guided tours, craft demonstrations and catering facilities for the many visitors who come to gorge on the local speciality.

through the area takes in plantations, natural woodland and rough downland. This is a place that draws rock climbers, but the less ambitious may like to take the 322 steps of **Jacob's Ladder** that lead up the side of the gorge to the site of **Pavey's Lookout Tower**, a novel vantage point that offers yet more spectacular views of the surrounding area.

While the gorge is undoubtedly everyone's idea of Cheddar, the village is also renowned for its caves and, of course, its cheese. Although much embellished by modern tourist paraphernalia, its two main show caves, **Gough's Cave** and **Cox's Cave**, are worth seeing for their sheer scale and spectacular calcite formations. In 1903 an almost complete skeleton, named 'Cheddar Man', was discovered in Gough's Cave and this can be seen in a nearby museum. There is also further

AROUND CHEDDAR

CONGRESBURY

6 miles N of Cheddar on the A370

This sizable village, which today appears to be just another commuter town, has a long and eventful history that goes back to Roman times. Around 2,000 years ago a settlement stood here at the end of a spur of the Somerset marshes. Fragments of Roman and pre-Saxon pottery have been found on the site of the ancient hill that overlooks the present village.

The early Celtic missionary, St Congar, is believed to have founded an early wattle chapel at Congresbury in the 6th century. A tree bound by an iron hoop, on the eastern side of the church, is still referred to as 'St Congar's Walking Stick'. This is reputed to have grown from the saint's staff that miraculously sprouted

WALK NUMBER 10

Yatton

Distance:	4.6 miles (7.3 kilometres)
Typical time:	120 mins
Height gain:	40 metres
Map:	Explorer 154
Walk:	www.walkingworld.com ID:1267
Contributor:	Joy and Charles Boldero

Access Information:

Train service ring 08437 4844950. Bus service ring 0800 260 270. Free car parking at the railway station where the walk begins. Yatton is situated on the B3133 16 miles south of Bristol.

Description:

This walk is also along a part of the Strawberry Line track, the route goes through woodland and along tracks, over meadows and along country lanes.

Additional Information:

Waymark1: This old railway line is part of the Old Strawberry line. Now a nature reserve, short tailed field voles are found here as well as many wild flowers including the marsh marigold. Yatton station is still in use, but the main line used to serve two other junctions, the Cheddar Valley line and Clevedon line.

Waymark 2: This attractive and unusual seat was made by Yatton Junior School to celebrate the finds of the Roman remains near this spot.

Waymark 7: Cadbury Hill is a local nature reserve where green woodpeckers can be seen. The Hill fort is a scheduled ancient monument. Once a defended settlement of the Iron Age 500 BC.

Features:

Pub, toilets, church, wildlife, birds, flowers, great views, butterflies, food shop

Walk Directions:

1 From the station car park go to barrier and along the old railway line path westwards.

2 With the church on the far left turn left to five bar gate with, 'Batts Five Acres' on it. The path goes across the meadow. It is a permissive route. Keep to the track of sorts as it winds around going over a wide earth bridge towards the farm. Climb stile on left, cross grass area.

3 Turn right along road. At T junction turn right.

4 At the end of Mendip Road turn left along pavement.

5 Cross road with bus stop opposite near the bend, turn right along the 'No thro road'.

6 Turn right at white cricket notice board sign. Climb stile, cross car park and country lane. Climb stile by notice board and go diagonally left uphill over meadow. The path narrows with wood on left. Go through kissing gate, later keep to the right hand path by fence line.

7 Go though barrier and follow path upwards. Halfway up by two trees turn left to woodland. Follow path through woodland as it goes over tree roots and boulders. Ignore paths left. Go though kissing gate. Continue along path to top. Go down left along sunken path, go through gate, it becomes a lane.

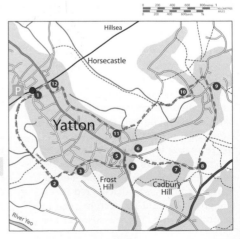

8 Turn left at sign through iron gateway. Go down path. (this after heavy winter rain has a stream and horses use this path too, so it can be very muddy!) At end it becomes a tarmac lane.

9 At crossroads go straight ahead along High Street, with a Post Office on the right hand corner. Turn left into Chestnut Drive. Turn left at T junction.

10 Turn right along hedged track at finger post sign to farm. Go through farmyard, cross stream and meadows, stiles, keep along meadow with houses on left. Climb stile.

11 Turn right along road. This curves left at the No thro road sign.

12 At T junction turn right back to start of walk.

CHURCH HOUSE DESIGNS

Broad Street, Congresbury, Bristol, North Somerset BS49 5DG
Tel/Fax: 01934 833660
website: www.churchhousedesigns.co.uk

When Robert and Lorraine Coles opened **Church House Designs** in 1986 it was to sell Robert's bespoke furniture, but it has since expanded into a contemporary craft gallery with a growing reputation for high-quality, imaginative work. The emphasis is particularly on ceramics, glassware, jewellery, wood and textiles, and the owners organise lively and varied exhibitions with a wide cross-section of artists represented. Visitors are encouraged to browse at leisure in the gallery, which is open from 10am to 1pm and 2.15pm to 5pm. Closed Wednesday, Sunday and Bank Holidays.

leaves after he had thrust it into the ground outside the chapel.

BARROW GURNEY

10 miles NE of Cheddar on the B3130

Before the construction of the reservoirs of Blagdon and Chew Valley, Bristol's fresh water came from the three small reservoirs at Barrow Gurney. The first was opened in 1852 but within two years it developed a leak and had to be drained, causing a serious disruption to the city's water supply. Like many of the villages to the southwest of Bristol, Barrow Gurney has undergone considerable change since World War II and is now becoming a dormitory settlement for the city's commuters.

CHEW MAGNA

9 miles NE of Cheddar on the B3130

Situated just to the north of Chew Valley Lake, this former wool village is a pleasant place with some handsome

BARLEYWOOD CRAFTS

The Walled Garden, Long Lane, Wrington, Somerset BS40 5SA
Restaurant Tel: 01934 863713 Workshop Tel: 0776 8543151

Visitors to **Barleywood Crafts** can look forward to a real treat. The restored Victorian walled kitchen garden produces organic fruit and vegetables, honey, apple juice and cider; the restaurant serves delicious home-cooked food; and the craft workshops sell a wide range of high-quality artwork and gifts. Jenny Davidson produces richly coloured pastel paintings, prints, scarves and jewellery; Ray Hopley is a potter and sculptor making functional domestic stoneware; Sandy Cocks specialises in abstracts and landscapes in oils; and Sylvia Owen produces ceramics of animals, birds and people for interiors and gardens.

WILLOW

South Parade, Chew Magna, Somerset BS40 8SH
Tel: 01275 333155

Beatrice de la Haye Arnoux studied interior design and
worked as a florist in Mayfair before returning to her roots
and opening **Willow** in 2002. Since then she has pleased
her customers with her cutting edge styles and ideas, and
her shop is filled with bright, inviting displays of gifts and
home accessories. The range includes fresh flowers, fabrics
and soft furnishings, wallpapers and paints, teapots and
mugs, lighting and home decorations, as well as everything needed for a wedding or any other special
occasion - both the function itself and a wide range of suitable presents. Free parking opposite.

Georgian houses. This, too, has become a
commuter village for Bristol. The nucleus
of the village is its three-sided green
whose surrounding shops and pubs are
linked by an unusual raised stone
pavement. At the top of the green is the
striking early 16th century **Church
House** that was originally intended to be
the venue for the annual church sales
and for brewing the ale and baking the
bread to be sold on these occasions. The
funds raised at this event were used to
maintain the parish church for the
coming year. These church houses, built
in the 15th or early 16th century, were
mainly confined to the counties of
Somerset and Devon. Close by is the
impressive parish Church of St Andrew, a
testimony to the former prosperity of
this village. Inside can be seen the
interesting double effigy of Sir John Loe,
a 15th century local squire reputed to be

seven feet tall, and his wife. Behind a
high wall adjacent to the churchyard lies
Chew Court, a former summer palace of
the bishops of Bath and Wells.

Just to the east of the village lies
Stanton Drew, an ancient settlement
that stands beside a prehistoric site of
some importance – a series of stone
circles over half a mile across that were
constructed by the Bronze Age Beaker
people between 2000 and 1600 BC. This
complex of **Standing Stones** consists of
three circles, a lone stone known as
Hauteville's Quoit and a large
chambered burial tomb called **The Cove**.
The stones are composed of three
different types of rock; limestone,
sandstone and conglomerate. They are
thought to have been erected for
religious, or perhaps astronomical,
purposes. In common with many stone
circles in western Britain, the origin of

WEST HARPTREE NURSERY

Bristol Road, West Harptree, Bath BS40 6HG
Tel: 01761 221370   e-mail: bryn@herbaceousperennials.co.uk
Fax: 01761 221989   website: www.herbaceousperennials.co.uk

At the foot of the Mendip Hills, Bryn and Helene Bowles have been running
their four acre nursery for approximately eight years and have a collection
of around 700 rare, unusual and hard-to-find plants. Many have been
awarded the Royal Horticultural Society's AGM and the collection includes
herbaceous perennials, grasses and shrubs. Visit between March and October,
and, after picking up a 'treasure', try a local pub lunch or afternoon tea
room. The plants list is on the website or you can telephone for a hard copy.

this stone circle is steeped in legend. The most widespread tale tells of a foolhardy wedding party who wanted to continue dancing into the Sabbath. At midnight, the piper refused to carry on, prompting the infuriated bride to declare that if she had to, she would get a piper from hell. At that point, another piper stepped forward to volunteer his services and the party resumed its dancing. As the music got louder and louder and the tempo faster and faster, the dancers realised, too late, that the good natured piper was the Devil himself and, when his playing reached its terrifying climax, he turned the whole party to stone. To this day, this curious group of standing stones is still known as 'The Wedding'.

A couple of miles to the north of Stanton Drew, the line of the ancient **Wansdyke** runs in a roughly east-west direction around the southern fringes of Bristol. Built during the Dark Ages as a boundary line and defensive barrier against the Saxons, short sections of this great earthwork bank can still be seen, notably at Maes Knoll and along the ridge adjoining the Iron Age hill fort on Stantonbury Hill.

To the south of Chew Magna are the two reservoirs constructed to supply Bristol with fresh water but that also provide a first class recreational amenity. The smaller **Blagdon Lake** was completed in 1899 and **Chew Valley Lake** in 1956. Together they have around 15 miles of shoreline and attract visitors from a wide area who come to fish, take part in watersports and observe the wide variety of waterfowl and other bird life that is drawn to this appealing habitat.

CHARTERHOUSE

2½ miles NE of Cheddar off the B3134

Rising, in some places, to over 1,000 feet above sea level, the **Mendips** form a landscape that is like no other in the region and, although hard to imagine today, lead and silver were once mined from these picturesque uplands. The Mendip lead-mining activity was centred around the remote village of Charterhouse and the last mine in the district, at Priddy, closed in 1908.

Charterhouse takes its name from a Carthusian monastery, **Witham Priory**, which owned one of the four Mendip mining sectors, or liberties. This area has been known for its mineral deposits since the Iron Age and such was its importance that the Romans declared the mines here state property within just six years of their arrival in Britain. Under their influence, silver and lead ingots, or pigs, were exported to France and to Rome, and the settlement grew into a sizable town with its own fort and amphitheatre, the remains of which can still be seen today. Centuries later, improved technology allowed the original seams to be reworked and the area is now littered with abandoned mine buildings and smelting houses.

A footpath from Charterhouse church leads up onto **Black Down** that is, at 1,067 feet, the highest point in the Mendips. From here, to the northwest, the land descends down into **Burrington Combe**, a deep cleft said to have inspired the Reverend Augustus Toplady to write the hymn *Rock of Ages*.

BURNHAM-ON-SEA

10 miles SW of Cheddar on the B3140

In the late 18th century, mineral springs were discovered, and an attempt was made to turn Burnham-on-Sea into a spa town to rival Cheltenham and Bath. However, the efficacious effects of its waters were never properly realised and, in the end, the town depended on its wide sandy beach to attract visitors. It is a large and popular seaside resort today with, particularly at low tide, a vast expanse of beach. Burnham's most distinctive landmark is the **Low Lighthouse**, a curious square structure raised above the beach on tall stilts. Another of the town's buildings that has fared less well on its sandy foundations is the church, whose 80-foot tower leans three feet from the vertical. The structure is quite stable and has not moved for many decades. Inside the church there are some reredos, designed by Inigo Jones and made by Grinling Gibbons, that were originally intended for the chapel at Whitehall Palace but were presented to the vicar of Burnham by George IV in 1820.

To the southeast of Burnham is the small town of **Highbridge**, once a busy coastal port on the Glastonbury Canal. To the northeast lies **Brent Knoll**, a conspicuous landmark that can be seen from as far away as South Wales. Before the Somerset Levels were drained, this isolated hill would almost certainly have been an island. Like many other natural features that appear out of place in the landscape, there are several stories that suggest that the knoll owes its existence to the Devil. The 445-foot summit is crowned with the remains of an Iron Age hill fort. Several hundred years later, Brent Knoll's southern slopes are said to have been the site of a battle that King Alfred fought and won against the Danes. The summit, which can be reached by footpaths beginning near the churches at East Brent and Brent Knoll, offers walkers a spectacular view out over the Bristol Channel, the Mendips and the Somerset Levels.

AXBRIDGE

2 miles W of Cheddar off the A371

A fortified market town that had its own mint during Saxon times, by the late medieval period Axbridge had developed into a prosperous wool centre that made

its living processing the Mendip fleeces into woven cloth. A small town today with a delightful centre, the old market square is home to an exceptional example of a half-timbered merchant's house dating from around 1500. **King John's Hunting Lodge**, now in the ownership of the National Trust, was extensively restored in the early 1970s and is home to an excellent **Local History Museum**. Although it has nothing to do with King John or hunting, its name is a reminder that the Mendip hills were once a royal hunting ground. Elsewhere in the centre of Axbridge there are many handsome Georgian shops and town houses.

To the east of the town is Cheddar's curious circular reservoir while, to the west, lies the hamlet of **Webbington Loxton**, home to the **Wheelwright's Working Museum** and the **Gypsy Folklore Collection**.

BREAN

10 miles W of Cheddar off the A370

This elongated, mainly modern resort village is sheltered, to the north, by the 320 foot **Brean Down**, an imposing remnant of the Mendip hills that projects out into the Bristol Channel. Another fragment can be seen in the form of the offshore island **Steep Holm**. A site of settlement, ritual and defence for thousands of years, the remains of an Iron Age coastal fort and a Roman temple have both been found on the down along with some medieval 'pillow' mounds. However, the tip of the promontory is dominated by the Palmerston fort of 1867, built as part of the defences to protect the Bristol Channel. There are also some 20th century gun emplacements. As well as its archaeological and geological interest, this peninsula has been designated a Site of Special Scientific Interest for its habitats. Oystercatcher and dunlin can be seen along the foreshore and estuary; the scrubland is an important habitat for migrating birds such as redstart, redpoll and reed bunting; rare plants take root in the shallow and exposed soil, and the south-facing slopes are home to a variety of butterflies. With one of the widest tidal ranges in Europe, the currents around the headland can be dramatic and very dangerous.

Uphill Harbour, nr Weston-super-Mare

BANWELL

5 miles NW of Cheddar on the A368

This pleasant village was once the site of a Saxon monastery and the parish church here is certainly ancient. **Banwell Castle**, on the other hand, is a relatively recent addition to the village and is, in fact, a Victorian mansion house. Just to the west of the village, on Banwell Hill, a remarkable discovery was made in 1821. A series of caverns were found containing the remains of prehistoric animals including bison, bear and reindeer. They are now known as the **Bone Caves**. Some years after the discovery the local bishop created an extravagant romantic park, which he filled with pyramids, a monk's cell, fairy cottages and other fanciful buildings.

A couple of miles north of Banwell is the village of **Puxton**, noted for its eccentric church tower that leans at such an angle that it looks as if it might topple at any moment, causing its weathercock to nosedive into the churchyard.

WESTON-SUPER-MARE

10 miles NW of Cheddar on the A370

This traditional seaside resort, whose greatest asset is undoubtedly its vast expanse of sandy beach, has, in recent years, also developed as a centre of light industry. Weston-super-Mare was, as late as 1811, just a fishing hamlet, with only 170 residents. Within 100 years, it grew to become the second largest town in Somerset. Despite is relatively modern appearance, this area has been inhabited since prehistoric times and the wooded promontory at the northern end of Weston Bay was the site of a sizable Iron Age hill settlement known as **Worlebury Camp**. In the 1st century AD this is said to have been captured by the Romans after a bloody battle. Recent excavations, which revealed a number of skeletons showing the effects of sword damage, provided confirmation. A pleasant walk from the town centre now leads up through attractive woodland to this ancient hilltop site from where there are magnificent views out across the mouth of the River Severn to Wales. At the southern end of Weston Bay, another spectacular view can be found from the clifftop site of the semi-ruined church at **Uphill**. This village lies at the start of the sometimes demanding **Mendip Way**, a 50-mile footpath that takes in the whole length of the Mendip Hills, including the broad vale of the Western Mendips, the high plateau of the central part and the wooded valleys in the eastern region.

The development of Weston began in the 1830s around the Knightstone, an islet joined to the shore at the northern end of the bay, and here were eventually built a large theatre and swimming baths. The arrival of the railway in 1841 saw the town's rapid expansion, and in 1867 a pier was built on the headland below Worlebury Camp connecting Birnbeck Island with the mainland. Intended as a berth for steamer traffic, the pier was found to be slightly off the tourist track. Later, a more impressive pier was built nearer the town centre. Prior to serious fires in the 1930s and during World War II, it was approximately twice its current length. The **Grand Pier** now stands at the centre of an area crammed with souvenir shops, ice cream parlours, cafés and assorted attractions that are part and parcel of a British seaside resort. There are also the indoor attractions of the **Winter Gardens**, along the seafront, and the fascinating **North Somerset Museum**.

For anyone wishing to explore Weston on foot, the Museum Trail begins on the seafront and follows a trail of carved stones created by the artist Michael Fairfax. The **Seaquarium** has over 30 interesting marine displays, along with feeding times and demonstrations, to amuse the whole family. The **Weston Miniature Railway** provides a leisurely way to see something of Weston's seafront.

An excellent viewpoint to the north of the resort is **Sand Point**, a ridge overlooking a lonely salt marsh that is home to a wide variety of wading birds. Just back from the headland is **Woodspring Priory**, a surprisingly intact medieval monastery founded in the early 13th century by a grandson of one of Thomas à Becket's murderers, William de Courtenay. The priory fell into disrepair following the Dissolution when the buildings were given over to agricultural use but the church, tower, refectory and tithe barn have all survived and the outline of the cloister can also still be made out.

Just to the southeast of the town lies Weston Airport, home to the world's largest collection of helicopters and autogyros. The only museum in Britain dedicated to rotary wing aircraft, the **International Helicopter Museum** has over 40 exhibits ranging from single-seater autogyros to multi-passenger helicopters. Visitors can see displays on the history and development of these flying machines and a conservation hangar where the aircraft are restored.

CLEVEDON

12 miles NW of Cheddar on the B3133

Developed in the late 18th and early 19th century as a resort, the lack of a railway prevented the town from expanding further and so it was overtaken by Weston-super-Mare as the leading seaside town along this stretch of coast. As a result there are few of the attractions that are normally associated with a holiday resort, although the exception is **Clevedon Pier**, a remarkably slim and elegant structure that was built in the 1860s from iron rails intended for Brunel's ill-considered South Wales Railway. When part of the pier collapsed in the 1970s, its long term future looked bleak but, following an extensive restoration programme, the pier is now the landing stage, during the summer, for large pleasure steamers such as the *Balmoral* and the *Waverley*, the only surviving sea-going paddle steamers in the world. Unusually for a holiday resort Clevedon has a **Market Hall** that was built in 1869 to provide a place for local market gardeners to sell their produce.

Beginning at Clevedon promenade and leading up to Church and Wain's Hills is the **Poet's Walk**, a flower-lined footpath that is said to have been popular with Victorian poets. On the top of Wain's Hill, are the remains of an Iron Age coastal fort, from which walkers can look out over the town, the Somerset Levels and the Severn Estuary.

However, it is **Clevedon Court**, an outstanding 14th century manor house that brings most people to this town. One of the earliest surviving country houses in Britain, this house displays many of its original 14th century features still intact and incorporates a massive 12th century tower and a 13th century great hall. Once partly fortified, this imposing manor house has been the home of the Elton family since 1709. As longstanding patrons of the arts, the family invited many of the countries finest poets and writers to Clevedon in the early 19th century. These included Coleridge, Tennyson and Thackeray. It was while staying here that Thackeray fell in love with one of his host's daughters, Mrs Brookfield. He was to spend some time here seeing her and writing *Vanity Fair*. Another member of the Elton family was Arthur Hallam, a student friend of Lord Tennyson who showed great promise as a poet but who died very young. Tennyson never got over his friend's untimely death and he visited his grave in 1850, the same year that his poem, *In Memoriam, AHH*, was published.

Although the Elton family is closely associated with the arts, one member of the family in the Victorian era invented a special technique for making the type of brightly coloured pottery that was to become known as Eltonware. Particularly popular in the United States, there are many fine examples on display in the house, along with a collection of rare glass from the works at Nailsea. Now owned by the National Trust, Clevedon Court is an impressive place housing some fine treasures and is surrounded by beautiful 18th century terraced gardens. A footpath leads through nearby woodland on to a ridge overlooking the low and once marshy Gordano valley.

Just to the east of Clevedon lies the tiny village of **Walton-in-Gordano** where the wonderful gardens of the **Manor House** are planted with rare shrubs, trees and herbaceous plants.

WELLS

This ancient ecclesiastical centre derives its name from a line of springs that rise up from the base of the Mendips. The first church here is believed to have been founded by King Ine in around 700 and, after a diocesan tussle with Bath, the present **Cathedral of St Andrew** was begun in the 12th century. Taking over three centuries to complete, this magnificent cathedral demonstrates the three main styles of Gothic architecture. Its 13th century west front, with over 100 statues of saints, angels and prophets gazing down on the cathedral close, is generally acknowledged to be its crowning glory, although it was defaced during the English Civil War. Inside there are many superb features including the beautiful scissor arches and the great 14th century stained glass window over the high altar. However, the cathedral's

Wells Cathedral

most impressive sight is its 14th century **Astronomical Clock**, one of the oldest working timepieces in the world, that shows the minutes, hours and phases of the moon on separate inner and outer dials and marks the quarter hours with a lively battle between knights.

The large cathedral close is a tranquil city within a city and for centuries the ecclesiastical and civic functions of Wells have remained separate. The west front of the cathedral has an internal passage with pierced apertures and there is a theory that choirboys might have sung through these openings to give the illusion to those gathered on the cathedral green that the then lifelike painted statues were singing. The cathedral green is surrounded by a high wall breached at only three castellated entrance points. One of these, the gateway into the Market Place, is known as **Penniless Porch**. It was here that the bishop allowed the city's poor to beg for money from those entering the cathedral close. Set in the pavement here is a length of brass that extends

over the prodigious distance leapt by local girl Mary Rand when she set a world record for the long jump.

To the south of the cathedral's cloisters is the **Bishop's Palace**, a remarkable fortified medieval building, enclosed by a high wall and surrounded by a moat fed by the springs that give the city its name. In order to gain access to the palace from the Market Place, visitors must pass under a 13th century stone arch known as the **Bishop's Eye** and then cross a drawbridge that was last raised for defensive purposes in 1831. Although it is still an official residence of the Bishop of Bath and Wells, visitors can tour the palace's chapel and its Jocelin's hall. On the northern side of the cathedral green is the **Vicar's Close**. This 14th century cobbled thoroughfare is one of the oldest planned streets in Europe.

There is, of course, much more to Wells than its ecclesiastical buildings and heritage. A visit to the **Wells Museum**, found near the west front of the cathedral, explains much of the history

Bishop's Palace

POTTING SHED HOLIDAYS

Harter's Hill Cottage, Pillmoor Lane, Coxley,
Nr Wells, Somerset BA5 1RF
Tel: 01749 672857 Fax: 01749 679925
e-mail: info@pottingshedholidays.co.uk
website: www.pottingshedholidays.co.uk

Chris and John van Bergen have created something very
special at **Potting Shed Holidays**, where two beautifully
renovated self-catering cottages offer respite from the
stress of everyday life, a place to relax and restore the
spirits. Spiders End, dating from about 1670, provides
up-to-date comforts in a setting of old-world charm that includes original features such as beams,
sturdy stone and a section of ancient wattle and daub walls, all newly restored by local craftsmen

using local materials. This cottage has one double and
one twin bedrooms, two bathrooms, a fully equipped
modern kitchen, dining room and sitting room.

The Potting Shed, originally a farmhand's shed
and animal shelter, is now a cosy retreat for two, and
among its many attractions is a luxurious emperor-
size double bed. Guests at the cottages have the use
of a lovingly cared-for garden full of interesting
botanical specimens and a haven for wildlife. The
surprise feature is a garden spa in its own fully heated
cabin. No smoking in the cottages; pets by
arrangement. Bed & breakfast by arrangement.

of the city and surrounding area through
a collection of interesting locally found
artefacts. The city also remains a lively
market centre, with a street market held
every Wednesday and Saturday. For those
wanting to view Wells from a distance,
there is an attractive footpath that starts
from the Moat Walk and leads up the
summit of Tor Hill.

AROUND WELLS

CAMELEY

8½ miles NE of Wells off the A37

This attractive village is home to a
church referred to by John Betjeman as
"Rip Van Winkle's Church" because of
the remarkable series of medieval wall
paintings that were discovered here,
under layers of whitewash, in the 1960s.
The murals are believed to have been

painted between the 11th and the 17th
centuries and feature such diverse images
as the foot of a giant St Christopher
stepping through a fish and crab infested
river, a charming 14th century jester
complete with harlequin costume and a
rare coat of arms of Charles I.

GLASTONBURY

5½ miles SW of Wells on the A39

Today this ancient town of myths and
legends, of tales of King Arthur and the
early Christians, is an attractive market
town still dominated by the ruins of its
abbey, which continues to attract
visitors. The dramatic remains of
Glastonbury Abbey lie in the heart of
the old town and, if the legend of Joseph
of Arimathea is to be believed, this is the
site of the earliest Christian foundation
in the British Isles (see panel on page
332). The abbey wielded considerable
power until the Dissolution forced its

Glastonbury

Distance:	3.0 miles (4.8 kilometres)
Typical time:	120 mins
Height gain:	50 metres
Map:	Explorer 141
Walk:	www.walkingworld.com ID:1081
Contributor:	Tony Brotherton

Access Information:

Park in Magdalene Street, next to Glastonbury Abbey grounds (current charge £3 all day).

Description:

A short tour of the town, allowing optional visits to the Abbey Ruins and Glastonbury Thorn, the Chalice Well and other points of religious interest, plus the 'obligatory pilgrimage' to Glastonbury Tor and a suggested visit to the Rural Life Museum and its tea room.

Additional Information:

Glastonbury was the first Christian sanctuary in Great Britain and is the legendary burial-place of King Arthur. The legend of the Glastonbury Thorn and Joseph of Arimathea's visit is well-known.

Chalice Well is open every day of year, 10am - 6pm or 11am - 5pm or noon - 4pm according to season.

Somerset Rural Life Museum is open 10am - 5pm on Tuesday to Friday between April and October and at weekends from 2 - 6pm; tea shop.

The abbey ruins may be visited every day (except Christmas Day). Open 9:30 am to 6pm (or dusk if earlier).

Features:

Hills or fells, pub, toilets, museum, National Trust/NTS, wildlife, birds, flowers, great views, Butterflies, food shop, tea shop

Walk Directions:

❶ From car park in Magdalene Street may be seen 14th Century Abbot's Kitchen in grounds of Glastonbury Abbey. Turn right along street, passing entrance to Abbey, to reach bottom of High Street. Go right to see on left, historic George & Pilgrims Hotel, founded in 1300s.

❷ Walk up High Street. Tourist Information Office is located on left, in 15th Century Tribunal: here is housed also, Lake Village Museum. Further up on left is St John's Church. This contains stained glass window depicting Joseph of Arimathea. Carry on up High Street and turn right along Lambrook Street, as far as imposing gateway of Abbey House on right.

❸ Now turn up Dod Lane and take driveway on right signed 'Footpath to Tor', to reach squeeze-stile. Follow path uphill through fields to lane and continue ahead to see tor at bend.

❹ Turn left to follow Bulwarks Lane to end. At road (Wick Hollow) turn uphill to crossroads.

❺ Take lane to right, with tor visible ahead, to reach lane junction. Here turn left as far as footpath to tor.

❻ Follow path into field, soon to climb past information board and squeeze-gate, through trees and onto stepped path. Path rises steeply around tor to summit and monument. Here are superb views over surrounding countryside.

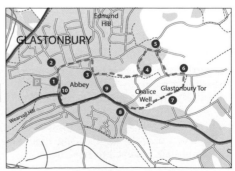

7 Continue walk by descending Glastonbury Tor to metal gate. Take footpath running downhill to reach Well House Lane. Turn left, then right at main road to arrive at Chalice Well. Chalybeate waters of Chalice Well were considered curative.

8 Turn right along Chilkwell Street to reach, on left at junction with Bere Lane, Somerset Rural Life Museum.

9 To continue the walk, turn left on Bere Lane and then right downhill at crossroads to return to Magdalene Street, to visit Almshouses Chapel. The tiny chapel and garden of almshouses afford a quiet place for meditation.

10 To complete the walk, turn left along the street, past a former pumphouse (Glastonbury was once spa-town) to return to start.

closure. Today, the picturesque ruins, with their associations with the legend of King Arthur, remain a great tourist attraction.

During the Middle Ages, Glastonbury Abbey was an internationally renowned centre of learning, and scholars and pilgrims from all over Christendom, made their way here. Eventually the numbers of visitors became so great that a guest house was built outside the abbey walls. Originally constructed in 1475, the **George and Pilgrim Hotel** is a striking building whose old timber beams are adorned with carved angels and whose interior is guarded by a series of curious monks' death masks. Close by is another 15th century building, the handsome **Tribunal** that is home to the town's Tourist Information Centre. Even the

town's **Somerset Rural Life Museum** (see panel below), which explores the life of farmers in this area during the 19th and early 20th centuries, cannot escape from the influence of the abbey. Although the museum is housed in a Victorian farmhouse, there is an impressive 14th century barn here that once belonged to Glastonbury Abbey.

To the east of the town lies another site renowned for its ecclesiastical, secular and legendary connections. **Glastonbury Tor** is a dramatic hill that rises above the surrounding Somerset Levels that were drained in the 18th century. One of the earliest visitors to the tor was the early Christian trader, Joseph of Arimathea, who is said to have arrived here in around AD 60. Many legends abound but one tells that, while

---

SOMERSET RURAL LIFE MUSEUM

Abbey Farm, Chilkwell Street, Glastonbury BA6 8DB
Tel: 01458 831197 Fax: 01458 834684
e-mail: county-museums@somerset.gov.uk
website: www.somerset.gov.uk/museums

The **Somerset Rural Life Museum** is housed in an attractive Victorian farmhouse and farm buildings and includes a magnificent 14th century barn. Traditional farming practices of the 19th and early 20th centuries are illustrated through displays, as are the local industries of peat cutting, withy growing and cider and cheese making. The life of John Hodges, a 19th century farm labourer, and his family is told through images and objects, whilst outside you will find the cider apple orchard, home to bee hives and rare breeds of poultry and sheep. Farming and craft demonstrations are held throughout the summer and special activities for families and children are a regular feature, as are the exhibitions. The Museum is open all year and facilities include a shop, free car park, tea room and disabled access.

GLASTONBURY ABBEY

Glastonbury, Somerset BA6 9EL
Tel: 01458 832267 Fax: 01458 832267
e-mail: glastonbury.abbey@dial.pipex.com
website: www.glastonburyabbey.com

Set in the middle of the old market town, **Glastonbury Abbey** has been an influence on the lives of those who have lived in this part of the world for the past 1,950 years and there are many people who believe that the 'Somerset Tradition' makes the association even longer than that. It is said that it was here that the followers of Jesus landed shortly after His death and set up the first Christian settlement with its own church in Britain, whilst some traditions go further and suggest that Christ Himself came to Glastonbury as a boy on one of the boats of his great uncle, Joseph of Arimathea. The legends around Glastonbury would certainly indicate that it was Joseph of Arimathea, and not St Augustine centuries later, who started the Christian conversion of Great Britain in the 1st century.

What, however, can be said with more certainty is that Glastonbury Abbey was a major Christian sanctuary during the 5th and 6th centuries and, by the time of the Norman Conquest, it was considered to be the wealthiest and grandest abbey in the country. Such was its status within England during the Dark Ages that it would have been logical that the great Celtic monarch, King Arthur, should be buried here after his long struggle against the Saxons.

Following the Dissolution in the 16th century, the abbey fell into ruins and, along with it, King Arthur's tomb was destroyed. Nevertheless, a number of impressive remains have survived and these include **St Mary's Chapel**, the shell of the great church, and the 14th century **Abbot's Kitchen**.

However, people coming here today come for three main reasons: to see where the first church might have existed; to see where King Arthur and Queen Guinevere might have been buried; and to enjoy the beautiful and peaceful parkland that surrounds the ruins.

The abbey is a private organisation run by trustees and, although a small concern, the abbey remains open throughout the year. Along with the ruins and the parkland, there is an award-winning museum and a small abbey shop and visitors may also come across Brother Thomas Cleeve, the Guestmaster of 1538.

MIDDLEWICK HOLIDAY COTTAGES

Wick, Glastonbury, Somerset BA6 8JW
Tel/Fax: 01458 832351
e-mail: info@middlewickholidaycottages.co.uk
website: www.middlewickholidaycottages.co.uk

In the shadow of Glastonbury Tor, **Middlewick Holiday Cottages** offer a choice of self-catering and bed & breakfast accommodation. The eight self-catering cottages, converted from old farm buildings, sleep from two to six guests, and all have full kitchen facilities. Meadow Barn has two en suite rooms for B&B, with breakfast served in a conservatory that links the two self-contained rooms. Set in eight acres of gardens and orchards, all the accommodation enjoys lovely views. Guests have the use of an indoor heated swimming pool. No smoking; no pets.

he was walking on the tor, Joseph drove his staff into the ground whereupon it took root and burst into leaf. Taking this as a sign that he should build a church, Joseph erected a simple church on the site now taken by the abbey. His staff is reputed to have grown into the celebrated Christmas-flowering Glastonbury Hawthorn.

The 520-foot tor has been inhabited since prehistoric times and excavations on the site have revealed evidence of Celtic, Roman and pre-Saxon occupation. Because of its unusually regular conical shape the hill has long been associated with myth and legends and, in its time, it has been identified as the Land of the Dead, the Celtic Otherworld, a Druid's temple, a magic mountain, an Arthurian hill fort, a ley line intersection and a rendezvous

Glastonbuty Tor

point for passing UFOs. Along with its mystical energy, the tor also offers magnificent views across Somerset to Wells, the Mendips, the Quantocks and the Bristol Channel. The striking tower at the summit is all that remains of the 15th century **Church of St Michael**, an offshoot of Glastonbury

---

HEARTFELT TRADING

3 Market Place, Glastonbury,
Somerset BA6 9HD
Tel: 01458 833910
Fax: 01458 830227
e-mail: ask@heartfelt.co.uk
website: www.heartfelt.co.uk

Heartfelt Trading, in the heart of the historic town of Glastonbury, is a very interesting and very different gift shop specialising in promoting British craftwork.

Opened in 1994 by Lesley Wright, a qualified artist whose field is ceramics and sculpture, the stock at this particularly attractive and charming

shop comprises 'Unusual Gifts from the Three Realms', the realms being the Angel Room, the Greenwood and the Faerie Room. In the Faerie Room customers can be sprinkled with faerie dust and given the faerie stick from the faerie wood; they then make a wish, which will be granted as long as they are good all day – and it's not only children who are captivated by this magical place!

Well known for its highly individual range of handcrafted jewellery, Heartfelt Trading also has for sale a selection of unusual Celtic bronze and wood gifts, mobiles, ceramics, crystals, pictures and cards. For an imaginative gift that's certain to delight, Heartfelt Trading is *the* place to explore, and Lesley has plans to make it even more irresistible by opening a Tolkien Room in 2005.

Abbey. Between the tor and the town lies the wooded rise of **Chalice Hill**, where, it is said, Joseph buried the Holy Grail, the chalice used at the Last Supper.

To the northwest of the town is the site of a prehistoric **Lake Village** discovered in 1892 when it was noticed that the otherwise level fields was studded with irregular mounds. Thought to date from around 150 BC, the dwellings were built on a series of tall platforms that raised them above the surrounding marshland.

STREET

7 miles SW of Wells on the A39

The oldest part of this now sprawling town lies around the 14th century parish Church of the Holy Trinity although most of the town itself dates from the 19th century when it began to expand from a small rural village into the light industrial town of today. Much of this growth was due to one family, the Clarks. In the 1820s, the Quaker brothers, Cyrus and James Clark began to produce sheepskin slippers from the hides of local animals. Many of the town's older buildings owe their existence to the family and, in particular, there is the **Friends' Meeting House** of 1850 and the building that housed the original Millfield School. The oldest part of the Clark's factory has now been converted into a fascinating **Shoe Museum** and, although the company is one of the largest manufacturers of quality footwear in Europe, it continues to keep its headquarters in the town.

MEARE

6½ miles SW of Wells on the B3151

Just to the east of this attractive village is an unusual medieval building known as the **Abbot's Fish House**. Before 1700, this isolated building stood on the edge of **Meare Pool**, once a substantial lake

that provided nearby Glastonbury Abbey with a regular supply of freshwater fish.

Before the lake was drained, this early 14th century building was used for storing fishing equipment and salting the catches.

To the southwest of Meare, in terrain scarred by years of peat extraction, is the **Shapwick Heath Nature Reserve**, which provides a safe haven for rare plants and wildlife. To the northwest, at **Westhay**, is the **Peat Moor Visitor Centre**, which offers visitors a fascinating insight into the history and ecology of the Somerset Levels and, through a series of imaginative displays, describes the development of commercial peat digging, the special trades that have grown up in this unique environment and the measures that have been taken to conserve the area's flora and fauna.

WEDMORE

7½ miles W of Wells on the B3139

This remote village was the ancient capital of the Somerset marshes, where King Alfred is said to have brought the newly baptised Danish King Guthrum to sign the Peace of Wedmore in 878. This treaty left Wessex in Alfred's hands but gave East Anglia, East Mercia and the Kingdom of York to the Danes. The village's main street, the Borough, is lined with fine stone buildings, including a lovely old coaching inn. The parish church's spectacular Norman south doorway is thought to have been carved by the craftsmen who built Wells Cathedral.

WOOKEY HOLE

1½ miles NW of Wells off the A371

The village, in the rolling uplands of the Mendip Hills, is a popular place with walkers, cavers and motorised sightseers who are drawn by the natural formations found here. Throughout the centuries,

THE SEXEY'S ARMS

Blackford, Wedmore, Somerset BS28 4NT
Tel: 01934 712487 Fax: 01934 712447
e-mail: thierrylacassin@aol.com
website: www.thesexeysarms.co.uk

Frenchman Thierry Lacassin and his wife Philippa have injected new life into the **Sexey's Arms** since taking over towards the end of 2003. This is their first venture into the licensed trade, and they have quickly won friends with their warm welcome, Thierry's abundant Gallic charm, the quaint rural ambience and food that tempts and tantalises the taste buds. Fresh local produce gets expert treatment on an ever-changing menu that draws its influences from near and far. Typical dishes might include warm pigeon breast salad with pan-fried figs; fillet of Somerset beef with pancetta, Stilton and a rich port gravy; and seared scallops with a warm salad of pak choi, beansprouts and glass noodles. Delectable puddings and a fine French and English cheeseboard round off a meal in style, and the great food is complemented by an extensive wine list.

Bar meals are served Tuesday to Saturday from 12pm - 2pm. The à la carte menu is available Tuesday to Saturday evenings, and the Sunday lunch menu, including a traditional roast, is served from noon to 3pm. Closed Monday lunchtime. The inn has a large garden and two car parks. Children are welcome.

the carboniferous limestone core of the hills has been gradually dissolved away by the small amount of carbonic acid in rainwater. This erosion has created over 25 caverns around Wookey Hole, of which only the largest half dozen or so are open to the public. The **Great Cave** contains a rock formation known as the Witch of Wookey that casts a ghostly shadow and is associated with gruesome legends of child-eating. During prehistoric times, lions, bears and woolly mammoths lived in the area. In a recess known as the **Hyena's Den**, a large cache of bones have been found, many of them showing signs of other animal's tooth marks. The river emerging from Wookey Hole, the River Axe, has been

harnessed to provide power since the 15th century and the present building here was originally constructed in the early 17th century as a paper mill.

Just to the northwest lies the dramatic **Ebbor Gorge** now a National Nature Reserve managed by English Nature.

Wookey Hole

ENIGMA CONTEMPORARY ARTS & CRAFTS

15 Vicarage Street, Frome, Somerset BA11 1PX
Tel: 01373 452079 Fax: 01373 469810
e-mail: info@enigma-gallery.com
website: www.enigma-gallery.com

Easy to find between the historic town centre and the railway station, **Enigma Contemporary Arts & Crafts** is owned and run by the very talented resident

ceramicists Jenny Barton and Everton Byfield. Jenny, who spent a large part of her life on the Isle of Wight, creates thrown and press-moulded earthenware products inspired by the ocean. Everton creates hand-built, carved, burnished and smoke-fired ceramic vessels; inspired by traditional African designs, his carving technique is a development of his passion for woodcarving. Their work, produced in their workshop in the garden, can be seen in the Main Gallery, along with that of many regular artists/makers of quality, and an ongoing programme of eyecatching window exhibitions that is booked for many months ahead.

The Georgian Room, in contrast, is an intimate space where visitors can relax and admire the work of the invited artists/makers of the month. Between May and September visitors can wander among the sculptures and garden pots in the secluded walled garden. Enigma, which is fully accessible to wheelchair users, is open from 10am to 5pm Tuesday to Saturday, or by appointment.

THE GOLDEN GOOSE

24-25 Catherine Hill, Frome, Somerset BA11 1BY
Tel: 01373 466681

An eyecatching double window display tempts passers-by into **The Golden Goose**, a design-led gift shop situated in a quaint cobbled street tucked away in the heart of Frome. With many years of experience as designers, owners Mary and Tony Gibson aim to choose high-quality, well-produced gifts and are always

looking for something just that little bit different to add to the stock. As a result, their friendly shop is full of beautiful things that are a delight either to give or receive, and the gift-wrap and ribbons they sell add the finishing touches to a special present.

The range caters for all occasions and includes toiletries and aromas, outfits for babies and young children, soft toys, games and puzzles to tease or boggle the mind, jewellery, Bridgwater pottery, cards and books on the nice things in life. Visitors are welcome to browse at leisure in The Golden Goose, which is open from 10am to 5pm Monday to Friday and from 9.30am to 5.30pm on Saturday. With more listed buildings than any other town in Somerset, Frome is well worth taking time to explore, and for anyone looking to combine historic interest with an enjoyable shopping experience, The Golden Goose is a must on their itinerary.

There are two walks here, the shorter one suitable for wheelchairs accompanied by a strong pusher. The longer walk involves a certain amount of rock scrambling. However, the hard work is rewarded as there is a wealth of wildlife here, including badger and sparrow hawk in the woodland, lesser horseshoe bats in and around the caves and buzzards flying overhead.

Cheap Street, Frome

FROME

Situated beside the river from which it takes its name, the first permanent settlement at Frome was founded in around 685 when St Aldhelm, the Abbot of Malmesbury, set up a mission station on the river banks. Then on the edge of Selwood Forest, this was a suitable river crossing close to the tracks through the Mendip Hills and the Salisbury Plain gap. Such was the expansion around St Aldhelm's stone **Church of St John** that, by the time of the Domesday Book, the settlement had a market, which suggests that it had become a place of some importance.

Frome continued to prosper during the Middle Ages on the back of its cloth industry but competition from the woollen towns of the north in the 19th century saw the industry begin to decline although the trade did not vanish from Frome completely until the 1960s. Since then other industries, and in particular printing, have flourished. Fortunately,

this new growth has not spoilt the charm of the town's old centre. Best explored on foot the town's old quarter is an attractive conservation area where, amidst the interesting shops, cafés and restaurants, can be found the **Blue House**. Built in 1726 as an almshouse and a boy's school it is one of the town's numerous listed buildings. In fact, Frome has more listed buildings that any other town in Somerset. Across the River Frome, the **Bridge**, a contemporary of Bath's Pulteney Bridge, dating from 1667, has buildings along its length.

Surprisingly, this charming place, with its steep cobbled streets, wealth of architecture and lively market, is the fourth largest town in Somerset. Visitors should take time to discover the local history collections at **Frome Museum**.

AROUND FROME

LULLINGTON
2½ miles N of Frome off the B3090

A footpath leads southwards from this peaceful riverside village to

TULSI

Weavers Cottage, 33 Sturford Lane, Temple, Nr Corsley,
Wiltshire BA12 7QR
Tel/Fax: 01373 832856
e-mail: pie@tulsi.uk.com website: www.tulsi.uk.com

With Pie Chambers at the helm, **Tulsi** deals in old and rare textiles,
organises craft and textile tours to India, and runs textiles workshops
in a delightful restored weaver's cottage on the edge of the Longleat
Estate. Pie began her career in textiles in 1974 as a weaver, and soon

developed an interest in kilim
weaving. Since visiting India and
later living and working there she
started a passionate love affair
with indigo, and her skills have
spread to block printing and resist dyeing.

Tulsi specialises in old and rare textiles and embroideries from
the East, and other interests include antique tribal silver and Indian
and Afghani carved furniture. Pie leads textile and cultural holiday
tours in the winter months to lesser-known rural areas of India
and the sub-continent, and in the summer conducts textile
workshops at her home, covering shibori techniques, kilim weaving
and indigo dyeing. Accommodation for these courses is available
in charming rooms in the cottage or in a nearby B&B. The cottage
is decorated with Pie's work, which she also exhibits in various
galleries and museums.

PICKFORD HOUSE

Bath Road, Beckington, Bath BA11 6SJ
Tel/Fax: 01373 830329
e-mail: ampritchard@aol.com
website: www.pickfordhouse.com

For 20 years, **Pickford House** has been the home of Ken and Angela
Pritchard, who invite guests to stay and enjoy the civilised, relaxed
atmosphere, to see the beautiful Somerset countryside and to savour
the delights of Angela's cuisine and Ken's cellar. The Regency-style
house, lovingly maintained in keeping
with its age and tradition, stands on
top of a hill overlooking the
surrounding countryside and although
near the main road it is quiet and
secluded, with a stone-walled garden ensuring complete privacy.

Guest accommodation comprises double and family bedrooms with
or without private facilities; all rooms have central heating, hot and cold
water, TV, tea/coffee making facilities and folders of local information.
Breakfast includes a traditional English platter or a choice from the menu,
and Angela's three-course evening meals should definitely not be missed.
Her cooking is superb, and a memorable meal is made even more special
when accompanied by something from Ken's expertly compiled wine list.
Special diets can be catered for, and packed lunches are available on
request. Pickford House has its own outdoor swimming pool, and tennis,
squash, putting and riding can be arranged.

Orchardleigh Park, an imposing Victorian mansion built in the mid-19th century. In the grounds of the house is a lake with an island that is home to a small church whose churchyard contains the grave of Sir Henry Newbolt, the author of *Drake's Drum*.

On the opposite bank of the River Frome lies the former wool village of **Beckington** where, among the fine stone houses, can be found the **Cedars**, which was possibly once an ecclesiastical hospice for Augustinian canons. Here, too, is **Seymour Court** that takes its name from the St Maur family who became the lords of the manor of Beckington by marriage.

North of Lullington and, again on the banks of the river, is the famous **Rode Bird Gardens**, an impressive park of some 17 acres that is home to over 200 different species of exotic birds from around the world, many of which are allowed to fly freely. The grounds incorporate a miniature woodland steam railway, a pets' corner and a series of lakes inhabited by flamingos, penguins and other species of waterfowl.

BATCOMBE

8 miles SW of Frome off the A359

This secluded community, whose name comes from the Saxon for 'Bata's Valley', is surrounded by an Area of Outstanding Natural Beauty. It has one of the finest church towers in the whole of the county, built in the 16th century on the proceeds of the village's thriving wool

---

CHRISTINE-ANN RICHARDS

Chapel House, High Street, Wanstrow,
Nr. Shepton Mallet, Somerset BA4 4TE
Tel/Fax: 01749 850208
e-mail: mail@christineannrichards.co.uk
website: www.christineannrichards.co.uk

Christine-Ann Richards lives and works in a converted Methodist Chapel just outside Frome, where both her thrown porcelain and large garden pots are permanently on display. Much of her work is influenced by her

journeys to the Far East, and especially by her first visit to China, with other potters in 1978. Since 1985 she has co-ordinated and accompanied people from throughout the world on visits to other artists in China and Central Asia, as well as visiting archaeological sites and places of cultural interest.

Her classical oriental style thrown porcelain vases and bowls are glazed in transparent, dark green crackle and copper red glazes. Her later black on white splash decorated wares remind one of her interest in Chinese calligraphy and painting. Her work is used by both interior and garden designers and over the years other pieces have found their way to auction at Christie's and Sotheby's.

During the last decade she has also been making large pots, water features and sculptures for the garden. A Winston Churchill Travelling Fellowship to Japan in 1996 to 'look at the way that water is used in landscape and architecture' has been an ongoing source of inspiration for these works.

Her current work, as well as future tours to the East, are to be found on her website. Visitors welcome by appointment.

SALLY POLLITZER

Batcombe Lodge Studio, Batcombe, Somerset BA4 6BZ
Tel: 01749 850589 Fax: 01749 850900
e-mail: mail@sally-pollitzer.co.uk
website: www.sally-pollitzer.co.uk

Sally trained first as a painter, studying at the Central
and Byamshaw Schools of Art in London. She has built
an enviable wide-reaching reputation as a master of her
craft in the years since, and for over 20 years she has
worked mainly in the medium of architectural glass
(traditionally known as stained glass). She combines her
skills in this field in making windows and screens for a
wide variety of settings - domestic, commercial and
ecclesiastical. She works from a large, well-equipped
studio in the grounds of her Somerset home, where she
employs a variety of techniques such as leading and
laminating, enamelling and acid etching, using the best
'antique' glass. She is equally at home with traditional
and modern methods, and each work that she produces

is unique;
the client's taste and the location are always carefully
considered in her original designs.

Past commissions have included work for the Lord
Chancellor's residence and for the Princess of Wales
Conservatory in Kew Gardens, three screens, each
comprising 10 panels set in penny bronze frames, for the
Lloyds TSB Headquarters in the City of London, the
baptistery window in the Church of the Good Shepherd at
Tadworth, and the Millennium Window at St James's
Church, Rowledge. Many of her works are on an impressively
large scale, for example staircase lights reaching up four
metres in a converted warehouse. The cost of commissioned
work naturally depends on several factors, including the
size of the work, the materials used and the amount of labour

involved. Sally
has also written
and lectured on
the subject of
stained glass
and is a
member of the
Art Workers'
Guild, the
British Society

of Master Glass Painters and the Society of Designer-
Craftsmen.

Sally's studio can be visited by appointment, and
visitors to Batcombe, which is surrounded by a designated
Area of Outstanding Natural Beauty, should take time to
visit the village's other famous attraction: the Church of
St. Mary the Virgin, where the main feature is the mighty
16th century tower, one of the finest in the whole county.

VALLEY VIEW FARM BED & BREAKFAST

Batcombe, Shepton Mallet, Somerset BA4 6AJ
Tel: 01749 850302
e-mail: valleyviewfarm@lineone.net
website: http.//mysite.freeserve.com/valleyviewfarm/

Since the year 2000, Bryan and Gladys Mead have been sharing their family home in a beautiful valley setting with bed & breakfast guests. The choice of accommodation at their well-designed modern house comprises a family room for four with private bathroom, an en suite double, and en suite twin and a standard twin, all warm, comfortable and well furnished. Guests can stroll in the extensive gardens and enjoy the tremendous views, and another treat is sampling the excellent home made cider!

industry. At that time, there were nine cloth mills in the district that produced more woven fabric than those along the River Avon between Bath and Bristol.

SHEPTON MALLET

10 miles SW of Frome on the A371

Situated on the banks of the River Sheppey, just to the west of Fosse Way, this old market town has been an important centre of communications since before the time of the Romans. The settlement's name is Saxon and it means, quite simply, 'sheep town'. This reveals its main commercial activity from before the Norman Conquest to the Middle Ages, when Shepton Mallet was a centre of woollen production and then weaving. The industry reached its peak in the 15th century. It was around this

BOWLISH HOUSE HOTEL & RESTAURANT

Wells Road, Shepton Mallet, Somerset BA4 5JD
Tel: 01749 342022 Fax: 01749 345311
e-mail: enquiries@bowlishhouse.com
website: www.bowlishhouse.com

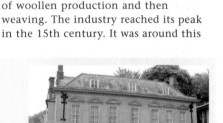

The ancient market town of Shepton Mallet is full of interesting things to see, and **Bowlish House Hotel** is an ideal base for visitors. Built in 1732 for a prosperous clothier, it was subsequently the home of generations of top brass from the local brewery. It passed into private hands in 1954 and so began its latest phase as a hotel and subsequently a restaurant. The current proprietors Jason Goy and Darren Carter are undertaking a major restoration programme on the interior of the building, creating a natural blend of Georgian architecture and colour schemes with contemporary art.

The result is both stylish and charming, and the three en suite guest bedrooms combine their original splendour with modern features. Food is very much part of the appeal of Bowlish House. Lunch offers the choice of à la carte and set menus, while dinner is a grander affair with a seasonal two- or three-course table d'hote menu; the excellent food is enhanced by well-chosen wines and friendly, efficient service. The hotel is open to residents and non-residents for lunch, dinner, morning coffee and afternoon tea, and a function suite is available for special occasions. All rooms at the hotel are strictly non-smoking.

time that the town's most striking building, its magnificent parish church, was constructed. Other reminders of Shepton Mallet's past can be seen around its market place where there is a 50 foot **Market Cross**, dating from around 1500 and restored in Victorian times. There is also **The Shambles**, a 15th century wooden shed where meat was traded. After the Duke of Monmouth's ill-fated Pitchfork Rebellion, several of his followers were executed at the Market Cross in 1685 on the orders of the infamous Judge Jeffreys. Although it is a relatively nondescript building, Shepton Mallet's old prison was thought to be so well away from the threat of enemy bombing that it was here that the Domesday Book was hidden during World War II.

Today, Shepton Mallet is a prosperous light industrial town that has a good selection of shopping and leisure activities. Each year the town plays host to two agricultural shows. The **Mid-Somerset Show** is in August and, in May, the **Royal Bath and Wells Show** has a permanent showground to the southeast of the town.

To the southwest of the town lies a former residence of the abbots of Glastonbury, **Pilton Manor**, whose grounds have been planted with vines, mostly of the German Riesling variety. Visitors are encouraged to stroll around the estate and also take the opportunity of sampling the vineyard's end product. Another legacy of Glastonbury Abbey can be found at **Pilton** village where there is a great cruciform tithe barn that stands on a hill surrounded by beech and chestnut trees. Unfortunately, the barn lost its arch-braced roof when it was struck by lightning in 1963.

Further evidence of this area's great reliance on the woollen textile industry

MONET

The Old Coach House, The Charlton Estate, Shepton Mallet, Somerset BA4 5QE
Tel/Fax: 01749 346479
e-mail: monet@wgartpartners.co.uk
website: www.monetfineart.com

Collectable art and fine framing are the two main areas of interest and expertise at **Monet Fine Art Gallery**, which is situated on the award-winning Charlton Estate in the heart

of Somerset. The aim of owners Steve and Lin Butt together with their daughter Lisa is to make art buying as easy as possible, and they are delighted to welcome new collectors into their gallery and to offer help and advice on buying art, whether for the first time or to add to a collection. Established in 1997, Monet has built up a reputation as one of the southwest's leading commercial galleries and is a showcase for a diverse range of paintings and limited edition prints by some of the most talented and sought after contemporary artists.

The go-ahead owners produce a quarterly magazine that illustrates the latest releases from the gallery artists, together with introductions of new painters and sculptors, and details of future events and exhibitions. As accomplished framers, Monet also offer a friendly, competitive and professional service, backed by the Fine Art Trade Guild supplying a superb choice of quality frames to enhance and complement any work of art.

KNOWLE FARM COTTAGES

West Compton, Shepton Mallet, Somerset BA4 4PD
Tel: 01749 890482 Fax: 01749 890405
e-mail: info@knowle-farm-cottages.co.uk
website: www.knowle-farm-cottages.co.uk

In a quiet rural location at the end of a private drive, **Knowle Farm Cottages** provide comfortable, characterful self-catering accommodation. Built of Dulcote stone and dating back 200 years, the four cottages sleep from two to six and are equipped with everything needed for a relaxed holiday, including fully fitted modern kitchens. The cottages are set around the original farmyard, which is now an attractive communal garden. Shepton Mallet and many other places of interest are within easy reach. No pets.

through the ages can be seen in the former weaving village of **Croscombe** to the west of Shepton Mallet. To the east is **Doulting**, an ancient village dating back to the 8th century, when King Ine gave the local estate to Glastonbury Abbey after his nephew, St Aldhelm, died here in 709. The saint's body was taken back to Malmesbury, where he was abbot, via a circuitous route marked by a series of tall stone crosses. In the garden of the village's former vicarage is a spring that, along with the church and a statue, is dedicated to St Aldhelm. The village's 15th century **Tithe Barn** is a reminder that the local tenant farmers paid a proportion of the crops each year to their ecclesiastical landlords.

Doulting is also one of the stations on the **East Somerset Railway** founded by the wildlife artist David Shepherd in 1975 on the original broad gauge line dating from the 1850s (see panel).

NUNNEY

3 miles SW of Frome off the A361

This picturesque old market town is dominated by its dramatic moated **Castle** begun in 1373 by Sir John de la Mare on his return from the French wars. Thought to have been modelled on the Bastille, the fortress consists of four solidly built towers that stand on an island formed by a stream on one side and a broad water-filled moat on the other. The castle came under attack from Parliamentarian forces during the English Civil War and, despite having a garrison of only one officer, eight men and a handful of civilian

EAST SOMERSET RAILWAY

Cranmore Railway Station, Shepton Mallet, Somerset BA4 4QP
Tel: 01749 880417 Fax: 01749 880764
e-mail: info@eastsomersetrailway.org
website: www.eastsomersetrailway.org

East Somerset Railway is run by a charitable trust and based just outside Shepton Mallet at Cranmore Railway Station. The engine shed and workshops are open to the public where you can see how to prepare and maintain the steam engines and rolling stock. The workshops contain engines and stock in the process of restoration. A picnic area and children's playground are next to the station and there is ample parking for cars and coaches. Disabled facilities include station access, toilets and ramps onto the trains. The Whistlestop Restaurant offers a range of snacks, meals and drinks for all the family and is open every day trains are running.

refugees, the castle held out for two days. However, the bombardment damaged the building beyond repair and it had to be abandoned, leaving the romantic ruins that can still be seen today. One of the 30-pound cannonballs that were used by Cromwell's forces can be seen in the village's 13th century church.

MELLS

3 miles NW of Frome off the A362

Located at one time on the easternmost limit of the lands belonging to Glastonbury Abbey, in the 15th century Abbot Selwood drew up plans to rebuild the village in the shape of a St Anthony's cross, with four arms of equal length. However, only one street, New Street, was ever completed. This architectural gem can still be seen to the south of St Andrew's parish church. While the exterior of the church is certainly imposing, the main interest lies inside where there is a remarkable collection of monuments designed by masters such as Lutyens, Gill, Munnings and Burne-Jones. One of the memorials is to Raymond, the eldest son of Herbert Asquith, the Liberal Prime Minister. Raymond was killed in the First World War. Raymond's sister was Violet Bonham Carter, whose grave is in the churchyard. Another memorial in the churchyard honours the pacifist and poet Siegfried Sassoon.

According to legend, the Abbot of Glastonbury, in an attempt to stave off Henry VIII's Dissolution of the Monasteries, dispatched his steward, John Horner, to London with a gift for the king consisting of a pie into which was baked the title deeds of 12 ecclesiastical manor houses. However, rather than attempting to persuade the

---

THE TALBOT INN

Mells, Nr Frome, Somerset BA11 3PN
Tel: 01373 812254 Fax: 01373 813599
e-mail: roger@talbotinn.com
website: www.talbotinn.com

Situated in a beautiful village on the edge of the Mendip Hills, **The Talbot Inn** is a privately-owned 15th century coaching inn with an abundance of old-world charm, comfortable overnight accommodation and an award-winning restaurant. The inn is reached through large double doors under an archway and into an attractive courtyard with a beautiful vine-covered pergola. To the left of the courtyard is the restaurant, where Head Chef Mark Jones and his team use fresh local ingredients to create tempting dishes with English and French influences. An excellent worldwide selection of wines complements the fine cooking.

The restaurant has low oak-beamed ceilings hung with hops, stripped pews and wheelback chairs, candles in bottles, fresh flowers on the tables and sporting pictures on the walls. The front restaurant is equally appealing, and across the courtyard the old tithe barn is now an atmospheric bar. Apart from being an ideal setting for a lunch or dinner, the Talbot is the perfect choice for a small wedding reception or party. It's also a great place to stay, with en suite bedrooms that combine traditional furnishings with up-to-date amenities. Top of the range is the Manor Suite, with a luxurious mahogany four-poster bed.

king, Horner returned to Somerset the rightful owner of three of the manors himself. He paid a total of £2,000 for Mells, Nunnery and Leigh-upon-Mendip. This blatant act of disloyalty is, supposedly, commemorated in the nursery rhyme *Little Jack Horner* that describes how Jack 'put in his thumb and pulled out a plum'. The manor house at Mells remained in the hands of the Horner family until the early 20th century, when it passed to the Asquith family by marriage.

OAKHILL

9 miles W of Frome on the A367

Although the original brewery in this old brewing village has long since disappeared, the renewed interest in real ales in the last few decades has seen a new brewery established here to provide the local pubs and inns with traditional ales. Just to the west of the village lies **Oakhill Manor**, a small country mansion that has been developed as a popular tourist attraction, with a scaled down version of Cheddar Gorge and a scenic miniature railway. The house itself contains an extraordinary collection of models and pictures relating to historic forms of land, sea and air transport.

STRATTON-ON-THE-FOSSE

7½ miles NW of Frome on the A367

This former coal mining village is home to the famous Roman Catholic boys' public school, **Downside Abbey**, which occupies the site of a monastery founded in 1814 by a group of English Benedictines. The steady expansion of the school during the 20th century encouraged the monks to move to a new site on higher ground near the existing abbey church, an impressive building that took over 70 years to complete and numbered among its architects Sir Giles Gilbert Scott.

MIDSOMER NORTON

8 miles NW of Frome on the B3355

The history of the area around this town is one of mining, with coal being hewn from nearby Norton Hill until as recently as the 1970s. In the churchyard of the town's parish church is a memorial to the 12 miners who were killed in an accident at Wellsway coal works in 1839. The surrounding countryside is beautiful and the sights and sounds of collieries have long since been replaced with that of open farmland. Midsomer Norton itself is a pleasant mix of old and new. There are excellent shopping facilities along with attractive Georgian buildings and a late medieval tithe barn.

At the interesting **Radstock, Midsomer North and District Museum**, housed in a converted 18th century barn, more information can be sought about the Somerset coalfield as the museum is devoted to the people of the local coal mines although there are other exhibits relating to the railways, farms and schools of the area.

BATH

Since time immemorial over half a million gallons of water a day, at a constant temperature of 46°C, have bubbled to the surface at Bath. The ancient Celts believed the mysterious steaming spring was the domain of the goddess Sulis and they were aware of the water's healing powers long before the invasion of the Romans. However, it was the Romans who first enclosed the spring and went on to create a spectacular health resort that became known as Aquae Sulis. By the 3rd century, Bath had become so renowned that high ranking soldiers and officials were coming here from all over the Roman Empire. Public buildings and temples were constructed

THE WINDSOR HOTEL

69 Great Pulteney Street, Bath BA2 4DL
Tel: 01225 422100 Fax: 01225 422550
e-mail: sales@bathwindsorhotel.com
website: www.bathwindsorhotel.com

One of the most recently opened townhouse hotels, **The Windsor Hotel** enjoys a magnificent setting in Great Pulteney Street, widely considered to be among the finest and most elegant boulevards in Europe. The hotel, which was completely refurbished in 2000, is owned by Cary Bush, who spent many years as a banker in the Far East, and his Japanese wife Sachiko, whose eye for design is evident in the bedrooms and the restaurant. Each of the 14 bedrooms has been individually designed by Sachiko, based on a mix of original Georgian and traditional English patterns using the finest local fabrics. The rooms range from singles to doubles, suites and four-posters - the front-facing Windsor Room on the second floor is dominated by a large, Georgian mahogany four-poster, and the Princess Room also has

a four-poster. All rooms have en suite facilities, direct-dial telephone, satellite TV and broadband access.

A unique feature of the hotel is its Japanese restaurant Sakura, which means 'cherry blossom'. Overlooking its own beautifully designed garden with bamboo trees and giant pebbles, it offers the choice of the two main styles of authentic Japanese cooking - Shabu Shabu and Sukiyaki. The set meals both start with a green salad, yakitori (chargrilled chicken pieces on a stick) and miso soup. Shabu Shabu consists of wafer-thin slices of beef or pork and Oriental vegetables which the diner cooks at the table in a delicate simmering stock and eats with a selection of sauces, pickles and rice. With the Sukiyaki menu, the meat is first browned then simmered with the vegetables. A variety of appetisers can be ordered in addition to the set meal, and green tea can be served throughout the meal. The traditional drink is sake, served either hot or at room temperature, and Japanese lagers and fine wines are also available. Tea and coffee are complimentary throughout the guests' stay, served either in the lounge or from room service. The hotel is strictly non-smoking throughout. Children aged 12 or over are very welcome.

Great Pulteney Street, which was designed and built by Thomas Baldwin in 1794, leads on to the exquisite Pulteney Bridge, the work of Robert Adam, and is in easy reach of all the numerous attractions of Bath.

and the whole city was enclosed by a stone wall. By AD 410, the last remaining Roman legions had left and, within a few years, the drainage systems failed and the area returned to marshland. Ironically, the ancient baths remained hidden throughout the entire period of Bath's 18th century renaissance and were only discovered in the late 19th century. The restored Roman remains can be seen today. They centre around the **Great Bath**, a rectangular lead-lined pool standing at the centre of a complex system of buildings that took over 200 years to complete. It comprised a swimming pool, mineral baths and a series of chambers heated by underfloor air ducts.

Roman Baths

The population of Bath fell during the Dark Ages until the 8th century when the Saxons founded a nunnery here that was later elevated to monastic status when King Edgar of Wessex chose to be crowned King of all England here in 973. The present great church was begun in 1499, after its Norman predecessor had been destroyed by fire. Building work was halted at the time of the Dissolution and

THE BATH SWEET SHOP

8 North Parade Passage, Abbey Green, Bath BA1 1NX
Tel: 01225 428040
e-mail: welovetotalk@thebathsweetshop.com
website: www.thebathsweetshop.com

The Bath Sweet Shop offers visitors the chance to take a walk down memory lane to re-live the days when sweets tasted like they should. Since opening seven years ago in this historic Bath stone building in the shadow of the Abbey, proprietors Glenys Greenaway and James Sherman

have watched the smiles of delight on the faces of thousands of customers as they contemplate the 250 jars of sweets and wonder which they will have weighed out for them.

Youngsters will perhaps be experiencing the taste of old-fashioned sweets and candy for the first time, while for the older generation there is the added thrill of being able to ask for sticky toffees and sherbet lemons and gobstoppers and chocolate cigars! The sweets in the jars are priced per 113 grams (the good old quarter) and everything is available by mail order. The Bath Sweet Shop also offers beautifully wrapped gifts for all occasions, including miniatures in tiny carrier bags, as well as preserves, soft drinks and postcards. Definitely a place not to be missed, the ultimate in retail therapy!

LOCH FYNE RESTAURANT & MILSOMS HOTEL

24 Milsom Street, Bath BA1 1DG
Hotel Tel: 01225 750128 Fax: 01225 750129
e-mail: reservations@milsomshotel.co.uk
website: www.milsomshotel.co.uk
Restaurant Tel: 01225 750120 Fax: 01225 750121
e-mail: bath@lochfyne.net

The elegant beauty of Bath's architecture and the best of contemporary design come together at **Milsoms Hotel**, which offers a prime city-centre location, excellent hospitality, comfortable accommodation and the very considerable bonus of a top-class seafood restaurant on the premises. The sympathetically restored Grade II listed Bath stone building has nine light, airy Standard and Executive bedrooms with a fresh modern feel, all with en suite facilities, TV, telephone, hairdryer, tea makers and mineral water. Irons, boards and travel cots are available on request.

A splendid breakfast featuring traditional English, Scottish or Continental dishes is served in the **Loch**

Fyne Restaurant beneath the hotel, setting up guests in fine style for a day exploring the sights of Bath. The restaurant is also open to non-residents for breakfast and throughout the day, seven days a week, when the full menu for which Loch Fyne restaurants have become renowned is served. Fresh seafood served simply has been the watchword of Loch Fyne Restaurants Ltd, owners of the hotel, since it was founded to develop a group of seafood restaurants throughout the UK. All the menus are created using the freshest ingredients with zest, style and

simplicity. This is a sister company to Loch Fyne Oysters Ltd, which operates at the head of Loch Fyne; the Oyster Bar, Shop and Smokehouse are housed in a former cattle byre beside the Inverary road. A mile across the water at Ardkinglass lies the mussel and oyster fishery. Both companies are dedicated to the protection of our seas, our maritime communities and all forms of marine life.

Milsom Street is in the very heart of Bath, among the best shops and very close to the wonderful Abbey, the Roman Baths and the stately Pump Room.

the church remained without a roof for 75 years and, indeed, it was not finally completed until 1901. However, **Bath Abbey** is now considered to be the ultimate example of English Perpendicular church architecture. Inside, there is a memorial to the Richard 'Beau' Nash, one of the people responsible for turning Bath into a fashionable Georgian spa town.

Bath Abbey

Prior to Nash's arrival in the early 18th century, Bath was a squalid place with farm animals roaming the streets within the confines of the old Roman town. Notwithstanding, the town had continued to attract small numbers of rich and aristocratic people. Eventually, the town authorities took action to improve sanitation and their initiative was rewarded, in 1702, when Queen Anne paid Bath's spa a visit. The elegant and stylish Beau Nash, who had only come to the town to earn a living as a gambler, became the Master of Ceremonies and, under his pressure, the town became a

THE BRITISH HATTER

9-11 Walcot Street, Bath BA1 5BN
Tel: 01225 339009
e-mail: pamelabromley@lineone.net
website: www.thebritishhatter.co.uk

Pamela Bromley is a very experienced and widely respected milliner who designs and makes hats that put the finishing touches on many a well-dressed lady's outfit - and many a man's, too. Her creations, all handmade with natural materials, all range over quite different styles, and visitors to her delightful little shop will find something suitable for any mood and occasion, from frivolous to formal, from everyday wear to the Royal Enclosure at Ascot.

An open fire greets customers as they enter the premises, and the feel throughout is one of friendly relaxation. It's very cosy and congenial, creating a pleasant ambience for the serious business of choosing exactly the right hat.

The hats and headpieces - some designed by Pamela, others by a variety of other leading milliners - are stylishly displayed on wrought iron stands in the shape of trees, and there's a selection of bags, shoes, wraps and other accessories to complement the hats. The range of hats also includes many for gentlemen, displayed in their own room at the back. Opening times are 10-5.30 Monday to Saturday. Walcot Street 'The Artisan Quarter' is at the very heart of the historic and bustling city of Bath, close to the River Avon and many of the major attractions.

Royal Crescent

neoclassical squares and terraces. Among these is the **Royal Crescent**, John Wood the Younger's Palladian masterpiece and one of the first terraces in Britain to be built to an elliptical design. Bath's other 18th century founding father was Ralph Allen, an entrepreneur who made his first fortune developing an efficient postal system for the provinces and who went on to make a second as the owner of the local quarries that supplied most of the honey-coloured Bath stone to the city's Georgian building sites.

relaxing place for the elegant and fashionable of the day's high society. Among the entrepreneurs and architects who shared Nash's vision was the architect John Wood who, along with his son, designed many of the city's fine

Famed for its wealth of Georgian architecture, Bath is a delightful city to

BATH PARADISE HOUSE HOTEL

86-88 Holloway, Bath BA2 4PX
Tel: 01225 317723 Fax: 01225 482005
e-mail: info@paradise-house.co.uk
website: www.paradise-house.co.uk

The discovery of an elegant 18th century mansion set in its own grounds close to the centre of Bath is an unexpected delight, so it is no surprise that many first-time guests at **Bath Paradise House Hotel** resolve to return at the earliest opportunity. David and Annie Lanz ensure that guests receive the warmest of welcomes, and, lovingly restored to its former glory, the house offers the highest standard of comfort while retaining many of its gracious original features. Bath Paradise has 11 delightfully appointed guest bedrooms, each one with its own special appeal, and all with en suite facilities, TV, telephone, radio-alarm, hospitality tray and hairdryer.

The four-poster garden room is the perfect choice for a special occasion. Breakfast brings a choice of traditional English or Continental (the latter can be served in the rooms), and guests can relax and plan their days in the magnificent drawing room with its classic arched windows, winter fire and views over the gardens and beyond. Overlooked only by the ancient Magdalen Chapel, the gardens offer a haven of peace and tranquillity away from the bustle of the city below, and in summer guests can while away an hour or two with a gentle game of boules.

Pulteney Bridge

wander around and marvel at the buildings. Beside the original Roman Baths is the **Pump Room**, which looks much as it did when it was completed in 1796. The National Trust owned **Assembly Rooms**, one of the places where polite 18th century society met to dance, play cards or just be seen, were severely damaged during World War II and not re-opened until 1963. They now incorporate the interesting **Museum of Costume**. Spanning the River Avon, in the centre of the city, is the magnificent **Pulteney Bridge**, designed by Robert Adam and inspired by Florence's Ponte Vecchio. The **Holburne Museum** is housed in one of the city's finest examples of fine Georgian architecture and set in beautiful gardens. Originally a spa hotel, it was converted into a museum in the early 20th century and it now contains the superb collection of decorative and fine art put together by Sir William Holburne in the 19th century. Of the town's other museums the **Building of Bath Museum** holds a fascinating collection that chronicles the city's unique architectural evolution; the **Museum of East Asian Art** displays artefacts from China, Japan, Korea and Southeast Asia; and the **Bath Postal**

Museum has a reconstruction of a Victorian sorting office. The city is synonymous with Jane Austen and her novels and, at the **Jane Austen Centre**, enthusiasts can learn more about the Bath of her time and the importance of the city to her life and works.

An ideal way to gather a general impression of this magnificent city is to take the **Bath Skyline Walk**, an eight mile footpath, through National Trust owned land, taking in some superb landscaped gardens and woodland to the southeast of the city and from where there are extensive views out over Bath.

To the northwest of the town, in a beautiful rural setting, is **Bath Racecourse** where visitors and local people can enjoy a relaxed day's flat racing in pleasant surroundings at various meetings in the summer.

AROUND BATH

BATHFORD
3 miles NE of Bath off the A363

This residential community once belonged to Bath Abbey and among the many fine 18th century buildings to be seen here is **Eagle House**, a handsome residence that takes its name from the great stone eagle that stands with its wings outstretched on the gabled roof. On the hill above Bathford, there is a tall Italianate tower known as **Brown's Folly** built following the Napoleonic Wars to provide local craftsmen with work during the economic depression of the 1830s.

NAILEY COTTAGES

Nailey Farm, St Catherine's Valley,
Bath BA1 8HD
Tel/Fax: 01225 852989
e-mail: cottages@naileyfarm.co.uk
website: www.naileyfarm.co.uk

In the heart of the stunning St Catherine's Valley, a short drive from historic Bath, **Nailey Cottages** are the ideal choice for a relaxed, peaceful self-catering holiday. The location is a designated Area of Outstanding Natural Beauty, and the unspoilt landscape provides a haven for wildlife. The accommodation comprises three cottages and a shared laundry room stylishly converted from redundant farm buildings, originally built as a cattle byre and latterly used for stabling and storage. They take their names from three

woods in the valley - Trulls, which sleeps up to eight plus a cot, and the interconnected Dicknick and Longley, each of which can accommodate up to six plus a cot.

The cottages are notably light, airy and spacious and at the same time warm and cosy; natural materials are a feature throughout, including cherrywood kitchens, English oak floors, slate tiles and gleaming white porcelain in the shower rooms and bathrooms, and bespoke furniture made by local craftsmen. The kitchens are fitted with all the latest equipment, and other standard features include TV/videos, CD/radios, hairdryers, books and games, maps, guides and tourist information. Baskets of logs are provided for the wood-burning stoves. Each cottage has a sunny south-facing terrace and access to the garden, and the courtyard to the rear offers ample parking space. The cottages are non-smoking, and do not accommodate pets.

In the laundry room are a washing machine and tumble dryer, freezer, drying space, shoe cleaning kit and many other thoughtful touches that typify the care taken by the Gardner family. The farm and garden lead on to 200 acres of farmland that offer endless locations for leisurely strolls and picnics.

The family also farm here, producing Farm Assured British beef and lamb; the farm is in the Countryside Stewardship Scheme. Ducks, chickens and the younger Gardners roam freely, and the sheepdogs Ruby and Kate and the Jack Russell Jasper are great favourites. New stables provide accommodation for livery and the owners' horses and Pixie the pony. The farm is at its busiest in March-April, the lambing season. The thriving market town of Marshfield is about two miles away, and Bath can be reached by car in 15 minutes.

To the west lies **Bathampton** whose church is the last resting place of Admiral Arthur Phillip, the first governor of New South Wales, who took the initial shipload of convicts out to the colony and established the settlement of Sydney. Considered by some to be the founder of modern Australia, a chapel in the south aisle, known as the Australian Chapel, contains memorials to the admiral's family. Above the village lies **Bathampton Down**, which is crowned with an ancient hillfort that, according to some historians, was the site of the 6th century Battle of Badon in which the forces of King Arthur defeated the Saxons.

CLAVERTON

2 miles E of Bath on the A36

Just to the west of the village lies the 16th century country mansion, **Claverton Manor**, bought in 1764 by Ralph Allen, the quarry-owning co-founder of 18th century Bath. The mansion that Allen knew has been demolished, leaving only a series of overgrown terraces, but some of the stone from the old house was used in the construction of the new mansion on the hill above the village. It was here, in 1897, that Sir Winston Churchill is said to have given his first political speech. Claverton Manor is best known as the **American Museum and Gardens**. Founded in 1961, it is the only establishment of its kind outside the United States, and the rooms of the house have been furnished to show the gradual changes in American living styles from the arrival of the Pilgrim Fathers in the 17th century to New York of the 19th century. The arboretum contains a collection of native American trees and shrubs.

HINTON PRIORY

3½ miles SE of Bath off the B3110

All that remains of the early Carthusian monastery founded here by Ela, Countess of Salisbury, are atmospheric ruins. As in other religious houses belonging to this order, the monks occupied their own small dwellings set around the main cloister, often with a small garden attached. These communities were generally known for their reclusiveness. However, one outspoken monk from Hinton Priory, Nicholas Hopkins, achieved notoriety in Tudor times as the confessor and spiritual adviser to the 3rd Duke of Buckingham and his story is recounted by Shakespeare in *Henry VIII*. Several sections of the old priory remain, including the chapter house, parts of the guest quarters and the undercroft of the refectory.

To the west of the priory is the village of **Wellow** that is today home to a pony trekking centre as well as having some fine old houses and a charming medieval circular dovecote. On the southern edge of the village the road descends steeply to a ford on the **Wellow Brook**, across which is a handsome medieval packhorse bridge. Close by can be found one of the finest examples of a Neolithic monument in the west of England, **Stoney Littleton Long Barrow**, built over 4,000 years ago. A striking multi-chambered tomb, now restored, the interior can be inspected by obtaining a key from nearby Stoney Littleton Farm.

FARLEIGH HUNGERFORD

5 miles SE of Bath on the A366

This old fortified settlement is still overlooked by the impressive remains of **Farleigh Hungerford Castle** that stands on a rise above the River Frome to the northeast of the village. It was built by

Sir Thomas Hungerford, the first Speaker of the House of Commons, on the site of an old manor house that he acquired in the late 14th century. Legend has it that Sir Thomas failed to gain the proper permission from the Crown for his fortification and this oversight led to his downfall. The castle changed hands in the early 18th century and the incoming family saw it as a quarry for building stone rather than as a place to live. Much of the castle was left to go to ruin while the family built a new mansion on the other side of the village. Nevertheless, an impressive shell of towers and perimeter walls has survived intact, along with the castle's **Chapel of St Leonard**. This contains a striking 15th century mural of St George, some fine stained glass and a number of interesting monuments, including the tomb of Sir Thomas Hungerford himself.

Farleigh Hungerford Castle

Just to the north, just in Wiltshire, lies **Ilford Manor**, home to **The Peto Garden**, a Grade I listed Italian style garden famed for its tranquil beauty. A unique hillside garden, it was the creation of architect and landscape gardener Harold Peto, who lived at the manor from 1899 until 1933.

NORTON ST PHILIP

5½ miles S of Bath on the A366

A former wool village recorded in the Domesday Book in the 13th century, the Carthusian monks were given some land near here, where they founded a Priory that was completed in 1232. The monks were also responsible for building the village's most famous landmark, the splendid **George Inn**, originally established as a house of hospitality for those visiting the priory. Still a hostelry today, the timber framed upper floors were added in the 15th century when the inn doubled as a warehouse for storing the locally produced woollen cloth. In 1668, the diarist Samuel Pepys stayed here while on his way to Bath with his family and noted, "Dined well. 10 shillings." Just a short while later, the inn played host to the Duke of Monmouth, who made the George his headquarters shortly before his defeat at the Battle of Sedgemoor in 1685. According to a local story, 12 men implicated in the uprising were imprisoned here after the battle, in what is now the Dungeon Bar, and later were taken away to be hung, drawn and quartered at the local market place. Virtually unaltered today, this ancient inn is a wonderful fusion of medieval stonework, oriel windows and timber framing.

PRISTON

4½ miles SW of Bath off the B3115

The earliest mention of **Priston Mill**, on the northern outskirts of the village, is in the Domesday book and it has continued to supply flour to the people of the city of Bath ever since. Powered by a spectacular 25-foot overshot water wheel, the millstones still produce genuine stoneground flour for retail sale. Visitors to the mill can learn about its history and workings and take a trailer ride around the adjoining working farm. Moreover, the site incorporates an award winning nature trail and an adventure play area for children.

KEYNSHAM

6½ miles NW of Bath on the A4175

A former industrial centre, Keynsham is also a dormitory town for Bristol. Despite its modern appearance, it has ancient roots and, during the excavations for a chocolate factory, the remains of two Roman villas were discovered. These remains have since been incorporated into an interesting small **Museum** near the factory entrance. In the late 12th century an abbey was founded here, close to the River Chew, but it seems that the medieval monks were not as pious as they should have been. Eventually, they were banned from keeping sporting dogs, going out at night, employing private washer-women and entertaining female guests in the monastery. Today, the abbey buildings lie under the bypass but the part 13th century parish church has survived and, along with being a good example of the Somerset Gothic architectural style, it contains some impressive tombs to members of the Bridges family.

Much later, two large brass mills were established at Keynsham during the town's 18th century industrial heyday, one on the River Avon and the other on the River Chew. Though production had ceased at both mills by the late 1920s, they are still impressive industrial remains.

BRISTOL

Situated at a strategically important bridging point at the head of the Avon gorge, Bristol was founded in Saxon times and soon became a major port and market centre. By the early 11th century, it had its own mint and was trading with other ports throughout western Europe, Wales and Ireland. The Normans quickly realised the importance of the port and, in 1067, began to built a massive stone keep. Although the castle was all but destroyed at the end of the English Civil War, the site of the fortification remains as **Castle Park**. Situated just to the west of the castle site stands **Bristol Cathedral** founded in around 1140 by Robert Fitzhardinge as the great church of an Augustinian abbey. While the abbey no longer exists, several original Norman features, such as the chapter house, gatehouse and the east side of the abbey cloisters, remain. Following the Dissolution in 1539, Henry VIII took the unusual step of elevating the abbey church to a cathedral and, soon after, the richly-carved choir stalls were added. However, the building was not fully completed until the 19th century, when a new nave was built. Among the treasures, is a pair of candlesticks donated to the cathedral in 1712 by the rescuers of Alexander Selkirk, the castaway on whom Daniel Defoe based his hero Robinson Crusoe.

During the Middle Ages, Bristol expanded as a trading centre and, at one time, it was second only to London as a seaport. Its trade was built on the export of raw wool and woollen cloth from the Mendip and Cotswold Hills and the import of wines from Spain and southwest France. It was around this time that the city's first major wharf development took place when the River Frome was diverted from its original course into a wide artificial channel now known as **St Augustine's Reach**. A remarkable achievement for its day, the excavation created over 500 yards of new berthing and was crucial in the city's development. Later, in the early 19th century the harbour was further increased when a semi-artificial waterway, the **Floating Harbour**, was created by diverting the course of the River Avon to the south. Another huge feat of engineering, the work took over five years to complete and was largely carried out by Napoleonic prisoners of war using only picks and shovels. Today, the main docks have moved downstream to **Avonmouth** and the Floating Harbour has become home to a wide assortment of pleasure and small working craft.

Much of Bristol's waterfront has now been redeveloped for recreation and down on the harbour side is @ **Bristol**, the home of three spectacular attractions. **Explore** is a hands-on centre of science and discovery; **Wildwalk** takes a breathtaking journey through the natural world; and the **Imax Theatre** promises the ultimate cinematic experience. Also clustered around the old port area of the city is the **Bristol Industrial Museum**, which presents a fascinating record of the achievements of the city's industrial and commercial pioneers, including those with household names such as Harvey (wines and sherries), McAdam (road building), Wills (tobacco) and Fry (chocolate). Visitors can also find out about the port's history, view the aircraft and aero engines that have been made here since 1910 and inspect some of the many famous vehicles that have borne the Bristol name since Victorian times. The city's connections with the sea are remembered at the **Maritime Heritage Centre** dedicated to the history of shipbuilding in Bristol where a number of historic ships line the wharf, including Brunel's mighty *SS Great Britain*, the world's first iron-hulled passenger liner launched in 1843. A new exhibition called 'Extreme Iron: Science and the Future of Brunel's Steam Ship'

tells of the history of the *SS Great Britain* and the technology that is now being used to conserve her.

Beyond the old waterfront there is much to see in Bristol and, as well as being a modern city with an excellent array of facilities for both residents and visitors, there are numerous fine buildings to discover. With their increasing wealth the city's medieval merchants founded one of the most impressive parish churches in the country. **The Church of St Mary Redcliffe** was described by Queen Elizabeth I as "the fairest, goodliest and most famous Parish Church in England." Along with its wonderful exterior, the church contains monuments to John Cabot, the maritime pioneer who, in the 15th century, was the first non-Scandinavian European to set foot on Newfoundland, and Admiral Sir William Penn, whose son founded the state of Pennsylvania in the United States. The sandstone beneath the church is riddled with underground passages known as the **Redcliffe Caves** and there are occasional guided tours of these unusual natural subterranean caverns.

Elsewhere in the city there is **Llandoger Trow**, the striking timber framed merchant's house of 1669, **The Red Lodge**, the only remaining Tudor domestic interior in Bristol, the elegant **Georgian House** originally built in 1791 and **John Wesley's Chapel**, the oldest Methodist chapel in the world that was constructed by the preacher in 1739. The city is also home to one of the oldest theatres in the country that is still is use. The **Theatre Royal** was built in the 1760s and is the home of the famous Bristol Old Vic theatre company.

Down by the waterfront, there is the **British Empire and Commonwealth Museum**, which traces the history of British discovery and colonisation of

Clifton Suspension Bridge

which dates from the 1730s. The walls of this fantastic labyrinth, filled with spectacular rock formations, foaming cascades and a marble statue of Neptune, are covered with thousands of seashells and 'Bristol diamonds', fragments of a rare quartz found in Avon gorge.

To the north of Clifton is the suburb of **Westbury on Trym**, the home of **Westbury College Gatehouse**, a 15th century gatehouse to the now demolished College of Priests founded in the 13th century. A little further to the north is **Blaise Hamlet**, a tiny hamlet of nine detached and individual stone cottages designed in a romantic rustic style by John Nash in 1809.

foreign lands and the rich cultural legacy of the Commonwealth, and the **City Museum and Art Gallery**, which has among its fine collections some exceptional Chinese glass.

However, for most people, Bristol's most famous feature is the graceful **Clifton Suspension Bridge** that spans the Avon gorge to the west of the city centre. Opened in 1864, five years after the death of its designer, Isambard Kingdom Brunel, the bridge continues to be a major route into the city. Suspended more than 200 feet above the river, it provides magnificent views over Bristol and the surrounding countryside. A new Visitor Centre, adjacent to the bridge on the Clifton side, is due to open late 2004. The land just to the west of the bridge is now the **Avon Gorge Nature Reserve** and there are some delightful walks here through Leigh Woods up to the summit of an Iron Age hill fort. On the eastern side of the gorge an old snuff mill has been converted into an observatory whose attractions include a camera obscura. Once a genteel suburb, **Clifton** is now an attractive residential area of elegant Georgian terraces. Here too is **Goldney House**, now a university hall, but also the home of the unique subterranean folly, **Goldney Grotto**,

Blaise Hamlet

LOCATOR MAP

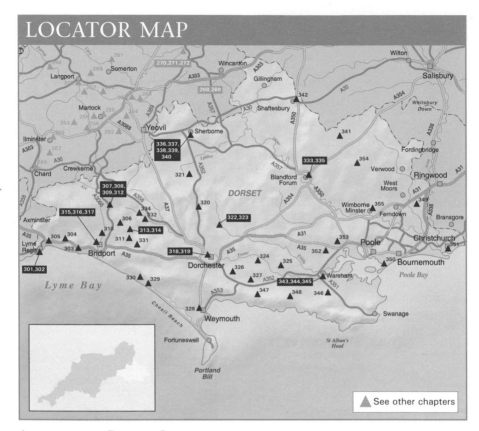

△ See other chapters

ADVERTISERS AND PLACES OF INTEREST

301 The Nags Head, Lyme Regis — page 361

302 Dinosaurland & Fossil Museum, Lyme Regis — page 362

303 Chideock House Hotel, Chideock — page 364

304 Moores Dorset Biscuits, Morecombelake, Bridport — page 364

305 Charmouth Heritage Coast Centre, Charmouth — page 365

306 Garden Cottage, Loscombe, Bridport — page 366

307 Country Seats, Beaminster — page 366

308 @ Home, Beaminster — page 367

309 21, Beaminster — page 367

310 Anglo Longbow & Gallery, Pymore, Bridport — page 368

311 Marquis of Lorne, Nettlecombe — page 368

312 Mapperton Gardens, Beaminster — page 369

313 David Risk Kennard, Powerstock — page 370

314 Three Horseshoes, Powerstock — page 370

315 Partners Wine Bar & Restaurant, Bridport — page 371

316 No. 38 Lifestyle Deli, Bridport — page 372

317 Pierrepoint Gallery, Bridport — page 372

318 6 North Square, Dorchester — page 373

319 Kingston Maurward Gardens & Animal Park, Dorchester — page 374

320 Abbots, Cerne Abbas — page 376

321 White Horse Farm, Middlemarshe — page 377

322 Higher Waterston Farm, Piddlehinton — page 378

323 Muston Manor, Piddlehinton — page 379

324 Moreton Gardens, Tea Rooms & Licensed Restaurant, Moreton — page 381

325 The Tank Museum, Bovington — page 382

326 Yoah Cottage, West Knighton — page 383

327 Dorset Collection of Clocks, Owermoigne, Dorchester — page 384

328 Brewers Quay, Weymouth — page 385

DORSET 10

Although Dorset is by no means a large county, it does provide an extraordinary variety of attractions for the visitor. There are the dramatic cliffs of the western coastline and the more gentle harbours and bays and major resorts to the east, while, inland, there is chalk upland and heathland that support a wide range of bird, animal and plant life. Ancient monuments litter the landscape, many of the towns and villages date from Saxon and Roman times and, throughout, there are connections with the life and works of the county's best-known son – Thomas Hardy. Many of the towns and villages in this Guide were well known to Hardy, and today's visitors will recognise many of the buildings and geographical features that appear in the novels. The Thomas Hardy Society have devised Hardy tours, and the major points, with the equivalent names used by Hardy and the stories in which they appear, include the following:

Dorchester:	Casterbridge:	*The Mayor of Casterbridge*
Bere Regis:	Kingsbere:	*Tess of the d'Urbervilles*
Weymouth:	Budmouth Regis:	*Under the Greenwood Tree*
		Far From the Madding Crowd
Swanage:	Knollsea:	*The Hand of Ethelberta*
Bournemouth:	Sandbourne:	*The Hand of Ethelberta*
Poole:	Havenpool:	*The Mayor of Casterbridge*
Shaftesbury:	Shaston:	*Jude the Obscure*
Sherborne:	Sherton Abbas:	*The Woodlanders*
Bridport:	Port Bredy:	*Fellow-Townsmen*

ADVERTISERS AND PLACES OF INTEREST

329 Abbotsbury, Abbotsbury — page 386
330 The Manor Hotel, West Bexington — page 388
331 Badgers & Barn Owls, Askerswell — page 388
332 Gray's Farmhouse B&B/Paintings & Art Courses, Toller Porcorum — page 389
333 Papyrus, Blandford Forum — page 390
334 The Old Barn & Sunnyside Farm, Lower Kingscombe, Toller Porcorum — page 391
335 Offspringz, Blandford Forum — page 392
336 Sherborne Castle, Sherborne — page 393
337 Dodge & Son, Sherborne — page 395
338 Diva, Sherborne — page 396
339 The Green Restaurant, Sherborne — page 396
340 Melbury Gallery, Sherborne — page 397
341 Farnham Farm House, Farnham — page 398
342 Shaftesbury Abbey Museum & Garden, Shaftesbury — page 399

343 Mainly Blue, Wareham — page 400
344 The Stables, Camp Cottage, Wareham — page 400
345 Culeaze, Wareham — page 402
346 Barbrook Blue Pool, Furzebrook — page 402
347 The Sailors Return, East Chaldon — page 404
348 Lulworth Castle, East Lulworth — page 406
349 Avon Heath Country Park, St Ives — page 409
350 Campton Acres, Canford Cliffs, Poole — page 410
351 The Museum of Electricity, Christchurch — page 411
352 The Old Post Office Tea Room, Organford — page 412
353 The Courtyard Craft Centre, Lytchett Minster — page 412
354 The Drovers Inn, Gussage All Saints — page 414
355 Kingston Lacy House, Wimborne — page 415

Bournemouth Beach

Dating back to AD 74, when the Romans established a settlement called Durnovaria, the county town of Dorchester has a long and interesting history. It will be forever best known for the Thomas Hardy connection, as it was in the town that he wrote many of his novels and entertained the literary greats of the day. North of Dorchester is one of the most striking images in the whole country, the famous Cerne Abbas Giant cut into a hillside north of the village. To the south lies the pleasant town of Weymouth, and beyond this the Isle of Portland, where the famous Portland stone is still quarried, and the vast pebble bank of Chesil Beach. At the most westerly point are the town of Lyme Regis and a stretch of coast that has attracted fossil hunters since the early 19th century.

North Dorset represents rural England at its most appealing - a peaceful area with several small market towns and a large number of picturesque villages. Blandford Forum, the administrative centre, has a strong military connection, and to the north lies King Alfred's Shaftesbury. To the west is Sherborne, one of the most beautiful towns in the country, with an abbey, two castles and a famous school.

Weymouth Harbour

The county's two largest towns, Bournemouth and Poole, are in this part of Dorset, which boasts some of the finest beaches in the country. There are several islands in Poole Harbour, the largest of which, Brownsea, is famous as being the birthplace of the Boy Scout Movement. To the south is the Isle of Purbeck, famous for its stone, and the charming seaside resort of Swanage. In the centre of the Isle is historic Corfe Castle, while to the west is the beautiful and dramatic Lulworth Cove.

LYME REGIS

Although the first record of the town occurred in 1294, when Edward I granted Lyme a charter to allow it to add 'Regis' to its name, it is known that there was a saltworks here at least 500 years earlier. In 1588 Sir Francis Drake's fleet fought a small battle with the Spanish Armada in Lyme Bay. During the English Civil War, surprisingly, the town was staunchly anti-Royalist and the forces of Prince Maurice suffered a heavy defeat here when over 2,000 of the king's followers were killed. Just a few decades later, in 1685, the Duke of Monmouth landed at Lyme Regis and began his unsuccessful rebellion that would lead to the Bloody Assizes of Judge Jeffreys. James, Duke of Monmouth, Duke of Buccleuch, Earl of Doncaster and Baron Tyndale was born in Rotterdam in 1649, the illegitimate son of Charles II and Lucy Walter. When Charles died and

Lyme Regis

THE NAGS HEAD

Silver Street, Lyme Regis, Dorset DT7 3HS
Tel: 01297 442312

Debbie and Robin Hamon - she's a local girl, he's originally from Sark - are continuing a tradition of hospitality that goes back several centuries at **The Nags Head**, which stands on one of the main roads running up from the town centre. This fine old hostelry is everything a good local should be, and the tenants are the most friendly and welcoming of hosts. Four real ales are always on tap in the two cosy main bar areas, which are adorned with

an amazing collection of bric a brac and ornaments - mugs and tankards, framed photographs, sporting prints and cartoons, cigarette cards, a cricket bat, a plaque from Deauville races, a list of Goodwin Sands shipwrecks, rolls of honour of the Royal Antediluvian Order of Buffaloes.

Appetising home-cooked food is served Sunday lunch times with a choice of roasts which are always popular. When the sun shines, the beer garden overlooking the coast comes into its own. There's plenty to see and do in Lyme Regis, and The Nags Head makes an excellent base, with three cosy en suite bedrooms for bed & breakfast guests.

DINOSAURLAND & FOSSIL MUSEUM

Coombe Street, Lyme Regis, Dorset DT7 3PY
Tel: 01297 443541
e-mail: steve@dinosaurland.co.uk
website: www.dinosaurland.co.uk

Dinosaurland is housed in an 18th century building that was previously a church where the renowned fossil hunter Mary Anning worshipped. It features a spectacular collection of local Jurassic marine fossils large and small and a Time Gallery chronicling the history of the Earth and showing how the continents and life have changed over time. The animal room, with its array of shells and skeletons, shows how present-day life evolved and how dinosaurs fit into the jigsaw.

It also has a shop and a clinic where visitors can bring their own fossil finds for expert analysis. Regular fossil hunts are arranged by the Museum. Open every day except Christmas Day and Boxing Day.

his brother, James II, succeeded to the throne in 1685 the Duke of Monmouth, a committed Protestant, began to conceive a plot that would oust the new Roman Catholic king. Landing at Lyme with just 80 supporters, his followers grew to some 3,500 by the time that they were defeated at the Battle of Sedgemoor. The rebellion, which became known as the Pitchfork Rebellion, was quashed. The duke was captured at Hopton, taken to London and beheaded by the state executioner, Jack Ketch, who was notorious for his barbaric incompetence; it is said that he took eight strokes before finally beheading Monmouth.

Maybe this was a sign of the barbarism that was to come as the end of the rebellion heralded the beginning of the infamous Bloody Assizes, the trials of the followers of the duke that were presided over by Judge Jeffreys, later the 1st Baron Jeffreys of Wem, and four others. Held throughout the West Country, the trials started at Winchester before moving to Salisbury and then to Dorchester. By the time the trials had finished, more than 300 men had been hanged, 800 transported to Barbados and hundreds of others had been fined, flogged or

imprisoned. Judge Jeffreys made sure that each town witnessed the hanging of some of the supporters, hence his nickname of the Hanging Judge. Twelve men were hanged in Lyme Regis. However, the end of the trials was not the end of the judge. Although he was a Protestant, James II placed him in charge of implementing his unpopular religious policies. When James was overthrown in 1688 by the Protestant William of Orange, Jeffreys tried to escape disguised as a sailor but he was arrested and imprisoned in the Tower of London, where he later died.

A place of turmoil during the late 17th century, Lyme Regis developed during the 18th century into a fashionable seaside resort famed for its clean sea air. Although without a pier, the town's most famous landmark is undoubtedly **The Cobb**, built in medieval times to protect the harbour and sandy beach from the southwesterly storms, but finally joined to the mainland in 1756. This was the location for one of cinema's most enduring images, of a lone woman standing on the wave-lashed Cobb. The film, *The French Lieutenant's Woman*, was based on the novel of the same name by

Lyme resident John Fowles. This is not the town's only literary connection as Jane Austen and her family visited here in 1803 and part of her novel, *Persuasion*, is set in Lyme Regis. The **Jane Austen Garden** on Marine Parade commemorates her holiday here. In the centre of the town, beside the River Lym, is the old **Town Mill** saved from demolition in 1991. There has been a mill here for centuries but the present building dates from the 17th century, when it was rebuilt after being burnt to the ground during the Civil War. Today, the restored mill is one of the town's major attractions and it houses two art galleries that stage regular exhibitions, concerts, poetry readings and other live performances. The town is an elegant blend of charming Georgian and Regency houses as well as being the venue for an annual, week long **Regatta and Carnival** and an annual **Town Criers' Open Championship**. There has been a town crier in Lyme Regis for over 1,000 years.

Along with its history and its literary connections, Lyme Regis is famous for its fossils first discovered by Mary Anning in the early 19th century. While wandering along the shore, the 12-year-old girl noticed bones protruding from the cliffs. They turned out to be the first ichthyosaur to be found in England. Later, as one of the first professional fossil collectors, Mary unearthed a plesiosaur and a pterodactyl from the same stretch of cliffs and many of the fine specimens discovered by her and other collectors are on display at the award winning **Philpot Museum**. There are also displays on the town's history, the Cobb, smuggling and literary Lyme. Meanwhile, at **Dinosaurland** (see panel opposite), there are, of course, dinosaurs but also a fossil clinic where visitors can bring their own fossil finds for expert analysis, a Time Gallery that chronicles the history of the Earth, a fossil shop and a natural history room with a collection of live animals.

The eight mile stretch of coast to the east of Lyme Regis includes the highest cliff on the south coast, **Golden Cap**, so called because golden sandstone can be seen on the cliff face. The cliffs are highly unstable and dangerous and, although they contain a large number of fossils, their extraction is discouraged. This part of the coast is now owned by the National Trust and, along with the wealth of wildlife, there are several historical sites here including a Bronze Age bowl barrow, a Roman road, medieval pillow mounds and an Admiralty signal station dating from the Napoleonic Wars.

AROUND LYME REGIS

CHARMOUTH
1½ miles NE of Lyme Regis off the A35

This peaceful coastal village, whose steep streets are lined with fine Regency properties, was a favourite with the novelist Jane Austen, who called it "sweet and retired". Visitors today will certainly share the same sentiments as this remains a quiet and attractive little place with a wide main street and a stretch of sandy beach that gradually merges into the shingle. The beach, foreshore and cliffs at Charmouth extend from Evans Cliff to the Spittles and they are divided by the River Char as it enters the sea. In 1925 a section of the river mouth was exposed to reveal various fossils, including the vertebrae, skull and antlers of a red deer, which are now all housed in the British Museum, London. Fossil hunters on Charmouth Beach should keep away from the cliffs as they have suffered major collapses in recent years.

CHIDEOCK HOUSE HOTEL

Main Street, Chideock, Dorset DT6 6JN
Tel: 01297 489242 Fax: 01297 489184
e-mail: c-l@chideockhouse.com
website: www.chideockhouse.com

Two miles west of Bridport, on the A35 road to Lyme Regis, **Chideock House Hotel** has for many years been owned and run by George and Anna Dunn. The house dates from the middle of the 15th century and still retains some of its original features, including a priest's hole in the drawing room and a hideaway in one of the bedrooms. Since 1995 the property has undergone extensive renovation, and the nine bedrooms, all individually decorated and furnished to a high standard, provide modern convenience while losing nothing of their period atmosphere. All have en suite facilities, TV, telephone, tea tray and hairdryer, and the de luxe rooms have king-sized beds - extra large in the premier room.

The cosy oak-beamed bar is an ideal place to unwind, and the restaurant, graced by a magnificent Adam fireplace, is a delightful setting for enjoying Anna's excellent cooking. The restaurant is open to non-residents Tuesday to Saturday evenings and can also be booked for private parties. Chideock House has a charming informal garden and ample off-road parking facilities. It has several times been touched by history, notably as the Headquarters of General Fairfax while the nearby Royalist castle was under siege.

MOORES DORSET BISCUITS

Morecombelake, Bridport, Dorset DT6 6ES
Tel: 01297 489253 Fax: 01297 489753

Moores Dorset Biscuits started life at Stoke Mills in the Marshwood Vale in the early Victorian era by making Dorset Knobs in the ovens where bread was baked. Butter and sugar were added to the bread dough and the small buns were baked in the dying heat of the oven. They became the traditional meal for local farm workers at the start of the day and received the seal of approval from none other than Thomas Hardy, who enjoyed them with Blue Vinny cheese (another local speciality). In about 1880 one of the sons of the founder Samuel Moores opened the bakery here at Morcombelake, starting as a general bakery but later specialising in the Dorset Knobs.

The business, carried on by the fourth generation, is now mainly concerned with the production of sweet biscuits, but the Knobs are still made in the traditional way between January and March each year. The Biscuit Bakery is open to visitors Monday to Friday throughout the year, and all the biscuits, along with many other West Country products, are on sale in the Dorset Shop. Also here is a little gallery featuring West Country paintings and bakery bygones. The premises are on the south side of the A35 four miles west of Bridport.

Just to the west of the mouth of the River Char, is the **Charmouth Heritage Coast Centre** (see panel below) established in 1985 in an old cement works. Designed to be an education and information centre, its aim is to further the public's understanding and appreciation of this area's scientific wealth, its natural beauty and the potential dangers posed by the unstable cliffs.

Whitchurch Canonicorum
4 miles NE of Lyme Regis off the A35

Delightfully situated on the edge of Marshwood Vale and in the steep valley of the River Char, this charming village of thatched cottages is home to the Church of St Candida and the Holy Cross, which is often referred to as the 'Cathedral of the Vale'. A handsome building dating from Norman times, with an imposing 13th century tower, the church is one of only two in the country that still has a shrine to a saint. The other is the shrine to Edward the Confessor in Westminster Abbey. A Saxon lady called Wite lived here as a hermit and was murdered during a Viking raid in 831. The Normans gave her the name Candida, the Latin for white, as they took her name to mean the same in Saxon. During the Middle Ages a cult grew up around her memory and a large shrine was built here of Purbeck stone. The lower level was pierced with three large ovals ('limb holes') into which the sick and maimed placed their affected limbs in order to receive the miracle cure that the saint was thought to be able to provide. The cult around St Wite continued up until the time of the Reformation when all such practices were swept away and along with them the saints' shrines. At the beginning of the 20th century the foundations of the church settled and cracked open a 13th century tomb chest inside which was a lead casket bearing the inscription 'Here rest the relics of St Wite' in Latin. Inside

Charmouth Heritage Coast Centre

Charmouth Seafront, Charmouth, Dorset
Tel: 01297 560772
website: www.charmouth.org

Charmouth Heritage Coast Centre is one of the country's leading coastal geological visitor centres. The Centre's displays introduce the visitor to the amazing geology and fossils of the West Dorset coast. There are fossils for you to look at and touch,

interactive fossil identification displays and a "fossil beach" to practice fossil hunting.

Two large aquariums house a variety of local marine life, while a computerised display lets you

dive into Lyme Bay and discover the secrets of the underwater world. For a small charge you can visit the Jurassic Theatre and discover "Finding Fossils at Charmouth" or "Secrets of the Sea". A wide selection of books, postcards and gifts are on sale.

The Centre is run by three wardens who organise a series of guided walks throughout the season. As well as the popular fossil hunting walks, there are rockpooling sessions and walks in the local countryside. Details are available from the Centre or from the website.

GARDEN COTTAGE

Pear Tree Farm, Loscombe, Bridport, Dorset DT6 3TL
Tel: 01308 488223
e-mail: poe@loscombe.freeserve.co.uk

Major Poë and his wife welcome guests into the civilised surroundings of Pear Tree Farm and the self-catering **Garden Cottage** in the grounds. The cottage was converted from part of the original stone outbuildings and combines period charm with all the expected home comforts and an atmosphere of total relaxation. Fully furnished to a very high standard, it has three bedrooms and a living area with dining and kitchen sections, TV and video and plenty of

books, magazines and board games. Cooking and hot water by electricity, heating by bottle gas in the living area and two bedrooms. The cottage also has a woodburning stove.

The cottage has its own secluded little garden, and the owners will happily tell guests about the several walks that start more or less on the doorstep. Loscombe is situated in a designated Area of Outstanding Natural Beauty, and the nearby valley is in the care of the Dorset Wildlife Trust. The farm is easily reached from the A3066 Bridport-Beaminster road - leave at Melplash. Beaminster is three miles away, Bridport four miles, and the coast at West Bay is just five miles away.

COUNTRY SEATS

The Square, Beaminster, Dorset DT8 3AX
Tel: 01308 863545 e-mail: khayball@tiscali.co.uk
website: www.countryseats.uk.com

Country Seats is a firm of interior furnishers offering the widest range of soft furnishings, fabrics and wallpapers in the area. They specialise in handmade curtains, soft furnishings, loose covers and a complete re-upholstery service, and owners Martin Ball and Katherine Hayball and their friendly, well-informed staff are always

ready with advice and help, including home visits. The curtain service could be anything from supplying curtains to be hung by the customer to fitting tracks and poles and making and hanging the curtains. All the curtains, loose covers and soft furnishings are made in the Beaminster workshop by skilled seamstresses, and all the work is overseen by Martin or Katherine.

The Beaminster shop, which opened in 1995, stocks fabrics and wallpapers from leading design houses, and customers can browse through the hundreds of sample books. A lovely selection of occasional furniture, gifts and accessories from table lamps and candle holders to photo frames and beautiful faux flowers and fruit is always available, as well as superior paints to order, and a range of painted distressed furniture.

The Bridport shop (18 South Street, Tel: 01308 427968) was opened in July 2003 to complement the Beaminster premises. It holds a similar stock, along with sofas from the local Madewell Furniture Company.

the casket were found the bones of a small woman. The shrine still attracts pilgrims today.

It is now obvious that the first part of this small village's name is derived from its church but the unusual suffix, Canonicorum, dates back to the days after 1242 when the Canons of Wells and Salisbury took the majority of the tithes from the village.

while and declared that there was no finer view in England. The three hills are covered with a mixture of habitats making them very rich in wildlife and flora. Now in the ownership of the National Trust, the three separate hills are connected by a network of footpaths that provide an ideal opportunity for some not too strenuous walking as well as nature hunting.

BROADWINDSOR
9 miles NE of Lyme Regis on the B3163

Just to the south of this pretty terraced village is a trio of hill forts, the **West Dorset Hill Forts**, for which the county is renowned. Each dates back to the Iron Age and, as they were all built on hill tops, **Pilsdon Pen, Lambert's Castle** and **Coney's Castle** all provide magnificent views out across the Marshwood Vale to the sea. The poet William Wordsworth took a house on Pilsdon Pen for a short

BEAMINSTER
10½ miles NE of Lyme Regis on the A3066

This attractive and ancient market town, whose name is pronounced 'Be'mi'ster', has few medieval buildings as it was destroyed by fire by the occupying Royalist forces during the English Civil War. After being rebuilt, Beaminster then suffered twice more from flames, in 1684 and in 1781. As a result the centre of the town is a handsome collection of 18th and 19th century buildings while the

21

@HOME

21/22 The Square, Beaminster, Dorset DT8 3AU
Tel: 01308 861382 Fax: 01308 863969
e-mail: athome@selwood-miller.co.uk

The Church of St Mary is just one of many attractions in the ancient market town of Beaminster, and when Annie and Mark Selwood-Miller opened **@Home** in the spring of 2002 they provided another very good reason to visit the town. Behind its small double-windowed frontage in a handsome period building, @Home reveals itself as a design-led contemporary shop selling everything for the home, from kitchenware, china and glass to furniture and soft furnishings, bathroom accessories, lighting and garden accessories from the courtyard.

Following on the success of @Home, which provides everything for the home, Annie and Mark opened **21** next door in February 2003. The premises are a charming blend of modern and traditional, and the chief stock in trade is beautiful ladieswear for the discerning woman. Clothes from many of the leading designers are on display, featuring the top houses of Isuchiko, Joyce Ridings, Oska, Sand, Marc O'Polo and Save the Queen. If the women of Beaminster and the surrounding area are now better dressed than before it is thanks in no small part to 21, and the same is true of the children of these smart women. 21 stocks a great range of children's wear from Osukosu, b'Gosh, Oilily, Tomina, Ikks, Le Phare de la Baleine, Claire Kids and Mini Minors.

ANGLO LONGBOW & GALLERY

No 2, Old Wooth Farm, Nr Pymore, Bridport, Dorset DT6 5LE
Tel: 01308 458137

Anglo Longbow and Gallery is the showcase for the unique talents of Michael Foote, whose paintings and handiwork occupy a delightful little gallery converted from the living room of the family home. Ever since he was a boy he has carved wood and painted wildlife, and the start of a distinguished career came about when he made an English longbow for a friend. He uses a variety of timbers from all round the world, the choice depending on the size, weight and individual specification of the bow commissioned.

He is one of only a handful of craftsmen engaged in the making of longbows, and he travels around the country lecturing on the subject. His talent for making longbows is unusual enough, but he combines it with equal skill as a painter, in which field he has for many years attracted attention far and wide. The works that hang in the gallery and in his house draw their inspiration from nature and from the culture and traditions of native Americans.

MARQUIS OF LORNE

Nettlecombe, Nr Bridport, Dorset DT6 3SY
Tel: 01308 485236
e-mail: enquiries@marquisoflorne.com
website: www.marquisoflorne.com

Julie and David Woodroffe and their staff welcome visitors to the **Marquis of Lorne**, a 16th century country hostelry in a superb location at the foot of Eggardon Hill. The setting is secluded, but visitors come from near and far to enjoy the winning combination of superb real ales from the Palmer's Dorset brewery and the outstanding food that David and his kitchen team prepare. Members of Taste of the West and the Campaign for Real Food, they set great store by the quality of produce, and almost all the raw materials for the daily changing selection of pub lunches and evening à la carte menus are sourced locally. The inn is also a popular place to stay, and the cottage-style bedrooms all offer en suite facilities, TV, telephone, adjustable central heating and hospitality tray; top of the range is a romantic four-poster room.

Each of the inn's three bars (one non-smoking) has its own particular charm, and the extensive gardens, with lawns, flower beds and a variety of trees and shrubs, include a children's play area with a living willow playhouse.

stone-roofed market cross, though an old symbol, dates from as late as 1906. However, some older buildings did survive the fires, including the 16th century Pickwick's Inn originally the King's Head and the 15th century Church of St Mary with its splendid 100-foot tower from which, it is said, a number of citizens were hanged during the Bloody Assizes.

Another religious house, the former Congregational chapel of 1749, is now the home of the **Beaminster Museum** where there are numerous displays that relate to the life of the town from medieval times to the present day. There are also exhibits that tell the stories of the families who influenced the town including the Daniels (one of whom fought with the Duke of Monmouth), the Hines (the founders of the cognac dynasty) and the Strodes.

Just to the south of the town lies **Parnham House**, a beautiful Elizabethan mansion enlarged and refurbished by John Nash in the 19th century, which was the Strode family home. Surrounded by glorious gardens, the house is certainly one of Dorset's finest Tudor residencies but, much more recently, in the 1970s, it came into the ownership of John Makepeace and his wife. Today, this glorious mansion is a showcase for the very best in modern furniture much of which is created by John and his students at the John Makepeace Furniture Workshops that he runs from here. John's wife Jennie, has undertaken the restoration of the gardens and here she has created a magical environment with unusual plants, a lake rich in wildlife and a play area for children. Anyone visiting here should call in at the house's old library now the studio shop from where a wide variety of gifts in wood, ceramics and textiles can be purchased.

MAPPERTON GARDENS

Beaminster, Dorset DT8 3NR
Tel: 01308 862645 Fax: 01308 863348
e-mail: office@mapperton.com
website: www.mapperton.com

Two miles from Beaminster, five miles from Bridport, **Mapperton Gardens** surround a fine Jacobean manor house with stable blocks, a dovecote and its own Church of All Saints. The grounds, which run down a gradually steepening valley, include an orangery and an Italianate formal garden, a 17th century summer house and a wild garden planted in the 1960s. The gardens, which are open to the public from March to October, are a natural choice for film location work, with *Emma* and *Tom Jones* among their credits.

To the southeast of Beaminster, **Mapperton Gardens** (see panel above) surround a fine Jacobean manor house with stable blocks, a dovecote and its own church. The gardens, which run down a gradually more steeply sided valley, have been a favourite choice for filmmakers and Mapperton Gardens have featured in both *Emma* and *Tom Jones*.

This western region of Dorset is, indeed, a horticulturists' delight as, just to the north of Beaminster is yet another lovely garden, **Horn Park Gardens**, laid out around an Edwardian country house. Full of unusual trees and shrubs, with terraced lawns, colourful herbaceous borders and water gardens, Horn Park is an ideal place for the budding gardener

DAVID RISK KENNARD

Merriott House, Powerstock, Bridport, Dorset DT6 3SZ
Tel: 01308 485529
e-mail: akennard@bigfoot.com website: www.dkennard.co.uk

The paintings of the renowned artist **David Risk Kennard** are quintessentially English. They are vivid evocations of landscape and architecture, light and atmosphere. David draws his inspiration and muse from West Dorset and from his travels in Europe and beyond.

Visitors are always welcome. On view is a large and changing display of framed and unframed works in different media. The spacious gallery is adjacent to the family home. Please ring to check opening times.

THREE HORSESHOES

Powerstock, Bridport, Dorset DT6 3TF
Tel: 01308 485328 Fax: 01308 485229
e-mail: info@threehorseshoesinn.com
website: www.threehorseshoesinn.com

Known affectionately as 'The Shoes', the **Three Horseshoes** is a Victorian stone inn tucked away in a peaceful part of West Dorset. Over the years, the inn has built up a great reputation for its excellent cuisine, a reputation that is being maintained and enhanced by tenants Andy and Marie Preece, here since the spring of 2003. Palmers real ales and a wide range of other drinks are served at the thatched counter in the bar, and in the pine-panelled dining areas Andy's menus provide a mouthwatering choice on the lunchtime and evening

menus. Fresh local produce is used wherever possible, and herbs from the inn's own garden add the finishing touches to many of the dishes.

The printed menus and specials board really do offer something for everyone, from classics such as coq au vin and pan-fried steaks to tarragon-braised rabbit, gurnard fillets with a spinach cream sauce or chestnut and feta-stuffed peppers. Desserts keep the enjoyment level high to the end, and the fine food is complemented by a great selection of wines. The Shoes also offers spacious overnight accommodation in three double en suite guest rooms, two with superb views overlooking the valley.

as many of the plants found here can be purchased in the garden shop.

BRIDPORT

8 miles E of Lyme Regis on the A35

Hemp has been grown in the area around Bridport for over 2,000 years and this crop has provided the town, and neighbouring Loders, with its industry, rope-making. Throughout the centuries the town's rope works have produced cables and hawsers for the Royal Navy, nets for fishermen and hangman's nooses known as Bridport Daggers. Rope production in the town declined severely when the Royal Navy built its own rope works but the industry is still in existence today, though on a much smaller scale; the nets for the tennis courts of Wimbledon are made here. The legacy of Bridport's most profitable industry can be seen in the town's unusually wide pavement and alleys as this is where the ropes were laid out for twisting and drying. Rope-making and Bridport feature in Thomas Hardy's novel *Fellow-Townsmen*, where he changes the name of the town to Port Bredy.

Along with rope-making, this has been a key market centre for centuries and, today, a lively street market still takes place every Wednesday and Saturday. Bridport, too, has close links with the non-conformists and here can be found two well-appointed chapels, the Unitarian Chapel of 1794 and the Methodist chapel of 1838. An altogether appealing town with some handsome 17th and 18th century buildings, including an elegant Georgian Town Hall, Bridport also has a fine Tudor building that is now home to the **Bridport Museum**, telling the history of the town and the surrounding area as well as the circumstances of two of the town's most distinguished visitors. Joan

PARTNERS WINE BAR & RESTAURANT

6 West Street, Bridport, Dorset DT6 3QP
Tel/Fax: 01308 458693

Tania Harmon brought a wealth of experience in the catering business when she moved from London to open **Partners Wine Bar & Restaurant** in 1995. The residents of Bridport and visitors to the area soon took the place to their hearts, and Partners remains a popular

place to drop in at any time of day, whether for a morning coffee

break from a shopping trip, a light lunch, a glass of wine or a full evening meal. Perfect for ones and twos, it is also an ideal spot for a larger gathering, families and children are very welcome, even a buffet spread to celebrate a wedding or other special occasion. Partners has always set great store by fresh local supplies, and the fish and seafood specials are particular favourites with many of the regular customers.

The choice varies with the seasons and the catch, but typical dishes might include sea bass, plaice and brill prepared simply to emphasise their freshness, Cornish rope-grown mussels, classic fish & chips, herring roes on toast, monkfish in ham parcels and the speciality crab and mushroom thermidor. Meat eaters and vegetarians are equally well provided for, and few can resist choosing something from the dessert board, perhaps caramel parfait, gooseberry crunch or a selection of sorbets.

No 38 Lifestyle Deli

38 South Street, Bridport, Dorset DT6 3NN
Tel: 01308 425333

On the corner of South Street and Cundry Lane, **No 38 Lifestyle Deli** was recently opened by the McLellan family, whose business connections with Bridport and Dorset go back many years (they also own and run 6 North Square in Dorchester). No 38 is full to the brim with top-quality delicatessen items and delightful gifts. Besides a wide range of cooked meats and shelf after shelf of tinned and bottled products, the Deli itself produces a frequently changing variety of items sold by weight or quantity to take away and enhance

the efforts of the serious home cook - draught olive oil, fragrant Thai rice, dried wild mushrooms, pine nuts, juniper berries, houmous, green pesto, a splendidly strong house cheese.

In addition to all this the deli sells the very best breads and cakes and a range of health products. They will make up hampers to individual instructions and also offer a local delivery service.

Pierrepoint Gallery

76 South Street, Bridport, Dorset DT6 3NN
Tel: 01308 421638
e-mail: thepierrepoint@aol.com

Chris Day brought many years' experience in various aspects of the art world when he came to Bridport in 2002 to open the **Pierrepoint Gallery**. Behind the double frontage of what had previously been a shop,

the gallery comprises several separate areas, each one filled with the work of talented artists, many of them from Dorset and the surrounding counties. Their work covers many themes and many media, including paintings in oils and watercolours - abstracts, still life, figurative - as well as pottery and ceramics, bronze sculptures and beautiful carved wooden figures.

Many of the works take animals and nature as their theme, while the Dorset coast is the inspiration for others. The ground floor ends with a display area in the enclosed garden, where tables and chairs are set out and interested customers can enjoy a chat with the owner over a cup of coffee. There are two more display rooms upstairs, and a workshop where a framing service is available. Bridport is a place of many attractions, and the Pierrepoint Gallery has quickly become one that should be on every visitor's itinerary.

of Navarre landed at Bridport while journeying to marry Henry IV and Charles II arrived here after his defeat at the Battle of Worcester. The future king was fleeing to France disguised as a groom and, as he attended to his horses in the yard of the George Inn, an ostler approached him thinking that he recognised him. Asking the king whether they had met before, the quick thinking future monarch asked where the ostler had been working and on hearing the reply "Exeter", Charles said, "Ay, that's where we must have met," before he hurried away.

In the early 18th century, Bridport's harbour began to silt up and so a new harbour was built at the mouth of the River Britt that is now called **West Bay**. During the 19th century, hundreds of ships docked here annually and, although it had its own shipbuilding industry, the largest boats of the day found that they could not be accommodated. An attractive place, a little off the beaten track, which never developed into a holiday resort, the story of West Bay's harbour is told at the **Harbour Life Exhibition**. However, people who have never visited here before may find it familiar as it was the location for the TV drama series, *Harbour Lights*.

DORCHESTER

After capturing the Iron Age hill fort of **Maiden Castle**, the Romans went on to found a settlement here called Durnovaria that is now one of the country's most attractive places. The hill fort, just to the southwest of Dorchester, is one of the biggest in England and the steep ramparts and ditches of this complex defensive structure are still visible today. Another ancient

6 North Square

6 North Square, Dorchester, Dorset DT1 1HY
Tel: 01305 267679

The McLellan family has long been associated with hospitality in this part of the world, and with chef-patron Stephen McLellan at the helm, **6 North Square** enjoys a reputation as one of the best places in Dorset for enjoying a meal. Just off the main road through town (the A35), the period building on a prominent corner site has a warm,

intimate ground-floor dining room preceded by an area with armchairs where diners can peruse the menus over a drink and nibbles. The kitchen sets great store by local suppliers, and Stephen's menus offer a fine choice that draws its inspiration from near and far, from traditional English to Mediterranean and the East.

Lunchtime offers open sandwiches, pasta and light dishes such as smoked mackerel, omelettes, Thai fish cakes and the popular Oliver Twist Special – soup of the day (top-ups welcome), bread and cheese. The evening menu typically runs from Dorset game terrine and roasted Mediterranean vegetables to roast sea bass, lamb chops with a classic Reform sauce, steaks and breast of chicken stuffed with soft cheese and spinach, served with a citrus salsa. A separate cheese menu offers such delights as Dorset Blue Vinney and charcoal-coated goats' cheese.

monument nearby was also utilised by the Romans who converted the Neolithic henge monument of **Maumbury Rings** into an amphitheatre for games, contests and gladiatorial combat. This site was later used for public hangings, the last one in 1705. During the Civil War, it was home to a gun emplacement.

As with so many towns in Dorset, Dorchester played host to the infamous Judge Jeffreys who presided over the trials of the followers of the Duke of Monmouth in 1685 sentencing over 70 men to death. Later, in the 1830s, the town was once again the scene of a famous trial, as it was here, in the **Old Crown Court**, that the Tolpuddle Martyrs were sentenced to seven years transportation to Australia for swearing an oath of allegiance to their newly-formed union. The Old Crown Court and its cells are now open to the public and provide an ideal opportunity for visitors

to gain an insight into over four centuries of trials and gruesome punishments. The **Keep Military Museum** tells the story of the men who fought and served in the County Regiments of Dorset and Devon.

As the county town of Dorset, Dorchester is the natural home of the excellent **Dorset County Museum** that contains a wealth of exhibits spanning the centuries, from fossils in the Geology Gallery to Roman mosaics and weaponry, Iron Age warrior skeletons, a 19th century cheese press and a stuffed great bustard, a bird often seen in Dorset before it became extinct in Britain in 1810. The museum's Writers Gallery - A Writer's Dorset - honours the town's two most famous adopted sons, Thomas Hardy and his friend, the dialect poet William Barnes. Pride of place here goes to the reconstruction of Hardy's study, complete with many of his personal

KINGSTON MAURWARD GARDENS & ANIMAL PARK

Dorchester, Dorset DT2 8PY
Tel: 01305 215003 Fax: 01305 215001
e-mail: events@kmc.ac.uk website: www.kmc.ac.uk

In a beautiful parkland setting on the eastern edge of the county town of Dorchester, **Kingston Maurward Gardens & Animal Park** offer a splendid day out for all ages. The grounds, which sweep down to an ornamental lake, include rainbow beds, herbaceous borders, stone terraces and balustrades, yew hedges, a walled garden, a Japanese-style garden with Chusan palms, bamboos and Japanese maples, a superb croquet lawn and a number of topiary animals; Kingston Maurward is particularly proud to be home to National Collections of Penstemons and Salvias.

In the Animal Park are donkeys, miniature Shetland ponies, rabbits, sheep, pigs and calves, and visitors can sometimes help with feeding. There

is also a large play area and plenty of space for picnics. The Grade I listed house, built by George Pitt, a cousin of the Prime Minister, in about 1717, is an exceptional venue for both social and business gatherings, and Kingston Maurward hosts a busy programme of events throughout the year, including lambing weekends, antiques and book fairs, computer shows, plays and concerts, teddy bear fairs, children's entertainment and lakeside fireworks.

possessions. To the northeast of the town, lies **Max Gate**, the house that Hardy designed and lived in from 1885 until his death in 1928. Although by this time Hardy was spending considerable amounts of time mixing with London society, he desired a Wessex retreat and this house, built on the site of Mack's Tollgate, from which it takes its name, provided an ideal place from which to write. The years that followed Hardy's move here saw the publication of many of his finest works. He also entertained many of the great celebrities of the day such as Robert Louis Stevenson, George Bernard Shaw and HG Wells. Visitors can tour the dining room and the drawing room, where several pieces of the great writer's furniture are on display.

Situated on the River Cerne, on the northern outskirts of Dorchester, is the attractive village of **Charminster**, where **Wolfeton House**, a splendid medieval and Elizabethan building surrounded by water meadows, lies close to the confluence of the Rivers Cerne and Frome. The home of the Trenchard family, this house contains some magnificent original features including a great stone staircase, superb carved oak panelling and glorious plaster ceilings. There is also a cider house here from where cider can be purchased.

Just to the east of Dorchester lies the village of **Stinsford** that appeared as Melstock in Hardy's *Under the Greenwood Tree*. It was inside the village's St Michael's Church that Thomas Hardy was christened and, throughout his life, he returned here to attend services. Although the building's minstrel's gallery was demolished during the novelist's lifetime, he was

able, years later, to draw from memory a sketch of the gallery showing the position of each player with his particular instrument. A copy of this drawing can be seen in the church. In the churchyard is the grave of Hardy's first wife, Emma, and the tomb of the Poet Laureate Cecil Day Lewis.

Just ouside the village lie **Kingston Maurward Gardens & Animal Park** (see panel opposite). The Edwardian gardens are listed on the English Heritage register of Gardens. The 35 acres of classical 18th century parkland and lawns sweep majestically down to the lake from the Georgian House. Stone terraces, balustrading and yew hedges have been used to create many intimate gardens and planned vistas.The walled demonstration garden is planted with a superb collection of hedges and plants suitable for growing in Dorset.

The Animal Park has an interesting collection of unusual breeds of animals and provides interest to all age groups. The Nature Trail follows the edge of the lake for approximately one mile providing the opportunity to see a wide variety of fauna and flora in stunning surroundings. Sixty-five different varieties of trees are described in the Tree Trail Guide.

River Frome, Dorchester

AROUND DORCHESTER

CERNE ABBAS

6½ miles N of Dorchester on the A352

This pretty village, beside the River Cerne, grew up around its Benedictine **Abbey** that was founded here in the 9th century. All that remains of the buildings are the imposing 15th century gatehouse and a 14th century tithe barn converted into a house. The village is home to the holy well of St Augustine who is said to have visited here during his travels around England. The abbey was the centre of village life for centuries and Cerne Abbas was once a thriving market town. After the Dissolution of the Monasteries, it became a manufacturing centre with a malthouse and a tannery where leather goods such as gloves and saddlery were produced. These industries declined in the late 19th century when the town was missed out of the growing railway system.

Once dominated by its monastic house, the village today is famous for the **Cerne Abbas Giant**, a colossal figure cut into the chalk hillside just to the north of the village. Brandishing a club, the giant is naked, uncensored and full frontal and is, undoubtedly, a powerful pagan symbol of virility although the precise reason for the figure is unclear. First mentioned in 1742, the giant has always been well looked after. At 182 feet tall he is certainly large, but the Wilmington Long Man in Sussex is taller. Connected with many local legends of fertility, until the mid-17th century a maypole was erected above the giant and courting couples are still known to make night-time journeys to the figure to ensure that their marriage is blessed with children. Some authorities believe the giant to be a depiction of one of the

---

ABBOTS

7 Long Street, Cerne Abbas, Dorset DT2 7JF
Tel: 01300 341349 Fax: 01300 348859
e-mail: abbots@3lambs.com

Fine food and comfortable overnight accommodation are the twin offerings at **Abbots**, a licensed establishment, which is owned and run by Bertie, Ann and Lindsay Lamb. Sandwiches, filled demi-baguettes and baked potatoes make satisfying quick meals, and the lunch menu runs from excellent home-made soups to ploughman's platters, omelettes, chicken in a choice of tasty sauces, grilled salmon and sirloin steak. Scones, toasted tea cakes, crumpets and a selection of Dorset cakes provide a delightful choice for a traditional afternoon tea (but available throughout the

day), and indulgent ice creams and home-made desserts such as treacle tart or Dorset apple cake round off a meal in style.

A good choice of teas, coffees and soft drinks accompanies the food. Baby changing facilities and a high chair are available on request. The sheltered garden at the rear is a boon is summer - dogs and smokers are welcome here. The tea room is open from 10am to 5pm Tuesday to Sunday and also on Bank Holiday Mondays. The bed & breakfast accommodation comprises four first-floor twin or double bedded rooms with en suite or private bathrooms.

Druids' brutal wicker men, the vast covered framework figures in which humans were sacrificed.

Just a couple of miles southeast of Cerne Abbas lies the beautiful village of **Piddletrenthide** believed to be have been the home of Alfred the Great's brother, Ethelred. To the northwest of Cerne Abbas lies **Minterne**, a house that was rebuilt in the Arts and Crafts style in around 1900. Although this is not open to the public, the splendid gardens, which are laid out in a horseshoe shape below the house, are open and they are a wonderful example of 18th century landscaping in the style of Capability Brown. Along with the garden's important collection of Himalayan rhododendrons and azaleas, there are maple, cherry and many other rare trees to be found here.

A little to the west of the village of **Minterne Magna**, on Batcombe Hill,

stands a stone pillar, known as the Cross and Hand, which is said to date from the 7th century. While the reason for this pillar is unclear, several explanations can be found within local legends. Some believe that it stands at the very spot that a priest found his lost holy relic. In *Tess of the d'Urbervilles*, Hardy quotes an altogether more gruesome story, that the pillar marks the grave of a criminal who was tortured and hanged here and whose ghost is still said to appear beside the pillar.

PUDDLETOWN

4½ miles NE of Dorchester off the A35

Formerly known as Piddletown ('piddle' is a Saxon word meaning 'clear water') this village's name was changed to its present form by the sensitive Victorians. This was the birthplace of Hardy's grandfather and great grandfather. Just to the southwest, in the woods above the

HIGHER WATERSTON FARM

Piddlehinton, Dorset DT2 7SW
Tel: 08704441901

Standing alongside the owners' handsome period farmhouse around an original stable yard, brick and flint conversions of stables provide a wonderful base for a family holiday. The Pole-Carew family have taken great care in renovating the properties at **Higher Waterston Farm**, retaining many of the best 18th century features while providing all the up-to-date amenities and conveniences needed for a relaxing, self-catering stay. **Barn Cottage**, which sleeps up to six, has a spacious living/dining room with wood-burning stove, modern fitted kitchen and French doors leading to the garden. On the first floor are a double bedroom, two

twin-bedded rooms and bathroom. **Livery House**, which sleeps up to 11, has a beamed sitting room with wood-burning stove and French doors, a modern fitted kitchen with large dining area and French doors to the garden and a twin-bedded room downstairs with its own shower room. Upstairs are four bedrooms with beamed sloping ceilings, two bathrooms and an additional bed on the landing. Cots and high chairs are available on request. Both properties are very well heated, with electric heaters and night storage heaters as well as the wood-burning stoves (for which the first batch of logs is supplied). Purbeck stone terraces with garden furniture overlook a central enclosed area with lawns, shrubs and flower borders. The shared grounds include an all-weather hard tennis court and a games barn with table tennis, badminton and a basketball hoop. A flock of alpacas roam in the grounds, creating enormous interest, especially among younger guests. Also in the grounds is a borehole that provides natural spring water.

Situated in rolling countryside on the Dorchester-Piddlehinton road (B3143), the farm offers easy access to the many scenic, historic and tourist attractions of the area; notable among these are the Cerne Abbas Giant, Lawrence of Arabia's Clouds Hill and the Thomas Hardy connection - his cottage at Higher Bockhampton, St Michael's Church at Stinsford, where he worshipped, and a reconstruction of his study in the Dorset County Museum in Dorchester. Riding, golf and fishing are all available nearby, and the sea is only 10 miles away.

village of **High Bockhampton**, lies the small thatched cottage where Hardy himself was born in 1840. Built by his grandfather in 1801 and little altered today, it was at **Hardy's Cottage** that the novelist grew up and he continued to live here, on and off, until his marriage to Emma Gifford in 1874. Now in the care of the National Trust, Hardy featured his birthplace in his novel *Under the Greenwood Tree*. Visitors can see the very room in which his mother gave birth, only to hear her child proclaimed stillborn, before an observant nurse noticed that the infant was, in fact, breathing.

Meanwhile, to the east of Puddletown lies one of the country's finest examples of a 15th century house, **Athelhampton** that features magnificently furnished rooms including its Great Hall, Great Chamber and a State Bedroom with a Charles I tester bed. Also containing a

Athelhampton Gardens

MUSTON MANOR

Piddlehinton, Nr Dorchester, Dorset DT2 7SY
Tel/Fax: 01305 848242

Muston Manor is a delightful manor house built in the 17th century by the Churchill family and added to down the years. It remained in their ownership until bought by the present owners Paddy and Barry Paine, who offer comfortable bed & breakfast accommodation in two beautifully furnished, very spacious bedrooms with lounge areas, TV and tea trays.

Guests have the use of a charming lounge, and an excellent breakfast, full English or Continental, is served in the graciously appointed dining room.

The five acres of peaceful, mature grounds in which the manor house stands are home to a variety of wildlife, and a heated outdoor swimming pool is available in the summer months. Muston Manor lies in the midst of Hardy country one mile south of the village of Piddlehinton (just off the B3143), four miles from Dorchester and just 10 miles from the Dorset coast. This is fine walking country, with public footpaths all around, and the owners are happy to tell guests about all the many local attractions.

fine collection of art by Pugin, the wonderful grounds feature world-famous topiary pyramids, fountains and the Octagonal Garden designed by Sir Robert Cooke in 1971. Naturally, with a house of this age there are stories of ghosts but Athelhampton seems to have more than its fair share. There is a headless man, a grey lady and a black monk who is thought to have been an itinerant priest who visited the staunchly Catholic Martyn family sometime between 1350 and 1595.

TOLPUDDLE

7 miles NE of Dorchester off the A35

Like so many villages beside the River Piddle, Tolpuddle's name was changed by the Victorians from the original, Tolpiddle. A tiny village today it was here in the 1830s that the first trades' union was formed, when six villagers, in an attempt to escape from both grinding poverty and their harsh employers, banded together and took an oath of mutual support. Their leader was a Wesleyan Methodist preacher, George Loveless, and the others were his brother, James Loveless, James Brine, James Hammett, John Standfield and his father, Thomas Standfield, in whose cottage the union, the Friendly Society of Agricultural Labourers, was formed. Fearing a spreading uprising, the landowners acted quickly and invoked the Mutiny Act of 1797. The six men were found guilty in court, for swearing the oath, not for the formation of the union. That had been made legal in 1824. The six were transported to Botany Bay, Australia for seven years. However the harsh sentence caused such a public outcry, led by Dorchester's member of Parliament, that they were granted a free pardon and allowed to return home. However, only one of the six, James

Hammett, returned to Tolpuddle, the others went first to Essex, before seeking new lives in Canada. The story of the martyrs is told in the **Tolpuddle Martyrs Museum** housed in some memorial cottages built in 1934 by the TUC.

BERE REGIS

10 miles NE of Dorchester off the A35

It is the village church of St John here that draws many visitors to Bere Regis, whose suffix comes from the time when this was a favourite stopping place for kings on their way to the West Country. It was here that Queen Elfrida spent the rest of her days in penitence for her involvement in the murder of King Edward at Corfe Castle in 979. The church has a long history and several fine features, including figures of the Apostles in Tudor dress. However it is the crumbling tombs of the once powerful Turberville family that most people find interesting as it was their name, corrupted, that Hardy used in his novel *Tess of the d'Urbervilles*.

MILBORNE ST ANDREW

8 miles NE of Dorchester on the A354

The parish church in this picturesque riverside village is home to several monuments to the influential Morton family and it was one member of the family who gave his name to the expression 'Morton's Fork'. Born in 1420, John Morton became Archbishop of Canterbury but it was as Lord Chancellor to Henry VII that he devised a scheme for parting the rich, and the not so rich, from their money. Morton's system was simple: if a man was living in a grand style he clearly had money to spare but if he lived frugally he was obviously keeping his wealth hidden! Many citizens were caught by this vicious scheme but its simplicity and rich rewards so delighted the king that in 1493 he made John Morton a Cardinal.

MILTON ABBAS

10½ miles NE of Dorchester off the A354

In 935, King Athelstan founded an abbey here for 40 monks and, gradually, a settlement grew up around the monastic house. After the Dissolution, **Milton Abbey** fell into private hands and, in the late 18th century, it was the home of Joseph Damer, the Earl of Dorchester, who lived in the converted abbey buildings. In 1771, Damer decided he needed a large house, so he demolished the monastic buildings, built a new mansion and surrounded it with grounds landscaped by Capability Brown. Unfortunately, the village, which by now was a considerable size, spoilt the views from the earl's new home and gardens so he demolished the village and moved it and its people, a mile or so away. Today,

Milton Abbas is an attractive model village of simple thatched cottages in a beautiful setting. The one part of the original abbey that has managed to survive is the Abbey Church, which contains some superb Pugin glass and also the tomb of Joseph Damer.

To the north of the village lies **Bulbarrow Hill**, one of the highest points in Dorset, taking its name from the prehistoric burial mound that can be found not far from its summit.

MORETON

7 miles E of Dorchester off the B3390

Thought to have been inhabited since prehistoric days, this charming village of old cottages beside the River Frome is home to the 18th century Church of St Magnus and St Nicholas built on the site of an older church by the local Frampton family. Close by the church are **Moreton Gardens**, a tranquil place of woodland,

MORETON GARDENS, TEA ROOMS & LICENSED RESTAURANT

Moreton, Dorset DT2 8RF
Tel: 01929 405084/463647

Housed in the old school, the traditionally appointed **Moreton Tea Rooms & Licensed Restaurant** serve a wide variety of home-made, freshly preapred food, including breakfasts, lunches, a weekend carvery, cream teas, snacks and beverages. Friendly staff have a warm welcome for everyone, whether they drop in for a coffee and cake or stay for a full meal. The tea rooms are available for private functions and can cater for groups and coach parties. In the picturesque village of Moreton, the Church of St Magnus and St Nicholas is known for its unique engraved windows, the work of Lawrence Whistler, and as the site of the grave of T E Lawrence, Lawrence of Arabia, who lived nearby and was killed in a motorcycle accident close to his home.

Lawrence photographs, documents and other memorabilia fill one of the tea rooms. In **Moreton Gardens**, a path meanders past a variety of flower beds and round a pond to a peaceful woodland area. Visitors can enjoy the Fountain and Sundial Gardens, and a children's woodland walk includes 'Fairies at the Bottom of the Garden'. The Plant Centre sells a wide range of shrubs, conifers, perennials, roses, clematis, alpines and grasses. The Tea Rooms are open daily, the gardens daily from March to September.

THE TANK MUSEUM

Bovington, Dorset BH20 6JG
Tel: 01929 405096
Fax: 01929 405360
e-mail: info@tankmuseum.co.uk
website: www.tankmuseum.co.uk

The Tank Museum, defined by the Government
as a Designated Collection, houses the world's finest
and most extensive indoor collection of armoured
fighting vehicles. It tells the story of tanks and
armoured warfare illustrated through scientific
and technological developments, woven together with the stirring story of human endeavours on
the battlefield.

In 1919 the tanks came back from France and hundreds of them, awaiting scrap, filled the fields
around Bovington, where tank training had started in 1916. A few were rescued from the scrapman
and fenced off from the rest. The plan was to provide young Tank Corps soldiers with an idea of their
heritage and tank designers with historical references. When Rudyard Kipling visited Bovington in

1923 he suggested that a proper tank
museum be established, and the museum,
its stock much expanded after the Second
World War, opened to the public in 1947.

The display of over 150 vehicles has
continued to expand ever since, ranging
from a unique collection of First World War
tanks, starting with Little Willie from 1915
and the nimble Renaults; through to the
awesome machines of the Second World
War - the Tiger, the Sherman and the T34 -
and modern-day battle tanks that saw
action in the Gulf. These include the
superb Centurion, which was developed
over the years from the first version, which appeared in 1945. 'The Trench - Tanks on the Somme
1916' is one of many enthralling exhibitions ('Take a walk from the recruiting office, arrive on a
railway platform in France then head straight for the trenches'), and the new TE Lawrence exhibition
is proving a great attraction. Lawrence was called Shaw while serving with the Tank Corps at Bovington
in 1922-23. In addition to the 150 vehicles assembled from 26 countries the Museum has displays of
medals, uniforms and personal articles.

The library and archive are available for research and there is an education service. A free audio-
guided tour of the Museum is available in three languages, and there are regular Vehicle Rides, Tanks
in Action displays and School Holiday special events. The Museum has a large model, book and gift
shop, fully licensed restaurant, grass picnic area, outdoor play area and ample car and coach parking.
Bovington still trains all branches of the Army in tracked vehicle driving and its tank repair workshops
are one of the largest employers in the county.

lawns, streams and ponds, which were
originally the kitchen gardens to
Moreton House, the home of the
illustrious Frampton family. It was
Tregonwell who founded Newmarket
racecourse, James who built the grand
house and founded the Dorset Yeomanry
and another James who led the
prosecution against the Tolpuddle
martyrs. However, the village is best
remembered as the last resting place of TE
Lawrence, whose funeral was held at the
village church in 1935 following his fatal
motorcycle accident on the nearby

country lanes. The distinguished list of mourners at his funeral included Winston Churchill and the King of Iraq and his headstone was made by his great friend Eric Kennington. The life of Lawrence was memorably chronicled in the film *Lawrence of Arabia*, starring a young, dashing Peter O'Toole (of whom one wag said that if he had been any prettier the film would have been called *Florence of Arabia*).

Just to the northeast of the village is **Cloud's Hill**, a tiny redbrick cottage now owned by the National Trust, where TE Lawrence lived after retiring from the RAF in 1935. To the east of Moreton, lies **Bovington Camp** which has been used as a training area by the army since World War I and where Lawrence served as a private in the Royal Tank Corps. Tanks are still a common sight on the surrounding heathland and this is therefore the obvious place for the **Tank**

Museum (see panel opposite), an impressive collection of over 150 tanks and armoured vehicles from over 26 countries. From Britain's first tank of 1915, Little Willie, to modern day battle tanks that saw action in the Gulf conflict of the 1990s, there is plenty of interest here, including the TE Lawrence exhibition and the fascinating 'The Trench – Tanks on the Somme 1916' attraction.

Just to the southeast of the army camp and tank workshops is an altogether different family attraction – the award-winning **Monkey World** established in 1987 to provide a permanent home for abused Spanish beach chimpanzees. Along with rescuing chimps from all over the world and rehabilitating them into social groups, Monkey World is home to numerous other primates; its conservation and rehabilitation work is described at the visitor centre.

Yoah Cottage

West Knighton, nr Dorchester, Dorset DT2 8PE
Tel: 01305 852087

Rosemary and Furse Swann welcome guests to their beautiful 17th century thatched cottage a short drive from Dorchester, with lovely views over the romantic garden and rolling farmland. Overnight accommodation comprises two very comfortable twin-bedded rooms with a guest bathroom and a sitting room with a log fire. Delicious breakfasts featuring Furse's home-made preserves start the day, and in the evening Rosemary's superb three-course dinners or light suppers are available by arrangement. In every room of the cottage are delightful

ceramics made by Rosemary and Furse, including pigs (Rosemary's favourite), sheep (Furse's number one), and many other animals and birds, as well as Green Men,

Gardens of Eden and pieces based on the story of Noah.

In addition to their own work, they have filled the cottage with all sorts of treasures, from pictures of Borzoi dogs by Weschke to metal animals, green Bristol glass and Oriental rugs. Rosemary and Furse have both exhibited in London, the Midlands, Sweden (where Rosemary lived and worked for several years) and a variety of local galleries. **Yoah Cottage** lies next to the friendly 18th century New Inn in the village of West Knighton, off the A352 three-and-a-half miles east of Dorchester.

DORSET COLLECTION OF CLOCKS

Owermoigne, nr Dorchester, Dorset DT2 8HZ
Tel: 01305 852220

The **Dorset Collection of Clocks** is an intriguing museum with a display
of 50 longcase clocks showing their development from 1695 to 1850
and the way they work. Turret clocks demonstrate mechanisms, and
landmark experiments, and models of notable developments include
the Foliot balance, Galileo's escapement and the verge escapement. Also
here is a cider museum with a video of the antique equipment in use.
For both attractions, follow the brown and white Cider Museum signs
from the A352.

Close by, and beside the River Frome,
is the Jacobean house, **Woodbridge
Manor**, once the home of the Turberville
family. It is said that a ghostly coach
drawn by four horses, that can only be
seen by those with Turberville blood,
leaves the manor around twilight and
the sighting foretells disaster. It is this
story that Hardy adapted for his tale, *Tess
of the d'Urbervilles*, in which his heroine
believes that she has seen the coach and
disaster does indeed follow.

The land to the southwest of
Bovington Camp is **Winfrith Heath**,
which supports a wide range of plants,
animals and birds, including sand lizards,
smooth snakes and Dartford warblers.
The heathland is now in the care of the
Dorset Wildlife Trust.

WEYMOUTH

7 miles S of Dorchester on the A354

Originally two ports dating back to
Roman times, Weymouth and Melcombe
Regis, on either side of the mouth of the
River Wey, owed their early prosperity to
the woollen trade. As elsewhere, the
woollen trade suffered a rapid, if
temporary, decline during the Black
Death. The years following the plague saw
further expansion but Weymouth received
a great boost when Henry VIII built
Sandsfoot Castle here as part of the
south coast's defences. Like many coastal
towns and villages in the late 18th

century, Weymouth began to develop as a
resort for those looking for fresh sea air
and sea-water bathing and, in 1789,
George III came here to try out the newly
invented bathing machine. The king was
to return to Weymouth frequently
between then and 1805, as he had been
told that sea bathing would help to cure
his nervous disorder and fashionable
society followed in his wake. The grateful
town thanked the king for his patronage
by erecting an unusual painted statue of
their frequent visitor in 1810. Close by,
the colourful Jubilee Clock was put up in
1887 to celebrate the Golden Jubilee of
the king's granddaughter, Queen Victoria.

A pleasing, attractive and genteel town
today, with plenty of leisure activities for
visitors, Weymouth's harbour is always
busy with a profusion of boats, from little
yachts and small fishing boats to sea-
going catamarans and even tall ships,
bustling in and out. One of the town's
most popular tourist attractions is
Brewers Quay (see panel opposite), an
imaginatively converted Victorian
brewery close to the harbour that is home
to a shopping village of over 20 specialist
shops and superb attractions. Nearby
Weymouth Museum holds a fascinating
collection on local and social history as
well as the important Bussell Collection.

Not far from Brewers Quay is **Nothe
Fort**, built between 1860 and 1872 as part
of the defences of the new naval base

Brewers Quay

Old Harbour, Weymouth,
Dorset DT4 8TR
Tel: 01305 777622 Fax: 01305 761680
website: www.brewers-quay.co.uk

Brewers Quay is an imaginatively converted Victorian brewery in the heart of the picturesque Old Harbour. Amid the paved courtyards and cobbled alleys is a unique under-cover shopping village with over 20 specialist shops and attractions.

The Timewalk tells the fascinating story of the town as seen through the eyes of the brewery cat and her family, and in the Brewery Days attraction Hope Square's unique brewing heritage is brought to life with an interactive family gallery, audio-visual show and Victorian-style Tastings Bar.

Weymouth Museum contains an important record of local and social history; its latest exhibition is called Marine Archaeology and Associated Finds from the Sea. The Discovery Hands-on Science Centre has over 60 interactive exhibits, and this entertaining complex also has a bowling alley, gift shops, a traditional pub and a self-service restaurant.

that was being established at nearby Portland and from where 10 huge guns faced out to sea while two smaller ones were trained inland. The fort remained in active service until 1956 and is now the home of the **Museum of Coastal Defence** illustrating the past life of the fort and the part that the people of Weymouth played during the dark days of World War II. One of the harbour's imposing Victorian grain warehouses is now the home of **Deep Sea Adventure**, a wonderful family attraction that tells the story of deep-sea exploration and marine exploits down the centuries.

Another tribute to George III can be found carved into the chalk hills above the village of **Osmington**, just a short distance northeast of Weymouth. One of many **White Horses** caved into hillsides around the country this particular one is different as, besides being the largest, it is the only one that carries a rider, although it is unrecognisable as a likeness of the king. An excellent walk leads from Osmington village, where John Constable spent his honeymoon, along a coastal path to Osmington Mills.

Isle of Portland

11 miles S of Dorchester on the A354

The Isle of Portland is not, strictly speaking, an island but a peninsula joined to the mainland by the amazing **Chesil Beach**, a vast bank of pebbles worn smooth by the sea, stretching for 18 miles from the island westwards to Abbotsbury. The effect of the tides here is such that the pebbles along the bank are graded in size from west to east and fishermen and smugglers reckoned that they could tell exactly where they were along the bank by the size of the pebbles. The beach has long been the bane of sailors and many ships have come aground on the pebbles.

This island is also famous for its Portland stone, a building material that has been quarried here for centuries and that has gone into the construction of some of the country's most famous buildings including St Paul's Cathedral and Buckingham Palace. The island's most famous building is, undoubtedly, **Portland Castle**, constructed by Henry VIII as part of his south coast defence. It

ABBOTSBURY

Abbotsbury Tourism Ltd, West Yard Barn, West Street, Abbotsbury, Dorset DT3 4JT
Tel: 01305 871130 Fax: 01305 871092
e-mail: info@abbotsbury-tourism.co.uk website: www.abbotsbury-tourism.co.uk

Surrounded by hills, with the sea close at hand, **Abbotsbury** is one of the county's most popular tourist spots and by any standards one of the loveliest villages in England. Very little remains of the Benedictine Abbey that gives the village its name, but what has survived is the magnificent Great Abbey Barn, a tithe barn almost 250ft long that was built in the 14th century to house the Abbey's tithes of wool, grain and other produce.

The village's three main attractions, which bring the crowds flocking in their thousands to this lovely part of the world, are the **Swannery**, the **Sub-Tropical Gardens** and the **Tithe Barn Children's Farm**. The most famous of all is Abbotsbury Swannery, which was established many centuries ago, originally to provide food for the monks in the Abbey. For at least 600 years the swannery has been a sanctuary for a huge colony of mute swans. The season for visitors begins in earnest in March, when the swans vie for the best nesting sites. From May to the end of June cygnets hatch by the hundred and from then until October the fluffy chicks grow and gradually gain their wings. Cygnets who have become orphaned are
protected in special pens until strong enough to fend for themselves. By the end of October many of the swans move off the site for the winter, while other wildfowl move in. An audio-visual show is run hourly in the old swanherd's cottage, and a few lucky visitors are selected to help out at the spectacular

twice-daily feeding sessions. The swans' feed includes eelgrass from the River Fleet. Recently the Swanherd, who has looked after the colony for 40 years, Dick Dalley, retired. When he first started the birds were still being raised for the table, but today, the 159 breeding pairs - including two black swans - are protected by law. Also on site are a shire horse and cart service, a gift shop and a café housed in a delightful building that was converted from Georgian kennels.

At the western end of the village, Abbotsbury Sub-Tropical Gardens, established by the first Countess of Ilchester as a kitchen garden for her nearby castle, occupy a 20-acre site close to Chesil Beach that's largely protected from the elements by a ring of oak trees. In this micro-climate a huge variety of rare and exotic plants and trees flourish, and the camellia groves and the collections of rhododendrons and hydrangeas are known the world over.

There's a woodland trail, a children's play area, visitor centre, plant nursery, gift shop and restaurant with a veranda overlooking the sunken garden. Most of the younger children will make a beeline for the Tithe Barn Children's Farm, where they can cuddle the rabbits, bottle feed the lambs, race toy tractors, feed the doves and meet the donkeys and horses. The Farm's latest attraction is the Smugglers Barn, where the little ones can learn and play at the same time.

remains one of the best examples of his coastal fortresses. From then, until the 20th century, when the castle was used as a D-Day embarkation point for British and American soldiers, the castle has been in constant use. It acted as a prison under Cromwell. Visitors to the castle, today, can see Henry VIII in his Great Hall and climb up to the battlements from where there are superb views out over Portland harbour. The breakwaters here were constructed by convict labour to create the second largest man-made harbour in the world. Close to the castle, and housed in a charming pair of thatched cottages, is the **Portland Museum**, founded by the birth control pioneer, Marie Stopes, in 1930. The history of this fascinating area of land is told here.

The tip of the island, **Portland Bill**, is now a base for birdwatchers, who congregate around the now decommissioned lighthouse. Also of interest here is the tall, upright Pulpit rock, which can be scaled.

MARTINSTOWN

3 miles SW of Dorchester on the B3159

In a county that is so dominated by the life and works of Thomas Hardy, it is easy to think that **Hardy's Monument**, on Black Downs to the southwest of this village, must be a memorial to the writer. However, it is actually a memorial to Sir Thomas Masterson Hardy, the flag captain of *HMS Victory* at Trafalgar and the man to whom the fatally wounded Nelson said, "Kiss me, Hardy." Born in Portesham, a village just below the monument, Hardy the sailor was, like Hardy the writer, descended from the Hardys of Jersey. Of course, they could never have met even if they were related because the sailor died the year before the writer was born. After Nelson's death, Hardy escorted his body home and, some

time later, he rose to become the First Sea Lord. On retirement from active duty he took over the running of Greenwich Hospital, where he died in 1839. The monument has been likened to a 'peppermill' and a 'factory chimney wearing a crinoline'. From its summit, there are panoramic views out over Weymouth Bay.

LANGTON HERRING

7 miles SW of Dorchester off the B3157

This village, along with neighbouring **Chickerell**, stands close to an inlet of the stretch of shallow water between Chesil Beach and the mainland. Known as **The Fleet**, this area is now a nature reserve that is home to a wide variety of waterfowl and plants as well as fish that can be viewed by taking a glass-bottomed boat trip along the narrow stretch of water.

ABBOTSBURY

8 miles SW of Dorchester on the B3157

Almost nothing remains of the Benedictine Abbey, founded here in the mid 11th century by Orc, a follower of Canute, except its tithe barn built in the 14th century to store the abbey's tithes of wool, grain and other produce. With its thatched roof and stonewalls, the barn is a glorious sight and one of the largest and best preserved barns in the country. A popular tourist destination today Abbotsbury is, by any standards, one of the country's loveliest villages but, before it developed into a small and select resort, Abbotsbury was a fishing village. Right up until the beginning of the 20th century an ancient custom continued to be observed here when the fishermen's families would make large garlands of flowers, take them down to the beach to be blessed and then carry them out to sea where they would be cast overboard. The garland procession still takes place here

THE MANOR HOTEL

West Bexington, Nr Dorchester, Dorset DT2 9DF
Tel: 01308 897616 Fax: 01308 897035
e-mail: themanorhotel@btconnect.com
website: www.themanorhotel.com

The Manor Hotel stands down a winding country lane in a delightful garden on a slope near Chesil Bank shingle beach, overlooking Lyme Bay. Seclusion, scenic splendour, comfort, service and good food have long been the trademarks of this very special place, and the tradition of hospitality is being continued by business partners Peter King and Sheree Lynch, who brought years of experience in the hotel trade when they recently moved from London. Bedrooms, ranging from singles to doubles/twins and four-poster rooms, are handsomely

decorated and furnished, and all have bath or shower en suite, TV and tea/coffee-making facilities.

The lounge is a perfect spot to unwind or enjoy a quiet read, and guests can relax with a drink in the cosy cellar bar. Traditional bar meals are served here, while the full menu is available in the elegant dining room (non-residents welcome). The kitchen sets great store by local produce, so fish and seafood feature strongly on the multi-choice fixed-price menus. Bookings at this outstanding hotel can be made on a bed & breakfast or dinner, bed & breakfast basis, on daily, two-day, three-day, five-day or seven-day terms. No pets.

BADGERS & BARN OWLS

West Hembury Farm, Askerswell, nr Dorchester,
Dorset DT2 9EN
Tel: 01308 485289 Fax: 01308 485041
e-mail: farm@westhembury.com
website: www.westhembury.com

Eighteenth century stone barns have been stylishly converted to provide top-quality self-catering accommodation on a working organic farm in a designated Area of Outstanding Natural Beauty. The larger property is **Barn Owls**, which has three upstairs bedrooms – a double with ensuite bathroom and two twins – and a separate bathroom with shower. Downstairs are a hall, another toilet, a well-equipped kitchen/breakfast room and a lounge-diner with French doors opening on to a patio and private enclosed garden.

The single-storey **Badgers**, one of a pair of barns in the courtyard of the farm, has a twin bedroom and shower room and an entrance lobby leading to a lovely triple-aspect living room with a kitchen area overlooking the garden and courtyard. Both properties have laundry areas and full central heating (Barn Owls also has a wood-burning stove in a stone fireplace); other amenities include ample parking, storage for bicycles, stabling for horses, and a supply of spring water. Organic meat and eggs are available from the farm, where rare-breed White Park cattle and Sussex chickens are raised. No pets; no smoking except in the garden.

each May although the flowers are not carried out to sea but placed on the war memorial.

The village has three main attractions that draw holidaymakers here in their thousands each year – **The Swannery**, the **Sub Tropical Gardens** and the **Tithe Barn Children's Farm**. While each is very different, the combination, in close proximity, makes a visit to Abbotsbury ideal for all the family (see panel on page 386).

PUNCKNOWLE
9½ miles W of Dorchester off the B3157

This village's name rhymes with 'tunnel' and it is best known as being the birthplace, in 1761, of Henry Shrapnel, an English artillery officer who invented a bomb that was first used in the Crimean War. To the east of the village are two of the area's many ancient monuments:

Kingston Russell Stone Circle, a Bronze Age circle of around 80 feet in diameter, and **Poor Lot Barrows**.

TOLLER PORCORUM
9 miles NW of Dorchester off the A3066

Nestling in the valley of the River Hooke, this village, whose name is derived from the pigs for which this area was once famous, is the starting point for several good walks. In particular, there is the village's own trail that takes in the site of the dismantled station of the old Bridport branch line. The station was rebuilt on the Dart Valley Line in Devon. The trail continues through some attractive woodland to the neighbouring hamlet of **Toller Fractum**, where the Knights Hospitalers founded a monastery in the 11th century.

Just to the northeast lies the village of **Cattistock** whose chiefly Victorian

---

GRAY'S FARMHOUSE B&B/PAINTINGS & ART COURSES

Toller Porcorum, Dorchester, Dorset DT2 0EJ
Tel: 01308 485574
e-mail: rosie@farmhousebnb.co.uk
web: www.farmhousebnb.co.uk

Idyllically tranquil and warmly welcoming, **Gray's Farmhouse Bed & Breakfast** is a former shooting lodge with chunky beams, enormous flagstones and spacious rooms. Full English breakfast, with home-baked bread, free-range eggs and organic yoghurt, is served in a dining room with expansive views across the lovely garden to a stream, with Powerstock Common and Eggardon Hill Fort beyond.

Accomplished artists Rosie and Roger Britton also offer **painting courses** described in the national press as amongst 'the best residential courses in the UK'. The richly coloured walls provide a glowing backdrop to their sought-after paintings, which can be seen by arrangement or during **Dorset Art Weeks**, **Bridport Open Studios**, or their **Christmas Craft Show**.

Wildflower meadows and ancient bluebell woods adjoin the lovingly tended grounds from which

hidden paths and primrose-fringed lanes thread through the county's richest wildlife habitats. Bumpy hills, intimate valleys, strip lynchets and tiny hamlets of thatched honey-coloured cottages nestle undisturbed beneath the crowning glory of Eggardon, whose dramatic iron-age ramparts overlook Lyme Bay and distant South Devon. For painter, walker and naturalist, this is paradise, and it's an excellent base for exploring the attractive old towns and villages of West Dorset and the World Heritage Coast from Lulworth to Lyme Regis.

Papyrus

8 Salisbury Street, Blandford Forum, Dorset DT11 7AR
Tel: 01258 455118 Fax: 01258 453346
e-mail: harmans@tesco.net

Located in one of Blandford Forum's beautiful Georgian buildings is **Papyrus**, whose bright and imaginative window displays are so inviting that they are a point of local interest. The shop was originally a gentlemen's outfitters and still retains its Victorian

fittings. Heather and Rob changed the decor but retained the original dressers and deep drawer units as they are perfect for displaying the wealth of items stocked. Papyrus has been established for 10 years and constantly evolves to create an exciting environment in which to shop. Rob and Heather have always understood the importance of a strong identity. Papyrus has just that. From small beginnings to the present location in Blandford, their secret is not to lose the personal feel of the shop as the business grows. From special presents, beautiful cards, stunning jewellery and accessories and a co-ordinated range of ladies' clothing, there is something here at Papyrus for everyone. They have a loyal following of regular customers as there is always something new to discover. All the items are unusual pieces that they have sourced to retail at reasonable prices and displayed here in the couples stylish and unique manner. The couple make a successful team, their previous retail experience and background in visual presentation makes them aware of how helpful good merchandising can be to the customer. They have a team of knowledgeable, friendly and helpful staff as customer service is of great importance. The Christmas ideas are no exception and in the run up to Christmas, Papyrus devotes an additional area of the shop to seasonal gifts and decorations, creating a very special Christmas shop.

Adding women's clothing to their original stock was a natural progression, as the family have had fashion in their blood for three generations. The distinctive brands they stock combine well with each other, appealing to women of all ages, and are completed with a large range of jewellery and accessories. Seasonal collections of ladies clothing include linen garments from FLAX and co-ordinated pieces from the very individual labels of EAST ADINI and NOA NOA.

NOA NOA at Papyrus

'All things start small - but nurturing helps them grow.'

In March 2003 Rob and Heather were pleased to work in conjunction with NOA NOA to open their 'shop within a shop' offering their customers an even greater selection from this stunning brand. NOA NOA's beautiful white Scandinavian fittings complement the wonderful range of colours each season and fit remarkably well with the period interior of Papyrus. The response has been so positive that each season the collection has grown. NOA NOA perfectly reflects the identity of Papyrus and offers a spectrum of choice to women of all ages. The eclectic designs appeal to creative, sensitive, independent individuals: their appreciation of these beautiful clothes, subtle and vibrant colours, original designs and wonderful accessories enables them to express their own personality.

The Old Barn & Sunnyside Farm

Lower Kingscombe, Toller Porcorum, Dorset DT2 0EQ
Tel: 01300 321537
e-mail: mandiefletcher@sunnyside95.fsnet.co.uk

Twin attractions on the same site in the Kingcombe Valley amid 400 acres of the Dorset Wildlife Trust and next door to the Kingcombe Centre. **The Old Barn** is a luxury holiday cottage on **Sunnyside Farm**, a working organic farm with a small shop attached. Downstairs in the cottage is a large farmhouse kitchen linking to a large and very

comfortable living area with a wood-burning stove, TV and video. Upstairs are two double bedrooms, both en suite. The second bedroom has a king-size bed which can be converted in to two singles if required. One of the sofas can be converted in to a double bed (at an extra cost) if necessary. To start a holiday on a really special note, owners Mandie and Sweetpea can arrange for the fire to be lit, a bottle of wine opened on the kitchen table and a casserole made from organic ingredients in the oven.

The Wessex Ridgeway and the Jubilee Trail cross the 85-acre farm, making it an ideal base for a walking holiday. The shop, housed in an ancient stone barn, sells the farm's fresh and frozen produce, including joints, mince and burgers from Aberdeen Angus, Beef Shorthorn and Red Devon herds; legs, shoulders, chops and neck fillet of lamb and seasonal vegetables from the market garden. Also on sale are paintings and prints by a local artist, Carol Biss, and a range of locally made crafts.

church was built by Gilbert Scott, father and son, and where some fine stained glass by Morris and Burne-Jones can be seen. To the east of Toller Porcorum is the little village of **Maiden Newton** that straddles the River Frome.

BLANDFORD FORUM

Beautifully situated in the wooded valley of the River Stour, this attractive town is the administrative centre for North Dorset. After being granted a market charter in 1605, it prospered as the market centre for the Stour valley and was also known for its production of lace and buttons. The handsome and elegant Georgian buildings that grace the town today were mostly designed by two talented architect-builders, the brothers John and William Bastard, and they were

charged with rebuilding much of the town after a devastating fire in 1731. However, three important buildings escaped the flames: the Ryves Almshouses of 1682, the Corn Exchange and the splendid 15th century Old House in the Close built to house Protestant refugees from Bohemia.

To mark the completion of the town's rebuilding in 1760, the **Fire Monument**, disconcertingly known locally as the Bastards' Pump, was erected in front of the church. This had a dual purpose – to provide water for fire-fighting and as a public drinking fountain. Inside the church, there is a memorial tablet listing all the buildings created by the Bastard brothers.

Opposite the church is the **Blandford Museum** that depicts the history, culture and industry of this town as well as having a special display on Blandford's

OFFSPRINGZ

22 Salisbury Street, Blandford Forum,
Dorset DT11 7AR
Tel/Fax: 01258 488555
website: www.offspringz.co.uk

If the younger generation of Blandford Forum residents seem unusually smart and chic nowadays, it might well be because they've shopped at **Offspringz**.

In a town centre location, with ample parking nearby, this splendid shop is stocked with an impressive range of 'clothing for boyz and girlz', and proprietor Rachel Robson, mother of three of the best dressed kidz in town, has many years experience in the retail sales business. Her shop is crammed with stylish clothes in sizes to fit children from newly born to pre-teen, and beside the clothes there are all kinds of fashionable accessories, from animal backpacks to colourful wellies; the Lego Wear range is the largest in the region. Shopping for children, with children, has to be fun, and the changing room at Offspringz, in the shape of an Arabic-style tent, is tempting enough to make any youngster happy to try on a few clothes for size. Shop hours are 9.30am to 5pm Monday to Friday, 9.30am to 4pm Saturday.

great fire. Nearby **Stour House** has a beautiful town garden, occasionally open to the public, part of which is a romantic island in the River Stour.

To the northeast of the town lies **Blandford Camp** and the **Royal Signals Muscum**, where there is a wealth of interactive displays on communication, science and technology and, in particular, on codes and code breakers, animals at war and the SAS.

AROUND BLANDFORD FORUM

SHERBORNE

16½ miles NW of Blandford Forum on the A352

It was here, in 705, that St Aldhelm founded **Sherborne Abbey** as the

Mother Cathedral for the whole of the southwest of England and this is a status that it retained until 1075.

Unfortunately, there are few traces of the original Saxon church but the present building, which dates chiefly from the mid-15th century, is noted for its wonderful fan vaulting that is among the earliest and the finest in the country. Of the many other treasures to be seen here there are the two enormous stone coffins in the north aisle containing, according to legend, the remains of two Saxon kings, Ethelbald and Ethelbert, who were the elder brothers of Alfred the Great and Ethelred. Ethelbald and Ethelbert, and perhaps even Alfred himself, were among the earliest pupils at what was eventually to become, in 1550,

Sherborne School, whose more recent old boys include Cecil Day Lewis, the poet laureate, and the writer David Cornwell, best known as John Le Carré. The school, which is housed in some of the old abbey buildings, may be familiar to cinemagoers as the setting for three major films: *The Guinea Pig* (1948), *Goodbye, Mr Chips* (1969) and *The Browning Version* (1994).

Sherborne's best-known resident was Sir Walter Raleigh who, while enjoying the favouritism of Elizabeth I, asked for and was granted the house and estate of **Sherborne Old Castle** in 1592. This was a stark and comfortless residence, especially for someone of Raleigh's sophistication and ambition, and he chose to build a new castle rather than

The Conduit, Sherborne

refurbish the old. The result is the splendid **Sherborne Castle** (see panel below), which Raleigh called Sherborne Lodge to distinguish it from its predecessor. This remains today one of the grandest of Dorset's country houses, a distinctive rectangular, six-turreted structure. The Castle was enlarged

Sherborne Castle

Sherborne, Dorset DT9 3PY
Tel: 01935 813182
e-mail: enquiries@sherbornecastle.com
website: www.sherbornecastle.com

As soon as Sir Walter Raleigh was given the Old Castle and its estates by Queen Elizabeth I, he realised that the stark, comfortless castle was not his ideal residence, and instead of restoring it he built a new castle alongside the old one. He called it Sherborne Lodge to distinguish it from the Old Castle, and this unusual rectangular, six-turreted building became his home.

Upon Sir Walter Raleigh's death his estates were forfeited to the Crown, but in 1617 King James I allowed Sir John Digby to purchase the new castle and this gentleman added four wings in a similar style to the old building. During the Civil War, the Old Castle was reduced to a ruin by Cromwell's Parliamentary forces - the siege in 1645 lasted 16 days and prompted Cromwell to talk of this 'malicious and mischievous castle'. The name Sherborne Castle came to be applied to the new building, where today splendid collections of Old Masters, porcelain and furniture are on display.

Other attractions at the castle, which is still in the care of the Digby family, include the library, a Tudor kitchen and an exhibition of finds from the Old Castle. Lancelot 'Capability' Brown was called in to create the lake in 1753 and gave Sherborne the very latest in landscape gardening. The Castle, which was a Red Cross Hospital for wounded soldiers in the First World War and the HQ for D-Day Commandos in the Second, was opened to the public in 1969 and hosts a variety of events in the summer season. The gardens, tea room and shop are open every day except Mondays and Fridays (open Bank Holiday Mondays), from April to October.

Sherborne

Distance:	5.0 miles (8.0 kilometres)
Typical time:	120 mins
Height gain:	75 metres
Map:	Explorer 129
Walk:	www.walkingworld.com ID:582
Contributor:	Pat Mallet

Access Information:

Park in Sherborne station car park.

Description:

A delightful walk through fields, woods and farms with views of Sherborne's two famous castles and their lake as well as panoramas of the gentle hills of Dorset. It is mainly undulating countryside with just one short hill.

Features:

Lake/loch, castle, great views

Walk Directions:

1 From the station car park, cross the railway tracks and walk up Gas House Hill to the main road at the top.

2 From the top of Gas House Hill, turn left at the waymarked path up the gentle slope to the swing-gate at the top.

3 Follow the well-walked path through the fields with Sherborne Castle and beautiful lake on your left in the distance.

4 Go through the gate and continue in the same direction, along the path straight ahead. You climb a little here, towards the deer-park at the top of the hill.

5 Go through the high deer-gate, past a boarded-up thatched gatehouse and on up the hill. Look for the deer in the trees.

6 Exit the deer park at the top of the hill and follow the path as it goes through the woods past the overgrown foundations of a Second World War army camp. You reach some corrugated iron farm buildings after about ½km.

7 Turn right in the middle of the group of farm buildings, along a tarmac road. Continue to a small crossroads, about 200m away.

8 Turn sharp left here so that you are facing a farm cottage up the track. Walk towards the cottage as far as the waymark on the side of the road and there turn right, only about 50 metres. Follow the edge of the field with the fence on your left, to a stile on your left. Climb the stile and follow the path (sometimes muddy) through the trees to another deer-gate.

9 You are now back in the deer-park. Follow the telegraph poles down the hill towards Pinfold Farm, straight ahead in the valley. Apart from the farm, can you see another building? Keep a straight line for the farm, across a stile and a wooden bridge over the River Yeo. On your left, you may see just the end of the artificial lake created by Capability Brown in the grounds of the castle.

10 At the waymark on the gate to the left of the main farm buildings, turn left and walk along the farm road for about 100 metres, through another gate with a waymark just beyond on a post on the right. Turn right here and walk through the field towards the two imposing stone gate pillars up the slope.

11 Walk between the gate pillars and take the second path on the left, through the trees. Immediately turn right and follow a narrow path in the trees, NOT the obvious track which veers left. Follow the path until it reaches a stile, coming out of the woods.

12 Climb the stile, go straight ahead across the fields towards the railway line, setting your sights on the rail track lights in the distance. The tunnel under the railway line lies to the right of the rail lights. Go through the tunnel, keeping to the right and look for a stile, which at times is hidden behind a farm manure pile!

13 Climb the stile, go up to the main road and turn left. A detour can be made here to the tiny village of Oborne (signposted from the road).

14 Walk back towards Sherborne along the main road for a distance of about 1/4km, then take the left fork onto the B3145. Continue along the road past the Castleton Waterwheel on the left (sometimes open for tours).

15 Fork left here towards the castle, cross the bridges over the railway and the River Yeo and see the next waymark on a gate to the right.

16 Turn through the gate and follow the river back to the station and the car park. As a pleasant extension to the walk, take a stroll through the gardens opposite the station. Veering left, exit the gardens on the north west side, walk up Digby Road to the Abbey (about 200m) and visit this one-thousand-year-old church. From there it is a short stroll to the delightful shops and teashops of Sherborne.

shortly after Raleigh's execution by Sir John Digby, a member of the family who have owned the Castle since 1617 and still do so. The huge windows let light flood into the gracious rooms with their elaborately patterned ceilings and superb collections of porcelain, paintings and furniture. Other attractions include the library, a Tudor kitchen and an exhibition of finds from the Old Castle. Lancelot 'Capability' Brown created the lake in 1753 and gave Sherborne the very latest in landscape gardening.

The abbey and the castle are not the only attractions in this appealing town, which still retains something of the air of a cathedral city though it has not enjoyed that status for nearly 1,000 years. The **Almshouse** near the abbey was founded in 1437 to house 12 men and four women and, although it has been considerably extended, it continues to fulfil this role. Close by is the attractive, early 16th century hexagonal **Conduit House** that was originally used as a washroom by the monks. Moved to its present position after the Reformation, this building has, over the years, been used as a public fountain and a police

DIVA

Long Street, Sherborne, Dorset DT9 3BS
Tel/Fax: 01935 816488

When Lindi Hunt opened **DIVA** she created a calm, unhurried and spacious shop with a style that reflects the quality of DIVA's beautiful clothes and accessories. From some of the country's leading designers there are clothes which are 'classic for when you need to impress; elegant when you need to turn heads; frivolous when you feel like fun; understated when you need to relax; simple when you just need to look good.'

Labels include Caroline Charles, Magaschoni, Ghost, Saltwater, Marilyn Moore, Jean Muir, Paul Costelloe, L K Bennett, Lola Rose and Angie Gooderham. Sherborne has many attractions to appeal to historians, including the abbey, the castle and the renowned school. And with the opening of Diva, Lindi Hunt has provided a reason why fashion conscious ladies should make a beeline for the heart of this historic town: opening hours are 9.30am to 5pm Monday to Saturday.

THE GREEN RESTAURANT

The Green, Sherborne, Dorset DT9 3HY
Tel: 01935 813821
website: www.thegreen.info

By insisting on the best and freshest seasonal produce and the highest standards of service, family owners Michael and Judith Rust have made **The Green** one of the best places to eat out in the West Country. The atmosphere in the handsome dining room is easy and stylish, with antique wooden tables and chairs, linen napkins and candlelight, and this combination of ambience and Michael's skills in the kitchen makes a meal here an occasion to remember. The menus follow the seasons, and local producers and suppliers are used whenever possible. Fish is from West Bay and the South Coast, meat and poultry from the Quantocks and surrounding Dorset estates. Fruit and vegetables are sourced locally or delivered overnight from London, and the very special cheese list features small

but excellent local producers. Typical dishes on the mouthwatering menus range from pan-fried West Bay scallops on saffron and herb couscous with red peppers to fillet of brill with langoustines, crab and basil butter; loin of Dorset venison with celeriac, chestnuts, French beans, bacon and port, and, for dessert, dark chocolate mousse with cherry ice cream and compote of cherries. Wine is taken every bit as seriously as food at this outstanding restaurant, and the wide-ranging list is particularly well annotated.

The Green, a non-smoking establishment, is open for lunch and dinner Tuesday to Saturday. A private room for up to 21 is available for business or special occasions.

MELBURY GALLERY

Half Moon Street, Sherborne, Dorset DT9 3LN
Tel/Fax: 01935 814027

Situated in the heart of Sherborne, **Melbury Gallery** is a
unique and enchanting shop that stocks a colourful array
of clothes, jewellery, soft furnishings, a distinctive range
of lighting and literally hundreds of gifts. Thelma Drabik
established Melbury Gallery in 1980, and over the years
she has expanded and developed it into the wonderful
emporium it is today. Thelma's lively personality is mirrored
in the shop's decor, and throughout the two floors there

are unusual and interesting things to discover. The range of beautifully made clothes have a style and
simplicity that make them suitable for almost any occasion, and to complete the look, the Melbury
Gallery stocks a range of scarves in a kaleidoscope of colours that blend or contrast with the clothes.

The display cases of jewellery provide a
bewildering choice of necklaces, bracelets, rings and
earrings in plain silver and semi-precious stones;
ideal jewellery for day and evening wear, and perfect
presents for a friend or relation. Upstairs, customers
will find rugs of all shapes and sizes, a huge
collection of sumptuous cushions and large items
for the home. Thelma sources her stock from over
100 suppliers, and the combination of range and
quality has gained the Melbury Gallery a large
following in Sherborne and for miles around.

telephone box. It is mentioned,
specifically, in Hardy's *The Woodlanders*
as the place where Giles Winterborne,
while seeking work, stood in the market
place "as he always did at this time of
the year, with his specimen apple tree".

The year 1905 was the 1,200th
anniversary of the founding of the town
and, to mark this historic event, a
pageant was held. This successful event
raised the money for the creation of the
Pageant Gardens to the south of the
town centre. Finally, housed in the
former Abbey Gatehouse is the
Sherborne Museum, where the whole
history of the town and surrounding
rural area, from prehistoric times to the
present day, is told through a wide range
of interesting and imaginative displays.

STURMINSTER NEWTON

7½ miles NW of Blandford Forum on the B3092

An unspoilt market town on the River

Stour at the heart of the rich agricultural
area of Blackmore Vale, Sturminster and
Newton were separate communities on
opposite riverbanks until Elizabethan
times. Shortly after the graceful Town
Bridge was constructed to link the two
communities, a mill was built a little way
upstream. Now fully restored and
powered by a 1904 turbine, **Newton Mill**
is once again producing flour and is an
ideal place to find out more about the
milling process.

It was here that Thomas Hardy and his
wife Emma had their first home, between
1876 and 1878, and, while here, he wrote
The Return of the Native. He often referred
to this period of his life as "our happiest
time". Two other writers made their
home at Sturminster: William Barnes, the
19th century poet who wrote about
Dorset in dialect and his fellow poet
friend, Robert Young, who died at the
age of 97 in the house that his family

FARNHAM FARM HOUSE

Farnham, Nr Blandford,
Dorset DT11 8DG
Tel: 01725 516254 Fax: 01725 516306
e-mail: info@farnhamfarmhouse.co.uk
website: www.farnhamfarmhouse.co.uk

Nestling in the heart of Cranborne Chase, **Farnham Farm House** combines the twin attractions of a luxurious country house retreat and a spa offering a wide range of natural therapies. A private drive leads to the pretty mid-19th century farmhouse, where the beautifully appointed and traditionally furnished bedrooms all feature en suite bath or shower, TV, beverage trays and extensive views of the surrounding countryside. The day rooms have flagstone floors and open fires, and in the garden is a heated swimming pool. There are lovely walks on the 350-acre working farm, which is part of a private estate owned by the descendants of General Augustus Pitt-Rivers, a prominent landowner and noted archaeologist of the 19th century.

The daughter of the owners John and Pat Benjafield offers what is surely a unique attraction on a farm - a natural therapies centre adjoining the main house, where visitors can spend a day or stay for a retreat. Sarpenela Natural Therapies Centre (Tel/Fax: 01725 516942, web: www.sarpenela.com) has on offer an extensive range of natural therapies and spa body treatments using the services of experts, among them holistic therapists, a hypnotherapist and psychotherapist and a make-up artist and beauty consultant. They apply their skills to a wide variety of treatments: therapeutic, remedial, sports and Indian head massages; reflexology; reiki; Hopi ear candles; help in stopping smoking, reducing stress and improving confidence; make-up techniques and beauty treatments; essential skin care; body wraps and therapeutic baths. Whether here for a few days in the country or for treatment at the Centre, a stay at Farnham Farm House is certain to be a relaxing, revitalising experience. The lovely, unspoilt village of Farnham is well worth taking time to explore, as are the many other delightful villages hereabouts, including the eight Tarrants and Tollard Royal, the old capital of the ancient royal hunting ground of Cranborne Chase.

Shaftesbury Abbey Museum & Garden

Park Walk, Shaftesbury, Dorset SP7 8JR
Tel/Fax: 01747 852910
e-mail: anna@shaftesburyabbey.fsnet.co.uk

Visitors can explore the site of Saxon England's foremost Benedictine nunnery, founded by King Alfred, who installed his daughter as the first prioress. The excavated remains of the original abbey church lie in a peaceful walled garden, and a nearby state-of-the-art museum, decorated in dramatic medieval colours chosen to reflect the original colours of the church, houses a fascinating collection of carved stonework, medieval floor tiles and other excavated objects. There's also an interactive touch-screen exhibition and a gift shop.

had rented to the Hardys.

Just to the north of Sturminster Newton, near the village of **Hinton St Mary**, a large Roman mosaic pavement was discovered in 1960 that can now be seen at the British Museum, London.

SHAFTESBURY

10 miles NW of Blandford Forum on the A350

This hill top town, which stands over 700 feet above sea level, was founded in 880 by King Alfred who fortified the settlement here and established a Benedictine abbey for women installing his daughter as the first prioress. Just a hundred years later, King Edward, who was murdered at Corfe Castle, was buried at **Shaftesbury Abbey** and it soon became a place of pilgrimage. There is a local story that tells that the abbey treasure remains where it was hidden at the time of the Dissolution, when the abbess asked one of the monks to bury the valuable items. Unfortunately, before he could tell the abbess where he had dug the hole he had a massive heart attack and died. No treasure has ever been found but the ghost of the monk has been seen wandering the abbey ruins. Today, the abbey remains have been excavated and they lie in a

quiet, peaceful walled garden. The nearby **Shaftesbury Abbey Museum** (see panel above) houses many of the finds from the abbey's excavations and state of the art, touch screen displays bring the ancient religious house to life.

The town has other royal connections as it is said that King Canute died here in 1035; Elizabeth, the wife of Robert the Bruce, was imprisoned here for two years; and Catherine of Aragon, Henry VIII's first wife, stayed here on her way to London to marry Henry's brother, Prince Arthur.

Apart from the abbey, there are some interesting buildings here, such as the Tudor style **Town Hall** dating from the 1820s and 17th century **Ox House** that receives a mention in Hardy's *Jude the*

Gold Hill, Shaftesbury

MAINLY BLUE

3 Seymour Place, St Johns Hill (off South Street), Wareham,
Dorset BH20 4LR   Tel/Fax: 01929 550897
website: www.mainlyblue.co.uk

Opened in July 2003, Mainly Blue manages to offer a wide
selection within its compact shop space. Most eye-catching
are the genuine Native American pieces: the combination of
turquoise and silver used in Navajo work is stunning. Equally
striking is the inlaid jewellery produced by the Zuni,

employing materials such as coral, jet, lapis, malachite, onyx, opal and shell.
The Zuni are also renowned for their skill in working with "needlepoint"
turquoise. The silver designer jewellery includes original pieces crafted in
Orkney by Sheila Fleet and her team, reflecting nature and celebrating the
colours of sea and sky in a wonderful range of enamels. Inspiration comes
from history and folklore too, with modern renditions of the "endless knot"
design, symbol of continuity and the quintessential lover's knot.

Earrings and pendants carved from caribou bone and decorated in the
scrimshaw technique in Newfoundland hark back to the ancient shamanic
cultures of northeastern Canada. Some of the designs incorporate local
gemstones: red and variegated jasper, labradorite and garnet. All this, plus
charming gemstone and freshwater pearl jewellery, animal carvings,
benevolent Buddhas, stress-relieving palmstones and other inexpensive gift
ideas. New for 2004: silver and gemstone jewellery sets with motifs that
highlight Wareham's status as a gateway to the "Jurassic Coast". Browsers
welcome.

THE STABLES, CAMP COTTAGE

Sandford Road, Wareham, Dorset BH20 7AG
Tel/Fax: 01929 552686
e-mail: stables@campcottage.fsnet.co.uk website: www.campcottage.info

The Stables is a stylish and sympathetic conversion of a Grade II listed building situated in the secluded
three-and-a-half acre grounds of a beautiful Regency cottage. Mr & Mrs Watkins-Jones offer The Stables
as self-catering accommodation throughout the year. The downstairs twin and double bedrooms with
the sleeping loft have room for up to six guests with style and quality the keynotes in all the
rooms: timber from beech and cedar trees that once stood in the garden is used for the floors in the

living room and bedrooms.
Carrera marble floors in the two
ensuite bathrooms, Purbeck
stone in the kitchen and lobby.
Two of The Stable walls are of
Cobb construction as in the
main house.

The Stables is south off the
A351 at Sandford and has ample
private parking. Wareham Forest
is within a five-minute walk
and the Saxon town of Wareham
is three miles away. Detailed
information and pictures of
this exceptional property are on
our web site.

Obscure. However, the town's most famous sight is **Gold Hill**, a steep cobbled street, stepped in places and lined with delightful 18th century cottages. Many people who have never visited the town will recognise this thoroughfare as it was made famous through the classic TV advertisement for Hovis bread. The cottage at the top of the hill is home to the **Shaftesbury Museum** and each of the former dwelling's little rooms is filled with objects of local interest while, outside, there is a cottage-style garden. Button-making was once an important cottage industry in the town and some of the products can be seen here including the decorative Dorset Knobs, which share their name with a famous, also locally-made, biscuit.

IWERNE MINSTER
5 miles N of Blandford Forum on the A350

This village is surrounded by **Fontmell** and **Melbury Downs**, two estates that cover an important stretch of chalk downland cut by steep-sided valleys, or combes. Little changed over the centuries, sheep graze the uplands and, all around, there are ancient monuments, including two Iron Age cross-ridge dykes. These two estates, now owned by the National Trust, evoke the landscapes of Thomas Hardy as well as being important for their butterfly populations and a joy to walk around.

Cranborne Chase, an ancient royal hunting ground, stretching out northeastwards across the county as it borders into Wiltshire, became a hiding place for smugglers and is now an important habitat for plant, animal and bird life. Thousands of acres of the woodland celebrated by Hardy are being restored to their former splendour by the Forestry Commission, who are weeding out non-native species from the woods.

Spruces, firs, pines and the Western Red Cedar will be replaced by ash, beech, hazel, field maple and hawthorn to return the woods to the way they looked immediately after World War I, when imported species were planted to ensure a plentiful supply of wood should hostilities resume. The scheme will make the woodland better for recreation and also be good for native animals and plants.

WAREHAM

Situated between the Rivers Frome and Piddle (or Puddle), Wareham lies within the earthworks of a 10th century encircling wall and was an important port until the River Frome silted up the harbour approaches. However, Wareham's history goes back much further, to the days of the Romans, and it was these invaders who laid out its street plan – a grid of streets that faithfully follow the points of the compass. Having lost its direct links with the sea, the town was hit, in 1726, by a devastating fire that destroyed all but a few of its buildings. Fortunately for today's visitors, the town was rebuilt and is now dominated by elegant Georgian stone houses.

The town's **Museum** has a special section devoted to TE Lawrence, who lived for the last few months of his life at nearby Clouds Hill and who was trained at Bovington Camp close by. The **Rex Cinema** here is a fine period building now restored. This Victorian building has a gas lit auditorium and the original carbon arc projectors that are still in use.

The town still remembers the ancient customs of the Court Leet, which, in Norman times, was the main judicial court in many parts of the country. On four evenings in November, strangely dressed men visit the town's inns to check the quality and quantity of food

and ale that is supplied by the landlords. The officials include ale-tasters, bread weighers and carnisters, who taste the meat. While they have no powers today it is a quaint tradition.

Just to the south of the town, at **Furzebrook**, lies a rare of oasis of peace in today's hectic world, **The Blue Pool** (see panel), which has been welcoming visitors to this unique, tranquil beauty spot for over 65 years.

AROUND WAREHAM

CORFE CASTLE

4½ miles SE of Wareham on the A351

This greystone village is dominated by the majestic ruins of **Corfe Castle** high on a hill. An important stronghold that protected the gateway through the Purbeck Hills, the castle was constructed in the years immediately following the Norman Conquest. There was a royal residence here in the 10th century and it was at Corfe that Queen Elfrida murdered her stepson, King Edward the Martyr in 978. Additions were made to the fortification during the reigns of King John and Edward I, and on one occasion King John is said to have thrown 22 French knights into the dungeons from a hole in the ceiling and

left them to starve. Later, Edward II was imprisoned here before being sent to his horrible death at Berkeley Castle. During the English Civil War, the castle withstood two sieges but the Royalist garrison finally fell to the besieging Parliamentarian forces in the winter of 1644-5. Its ruinous state was due to the victors' deliberate demolition. Now owned by the National Trust, the castle is part of an extensive estate, with a network of footpaths taking in both the

coastline and the inland heath, and encompassing important habitats for many rare species, including all six species of British reptile. Today, the **Castle Museum** shows a collection of domestic and agricultural implements and a set of dinosaur footprints – a gentle reminder that this is still fossil country. Almost in the shadow of the ruins of the Castle lies **Corfe Castle Model Village & Gardens**, a wonderfully detailed work in 1/20th scale that took Eddie Holland two years to complete.

Corfe Castle

SWANAGE

8½ miles SE of Wareham on the A351

This seaside town, complete with its fully restored Victorian pier and its little exhibition, built its early fortune on Purbeck stone and the gentleman who really put Swanage on the map was John Mowlem, a quarryman, who built the town's first roads. With the aid of his nephew and partner, George Burt, they built several civic buildings and even gave the town piped water. However, the Town Hall's magnificent front facade was not their work but that of Christopher Wren who had originally designed the front for Mercers Hall in the City of London. When the building was demolished, the facade was taken down, piece by piece, and reconstructed here. This was not the only building in the town to make use of architectural salvage from London and even George Burt's home, Purbeck House, did not escape additions from the metropolis.

There is, though, one monument in the town that is purely Swanage: the

King Alfred Column, on the seafront, records that this was where the king fought and saw off the Danish fleet in 877. The column is topped by cannonballs that would, undoubtedly, have been a great help to King Alfred, had they been invented at the time. These particular cannonballs date from the Crimean War. Housed in the late 19th century market hall is the **Swanage Heritage Centre** that tells the story of the town and, in particular, features the Jurassic coast, Purbeck stone and the two men, Mowlem and Burt, who transformed the town. Next to the parish church is the **Tithe Barn Museum and Art Centre**, which has reconstructions of stone quarrying, an old-time grocer's shop and a Lloyds chemist. Another attraction not to be missed is the **Swanage Railway**, which uses old Southern Region and BR Standard locomotives to pull trains on a six-mile scenic journey to Norden, just north of Corfe Castle.

To the north of Swanage lies **Studland** whose fine sandy beach stretches from Handfast Point to South Haven Point and the entrance to Poole Harbour. The heathland behind the beach is a haven

THE SAILORS RETURN

East Chaldon, Dorchester, Dorset DT2 8DN
Tel: 01305 853847 Fax: 01305 851677
e-mail: clairevkelly@msn.com
website: www.sailorsreturn.com

What started life in the 18th century as a thatched cottage has been extended at either end to become one of the most delightful country pubs in the region. Old flagstones, low ceilings and ancient scrubbed pine tables contribute to the old-world atmosphere at the heart of **The Sailors Return**, and the bars and dining areas are filled with all sorts of mainly nautical bric-a-brac, from brass and copper

ornaments to mugs and tankards, ships' ropes and tackle, lanterns, mounted oars, a lobster pot, a framed display of ships' knots in miniature - even a dartboard framed by a rope. The decor is certainly eyecatching, but what takes the eye of many visitors is the impressive blackboard that lists the day's dishes.

Food has always been taken very seriously here, and never more so than under the present tenant Mike Pollard and his family. Classic starters such as prawn cocktail, breaded brie and smoked salmon could precede a choice of at least two dozen main courses typified by goujons of haddock or plaice, fisherman's pie, gammon steak topped with stilton, half a shoulder of lamb with a garlic, honey and rosemary sauce, sizzling chicken with ginger and spring onions, and the mighty 'Belly Buster' - a full rack of BBQ pork spare ribs. The selection of sweets and desserts is equally mouthwatering, and this terrific food is complemented by an equally fine range of real ales, draught and bottle beers, wines and spirits.

Outside, there's ample off-road parking and a choice for soaking up the sun between a bench-filled terrace at the front and a sheltered garden at the rear. Standing all on its own on a little green is the pub sign, which illustrates the delights - and the surprises - that could lie in wait for

a sailor returning to his loved one. East Chaldon, also known as Chaldon Herring, is located a short distance south of the A352 Wareham-Dorchester road. It lies on the waymarked Three Villages Trail that takes in East Knighton and Winfrith. Walking this trail is a fine way to build up a thirst and an appetite which The Sailors Return is more than happy to satisfy.

Towards Old Harry Rocks, Swanage

for rare birds and is a National Nature Reserve. This glorious area of National Trust owned land incorporates bird hides, several public footpaths and two nature trails. To the south lies **Durlston Country Park**, where George Burt built a castle in 1887. One of the footpaths leading from here along the coast takes in **Tilly Whim Caves**, named after the owner, Mr Tilly, who used a whim, or wooden derrick, to load stone into barges for transportation to Swanage.

WORTH MATRAVERS

7 miles SE of Wareham off the B3069

Worth Matravers is a former centre of the stone-quarrying industry. Just to the south of the village is the cliff top Church of St Aldhelm said to have been built by a local man, who watched from here as his daughter and her new

husband were swamped by a huge wave and drowned as they set sail for their new home along the coast. In the churchyard of the parish Church of St Nicholas is the grave of Benjamin Jesty, a farmer who, it is claimed, developed an inoculation against smallpox years before the physician Jenner.

To the northwest of the village, close to **Kimmeridge**, lies **Smedmore House**, a handsome 18th century Portland stone mansion housing some fine period furniture where visitors can also see its original kitchen and a small museum.

EAST LULWORTH

5 miles SW of Wareham on the B3070

This charming little village stands on a minor road leading down to one of the country's best loved beauty spots, **Lulworth Cove**, an almost perfectly circular bay surrounded by towering cliffs. Over the centuries, the sea has eaten away at the weak points in the limestone creating a breathtakingly beautiful scene. East Lulworth is home to **Lulworth Castle** (see panel on page 406), built as a hunting lodge in the first few years of the 17th century.

Close to the castle, and housed in St Andrew's Church, is a permanent

Lulworth Cove

exhibition of Thomas Hardy's life and works. This is an ideal setting for such a display as the writer worked here, with the architect John Nicks, during the restoration of the building. About a mile west of Lulworth Cove stands a remarkable natural feature, **Durdle Door**, a magnificent archway carved out from the coastal limestone by wind

Durdle Door

and sea erosion. There is no road to the coast at this point but it can easily be reached by following the South West Coast Path from the cove.

LULWORTH CASTLE

East Lulworth, Wareham, Dorset BH20 5QS
Tel: 01929 400352 Fax: 01929 400563
website: www.lulworth.com

Lulworth Castle was built primarily as a hunting lodge in the first decades of the 17th century and down the years has played host to no fewer than seven monarchs. It was reduced to a virtual ruin by a devastating fire in 1929, but in the 1970s restoration work was begun with the help of English Heritage. The exterior is now exactly as it was before the fire, and visitors can climb the tower to enjoy some spectacular views. A video presentation brings the history of the castle to life, and interior features including a gallery concerning the Weld family, owners of the estate since 1641, a Victorian kitchen, dairy, laundry and wine cellar. There is also a children's activity room.

Lulworth Castle House, the modern home of the Weld family, contains 18th century sculptures as well as portraits and furniture rescued from the castle fire. In the grounds of the castle are a delightful walled garden and a curious circular building dating from 1786. This was the first Roman Catholic Church to be established in Britain since Henry VIII's defiance of the Pope in 1534. Permission to build it was given to Sir Thomas Weld by King George III; the King cautiously added the proviso that Sir Thomas' new place of worship should not offend Anglican sensibilities by looking like a church - so it doesn't! The beautifully restored chapel contains an exhibition of 18th and 19th century vestments, a collection of church silver and a wonderful Seede organ. A short walk from the Castle and Chapel are the animal farm, play area and woodland walk. The old castle stables house the licensed café serving morning coffee, light lunches and cream teas, and the courtyard shop offers a wide range of gift ideas. Special events, including horse trials, country fairs and jousting shows, are held regularly throughout the season. Lulworth Castle Park is open all year Sunday to Friday, Lulworth Castle House on Wednesday afternoons in summer.

BOURNEMOUTH

At the end of 18th century, Bournemouth, now considered to be one of England's most exotic resorts, was a mere satellite of Poole. It was just the tiny village of Bourne, whose empty coastline was the haunt of smugglers and the Revenue men who were posted to patrol the area. One of these men, Louis Tregonwell, was so taken with the village's setting at the head of three deep valleys, that he and his wife bought some land here, built a house and planted the valleys with

Bournemouth

the pine trees that today give this town its distinctive appearance. The fresh pine-scented sea air was considered to be an effective treatment of tuberculosis. One of the many sufferers who sought relief here was Robert Louis Stevenson, who wrote *Kidnapped* while in the town.

Already established as a resort by the 1830s, Bournemouth continued to expand during the Victorian age and blossomed into a place of wide boulevards, grand parks and handsome public buildings. The splendid pier built in 1855 was later rebuilt and extended in 1880, when a theatre was erected at the sea end. Above the Cliff Gardens is **Shelley Park** named after Sir Percy Florence Shelley, son of the poet, and sometime lord of the manor of Bournemouth. The poet's heart is said to have been saved from his funeral pyre in Italy and is buried, along with the body of his wife Mary, in a tomb in the marvellous **Church of St Peter**, where, in 1898, the ailing Prime Minster William

Gladstone took his last communion.

The town is home to several other museums, including the **Rothesay Museum**, which maintains a mainly nautical theme, the **Teddy Bear Museum**, where life-size teddy bears are making smaller teddies, and the **Russell-Cotes Art Gallery and Museum**, an award-winning museum and art gallery named after the globetrotting Sir Merton Russell-Cotes.

As elsewhere in Dorset, Bournemouth has a strong connection with Thomas Hardy. It is mentioned in *Tess of the d'Urbervilles* and *Jude the Obscure* as Sandbourne, and also features in a less well-known work, *The Hand of Ethelberta*. However, the town's connection with Winston Churchill is much less well documented. It was while staying here as a young man, in 1892, that he fell off the town's Suspension Bridge and, after lying unconscious for three days, had to spend a further three months in bed with a ruptured kidney.

Hengistbury Head

Distance:	3.8 miles (6.0 kilometres)
Typical time:	95 mins
Height gain:	35 metres
Map:	Outdoor Leisure 22
Walk:	www.walkingworld.com ID:719
Contributor:	Peter Salenieks

Access Information:

Cars can be parked in Hengistbury Head Car Park. This is approached from the A35, turning south onto the B3059 and then east onto the Broadway to the west of Tuckton. Hengistbury Head is also accessible by bus during the summer months. Open Top Coastal Service 12 runs between Sandbanks and Christchurch Quay from 28 May to 30 September. It is possible to shorten the walk by catching the Land Train which runs between the Ranger Office and Sandspit. Whilst the service is operating, land trains run from 10am to 4pm. For a longer day, consider combining this walk with a ferry boat trip from Sandspit to Mudeford Quay.

Description:

Hengistbury Head has witnessed 11,000 years of human history, including a Stone Age camp on Warren Hill, an Iron Age port and 18th century quarrying. Nowadays it is a popular tourist spot, including a Local Nature Reserve which is home to a variety of birds, insects and small mammals.

This walk starts at the Ranger Office and Land Train terminus. There are good views of Christchurch Harbour and Christchurch Priory. In clear weather, the Purbecks can be seen across Poole Bay, with the Needles and the Isle of Wight lying to the south-east. The walk reaches the southern tip of Hengistbury Head, before descending to the beach. The return passes Holloway's Dock, a Site of Special Scientific Interest. The walk includes a short, optional detour to the wildlife pond in the quarry. A cafe and toilets are situated at the end of the walk.

Features:

Sea, toilets, wildlife, birds, great views, nature trail, ancient monument

Walk Directions:

1 Start with the Ranger Office and Land Train terminus behind you and walk about fifty metres east along the tarmac road, until you reach a junction with the track just before the Double Dikes. Bear right (south) and go along the track, which runs parallel to the Double Dikes, until you reach the seaward end of the dikes.

2 Turn left (east) at the seaward end of the Double Dikes and walk along a tarmac path that goes along the clifftop towards Hengistbury Head. The path takes you towards Warren Hill, passing Barn Field and two paths on your left. Ascend steadily, keeping the wildlife pond on your right, to reach the triangulation pillar on top of Warren Hill.

3 Continue east along a gravel track, passing a toposcope to reach the coastguard lookout station.

4 The track continues beside the coastguard lookout station, passing a path junction on the left, to reach a crossroads. Ahead, the Isle of Wight can be seen in the distance.

5 Turn right at the crossroads and follow the track along the clifftop, passing the southern end of the wildlife pond in the old quarry on your left. The track takes you to the southern tip of Hengistbury Head, before turning north-east to reach broad steps that lead down to the beach. There are several seats where you can sit and admire the view.

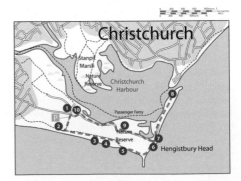

6 Descend the steps and bear left to pick up a broad path which leads inland from the beach huts at Sandspit. Follow the broad path about 100 metres north-west from the beach huts, until you reach the road.

7 Turn right (east) and follow the road towards Sandspit. Pass the Land Train terminus and the pontoon for the ferry boat to Mudeford Quay on your left. When you reach The Hut Cafe, cross between it and the beach office to reach the seaward side of Sandspit and walk north towards the end of the spit, where Avon Run marks the outflow from Christchurch Harbour into the sea. Do not enter the water as there are very strong currents.

AROUND BOURNEMOUTH

CRANBORNE

14 miles N of Bournemouth on the B3078

This pretty village has a glorious setting, beside the banks of the River Crane, and, with its fine church and manor house, it creates a charming picture of a traditional English village. The imposing Church of St Mary is noted for its fine Norman doorway and exquisite 14th century wall paintings. **Cranborne Manor**, the home of the Cecil family, stands on the site of a royal hunting lodge built by King John for use during his excursions into Cranborne Chase.

Just to the southwest, in the village of **Wimborne St Giles**, there can be found, in the church, a marvellous monument to the 7th Earl of Shaftesbury, who is even more memorably honoured by the statue of Eros in London's Piccadilly Circus.

ST IVES

9 miles NE of Bournemouth off the A31

Situated close to the county border with Hampshire and on the edge of the New Forest, this village is also close to **Avon Heath Country Park**, the county's largest country park that provides the

8 Retrace your route from Avon Run to Waymark 7 and go west along the road, passing Holloway's Dock (a Site of Special Scientific Interest) on your right. Pass a track on your left before entering woodland and continue until you see a wooded track on your left which leads gently uphill.

9 Follow the track uphill for about fifty metres to reach the wildlife pond (this detour can be omitted if you are short of time). Retrace your route back to the road and turn left. Walk about a kilometre west to reach the Land Train terminus and Ranger Office.

10 The walk ends at the Ranger Office and Land Train terminus. There are toilets and you can buy snacks at the Hungry Hiker Cafe.

opportunity to explore some of Dorset's ecologically important heathland and the wildlife that it supports (see panel below).

AVON HEATH COUNTRY PARK

Birch Road, St Ives, Ringwood, Dorset BH24 2DA
Tel/Fax: 01425 478082

Dorset's largest country park offers a unique opportunity to explore some of the county's internationally important heathland and its rare wildlife. There are miles of tracks for walking and cycling, kids' fun trails, activities and playground; regular events are run throughout the year. Easy to find along the A31, North Park has all the facilities for visitors including the Visitor Centre (Tel: 01425 478470), gift shop, café, BBQ hire and toilets (all are wheelchair accessible). Visitors can join in the family fun or explore deeper and experience the tranquillity and wildness of the Park.

COMPTON ACRES

Canford Cliffs Road, Canford Cliffs,
Poole, Dorset BH13 7ES
Tel: 01202 700778 website: www.comptonacres.co.uk
Fax: 01202 707537 e-mail: sales@comptonacres.co.uk
Opening times: 9am - 4pm Winter, 9am - 6pm Summer

A visit to the Gardens at **Compton Acres** will be a memorable experience. For those who have not been for several years, there is much to see.

Two years ago new owners purchased the 10 acre estate and brought together a team of highly skilled garden staff, under the leadership of Chris Allen. They have begun the huge task of bringing the gardens up to their past high standard of horticultural content and beauty.

Prior to the extensive new planting programmes being carried out, large quantities of overgrown shrubs and weeds have been pruned and cleared. This has allowed sunlight to come flooding back into the gardens. The result is a dramatic increase in the wildlife population. Bird song can once again be heard throughout the gardens.

The major project last winter was the re-designing, construction and planting of the formal Italian Garden. The work is now complete; time will give maturity to the specimen Yew trees and low hedges. Spectacular seasonal bedding strengthens the vibrant Italian feeling within the garden.

Work is also under-way in the Wooded Valley to create a new garden in association with a well-known garden publication. Watch this space for the official opening in Spring/Summer 2004.

A brand new retail facility, the 'Ark' and the newly refurbished craft shop called 'Something Different' sell a wide range of gifts for the home and garden, plus holiday souvenirs.

The catering venues within the gardens offer a wide range of food and refreshments. Staff will be pleased to serve a full lunch from the menu, a snack to eat in the garden, or a cup of tea. A new Italian Restaurant called 'Sorridi' is open throughout the day and in the evenings with mouth watering menus and wine lists.

Take time to explore Compton Acres, there really is something around every corner and over every hedge and through every gate and.....

CHRISTCHURCH

5 miles E of Bournemouth on the A35

Situated at the junction of the Rivers Avon and Stour, Christchurch began life as a Saxon village. In 1094, Ranulf Flambard began the construction of the magnificent **Christchurch Priory** that has ever since been in use as a place of worship. Said to be the longest parish church in England, it has many treasures, including a memorial to the poet Shelley and the **St Michael's Loft Museum**, above the Lady Chapel, which contains a fascinating exhibition on the history of the priory. While time has certainly been kind to the priory and to the Saxon mill and quay found here, the same cannot be said of the town's Norman castle of which all that can be seen today is a section of the massive keep wall.

The **Red House Museum**, housed in a charming Georgian building, follows a local history and natural history theme, while the **Museum of Electricity** is an exciting and interesting place containing only items that have a connection with this invisible power source (see panel below). The **Christchurch Motor Museum** houses rare cars and memorabilia, and its shop stocks a wide range of Formula 1 merchandise. Christchurch, according to the Guinness Book of Records, boasts the most modern of all the country's Scheduled Ancient

Monuments, a World War II pillbox and anti-tank obstacles.

Along the coast to the east lies the village of **Mudeford**, a former smugglers haunt and also the scene of a famous battle between the smugglers and excise men in which the men of the law were defeated. On nearby Hengistbury Head are the ancient ditches called the **Double Dykes**. This area is also well known for its superb walking and wonderful views. Britain's first air show took place here in 1910 and the historic event was attended by many of the great names of early aviation, including Wilbur Wright, Blériot and the Hon Charles Rolls, who was killed when he crashed his plane during the show.

SANDBANKS

3½ miles SW of Bournemouth on the B3369

This spit of land, along with Studland to the southwest, almost cuts off the harbour at Poole from the sea but it is these two headlands that provide the harbour with its shelter. Just at the top of the headland lies **Compton Acres** (see panel opposite), a series of themed gardens separated by paths, steps, rock walls and terraces that have been delighting visitors for years. The opening of the gardens was the realisation of a dream for their creator, Thomas William Simpson, who, in the 1920s, spent the

THE MUSEUM OF ELECTRICITY

The Old Power Station, Bargates, Christchurch, Dorset BH23 1QE
Tel: 01202 480467 Fax: 01202 480468

Only five minutes walk from the centre of Christchurch, in the setting of a genuine Edwardian Power Station, the **Museum of Electricity** is a must for all ages. Everything here is electric, from an old Bournemouth tram to a pair of boot warmers! There really is something to interest everyone, with hands-on exhibits and the demonstrations for children tie in with the national curriculum. Car parking is free on site and picnic tables are available.

THE OLD POST OFFICE TEA ROOM

Palmerston Place, Wareham Road, Organford,
Dorset BH16 6LB
Tel: 01202 622440
e-mail: organfordtearoom@tiscali.co.uk
website: www.organford-tearooms.com

At the beginning of the 20th century, the Post Office
and Stores was a place where villagers could buy

anything from
patent medicines
to paraffin, black
lead to long leather laces. It fulfilled this role until the 1990s, and
today the **Old Post Office** continues as the hub of village life in its
current role as Tea Room and B&B. It is owned and run by the Stark
family, with Pete looking after the tea room and Nicola in charge of
the accommodation.

Teas and coffees, sandwiches, toasties and snacks, cakes,
confections, lunches and cream teas are served in the traditionally
appointed, tea room, and when the weather is kind the tables in the
garden are a popular alternative. The bed & breakfast accommodation,
available all year round, comprises four en suite bedrooms (non-
smoking) with TV and tea trays. A choice of full English or Continental
breakfast is served in the Tea Room, and vegetarians can be catered
for. Organford is situated close to the A35 and A353, four miles from
Poole and three miles from Wareham.

THE COURTYARD CRAFT CENTRE

Lytchett Minster, Dorset BH16 6BA
Tel: 01202 623423 Fax: 01202 649422

Old farm buildings were renovated,
extended and converted to make one of
the most interesting and versatile
country arts and crafts centres in the
whole county.

The Courtyard Centre is a focal
point for a wide range of crafts and
hobbies and provides a relaxing day in
the country for all the family. Gordon

Batchelor seized the chance to buy the property while he was managing the restaurant, where the
extensive menu of home-made dishes includes speciality cream teas.

Gordon also has his own leather business on the premises, and other units in this unique complex
include Candles 'n' Cards - quality candles and hand-crafted cards and toys; Emmaculate - curtains
and cushions made to order; Over the Rainbow - crystals and faeries; Trad Pots - hand-made pottery;
The Engraving Room - trophies, watches, gold jewellery; Wisteria - cottage crafts, dolls houses; Lytchett
Minster Mirror Centre - custom-made mirrors; the Courtyard Garden Centre; and Three Oaks Animal
Kabin & Mini Farm - birds, poultry and animal needs and supplies; Bears in Mind - a large selection of
Teddy Bears.

The Centre, which is open every day, is located three-and-a-half miles west of Poole, off the
Dorchester Road between Upton and the Bakers Arms roundabout.

equivalent of £10 million in today's money, designing and planting the gardens that range from Roman and Old English to Canadian, Indian and Egyptian. Described as ten gardens in one, Compton Acres is a glorious place that has been restored following its decline after World War II.

Brownsea Island

POOLE

4 miles W of Bournemouth on A350

Once the largest settlement in Dorset, Poole has a huge, natural harbour that is actually a drowned river valley. Its history goes back to the time of the Romans. The silting up of the River Frome might have been the downfall of Wareham as a port but it was the making of Poole and by the mid 13th century it was well established as a town and port. Trade has continued from here ever since and, today, the town happily combines its dual functions as a commercial port and ancient town. Still proud of its long maritime history, the **Waterfront Museum**, housed in an 18th century warehouse and the adjoining medieval town cellars, tells the 2,000-year story of the port. The town has also lent its name to **Poole Pottery** and this expanding complex, where the famous red tiles for London Underground were made, is Poole's third major attraction. Poole lies at beginning of the 630-mile **South West Coast Path** that runs continuously from here around the coastlines of Devon and Cornwall to Minehead in Somerset. A spectacular walk, which takes in Land's End, it can be arduous at times and is best tackled in weekend or week-long chunks.

Out in the harbour are several islands, the largest of which is the National Trust's **Brownsea Island**. With its mixed habitat of heath and woodland it is home to a wide variety of wildlife and, in particular, it has one of the few remaining colonies of red squirrels in England. Footpaths traverse the island in all directions, there are spectacular views of Poole Harbour, and there is a café and a shop. In 1907, General Robert Baden-Powell carried out an experiment, to test his idea of teaching boys of all social classes the scouting skills he himself had refined during the Boer Wars, when he brought a party of 20 boys to the island. The venture was a great success and a year later Baden-Powell put his thoughts into words by writing *Scouting for Boys* and creating the Boy Scout movement. Two years later he and his wife founded the Girl Guides. A stone at the western end of the island commemorates the first camp. Just to the north of Poole lies **Upton Country Park**, a large estate where parkland, gardens and meadows surround a handsome early 19th century manor house.

LYTCHETT MINSTER

7½ miles NW of Bournemouth on the A35

In the churchyard of the church of St Peter ad Vincula is the grave of the great explorer Sir Francis Younghusband (1863-1942), the first European to cross the Gobi Desert and the first white man to see the northern slopes of K2. He made several expeditions to Tibet and his headstone has a unique relief carving of

WIMBORNE MINSTER

A wonderful old market town set among meadows beside the Rivers Stour and Allen, Wimborne is dominated by its **Minster**, a glorious Norman building of multi-coloured stone that is undoubtedly the best example of its kind in the county. However, the foundations of the minster are much older, going back to 705 when Cuthburga, sister of the king of the West Saxons, founded a nunnery that was destroyed in 1013 by the Danes. A few centuries later, in 1497, Margaret Beaufort, the mother of Henry VII, founded a school at the minster, and in 1686 one of the country's first libraries was established here though its great

tomes were chained to the desks. Close by the minster, in the High Street, is the **Priest's House**, a 16th century town house now home to a Museum. Outside, behind the house, there is a charming walled garden.

AROUND WIMBORNE

GUSSAGE ST ANDREW
7 miles N of Wimborne off the B3078

Situated in the picturesque valley of the River Gussage, this village has a pretty 12th century flint church with an exceedingly rare depiction of the hanging of Judas.

To the east of Wimborne, at **Hampreston**, is **Knoll's Garden and Nursery**, a delightful, informal and typically English garden planted over 30 years ago with a collection of

THE DROVERS INN

Gussage All Saints, Nr Wimborne, Dorset BH21 5ET
Tel: 01258 840084
e-mail: info@thedroversinn.net

Deep in the lovely Dorset countryside, **The Drovers Inn** is well worth seeking out for its outstanding food and drink and for the super atmosphere generated by the young, enthusiastic tenants Catherine and Jason Anthony. The 17th century facade is part thatched, part creeper-clad and the bar areas are no less appealing, with beams, open fires, and a wealth of brass and copper ornaments. Handsome wood-

framed blackboards announce the day's dishes, which really do offer something for all tastes and appetites, from sandwiches, ploughman's platters and jacket potatoes to prawns in filo pastry, salmon and leek tart, chicken breast with bacon and brie, steaks, curries, liver & bacon casserole and a selection of sweets are equally enticing, with such delights as home-made jam sponge, blood orange torte and 'nuts about praline' cake on offer.

Ringwood supplies its range of excellent real ales, and the wines are available by bottle or two sizes of glass; a special feature is a selection of country wines by Gales. Very much the hub of the local community, the Drovers Inn has a beer garden and parking space front and rear.

KINGSTON LACY HOUSE

Wimborne, Dorset BH21 4EA
Tel: 01202 883402 Fax: 01202 882402
website: www.nationaltrust.org.uk

The 3,440 hectare Kingston Lacy estate was bequeathed in 1981 to the National Trust, along with 3,000 hectares on the Isle of Purbeck, in the will of Ralph Bankes. Much of the land has been declared inalienable, meaning that it can never be sold, developed or mortgaged. Kingston Lacy House, home of the Bankes family for over 300 years, is a beautiful 17th century building with an outstanding collection of Old Masters, Egyptian artefacts and the amazing Spanish room with gilded leather hanging on the walls. All four floors are open to visitors, and the Edwardian laundry gives a fascinating insight into life below stairs 100 years ago.

The garden has two formal areas, the parterre and the sunken garden. The Victorian Fernery supports over 25 types of fern, the Blindwalk contains flowering shrubs and groundcover plants, and the 18th century Lime Avenue leads to Nursery Wood, where specimen trees, rhododendrons, azaleas and camellias grow. The landscaped park covers 250 acres and is home to the North Devon herd of cattle. There are lovely walks through the woodland areas, some suitable for wheelchairs, and Coneygar Copse has three different areas of woodland play equipment.

rhododendron and Australasian plants; further east again, is **Stapehill**, a 19th century Cistercian nunnery that is now a craft centre and countryside museum.

However, by far the finest example of the country house in the area lies to the west of Wimborne. **Kingston Lacy House**, set in wooded parkland with attractive waymarked walks, contains an outstanding collection of paintings and other works of art (see panel above).

Elsewhere on the estate the Iron Age hill fort of **Badbury Rings**, three concentric rings of banks and ditches were cut and raised by the Celtic tribe of Durotriges. Built beside the River Stour, on the site of a mill mentioned in the Domesday Book, the 18th century **White Mill** was extensively repaired in the 1990s. Although it still contains its original machinery, this is far too fragile to be put to milling.

TOURIST INFORMATION CENTRES

CORNWALL

BODMIN

Shire Hall
Mount Folly
Bodmin
Cornwall
PL31 2DQ
Tel: 01208 76616
Fax: 01208 76616

BUDE

Bude Visitor Centre
The Crescent
Bude
Cornwall
EX23 8LE
e-mail: budetic@visit.org.uk
Tel: 01288 354240
Fax: 01288 355769

CAMELFORD

North Cornwall Museum
The Clease
Camelford
Cornwall
PL32 9PL
Tel: 01840 212954
Fax: 01840 212954

FALMOUTH

28 Killigrew Street
Falmouth
Cornwall
TR11 3PN
Tel: 01326 312300
Fax: 01326 313457

FOWEY

4 Custom House Hill
Fowey
Cornwall
PL23 1AB
e-mail: foweytic@visit.org.uk
Tel: 01726 833616
Fax: 01726 833616

HELSTON & LIZARD PENINSULA

79 Meneage Street
Helston
Cornwall
TR13 8RB
Tel: 01326 565431
Fax: 01326 572803

LAUNCESTON

Market House Arcade
Market Street
Launceston
Cornwall
PL15 8EP
Tel: 01566 772321
Fax: 01566 772322

LOOE

The Guildhall
Fore Street
East Looe
Cornwall
PL13 1AA
Tel: 01503 262072
Fax: 01503 265426

NEWQUAY

Municipal Offices
Marcus Hill
Newquay
Cornwall
TR7 1BD
e-mail: info@newquay.co.uk
Tel: 01637 854020
Fax: 01637 854030

PADSTOW

Red Brick Building
North Quay
Padstow
Cornwall
PL28 8AF
e-mail: padstowtic@visit.org.uk
Tel: 01841 533449
Fax: 01841 532356

PENZANCE

Station Road
Penzance
Cornwall
TR18 2NF
Tel: 01736 362207

ISLES OF SCILLY

The Old Wesleyan Chapel
St Marys, Well Lane
Isles of Scilly
Cornwall
TR21 OHZ
e-mail: steve@scilly.demon.co.uk
Tel: 01720 422536
Fax: 01720 422049

ST IVES

The Guildhall
Street-an-Pol
St Ives
Cornwall
TR26 2DS
Tel: 01736 796297
Fax: 01736 798309

TRURO

Municipal Building
Boscawen Street
Truro
Cornwall
TR1 2NE
Tel: 01872 274555
Fax: 01872 263031

WADEBRIDGE

Wadebridge Town Hall
The Platt
Wadebridge
Cornwall
PL27 7AQ
Tel: 01208 813725
Fax: 01208 813781

DEVON

AXMINSTER

The Old Courthouse
Church Street
Axminster
Devon
EX13 5AQ
Tel: 01297 34386

BARNSTAPLE

36 Boutport Street
Barnstaple
Devon
EX31 1RX
Tel: 01271 375000
Fax: 01271 374037

BIDEFORD

Victoria Park
The Quay
Bideford
Devon
EX39 2QQ
e-mail: bidefordtic@visit.org.uk
Tel: 01237 477676
Fax: 01237 421853

BRAUNTON

The Bakehouse Centre
Caen Street
Braunton
Devon
EX33 1AA
e-mail: brauntontic@visit.org.uk
Tel: 01271 816400
Fax: 01271 816947

BRIXHAM

The Old Market House
The Quay
Brixham
Devon
TQ5 8TB
Tel: 0906 680 1268
Fax: 01803 852939

BUDLEIGH SALTERTON

Fore Street
Budleigh Salterton
Devon
EX9 6NG
Tel: 01395 445275
Fax: 01395 442208

COMBE MARTIN

Seacot
Cross Street
Combe Martin
Devon
EX34 0DH
e-mail: combemartintic@visit.org.uk
Tel: 01271 883319
Fax: 01271 883319

CREDITON

The Old Town Hall
High Street
Crediton
Devon
EX17 3LF
Tel: 01363 772006
Fax: 01363 772006

DARTMOUTH

The Engine House
Mayor's Avenue
Dartmouth
Devon
TQ6 9YY
e-mail: enquire@dartmouth-tourism.org.uk
Tel: 01803 834224
Fax: 01803 835631

DAWLISH

The Lawn
Dawlish
Devon
EX7 9PW
Tel: 01626 863589
Fax: 01626 865985

DEVON

Po Box 55
Barnstable
Devon
EX32 8YR
Tel: 0870 6085531

EXETER

Civic Centre
Paris Street
Exeter
Devon
EX1 1JJ
Tel: 01392 265700
Fax: 01392 265260

EXMOUTH

Alexandra Terrace
Exmouth
Devon
EX8 1NZ
Tel: 01395 222299
Fax: 01395 269911

HONITON

Lace Walk Car Park
Honiton
Devon
EX14 1LT
Tel: 01404 43716
Fax: 01404 43716

ILFRACOMBE

The Landmark
The Seafront
Ilfracombe
Devon
EX34 9BX
Tel: 01271 863001
Fax: 01271 862586

IVYBRIDGE

St Leonards Road
Ivybridge
Devon
PL21 0SL
Tel: 01752 897035
Fax: 01752 690660

KINGSBRIDGE

The Quay
Kingsbridge
Devon
TQ7 1HS
Tel: 01548 853195
Fax: 01548 854185

LYNTON

Town Hall
Lee Road
Lynton
Devon EX35 6BT
Tel: 01598 752225
Fax: 01598 752755

MODBURY

Poundwell Meadow Car Park
Modbury
Devon PL21 0QL
Tel: 01548 830159
Fax: 01548 830129

NEWTON ABBOT

6 Bridge House
Courtenay Street
Newton Abbot
Devon
TQ12 4QS
Tel: 01626 367494
Fax: 01626

OKEHAMPTON

Museum Courtyard
3 West Street
Okehampton
Devon
EX20 1HQ
e-mail: oketic@visit.org.uk
Tel: 01837 53020
Fax: 01837 55225

OTTERY ST MARY

10b Broad Street
Ottery St Mary
Devon
EX11 1BZ
e-mail: info@cosmic.org.uk
Tel: 01404 813964
Fax: 01404 813964

PAIGNTON

Victoria Car Park
Garfield Road
Paignton
Devon
Tel: 0906 6801268
Fax: 01803 551959

PLYMOUTH (DISCOVERY CENTRE)

Plymouth Discovery Centre
Crabtree
Plymouth
Devon
PL3 6RN
Tel: 01752 266030
Fax: 01752 266033

PLYMOUTH (THE BARBICAN)

Island House
9 The Barbican
Plymouth
Devon PL1 2LS
Tel: 01752 304849
Fax: 01752 257955

SALCOMBE

Market Street
Salcombe
Devon
TQ8 8DE
e-mail: info@salcombeinformation.co.uk
Tel: 01548 843927
Fax: 01548 842736

SEATON

The Underfleet
Seaton
Devon
EX12 2TB
e-mail: info@seatontic.freeserve.co.uk
Tel: 01297 21660
Fax: 01297 21689

SIDMOUTH

Ham Lane
Sidmouth
Devon
EX10 8XR
Tel: 01395 516441
Fax: 01395 519333

SOUTH MOLTON

1 East Street
South Molton
Devon
EX36 3BU
Tel: 01769 574122
Fax: 01769 574044

TAVISTOCK

Town Hall
Bedford Square
Tavistock
Devon PL19 0AE
e-mail: tavistocktic@visit.org.uk
Tel: 01822 612938
Fax: 01822 618389

TEIGNMOUTH

The Den
Sea Front
Teignmouth
Devon TQ14 8BE
Tel: 01626 779769
Fax: 01626 779770

TIVERTON

Phoenix Lane
Tiverton
Devon EX16 6LU
Tel: 01884 255827
Fax: 01884 257594

TORQUAY

Vaughan Parade
Torquay
Devon TQ2 5JG
e-mail: torbay.tic@torbay.gov.uk
Tel: 0906 680 1268
Fax: 01803 214885

TORRINGTON

Castle Hill
South Street Car Park
Great Torrington
North Devon
EX38 8AA
e-mail: info@great-torrington.com
Tel: 01805 626140
Fax: 01805 626141

TOTNES

The Town Mill
Coronation Road
Totnes
South Devon
TQ9 5DF
Tel: 01803 863168
Fax: 01803 865771

WHIDDON DOWN

Little Chef
Whiddon Down
Devon
EX20 2QT
Tel: 01647 231375

WOOLACOMBE

The Esplanade
Woolacombe
Devon
EX34 7DL
e-mail: woolacombetic@visit.org.uk
Tel: 01271 870553
Fax: 01271 870553

DORSET

BRIDPORT

32 South Street
Bridport
Dorset DT6 3NQ
Tel: 01308 424901
Fax: 01308 421060

DORCHESTER

11 Antelope Walk
Dorchester
Dorset DT1 1BE
Tel: 01305 267992
Fax: 01305 266079

LYME REGIS

Guildhall Cottage
Church Street
Lyme Regis
Dorset
DT7 3BS
Tel: 01297 442138
Fax: 01297 444668

SHERBORNE

3 Tilton Court
Digby Road
Sherborne
Dorset
DT9 3NL
Tel: 01935 815341
Fax: 01935 817210

WEYMOUTH

The King's Statue
The Esplanade
Weymouth
Dorset DT4 7AN
e-mail: tourism@weymouth.gov.uk
Tel: 01305 785747
Fax: 01305 788092

SOMERSET

BATH

Abbey Chambers
Abbey Church Yard
Bath BA1 1LY
e-mail: bath_tourism@bathnes.gov.uk
Tel: 01225 477101
Fax: 01225 477787

BRIDGWATER

50 High Street
Bridgwater
Somerset TA6 3BL
e-mail: bridgwater.tic@sedgemoor.gov.uk
Tel: 01278 427652

BRISTOL

The Annexe
Deaney Road
Bristol BS1 5DB
e-mail: bristol@tourism.bristol.gov.uk
Tel: 0117 926 0767
Fax: 0117 922 1557

BRISTOL INTERNATIONAL AIRPORT

Bristol International Airport
Bristol
BS48 3DY
Tel: 01275 474444
Fax: 01275 474767

BURNHAM-ON-SEA

South Esplanade
Burnham-on-Sea
Somerset
TA8 1BU
e-mail: burnham.tic@sedgemoor.gov.uk
Tel: 01278 787852
Fax: 01278 781282

CHARD

The Guildhall
Fore Street
Chard
Somerset TA20 1PP
Tel: 01460 67463

CHEDDAR

The Gorge
Cheddar
Somerset BS27 3QE
e-mail: cheddar.tic@sedgemoor.gov.uk
Tel: 01934 744071
Fax: 01934 744614

FROME

The Round Tower
Justice Lane
Frome
Somerset BA11 1BB
e-mail: frome.tic@ukonline.co.uk
Tel: 01373 467271
Fax: 01373 451733

GLASTONBURY

The Tribunal
9 High Street
Glastonbury
Somerset
BA6 9DP
e-mail: glastonbury.tic@ukonline.co.uk
Tel: 01458 832954
Fax: 01458 832949

GORDANO

Welcome Break Services
Gordano, J19/M5, Portbury
Bristol
BS20 9XG
Tel: 01275 375516
Fax: 01275 373211

MINEHEAD

17 Friday Street
Minehead
Somerset
TA24 5UB
e-mail: mineheadtic@visit.org.uk
Tel: 01643 702624
Fax: 01643 707166

PODIMORE

South Somerset Visitor Centre
Services Area (A303)
Podimore, Nr Yeovil
Somerset BA22 8JG
e-mail: podimore.tic@ukonline.co.uk
Tel: 01935 841302
Fax: 01935 841294

SEDGEMOOR SERVICES

Somerset Visitor Centre
Sedgemoor Services, M5 South
Axbridge
Somerset BS26 2UF
e-mail: sominfo@msn.com
Tel: 01934 750833
Fax: 01934 750755

SHEPTON MALLET

70 High Street
Shepton Mallet
Somerset BA4 5AS
e-mail: sheptonmallet.tic@ukonline.co.uk
Tel: 01749 345258
Fax: 01749 345258

TAUNTON

Paul Street
Taunton
Somerset TA1 3XZ
Tel: 01823 336344
Fax: 01823 340308

WELLINGTON

30 Fore Street
Wellington
Somerset
TA21 8AQ
Tel: 01823 663379
Fax: 01823 667279

WELLS

Town Hall
Market Place
Wells
Somerset
BA5 2RB
e-mail: wellstic@ukonline.co.uk
Tel: 01749 672552
Fax: 01749 670869

WESTON-SUPER-MARE

Beach Lawns
Weston-super-Mare
Somerset
BS23 1AT
Tel: 01934 888800
Fax: 01934 641741

YEOVIL

Petter's House
Petter's Way,
Yeovil
Somerset
BA20 1SH
Tel: 01935 471279
Fax: 01935 434065

INDEX OF ADVERTISERS

NUMBERS

@ Home, Beaminster, Dorset 367

21, Beaminster, Dorset 367

2wentythree, Truro, Cornwall 42

6 North Square, Dorchester, Dorset 373

A

Abbots, Cerne Abbas, Dorset 376

Abbotsbury, Abbotsbury, Dorset 386

Alicium Ceramics, St Erth Praze, Hayle, Cornwall 13

Anglo Longbow & Gallery, Pymore, Dorset 368

Arlington Court, Arlington, Barnstaple, Devon 123

Arwyn Jones Ceramics, Modbury, Devon 169

The Ashburton Delicatessen, Ashburton, Devon 178

Avon Heath Country Park, St Ives, Dorset 409

B

Badcock's Gallery, Newlyn, Penzance, Cornwall 15

Badgers & Barn Owls, Askerswell, Dorset 388

Bahamas Hotel, Torquay, Devon 213

Barbrook Blue Pool, Furzebrook, Dorset 402

Barleywood Crafts, Wrington, Somerset 321

Bath Paradise House Hotel, Bath, Somerset 350

The Bath Sweet Shop, Bath, Somerset 347

The Bear and Dolls House Company, Wadebridge, Cornwall 74

The Bear Shop, Totnes, Devon 220

Becky Falls Woodland Park, Menaton, Devon 183

The Belfry Country Hotel, Yarcombe, Devon 248

Beside The Wave Gallery, Falmouth, Cornwall 30

Bickleigh Mill, Bickleigh, Tiverton, Devon 244

Bicton Park Botanical Gardens, East Budleigh, Budleigh Salterton, Devon 233

Black & White, Castle Cary, Somerset 314

Blue Reef Aquarium, Newquay, Cornwall 67

Blue, Salcombe, Devon 205

Bodrugan Barton, Portmellon, Cornwall 62

Bosinver Farm Cottages, Trelowth, Cornwall 57

Bowlish House Hotel & Restaurant, Shepton Mallet, Somerset 341

Brend Hotels, Devon 114

Brewers Quay, Weymouth, Dorset 385

The British Hatter, Bath, Somerset 349

The Brook Gallery, Budleigh Salterton, Devon 234

Browns Hotel, Wine Bar & Brasserie, Tavistock, Devon 156

Buckfast Butterflies & Dartmoor Otter Sanctuary, Buckfastleigh, Devon 170

Buckland Abbey, Yelverton, Devon 161

Buckland House, Buckland Filleigh, Devon 149

Bucklawren Farm, St Martin By Looe, Cornwall 98

Budleigh Salterton Riding School & Holiday Cottages, Budleigh Salterton, Devon 236

Burrow Farm Gardens, Dalwood, Devon 249

The Burton Art Gallery & Museum, Bideford, Devon 127

Bussells Farm Holiday Cottages, Stoke Canon, Exeter, Devon 232

The Busy Bee, Kingsbridge, Devon 192

C

C9, Wellington, Somerset 290

Cadhay Manor, Ottery St Mary, Devon 260

Caerhays Castle Gardens, Gorran, Cornwall 65

Callisham Farm, Meavy, Yelverton, Devon 162

Campton Acres, Canford Cliffs, Poole, Dorset 410

Caradon Country Cottages, East Taphouse, Cornwall 93

Castle Drogo, Drewsteignton, Exeter, Devon 153

Ceramics by Martin Pettinger, Williton, Somerset 274

Chambercombe Manor, Ilfracombe, Devon 133

Charmouth Heritage Coast Centre, Charmouth, Dorset 365

Chedzoy Farm Shop, Chedzoy, Somerset 280

Cheriton Guest House, Sidmouth, Devon 257

Chideock House Hotel, Chideock, Dorset 364

The China Matching Service, Frogmore, Devon 193

Christine-Ann Richards, Wanstrow, Somerset   339

Church House Designs, Congresbury, Somerset   321

Cliftons Guest House, Truro, Cornwall   40

Cofro, Mevagissey, Cornwall   60

Combe Martin Wildlife & Dinosaur Park, Combe Martin, Devon   136

Come to Good Farm, Feock, Truro, Cornwall   34

The Conker Shoe Company, Totnes, Devon   218

Constables Studio, Fowey, Cornwall   107

Coombe Farm Gallery, Dittisham, Devon   201

Core House Cottages, Sidford, Devon   258

Cornish Farm Holidays, Cornwall   5

Cornish Farm Holidays, Cornwall   73

Cornish Orchards, Duloe, Cornwall   100

Corrymoor Mohair Socks, Stockland, Devon   248

Cotmore Farm, Chillington, Devon   195

Country Antiques & Interiors, Uffculme, Devon   242

Country Seats, Beaminster, Dorset   366

Court Barton Farm, Aveton Gifford, Devon   207

The Courtyard Craft Centre, Lytchett Minster, Dorset   412

Coves Quay Gallery, Salcombe, Devon   204

Cowslip Cottage, South Hay, Shebbear, Devon   119

The Crooked Window Gallery, Dunster, Somerset   270

Culeaze, Wareham, Dorset   402

The Cunning Artificer, Wincanton, Somerset   312

Cyprians Cot, Chagford, Devon   152

D

The Dartmoor Wildlife Park, Sparkwell, Devon   167

Dartmouth Museum, Dartmouth, Devon   197

David Risk Kennard, Powerstock, Dorset   370

Days of Grace, Budleigh Salterton, Devon   234

Deer Park Country House Hotel, Buckerell, Devon   247

The Devon guild of Craftsmen, Bovey Tracey, Devon   173

The Devonshire Angel, Long Sutton, Langport, Somerset   303

Dingles Steam Village, Milford, Lifton, Devon   165

Dinosaurland & Fossil Museum, Lyme Regis, Dorset   362

Diva, Sherborne, Dorset   396

Docton Mill & Gardens, Lymebridge, Devon   117

Dodge & Son, Sherborne, Dorset   395

Dorset Collection of Clocks, Owermoigne, Dorset   384

Drewstone Farm, South Molton, Devon   137

The Drovers Inn, Gussage All Saints, Dorset   414

E

Earthcentric, Washford, Watchet, Somerset   273

East Somerset Railway, Shepton Mallet, Somerset   343

The Eden Project, Bodelva, St Austell, Cornwall   58

Ellishayes Farmhouse, Combe Raleigh, Devon   246

Encore Contemporary Homestyle, Tavistock, Devon   158

Endsleigh Gardens Nursery, Milton Abbots, Devon   166

Enigma Contemporary Arts & Crafts, Frome, Somerset   336

Enys Wartha Victorian Tea Rooms, Penzance, Cornwall   7

Esho Funi Interiors, Totnes, Devon   219

Ethera, Dartmouth, Devon   196

Exeter's Underground Passages, Exeter, Devon   230

Exmoor Sandpiper Inn, Countisbury, Lynton, Devon   142

F

F N Gardner Rocking Horses, St Martin, Cornwall   49

Farnham Farm House, Farnham, Dorset   398

Fifth Element, Totnes, Devon   222

Fingals at Old Coombe Manor Farm, Dittisham, Dartmouth, Devon   200

Finn's at the Old Boathouse, Newquay, Cornwall   66

Finn's, Polzeath, Wadebridge, Cornwall   75

Flambards Theme Park, Helston, Cornwall   54

Fleet Air Arm Museum, Yeovilton, Somerset   305

Fluxton Farm, Ottery St Mary, Devon   259

Forde Abbey, Chard, Somerset   307

Foxgloves, Ashburton, Devon   175

Fraddon Pottery, Fraddon, Cornwall   68

Frost Farm, Hennock, Bovey Tracey, Devon   174

Fusions - Barnstaple's Delicatessen, Barnstaple, Devon   122

G

Gages Mill, Ashburton, Devon   178

The Galley Restaurant with Cabins, Topsham, Exeter, Devon   239

Garden Cottage, Loscombe, Bridport, Dorset   366

The Garden Shop, Colyton, Devon   251

The Garrack Hotel & Restaurant, St Ives, Cornwall   10

Gaulden Manor Gardens & House, Tolland, Taunton, Somerset   279

The Gem & Jewellery Workshop, Pendeen, Penzance, Cornwall   25

The George Inn, Blackawton, Totnes, Devon   194

Gilbert & Dale Antiques, Ilchester, Somerset   304

Gili Trading, Truro, Cornwall   38

Glastonbury Abbey, Glastonbury, Somerset   332

Glen Cottage, Chudleigh, Devon   210

The Golden Goose, Frome, Somerset   336

The Goldfish Bowl, Penzance, Cornwall   6

Goutsford, Ermington, Ivybridge, Devon   166

The Granary, Boswinger, Mevagissey, Cornwall   62

Gray's Farmhouse B&B / Paintings & Art Courses, Toller Porcorum, Dorchester, Dorset   389

Great Sloncombe Farm, Moretonhampstead, Devon   182

The Green Lantern, St Mawes, Cornwall   47

The Green Restaurant, Sherborne, Dorset   396

Greenswood Farm, Dartmouth, Devon   200

Gulshan Indian Cuisine, Probus, Truro, Cornwall   64

Gunns Art Gallery, Lynton, Devon   144

H

Hall for Cornwall, Truro, Cornwall   41

The Harbour Tavern, Mevagissey, Cornwall   60

Hardy's Hill Bed & Breakfast, Colyton, Devon   253

The Harrabeer Country House Hotel, Yelverton, Devon   162

The Harris Arms, Lewdown, Devon   165

Hartshanger Holidays, Porlock, Somerset   267

Heartfelt Trading, Glastonbury, Somerset   333

Hemborough Farm, Blackawton, Totnes, Devon   195

Hestercombe Gardens, Cheddon Fitzpaine, Taunton, Somerset   287

High Cross House, Dartington, Totnes, Devon   223

Higher Beeson House, Beeson, Devon   203

Higher Bowden, Dartmouth, Devon   198

Higher Waterston Farm, Piddlehinton, Dorset   378

Hindon Organic Farm, Selworthy, Somerset   266

Holne Chase Hotel, Ashburton, Devon   176

Horriford Farm, Colyford, Colyton, Devon   253

I

Ilfracombe Aquarium, Ilfracombe, Devon   132

In Your Dreams, Mevagissey, Cornwall   61

J

Jalapeno Peppers, Barnstaple, Devon   121

Jamaica Inn & Museums, Bolventor, Cornwall   89

Jane Armour Trading, Taunton, Somerset   288

John Neusinger, Devon   241

Julia Mills Gallery & Workshop, Porthleven, Cornwall   56

K

Karslake House Hotel, Winsford, Somerset   268

Kate's Farm, Musbury, Axminster, Devon   250

Kingsbridge Inn, Totnes, Devon   222

Kingston Lacy House, Wimborne, Dorset   415

Kingston Maurward Gardens & Animal Park, Dorchester, Dorset   374

Knowle Farm Cottages, West Compton, Shepton Mallet, Somerset   343

L

Lambscombe Farm Cottages, North Molton, Devon   138

Lamerhooe Lodge, Horsebridge, Devon   160

Lamorna Cove, West Penwith, Cornwall   18

Lesquite Farm, Lansallos, Looe, Cornwall   104

Levelife, Langport, Somerset   301

Leworthy Farmhouse Bed & Breakfast, Pyworthy, Holsworthy, Devon   120

The Linen Press, Dunster, Somerset   269

Little Jem's Jewellers, Penzance, Cornwall   6

Loch Fyne Restaurant & Milsoms Hotel, Bath, Somerset   348

The Lost Gardens of Heligan, Pentewan, St Austell, Cornwall   63

Lower Meadows, Boscastle, Cornwall   84

Lufflands, Yettington, Devon   236

Lulworth Castle, East Lulworth, Dorset   406

M

Mainly Blue, Wareham, Dorset   400

Manor Farm, Shepton Beauchamp, Somerset   296

The Manor Hotel, West Bexington, Dorset   388

The Manor Mill, Waterrow, Taunton, Somerset   278

Mapperton Gardens, Beaminster, Dorset   369

Marquis of Lorne, Nettlecombe, Dorset   368

Marshall Arts Gallery, Totnes, Devon   221

Maryknowle Cottage, Salcombe, Devon   204

The Meeting House Arts Centre,
   Ilminster, Somerset   309

Melbury Gallery, Sherborne, Dorset   397

Mevagissey Model Railway, Mevagissey, Cornwall   63

Michael Burton, Martock, Somerset   298

Middlewick Holiday Cottages, Wick, Glastonbury,
   Somerset   332

Mill End Hotel, Chagford, Devon   152

The Minack Theatre, Porthcurno, Cornwall   20

Monet, Shepton Mallet, Somerset   342

Monocot Nursery, Littleton, Somerset   304

Montacute TV & Radio Museum,
   Montacute, Somerset   294

Moody Dragons, Bideford, Devon   126

Moonlight, Dunster, Somerset   270

Moores Dorset Biscuits, Morecombelake, Dorset   364

Moreton Gardens, Tea Rooms & Licensed Restaurant,
   Moreton, Dorset   381

Mount Tavy Cottage, Tavistock, Devon   159

Mowhay Gallery, Trebetherick, Cornwall   76

Muchelney Pottery (John Leach), Muchelney,
   Langport, Somerset   300

The Museum of Electricity, Christchurch, Dorset   411

Muston Manor, Piddlehinton, Dorset   379

N

The Nags Head, Lyme Regis, Dorset   361

Nailey Cottages, St Catherine's Valley, Somerset   352

The Narracott Hotel, Woolacombe, Devon   130

National Maritime Museum, Falmouth, Cornwall   31

Needful Things, Castle Cary, Somerset   313

The Net Loft Gallery, Porthleven, Cornwall   56

Netherton Vine Cottages,
   Drewsteignton, Devon   151

Nethway Farm Holiday Cottages, Kingswear,
   Dartmouth, Devon   216

The New Inn, Manaccan, Helston, Cornwall   51

New Millenium Gallery, St Ives, Cornwall   12

No. 13, Tavistock, Devon   158

No. 38 Lifestyle Deli, Bridport, Dorset   372

Norman Lockyer Observatory,
   Sidmouth, Devon   254

North Barn, Cornworthy, Totnes, Devon   201

North Inn, Pendeen, Penzance, Cornwall   24

Number One, Castle Cary, Somerset   314

O

Offspringz, Blandford Forum, Dorset   392

The Old Bakehouse, Colyton, Devon   252

The Old Barn & Sunnyside Farm, Lower Kingscombe,
   Toller Porcorum, Dorset   391

The Old Forge at Totnes, Totnes, Devon   219

Old House of Foye, Fowey, Cornwall   106

The Old Mill House, Little Petherick,
   Wadebridge, Cornwall   78

The Old Mill, Boscastle, Cornwall   85

The Old Post Office Tea Room,
   Organford, Dorset   412

The Old Rectory Cottages,
   Kings Nympton, Devon   140

The Old Rectory, Cricket Malherbie, Somerset   310

The Olde House, Chapel Amble, Cornwall   74

One World, South Petherton, Somerset   297

Ottery Antique Restorers, Wincanton, Somerset   311

P

Pandora Inn, Mylor Bridge, Falmouth, Cornwall   32

PaperWorks, Totnes, Devon   220

Papyrus, Blandford Forum, Dorset   390

Partners Wine Bar & Restaurant,
   Bridport, Dorset   371

Penhale Cottages, Feock, Truro, Cornwall   34

Phoenix, Truro, Cornwall   40

Pickford House, Beckington, Bath, Somerset   338

Pierrepoint Gallery, Bridport, Dorset   372

The Pilchard Works, Tolcarne, Newlyn, Cornwall   16

Pink Kite Interiors, Fowey, Cornwall 106

Pitney Farm Shop, Pitney, Langport, Somerset 302

Pitt House, Pelynt, Looe, Cornwall 102

Place Settings, Topsham, Exeter, Devon 238

Plantation House Hotel, Ermington, Devon 208

The Plume of Feathers, Mitchell, Truro, Cornwall 69

Plym Valley Railway, Plympton, Devon 188

Plymouth Dome, Plymouth, Devon 189

Porfell Animal Land Wildlife Park, Lanreath, Liskeard, Cornwall 94

Porlock Antiques, Porlock, Somerset 267

The Pottery (Ann Saward), Cockington, Devon 214

Potting Shed Holidays, Coxley, Wells, Somerset 329

Pound Court Cottage, Harbertonford, Devon 223

Probus Gardens, Probus, Truro, Cornwall 65

Prospect House, Penryn, Cornwall 35

Q

Quinceborough Farm & Cottages, Widemouth Bay, Bude, Cornwall 86

R

The Railway Inn, Princetown, Devon 171

Randell Cox Floral Design, Tavistock, Devon 157

Reka Dom, Topsham, Exeter, Devon 238

Restormel Castle, Lostwithiel, Cornwall 109

Ridgeway Farm B&B, Awliscombe, Devon 247

Ringrose Gallery, Modbury, Devon 168

The Rising Sun, St Mawes, Cornwall 46

Roborough House, Ashburton, Devon 177

Rocky Valley Gallery, Rocky Valley, Tintagel, Cornwall 81

The Romantic Englishwoman, Fowey, Cornwall 105

The Rose & Crown, Calverleigh, Devon 242

Roseland Holiday Cottages, Portscatho, Truro, Cornwall 45

Roskilly's, St Keverne, Helston, Cornwall 50

Rotorua Apartments, Carbis Bay, Cornwall 12

The Royal Glen Hotel, Sidmouth, Devon 256

The Royal Standard, Portscatho, Truro, Cornwall 45

S

Saffron, Truro, Cornwall 39

Sail & Oar, Dartington, Totnes, Devon 225

The Sailors Return, East Chaldon, Dorset 404

Sally Pollitzer, Batcombe, Somerset 340

The Salty Monk, Sidford, Sidmouth, Devon 258

Sandpiper Gallery, Mousehole, Cornwall 19

Sea Shanty Licensed Restaurant, Torcross, Devon 202

Seaview Villa, Lynmouth, Devon 143

The Sexey's Arms, Blackford, Somerset 335

Shaftesbury Abbey Museum & Garden, Shaftesbury, Dorset 399

The Shambles, Ashburton, Devon 177

Sherborne Castle, Sherborne, Dorset 393

Sidmouth Trawlers, Sidmouth, Devon 255

Small World of Toys and Hobbies, Washford, Watchet, Somerset 272

Smugglers Cottage of Tolverne, Philleigh, Truro, Cornwall 35

Smugglers Restaurant, Newlyn, Cornwall 17

Somerset Rural Life Museum, Glastonbury, Somerset 331

St Anthony Holidays & Sailaway St Anthony, Manaccan, Helston, Cornwall 48

St Kitts Herbery, Starapark, Camelford, Cornwall 83

St Olaves Hotel, Exeter, Devon 229

St Veep Riding Stables, St Veep, Lerryn, Cornwall 108

The Stables, Camp Cottage, Wareham, Dorset 400

Sterts Theatre, Upton Cross, Liskeard, Cornwall 92

Stewart Gallery & Studio, Dartmouth, Devon 197

The Sticky Prawn, Falmouth, Cornwall 29

Sunseed Wholefoods & Healthfoods, Wellington, Somerset 290

T

The Talbot Inn, Mells, Frome, Somerset 344

Tall Ships Trading, Falmouth, Cornwall 30

The Tank Museum, Bovington, Dorset 382

The Tannery Shop, Colyton, Devon 251

Tessdesigns, Ashburton, Devon 175

Three Horseshoes, Powerstock, Bridport, Dorset 370

Tidwell Manor, Knowle, Budleigh Salterton, Devon 235

Tinhay Mill, Tinhay, Lifton, Devon 164

Tintagel Castle, Tintagel, Cornwall 79

Tiverton Castle, Tiverton, Devon   240

Tom Clark Gallery, Hurst, Martock, Somerset   299

The Tony Warren Maritime Gallery,
    Falmouth, Cornwall   33

Torcross Apartment Hotel, Torcross, Devon   202

The Totnes Wine Company, Totnes, Devon   220

Trehaven Manor Hotel, East Looe, Cornwall   98

Trelawney Garden Leisure,
    Sladesbridge, Cornwall   72

Trenderway Farm, Pelynt, Looe, Cornwall   102

Trenona Farm Holidays,
    Ruan High Lanes, Cornwall   44

Trevor J Cottell, Burrow Wall,
    Burrowbridge, Somerset   280

Trewithen Gardens & Nurseries, Truro, Cornwall   43

Trudgian Farm Shop, Probus, Truro, Cornwall   64

Tulsi, Temple, Corsley, Wiltshire   338

Turn of the Tide, Teignmouth, Devon   212

Twelve Oaks Holiday Cottages,
    Teigngrace, Devon   209

U

Uniek, Dartmouth, Devon   199

Upcott House, Okehampton, Devon   148

V

Valley View Farm Bed & Breakfast, Batcombe,
    Shepton Mallet, Somerset   341

Veryan Gallery, Veryan Green, Truro, Cornwall   42

W

Watermouth Castle, Ilfracombe, Devon   135

Wayside Folk Museum, Zennor, St Ives, Cornwall   9

West Country Water Buffalo, Chilthorne Domer,
    Yeovil, Somerset   306

West Harptree Nursery, West Harptree, Somerset   322

White Hart Inn, Bridestowe, Devon   150

White Horse Farm, Middlemarsh, Dorset   377

Wild Goose Antiques, Modbury, Devon   168

Willow, Chew Magna, Somerset   322

Willowbrook Nursery & Garden Centre,
    West Buckland, Wellington, Somerset   292

The Windsor Hotel, Bath, Somerset   346

Woodside Cottage, Blackawton, Devon   194

Y

Yew Tree Gallery, Morvah, Penzance, Cornwall   21

Yoah Cottage, West Knighton, Dorset   383

INDEX OF WALKS

Start	Distance	Time	Page
1 BOSSLOW Bosslow Common	4.0 miles (6.5km)	3 hrs	22
2 TRELISSICK GARDENS Trelissick Gardens car park	4.4 miles (7.0km)	3 hrs	36
3 TINTAGEL CASTLE Bossiney car park	3.1 miles (4.8km)	2¾ hrs	80
4 LANHYDROCK HOUSE Lanhydrock House car park	4.1 miles (6.5km)	2½ hrs	96
5 SOUTH WEST COAST PATH AND WOODY BAY Car park at Hunters Inn	6.0 miles (9.7km)	3 hrs	134
6 HAYTOR RAMBLE Middle car park, nr Haytor	4.0 miles (6.4km)	3 hrs	180
7 WEMBURY Car park, Wembury	4.8 miles (7.6km)	2 hrs	190
8 DARTINGTON The Cider Press Craft Centre car park	4.8 miles (7.5km)	2 hrs	224
9 WIMBLEBALL LAKE South West Lakes Trust car park	4.4 miles (7.0km)	1¾ hr	276
10 YATTON Yatton railway station	4.6 miles (7.3km)	2 hrs	320
11 GLASTONBURY Magdalene Street car park, Glastonbury	3.0 miles (3.8km)	2 hr	330
12 SHERBORNE Sherborne railway station	5.0 miles (8.0km)	2 hrs	396
13 HENGISTBURY HEAD Hengistbury Head car park	3.8 miles (6.0km)	1½ hrs	408

Looking for more walks?

The walks in this book have been gleaned from Britain's largest online walking guide, to be found at *www.walkingworld.com*.

The site contains 300 walks across eastern England, so there is plenty more choice in this region alone. If you are heading further afield there are walks of every length and type across England, Scotland and Wales – ideal if you are taking a short break as you can plan your walks in advance.

Want more detail for the walks in this book? Next to every walk in this book you will see a Walk ID. You can enter this ID number on Walkingworld's 'Find a Walk' page and you will be taken straight to the details of that walk.

- Over **1850** walks across Britain
- **Print routes out as you need them**
- **No bulky guidebook to carry**

Walkingworld routes contain much more detailed instructions and mapping than can be given in a printed book. The walk descriptions have photographs at every major decision point to help you to navigate and each comes with an Ordnance Survey 1:50,000 scale map. Once you have found a walk you like, simply print it out on standard A4 paper and you are ready to go!

- **Convenient A4 sized maps**
- **Print copies for everyone in your party**
- **Find walks for holidays and short breaks**

A modest annual subscription gives you access to over 1850 walks, all in Walkingworld's easy to follow format. The database of walks is growing all the time and as a subscriber you gain access to new routes as soon as they are published.

Visit the Walkingworld website at *www.walkingworld.com*

Travel Publishing

The Hidden Places

Regional and National guides to the less well-known places of interest and places to eat, stay and drink

Hidden Inns

Regional guides to traditional pubs and inns throughout the United Kingdom

GOLFERS GUIDES

Regional and National guides to 18 hole golf courses and local places to stay, eat and drink

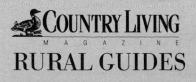

RURAL GUIDES

Regional and National guides to the traditional countryside of Britain and Ireland with easy to read facts on places to visit, stay, eat, drink and shop

For more information:

Phone: 0118 981 7777　　　　**Fax:** 0118 982 0077
e-mail: adam@travelpublishing.co.uk　**website:** www.travelpublishing.co.uk

Easy-to-use, Informative
Travel Guides on the British Isles

THE HIDDEN PLACES OF
Northumberland & Durham

An informative guide to the more secluded and less well-known places to visit
■ Places of interest ■ Accommodation ■ Food ■ Drink

HIDDEN INNS OF
YORKSHIRE
INCLUDING THE YORKSHIRE DALES AND MOORS

AN INFORMATIVE GUIDE TO THE MORE SECLUDED PUBS AND INNS OF YORKSHIRE

The Hidden Places of
SCOTLAND

● Food
● Drink
● Accommodation
● Places of Interest

An informative guide to the more secluded and less well-known places to visit in Scotland. Fully illustrated with detailed directions and maps
New in Full Colour

Second Edition

GUIDE TO RURAL ENGLAND
EAST ANGLIA

Norfolk, Suffolk, Essex and Cambridgeshire
Fully illustrated with detailed directions and maps
● Where to go ● What to see ● What to do
● Where to stay ● Where to eat ● Where to buy

THE GOLFERS GUIDE to Ireland

Packed with information on Golf Courses and where to stay, eat and drink

Dermot Gilleece

COUNTRY LIVING
GUIDE TO RURAL ENGLAND
THE NORTH WEST
Including Lancashire, Cheshire and Cumbria

● Where to go ● What to see ● What to do
● Where to stay ● Where to eat ● Where to buy
Fully illustrated with detailed directions and maps

Travel Publishing Limited

7a Apollo House • Calleva Park • Aldermaston • Berkshire RG7 8TN

ORDER FORM

To order any of our publications just fill in the payment details below and complete the order form. For orders of less than 4 copies please add £1 per book for postage and packing. Orders over 4 copies are P & P free.

Please Complete Either:

I enclose a cheque for £ [   ] made payable to Travel Publishing Ltd

Or:

Card No: [   ] Expiry Date: [   ]

Signature: [   ]

NAME: [   ]

ADDRESS: [   ]

TEL NO: [   ]

Please either send, telephone, fax or e-mail your order to:
Travel Publishing Ltd, 7a Apollo House, Calleva Park, Aldermaston, Berkshire RG7 8TN
Tel: 0118 981 7777   Fax: 0118 982 0077 e-mail: info@travelpublishing.co.uk

HIDDEN PLACES REGIONAL TITLES	PRICE	QUANTITY	HIDDEN INNS TITLES	PRICE	QUANTITY
Cambs & Lincolnshire	£8.99	....	East Anglia	£7.99	....
Chilterns	£8.99	....	Heart of England	£7.99	....
Cornwall	£8.99	....	Lancashire & Cheshire	£7.99	....
Derbyshire	£8.99	....	North of England	£7.99	....
Devon	£8.99	....	South	£7.99	....
Dorset, Hants & Isle of Wight	£8.99	....	South East	£7.99	....
East Anglia	£8.99	....	South and Central Scotland	£7.99	....
Gloucs, Wiltshire & Somerset	£8.99	....	Wales	£7.99	....
Heart of England	£8.99	....	Welsh Borders	£7.99	....
Hereford, Worcs & Shropshire	£8.99	....	West Country	£7.99	....
Kent	£8.99	....	COUNTRY LIVING RURAL GUIDES		
Lake District & Cumbria	£8.99	....	East Anglia	£10.99	....
Lancashire & Cheshire	£8.99	....	Heart of England	£10.99	....
Lincolnshire & Nottinghamshire	£8.99	....	Ireland	£10.99	....
Northumberland & Durham	£8.99	....	North East of England	£10.99	....
Sussex	£8.99	....	North West of England	£10.99	....
Yorkshire	£8.99	....	Scotland	£10.99	....
HIDDEN PLACES NATIONAL TITLES			South of England	£10.99	....
England	£11.99	....	South East of England	£10.99	....
Ireland	£11.99	....	Wales	£10.99	....
Scotland	£11.99	....	West Country	£10.99	....
Wales	£11.99	....			

Total Quantity [   ]

Total Value [   ]

READER REACTION FORM

The *Travel Publishing* research team would like to receive readers' comments on any visitor attractions or places reviewed in the book and also recommendations for suitable entries to be included in the next edition. This will help ensure that the *Country Living series of Rural Guides* continues to provide its readers with useful information on the more interesting, unusual or unique features of each attraction or place ensuring that their visit to the local area is an enjoyable and stimulating experience. To provide your comments or recommendations would you please complete the forms below and overleaf as indicated and send to:

The Research Department, Travel Publishing Ltd,

7a Apollo House, Calleva Park, Aldermaston, Reading, RG7 8TN.

Your Name:

Your Address:

Your Telephone Number:

Please tick as appropriate: Comments ☐ Recommendation ☐

Name of Establishment:

Address:

Telephone Number:

Name of Contact:

READER REACTION FORM

Comment or Reason for Recommendation:

....

....

....

....

....

....

....

....

....

....

INDEX TO TOWNS & PLACES OF INTEREST

A

Abbotsbury 387
Sub Tropical Gardens 389
The Swannery 389
Tithe Barn Children's Farm 386, 389

Aller 302

Allerford 268
Museum 268
Packhorse Bridge 268

Altarnun 90
Cathedral of the Moors 90

Appledore 129
North Devon Maritime Museum 129

Ashburton 175
Ashburton Museum 179

Athelney 289

Aveton Gifford 207

Axbridge 324
King John's Hunting Lodge 324
Local History Museum 324

Axminster 249
Axminster Museum 250

B

Baltonsborough 293

Bampton 241
Exmoor Pony Sale 241

Bantham 206

Banwell 325
Banwell Castle 325
Bone Caves 325

Barnstaple 121
Barnstaple Heritage Centre 122
Butchers' Row 121
Church of St Peter and St Paul 121
Horwood's Almshouses 121
Lynton and Barnstaple Railway Museum 122
Pannier Market 121
Queen Anne's Walk 122
St Anne's Chapel 121
Tarka Line 122
Tarka Trail 123

Barrington 296
Barrington Court 296

Barrow Gurney 321

Barwick 294
Barwick Park 294
Jack the Treacle Eater 294

Batcombe 339

Bath 345
Assembly Rooms 351
Bath Abbey 349
Bath Postal Museum 351
Bath Racecourse 351
Bath Skyline Walk 351
Building of Bath Museum 351
Great Bath 347
Holburne Museum 351
Jane Austen Centre 351
Museum of Costume 351
Museum of East Asian Art 351
Pulteney Bridge 351
Pump Room 351
Royal Crescent 350

Bathampton 353
Bathampton Down 353

Bathford 351
Brown's Folly 351
Eagle House 351

Beaminster 367
Beaminster Museum 369
Horn Park Gardens 369
Mapperton Gardens 369
Parnham House 369

Beckington 339
Cedars 339
Seymour Court 339

Beer 253

Beesands 203
South West Coast Path 203
Start Point 203

Belstone 150
Nine Stones 150

Bere Alston 163
Morwellham Quay 163

Bere Regis 380

Berry Pomeroy 217
Berry Pomeroy Castle 217

Berrynarbor 135
Watermouth Castle 135

Bickleigh 243
Bickleigh Castle 243
Bickleigh Mill 243

Bideford 125
Burton Museum and Art Gallery 127
Lundy Island 127
Pannier Marke 126
Royal Hotel 126
Statue of Kingsley 127
Tapeley Park Gardens 128
The Big Sheep 128

Bigbury on Sea 206
  Burgh Island 207
Bishop's Lydeard 282
  West Somerset Railway 282
Bishop's Nympton 138
Blaise Hamlet 357
Blandford Forum 391
  Blandford Camp 392
  Blandford Museum 391
  Fire Monument 391
  Royal Signals Museum 392
  Stour House 392
Blisland 97
  Blisland Manor Common 99
  Stipple Stone Henge Monument 99
Bodinnick 108
Bodmin 95
  Bodmin Beacon Local Nature Reserve 95
  Bodmin Jail 95
  Bodmin Town Museum 95
  Camel Trail 95
  Castle Canyke 95
  Duke of Cornwall's Light Infantry Regimental Museu
  * 95*
  Gilbert Memorial 95
  Lanhydrock House 95
  Saints' Way 95
  St Goran's Well 95
  The Courtroom Experience 95
Bodmin Moor 88
Bolventor 88
  Bodmin Moor 89
  Brown Willy 89
  Colliford Lake 90
  Dozmary Pool 89
  Jamaica Inn 88
  Rough Tor 89
Boscastle 83
  Museum of Witchcraft 84
  St Juliot 84
Bossiney 81
  Bossiney Common 81
  Bossiney Haven 81
Bournemouth 407
  Church of St Peter 407
  Rothesay Museum 407
  Russell-Cotes Art Gallery and Museum 407
  Shelley Park 407
  Teddy Bear Museum 407
Bovey Tracey 173
  Museum of Craftsmanship 174
  Parke 174
  Riverside Mill 173
Bovington
  Tank Museum 382

Branscombe 254
  Forge 254
  Manor Mill 254
  Old Bakery 254
  South West Coast Path 254
Braunton 129
  Braunton Burrows 129
  Braunton Great Field 129
Brean 324
  Brean Down 324
  Steep Holm 324
Brent Tor 160
  Church of St Michael of the Rocks 160
Bridgwater 278
  Admiral Blake Museum 281
  The Water Gate 279
Bridport 371
  Bridport Museum 371
  Harbour Life Exhibition 373
  West Bay 373
Bristol 355
  @ Bristol 356
  Avon Gorge Nature Reserve 357
  Avonmouth 356
  Bristol Cathedral 355
  Bristol Industrial Museum 356
  British Empire and Commonwealth Museum 356
  Castle Park 355
  City Museum and Art Gallery 357
  Clifton Suspension Bridge 357
  Explore 356
  Floating Harbour 356
  Georgian House 356
  Imax Theatre 356
  John Wesley's Chapel 356
  Llandoger Trow 356
  Maritime Heritage Centre 356
  Redcliffe Caves 356
  St Augustine's Reach 355
  The Church of St Mary Redcliffe 356
  The Red Lodge 356
  Theatre Royal 356
  Wildwalk 356
Brixham 215
  Berry Head 216
  Berry Head Country Park 216
Broadclyst 232
  Forest Cottage 233
  Killerton 232
  Marker's Cottage 233
Broadwindsor 367
  Coney's Castle 367
  Lambert's Castle 367
  Pilsdon Pen 367
  West Dorset Hill Forts 367
Brownsea Island 413

Bruton 315
  Patwell Pump 315
  The Dovecote 315
Buckfastleigh 169
  Buckfast Abbey 170
  Buckfast Butterflies and Dartmoor Otter Sanctuary 170
  Pennywell 170
  South Devon Railway 169
  Valiant Soldier Museum and Heritage Centre 169
Buckland Monachorum 162
  Buckland Abbey 162
  The Garden House 163
Bude 85
  Bude Canal 85
  Bude Canal Trail 86
  Bude Castle 86
  Town Museum 86
Budleigh Salterton 235
  Fairlynch Museum 237
  The Octagon 237
Burnham-on-Sea 323
  Low Lighthouse 324
Burrow Bridge 289
  Bridgwater and Taunton Canal 289
  Burrow Mump 289
  King's Sedge Moor 289
  Pumping Station 289
  Somerset Levels Basket and Craft Centre 289

C

Cadbury 245
  Cadbury Castle 245
  Fursdon House 245
Cadgwith 52
  Devil's Frying Pan 52
  Kynance Cove 52
  The Todden 52
Callington 111
  Cadsonbury Hillfort 111
  Kit Hill 111
  Mural Project 111
Calstock 110
  Cotehele House 111
  Cotehele Quay 111
  Railway Viaduct 111
  Tamar Valley Line 111
Camborne 28
  Geological Museum 28
  Godrevy Island 28
  Godrevy Point 28
  Navax Point 28
  School of Mining 28
Cameley 329

Camelford 83
  Arthurian Centre 83
  British Cycling Museum 83
  North Cornwall Museum and Gallery 83
  Slaughterbridge 83
Capton 193
Carhampton 272
Carn Euny 23
  Bartinney Downs 23
  Fogou 23
Castle Cary 313
  Castle Cary District Museum 314
  Round House 314
  War Memorial 314
Cattistock 389
Cawsand 103
  Cawsand Bay 103
Cerne Abbas 376
  Abbey 376
  Cerne Abbas Giant 376
  Minterne 377
Chagford 153
  Cranmere Pool 154
  Holed Stone 154
  Kestor Rock 154
  Market House 153
  Shovel Down 154
Challacombe 145
  Edgerley Stone 145
Chard 308
  Chard Museum 309
  Chard Reservoir Nature Reserve 309
  Hornsbury Mill 309
Charlestown 59
  Charlestown Shipwreck, Rescue and Heritage Centre 59
  Tregrehan Gardens 59
  Tregrehan Mills 59
Charminster 375
  Wolfeton House 375
Charmouth 363
  Charmouth Heritage Coast Centre 365
Charterhouse 323
  Black Down 323
  Burrington Combe 323
  Mendips 323
  Witham Priory 323
Cheddar 318
  Cheddar Gorge 318
  Cox's Cave 319
  Gough's Cave 319
  Jacob's Ladder 319
  Pavey's Lookout Tower 319
Cheddon Fitzpaine 289
  Hestercombe Gardens 289

Chew Magna 321
   Blagdon Lake 323
   Chew Court 322
   Chew Valley Lake 323
   Church House 322
   Hauteville's Quoit 322
   Standing Stones 322
   Stanton Drew 322
   The Cove 322
   Wansdyke 323

Chickerell 387

Chivelstone 203

Christchurch 411
   Christchurch Motor Museum 411
   Christchurch Priory 411
   Museum of Electricity 410, 411
   Red House Museum 411
   St Michael's Loft Museum 411

Chudleigh 209
   Ugbrooke House and Park 209

Chulmleigh 139
   Eggesford Forest 139

Clapton 307
   Clapton Court Gardens 307

Claverton 353
   American Museum and Gardens 353
   Claverton Manor 353

Clawton 120
   Clawford Vineyard 120

Clevedon 326
   Clevedon Court 327
   Clevedon Pier 326
   Market Hall 327
   Poet's Walk 327

Clifton 357
   Goldney Grotto 357
   Goldney House 357

Clovelly 117
   Fisherman's Cottage 118
   Kingsley Exhlbition 118
   Visitor Centre 118

Cockington 214
   Cockington Court 214

Colyton 251
   South West Coast Path 253

Combe Martin 135
   Combe Martin Museum 136
   Combe Martin Wildlife and Dinosaur Park 136
   The Pack o' Cards Inn 136

Compton 217
   Compton Castle 217

Congresbury 319

Corfe Castle 402
   Castle Museum 403
   Corfe Castle 402
   Corfe Castle Model Village & Gardens 403

Cornwood 171

Crackington Haven 85
   The Strangles 85

Cranborne 409
   Cranborne Manor 409

Crediton 138
   Church of the Holy Cross 139
   Lady Chapel 139

Cremyll 101
   Eddystone Lighthouse 103
   Mount Edgcumbe House 101
   Rame Head 103

Crewkerne 306
   River Parrett Trail 307
   Windwhistle Hill 307

Cricket St Thomas 308
   Cricket House 308
   Cricket St Thomas Wildlife and Leisure Park 308
   Crinkley Bottom 308

Croscombe 343

Croyde 129
   Baggy Point 129

Culmstock 243

D

Dalwood 247
   Burrow Farm Gardens 249
   Loughwood Meeting House 247
   Shute Barton 249

Dartington 223
   Dartington Hall 223
   High Cross House 225

Dartmeet 169
   Clapper Bridge 169
   Coffin Stone 169

Dartmouth 195
   Britannia Museum 199
   Britannia Royal Naval College 199
   Butterwalk 197
   Carnival 199
   Custom House 197
   Dartmouth Castle 196
   Dartmouth Museum 197
   Dartmouth Regatta 199

Dawlish 210
   Dawlish Museum 211

Dawlish Warren 211

Dean Prior 170

Delabole 82
   Delabole Slate Quarry 82
   Delabole Wind Farm 82
   Gaia Energy Centre 82

Doone Valley 144
   County Gate 145

Dorchester 373
  Dorset County Museum 374
  Keep Military Museum 374
  Maiden Castle 373
  Maumbury Rings 374
  Max Gate 375
  Old Crown Court 374
  The Animal Park 375
Doulting 343
  East Somerset Railway 343
  Tithe Barn 343
Drayton 301
  Midelney Manor 301
Drewsteignton 151
  Castle Drogo 153
  Cranbrook Castle 153
  Fingle Bridge 151
  Hunters' Path 153
  Prestonbury Castle 153
Dulverton 275
Dunkeswell 261
  Dunkeswell Abbey 261
  Dunkeswell Memorial Museum 261
Dunster 269
  Dunster Castle 269
  Dunster Priory 271
  Dunster Working Watermill 271
  Gallox Bridge 271
  Luttrell Arms 271
  Yarn Market 271
Durgan 49
  Trebah Garden 49

E

East Coker 296
East Lambrook 299
  Lambrook Manor Garden 299
East Lulworth 405
  Durdle Door 406
  Lulworth Castle 405
  Lulworth Cove 405
East Quantoxhead 283
  Court House 283
  Kilve 283
Enmore 282
  Barford Park 282
  Fyne Court 282
  Quantock Hills 282
  Wills Neck 282
Exeter 229
  Church of St Mary Steps 230
  Custom House 231
  Devon and Exeter Racecourse 232
  Devonshire Regiment Museum 231
  Exeter Historic Quayside 231
  Exeter Ship Canal 231

Exeter University Sculpture Walk 232
  Guildhall 231
  Museum 230
  Piazza Terracina 231
  Roman Bath House 229
  Rougemont Castle 230
  Rougemont House Museum 231
  Royal Albert Memorial Museum 231
  Seahorse Nature Aquarium 231
  St Nicholas' Priory 230
  St Peter's Cathedral 230
  Tucker's Hall 231
  Underground Passages 231
Exmoor National Park 274
  Alderman's Barrow 275
  Cow Castle 275
  Porlock Hill 275
  Tarr Steps 275
Exmouth 237
  A La Ronde 237
  East Devon Way 237

F

Falmouth 28
  Custom House Quay 31
  National Maritime Museum Cornwall 29
  Pendennis Castle 28
  Queen's Pipe 31
Farleigh Hungerford 353
  Chapel of St Leonard 354
  Farleigh Hungerford Castle 353
  Ilford Manor 354
  The Peto Garden 354
Feock 33
  Restronguet Point 33
Flushing 33
Fowey 104
  Coastal Footpath 107
  Gribbin Head 107
  King of Prussia 105
  Menabilly 107
  Museum 105
  Readymoney Cove 107
  Ship Inn 105
  St Catherine's Castle 107
  The Haven 107
Frome 337
  Blue House 337
  Bridge 337
  Church of St John 337
  Frome Museum 337

G

Galmpton 217
  Greenway 217
Gannel 67

Georgeham 131
Glastonbury 329
   Chalice Hill 334
   Church of St Michae 333
   George and Pilgrim Hotel 331
   Glastonbury Abbey 329
   Glastonbury Tor 331
   Lake Village 334
   Somerset Rural Life Museum 331
   Tribunal 331
Godolphin Cross 14
   Godolphin House 14
Golant 108
   Castle Dore Earthworks 108
Gorran Haven 63
   Dodman Point 63
Great Torrington 125
   Castle Hill 125
   Church of St Michael and All Angels 125
   Dartington Crystal 125
   May Fair 125
   Rosemoor 125
Gulworthy 163
Gunnislake 110
   New Bridge 110
Gussage St Andrew 414
   Badbury Rings 415
   Kingston Lacy House 415
   Stapehill 415
   White Mill 415
Gweek 53
   National Seal Sanctuary 53
   Woodland Nature Quest 53

H

Hampreston 414
   Knoll's Garden and Nursery 414
Harpford 259
   Aylesheare Common 259
Hartland 116
   Church of St Nectan 116
   Docton Mill 117
   Hartland Abbey 116
   Hartland Point 117
   Hartland Quay 117
   Museum 117
   Spekes Mill Mouth Coastal Waterfall 117
Haselbury Plucknett 308
   Haslebury Bridge 308
Hatch Beauchamp 291
   Hatch Court 291
   Staple Fitzpaine 291
Hatherleigh 140
   Hatherleigh Pottery 140
Hayle 13
   Paradise Park 14

Hele Bay 133
   Chambercombe Manor 135
   Old Corn Mill and Pottery 133
Helford 49
   Helford Passage 51
   Helford River Walk 51
Helston 53
   Angel House 54
   Culdrose 55
   Festival of the Furry 55
   Flambards 55
   Flora Dance 55
   Gardening Museum 55
   Guildhall 54
   Helston Folk Museum 54
   Loe Bar 55
   Loe Pool 55
   The Blue Anchor Inn 54
   Trevarno Estate and Gardens 55
High Bockhampton 379
   Hardy's Cottage 379
High Ham 302
   Stembridge Tower Mill 302
Highbridge 324
   Brent Knoll 324
Hinton Priory 353
Hinton St George 310
Hinton St Mary 399
Holford 283
   Beacon Hill 283
   Bicknoller Hill 283
   Dowsborough Fort 283
   Trendle Ring 283
Holsworthy 115
   Cadiho Well 116
   Dunsland 116
   Holsworthy Museum 116
   Pretty Maid Ceremony 115
   St Peter's Fair 115
   West Country Way 116
Holywell 67
   Holywell Bay Fun Park 67
Honiton 245
   Allhallows Museum 246
   Bishop's Tower 247
   Copper Castle 247
   Marwood House 246
   St Margaret's Hospital 247
Hope Cove 206
Huish Episcopi 302

I

Ilchester 305
   Ilchester Mace 305
   Ilchester Museum 305

Ilfracombe 132
  Ilfracombe Aquarium 133
  Ilfracombe Museum 133
  Landmark Theatre 133
  Lantern Hill 132
  South West Coast Path 133
  St Nicholas Chapel 132
  Tunnel Baths 132
Ilminster 309
  Dillington House 310
  Dowlish Wake 310
Ilsington 174
  Haytor Rocks 175
  St Michael's Cottages 174
Indian Queens 68
  Screech Owl Sanctuary 68
Instow 129
  North Devon Yacht Club 129
Isle of Portland 385
  Chesil Beach 385
  Portland Bill 387
  Portland Castle 385
  Portland Museum 387
Ivybridge 166
  Dartmoor Wildlife Park 167
  Two Moors Way 167
  West Country Falconry Centre 167
Iwerne Minster 401
  Cranborne Chase 401
  Fontmell 401
  Melbury Downs 401

K

Kenton 210
  Powderham Castle 210
Keynsham 355
  Museum 355
Kilkhampton 87
Kimmeridge 405
  Smedmore House 405
Kingsand 103
Kingsbridge 192
  Cookworthy Museum of Rural Life 193
  Kingsbridge Estuary 193
  The Shambles 193
Kingswear 216
  Coleton Fishacre House and Garden 217
  Kingswear Castle 216

L

Landkey 124
  Bishop's Tawton 124
Land's End 20
  Longships Lighthouse 21
  Wolf Rock Lighthouse 21

Laneast 90
Langport 301
  Langport and River Parrett Visitor Centre 302
  Langport Gap 302
Langton Herring 387
  The Fleet 387
Lanreath 109
  Lanreath Folk and Farm Museum 109
Launcells 87
Launceston 109
  Launceston Castle 109
  Launceston Steam Railway 110
  Lawrence House 110
  Museum 110
  St Thomas' Church 109
  Tamar Valley Discovery Trail 110
Lelant 14
Lerryn 108
Lewdown 160
Lifton 163
  Dingles Steam Village 165
Liskeard 93
  Dobwalls Family Adventure Park 93
  Guildhall 93
  Looe Valley Line 93
  Museum 93
  Pipe Well 93
  Porfell Animal Land Wildlife Park 93
  Public Hall 93
  Stuart House 93
Lizard 52
  Lighthouse 52
  Lizard Peninsula 52
  Lizard Point 52
  South West Coast Path 52
Loddiswell 208
  Loddiswell Vineyard 208
Looe 99
  Aquarium 99
  Banjo Pier 99
  Looe Island 99
  Looe Valley Line Footpath 99
  Old Guildhall Museum 99
  South East Cornwall Discovery Centre 99
Lostwithiel 108
  Bonconnoc Estate 108
  Coulson Park 108
  Great Hall 108
  Guildhall 109
  Lostwithiel Museum 109
  Restormel Castle 109
Lullington 337
  Orchardleigh Park 339
  Rode Bird Gardens 339
Lulworth
  Lulworth Castle 406

Lustleigh 181
  Becky Falls Woodland Park 182
  Yarner Wood Nature Reserve 182
Lydford 155
  Devil's Cauldron 155
  Lydford Castle 155
  Lydford Gorge 155
Lyme Regis 361
  Dinosaurland 363
  Fossil Museum 362
  Golden Cap 363
  Jane Austen Garden 363
  Philpot Museum 363
  Regatta and Carnival 363
  The Cobb 362
  Town Criers' Open Championship 363
  Town Mill 363
Lyng 291
Lynmouth 141
  Exmoor Brass Rubbing and Hobbycraft Centre 143
  Flood Memorial Hall 143
  Lynmouth Pottery 141
  Lynton-Lynmouth Cliff Railway 141
  Rhenish Tower 143
  Watersmeet House 143
Lynton 144
  Exmoor Museum 144
  Valley of the Rocks 144
Lytchett Minster 413

M

Madron 8
  Trengwainton Gardens 8
Maiden Newton 391
Malborough 206
Manaccan 51
Marazion 14
  Marazion Marsh & RSPB Reserve 14
  St Michael's Mount 14
  St Michael's Mount Castle 15
Martinstown 387
  Hardy's Monument 387
Martock 298
  Old Court House 298
  Treasurer's House 298
Marwood 123
  Marwood Hill Gardens 123
Mary Tavy 161
  Wheal Betsy 161
Mawnan 48
Mawnan Smith 48
  Giant's Stride 48
  Glendurgan Garden 48
  Heade Maze 48

Meare 334
  Abbot's Fish House 334
  Meare Pool 334
  Shapwick Heath Nature Reserve 334
Meeth 141
  Tarka Trail 141
Mells 344
Mevagissey 59
  Caerhays Castle Gardens 63
  Inner Harbour 59
  Lost Gardens of Heligan 61
  Mevagissey Folk Museum 59
  Outer Harbour 59
  The Aquarium 61
  World of Model Railway Exhibition 61
Midsomer Norton 345
  Radstock, Midsomer North and District Museum 345
Milborne St Andrew 380
Milton Abbas 381
  Bulbarrow Hill 381
  Milton Abbey 381
Minehead 264
  North Hill 264
  North Hill Nature Reserve 264
  Somerwest World 265
  West Somerset Railway 265
Minions 90
  Cheesewring 91
  Hurlers Stone Circle 91
  Minions Heritage Centre 90
Minterne Magna 377
Modbury 167
Molland 138
Monksilver 275
  Brendon Hills 277
  Combe Sydenham Hall 275
  Nettlecombe Court 277
Montacute 295
  Montacute House 295
  TV and Radio Memorabilia Museum 295
Moreton 381
  Bovington Camp 383
  Cloud's Hill 383
  Monkey World 383
  Moreton Gardens 381
  Tank Museum 383
  Winfrith Heath 384
  Woodbridge Manor 384
Moretonhampstead 182
  Almshouses 183
  Mearsdon Manor Galleries 183
Mortehoe 131
Morwenstow 87
  Higher and Lower Sharpnose Points 88

Vicarage Cliff 88
Welcombe and Marsland Valleys 88
Welcombe Mouth 88

Mousehole 17
Merlin's Rock 19

Muchelney 300
Muchelney Abbey 300
Priest's House 300

Muddiford 123
Arlington Court 123

Mudeford 411
Double Dykes 411

Mullion 53
Earth Satellite Station 53
Goonhilly Downs 53
Marconi Monument 53
Mullion Cove 53
Poldhu Cove 53

Murrayton 103
Monkey Sanctuary 103

Mylor 33
Mylor Bridge 33
Mylor Churchtown 33

N

Nether Stowey 282
Coleridge Cottage 283
Dodington Hall 283
Stowey Court 283

New Polzeath 75

Newlyn 15
Newlyn School 17
Pilchard Works Heritage Museum 17

Newquay 65
Blue Reef Aquarium 66
East Wheal Rose 67
Fistral Beach 67
Huer's Hut 66
Newquay Zoo 66
Porth Island 65
Towan Beach 67
Trenance Heritage Cottages 66
Tunnels Through Time 66
Water World 67

Newton Abbot 208
Bradley 209
Forde House 208
Hedgehog Hospital 209
Newton Abbot Racecourse 209

Newton Ferrers 191
The Old Mill 192

North Bovey 183

North Molton 137
Court Barton 137

North Newton 289
Firepool Lock 291
Maunsel House 291

North Petherwin 111
Tamar Otter Park 111

North Tawton 139
Bathe Pool 140
Broad Hall 140

Northam 127
Bloody Corner 128

Northlew 120

Norton Fitzwarren 292

Norton St Philip 354
George Inn 354

Nunney 343
Castle 343

O

Oakhill 345
Oakhill Manor 345

Oare 145

Okehampton 148
Chapel of Ease 149
High Willhays 148
Museum of Dartmoor Life 149
Okehampton Castle 149
Town Hall 149
Yes Tor 148

Osmington 385
White Horses 385

Otterton 233
Bicton Park Botanical Gardens 235
Otterton Mill 233

Ottery St Mary 259
Cadhay 261
Church of St Mary 259
Escot Park and Gardens 261
Tumbling Weir 260

Over Stowey 283
Quantock Forest Trail 283

P

Padstow 77
Harbour Cottage 78
May Day 78
National Lobster Hatchery 78
Prideaux Place 79
Raleigh Cottage 78
Saints' Way 77

Paignton 214
Oldway Mansion 215
Paignton and Dartmouth Steam Railway 215
Paignton Zoo 214
Quaywest 215

Parracombe 145
    Church of St Petroc 145
    Heddon Valley 145
Pendeen 25
    Geevor Tin Mine and Heritage Centre 25
    Levant Steam Engine 25
    Pendeen Lighthouse 25
    Pendeen Watch 25
Penhallow 27
    Cider Farm 27
    Cider Museum 27
Penzance 5
    Cornwall Geological Museum 8
    Egyptian House 5
    Jubilee Swimming Pool 5
    Maritime Museum 7
    Market House 5
    Penlee House Art Gallery and Museum 8
    The Union Hotel 7
    Trinity House Lighthouse Centre 7
Perranporth 27
    Lowender Peran Festival 27
    St Piran's Oratory 27
Peter Tavy 161
Piddletrenthide 377
Pilton 342
Pitminster 291
    Poundisford Park 291
Plym Bridge 189
    Plym Bridge Woods 189
Plymouth 187
    Arts Centre 188
    Barbican 187
    Drake's Island 187
    Eddystone Lighthouse 187
    Elizabethan House 188
    Jacka's Bakery 188
    Mayflower Stone 188
    Merchant's House 188
    Museum and Art Gallery 188
    National Marine Aquarium 188
    Pavilions 188
    Plymouth Breakwater 187
    Plymouth Hoe 187
    Plymouth Sound 187
    Prysten House 188
    Smeaton's Tower 187
    The Citadel 188
    Theatre Royal 188
Plympton 189
    Plym Valley Railway 189
    Saltram House and Park 189
Polkerris 107
Polperro 103
    Couch's House 104
    House on Props 104
    Museum of Smuggling 104
Polruan 107
    Polruan Blockhouse 107
Polzeath 75
    Church of St Enodoc 76
    Pentire Point 75
    Rumps Cliff Castle 75
    Rumps Point 75
Pool 27
    Cornish Mines and Engines 27
    Industrial Discovery Centre 27
Poole 413
    Brownsea Island 413
    Poole Pottery 413
    South West Coast Path 413
    Upton Country Park 413
    Waterfront Museum 413
Porlock 265
    Dovery Manor 265
    Porlock Hill 267
Porlock Weir 265
    Culbone Church 265
    Submerged Forest 265
Port Gaverne 82
Port Isaac 82
    Long Cross Victorian Gardens 82
    Tregeare Rounds 82
Port Quin 76
    Doyden Castle 76
Porthcothan 77
    Bedruthan Steps 77
    Constantine Bay 77
    Porth Mear 77
    South West Coast Path 77
    Trevose Head 77
    Trevose Lighthouse 77
Porthcurno 19
    Cribba Head 19
    Gwennap Head 19
    Minack Theatre 19
    Porthcurno Wartime Telegraph Museum 19
Porthleven 55
Porthtowan 26
Portloe 47
    Carne Beacon 47
Portreath 26
Portscatho 47
Portwrinkle 103
Postbridge 154
    Clapper Bridge 154
    Crockern Tor 154
    Powder Mills 154
    Warren House Inn 154
Princetown 171
    Dartmoor Prison 171
    High Moorland Visitors' Centre 172

Priston 354
   Priston Mill 354
Probus 63
   Probus Gardens 63
   Trewithen House and Gardens 63
Prussia Cove 14
Puddletown 377
   Athelhampton 379
Puncknowle 389
   Kingston Russell Stone Circle 389
   Poor Lot Barrows 389
Puxton 325

R

Redruth 25
   Carn Brea 26
   Gwennap Pit 26
Rinsey 14
   Praa Sands 14
   Wheal Prosper 14
   Wheal Trewavas 14

S

Salcombe 205
   Batson Creek 205
   Overbecks Museum and Garden 205
   Prawle Point 206
   South Devon Way 205
Saltash 101
   Guildhouse 101
   Mary Newman's Cottage 101
   Royal Albert Bridge 101
   Tamar Bridge 101
Sampford Brett 273
Sancreed 21
   Blind Fiddler 21
   St Credan's Church 21
   Two Sisters 21
Sandbanks 411
   Compton Acres 411
Seaton 250
   Seaton Tramway 250
Selworthy 267
   Dunkery Beacon 267
   Holnicote Estate 267
   Horner and Dunkery National Nature Reserve 267
   Selworthy Beacon 267
Shaftesbury 399
   Gold Hill 401
   Ox House 399
   Shaftesbury Abbey 399
   Shaftesbury Abbey Museum 399
   Shaftesbury Museum 401
   Town Hall 399

Shaldon 212
   Shaldon Wildlife Trust 212
Shebbear 118
   Devil's Stone 118
Sheepwash 119
Shepton Beauchamp 297
Shepton Mallet 341
   Market Cross 342
   Mid-Somerset Show 342
   Pilton Manor 342
   Royal Bath and Wells Show 342
   The Shambles 342
Sherborne 392
   Almshouse 395
   Conduit House 395
   Pageant Gardens 397
   Sherborne Abbey 392
   Sherborne Castle 393
   Sherborne Museum 397
   Sherborne Old Castle 393
   Sherborne School 393
Shirwell 123
Sidbury 259
   Sidbury Castle 259
Sidmouth 254
   Norman Lockyer Observatory 257
   Sidmouth Museum 257
Slapton 201
   Slapton Ley 201
Somerton 303
   Hext Almshouses 303
   Lytes Cary Manor 303
   Market Cross 303
South Brent 171
South Molton 136
   Guildhall 137
   Market Hall and Assembly Rooms 136
   Medical Hall 136
   Quince Honey Farm 137
South Zeal 150
Sparkford 312
   Cadbury Castle 313
   Haynes Motor Museum 312
St Agnes 26
   Engine House 26
   St Agnes Beacon 27
   St Agnes Head 27
   St Agnes Parish Museum 26
   Stippy-Stappy 26
   Wheal Coates 26
   Wheal Kitty 26
St Allen 27
St Anthony 47
   St Anthony Head 47
   St Anthony's Lighthouse 48

St Austell 57
  Cornish Alps 57
  St Austell Brewery Visitor Centre 59
  Wheal Martyn China Clay Museum 59
St Blazey 59
  Eden Project 59
St Breock 75
  St Breock Downs Monolith 75
St Buryan 19
  Boscawen-Un Stone Circle 19
St Cleer 91
  Golitha Falls 91
  King Doniert's Stone 91
  St Cleer's Holy Well 91
  Trethevy Quoit 91
St Clether 90
St Columb Major 69
  Castle Downs 69
  Castle-an-Dinas 69
  Old Rectory 69
St Germans 100
  St Germans' Church 100
St Ives 9, 409
  Avon Heath Country Park 409
  Barbara Hepworth Sculpture Garden and Museum 11
  Carbis Bay 13
  St Ives Museum 11
  Tate Gallery 11
  The Island 11
St Just 23
  Botallack 25
  Cape Cornwall 23
  Priest's Cove 23
  South West Coast Path 23
  The Tinners' Way 25
St Just in Roseland 47
St Keverne 51
  Cornish Rebellion 51
  The Manacles 51
St Keyne 99
  Paul Corin's Magnificent Music Machines 100
  St Keyne's Well 99
  Stone Circle 100
St Mawes 47
  St Mawes Castle 47
St Neot 93
  Carnglaze Slate Caverns 94
Starcross 211
  Atmospheric Railway 211
Sticklepath 150
  Finch Foundry 150
Stinsford 375
  Kingston Maurward Gardens & Animal Park 375

Stoke Fleming 201
  Blackpool Sands 201
Stoke sub Hamdon 297
  Ham Hill 297
  Stoke sub Hamdon Priory 297
Stratton 87
  The Tree Inn 87
Stratton-on-the-Fosse 345
  Downside Abbey 345
Street 334
  Friends' Meeting House 334
  Shoe Museum 334
Studland 403
  Durlston Country Park 405
  Tilly Whim Caves 405
Sturminster Newton 397
  Newton Mill 397
Swanage 403
  King Alfred Column 403
  Swanage Heritage Centre 403
  Swanage Railway 403
  Tithe Barn Museum and Art Centre 403
Swimbridge 124

T

Tamerton Foliot 191
Tatworth 308
  Forde Abbey 308
Taunton 286
  Bridgwater and Taunton Canal 287
  Castle 286
  National Hunt Racecourse 289
  Somerset County Cricket Museu 287
  Somerset County Museum 286
  Somerset Military Museum 286
Tavistock 157
  Fitzford Gate 159
  Goose Fair 159
  Guildhall 157
  Pannier Market 159
  Tavistock-Morwellham Cana 159
Teignmouth 211
  Assembly Rooms 211
  Church of St James 211
  The Quay 211
Templecombe 312
  Gartell Light Railway 312
  Templecombe Railway Museum 312
Tintagel 79
  King Arthur's Great Hall 79
  Old Post Office 81
  Rocky Valley 81
  Rocky Valley Carvings 81
  St Nectan's Kieve 81
  The Island 79
  Tintagel Castle 79

Tintinhull 299
  Tintinhull House Garden 299
Tiverton 239
  Great House 240
  Great Western Canal 240
  Knightshayes Court 240
  Old Blundell's School 240
  Slee Almshouses 240
  Tiverton Castle 239
  Tiverton Museum of Mid-Devon Life 240
Tolland 278
  Gaulden Manor 278
Toller Porcorum 389
  Toller Fractum 389
Tolpuddle 380
  Tolpuddle Martyrs Museum 380
Tolverne 33
  Smugglers Cottage 33
  Trelissick 37
Topsham 237
Torbay 214
Torcross 203
Torpoint 101
  Antony House 101
  Antony Woodland Gardens 101
  Hamoaze 101
Torquay 212
  Agatha Christie Memorial Room 213
  Babbacombe Model Village 213
  Kents Cavern 213
  Spanish Barn 212
  Torquay Museum 213
  Torre Abbey 212
Totnes 217
  Brutus Stone 219
  Guildhall 221
  Totnes Castle 221
  Totnes Museum 222
Treen 19
  Logan Rock 19
  Tretyn Dinas 19
Tregony 65
  Carrick Roads 65
Trerice 67
  DairyLand Farm World 68
  Lawnmower Museum 68
Treskillard 27
  Shire Horse Farm and Carriage Museum 27
Trevellas 26
  Blue Hills Tin Streams 26
Trewint 90
  Wesley Cottage 90

Truro 39
  Art Gallery 43
  Royal Cornwall Museum 43
  Truro Cathedral 43
Turnchapel 192
  Abraham's Garden 192

U
Uffculme 243
  Coldharbour Mill 243
Uphill 326
  Mendip Way 326
Upton Cross 91
  Cornish Yarg Cheese 91

V
Veryan 43
  Roundhouses 43

W
Wadebridge 73
  Bridge on Wool 73
  Camel Trail 75
  John Betjeman Centre 73
  Royal Cornwall Agricultural Show 73
Walton-in-Gordano 327
  Manor House 327
Wambrook 309
  Ferne Animal Sanctuary 309
Wareham 401
  Furzebrook 402
  Museum 401
  Rex Cinema 401
  The Blue Pool 402
Warleggan 94
  Cardinham Woods 94
Washford 272
  Cleeve Abbey 272
  Tropiquaria 273
Watchet 273
  Museum 274
Weare Gifford 125
  Weare Gifford Hall 125
Webbington Loxton 324
  Gypsy Folklore Collection 324
  Wheelwright's Working Museum 324
Wedmore 334
Wellington 291
  Town Hall 292
  Wellington Monument 292
Wellow 353
  Stoney Littleton Long Barrow 353
  Wellow Brook 353

Wells 327
  Astronomical Clock 328
  Bishop's Eye 328
  Bishop's Palace 328
  Cathedral of St Andrew 327
  Penniless Porch 328
  Vicar's Close 328
  Wells Museum 328
Wembury 192
  Great Mew Stone 192
Wendron 57
  Poldark Mine Heritage Complex 57
West Anstey 138
  The Two Moors Way 138
West Coker 295
  Brympton d'Evercy Manor House 295
Westbury on Trym 357
  Westbury College Gatehouse 357
Westhay 334
  Peat Moor Visitor Centre 334
Weston-super-Mare 325
  Grand Pier 326
  International Helicopter Museum 326
  North Somerset Museum 326
  Sand Point 326
  Seaquarium 326
  Weston Miniature Railway 326
  Winter Gardens 326
  Woodspring Priory 326
  Worlebury Camp 325
Westonzoyland 281
  King's Sedgemoor Drain 281
  Pumping Station 281
Westport 297
Westward Ho! 128
  Northam Burrows Country Park 128
  Pot Walloping Festival 128
Weymouth 384
  Brewers Quay 384
  Deep Sea Adventure 385
  Museum of Coastal Defence 385
  Nothe Fort 384
  Sandsfoot Castle 384
  Weymouth Museum 384
Whiddon Down 150
  Spinster Rock 150
Whitchurch Canonicorum 365
Whitsand Bay 103
Widecombe in the Moor 179
  Cathedral of the Moors 179
  Church House 179
  Glebe House 179
  Grimspound 181
  Widdecombe Fair 179

Williton 273
  Bakelite Museum 273
Wimborne Minster 414
  Minster 414
  Priest's House 414
Wimborne St Giles 409
Wincanton 311
  Hadspen House Gardens 312
  Wincanton National Hunt Racecourse 311
Winfrith Newburgh
  Lulworth Castle 406
Winnards Perch 69
  Cornish Birds of Prey Centre 69
Winsford 268
Wiveliscombe 278
  Clatworthy 278
  Wimbleball 278
Woodford 275
Wookey Hole 334
  Ebbor Gorge 335
  Great Cave 335
  Hyena's Den 335
Woolacombe 131
Woolfardisworthy 118
  Milky Way Adventure Park 118
Worth Matravers 405

Y

Yelverton 161
Yeovil 293
  Church of St John the Baptist 293
  Museum of South Somerset 293
Yeovilton 306
  Fleet Air Arm Museum 306
Yettington 233
  Hayes Barton 233
  Woodbury Common 233

Z

Zelah 27
  Chyverton Garden 27
Zennor 8
  Chysauster Ancient Village 9
  Wayside Folk Museum 8
  Zennor Quoit 9